A TEXTBOOK OF HISTORIOGRAPHY

A TEXTBOOK OF HISTORIOGRAPHY

500 BC to AD 2000

E. SREEDHARAN

Orient BlackSwan

A TEXTBOOK OF HISTORIOGRAPHY

ORIENT BLACKSWAN PRIVATE LIMITED

Registered Office
3-6-752, Himayatnagar, Hyderabad 500 029, Telangana, India
e-mail: centraloffice@orientblackswan.com

Other Offices
Bengaluru, Chennai, Guwahati, Hyderabad, Kolkata, Mumbai, New Delhi, Noida, Patna

First published 2004
Reprinted 2004 (Twice),2005, 2009, 2010, 2011, 2012, 2013, 2014, 2016, 2017, 2018, 2019, 2021, 2022, 2023, 2024, 2026

ISBN 978-81-250-2657-0

Printed in India at
B.B Press, Tronica City, Ghaziabad, U.P. 201 103

Published by
Orient Blackswan Private Limited
3-6-752, Himayatnagar
Hyderabad 500 029, Telangana, India
e-mail: info@orientblackswan.com

We might be standing on the threshold of an age in which history would be as important for the world as natural science had been between 1600 and 1900.

R.G. COLLINGWOOD

Contents

CHAPTER 10

CHAPTER 11

CHAPTER 12

CHAPTER 15

CHAPTER 16

Preface

Historiography is a comparatively new area of historical study introduced at the graduate and postgraduate levels in several Indian universities. But confronted with the task of learning a new subject and taking an examination in it in a specified time, the student looks for support and guidance entirely to the teacher who, having to learn the subject and teach it in a manner intelligible and easily comprehensible to the student, finds himself in a position not very different from that of the student. The student seeks easy comprehension, clear and precise guidance, and immediate utility. To weave out of the several books recommended for study and reference, material which would meet the requirements of the syllabus as well as of the examination without sacrificing scholarliness is a problem which students and teachers cannot by themselves solve. The total lack of a dependable volume between whose covers they can find a sizeable part of their reading material in historiography has resulted in anomalies sometimes seen at their worst in the kind of the questions set and answers given at examinations. In the circumstances a textbook should be considered an important element in the study of the subject, be it only an initiation into it.

Textbook writing is a job where neither the topic nor the period can be properly delimited. But there can be little doubt that its basic task is to provide a solid minimum of reliable information on the subject concerned, to present a balanced view of competing ideas, and not to back some thesis to the detriment of others. The present venture is a critical survey of the development of historiography from 500 BC to AD 2000. Its content is the irreducible minimum of what I think to be essential for a classroom textbook which by expectation should include everything but not so much as to make it unmanageably bulky. I have followed in the main the postgraduate historiography syllabi of some Indian universities. To this, however, significant additions have been made to make the account more comprehensive, exhaustive and up-to-date of post-Second World War developments in history writing – generally labeled 'structuralist' and 'postmodernist' – and also to give relatively full coverage to ancient, medieval and modern Indian historiography. Even as such it is only a sketchy outline of the long evolution, the slow development, of history writing and of the changing attitudes towards it during the 2500 years from Herodotus to our own 'postmodernist' days. I have taken care to stress the philosophical, religious, scientific, ideological and linguistic influences bearing on this evolution and to indicate the development of historical criticism – methodology – and the ever-widening scope of the subject itself. Yet I feel I have only furnished something in the nature of a map situating a number of leading figures and movements in their appropriate places in the historiographical landscape.

The book is one of transmission, not of creation. It does not carry any central thesis. Nor is it one of original method, scholarship or interpretation. A textbook of historiography critically surveying the development of the subject from beginning to end and constrained by the dictates of syllabi can scarcely be original, particularly in the Indian context. The material of the many different parts of the present work has been excerpted from many different works and abridged or summarized or paraphrased or quoted. Chopping the material and cutting it and piecing the parts together have all been a problem. The cuts and seams – the cobbling marks – may well tell the manner in which the material has been processed and absorbed into the fabric of the text.

I wish to thank the many friends and erstwhile colleagues without whose help the book would have been much more difficult to prepare. I record my gratitude to E.V. Ramakrishnan and Dr. Thankkappan Nair in Calcutta, Principal S. Somasekharan Nair of the Law Academy, Trivandrum, Principal Madhavan Nair of the Sanskrit College, Trivandrum, Dr. Rajan Gurukkal, Professors K.K. Kusuman, P. Vijayakumar, T.P. Sankaran Kutty Nair, Salim Balakrishnan, Ajayakumar, Gopakumar, Dr. A. Ubaid, M.M. Sacheendran andP. Govinda Pillai for making available books and material of crucial importance. Prof. Vishnu Narayanan Nambudiri helped me with his translation into English of two slokas – one on *itihasa* and the other on *purana* – from their Sanskrit original while the late Dr. Bernard Fenn rendered many a term from French and German into English. I owe a deep debt of gratitude to Dr. M.P. Sreekumaran Nair not only for his valuable suggestions but also for reading my account of European historiography in typescript. I would especially like to thank Dr. S. Ramachandran Nair who patiently helped me prepare a list of references to each of the sixteen chapters of the book as also a bibliography and to S. Vinayakumar and K. Gopalakrishnan, Professors of English, who, amidst countless cares, went through the entire thousand-page manuscript correcting it all the way. Again, in providing the information support required for the preparation of this volume and in its computer typesetting the Centre for South Indian Studies rendered all kinds of help which it is difficult to list separately. I am deeply indebted to C. Mukundan, a marine scientist in retirement, whose encompassing interest extended to preparing in free hand drawing a good number of the pictures included in the book. I wish to place on record the invaluable help so ungrudgingly rendered by the staff of the Kerala University Library, the C.D.S. Library and the British Council Library, Trivandrum. Since the help I have received from the academic community cannot be requited in any way, I shall only keep it in grateful remembrance. And, finally, I am deeply indebted to my wife, Sathya, for her cooperation, forbearance and quiet encouragement.

E. SREEDHARAN
August 2003

1

PRELIMINARIES

1. History

The English word 'history' is derived from the Greek word *istoria* meaning inquiry, research, exploration or information. In a broad sense history is a systematic account of the origin and development of humankind, a record of the unique events and movements in its life. It is an attempt to recapture however imperfectly, that which is, in a sense, lost forever.

History is the result of the interplay of man with his environment and with his fellowmen. Man has always expressed himself in terms of certain basic needs such as food, clothing and shelter, social and political organization, knowledge of his environment and transmission of such knowledge, self-expression, and religious and philosophical beliefs. Such activities together make up the universal culture pattern.[1] When men come to share the same institutions and ways of life they may be said to possess the same 'culture'. Fundamental differences between groups are essentially differences in their cultures. Cultures do not remain wholly static or isolated, but change over periods of time and interact with other cultures. Cultures interact both in peace and war. When a people come to have a highly complex cultural pattern resting upon an intricate social organization and exerting wide control over nature, they may be said to have achieved what is called 'civilization'.[2] Civilization in all its varied aspects constitutes the subject matter of history. Such a cultural approach to history would make it a biography of civilization.

History is the living past of man. It is the attempt made by man through centuries to reconstruct, describe and interpret his own past. In modern times, particularly from the period of Niebuhr and Ranke, it has come to mean the attempt to reconstruct the past in "a scholarly fashion, sticking to certain definite rules of establishing fact, interpreting evidence, dealing with source material, etc."[3]

2. Historiography

Historiography literally means the art of writing history. It is the history of history, or the history of historical writings. Historiography tells the story of the successive stages of the evolution or development of historical writings. It has come to include the evolution of the ideas and techniques associated with the writing of history, and the changing attitudes towards the nature of history itself. Ultimately it comprises the study of the development of man's sense for the past.[4]

There have been differences in the nature and quality as well as the quantity of historical literature in the different ages and among different peoples. These differences have generally reflected changes in social life and beliefs and the presence or absence of a sense of history. The spirit that moved the Greek and Roman historians was different from that which inspired the Christian historians of the Middle Ages. The historical writings of the Italian Renaissance, particularly that of Machiavelli, represented a harsh reaction to religious influence in history writing. The reaction reached its climax in the historians of the Enlightenment—Voltaire, Gibbon, Hume and Robertson. The pace of change has been greater ever since as the study of the past has increasingly come under the influence of manifold ideas. Historiography, as a special branch of history, traces these changes through the centuries.

While history proper is the historian's reconstruction of the past, historiography, says Arthur Marwick, is really the history of historical thought—it is not only the theory or practice of history. It began with the early compositions of advanced literate peoples like the Greeks and the Chinese of ancient times when, however, the absence of a system of chronology and method of criticism made the historian's task extremely difficult and uncertain. From those crude beginnings history writing has made tremendous strides towards complex and sophisticated developments in our own times. A unique branch of history, the study of historiography, says Marwick, is of particular value to researchers and professionals, a preliminary to any important historical endeavor, but of only remote concern to the general reader. By holding up models of how history has been written through the centuries, it guides the research scholar and the professional historian.

3. Preconditions of Historiography

Records

History is the historian's reconstruction of the past. The principal materials of reconstruction at the disposal of the historian are records or remains that the past has left behind. They serve him as evidence of the facts that he establishes. The records are of a rich variety—buildings, inscriptions, medals, coins, edicts, chronicles, travelogues, decrees, treaties, official correspondence, private letters and diaries. It is through the study of such history-as-records that the historian gains knowledge of history-as-events. History deals with evidence. Hence the dictum 'No records, no history.'

Critical Method

Because history deals with evidence, the material that the past leaves behind as records has to be used with great care for the simple reason that they may not be wholly authentic or genuine. Far from completely trusting his sources the historian should presume that all data are doubtful unless otherwise proved. There have been instances of spurious documents like the *Donation of Constantine* passing as authentic for centuries. The historian should aim at presenting as true a picture of the past as possible. The technique evolved to arrive at the truth of past events is called historical method. This method is largely analytical, consisting of *external* and *internal* criticism. External criticism or critical scholarship determines the authorship, the place, and the time of a document. Such information is crucial in determining the value of a document. Internal or interpretative or higher criticism finds out whether the contents of a document can be accepted as true or not. External and internal criticism together pronounce the verdict on the authenticity or veracity of facts as presented in the records. From the time of Niebuhr and Ranke, the German historians of the nineteenth century, historical method has been developed to a level where the possibility of error in arriving at the truth of a past event has been brought down to the minimum. Indeed, J.B. Bury in his inaugural lecture at Cambridge declared history to be a science 'no less and no more'. But it is to be admitted that the subjective element in history makes such an ideal impossible to realize.

Historical Sense

A keen sense of the past, i.e., historical sense, has not been uniformly present among the different peoples of the world, and at different times. Ancient Greece and Rome as well as Judaism and Christianity have bequeathed to the European a strong sense of history. Ancient Chinese and medieval Muslim schools of history have been central elements in their civilizations. In comparison, the historical sense of the Hindus of the ancient and medieval times was negligible.

But 'historical sense' means much more. Like history, the other social sciences, whether sociology, anthropology, political science or economics, study man in society and they do deal with the problem of change. But, writes Arthur Marwick,

> the characteristic which marks history out from these other disciplines is a specific concern with the element of change through time...the social scientist looks for the common factors, the regular patterns, discernible in man's activities in society; the historian looks at the way societies differ from each other at different points in time, how through time societies change and develop.[5]

It is his basic concern with change through time that makes it absolutely necessary for the historian to know when exactly the events which he describes took place. To narrate, analyze and interpret events, he must know the order of their occurrence.

2

I. GREEK HISTORIOGRAPHY

1. Historiography of Pre-classical Times

Herbert Butterfield distinguishes mainly three types of compositions in the pre-classical times in the West that may be said to contain historical information of some kind: ballads and epics, annals commemorating rulers, and the Hebrew scriptures.[1]

Ballads and Epics

Amongst animals man alone recollects his past experience and stores it in memory. But a society, unlike an individual, cannot have an organic memory. A primitive society's knowledge of its own past was only through tales told among its members of its own experience. Such tales, when repeated, became the tradition of the tribe and were turned into local ballads. Oral transmission of such ballads over long periods led to alteration of the material by addition of legend matter. Some of the ballads came to be organized into an epic, such as *Gilgamesh* of the ancient Babylonians or *Iliad* of the Greeks. Transmitted through professional storytellers or minstrels, the ballad and the epic, though not history as we define it now, served to stimulate an interest in the past and provided a narrative technique.

Annals of Rulers and Dynastic Lists

Another kind of historical composition in the pre-classical times are the annals produced for the rulers of great empires such as the Egyptian, Hittite and Assyrian. Engraved on the walls of palaces and temples, these annals tell us of the various activities of the monarchs but are chiefly about their military successes. Such annals represented history of the commemorative kind. The Hittite annals were perhaps the most distinguished among them. A more authenticated kind of history are the dynastic lists of the ancient Sumerians and Egyptians. While commemorative records are liable to be exaggerated, dynastic lists are far less liable to be so distorted. In the list of the first Babylonian empire the years would be named after some event—one event for each year. Such 'date-lists' may be reckoned as the ancient forerunner of the medieval chronicle. Again, the handsome and impressive reliefs of the ancient Assyrians provide excellent examples of illustrative history.

Hebrew Scriptures

Like all primitive tribes, the ancient Hebrews had for centuries told tales, sung songs, and related popular legends to their children. In this way, at least from the time of David (c. 1000 BC) there seems to have been a continuous oral tradition in which some clear division can be made between legend and history. This tradition forms the basis of the books of the *Old Testament*, the scripture of the ancient Hebrews. Though not primarily composed for historical purposes, they nevertheless contain an immense amount of historical information. Of the 39 books of the Hebrew scripture, 17 are manifestly historical, and the five major and twelve minor prophets are largely so. The ancient Hebrews were the first to produce anything like a national history, and attempting to describe the history of mankind from what they thought to be the 'Creation', they were also the first to conceive of the idea of universal history.

2. The Quasi-historical Nature of Pre-classical Compositions: Theocratic History and Myth

Can these compositions – the ballads and the epics, the annals and the dynastic lists, and the Hebrew scriptures – be regarded as history? R.G. Collingwood contends that all true history should partake of four characteristics.[2] The first of these is that history is a *science*. Science consists in discovering things which we do not know, for example, the cause of cancer, the chemical composition of the sun, etc. In this sense history is a science, for it begins not with the collection of known facts but with efforts to discover them, e.g., the origin of the parliament in England, or the origin of the caste system in India. The second characteristic of history is that it is *humanistic*. Every science has an object. The object of the science of history is to find out actions of human beings that have been done in the past. The third is that every science has an *inquiry procedure*. History proceeds by the interpretation of evidence in the form of documents. And the fourth characterestic is that every human endeavor has a *purpose* behind it. The purpose of history is human self-knowledge. The value of history is that it teaches us what man has done, and thus what man is. "History is," as Droysen has put it, "Humanity's knowledge of itself."[3]

Collingwood thinks that true history as he defines it did not exist four thousand years ago, say, for example, among the Sumerians. Taking the example of an official inscription of the Sumerians dated c. 2500 BC, he contends that the facts recorded, though in certain ways resemble history, do not constitute history, because the recorded facts lack the character of science as they do not attempt to answer questions. Also, the facts recorded are not about human actions, but those of the gods. The method used is unhistorical, for there is no interpretation of evidence. And lastly, the record cannot be qualified as historical in respect of its use or value, since it is not meant for man's knowledge of man, but man's knowledge of the gods. "The ancient Sumerians," concludes Collingwood, "left behind them nothing at all that we should call history. If they had such a thing as a historical consciousness, they have left no record of it."[4] The facts recorded in the document, he says, might be called *quasi-history,* as they resemble history by making statements about the past. History of this kind is *theocratic history*. There is another kind of quasi-history, namely *myth*, of which too we find examples in Mesopotamian, Egyptian, Chinese and Indian literatures. Myth is not concerned with human actions at all. It is in the nature of theogony, of which the Babylonian *Poem on the Creation* is a good example. Thus viewed, pre-classical compositions like ballads and epics, annals and dynastic lists, and the Hebrew scriptures belong to one of the two types of quasi-history, that is, theocratic history or myth. Collingwood writes that these two types dominated the whole of the Near East until the rise of Greece. The Moabite stone of the ninth century BC, a perfect document of theocratic history, shows that little change had taken place during that long interval.

3. The Difficulty of the Greeks

All historical writing in the West rests on the foundations laid by Herodotus and Thucydides whose works marked the decisive transition from theocratic history and myth to a genuine historical literature. Their achievements stand in great relief against the background of two great constraints with which they began. The first of these was an almost complete ignorance of the history that lay behind them, and the second was an anti-historical metaphysics.

The classical Greeks had behind them – behind Homer – a brilliant civilization which we call Mycenaen. But they had little knowledge of it. Of Greek history since the Trojan War they knew hardly anything and they were astonishingly late in producing any documents at all. The Jewish writer Josephus, in the first century AD, taunted the Greeks for these defects.[5]

Moreover, as Collingwood shows,[6] ancient Greek thought as a whole was uncongenial to the growth of historical thought, for it was based on a rigorously anti-historical metaphysics. History is a science dealing with human actions in the past; human actions in the past belong to a world of change, a world where things come to be and cease to be. Such things, according to the prevalent Greek metaphysical view, ought not to be knowable, and therefore history should be impossible. An object of genuine knowledge must be determinate, permanent and have a character of its own. This *substantialism* was anti-historical. Things which are transient do not have the above qualities. Since human actions in the past belong to a world of change, there cannot be anything of permanent value in them for the mind to grasp. True knowledge must hold good not only here and now, but always and everywhere, and history cannot partake of this character.

4. Influences behind Greek Historiography

A Period of Intellectual Transition

The sixth century BC was an epoch of intellectual transition in Greece. One great development was the growth of prose by the side of poetry, and with this development the Greek mind began to be more reflective and less imaginative. The new intellectual attitude acted as a check on the imaginative treatment found in poetic thought.

Geography and chronology slowly became distinct and the first philosophy and science appeared.

Ionia's Predominance

In this intellectual transition Ionia led the rest of Greece. Ionia was the home of the *Iliad* and it became the home of Greek prose, philosophy and science. There the scientific mentality, already developed, also applied itself to history.

Development of an Ethnographical Literature

Geographically, Ionia was the meeting place of all the eastern Mediterranean civilizations. Greek historical writing developed to a considerable degree out of the attempt to describe and understand neighboring peoples like the Lydians and the imperial Persians. As a result of their overseas trade and travel, especially under the Persian empire, the Ionians developed an ethnographical literature.

Logographers

In trying to know about neighboring peoples, the Greeks recognized the importance of first-hand inquiry, which is the root meaning of history. Writers in this style, known as the 'logographers', produced in simple prose the oral traditions and legends relating to the origin of towns, peoples, princes, temples, etc. Of the logographers, the more important were Hecataeus, Hellanicus, Charon and Dionysius. The logographers mark the transition from myth to history. Their subject was local history, their source of information local myths. Yet they excluded from these myths what was too incredible. Hecataeus omitted in his *Genealogies* stories which he thought to be ridiculous. The narrative compositions of the logographers, in part recited publicly on festive occasions, were designed to give artistic pleasure to the hearers. Narrative history is the oldest species of history, one destined to last, for narration of past events is the unchangeable essence of history. Narration meets the enduring need for preserving the memory of historical events. Logography developed in the fifth century BC into full-fledged history in the works of Herodotus and Thucydides.

Stimulus of Wars

Wars have always acted as a stimulus to history writing. Hecataeus and Herodotus were stirred by the Graeco-Persian conflicts (499–479 BC), and later, in the same century, Thucydides was moved by the Peloponnesian war (431–404 BC). War, down to our own times, has been a stimulus to the writing of history.

5. Herodotus (c. 484–430 BC)

The historical genius of Herodotus and Thucydides triumphed over two apparently insurmountable difficulties, namely, the absence of records, and an anti-historical philosophy which held history to be a hopeless endeavor.

Herodotus was born in an exalted family in Halicarnassus about 484 BC. His uncle's adventures earned him an exile at the age of thirty-two. The future historian profitably spent his undeserved exile in far-reaching travels. These took him to Phoenicia, Egypt, Cyrene, Susa, and finally to the Greek city-states on the Black Sea. Writes Will Durant:

> Wherever he went he observed and inquired with the eye of a scientist and the curiosity of a child; and when in 447, he settled down in Athens, he was armed with a rich assortment of notes concerning the geography, history, and manners of the Mediterranean states. With these notes and a little plagiarizing of Hecataeus and other predecessors, he composed the most famous of all historical works, recording the life and history of Egypt, the Near East and Greece from their legendary origins to the close of the Persian war.[7]

Theme and Content

The man known as the 'Father of History' announces in his introduction that the purpose of his *Histories* was to preserve for future generations the great deeds of the Greeks and the Barbarians (Persians), and lay bare the causes for which they waged war. Written in nine parts, each of which is dedicated to one of the nine muses, the work has for its main theme the Graeco-Persian conflict which comes to its epic end at Salamis in 480 BC. But Herodotus also brought into his narrative interesting descriptions of the customs, dress, manners, morals and beliefs of some twenty-four different peoples of the eastern Mediterranean. The immense framework of the book makes it, in a limited sense, a universal history.

Method

Herodotus's method was to write of far-off events reported to him at second or third hand. With curiosity and keen powers of observation he tried to know how things happened. He looked for rational explanations, showing the influence of climate and geographical factors. But he was liable to impute important events to trivial incidental causes, the influence of women, and purely personal factors. His belief in supernatural influences led him to introduce into his narrative dreams, oracles, visions and divine warnings of approaching evil. His childlike curiosity sometimes led to childlike credulity. Indeed, Strabo wrote that there was "much non-sense in Herodotus."[8] He thought that—the semen of Ethiopians was black; Egyptian cats jumped into fire; Danubians got drunk on mere smells; the priestess of Athena at Pedasus grew a mighty beard; Nebuchadnezzar was a woman; and that the Alps were a river! But he wrote in self-defence, "I am under obligation to tell what is reported, but I am not obliged to believe it; and let this hold for every narrative in this history."[9]

Style

Herodotus is patriotic in the treatment of fellow Greeks but he justly gives both sides of most political disputes and testifies to the heroism, honour and chivalry of the Persians. The father of history is also the father of prose composition and, as a narrator, he has never been surpassed. He wrote in a style which was at once loose, easygoing, romantic and fascinating, satisfying men's need for entertainment, for marvellous stories. And writing in terms of personalities rather than processes, he presented excellent portrayals of character.

Assessment

Whatever his faults, Herodotus was the first to have sought a perspective of man in time. Cicero called him the 'Father of History', and Lucian, like most of the ancients, ranked him above

Thucydides.[10] Shotwell describes him as the 'Homer of the Persian Wars'. H.E. Barnes looks upon him as "the first writer to imply that the task of the historian is to reconstruct the whole past life of man and was one of the most absorbing story-tellers in the entire course of historical writing."[11]

Collingwood credits Herodotus with the creation of scientific history. He puts Herodotus to all the four tests of modern historiography and finds him wanting only in not basing his narrative on rational evidence and interpretation. It was Herodotus who created real history. By skilful questioning he made it possible to obtain scientific knowledge of past human actions which had been thought to be impossible. "It is the use of this word ('history'), and its implications, that make Herodotus the father of history. The conversion of legend-writing into the science of history...was a fifth century invention, and Herodotus was the man who invented it."[12]

6. Thucydides (c. 460–396 BC)

Born to an Athenian father and Thracian mother, Thucydides received all the education that Athens could give. In 430 BC he suffered from the plague but death spared him for history. When the Peloponnesian war broke out, he kept a record of it from day to day. In 424 BC he was chosen as one of the two generals to command a naval expedition to Thrace, but a military failure earned him an exile from Athens. This misfortune proved fortunate for history, for Thucydides spent the next twenty years of his life in travel especially in the Peloponnessus. The oligarchic revolution of 404 BC ended his exile, and he returned to Athens. He died – some say by murder – about 396 BC leaving unfinished his *History of the Peloponnesian War.*

Theme and Content

As a young man Thucydides had heard Herodotus's public readings of his *History of the Persian Wars* in Athens. Unlike Herodotus who ranged from age to age and place to place, Thucydides confined himself to the narrower scope of the Peloponnesian war, forcing his story into a rigid chronological framework of seasons—the 'summer and winter' system. The *History of the Peloponnesian War* comprises eight books, the eighth book ending abruptly in the middle of a campaign in 411 BC. Thucydides wrote to furnish information for future historians and guidance for future statesmanship. He wrote for "those inquirers who desire an exact knowledge of the past as an aid to the interpretation of the future which, in the course of human affairs, must resemble the past."[13] The honest and severe Thucydides meant his work "not as an essay which is to win the applause of the moment, but as a possession for all time."[14] Since in his view human nature and human behavior would be forever the same, he held that similar situations and problems recur, so lessons of one period would be useful in another.

Method

The aim of writing an accurate and trustworthy account called for a rigid method. Unlike the credulous Herodotus, Thucydides subjected his sources to a rigorously scientific methodology and proceeded upon the clearest data. Believing that the historical process was a rational process uninfluenced by supernatural or extra-human agencies, he refused to trust the oracles and ran full tilt at myths and legends, marvels and miracles. He wrote as an eyewitness of most of the events of the war which he described. Herodotus may be the father of history, but Thucydides's conscientious accuracy and truthfulness make him "the father of scientific method in history".[15] And though recognizing the role of exceptional individuals in history, Thucydides leaned rather towards impersonal recording, and the consideration of causes, developments and results. Yet he compromised with truth and accuracy when he put elegant speeches – and this quite often – into the mouths of his characters. It was a means of explaining and vivifying personalities, ideas and events. Thucydides frankly admits that such orations are largely imaginary, but he claims that each speech represents the substance of an address actually given at the time.

Style

Thucydides's impressive impartiality is an example to future historians. He recounts the story of Athens and Sparta of his time with fairness to both sides. His desire to impart exact knowledge of the past conditioned his language and style as his scientific method and devotion to truth would not permit romance and exaggeration. However, this style is terse and vivid, sometimes rising to a dramatic power. Intending his *History* as a guide of conduct particularly useful to men in power and authority, Thucydides illumined his pages with many moral maxims. Some of these inform us that nemesis follows upon good fortune; that love often lures men to destruction; and that might does not make right.

Assessment

The strictly rational basis of Thucydides's historical thinking had important consequences for modern historical thought. The analytical depth which this ancient Athenian historian brought to historiography had an abiding influence. He wished to know not merely the *what* but the *how* and *why* of the historical process, while Herodotus had confined in the main to the first of these inquiries. Thucydides wanted to probe deeper, discover the motives and explain the processes behind human action. Influenced by the science of the time, he tried to apply the principles and methods of Hippocratic medicine to politics, so that everything could be covered by rational explanation. Analytical power enabled him to separate the deeper causes from the immediate occasion of an event and to proceed to general conclusions, as for instance when he analysed the relationship between wealth and power, or the remorseless logic behind Athenian imperialism. To Thucydides history is an organic process; it is the study of events that are connected with one another in a rational, systematic and permanent order. The belief reminds us of what in the twentieth century would be labeled *historicism.* Again, he was the first to employ what modern historical methodology calls *constructive reasoning.* When positive sources of information failed, Thucydides applied Anaxagoras's method of inverse reasoning, i.e., arguing backwards in a regressive fashion from the known to the unknown to locate the probable cause or causes of an event.

J.B. Bury rates Thucydides's work as the most decisive step taken by a single man towards making history what it is today. To David Hume the first page of Thucydides was the beginning of all true history. But Will Durant finds fault with him for his absorption in war to the exclusion of culture. Yet he concludes:

> Here at least is an historical method, a reverence for truth, an acuteness of observation, an impartiality of judgement, a

passing splendour of language and fascination of style, a mind both sharp and profound, whose truthless realism is a tonic to our naturally romantic souls. Here are no legends, no myths, and no miracles.[16]

Collingwood compares the two great Greek pioneer historians. Three of the four characteristics of genuine history which we see in Herodotus reappear in the preface of Thucydides; but the latter definitely steals a march over the father of history by explicitly stating that *history bases all its conclusions on rational evidence.* But the greatness of Herodotus, Collingwood affirms, stands out in the sharpest relief when he is set against the anti-historical substantialistic tendency of Greek thought which held that only what is unchanging can be an object of true knowledge. The genius of Herodotus triumphed over this substantialistic tendency by showing that, by skilful questioning, it was possible to attain dependable knowledge of past human actions. The British philosopher-critic goes on to show that there is a difference between the scientific attitudes of the two fifth-century giants, a difference reflected even in their styles. The "easy, spontaneous, and convincing" style of Herodotus gives way to the "harsh, artificial, and repellent" style of Thucydides. The latter style, Collingwood attributes, to a "bad conscience."[17] The dominant influence on Thucydides was that of Hippocratic medicine. Hippocrates was not only the father of medicine, he was also the father of psychology and Thucydides, his spiritual child, is the father of psychological history. Now, Collingwood affirms, psychological history is not history at all, but natural science of a special kind. The chief function of history is to narrate events and facts of the past, but the chief purpose of psychological history is to affirm psychological laws. A psychological law is not an event, nor even a complex of events—it is an unchanging rule which governs the relation between events. Herodotus was primarily interested in the events themselves; Thucydides was more interested in the laws according to which they happen, laws which are eternal and unchanging.[18] Collingwood cites as evidence for such a conclusion the speeches that Thucydides puts into the mouths of his characters. He asks: "Is it not historically speaking, an outrage to make all these very different characters talk in one and the same fashion...?"[19] The style betrays a lack of interest in the question what those different characters actually said on particular occasions.

The speeches themselves are imaginary – they are Thucydidean reconstructions of the speakers' motives and intentions – a bad convention for a historian to establish.

7. Greek Historical Method and its Limitations[20]

To Herodotus and Thucydides historical sources meant the reports of facts given by eyewitnesses, and historical method consisted in eliciting these narratives. The two historians must have thoroughly cross-questioned the witnesses, as in a court of law, for the ascertainment of the facts. Collingwood attests that this method of using the testimony of eyewitness accounts for the extraordinary solidity and consistency of the narratives of Herodotus and Thucyides. But he points out that this method, the only available one then, had three limitations. 1. It imposed on its users a *shortness of perspective.* Eyewitness accounts could not go beyond living memory. The method tied its users on a tether whose length was the length of living memory. For this reason what Herodotus or Thucydides tell us of things beyond living memory – say, about the sixth century BC – cannot be relied upon as scientific, because their sources and method could not reach remote periods of the past. But this was not a failure. The significant achievement of fifth century Greek historiography was to have definitely brought the recent past, if not the remote past, within the scope of scientific history. Scientific history had been invented. 2. The second limitation in the method was that *it precluded the historian from choosing his subject.* The only things he could write about were the events which had happened within living memory. The comic irony of the situation is well brought out by Collingwood when he says that "instead of the historian choosing his subject, the subject chooses the historian...."[21] The historian was not a historian in the true sense of the term; he was "only the autobiographer of his generation."[22] 3. The ancient Greek historical method made it *impossible to criticize, improve upon, or rewrite a history once written.* If any given history is the autobiography of a generation, the evidence on which it is based will have perished. It is impossible also for such a work to be absorbed into a larger whole, "because it is like a work of art, something having the uniqueness and individuality of a statue or a poem."[23] An ancient Greek historical work could only be complete in itself, incapable of being incorporated into a larger whole, say, a universal history.

8. Greek Conception of the Nature of History and its Value[24]

Sensitivity

Collingwood observes that there was in the Greek attitude towards life and knowledge an important pro-historical element which qualified the anti-historical tendency of Greek metaphysics. The Greeks lived at a time when history was moving with extraordinary rapidity and in a country where earthquakes and erosion changed the face of the land with unusual violence. These spectacles of incessant change gave to Greek thought "a peculiar sensitiveness to history".[25] The Greeks knew that it must have been such changes in the past that had brought the present into existence. Though Greek thought was engaged in the pursuit of the eternal, it had a vivid sense of the temporal.

Cyclic View

The ancient Greeks further thought that changes in human life – in history – itself followed a certain rhythm. Herbert Butterfield writes that they conceived of history as involving great progress upto a certain point and then decline or collapse. They thought that there must have been many such swings up and down, so that civilization repeatedly had to start over again and again almost from the beginning. For this reason Greek philosophy easily ran to a cyclic view of history. The cyclic view is 'anti-historical' as it held that history somewhat repeated itself. The Greeks lacked the Jewish feeling that the whole creation is moving to some great end, as well as the modern feeling that time itself is generative of progress.[26]

Pragmatic and Humanistic View

From the cyclic view, perhaps, the ancient Greeks conceived their pragmatic value of history. In the pragmatic view history is a repository of instances or lessons which are likely to be useful in the present and the future because history sufficiently repeated itself. Anything that repeats can be roughly foreseen (e.g., a tragedy) and guarded against. For this reason, historical knowledge, though only empirical semi-knowledge or 'opinion' not comparable to scientific knowledge, had, for the Greeks, a definite value for human life. History of notable events would serve as a basis for prognostic judgements, not demonstrable as in science, but probable, laying down not what will happen but what is likely to happen.[27]

Such a conception of history, affirms Collingwood, is not deterministic but humanistic—the Greeks regarded the course of history as flexible and open to salutary modification by the well-instructed human will. Nothing that happens is inevitable. The Greeks had a lively and indeed a naïve sense of the power of man to control his own destiny, and thought of this power as limited only by the limitation of his knowledge. This view of man as capable of moulding his own destiny is humanistic, not deterministic.[28]

II. HISTORIOGRAPHY IN THE HELLENISTIC PERIOD

1. Influences behind Hellenistic Historiography

The Hellenistic period in history roughly covers the two hundred years between the conquests of Alexander and the Roman conquest of Egypt. Collingwood attests that during this period Greek historiography overcame three of its limitations.[29]

The first of these was that the Greeks slowly shed their *cultural particularism*, i.e., the parochial outlook based on the linguistic and cultural distinction between the Greek and the Barbarian. Greek culture spread over the empire Alexander's arms had won, and many cities like Alexandria, Pergamum, Antioch and Rhodes became great centres of Greek civilization. It was found that the Barbarians could become Greeks by learning the Greek language and adopting Greek manners and customs. Alexander and ten thousand of his soldiers took Asiatic wives; thirty thousand Persian boys were to be taught the Greek language and Macedonian military tactics. The Greeks, too, took to some Asiatic ways, the conqueror himself setting the pace in adopting oriental dress, customs and manners. The contact of the Greeks with the non-Greeks in the Hellenistic period resulted in cultural fusion.

The second was that through the conquests of Alexander, the Greeks shed their *city-state particularism.* Greek thought had, with Alexander's phalanxes, set out to conquer the world. The 'world' became something more than a geographical expression; it became a historical expression as well. The whole empire of Alexander – from the Adriatic to the Indus and from the Danube to the Sahara – now shared a single history, that of the Greek world. The idea of the whole world as a single historical unit, says Collingwood, is a typically Stoic idea, and Stoicism was a typical product of the Hellenistic period. Greek historical consciousness reflected the above changes. The old conception of history as the history of one particular social unit or city at a particular time changed and developed into a world view with a corresponding amplification in time. It was Hellenism, affirms Collingwood, that created the idea of oecumenical or universal history.

The third limitation that Greek historiography overcame in the Hellenistic period was in the matter of *method.* A world history could not be written on the strength of testimony of eyewitnesses, dictated by the limits of human memory. A new method was sought, namely, *compilation,* for which materials were to be drawn from 'authorities', i.e., from previous historians who had already written histories of particular societies at particular times. Collingwood calls this the "scissors-and-paste"[30] historical method which as a method is indeed far inferior to the fifth century Socratic method of cross-questioning eyewitness data. It now became possible to write a new kind of history of any size, if the historian could collect materials and weld the information into a unified history. This new kind of history is fully demonstrated in Polybius.

2. Polybius (c. 208–126 BC)

Polybius was the greatest of the Hellenistic historians, and the only Greek fit to make a triad with Herodotus and Thucydides.[31] His immense *Histories* is the story of the expansion of Rome to a world power.

Theme and Content

Like all historians, Polybius has a story to tell. The period between 219 and 167 BC saw great changes in the Mediterranean world when Rome conquered and brought that world under its sway. Polybius ascribed this spreading power of Rome to Roman character, "the natural result of discipline gained in the stern school of difficulty and danger...."[32] He conceived his work on a grand scale and proposed to tell the story of the whole Mediterranean world from 221 to 146 BC which in effect covered the period of the expansion and constitutional development of Rome. Since Rome had become the centre of political history then, he gave his book unity by making Rome the focus of its events. Of the forty books into which Polybius divided his *Histories*, five have been preserved, and substantial fragments of the rest have been rescued. The language is degenerate Greek and the style so dull and lacking in literary taste that "No one," said Dionysius of Halicarnassus, "ever read him (Polybius) through."[33]

Qualifications

Not many could have written history from a more varied and rich background of education, travel and experience than Polybius. He insists that history should be written by those who have seen – or have directly consulted others who have seen – the events to be described. The historian should be a man of affairs, versed in statesmanship, politics and war; otherwise, he will never understand the behavior of states or the course of history. The historian should have geographical knowledge, and Polybius speaks with pride of his own travels in search of data, documents and geographical veracity. Personal investigation, he stresses, is the very cornerstone of history. Our historian himself gathered data from the study of inscriptions and documents. Trying to make his history as accurate as possible he subjected his sources to critical examination and quoted texts of several documents.

Causal Element

Polybius elaborates the causal element in history to great lengths. A "bare statement of an occurrence," he says, "is interesting indeed, but not instructive; but when this is supplemented by a statement of cause, the study of history becomes fruitful."[34] He distinguishes between the historical causes of wars and their occasions or pretexts. Cause, in general, he argues, has nothing mysterious and divine about it. Cause is natural and should be studied in a positive manner. Though he subscribes to the Stoic theology of a divine providence, he is too much of a realist and rationalist to give credence to stories of supernatural intervention. Yet he does not exclude the fortuitous in human affairs, but regards chance or the operation of the unexpected as part of the very constitution of history.[35] Although he recognizes the occasional efficacy of great men, in general he resolved to lay bare the factual and impersonal chain of cause and effect. Polybius's discussion of the guiding principles of history writing is worthy of the greatest theorists of history.

How to Study History

Polybius thought that the best method of studying history is that which sees the life of a nation as an organic unity and weaves the story of each part into the life history of the whole. He felt that studying isolated histories is like looking at the dissevered limbs of a dead animal.[36] A comprehensive account of human development can be obtained only from the study of universal history.

Cyclic Succession and the Mixed Constitution

Though not the originator of the idea of cyclic succession in history or that of a mixed constitution, Polybius was inclined to view political history as a repetitious cycle of monarchy, aristocracy and democracy, with their corresponding corrupt forms of despotism, oligarchy and mob rule. The best escape from this cycle seemed to this admirer of Roman institutions to be through a 'mixed' constitution like that of Lycurgus or Rome. Polybius saw in the Roman constitution the great virtue of a simultaneous expression of the monarchical, aristocratic and democratic elements of government. It was from this point of view that he wrote the record of his times.

History as Educator

By insisting that history should be written by men of affairs versed in the actual processes of war and government, Polybius was only stressing the didactic and pragmatic character and value of the subject. Like Dionysius of Halicarnassus, he reiterates that history is philosophy teaching by example. The subject is described as a lantern of understanding held up to the present and the future, a subject which alone will mature our judgement and prepare us to take right views. "There is no more ready corrective of conduct than knowledge of the past," and "the soundest education and training for a life of active politics is the study of history." [37]

Assessment

Polybius is 'the historians' historian'. Here is how Will Durant in the twentieth century estimates that historian of the second century BC:

> ...historians will long continue to study him (Polybius) because he was one of the greatest theorists and practitioners of historiography; because he dared to take a wide view and write a 'universal history'; and because, above all, he understood that mere facts are worthless except through their interpretation, and that the past has no value except as our roots and illumination.[38]

Collingwood sees in the conquest of the Mediterranean world by Rome and Polybius's treatment of it, important consequences for historiography.[39] It is to the ancient Romans, says he, that we owe the conception of history both as oecumenical and national—the unification of the world under the leadership of a people moved by a corporate spirit. Polybius begins his story at a point more than 150 years before the time of writing. With this larger conception of the field of history comes a more precise conception of history itself. Polybius uses the word *istoria* not in its original sense meaning any kind of inquiry but *in its modern sense of history*: it is now conceived as a special type of research needing a special name of its own. He advances the claim of this new science to universal study for its own sake, and thinks of himself as the first person to conceive of history as a form of thought having universal value. But the way he expresses this value is in consonance with the anti-historical substantialistic tendency of the Greeks. The value of history is not theoretical or scientific, but practical. History for Polybius is worth studying not because it is scientifically true but because it is a school and training ground for political life. It is only the study of history that equips men to take right views without involving them in actual danger; yet Polybius did not think that such study would enable men to avoid the mistakes of their predecessors and surpass them in worldly success. The study of history can lead to an inner success, a victory not over circumstances but over the self. What we learn from the tragedies of history's heroes is not to avoid such tragedies in our own lives, but to bear them bravely when fortune brings them. The idea of fortune bulks large in this conception of history and imports into it a new element of determinism. Fate is the master of man.

III. ROMAN HISTORIOGRAPHY

The early Romans had a somewhat special feeling of piety towards the past promoted by traditional devotion of the aristocratic families to their ancestors. Their early records were annalistic in form and flavored by religious and superstitious practices. Also, the Romans were more practical than the Greeks and their genius was more adapted to history than to philosophy. Yet, Roman historiography owed its origin to Greek influence.

1 (a). Cato (234–149 BC)

The *Origines* of Cato the Elder or Cato the Censor revolutionized Roman historiography. The work, written in seven books and carried down to the last year of the author's life (149 BC), is lost for the most part. J.W. Thompson writes that judging from what has come down to us, the *Origines* must have been one of the most instructive and interesting histories ever written, a work whose loss is a literary calamity.[40] In his introduction, Cato discusses the nature and value of education and the place of history in that education. He was profoundly convinced of the didactic purpose of history as inculcating patriotism, teaching morals, and shaping the character of the young. Accordingly the *Origines* abounded in moral reflections and wise sayings so much that the *Distichs* of Cato, a series of pungent quotations from his writings, was widely circulated after his death. Cato's work contained a vast amount of information of an ethnographic, topographic and economic nature. Books III and IV are remarkable surveys of the tribes of Italy dealing with anthropology, geography, custom and law, language, institutions, religion, culture and civilization. Thompson notes another peculiarity of the *Origines* as absolutely characteristic of

Cato. A downright plebeian, he held that Rome's battles were won by common soldiers and that it was unjust to give the glory to the generals. In an age redolent with the deeds of great men, Cato, throughout his entire work, does not mention any man by name. The one proper name that occurs in the *Origines* is that of an elephant in the Roman army, named Surus, who behaved so valiantly in battle against the Carthaginians that Cato condescended to mention him!

1 (b). The Historical Memoir

The Latin historical memoir appeared during the last century of the Roman republic. This genre of history had as its motive political vindication, the writers, mostly soldiers and statesmen, seeking to defend their policies.

Sempronius Asellio wrote his fourteen books in the time of Sulla, between 90 and 80 BC. Asellio wanted to know the *how* and *why* of events as well as their results. But he too adhered to the tradition that history should inculcate morals and teach patriotism. Sulla wrote his memoir in twenty books, all of which are lost. Plutarch in the second century AD used Sulla's books. Cornelius Sisenna wrote a memoir in twenty-three books which in effect was a history of the Social war (90–88 BC) and the Civil war between Sulla and Marius. Two brilliant memoir writers – nay, historians – were Sallust and Julius Caesar. Sallust's (86–34 BC) two remarkable works are *Conspiracy of Catiline* and *The Jugurthine War*. While the first is a partisan pamphlet, the second, according to J.W. Thompson, is matchless history. Caius Julius Caesar's (100 BC) *Commentaries on the Gallic War* in seven books, and *Commentaries on the Civil War* in three books are political propaganda designed to influence public opinion in his favor. Thompson warns the reader against being deceived by Caesar's apparent truthfulness.

2. Livy (59 BC–AD 17)

With Octavian's victory at Actium in 31 BC the temple of Janus was closed. Virgil began the composition of the *Aeneid* in 29 BC; and in the same year, Titus Livy began to write his *History of Rome.* Both the poet and the historian were inspired by a conviction of the greatness and grandeur of Rome, and both believed that a new and golden age had dawned.

Theme and Content

"Rome's historian," says Taine, "has no history."[41] Livy was born in Padua, came to Rome, devoted himself to rhetoric and philosophy, and gave the last forty-six years of his life to the writing of the great history. The *History of Rome* was planned and completed on a majestic scale. But of the 142 books, only thirty-five survive; as these fill six volumes, we may judge the magnitude of the whole. Indeed, its colossal dimension made it impossible for libraries to possess it.

Livy traced Rome's history from the city's foundation to his own times (753 BC–AD 9). What Livy wrote was, in effect, a history of the city of Rome, or, at most, of Italy. Its contents are in the main the Punic, the Social, and the Civil wars. There are only brief references to the Roman constitution, financial questions and economic conditions. Roman literature finds no mention at all. Livy, like all Roman historians, set before him a moral purpose. History, he believed, should inculcate morals, teach civic virtues, and promote patriotism. In an eloquent preface he deplores the immorality, luxury and effeminacy of the age. He would set forth through history the virtues that had made Rome great. "Polybius," comments Will Durant, "had ascribed Rome's triumph to its form of government; Livy would make it a corollary of the Roman character."[42] No wonder, Augustus forgave the book's republican sentiments and heroes, for its religious and moral tone accorded well with the emperor's policies. He took Livy into friendship and encouraged him as a prose Virgil.[43]

Method

For his sources, Livy must have had all the Roman historians before him. Polybius he paraphrases for pages, not always giving credit. For the period 753 to 391 BC there were no documents but only legends which, he says, are difficult to distinguish from history. He tries to escape the difficulty by writing frequently: "I neither affirm nor deny"; "I hesitate..."; and "It is not the price of labour to investigate."[44] So great is his respect for religion that he accepts any superstition and fills his pages with omens, portents and oracles.

He rarely consults original documents or monuments; he is no critical or scientific scholar who would probe, synthesize or organize his material in any systematic way. There is no inquiry into conditions, causes and processes. Livy's *History* is an eloquent literary panorama of historical personages and episodes. Added to these defects of method and approach are his patriotic and patrician prejudices which could often distort the narrative in favour of Rome and her aristocratic class.

Style

Livy's historical epic was a masterpiece of Augustan prose. His readers did not look for critical history and forgot all his inaccuracies and bias. They remembered only his story and the style, "the vigour of his characterisations, the brilliance and power of his descriptions, the majestic march of his prose."[45] Through the centuries it has continued to invite readers, and shaped their conception of Rome's history and character.

Assessment

Collingwood notes that while Polybius had depended on the 'scissors and paste' method only for the introductory phases of his work, the immensity of the *History of Rome* forced Livy to construct the whole body of his work by that method. Livy is clear that history is humanistic and that the historian's task is to paint the actions of men. He makes no claims to original research or original method, but says Collingwood, the Roman historian, like Herodotus, has been wrongly charged with the grossest credulity. He tries to be critical but methodical criticism had not been invented. Fables he repeated with a caution but when he comes to the foundation of Rome he accepts the tradition as he found it. What is outstanding in Livy is the literary quality which none has denied these 1900 years.

Censorship

Irritated by the republican sentiments of the historians and other writers, Emperor Augustus clamped down a censorship. The suppression, begun in 31 BC, lasted long after Augustus's death—till AD 96. Writes J.W. Thompson:

All kinds of literature suffered in this sharp transition from indulgence to severity, but history the most; for history dealt with politics and the emperors. Accordingly all history had to be written with prudence and much of it had to be written with flattery.[46]

A Roman History, by Velleius Paterculus extending down to AD 30, thus flattered the powers that be. The abrupt end of the work may have been due to the execution of its author. Tacitus disdained and scorned such measures.

3. Tacitus (c. AD 55–120)

Cornelius Tacitus, the greatest name in Roman historiography, was born about AD 55 and died about AD 120. An aristocrat by birth, character and education, he was trained in oratory and destined for the law—particulars which powerfully influenced the character of his work and method of exposition. He was a man of affairs who served the Roman government in various capacities.

Works

We must pass over the lesser works of Tacitus like the *Dialogues on Orators, Agricola* and *de Germania* and come to the two great ones—the *Histories* and the *Annals.* The *Histories,* which was the first to appear, is an account of the Roman emperors from Galba to the death of Domitian (AD 68 to 96). It is a history of the Flavian dynasty. Of the original fourteen or probably twelve 'books' of the *Histories,* only four and a half remain. The *Annals* carry the story further back and record the history of the emperors of the Julian house: Tiberius, Caligula, Claudius and Nero (AD 14–68). Of an original sixteen or eighteen of the *Annals*, twelve books survive.

Sources and Method

Tacitus's sources consisted of other histories, speeches, letters, *Acta Diurna, Acta Senatus* and the traditions of old families. These sources he often cites, and sometimes critically examines. He is cautiously ambiguous on matters of faith and he rejects most astrologers, auguries, portents and miracles though he is not above accepting some of them. Again, as in the case of Livy, Tacitus's moral purpose obscures much historical truth. Inimical to historical veracity, too, is his method of exposition. Comparable to that of an orator in the Roman courts, this method often turns the narrative into direct discourse putting the historian's own words into the mouths of interlocutors. The history that Tacitus wrote is to be read with extreme caution.

Theme and Content

Tacitus held a rather moral view of the function of history. The chief duty of the historian, according to him, is to judge the actions of men, preserve from oblivion the deeds of good men, and hold up evil men for posterity's condemnation. To him the Roman emperors whom he indicted were all evil men. Here is Durant's eloquent comment:

> It is a strange conception which turns history into a Last Judgement and the historian into a God. So conceived, history is a sermon – ethics teaching by horrible examples – and falls, as Tacitus assumed, under the rubric of rhetoric. It is easy for indignation to be eloquent but hard for it to be fair; no moralist should write history.[47]

Tacitus's moral indignation results in two defects—narrowness of scope and partiality. The surviving books of the *Histories* and the *Annals* would make the reader wonder whether Tacitus wrote the history of the Roman empire or the city of Rome. Tacitus's narrowness of view accounts for his failure to produce the larger history of the empire and of imperial policy, and the inability to perceive the excellent administration and growing prosperity of the provinces under the imperial monsters whom he indicts. He has no idea of economic influences upon political events, no interest in the life and industry of the people, the flow of trade, the condition of science, the status of women, the vicissitudes of belief, the achievements of poetry, philosophy or art. Apart from striking personalities and events; forces, causes, ideas and processes have no place in his narrative.[48]

Equally grievous is Tacitus's pronounced partiality. Flagrantly biased in favour of the senatorial opposition, his primary interest is to indict the emperors. Butterfield informs us:

> In his bitterness, he (Tacitus) painted some of these emperors as worse than modern scholars would regard them, worse than

would be suggested by the facts that he himself adduced; and sometimes where he recognized their good deeds he connected even these with malignant motives.[49]

J.W. Thompson writes that modern scholarship has vindicated the emperors Tiberius and Claudius whom Tacitus has pictured as human monsters.

Style

But with all such faults as a historian, few writers are more worth reading than Tacitus. There is nothing in all historical literature to compare with the clear living portraits that he paints. Few could match the splendor of his style, at once pithy, epigrammatic and ironic. This splendour of style is wedded to an abundance of ideas. No Roman author except Horace is so eminently quotable as Tacitus. Here are some examples:

> In war every commander claims the credit of victory, but none admits the blame for defeat.
>
> No hatred is so bitter as that of near relations.
>
> The more corrupt the state, the more numerous the laws.
>
> Tyrants merely procure infamy for themselves and glory for their victims.[50]

Assessment

J.W. Thompson writes:

> A masterly analytic power, especially of psychology and character, combined with irony of superlative degree and a trenchant style made Tacitus what he is: one to be read as a great writer—Macaulay for example—is yet read, as a literary genius, but not as an historian. As to historical fidelity Tacitus must be read with infinite caution.[51]

Collingwood observes that all of Tacitus's defects as a historian flowed from taking over the current pragmatic view of the purpose of history.[52] Tacitus was a rhetorician and not a serious thinker who would think out philosophically the fundamental problem of his enterprise. This defect led him to distort history systematically by representing it as essentially a clash of characters, the exaggeratedly good with the exaggeratedly bad. They are spectacles of virtue or vice. Nor can Tacitus be praised, says Collingwood, for character-drawing as is often done. This is because the principle on which he draws character is fundamentally vicious; the way he draws character is an outrage on historical truth. The Stoic and Epicurean philosophies make him believe the actions of a historical figure as originating only from his personal character; he forgets that a man's action may be determined partly by his environment, and only in part by his character. Tacitus's psychological-didactic approach, instead of being an enrichment of historical method was really an impoverishment, and indicated a declining standard of historical honesty. "As a contributor to historical literature," Collingwood concludes, "Tacitus is a gigantic figure; but it is permissible to wonder whether he was an historian at all."[53] "Livy and Tacitus," observes the same critic, "stand side by side as the two great monuments to the barrenness of Roman historical thought."[54]

4. Graeco-Roman Historians after Tacitus

After Tacitus there was a marked decline in Greek and Roman historiography first typified by Suetonius. Appian (c. AD 116–170), a contemporary of Plutarch and a Greek native of Alexandria, wrote the voluminous *Roman History* in twenty books, covering the history of the Roman republic and the empire down to his own times. Half the work has perished. Appian's method consisted in grouping events by nations so that his *Roman History* is a series of separate monographs. J.W. Thompson notes that Appian is indifferent to chronology, gives no indication of his sources and lacks critical ability. Yet, writes that critic, Appian's work has great value in that it enables us to check other historians of the same events, and particularly to know the administration, law and institutions of Rome.

Fronto (c. AD 100–170), the author of *De bello Parthico* and *Principia Historiae*, was a native of Africa. The most valuable of his writings are his *Letters* written to Antoninus Pius and Marcus Aurelius. Flavio Arrian (c. AD 95–175), like Plutarch and Appian, was a Romanized Greek. In AD 126 he had the good fortune to meet the Emperor Hadrian who was so impressed with him that he persuaded the historian to enter the government service. Arrian wrote many works all of which except his masterpiece, *Anabasis of Alexander the Great*, have been lost. To Thompson

> Arrian's work is distinguished for sedulous regard for truth, critical handling of materials, wide geographical knowledge, understanding of military technique and administrative questions, besides a sympathetic appreciation of his subject. The account of the last days and death of Alexander the Great was one of the moving descriptions of history.[55]

The *Roman History* of Dio Cassius (c. AD 155–235) originally consisted of eighty books and covered the whole field of Rome's history down to AD 235. But many books are lost, though summaries of some have been made. We have Dio's own work for the period only from 69 BC to AD 53, i.e., from Pompey to Claudius. Thompson observes that Dio largely follows the other Roman historians in his rhetoric, moralizing and biographical methods. Anecdotes abound and epigrammatic sayings are quoted. One such is Augustus's famous boast: 'I found Rome of clay, I leave it to you of marble.' Errors are numerous one of which makes the Nile rise in Mount Atlas! Aurelius Victor (c. AD 325) was the author of *Caesars* and the *Epitome*. Eutropius's *History of Rome* in ten parts had many qualities which made it a favourite book even in the Middle Ages. Another historian of merit was Ammianus Marcellinus (c. AD 330–401). Of his *Roman History*, only Books 14–31, covering the years AD 352–378, are extant. A man of intellectual honesty, Ammianus made careful and complete use of his sources. Giving information of various kinds, it is as a historian of culture that he is most valuable. Like all Roman historians he was a moralist exalting the old-fashioned virtues and denouncing current vices. With Ammianus, Latin and pagan historiography came to an end. "The libraries were closed for ever," wrote Ammianus.

Universal History

If the concept of universal history had its origin in the enormous conquests of Alexander, it became an established form of historiography in the first century BC. It was the combined result of Rome's world empire and the influence of the Stoic idea of the brotherhood of man. Trogus Pompeius, a contemporary of Livy, attempted to write a universal history, the *Historiae Philippicae*, in forty-four books. Symbolizing the concept of universal history cherished by the Stoics, Pompeius declared that the inhabitants of the Roman empire were all one people, the world was a wider Rome, and history had a right to be interested in the achievements of every people. Another universal history was the *Bibliotheca Universalis* of Diodorus of Sicily, written in the reign of Augustus. To Diodorus universal historians who record the common affairs of the inhabited world are ministers of divine providence. An immense work, the *Bibliotheca* comprises forty books of which only the first five and fragments of the rest survive. It spans the history of the Mediterranean world and the Middle East from mythical origins to Caesar's conquest of Gaul. J.W. Thompson calls the *Bibliotheca* a mine of information on many ancient Greek historians who are otherwise unknown. Nicholas of Damascus coming to Rome and winning the regard of Augustus, wrote, among other works, a great *Universal History* in one hundred and forty-four books. Of this, however, only a few fragments remain.

*History as Biography: Plutarch (*AD *46–126)*

The influence of great men upon history is a subject discussed throughout the centuries and the biographical method of historical interpretation is certainly an attractively popular method of presentation. Biographies of antiquity, unlike their modern counterparts, were intimately associated with the history of a country or culture. Nicholas of Damascus, mentioned earlier, had written a *Life of Caesar*, a *Life of Augustus,* and his own *Autobiography*. Suetonius's (c. AD 75–160) *Lives of the Twelve Emperors from Caesar to Domitian* brought into style the writing of history in the form of biography. Cornelius Nepos' *Lives of Great Captains*, and Diogenes Laertes's *Lives of the Philosophers* were other works of the kind. Such biographies, like all history in ancient times, were inclined to moralize and set patterns to be imitated. This vogue for biography reached its climax in Plutarch's *Parallel Lives*, one of the world's classics. Travelling in Asia Minor, Egypt and Italy, Plutarch resided in Rome during the Flavian rule and devoted himself to research in the libraries and archives of the imperial city. Shortly before the death of Domitian in AD 96 he returned to his native Chaeoronea where he lived until a ripe old age, much honoured by his fellow citizens. One of the most prolific writers of antiquity, Plutarch's extant works are forty-eight biographies and seventy-eight treatises or dialogues. In the *Parallel Lives* by which he is known to mankind, he compared great Romans with great Greeks, as a stimulus to virtue and heroism in his readers. Plutarch is to be regarded as more of a moralist than a historian. He warns us in his 'Alexander' – a chapter in *Parallel Lives* – that he is more interested in character than in history. Plutarch's book has been a stimulus to heroism and a pasture to writers of all kinds, including historians.

5. The Character of Graeco-Roman Historiography:[56] Humanism and Substantialism

Humanism

Collingwood observes that classical or Graeco-Roman historiography had firmly grasped one of the four characteristics of history—that history should be humanistic. Graeco-Roman historiography is a narrative of man's deeds, man's purposes, man's successes and failures. Though it admits divine agency into the deeds of men, the function of that agency is strictly limited. The will of the gods rarely manifests. Such a position meant that the cause of all historical events must be sought in the personalities of human agents. The philosophical idea underlying it was the belief in the ability of the human will to choose and pursue its own ends. This implied that whatever happens in history happens as a direct result of human will; man became entirely responsible for his own actions.

Substantialism

If humanism was the chief merit of Graeco-Roman historiography, its chief defect was substantialism. A substantialistic metaphysics implies a theory of knowledge according to which only that which is unchanging is knowable. But what is unchanging is not historical; it is the transitory event that is historical. The substance from whose nature an event proceeds is nothing to the historian.

For Herodotus events were important in themselves and knowable by themselves. But in Thucydides such a historical point of view got dimmed by substantialism. For Thucydides the events are important chiefly for the light they throw on eternal and substantial entities of which they are mere accidents. Collingwood says that the stream of historical thought which flowed so freely in Heredotus thus began to freeze up, a process which continued until, by the time of Livy, history was frozen solid.

Collingwood gives two examples of how the influence of substantialism appears in the two great Roman historians. First, in Livy: In writing a history of Rome, Livy did not trace or describe the process, the steps, by which Rome became what it came to be. Rome appears on the stage of history as a goddess or a ready-made heroine whose action Livy described. Rome is a substance, changeless and eternal. There is no origin, no development. In the very first years of its being, Rome had such institutions as augury, the legion, the senate, and so forth, and it was assumed that they remained thereafter unchanged. The origin of Rome, as Livy described it, was a kind of miraculous leap into existence of the city, full-fledged and complete as it existed at a later date. It is in the substantialistic and non-historical sense that Rome is still called, as Livy thought it to be, 'the eternal city'. Secondly, in Tacitus: The same substantialism operated in Tacitus's portrayal of historical personages. When Tacitus describes the way in which the character of a man like Tiberius broke down beneath the strain of empire, he presents the process not as a change in the structure of a personality, but as revelation of features in it which had hitherto been hypocritically concealed. It is not simply out of spite that Tacitus so misrepresents facts. It is because the idea of development in a character, an idea so familiar to us, is to him a metaphysical impossibility. A good man cannot become bad.

Graeco-Roman historiography, Collingwood concludes, can never show how anything comes into existence; all the agencies that appear on the stage of history have to be assumed ready-made before history begins. The nemesis of this substantialistic attitude was historical skepticism: What was the use of history? Since it did not have a substantialistic validity, it could not have a substantialistic value—a value in itself; it could only have a pragmatic value.

IV. ANCIENT CHINESE HISTORIOGRAPHY

One achievement of the eighteenth century European Enlightenment was the intellectual discovery of China. Indeed, Chinese life and civilization so much caught the imagination of the Europeans that Francois Quesnay, the physiocrat, elevated China to a model of Europe in rationality, good government, and good taste.

1. Circumstances Favorable for the Growth of Historiography in Ancient China

A significant element in the Chinese civilization, unlike the Indian, is its abiding taste for history. China has been called "the paradise of historians".[57] Chinese historical tradition is unparalleled in its length, in its internal consistency, prestige, and the bulk of its literary output.[58]

Chinese historiography developed independent of all outside influence. Certain circumstances did much to shape the Chinese mentality and dispose it towards the practice of history.[59] First, from very early times the recording of past events was regarded as important for writing itself seems to have been thought by the Chinese as a way of communicating with the divine order. Every temple had its archivist who looked after such documents as the registers, family trees, records of contracts, and decisions of the oracles. Princely houses similarly kept officials whose duty it was to draw up treaties, record edicts, draft documents, divine and decide the day for making a journey, holding a ceremony or beginning a war. From an early date these archivist-astrologers – whether in the temples or in the princely courts – recorded events, too. The archivist-astrologer acquired great influence at the imperial court and acted as secretary to the emperor or went as his emissary on diplomatic missions. Secondly, there was in ancient China a growing movement which we may label 'rationalist', which brought incidental support to history by insisting on the 'immortality' that men might secure in the memory of future ages.[60] During the period from the fifth to the third century BC, known as the period of the Warring (or Contending) States (403–221 BC), this movement culminated in a brilliant flowering of culture which brought philosophical thought to its climax. This greatly helped history, for in China philosophy was neither cosmological theory nor metaphysical speculation; it meant the kind of wisdom that is necessary for the conduct of life, particularly the conduct of government. It resorted not to deductive reasoning, but to the exploitation of historical examples. Again, after Szuma Ch'ien, the specialized role of the historiographer became recognized as part of the Chinese civil service. Under the T'ung dynasty from the early seventh century there emerged a history office which was an organ of the government, and history became an important subject in the civil service examinations. Such, in brief, were the factors which made history the most popular and respectable form of literature in China.

2. Some Chinese Historians

Confucius (c. 551–478 BC*)*

The Chinese would claim a history reaching back to 3000 BC, but anything going further back than 776 BC cannot be treated as trustworthy. Confucius particularly stressed the importance of history in promoting reverence for the past and respect for the examples set by ancestors. The three subjects which formed the curriculum for his pupils were history, poetry and the rules of propriety. He left behind him, apparently written and edited by his own hand, the *Five Ching* or Canonical Books which are deemed to constitute the surviving textual reflection of the golden age. Two of these books – the fourth and the fifth – are historical works. The fourth, the *Ch'un Ch'ieu* or *Spring and Autumn Annals*, is a brief chronicle of the reigns of twelve dukes of Confucius's own state of Lu from 722–484 BC. The *Annals* was also a guide to moral conduct. In the fifth, the *Shu-Ching* or *Book of History* or *Book of Documents* – which is a collection of royal speeches, edicts, memorials, feudal documents, etc – the great teacher sought to edify and inspire his pupils with the most important and elevating events of the early reigns. That was the period, thought Confucius, when China had been unified and civilized by heroic and unselfish heroes like the good king Yao who ruled for a hundred years. But Confucius cannot be regarded as so much an historian giving us an impartial account of times past, for he added to his record imaginary speeches and stories to promote morals and wisdom. He was a teacher who idealized his country's past to mould and inspire his young pupils with stories deliberately selected from legend and history.[61] But he promoted the study and writing of history by adding to its prestige.

History writing had become a prestigious activity in China and it advanced rapidly during the four centuries that separated Confucius and the great Szuma Ch'ien. Two works of this period may be mentioned—the first was the *Tso-chuan*, a commentary written about a century after Confucius's death to illustrate and enliven his *Book of History*; and the second was *Annals of the Bamboo Books*, found in the tomb of a king of Wei.

Szuma Ch'ien (c. 145–85 BC*)*

Confucius had invested Chinese historiography with a high moral tone which persuaded the Neo-Confucian philosophers to emphasize moral standards at the cost of the reality of the recent past. Against this was the historian who sought to draw strength from the reality of the past, and the connection between historiography and the bureaucracy. A history which served the interests of the bureaucracy and the ruling group may be just as pernicious as Confucian moralizing; but the bureaucratic insistence on the careful organization and the preservation of materials has left us copious, well-ordered sources. Szuma Ch'ien was the father of the historiography that sought to base itself on the reality of the past.[62]

Szuma Ch'ien was the son of Szuma T'an, the grand historian-astrologer at the court of the Han emperor, Wu. The young Szuma had travelled extensively before entering the civil service. He succeeded his father as the grand historian-astrologer. It was the dying wish of the historian's father that his son complete the historical record he had begun. But disaster occurred when, in coming to the aid of a defeated general, he drew upon himself the wrath of Emperor Wu. Szuma submitted to the worst of penalties – castration – in lieu of death so that he might live to complete the *Shih chi*. He first reformed the calendar and then devoted his life to the task which his father had laid upon him. His masterpiece, the *Shih chi* (*Historical Record*), ran to 526,000 Chinese characters patiently scratched on bamboo tablets.

Sources and Method

Despite its Confucian slant certain original features of the *Shih chi* may be noted.[63] First, unlike earlier histories which had dealt with particular regions or dynasties, the *Shih chi* is a history of the world as known by its author. Its 130 chapters cover the history of China and a number of lands on its borders from the time of the legendary Yellow Emperor to Szuma Ch'ien's own times—a period of about 3,000 years. Second, the book draws upon a more varied collection of source materials than its predecessors. Mythical in its early parts, the work becomes more detailed and precise from the middle of the third century BC; and, for this part – particularly for the fuller story of the Han dynasty down to the Emperor Wu – Ch'ien used more than seventy-five official records. He supplemented them by inscriptional data, examination of sites and relics, personal observation, and cross-questioning of individuals in the capital, and also by the information gathered during his extensive travels. He used his material with great care. He speaks with caution of the far-off days before the Ch'in dynasty as materials on that period are scanty. He refuses to swallow the information that is unbelievable. In Chapter 86, for instance, Szuma dismisses as 'ridiculous' the claim that Prince Tan was able to make the heavens rain grain, and horses sprout horns. Third, the *Shih chi* looks beyond the boundaries of the court. Finally, departing from the tradition of chronological arrangement Szuma Chi'ien organized his great history into five sections: 1. Basic Annals of the Emperors; 2. Chronological Tables; 3. Eight chapters or treatises, intended to be of particular use to officials—one each on rites, music, the pitch-pipes, the calendar, astrology, imperial sacrifices, water courses and political economy; 4. Annals of the Feudal Nobles; and 5. Biographies of Eminent Men. The chapterwise division is not arbitrary for each chapter is a significant formal unit whose contents have been selected and disposed with care and intention. The work mainly consists of a series of narratives inclusive of histories of famous individuals, and also some groups such as foreign peoples, the very rich, swordsmen, entertainers, and so on.

Absence of Causal Explanation, Interpretation of Data and Generalization

Szuma Ch'ien makes no serious attempt to explain and interpret. Nor does he see the need for connections, developments, underlying movements of causation—all that make a historical work organic. This is because he saw history as the product of man's will and did not seek to comprehend it. Events are presented as informed by the documents or reported by eyewitnesses, but they are not envisaged as a whole, or inquired into, to reveal the source and cause.[64]

Didacticism

Szuma Chi'ien's *Historical Record*, like Confucius's *Annals*, has a moral, didactic purpose. The grand historian, like Tacitus, passes judgments upon the events of the past. He makes the point that, although the wicked may sometimes prosper and the good suffer, wise historians will eventually restore the reputation of the good and condemn the wicked.[65]

With all physical strength gone, eyes dimmed, and few teeth remaining, the grand historian of China presented his great history to the Emperor Wu with the hope that he would deign to cast a sacred glance over the work "so as to learn from the rise and fall of former dynasties the secret of the successes and failures of the present hour."[66]

It was through Szuma Ch'ien's *Historical Record* that Chinese historiography came to exert a profound influence on Japanese, Korean and Vietnamese history writing.

*Standard Histories: Pan Ku (*AD *32–92) and Szuma Kuang (*AD *1019–1086)*

Pan Ku, the Chinese historian who lived in the first century AD, followed Szuma Ch'ien's pattern of organization for his *History of the Former Han Dynasty*. But in writing the history only of the former Han Dynasty, Pan Ku was unknowingly setting a pattern himself. Thereafter, it became a practice for each dynasty to compile historical materials for its successor. A proportion of officials would spend part of their careers in the History Bureau, and historical narratives came to be produced on the committee method, that is, collective, collaborative work. The *Diaries of Activity and Repose* reproduced the utterances of the emperor and the business that he transacted, day by day. These were abridged so that when the emperor died, there emerged the *Veritable Record*, a survey of his whole reign. When a dynasty came to an end, a comprehensive account of the former dynasty would be written under the succeeding dynasty. Such *Standard Histories* were produced for nearly two thousand years on the pattern set initially by Pan Ku.

The twenty-five *Standard Histories* now extant, if translated into English, is calculated to require 450 volumes of five hundred pages each; and this is only a small proportion of the vast historical production of China![67]

But this official history, written by civil servants for civil servants, did not pass without criticism. Liu Chih-chi's (AD 661–721) *Shih t'ung*, for example, contained a spirited plea on behalf of the individual historian and the chronicle form against the 'standard histories' of the committee method. The chronicle form and the role of the individual historian reached their culmination in Szuma Kuang who attempted again a universal history of China of the Szuma Ch'ien model. Kuang ransacked three hundred sources and the resultant material formed the basis of his *Tzu-chih t'ung-chien*. The book is a magisterial survey of almost fourteen centuries down to the author's own times—from the late Chow to the beginning of the Sung periods. It lists events year by year. This highly objective work tasted sour to the moralists, and the philosopher Chu Hsi (AD 1130–1200) charged his disciples with producing a summary, the *T'ung-chien kangmu*. Didactic in the extreme and given to much "praise and blame", this travesty of Szuma Kuang became established as the best known history textbook in China.[68]

3. A Critical Assessment of Chinese Historiography

West's Neglect of Chinese History

No nation has produced such voluminous, continuous, varied and accurate records of so long a past as China—imperial history, local and dynastic histories, gazetteers, chronicles on the dependencies of China, histories of non-Chinese peoples within China, histories of foreign relations, and specialist histories on different aspects of Chinese life. Yet, European historians and philosophers of history did not condescend to consider China even for purposes of comparison in matters historical.[69] Postulating the eternal stagnation of the Orient, Hegel's *Philosophy of History* (1830–31) gave classic expression to the West's thesis of the static and unprogressive nature of Chinese civilization. Ranke altogether excluded China from history proper by asserting that the Chinese sources are mythical, unreliable, secondary or unavailable to those ignorant of the Chinese language. Burckardt's lectures dismissed

China as unworthy of attention. Marx's theory of the Asiatic mode of production erroneously held that China suffered from the system of production and governmental despotism peculiar to Asia. In the twentieth century, however, works like H.G. Wells's *Outline of History* (1920), Oswald Spengler's *The Decline of the West* (1918–22), Arnold Toynbee's *A Study of History* (1934–61), and above all, William McNeill's *The Rise of the West* (1963), show that the West is making some amends in its estimate of China and its rich and unquenchably vital civilization.

Style

A great part of so rich a crop of historical literature as the Chinese have left must be of first-rate quality even when judged by the standards of modern Western historiography. Will Durant, however, has written that history in China did not rise from an industry to an art; that Chinese historians like the great Szuma Ch'ien did not care for beauty of style; and that they spent their energies upon truth, leaving nothing for beauty, perhaps thinking that history should be a science rather than an art.[70]

Absence of Causal Explanation, Interpretation of Data and Generalization

However, when Szuma Ch'ien indulged his passion for moralizing, he wrote passages of real literary beauty.[71] But moralizing does not go well with historical objectivity. Chinese historians deemed their objectivity as complete if their words coincided with the text of actual documents. They did not go beyond discrete facts; they did not attempt causal explanation; they did not interpret data, produce generalizations, describe the background, or examine processes.[72] But we cannot roundly conclude that Chinese historians were oblivious of the causes and effects of historical phenomena. Yuan-chu called his history *Tung chien-chishipenmo*, which means 'root causes and effects of affairs recorded in the universal mirror'.

Textual Criticism

The ancient Chinese historians excelled in textual criticism.[73] Few historical writings of the pre-Confucian days had survived and the genuineness and the textual accuracy of those that did survive had become a matter of controversy. And after Shih Hwangti's 'Burning of the Books' (212 BC), the recovery of the ancient writings became a definite objective. As a result of the vicissitudes that had been suffered by these texts, there emerged a subtle technique of textual criticism which developed greatly. As successive historians so often copied each other verbatim, the authenticity of ancient texts could be checked by comparing what had been reproduced by previous writers at various times. Thus it was that the exposition of forgeries and interpolations became an important aspect of Chinese criticism.

Internal Criticism

But this finesse in external criticism did not lead to like finesse in internal criticism. Chinese historians seem to have accepted as true any statement in chronicles or documents if it had not been contradicted anywhere. Should there be two contradictory accounts of an event, they would try to reconcile one with the other or produce a story that would explain both. Sometimes, if they opted for one of two documents, they would give no reasons for doing so and would leave the rejected document unmentioned. Even when satisfied about the genuineness of a document, they did not care to interpret it in terms of the people or situation behind it.

3

I. MEDIEVAL CHRISTIAN HISTORIOGRAPHY

1. Decline of Historiography in the West

The displacement of classical Greco-Roman culture with a Christian way of life in the West had a dampening effect on historiography. From the third century onward historiography both Greek and Roman showed signs of decline in quality, integrity, and dignity; it was degenerating to "sorry stuff."[1]

The rise of Christianity had a direct share in the decline of historiography in the West. Christianity wrought a fundamental change in the Western man's attitude toward life by shifting the centre of gravity from the present to a future life. By making eternal salvation of the soul superior to any other purpose of life, the ordinary life of mankind, the existence of the state, and the safety of the commonwealth – matters of the greatest concern to Graeco-Roman society – sank into insignificance.

> This indifference of early Christianity to public welfare was accentuated by the prevalent Christian belief that Christ would soon return to earth to establish his power....Why be interested in history, when all history would terminate shortly in a new heaven and new earth?[2]

As late as the middle of the third century the author of the *Didascalia Apostolorum* exclaims: "What does thou miss in God's word that thou does plunge into these pagan histories?"[3]

2. Growth of Christian Historical Consciousness

Thus, the earliest Christians, too otherworldly and intent upon spiritual life, seemed to have little place for mundane history. But it was a position difficult to maintain. For all its indifference to history, the early Christian church had need of it. It was important to assert the humanity as well as the divinity of Christ, and inquiries into his life were bound to be made. Christianity itself was making history and it became necessary to record and preserve its traditions for the instruction and edification of the faithful. There were decisions of the church in Jerusalem to be remembered, martyrs to be commemorated, and stories to be told about the missionary work in the Roman empire. Above all, it was necessary to answer pagan charges against the new faith. In this way, by the end of the third century, a Christian interpretation of large-scale mundane history was gradually developed.

But the historical consciousness that Christianity developed was not an interest in history as such. What the early Christian writers abstracted from the scriptures was a skeleton of supernatural or 'salvation history' that culminated in the crucifixion and resurrection. It has been pointed out that from its inception ecclesiastical history was violently distorted—first by the adoption of ancient Jewish history as pre-Christian history; secondly by its association of revelation and history; and thirdly by the vicious distinction made between 'sacred' and 'profane' history.[4] History so developed in the interests of theology invested it with a "protective halo", a "false guardianship of piety or authority", and prevented it from being treated and criticized as dispassionately as any other kind of history.[5] As late as the nineteenth century, Cardinal Manning branded the appeal to history as "treason to the Church".[6] As J.W. Thompson writes, belief in truth by revelation meant the distrust of reason; since no truth outside revelation was acknowledged, inquiry became sin, and the critical spirit blasphemy. The clean, critical, analytical faculty which had been the glory of Greek thinking disappeared.

3. Eusebius of Caesaria and Paulus Orossius

Universal History and Chronology

The earliest constructive achievement of Christian or ecclesiastical historiography was the formulation of the concept of universal history. St. Paul had a philosophy of history which was a compound of revelation and Neo-Stoicism—god had made all people of one blood, the children of Adam and Eve. Christian teaching dogmatically held that Christianity had been predestined from the foundation of the world to become the universal religion, the religion of all mankind. The concept of universal history at once called for a universal chronology. One of the first problems that the churchmen had to tackle was the problem of comparing the widely differing chronological systems in the ancient Mediterranean world, in the Roman empire. It was the task of synchronizing events in one region with events in another. About AD 221, Sextus Julius Africanus produced an important work in this field, the *Chronographia*. Africanus combined classical and biblical chronology, and his *Chronographia* was a primary source for Eusebius in the fourth century.

Eusebius of Caesaria (c. AD *260–340)*

Diocletian's fierce persecution of the Christians and Constantine's recognition of Christianity by the *Edict of Milan* (AD 313) alike accentuated the Christian Church's dawning inclination towards historiography. The history of this persecution is recorded in Lactantius's *De mortibus persecutorum*. The time was ripe for a genuine historian of the Church and he appeared in Eusebius, the founder of ecclesiastical history.

Eusebius lived and worked all his life in Caesaria in Palestine. Here was the foremost Christian library in the Roman world which had fortunately escaped destruction in the persecution under Diocletian. Here Eusebius wrote the *Chronographia*, *Ecclesiastical History*, *Lives of the Martyrs of Jerusalem*, and the *Life of Constantine*. The greatest of all church chronicles, Eusebius's *Chronographia* was a comparative chronology of all the peoples known to the author. Eusebius harmonized all the ancient chronological systems—Biblical, Egyptian, Assyrian, the Greek Olympiads, and the Roman consular fasti. The *Old Testament* is the core of the work; years are calculated from Christian 'Creation'; and every date in the end is calculated according to the chronology of the *Bible*. In the eighth century, when the Venerable Bede began to count the years from the incarnation of Christ, modern chronology was founded. Jerome translated Eusebius's *Chronographia* into Latin and it influenced all historical writings in the West. It is to Christianity that we owe the establishment of chronology as an auxiliary science to the study of history. Eusebius's *Historia Ecclesiastica* (*Ecclesiastical History*) "is a co-ordinated, sustained, critical, and interpretative history of the Church in ten books which grows deeper and fuller as the subject advances."[7] It is written with a remarkable temperateness and understanding. But the *Life of Constantine* is a panegyric suppressing and misrepresenting evidence adverse to the Roman emperor's character. Otto Seeck called the work a "Book of Lies".[8] Far less important for history is the *Lives of the Martyrs*. Full of miracles and wonder, it was to be emulated by many such *Lives of the Saints*. To Eusebius almost everything seemed to have been preordained—the Mosaic dispensation, and even pagan culture and philosophy, and the Roman empire are parts of the divine plan preparing for the coming of Christ. Eusebius is rightly regarded as the founder of ecclesiastical history.

Paulus Orossius (c. AD *380–420)*

Paulus Orossius was a disciple of St. Augustine from Spain. His *Seven Books of History against Paganism* written at the suggestion of his master is a violent anti-pagan tract vindicating Christianity against the pagan charge of the Christian responsibility for the fall of Rome. Orossius differed from Augustine in his excessive providentialism. He based history on the theory that ultimately the destinies of mankind – pagan, Jewish or Christian – are controlled by god. Orossius's work is important for the great influence it had in the Middle Ages which in fact followed Orossius's view of providence rather than St. Augustine's. Great was his share in establishing the patristic tradition in historiography or 'salvation historiography'. History came to be looked upon as the unfolding story of god's plan of salvation.

4. St. Augustine (AD 354–430)

St. Augustine, the greatest figure in the early Christian Church, was a pagan to whom Christianity had come as a profound emotional satisfaction. Augustine labored chiefly with his pen. Two of his books belong to the classics of the world. The *Confessions*, his autobiography, is written with great honesty and sincerity, and addressed directly to god. The *De Civitat Dei* (*City of God*) in twenty-two books composed between AD 413 and 426, is one of the greatest texts of the world. In AD 410 Rome was taken and sacked by the Goths under Alaric. The calamity that the city had suffered was attributed by pagans to Christianity—as a punishment for the neglect of the old gods. Augustine deeply felt the challenge to his faith and devoted all the powers of his subtle genius to convincing the Roman world that such catastrophes did not for a moment impugn Christianity. For thirteen years he labored on his book whose 1200 pages dealt with everything from the first sin to the Last Judgement.[9]

Augustine maintained against the pagan charge that Rome was punished not for its new religion but for its continued sins under paganism. But his more substantial answer took the form of a philosophy of history—an attempt to explain the events of recorded time on a universal principle. Here he appears as a political thinker taking for his main theme the contest between temporal and spiritual powers. There are two cities. The first city is the *Civitat Dei* or the 'City of God'. It is the divine city of the past, present and future worshippers of the one true god. This Heavenly City or Kingdom was founded by angels and its reflection is the holy Church, whose office was to realize that heavenly vision upon earth. The second is the *Civitat Terrena* or the Earthly City or Kingdom, also the city of man. Founded by the rebellion of Satan, the Earthly City is devoted to earthly affairs and joys. It is evil. The Earthly City is based on physical force, but the City of God is based on Divine Love. The City of Man is relative in importance, limited in scope, and transitory in nature; but the City of God is absolute in power, unlimited in scope, and permanent in nature, a city that enables man to attain higher knowledge and become perfect. Not until the Last Judgement will the two cities be wholly separated. "With this book," (the *Civitat Dei*), says Will Durant, "paganism as a philosophy ceased to be and Christianity as a philosophy began. It was the first definitive formulation of the medieval mind."[10] The book became the basis of Catholic theology and formulated the dominant political theory of the Middle Ages. It was the first effort to propound the relation between Church and State. The Catholic Church would eventually weave out of Augustine's theories the doctrines of a theocratic state, of the subordination of secular authority to spiritual authority.

The *City of God* controlled Catholic historiography ever since it was written. It put god in history, declaring that god ruled human affairs. Augustine represented the historical process as a struggle between good and evil, virtue and vice, the divine and the demonic, theocratic and secular. He saw history, sacred or salvation history, as conforming to a divine plan. The Graeco-Roman humanistic idea made man the wise architect of his own fortunes. But Christian doctrine based itself on human insufficiency, and held that man's unaided intellect and efforts cannot plan and achieve ends without divine grace. Human action is blind, a blindness derived from man's original sin. The human achievements are not due to forces of human will and intellect, but due to god's grace. God plans human actions and causes them to be executed. Such a view of history, placing god at the centre of human affairs, is variously called sacred history, salvation history, providential history, or patristic history. This view of history governed Europe throughout the Middle Ages.

In the *City of God*, observes Herbert Butterfield, we see Augustine arguing his way out of a cyclic view of history. He cannot allow that everything that happens will go on repeating itself endlessly through time. Such a belief would turn the incarnation of Christ into a puppet show.[11]

5. Gregory of Tours and the Venerable Bede

Pagan historiography disappeared in the fifth century. Most historical writing in the West for about eight hundred years thereafter was done by Christian writers almost every one of whom was a cleric. They wrote history according to a pattern which could be safely termed Christian and medieval. Lay-written historiography almost disappeared until the thirteenth century.

Gregory of Tours (AD *539–594)*

The sixth century was a century of hopeless disorder in Europe, yet, in Gregory of Tours, we have one of the most genuine of all medieval historians.

The Franks were an alloy of the three essential elements of medieval European culture – the Roman, Christian and German – their kingdom was destined to be the most enduring and constructive in the Middle Ages. Roman Gaul had preserved to a greater degree than elsewhere the classical literary tradition and the

Roman school system. Gregory was a model bishop of prodigious activity which also included the writing of history. His *Historia Regum Frankorum* (*History of the Kings of the Franks*) is the only history of the early Franks we have. Credulous of wonders, portents and miracles, Gregory had little critical sense; yet he was honest and sincere. Rough and incorrect though, his Latin has an elemental vigor and force. His book is a mine of information on matters relating to the civilization of the age: the Church, administrative matters and institutions, social classes, economic conditions, commerce and trade, slavery, manners and morals, education, the lapse of classical culture, and superstitions.[12]

The Venerable Bede (AD *673–735*)

At a time when learning and culture touched their lowest ebb in Europe, it is an academic surprise that a great scholar and historian, the Venerable Bede, should have emerged in England. The explanation is that the fusion of Latin, English and Irish cultures in the north of England resulted in a remarkably energetic intellectual movement of which the writing of history was the chief expression. With an intellectual honesty equalled only by his piety and fidelity to his monastic order, Bede encompassed every department of human thought. He wrote on theology, chronology, grammar, mathematics and science. But his enduring fame depends chiefly on his historical work, the *Historia Ecclesiastica* (*Ecclesiastical History of the English Nation*) (AD 731).

Bede's sources almost exhausted the available material of the age. He had all the documents available at the time in England; he collected others from Rome, Frankish Gaul and Germany. He specified his sources, sought first-hand evidence, and quoted pertinent documents. Particularly, Bede applied labour and ingenuity to problems of chronology. Since the Anglo-Saxon system of dating events by the regnal years in the various monarchies proved cumbrous, Bede originated in the *Ecclesiastical History* the practice of dating events from the incarnation of Christ—a system followed by Isidore of Seville in the seventh century. Written in Latin, the *Ecclesiastical History* is in five books. The work, so important, so charming and so readable, has earned the praise of all subsequent writers. J.W. Thompson writes:

> There is no other work in all early medieval literature

> comparable to it in depth and breadth of information combined with literary artistry. It is the greatest history written in the barbarian epoch.[13]

For the secular as well as the ecclesiastical events of the years from AD 597 to AD 731, it is our only authentic source, the source from which all later writers derive their information. Unlike many monastic histories, Bede's history is no dry chronicle, and though innocently credulous, it is a clear and captivating narrative, rising now and then to a simple eloquence, as in the description of the Anglo-Saxon conquest.[14] The noble ideal that Bede sets before him as a narrator of events is an example to future historians: "I would not," says he, "that my children should read a lie."[15] Bede knew the predicament that the conscientious historian always found himself in: "The hard condition of the historian is that if he speaks the truth he provokes the anger of men; but if he commits falsehoods to writings he will be unacceptable to God...."[16]

Bede was also the author of *Lives*, of Cuthbert, and of Benedict Biscop, his mentor; a treatise *On the Reckoning of Time*; and a wider work on universal history. Rightly called the father of English history, Bede had a stimulating effect on the Continent. His work on universal history, along with Jerome's version of the *Chronicle* of Eusebius, formed the basis of the historical writing of the subsequent period. Anglo-Saxon missionaries carried it to Germany, and it was prefaced to various Frankish annals.

6. The Annal and the Chronicle

Annal

The monastic annal was a type of medieval historiography of a unique nature, invented by early English monasticism. Annal originally meant annual information – literally a year's entry or record of events set in a strict chronological order – a year book. The annals grew out of a religious practice. At Easter time every year it was the duty of the abbot of a monastery to make up the calendar for the coming year, with the Sundays, the Saints' Days, and great church festivals indicated. Upon the margins of these tables, and sometimes between the lines, it became a practice in English monasteries, soon after the coming of Augustine in 596, to enter jottings of events of all sorts. By accretion and expansion the chronological information grew and this practice came to be imitated by other religious houses. Thus originated those monastic annals which contributed so much factual information to posterity. The English practice was imitated in the Continent, where it was introduced by English missionaries in the seventh century. Charlemagne was quick to see the value of the practice and required every monastery to keep an annual record of the doings of the time, especially those which happened in its own vicinity. The oldest English examples of monastic annals are those of Lindisfarn (AD 532–993). *The Annals of English History* by Richard Hoveden (thirteenth century) is a perfect example of what medieval annals could be.

Chronicle

Towards the end of the eighth century, in an obscure way, various local monastic annals in Northumbria began to be combined and fused into a larger whole. This fusion seems to have resulted in the composition of what is called the chronicle. The medieval contemporary chronicle was a detailed arrangement of events in the order of time. It was a record of acts and events which the actors and eyewitnesses thought worthy to be remembered.

The first chronicle of such a nature was the *Northumbrian Chronicle*, now lost. It appears that some annals composed at Winchester in the south of England that became the nucleus of the *Anglo-Saxon Chronicle*—the historiographical monument of early English literature and the oldest literary work composed in any Germanic tongue. Inspired by Alfred the Great, this most famous of all medieval chronicles seems to have been compiled sometime between AD 855 and 895. It was continued after that great king's time in different monasteries even after the Norman conquest down to the death of Stephen in AD 1154. It is the first continuous national history of a Western nation in its own national language, and the first substantial work of English prose. Most interesting are some character studies, of which the best example seems to be that of William the Conqueror. The *Chronicle of St. Albans* relates events from AD 1250 to 1422.

Annal, Chronicle and History

Annals and chronicles are mere lists of events with their dates of occurrence. They give authentic information on contemporary happenings, but not on past events as histories do. Unlike historians, annalists and chroniclers are merely recorders of events and do not generally trace their causal connections or results, or embark on historical disquisition. Historians make use of annals and chronicles. "The annals," says Bishop Stubbs, "are the ore, the chronicles are the purified metal out of which the historian elaborated his perfect jewel."[17] The chronicle retains its value for ever as record of facts; the history loses its importance as soon as the principles which it is written to illustrate, or which have guided its composition, become obsolete.

7. The Historiography of the Carolingian Renaissance

The Carolingian Renaissance

Charlemagne was not merely empire-builder; he was civilizer, too. Appalled by the illiteracy of the age, he brought the best scholars of the day to his court, to restore the schools of France—Alcuin, Paul the Lombard, Theodulf, Angilbert and Einhard. An ambitious scheme of general education was launched. A royal decree of AD 789 obliged every monastery and every abbey to have a school. The movement which spread throughout the realm was spearheaded by the famous Palace School which Charlemagne started in his own palace at Aix-la-Chappelle, the Carolingian capital. The most eager student at the Palace School was the barbarian emperor himself. His wife and children were also there to learn the three R's (reading, writing and arithmetic) and the rudiments of civilization. This revival of schools and of learning under Charlemagne is known as the 'Carolingian renaissance'. But it was too short-lived to be strikingly original or to have any bold intellectual or artistic adventure. What was important about the ninth-century revival was that it saved much knowledge from the wreckage of ancient learning. Many of the classical texts have come down to us from the monastic 'scriptoria' of the ninth century.

Einhard

The 'Carolingian renaissance' was important for historiography. Monastic annals multiplied in the reign of Charlemagne who required every monastery to keep an annual record of the doings of the time, especially those of the neighbourhood. Furthermore, we have histories which may be directly ascribed to the Carolingian revival of learning. Einhard, the most famous historian of the Carolingian period, was Charlemagne's secretary and biographer. His *Vita Caroli (The Life of Charlemagne)* though a slavish imitation of Suetonius's *Lives of the Caesars*, however, gives a real portrait of the Frankish emperor. It is mentioned in AD 820, and must have been written after AD 814 . The book was popular all through the Middle Ages and is the best known of the medieval biographies.

Paul the Deacon

The second important historian of the time was Paul the Deacon or Paul the Lombard whom Charlemagne met at the monastery of Monte Casino. Charlemagne was interested in his new conquest (Lombardy), and Paul, a Lombard, was interested as a patriot in his own people.[18] Thus came the *History of the Lombards*, in the year AD 774. Utilizing Lombard tradition for the earlier part of the work, Paul relates that the original home of the Lombards was in Scandinavia, that the migration was caused by the increase of population, and that in their great trek southwards they fell into a quivering morass, as the Goths had done in Russia. But as the author advances to later times, the saga element disappears and the narrative becomes more substantial. The account of the actual conquest of north Italy by the Lombards, the suppression of the native population there, and the land system is masterly.[19] Less credulous than Gregory of Tours, Paul also writes a less crude language.

Nithard

Another important work of history belonging to the Carolingian period is the *Four Books of History* by Nithard. Significantly, Nithard was a layman. His mother was Charlemagne's daughter, Bertha, his father, Angilbert, the statesman and scholar of the Carolingian court. For the value of the information and the forthrightness with which it is written, Nithard's work is the most remarkable history of the ninth century.[20] It ends abruptly in

AD 843, in which year the Treaty of Verdun, partitioning Charlemagne's empire, was signed. Before Nithard had had time to write an account of the treaty, he was called to the field in AD 844 and killed in battle.

8. The Crusades, Twelfth-Century Renaissance, and the Climax of Medieval Historiography

The Crusades and the Twelfth-Century Renaissance

The return of violence and disorder with the Viking attacks produced a decline in historiography, particularly in Germany. But in the tenth century Otto the Great secured stability again and, in the eleventh, the leaven of a new thinking and a distinct emergence of historical consciousness could be detected. It was aided by great history-making events such as the Norman conquests in England and Sicily, the religious reform movements, and the growth of papacy to portentous heights. But the first general historical event which excited the interest of all nations and all classes of society in Europe was the Crusades. The nature and novelty of these picturesque events roused the imagination of writers and shook Europe out of the narrow sphere in which annals, chronicles and biographies had been written previously. Again, the influence of Greek and Arabic culture on Europe in the eleventh century had led to an intellectual and aesthetic awakening in the twelfth. The awakening was so important as to be designated the Twelfth-Century Renaissance. The force of new thought broke the traditions of the old education and inspired an intellectual movement which culminated in the founding of the first universities. Important thinkers such as Albertus Magnus and Peter Abelard developed. The increasing study of Roman law, the growth of trade and town life, the development of Gothic art and the emergence of vernacular literature were factors which aided the Twelfth-Century Renaissance. It was impossible for historical writings to remain uninfluenced by the spirit of the times. The new consciousness meant a wider vision of things, as it drew attention to a wider world including Byzantium and the Near Eastern lands. In the twelfth century medieval history came to its climax.

Historians of the Twelfth-Century Renaissance

Sigibert of Gembloux

Sigibert of Gembloux (c. AD 1030–1112) carried this newer form of medieval historical writing to a height never previously attained. He wrote a world history based on wide reading, and so extensive in its political range as to include the first attempt to understand the history of Byzantium. Secular history was balanced against ecclesiastical history.

Otto of Freising

The best expression of the Twelfth-Century Renaissance in Germany is Otto of Freising's (d. AD 1158) chronicle of universal history titled *The Two Cities*. Otto was the uncle of Emperor Frederick I (Barbarossa), and the Bishop of Freising near Munich. Otto is still wholly medieval and Christian, but, in the *Two Cities*, he makes an attempt to synthesize sacred and profane history by dovetailing the latter to the former. The seven books of Otto's work trace European history from the Christian creation down to the First Crusade. Otto's narrative is most detailed and impressive when he comes to his own time, particularly the First Crusade. He explicitly says that Emperor Alexius of Constantinople appealed to Pope Urban II for help against the Turks. He believed that the end of the world is near at hand and the *Two Cities* concluded with an expression of that end. In this vast composition Otto laid bare practically all the historical sources known to the Middle Ages. He rarely alludes to miracles for he had a more critical faculty than most medieval historians. His constructive mind enables him to sort out and arrange his material effectively. "The first indication of real historical criticism," writes J.W. Thompson, "is when he (Otto) declares the Donation of Constantine to be forgery."[21] Herbert Butterfield thinks that there seems to have been none who could rise to the level of Otto's thought.[22] Otto's is a profound and philosophical interpretation of history. He views history as an immense and glorious pattern foreordained by god, a pattern into which fitted every single fact, however detailed.

Having completed his universal history in 1147, Otto embarked on another work describing the deeds of his nephew, the Emperor Frederick I. With its multitude of accurate details and fine potraiture of a number of historical personalities, the *History of Emperor Frederick I* is a historical monument of immense importance. The author treats Frederick's conflict with the Lombard cities with such insight and interpretation that J.W. Thompson thinks that "it would tax a modern historian to do better."[23] Again, Otto's account of Frederick's quarrel with the papacy is particularly valuable as he has inserted many original documents and Frederick's own speeches.

Guibert de Nogent

The French historian who is the most sensitive to the spirit of the Twelfth-Century Renaissance and the Crusades was Guibert de Nogent. Guibert wrote a history of the First Crusade in eight books, which was completed in 1106. His picture of the change that the First Crusade effected in the minds of the French is remarkable. Pope Urban II preached the crusade at a time when France was in the throes of a famine and avaricious merchants raised all prices that the poor ate roots and wild herbs. But the cry of the crusade made men sell so cheap things that they could not take on their journey to Jerusalem that one might have seven sheep for five pence! The famine turned into abundance. Guibert must have had, thinks F.W. Thompson, some understanding of mob psychology as he shows how the preaching of the crusade converted the economic and social unrest that prevailed at the time into action.

William of Tyre

By far the best historian of the Crusades is William of Tyre (c. AD 1130–1184) who was the archbishop of Jerusalem. William's *History of Jerusalem* in twenty-three books was begun in AD 1169. It was incomplete in AD 1184 when the author died. With his knowledge of Byzantine Greek, Latin and Arabic, William of Tyre gathered material from all quarters. But he was less critical and more credulous than a historian ought to be. Master of a fine Latin style, he had unusual narrative power. Butterfield observes that he had sufficient objectivity to commend even the Arabs and Turks, and potray a not unfavorable picture of Nureddin and Saladin.[24] Further, William recognized the importance of commerce, analyzed personal motives, and showed a breadth of view that was unusual in Europe at the time. A great and noble example of historical writing, William of Tyre's *History of Jerusalem* became so popular that it was translated from Latin to French completely, and in parts to various other tongues.

William of Malmesbury and William of Newburg

The spirit of the Twelfth-Century Renaissance and the impulse produced by the Norman Conquest combined to produce a new Norman-English historiography as practised by William of Malmesbury and William of Newburgh. There was an improvement in method, the former stressing the right use of authorities, and the latter the justification of authority by reason. Even the distinction between external and internal criticism are found in the work of both Williams.[25] William of Malmesbury was the son of a French knight and an English mother. He was a monk in the old West Saxon abbey of Wiltshire. His *Lives of the Kings of England 449–1125*, and *Lives of the Bishops and Abbots of England 601–1125*, were both completed in 1125. William had a high conception of the nature of history and a just pride in his own ability as a historian. He not only narrated, but embarked on historical disquisition.

Henry Huntingdon

Another British historian of the same quality and conception was Henry Huntingdon, archdeacon of Huntingdon and Hertfordshire. His *Historia Anglorum* in twelve books tells the history of England from Caesar's invasion of Britain to the anarchic reign of Stephen. The author used all available sources, chiefly Bede and the *Anglo-Saxon Chronicle*. Five recensions between AD 1130 and 1155 attest to the popularity of the work. Henry had a clear idea of the nature of history. "History," he wrote in the prologue, "mirrors to us the past as though it were the present; it gathers from things past the image of things to come."[26]

9. Assessment of Christian or Medieval European Historiography

How did Christianity influence historical writing? R.G. Collingwood's assessment of that influence takes the following lines:[27]

(a) Revolution in Historical Thinking

Collingwood informs us that Christianity revolutionized and remodelled historical writing by throwing overboard two of the leading ideas of Graeco-Roman historiography. The first was the humanistic idea that man's free will and unaided intellect enable him to plan and pursue worthy ends. The Graeco-Roman idea would make man the wise architect of his own fortunes. Against this basic idea of human self-sufficiency, Christianity advanced its basic doctrine of human insufficiency and dependence on god. Christian doctrine held that human action is blind and that man cannot plan and pursue worthy ends, because sin is inherent and proper to human nature—a condition which man owed to his original sin. It follows that man's achievements are not due to his own forces of will and intellect, but to god's grace. Achievements like the conquest of the Mediterranean world by Rome came about not because men conceived them, but because god wanted such plans to be executed. Man is only the agent of god. The second Graeco-Roman idea to be overthrown by Christianity was the metaphysical doctrine of substance. Against the Graeco-Roman doctrine of substance, Christanity advanced its doctrine of creation. Rome was not a substance, changeless and eternal as Livy believed. And, as Tacitus believed, personal character like that of a Tiberius or Nero was not a substance, incapable of change or development. The Christian doctrine of creation axiomatically held that nothing is permanent or eternal, except god, and he created all else. What he has created, he can modify, be it cities, empires, or personal character.

(b) Characteristics of Christian Historiography

Christian or medieval European historiography has been variously called patristic, providential or salvation historiography. Collingwood affirms that any history written on Christian principles will be of necessity universal, providential, apocalyptic and periodized.

Universal History

History written on Christian principles is bound to be a universal history or a history of the world, going back to the origin of man, the *Book of Genesis.* It will describe how the various races of men came into existence, how civilizations rose and fell. Graeco-Roman oecumenical history is not universal in this sense, because it has a particularistic centre of gravity – Greece or Rome – round which it revolves. In a sort of Copernican revolution, Christianity destroyed the very idea of such a centre of gravity.

Providential History

Christian historiography ascribed events not to their human agents but to the workings of providence, preordaining their course. For providential history there are no 'chosen people', as the Jews thought themselves to be, no favourites of god.

Apocalyptic History

Christian historiography attached a central importance to the historical life of Christ. It treated earlier events as leading up to it or preparing for it, and subsequent events as developing its consequences. It therefore divided history into two parts: the first part leading up to the birth of Christ has a forward-looking character consisting in blind preparation for an event not yet revealed; the second part has a backward-looking character depending on the fact that the revelation has been made. Collingwood calls a history thus divided into two periods – a period of darkness and a period of light – apocalyptic history.

History Periodized

Having divided the past into two, Christian historiography subdivided it again. Thus history was divided into epochs or periods, each with particular characteristics of its own, and each marked off from the one before by an epoch-making event.

(c) Strength of Christian Historiography

Collingwood enumerates the following points of strength in Christian historiography.

Christianity Overcame the Abstract, One-sided Humanism of Graeco-Roman Historiography

The new Christian attitude towards history overcame the abstract one-sided humanism of Graeco-Roman historiography which made man the sole agent, and end of the historical process. Christian thought as developed by Eusebius, Ambrose, Jerome and Augustine asserted on the other hand that the historical process is the development of God's purposes and not of man's. God's purpose is man's well-being to realize which man is used as an instrument. In such a position, however, Collingwood sees an important gain for the understanding of the historical process.

> By this new attitude to human action history gained enormously, because the recognition that what happens in history need not happen through anybody's deliberately wishing it to happen is an indispensable pre-condition of understanding any historical process.[28]

Christian Universalism Overcame the Particularism of Graeco-Roman History

The universalism of the Christian attitude made all men equal in the sight of God; there is no chosen people, no privileged race or class, no one community whose fortunes are more important than those of another. All persons and all peoples are involved in the evolution of god's purpose, and the historical process is everywhere and always of the same kind, and every part of it is part of the same whole. Collingwood observes:

> The Christian cannot be content with Roman history or Jewish history or any other particularistic history: he demands a history of the world, a universal history whose theme shall be the general development of God's purposes for human life.[29]

(d) Weakness of Christian Historiography

It is to be wondered whether the weakness of Christian historiography did not outweigh its strength.

Defective Method

The first and the greatest weakness of Christian historiography was its defective method. The medieval historian still depended on tradition for his facts, but he had no effective means of studying or criticizing tradition. His only criticism, observes Collingwood, was personal, unscientific and unsystematic, which often betrayed him into foolish credulity. There was no critical apparatus to scrutinize the Christian religious stories nor was any scrutiny attempted. Whenever an extraordinary situation arose, its explanation was sought in the notion of the Divine Will, and not on the basis of cause and effect. The great task of medieval historiography was the task not of establishing facts by means of a critical method, but of discovering and explaining the divine purpose or divine plan which was supposed to have an objective necessity of its own irrespective of human wishes. The aim dictated the method.

Defective Periodization

Medieval historiography conceived of historical ages or periods each initiated by an historical event. But the scheme of periods, for example, the 'Four Empires', was based not on accurate interpretation of facts but on an arbitrary scheme borrowed from the *Book of Daniel*. Collingwood illustrates the danger lurking in medieval Christian periodization with a single example. In the twelfth century, Jochim of Floris divided history into the following periods: the reign of the Father or unincarnate God, i.e., the pre-Christian age; the reign of the Son or the Christian age; and the reign of the Holy Ghost which was to begin in the future. If challenged to explain how he knew that there was an objective plan for the future at all, the simple, credulous medieval historian would reply that he knew it by revelation which gave the key to know what god was going to do in the future. Medieval historiography looked forward to the end of history as something foreordained by god and through revelation foreknown to man. The entire scheme, hinging on eschatology, was unhistorical.

Eschatology

But eschatology, the doctrine of the last or final things, or the ability to know the future in advance, says Collingwood, is always an intrusive element in history. This is because the historian's business is to know the past, not to know the future. A historian's claim to know the future in advance of its happening is a sure sign that something has gone wrong with his fundamental conception of history. That historian is in error who imagines that he can forecast the future. The root of the error could be traced back to providential or salvation history.

Providentialism

There is in medieval historical thought a complete opposition between the objective purpose of god and the subjective purpose of man. God's purpose appears to be an imposition of a certain objective plan upon history quite irrespective of man's subjective purposes. Man's purposes then make no difference to the course of history and the only force that determines it is the transcendent divine nature. Transcendence means that the divine activity is conceived not as working in and through human activity but as working outside it and overruling it; not immanent in the world of human action but transcending that world. The transcendentalist view looks for the essence of history outside of history, and is unhistorical.

Neglect of the Primary Duty of the Historian

Transcendentalism led the medieval Christian historians to neglect the primary duty of the historian. They exaggerated the work of providence in history to a point which left nothing for man to do. The result was that in their anxiety to detect god's plan in history, medieval Christian historians tended to look away from man's actions. For them consequently, the actual detail of human actions was relatively unimportant. In this they were neglecting, as Collingwood's searching eyes bring out, "that prime duty of the historian, a willingness to bestow infinite pains on discovering what actually happened."[30] And this is why medieval historiography was so weak in critical method. The weakness was not due to a limitation of source materials, but rather due to a conception of what medieval scholars wanted to do—detect god's plan, and narrate past events according to that supposed plan. What they wanted was not history but theology. For this reason medieval historiography was, in the words of Collingwood "deliberately and repulsively wrong-headed."[31]

(e) Impact of Christian or Medieval European Historiography on European Historical Thought

The Christian view of history had corrected three defects of Graeco-Roman historiography—an abstract one-sided humanism, substantialism and particularism. In a final assessment Collingwood discusses how the Christian reorientation of history "left its heritage as a permanent enrichment of historical thought."[32]

Firstly, *the Christian conception of history as the history of the world became a commonplace.* The symbol of this universalism was the adoption of a single chronological framework for all historical events. Eusebius in his *Chronicle* thus brought all events within a single chronological scheme instead of dating events in Greece by the Olympiads, events in Rome by the Roman consular fasti, and so on. The single universal chronology invented by Isidore of Seville in the seventh century and popularized by Bede in the eighth, dated everything forward and backward from the birth of Christ. The source was Christian.

Likewise, *the providential idea became a commonplace.* Collingwood cites the instance of how students in England are taught that in the eighteenth century the English conquered an empire in a fit of absent-mindedness. It means, says Collingwood, that what the English then did appears to us in retrospect as in accordance with a plan, but no such plan was present in their minds at the time. What did happen was not something which the executors had planned.

Again, *the apocalyptic idea also became a commonplace* although, as Collingwood points out, historians have placed their apocalyptic moments at many points of time: the Renaissance, the invention of printing, the scientific movement of the seventeenth century, the Enlightenment, the French Revolution, the Liberal movement of the nineteenth century, or even, as with Marxist historians, in the future.

And, finally, *the idea of epoch-making events became a commonplace.* With this idea the division of history into periods each with its own peculiar character has become a common practice.

All these elements, so familiar in modern historical thought, were totally absent from Graeco-Roman historiography and were consciously and laboriosly developed by the early Christians.

II. MEDIEVAL MUSLIM HISTORIOGRAPHY (WEST ASIAN TRADITION)

1. The Influences behind Islamic Historiography

Ta'rikh in Arabic means the organization of material by date and hence, by extension, history. In pre-Islamic Arabia the feeling for the past had expressed itself, as among any primitive people, in ballad or saga of the genealogies and tribes of the Arabian peninsula—half legend and half history. It was the life of Prophet Muhammad that marked the great dividing line in Arab history. But historiography was an acquired characteristic in Islam as the Arabs were not really historically minded.[33] The influence did not come from Greece. For all their contact with the Greeks and the peoples of the Near East, the Arabs did not discover the historians of classical Greece.

The first decisive influence behind Muslim historiography was the conquest of a vast empire. The Arabs, like the ancient Romans, built an empire spreading over Asia, Africa and Europe. The two cohesive forces that held this empire together were the Islamic religion and the Arabic language. Empire building and the propensity to write history go together. The second decisive influence came from conquered Persia.

> Although after the Muhammadan conquest of the East, Arabic was the only vehicle of literary expression, it is important to observe that most of the thinking in Islam and most of the literature was of the Persian mind.[34]

The inspiration for history writing seems to have come directly from Sassanid Persia where a historiographical tradition had taken roots under the stimulus of the exiled Greek scholars from Edessa and Athens. A considerable amount of Sassanid historical sources survived the Muslim conquest of Persia (the Battle of Nehawand, AD 641). Among the captured treasures of Ctesiphon was a copy of the important historical work, the *Kudai-Namak* (*Book of Kings*) which was sent to the Khalif in Damascus, where it was kept as a curio. In the middle of the eighth century, a Persian noble and convert to Islam translated this work into Arabic. It revealed to the Arabs the long and great history of the country which they had conquered. They now began to evince an interest in their own past and in the past of the peoples whom they had subjugated. A third factor which particularly aided Muslim historiography was a common chronology which began with the Hejira or the migration of the Prophet from Mecca to Medina in AD 622. The zeal instilled by the new religion and a common chronology were factors which proved to be of great stimulus to the writing of history.

Medieval Muslim (Arab and Persian) Historiography

Muslim history writing flourished with the foundation of the Abbasid Khalifate. It now established itself in the Islamic world as an independent branch of knowledge, and displayed a new vigor, dignity and magnitude. Not only the volume, but the variety of Muslim historical literature in the Middle Ages was great—universal histories of huge dimensions, histories of single countries under Muslim domination, dynastic histories, city chronicles, biographies, and travel literature. An outline of the immense corpus of this literature, which is bound to be narrowly selective, may be given under separate heads.

2. The Islamic East

Muhammad Ben Ishaq (d. AD 767) is said to have been the earliest recorder of Muhammad's campaigns. He also wrote a history of the Umayyad dynasty of Damascus (AD 661–750). Abu Ibn Yahya who died in AD 774 wrote thirty-three treatises on different persons and events, besides a *History of the Conquest of Iraq* which was his most important work. The last decades of the eighth and the early decades of the ninth century constituted a brilliant period in Abbasid historiography which corresponded to the Carolingian renaissance in Europe. To this period belonged Waqidi (AD 760–837), a native of Medina and a favourite of the great Harun al-Rashid. Waqidi's *Kitab-al-Maghazi* is a history of the military and missionary expansion of Islam. When Waqidi traveled – and he was always traveling – it required hundred and twenty camels to transport his library which he took with him everywhere. Of more eminence was Al-Madaini (d.c. AD 845), the author of the *Book of the Conquests from Abu Bekr to Othman, Book of the Khalifs*, two monographs on India, and *Tarikh al-Khulafa*. Al-Baladhuri (d. AD 892) was a prolific historian the titles of whose works would fill five printed pages! Baladhuri was principally interested in the westward expansion of Islam. His *History of the Conquests* covers the subjugation of Syria, Mesopotamia, Armenia, Egypt, Cyprus, Spain and Nubia. Selective in method, the work supplies a substantial narrative of the conquest of each province. One of the greatest of not only the Muslim historians but of all historians was Tabari (AD 838–923). Tabari was an indefatigable traveler and assiduous searcher for information. His *History of the Prophets and Kings* was the first universal history in the Arabic language. It was so vast in conception that Tabari did not live to complete it. A native of Baghdad, Al-Masudi spent years traveling through the Muslim world. He had written, before his death in AD 956, thirty-six works. Of these, the principal surviving work is the *Murudj* for whose composition he used 165 written sources including translations of Plato, Aristotle and Ptolemy as well as Arabic versions of the monuments of Pahlavi literature.[35] A work of encyclopedic range, the *Murudj* is written in a historico-geographical framework containing important references to rivers and seas and customs and religious practices of many people and countries, and a universal chronology. Masudi's compendium became a basic book of reference to future historians. Miskawaihi (d. AD 1032) was of Persian origin. His work, *The Experience of Nations*, is singularly valuable for matters of taxation and finance, and for economic and social conditions. Celebrated to the ends of the Muslim world was the *Obituaries of Eminent Men* by Ibn Khallikhan (AD 1211–1282). It is the earliest biographical dictionary in the Arabic language and a monument to the author's learning and literary industry. Abul Feda (AD 1273–1331), in spite of a long and active military and civil career, wrote a *Universal History* which extends to AD 1328. Of historians who wrote in Persian during this period was Minhaj-i-Siraj of Juzjan. In AD 1226 he was in India as the protege of Iltumish. In AD 1260 he completed a great universal history, the *Tabakati-i-Nasiri*, which began with the patriarchs and ended with the Mongol invasion of AD 1258. Rashid al-Din (AD 1247–1318) was born of Jewish parents in Hamadan in western Persia and was trained as a physician. Converted to Islam at the age of thirty he became *wazir* (prime minister), and from AD 1298 until his execution in AD 1318, was the leading statesman of the Mongol kingdom of Persia and Iraq, the Ilkhanate. Rashid's *Jami-al Tawarikh* (*Collection of Histories*) had been originally planned to cover only the Mongols and their conquests but later came to include all the peoples with whom the Mongols had come in contact. The first of the two parts of the lengthy work is said to be the most important single source in any language for the history of the Mongol world empire. Though not objective, the high bureaucrat's knowledge of affairs is exemplified in the information given. Historiographically the second part is more interesting. It includes accounts of China, India, the Turks, the Jews, the Franks, etc. and thus has claims to be regarded as a world history.

*Al-Biruni (*AD *973–1048)*

From the conquered Khwarazm in Persia, Mahmud of Ghazni had carried away Al-Biruni as a hostage (AD 1017). A scholar of encyclopedic range, Al-Biruni's *Surviving Monuments of Past Generations* is a comparative chronology. The scholar followed the conqueror to India where he lived for thirteen years studying Sanskrit and translating several books from Sanskrit into Arabic, as well as rendering several Arabic translations of Greek originals into Sanskrit.[36] Al-Biruni's most famous work, the *Kitab-ul-Hind* (*Book of India*) is a deep sociological study characterized by a rare spirit of inquiry, modern scientific attitude and sympathetic insight. The author studied Indian culture in its varied aspects – philosophy, mathematics, astronomy – and made keen observations. He noted the defective historical and chronological sense of the Hindus, their complacent sense of inherent superiority (born of ignorance of the outside world), and their supreme contempt for the learning of other peoples. Al-Biruni informs us:

> We can only say, folly is an illness for which there is no medicine, and the Hindus believe that there is no country but theirs, no nation like theirs, no kings like theirs, no religion like theirs, no science like theirs. They are haughty, foolishly vain, self-conceited, and stolid. They are by nature niggardly in communicating that which they know, and they take the greatest possible care to withhold it from men of another caste among their own people, still much more, of course, from any foreigner. Their haughtiness is such that, if you tell them of any science or scholar in Khurasan and Persis, they will think you to be both an ignoramus and a liar. If they travelled and mixed with other nations, they would soon change their mind, for their ancestors were not as narrow-minded as the present generation is....[37]

He appreciated Hindu intellectual achievements where they deserved such appreciation. The English translator of the *Kitab-ul-Hind*, Edward Sachau, writes:

> The work of Alberuni is unique in Muslim literature as an earliest attempt to study an idolatrous world of thought, not proceeding from the intention of attacking and refuting it, but uniformly showing the desire to be just and impartial....[38]

Al-Biruni's work, writes Jarret, was "like a magic world of quiet, impartial research in the midst of a world of clashing swords, burning towns and plundered temples"[39]—a spiritual retort to Mahmud's oppression and iconoclasm.

3. The Islamic West

Islamic Egypt did not give much evidence of its hoary historic past until the Fatimite period in the ninth century when Cairo became the capital of a state seceded from the Khalifate. Then a separate school of historical studies arose. The history of the Muslim conquest of Egypt is related by Al-Qurashi (AD 802–871) in his *Futuh Misr*. Divided into seven books, the work traces Egyptian history back to the Persian occupation under Darius I, and closes with the ninth century. El-Kindi (d. AD 961), another Egyptian historian, wrote a *History of the Judges of Egypt*. In Egypt under the Mamelukes in the fifteenth century there were many distinguished historians. The greatest of them all was Ibn Taghri Birdi. Birdi's *Annals* contain a number of subjects, all treated with careful objectivity. Philosophical by nature, Birdi had an astonishingly broad perception of what was of value in history along with unusual interpretative power. Of special importance are the economic data he provides. He makes numerous mentions of the price of commodities in the markets, of fluctuations of coinage, and of the ratio between gold, silver and copper coins. A school of historians arose in conquered Spain. The oldest known history of Muslim Spain was written by al-Razi (d. AD 937). The work is preserved only in a Spanish recension, the *Chronicle del Moro Rasis*. The other Spanish historians were Arib ben Sa'd (c. AD 996), author of the *History of the Founding of the Fatimite Dynasty*; and Ibn Adhari (d. AD 1292), who wrote a *History of Africa and Spain* at a time when the crescent was waning in the peninsula. Further, an important series of biographical works, commencing in the tenth and continuing into the thirteenth century, has been preserved, which compensates for the loss of other historical works pertaining to Muslim Spain.

4. Medieval Muslim Historians of the Crusades and of the Mongol Invasions

As in the West, the Crusades stimulated historical writing in the Muslim world too. The *Damascus Chronicle* of al-Qalanisi is an indispensable source for the First and the Second Crusades, particularly as it supplements the Latin and Byzantine narratives and enables us to check their veracity. The historical sources for the career of the great Saladin are abundant. The most valuable of the four biographies of Saladin was written by Baha-ad-Din (AD 1145–1234) of Mosul, who was a professor in the university there. He was Saladin's secretary and was by the conqueror's side when Jerusalem was captured in AD 1187.

Several writers have related the history of the earth-shaking invasions of the Mongols under Jingiz Khan in the thirteenth century. Ibn-al-Athir in his universal history based on Tabari, opens the account for the year AD 1220–21 with a description of the Mongols' appalling cruelty and the havoc they created. A new series of Mongol invasions came late in the fourteenth century with the appearance of Timur. By AD 1400, Timur's empire stretched from the confines of China and northwestern India to Hungary. The *Zafar-namah* (*Chronicle of Victory*) of Sharaf ud-Din Yazdi, a Persian and a close friend of the conqueror's son, Shah Rukh, had been popular from its appearance and was continued by various hands until as late as AD 1454. A *Life of Timurlane* by Ibn 'Arashah (AD 1392–1450), who as a child had been carried captive from Damascus by Timur, is naturally hostile to the Mongol conqueror. Interestingly enough, one of the sources on Timur is his own *Memoirs.*

5. Medieval Muslim Literature on Geography and Travel

The medieval Muslims produced remarkable literature on geography and travel which often contained significant material of historical interest. The far-flung nature of the Islamic empire, the universal practice of pilgrimage to Mecca, trade and commerce, and the necessities of administration and diplomacy were influences which stimulated travel. The postal system of the Abbasid empire was a continuation and extension of the former Persian and Byzantine systems, and it greatly facilitated communication between countries and peoples. The voyages of 'Sindbad the Sailor' in the *Arabian Nights*, though fictitious, must have added to this spirit of adventure and wanderlust. With travel went the development of a considerable geographical and, often, an ethnographical, literature. The more important of the great number of *rihla* (travelogues) and geographical works are—*Chain of Histories*, a volume of travelers' tales on China, India and Africa; the *Wonders of India* (AD 851), the author of which was Ramhurmuz, a Persian sea captain; Ibn Hawqal's (d. AD 966) *Book of Ways and Provinces*; the Spanish Muslim Abu-El-Bekri's (d. AD 1094) *Roads and Realms*; Spanish geographer El Idrisi's *Book of Roger* (twelfth century); still another Spanish Muslim Jubayer's (b. AD 1183) *Travels*; Yakut's (c. AD 1179–1229) *Geographical Dictionary*; Al-Qazwini's (AD 1203–80) *Monuments of the Lands;* and Ibn Batuta's *Rihla* (*Travels in Asia and Africa*).

Ibn Batuta (AD *1304–1377)*

As traveler and writer of travelogues few could rival Ibn Batuta. Batuta's travels, covering the period 1325–1354, took him to Egypt, Syria, Asia Minor, Byzantium (from where he made an excursion into Russia and saw the midnight sun), Persia, Arabia, Turkestan, India, Sri Lanka, the Malay Peninsula, Sumatra, Java, Borneo, the Philippines, and China. He returned home in 1349. Still restless and curious, he crossed to Spain and finally culminated his wanderings by penetrating the Sahara and visiting the Black Muslim lands on the Niger.[40]

It was from Transoxiana and Afghanisthan that Batuta crossed to the Indus valley. In 1334 he was in Delhi. Muhammad Tughlak appointed him *qazi* (judge) of the imperial city which position he occupied for eight years. Unfortunately he lost the sultan's favour and was imprisoned. Soon, however, he was released and was sent as Muhammad's ambassador to China in 1342. Shipwreck drove him to Maldives and thence he visited Sri Lanka and Madura.

Batuta's *Rihla* was completed in 1355. Its value has been recognized, particularly for his description of India. From his acquaintances in Delhi he had constructed an account of the sultans from Aibak to Ghiyas-ud-din Tughlak. But much of what he wrote about Muhammad Tughlak must have come from personal knowledge and experience. The Moroccan traveler's reliability is unquestionable. His picture of the Tughlak monarch is in perfect harmony with that of the historian of the Delhi sultanate, Barani. Batuta's *Rihla*, according to M. Husain, is a "mine of history".[41]

6. Ibn Khaldoun (AD 1332–1406)

The most celebrated thinker and historian of the Islamic world, Ibn Khaldoun, was born in Tunis in a Berber family of scholars and statesmen. He had a good though haphazard education. His perilously adventurous career took him to Egypt in 1382, where he died in 1406. For a glimpse of his true nature, one has to turn to the *Al-Taarif*, the short autobiography which the philosopher-historian attached to his *Kitab-al-Ibar* (*Universal History*). And, here, Khaldoun does not attempt to whitewash his nature and character. The author of the *Al-Taarif* is not a man above moral reproach but one recklessly pushing his way to grasp what he considered his due. Yet it is strange that this man who was politically unreliable, who changed sides as many times as he had masters to serve, should have kept steadfast all through his turbulent life to the occupation of thought.

Khaldoun's *Kitab-al-Ibar* consists of three great books. The first book treats of civilization, its essential characteristics, and its influence upon human beings; the second book tells the story of the Arabs with important and elaborate references to the history of all the nations from Central Asia to Italy; and the third book covers the history of the author's own Maghrib (northwest Africa and its Berber dynasties). Prefixed to these three books is the celebrated *Muqaddima* or *Prolegomena* (*Introduction*), which is an elaborate treatise on the science of history and the development of society; and suffixed to the three books of the *Ibar* is the *Al-Taarif*, a short autobiography of the author. Important as the *Ibar* is, it is, however, the *Muqaddima* which has engaged the attention of posterity. For it is in this part of his work that the Berber author expounds his philosophy of history, rather his sociological view of history. It is the book into which he pours all the powers of his subtle genius; the masterpiece which, even after six centuries, extorts the admiration of sociologists and theorists of history. It is the *Muqaddima* by which Ibn Khaldoun lives through the centuries.

Method

The *Muqaddima* (c. AD 1378), Khaldoun's lengthy methodological preface to his world history, is, in intention, an introduction to the historian's craft.[42] The historian should know his craft for the simple reason that the knowledge of the past comes to him bound up with much that is untrue. Khaldoun therefore set out to lay down, like Vico would in the eighteenth century, certain principles of historical criticism.

Belief

Belief in god did not deter our philosopher-historian from the study of processes. He restricted the influence of the divine to the unusual and the extraordinary in human affairs. Likewise, Khaldoun did not think of the supernatural as conditioning the ordinary course of man's life or "as a necessity in the historical drama".[43] He dismisses a thousand stories as being incompatible with the facts of the physical world and of human nature.

Historian's Qualifications

Khaldoun censures in strong terms previous annalists, chroniclers and historians for their lack of historical insight, their inability to think, to check, and to probe. This inability made many historical accounts "the vehicle of nonsensical statements".[44] To eliminate nonsensical stories and to inquire into the cause of events and conditions, the historian must have a skeptical mind which would not trust as true all that is transmitted to him. Lest he should lead himself astray from truth and land "in the desert of baseless assumptions and errors,"[45] he should equip himself with an abundance of sources and varied knowledge of the fundamental facts of politics, the nature of civilization, and the conditions governing human social organization.

Sources of Error

Khaldoun goes on to enumerate the sources of error which make objective history impossible. The first is bias or partiality. Partiality or sectarianism makes the historian unhesitatingly receive the information that is agreeable to him while impartiality leads him to investigate the information transmitted. "Prejudice and partisanship obscure the critical faculty and preclude critical investigation."[46]

A condition which makes falsehood unavoidable is ignorance of the nature peculiar to the essence of an event or a phenomenon different from its accidental circumstances. But the reason that makes untruth inevitable in historiography is an uncritical reliance on transmitters or informants. An informant may fail to know due to ignorance or inadvertence whether the picture he has of an event or condition conforms to reality or not. Again, susceptibility to flattery which is ingrained in human nature makes men indulge in false praise and encomiums which obscure historical truth. Personality criticism or an inquiry into the probity of the informant will help determine the reliability or unreliability of the information transmitted. Wrong information once accepted as true is believed, based on the authority of those who thus accept and transmit it.

Application of Sociology to History

To Khaldoun, a knowledge of the state of society and the degree of civilization, i.e., the conditioning circumstances of an age, was the means of weeding out the legends and untruths which encumbered history.[47] He was certain that the application of sociology to history could distinguish truth from falsehood, the possible from the impossible. For example, Al-Masudi and other historians report that Moses left Egypt with 600,000 soldiers. According to Masudi, Jacob and his followers entering Egypt 220 years before Moses, did not number more than seventy. How could the seventy Israelites have multiplied into such a large number in 220 years as to provide an army of 600,000—those able to carry arms? The information is incompatible with the facts of human life and the needs and resources of states. Israel of Solomon's time was at its most prosperous; and yet, Solomon had only 12,000 soldiers and 1,400 horses. The knowledge that a state's militia is directly proportional to the size of its administrative units enables the historian to avoid committing errors of this kind in using his sources.

Theme and Content: History as the Science of Culture and Civilization

In the *Muqaddima*, Ibn Khaldoun studied the general laws of historical development, expounded the cause of historical change, and presented a cyclic view of history.

What makes history a science worthy of study is its investigation of human social organization. "It should be known," writes Khaldoun, "that history, in matter of fact, is information about human social organization which itself is identical with world civilization."[48] History is the science of culture. Culture is the product of the cumulative impact of material, political, social, moral and philosophical elements. According to Khaldoun it is generated by material cause, formal cause, efficient cause, and final cause. By material cause, the first determinant of culture, Khaldoun meant environmental factors such as geography, climate, fertility of the soil and vegetation. These determine the ways in which men earn their living. His formal cause is the political factor, the state, the instrument through which culture actually takes shape. Khaldoun's efficient cause is an abstract idea, a teleological principle, like soul in a body. He regarded as its components such elements of social cohesion as solidarity, harmony, moderation and justice. The Berber historian's final cause is ethical and philosophical in nature—it is the idea of common good. Knowledge, itself a part of culture, accelerates its growth. Knowledge may be theoretical, practical, or productive, comparable to our humanities, sciences and technology.

Culture, like any living organism, is subject to the laws of birth, growth and decay. It is in the nature of every culture to undergo change. Khaldoun had such a sophisticated idea of the movement and change in human life that he considered the disregard of the fact of change as a hidden pitfall in historiography.

Sociological View of History

What makes the *Muqaddima* an independent work of striking originality is its author's attempt to explain the historical process in terms of the sociological phenomenon. Khaldoun rightly regarded his new approach as a new science, *al-umran*, meaning sociology or the science of human society, which he equated with human civilization.

The centre of Ibn Khaldoun's world is man. If Aristotle called man a 'political animal', it was this medieval Muslim thinker who gave to that phrase its full import of meaning by calling him a 'social animal'. Society is necessary because man cannot live by himself; he must seek the cooperation of his fellowmen in meeting the needs of his existence like food, shelter and defence. Mutual help is the law of human life without which the human species would vanish. Khaldoun describes man biologically. Despite his privileged rationality man remains instinctively an animal. The need for social organization is felt from the fact that, if left to his own animal instincts, man would eat man. Social organization is the first step in man's historical career, for it is the beginning of civilization. As soon as several human beings begin to cooperate with each other and to form some kind of social organization, *umran* results. *Al-umran* is a key word in the *Muqaddima* which Franz Rosenthal translates as 'civilization', and which, as Khaldoun meant it, is identical with social organization.

Another key word used in a very positive sense by the Berber thinker is *asabiyah*, which meant 'group feeling', natural solidarity, or a readiness and a desire to make common cause with others. *Asabiyah*, meant as a feeling or state of mind, is generated by ties of blood or by long and close contact. Beginning with man's physical environment and its influence upon him, Khaldoun discussed human society and its development from its primitive nomadic state to its settled condition in organized urban communities and states. The urban community, in comparison to desert or rural settlements, is to him, the highest form of social organization and civilization.

State as Political Authority

Herbert Butterfield writes that Ibn Khaldoun seems to stand alone among Islamic writers in his attempt to connect history with political science and forms of sociological inquiry.[49] In the *Muqaddima*, Khaldoun propounds a theory of state, again in the background of sociology.

Social organization based on cooperation could only be political in nature. The state is a natural growth. But its formation cannot come from within urban civilization, which lacks the essential ingredient, *asabiyah*. It is found in the more primitive kinds of social structures, such as that of the nomads and semi-nomads, since the conditions under which life is lived outside the cities require tribal organization. The nomads possess strength, courage and endurance, as well as *asabiyah* to a far higher degree than the more 'civilized' people. A nomadic community with a superior *asabiyah* and led by a *wazi* (leader) of native ability conquers an existing dynasty or state or founds a new one, the leader winning *mulk* (royal authority). For such a process, one further binding element is religion. The classic example is that of the early Muslim conquests. The Arabs, united under the rule of the Prophet and his successors by both a strong *asabiyah* and a divinely revealed religion, were invincible and set up the urban civilization of the Khalifate.[50] The state, once established, proceeds through a natural sequence of growth, maturity, decline and fall. No dynasty could expect to survive for more than three or at the most four generations. Civilization inevitably erodes tribal *asabiyah*. The ruler becomes absolute, and begins to rely on the paid army and bureaucracy, and no longer on his virile tribesmen. Luxury and leisure become the aims of life. Civilization attains a stage when the sciences are cultivated and when only luxuries are produced, and the dynasty or state enters a period of senile decay. Then a new dynasty or state is established only to suffer the same inexorable fate.

Economist

Khaldoun's idea of man's comprehensive development in society led him to a consideration of the influence exerted by lifestyle and methods of production on the evolution of social groups. Analyzing the role of labor, for example, he observes that when population increases, the amount of labor also increases, leaving a surplus. This surplus labor is channeled to the production not of necessities but of luxuries. There are even those who like to interpret Khaldoun in the spirit of Marxist dialectical materialism.[51]

Stylist

Khaldoun claims to have "tamed rude speech," and to his contemporaries the style of the *Muqaddima* appeared to be "more brilliant than well-strung pearls and finer than water fanned by the zephyr."[52] And Rosenthal, the translator of the *Muqaddima*, testifies to the pleasure of reading it or hearing it read aloud. Yet he observes that Khaldoun's style is discursive, meant for the lecturer and the classroom rather than for a general reading public. The *Al-Taarif* is considered a masterpiece of Arabic literature.

Assessment

It has been said in criticism that although Ibn Khaldoun's scheme fits the circumstances of North Africa in his own day, it is not for universal application. Again, it has been pointed out that having propounded an exciting new way of writing history, Ibn Khaldoun did not follow his own instructions in the *Kitab-al-Ibar*.[53] The Berber thinker had little influence on his immediate successors, though his pupil Maqrizi pursued his master's interest in economic and demographic factors.

Ever since Western scholarship discovered the *Muqaddima* in the nineteenth century, it has showered encomiums on its author. It is surprising that a medieval Muslim scholar, brought up in a religious and theocratic atmosphere, held out such original views – rational, scientific and secular – views which were to be expressed later by Machiavelli, Vico, Montesquieu, Adam Smith and Auguste Comte. The wealth of ideas provided in the *Muqaddima* makes it "one of the solemn moments of human thought;"[54] a wealth in which the early beginnings of a number of modern disciplines could be discerned. "If Thucydides is the inventor of history," writes Y. Lacoste, "Ibn Khaldoun introduces history as a science."[55] To Arnold Toynbee the *Muqaddima* is "undoubtedly the greatest work of its kind that has ever yet been created by any mind in any time or place."[56] Endless praise has been heaped on Ibn Khaldoun whose 'new science' was but a system of sociology. The ideas of the *Muqaddima* continue to exercise a considerable influence on the thought of contemporary writers such as Ernest Gellner;[57] to its English translator, Franz Rosenthal, it is "a work that ranks as one of mankind's important triumphs."[58]

7. Source Criticism in Islamic Historiography

The method of source criticism in Islamic historiography is called *isnad*. Little need was felt for stating one's authorities in the earliest times. But a strong need to state one's sources was realized as the first century of Islam advanced and the first important histories (in the sense of sustained narratives of important political events) came to be written in the ninth century. Among other kinds of material, these histories drew on *hadith* (tradition), that is, orally transmitted recollections of the sayings and deeds of the Prophet Muhammad.[59] The essential part of the transmission of tradition was a chain of authorities—*isnad. Isnad* as a method tries to ascertain an event by tracing it to the person who actually participated in it, or saw others participating in it. It insists that the veracity of all those persons who transmitted the fact relating to that event should be checked by investigating their conduct, character, circumstances and background. This was the essence of the principle of criticism evolved by scholars of *ahadis. Isnad*, in the words of Philip Hitti, "meets the most essential requirements of modern historiography."[60] The collections of traditions which were composed mainly from the ninth century onwards, give complete *isnads*.

There was nothing in Islamic historiography which can be said to have grown in preparation for Ibn Khaldoun's formulation of a system of source criticism. Khaldoun was a solitary figure with no predecessors or successors.

4

I. THE IMPACT OF THE RENAISSANCE ON HISTORIOGRAPHY

1. The Renaissance: Its Meaning

From the time of Petrarch (AD 1305–74) in the fourteenth century, the European mind began to experience changes of great magnitude. Scholasticism, the general name given to medieval education, slowly gave way to a new kind of learning signified by a spirit of inquiry, a spirit which affected every aspect of human thought and activity. An important aspect of the 'New Learning', as it was called, was the eager search for and an enthusiastic study of the works of the ancient Greeks and Romans. The culture of the ancients with its ideals of beauty, freedom and joy of life was imbibed, and the test of reason was applied to everything religious or profane. This fundamental change in the thought and taste of the Western man is designated by the term Humanism. The Humanists or those who took to the New Learning rejected the supernatural and put human interest and the mind of man paramount. They were concerned more with man than with god, with refinement of life here on earth than in the problems of life hereafter. The humanist movement reached its climax in the fifteenth century which ushered in the Renaissance, a great creative movement which emancipated Western thought from the shackles of medieval Christianity.

2. The Impact of the Renaissance on Historiography

The Renaissance represented a totally new spirit, a new confidence in man's limitless capacities. It was asserted that man was endowed with free will so that he could be his own maker and moulder.[1] Such confidence in the boundless capacity of man surely did not belong to the medieval period, but to the modern. The Renaissance spirit made a great impact on historiography. It could be seen in a return to the humanistic view of history, the emergence of the lay historian, a new interest in the remains of the past; an advance in historical criticism, and in the growth of a new school of humanistic historians such as Machiavelli and Guicciardini.

Return to the Humanistic View of History

The new interest in man and the world in the place of medieval otherworldliness led to a revival and reorientation of historical studies in the West. The Renaissance orientation represented a return to the humanistic view of life based on that of the ancient Greeks and Romans. Historical thought once more came to be focused on man.

Emergence of the Lay Historian

Closely related to the revival of interest in man and the world was a swing away from the medieval Christian tradition and a gradual secularization of life and thought which was reflected in the writing of history. Theological interpretations of history and the supernatural element in historiography disappeared as men ceased to believe in the operation of a providential plan in their affairs. History became purely mundane. Monastic annals and chronicles, universal histories and world chronicles, lives of saints and bishops, all went out of fashion with the emergence of the lay historian. This occurred first in Italy. Here the survival of some lay schools right down from Roman times – in spite of the ascendancy of the medieval Church in education – and the revived study of Roman law were factors which stimulated lay historical writing. Lay history was further promoted by the prevalence of political regimes in Lombardy, Piedmont and Tuscany, which unlike Naples and the papal states, were comparatively free as well from papal as from feudal influences. The cities of Lombardy, Piedmont and Tuscany were mostly independent republics and their societies predominantly bourgeois. Public offices were elective and the very intensity of local issues and party strife made for an intensely realistic history writing.

Interest in the Remains of the Past: Establishment of the Science of Archeology

A particular effect of humanism on Renaissance historiography was a newly awakened interest in archeological remains, succinctly described by Herbert Butterfield as an interest "in the sheer pastness of things past…".[2] The Italians were indifferent to the monuments of antiquity and even the humanist Pope Nicholas V (AD 1447–1455) had permitted a contractor to despoil the Coliseum of 2600 cartloads of cut stones![3] But there was now a definite change of attitude. Already in the fourteenth century historical writers had discovered the value of inscriptions, coins and medals as historical sources. In the fifteenth century was awakened a genuine sentiment for the surviving remnants of the past. There emerged a fervor for 'antiquities' which began to show itself in an eager search for ancient manuscripts, the founding of societies and museums, and in imposing publications. Tacitus's *Agricola* and *Germania* were recovered in 1455 and parts of his *Annals* were brought to light in 1506. In 1473 appeared a Latin translation of a great part of Polybius's work. Poggio Bracciolini, a historian of Florence, was a passionate manuscript hunter. Nicolao Nicoli, a Florentine merchant, was a pioneer in the collection and preservation of rare books. Lorenzo de Medici had a museum in one of his palaces. Pope Sixtus IV founded the Capitoline museum. Archeology as a science of scholarship was established by Flavio Biondo (1388–1463). "The new science of archaeology," writes J.W. Thompson, "not only furnished a valuable commentary to the classical revival, it contributed also to critical method and historical interpretation."[4]

Advance of Historical Criticism

Humanist historiography marked a general advance of historical criticism. The Italian humanists who had reached a high degree of critical awareness, achieved "a great clearing away of what had been fanciful and ill-founded in medieval historiography."[5]

1. A new form of criticism, *philological criticism*, was to liberate history writing from the grip of tradition and the binding force of authority. In AD 1440 Lorenzo Valla (1406–57) set out to prove that the *Donation of Constantine* had been a forgery. It was on the

authority of this document that the temporal power of the papacy had largely reposed. Valla was at the time in the service of Alfonso, King of Aragon and Sicily. His criticism, appearing at a time when King Alfonso was at war with the pope, was, in fact, part of a bitter publicity campaign.[6] In assailing the document, Valla employed not only the known evidence of history, but made brilliant use of philology, numismatics, psychology, and, common sense. Was it not against ordinary experience that an emperor would have disinherited his children? And how would the Roman Senate have agreed to such an alienation? From such arguments resting on common sense Valla proceeded to expose the absurdities and contradictions in the text, the barbarity of the Latin, and the mistakes in terminology.[7] The philologist came to the conclusion that the historical setting in which alone the document could be placed was AD 752–756, and therefore the document was a forgery. The first great triumph of humanist critical scholarship, the famous expose was the first achievement of textual criticism.

2. Jean Bodin in 1566 showed in his *The Method for the Easy Comprehension of History* that the accepted scheme of periods, the Four Empires, was based not on accurate interpretation of facts but on an arbitrary scheme borrowed from the *Book of Daniel*.[8] Bodin's ideas on criticism did not, however, go farther than ratifying Aristotle's view that authorities were likely to be unreliable if they were too ancient or too recent; yet, when they clashed with one another, he preferred the more recent. Again, he thought it better, where possible, to follow a writer who was intermediate, i.e., neither a hostile nor a friendly witness.[9]

3. Likewise, humanist scholars exploded many 'myths of origin'. Polydore Virgil, an Italian humanist in England, destroyed the legend about the foundation of Britain by Brutus the Trojan. The first to subject the sources of English history to real criticism, Virgil dismissed the legends about King Arthur and the tales of Geoffrey of Monmouth. In the mid-sixteenth century, again, the humanist L.V. de la Popeliniere, assailed the legend that the Franks were descended from the Trojans.

Yet, such works of the Italian humanists, though substantial, cannot be said to have established a general standard of historical criticism or brought new methods into general currency. Butterfield writes: "As yet...there could be no organic story of the development of historical technique, and the battles that had been won for a moment would have to be fought over again in the future."[10]

Humanist Historiography and the Territorial State

The new humanist historiography was from the beginning, connected with the development of modern political consciousness. Celebrating the glories of Florence was a particular function of the historiography that was developing in Florence under the stimulus of Bruni. Other governments of Italy following the example employed humanists as official historians. Indeed, between 1450 and the 1530s Italian humanists served like court historiographers in Germany, France, England, Spain, Poland and Hungary. The close identification of the new humanist historiography with the new kind of territorial state that was emerging, was to endure and develop into modern nationalist historiography.[11]

3. Renaissance Historians

Renaissance historiography was mostly a Florentine affair. From the fourteenth century onwards a tradition of historiography was developing in Florence which flowered under the stimulus of the humanist revival of classical learning. Rationalistic and mostly secular in character, this new historiography of the Italian Renaissance imitated the classical authors like Livy and Suetonius, and later Polybius and Tacitus.

Flavio Biondo (1388–1463) and Leonardo Bruni (d. AD *1444)*

Flavio Biondo was an historian as well as an antiquarian. His *Decades*, also called *History from the Decline of the Roman Empire*, is chiefly a history of southern Europe from the fall of Rome (AD 410–1440). This 'long' view along with the critical handling of sources, makes the *Decades* a milestone in modern historiography and an anticipation of Gibbon's *The Decline and Fall of the Roman Empire.*[12] Biondo anticipates specialists in medieval studies in the twentieth century when he reproaches Petrarch for his contempt for the Middle Ages.[13] He stresses the continuity of European history from the fall of Rome in the fifth century to the Renaissance in the fifteenth, thus suggesting the schematic division of history into the ancient, medieval and modern.

Analytical in method and constructive in reasoning, Leonardo Bruni has been called 'the first modern historian'. Bruni reflected the new humanist attitude in that he saw the history of Florence in relation to the broad background of classical antiquity and the rising importance of the Italian towns. Emphasizing humanist and psychological interpretation, his *History of the Florentine People* is a substantial work.

The budding historiography of Florence came into full bloom in Machiavelli and Guicciardini. Whereas Biondo, Bruni and Poggio Bracciolini wrote their histories in Latin, Machiavelli and Guicciardini wrote theirs in Italian.

Niccolo Machiavelli (1469–1527)

Diplomat, historian, dramatist, philosopher, the most cynical thinker of his time, and yet a patriot fired with a noble ideal—that was Niccolo Machiavelli, "a man who failed in everything that he undertook, but left upon history a deeper mark than almost any other figure of the age."[14] Such is Will Durant's sketch of the Florentine philosopher and historian.

Discourse on the First Ten Books of Livy

Machiavelli held that human nature remained the same in every age and clime and therefore human events must ever resemble those of preceding times. He also believed that for any given contingency, the ancient Romans were likely to have discovered the right policy. With a view to applying to modern situations the lessons drawn from the past, Machiavelli planned a comprehensive commentary on the first ten books of Livy's *History of Rome*, though he completed his commentary of only the first three. Machiavelli did not derive his political philosophy from history; he only selected from history incidents to support his conclusions towards which he had been led by his own experience and thought.[15]

The History of Florence

Machiavelli's second work was *The Prince* which wrought a revolution in political philosophy and which became a manual for all rulers. His third work, *The History of Florence*, written at the suggestion of the pope, likewise wrought a revolution in historiography. It began with the decline of Rome and carried the story in increasing political detail down to 1492. The work had vital defects[16]—it was inaccurate; it plagiarized substantial portions from previous historians; it showed itself to be more interested in the strife of factions than in the development of institutions; and it totally ignored cultural history. Yet, Machiavelli's approach represented a noteworthy contribution to historiography. The historian of Florence rejected the fables with which the city had embellished its origins. He further abandoned the medieval method of producing a mere chronicle of events, and gave instead a smooth-flowing and logical narrative. Viewing his city as a living organism, Machiavelli attempted to analyze particularly the importance of civil discords and internal enmities. As an historian he was concerned with tracing the causes and effects of events, just as much as the events themselves. He gives a clear analysis of the families, classes and interests of Florence. He spins his story on two unifying themes—that the papacy had kept Italy divided to preserve its temporal independence; and that all great advances had come under princes like Theodoric, Cosimo de Medici and Lorenzo de Medici. Machiavelli dedicated his book of such anti-papal tendencies to Pope Clement VIII and the Pope was gracious and liberal enough to accept the dedication without complaint and pay a sum to the author.

The History of Florence occupied its author for five years. It is written clearly in the humanist, secular spirit with no attention paid to the teachings of the Church fathers, nor to the metaphysical webs of the scholastics. Man's purpose so permeates the narrative that god's purpose has no place in it. The age that opened with St. Augustine was closed by Machiavelli, the theological authoritarianism of the Middle Ages gave way to the empiricism of the Renaissance.

Philosophy of History

If Machiavelli had a philosophy of history, it was identical with his political philosophy. The Florentine philosopher seems to have attempted a science of government based on a philosophy of history, and both were based on human nature which never changes. Thus he wrote in the *Discourses*:

> ...whoever wishes to foresee the future must consult the past; for human events ever resemble those of preceding times. This arises from the fact that they are produced by men...animated by the same passions; and thus they must necessarily have the same results.[17]

About a century and a half before Thomas Hobbes, Machiavelli described human nature as acquisitive, deceitful, pugnacious, cruel and corrupt. Men could be made to live with order in society only by the application of force, deceit and habit. Though religion and morality are to be completely divorced from politics and statesmanship, religion serves as the best means of habituating naturally wicked men to law and order.

Machiavelli died a disappointed man, leaving his family in the utmost poverty, and his dream of Italian unity unfulfilled. A handsome monument stands at the site of his burial with the words "No eulogy would do justice to so great a name."[18]

Francesco Guicciardini (AD *1483–1540)*

Machiavelli's greatest successor and his only rival as a historian was his contemporary Francesco Guicciardini, also a native of Florence. One of the sharpest minds of the age, Guicciardini had already written a *History of Florence* when he was only twenty-seven. It limited itself to a small segment of Florentine history, from 1378 to 1509. But Guicciardini treated that period, observes Will Durant, "with an accuracy of detail, a critical examination of sources, a penetrating analysis of causes, and a maturity and impartiality of judgement"—qualities that one misses in the work of his older and more famous contemporary, Machiavelli.[19] "With the *History of Florence*," says Fueter, "begins the modern analytical history, the political argument in history."[20] J.W. Thompson lists that the commendable features of the work are the clarity and precision of the narrative, a keen sense of affairs and the play of passions, penetrating analysis of characters and ambitions, the exactness of descriptions, and the clear judgements of the actions of princes, popular leaders, and of the masses.[21] Placing matter above the form, Guicciardini paid little attention to literary conventions. Yet the *History of Florence* is a vivid narrative in fresh, vigorous Italian.

Written in Italian, *The History of Italy*, with the subtitle, *History of the Wars*, in ten volumes, is Guicciardini's masterpiece. It surveys an entirely different and far wider field during the period 1492–1534. All Italy and all Europe as related to Italy is included. Dealing with a system of interacting states, it set a standard for political history and almost marked the beginning of diplomatic history. It is the first history to view the European political system as a connected whole. Besides his first-hand knowledge of many events (in some of which he himself had played a part), the author sedulously collected and ingeniously used a wide range of primary archival material. But sometimes he takes recourse to that ancient Graeco-Roman practice of inventing speeches for the persons of his tale, though he frankly admits that they are true only in substance. At any rate Guicciardini is far more accurate and reliable than Machiavelli. Herbert Butterfield rates Guicciardini's *History of Italy* "as the most impressive Renaissance achievement in this kind of literature."[22] Its popularity was very great. Before the end of the sixteenth century ten Italian editions were printed and translations appeared in Latin, French, English, German, Dutch and Spanish. The *History of Florence* and the *History of Italy* together make their author the greatest historian of the sixteenth century. Emperor Charles V, at Bologna, kept lords and generals waiting in an anteroom while he conversed at length with Guicciardini. "I can create a hundred nobles in an hour," said he, "but I cannot produce such an historian in twenty years."[23]

Jean Bodin (1530–1596) and Francis Bacon (1561–1626)

Jean Bodin, the French author of *The Method for the Easy Comprehension of History*, thought that the study of history was the beginning of wisdom and that it inspired men to virtue by showing the defeat of the wicked and the triumph of the good. Two hundred years after Ibn Khaldoun and hundred and fifty years before Montesquieu, Bodin outlined a philosophy of history based on geographical factors. The determinants of history are temperature, rainfall, soil and topography. These determine human character, and character determines history. Men differ in character and conduct according to whether they live on mountains, plains or coasts. In the north, men are strong in body and muscle, in the south nervous in sensibility and subtle of mind. Those in the temperate zone, as in the Mediterranean regions of France, unite the qualities of the north and the south. The government of a people should be adapted to its geographically determined character.

Francis Bacon, the man of science and philosophy, was also a historian. Bacon's main source for his *History of the Reign of King Henry VII* were Polydore Virgil and Hall. Bacon neither idealized nor flattered the Tudor monarch; rather, he was concerned about explaining the defects of the king's character. He presents in strong prose an illuminatingly real picture of the first Tudor monarch.

4. Humanist Historiography: An Assessment

Humanist historiography had broken new ground by thrusting god and theological interpretation out of history and making it completely secular. It had also arrived at an improved method of historical inquiry which dismantled many a fable and myth of origin. The budding sciences of textual criticism and archeology had come to its assistance. Not content with merely recording events, the humanist historian tried to trace their causes and effects.

But we must also refer, in summary, to the drawbacks of humanist historiography. In reviving the Graeco-Roman humanist view of history, the Renaissance historians also revived the didactic and pragmatic view of history. "Like the Greek and Roman historians," writes B.A. Haddock, "the humanist historian was intent upon learning from the past rather than presenting a true and full description."[24] The didactic and pragmatic aim led to certain defects: The first was that the humanist historian neglected detailed research since preoccupation with details was not indispensable for a history that had set political instruction as its aim. Histories of Florence like those of Bruni and Poggio had had to be panegyrics extolling Florentine liberties and fostering patriotism and civic pride. Machiavelli's *Discourses* had the avowed purpose of drawing practical lessons from the past and his overriding concern was to influence the conduct of affairs. The didactic end prevented the humanist historian from taking full advantage of the critical achievements of the philologists for an accurate portrayal of the past. "History, in short, could be either true or edifying but not both."[25] Again, Haddock observes that commitment to classical models made the humanist historian conform to good style decorum, which necessarily distorted the pattern of events. Even Machiavelli and Bacon, advocates of realism and objectivity, largely conformed to the conventional literary requirements in their purely historical works. In this Guicciardini was an exception not only in terms of purpose but of the method, too. In his *Considerations on the Discourses of Machiavelli* (1530), Guicciardini criticized Machiavelli's method of culling out examples from antiquity and applying them to situations of sixteenth-century Italy. And he explicitly rejected the humanist conception of an idealized antiquity, and with it the exemplar theory of history. In terms of method too Guicciardini deviated from his humanist predecessors. His extensive use of archive sources represented a technical advance on the method of the humanists. In Guicciardini, the humanist influence is manifest only in the carefully paired speeches in the *History of Italy*.

Thus if history was to be distinguished as a mode of knowledge, it required a fresh justification and epistemological foundation. To meet the skeptical challenge as that of Descartes, it was necessary to establish the theoretical character of history. This was what Vico did.

II. THE IMPACT OF THE SCIENTIFIC REVOLUTION: BACON AND DESCARTES

1. The Scientific Revolution

The Scientific Revolution is the name given to the fundamental change brought about in the seventeenth century in man's conception of the universe. The scientific awakening had started with Roger Bacon (1214–1292); it grew with Leonardo da Vinci (1442–1519), and reached the proportions of a revolution in the seventeenth century. It was made possible by the advance of mathematical knowledge.

The Scientific Revolution was inaugurated, as it were, by Copernicus (1473–1543), a Polish ecclesiastic of unquestionable orthodoxy. In his book, *The Revolution of the Heavenly Bodies* (1543), he propounded the notion that the sun is at the centre of the universe, and that the earth has a two-fold motion—a diurnal rotation and an annual revolution about the sun. The Copernican heliocentric theory acquired prominence when the German Johannes Kepler (1571–1630) discovered the laws of planetary motion and formulated them in mathematical terms. Galileo (1564–1642), one of the greatest of the founders of modern science, discovered the importance of acceleration in dynamics, established the true law of falling bodies, and studied projectiles. The Italian scientist became an ardent advocate of the Copernican heliocentric system, perfected the telescope and quickly made many important discoveries. But he was condemned by the Inquisition in 1633, and he recanted and promised never again to maintain that the earth rotates or revolves. Rene Descartes was a sincere and practising Catholic, but one who held many scientific heresies of the time. Descartes invented coordinate geometry which was his most valuable contribution to the Scientific Revolution. Again, his adumbration of the infinitesimal calculus was of fundamental importance to the development of science. Issac Newton (1642–1727) achieved the complete triumph of science for which Copernicus, Kepler and Galileo had prepared the way. In 1687 Newton published his *Principia Mathematica* which James Jeans regarded as "the greatest scientific work ever produced by the human intellect."[26] Starting with his three laws of motion, Newton proceeded to enunciate his law of universal gravitation, the law by which the heavenly bodies are held in their paths. From this he was able to deduce everything in planetary theory.

2. Transition to Modern Philosophy: Francis Bacon and Rene Descartes

Influenced by the attitude of the scientists, the leading philosophical spirits of the new age tended to reject the guiding hand of 'revealed' religion; philosophy now tended to associate itself with the viewpoint of mathematics and physics. Skepticism, characteristic of the Renaissance, now developed into a rejection of all supernatural explanations, as in Bruno. Bruno was burnt for his views in 1600. But the skeptical secular spirit persisted and became pronounced in Bacon and Descartes, both men of science, who stand on the threshold of modern philosophy.

Francis Bacon (1561–1626), more than any other, summed up in philosophy the spirit and resolve of modern science. Bacon's philosophy appeared before the Galilean and Newtonian triumphs in astronomy and physics. But it is imbued with the scientific spirit and wholly directed towards practical and utilitarian ends. Bacon is important in science and philosophy for devising a new method of inquiry and for formulating the ends of science. In his *Novum Organum* (*New Method*) he made a vigorous plea for the abandonment of Aristotelian deduction and the adoption of induction or the scientific or historical method of inquiry. Bacon was confident that his new method of induction would lead to "the knowledge of the causes and secret motions of things."[27] An important part of Bacon's philosophy is the enumeration of what he calls 'idols' or habits of mind that cause people to fall into error. To destroy these idols, he calls for the 'expurgation of the intellect'. It means that for any true scientific inquiry we must wash our minds clean "of all preconceptions, prejudices, assumptions, and theories...we must sweep out of our thoughts the 'idols' or time-honoured illusions and fallacies...."[28] Induction enables us to know the laws of nature, and by learning those laws, we can be nature's masters. An idea that runs through all of Bacon's writings is that knowledge is power, and utility is its end. In the *Advancement of Learning* he expressed the noblest passion of his age—the betterment of life through the extension of knowledge.[29] Scientific knowledge enables us to build a paradise on earth. Bacon drew a picture of this paradise in his *The New Atlantis.* It is a fancied utopia of a perfect social order which could be produced by controlling science itself.

Rene Descartes (1596–1650) was a scientist and a man of high philosophic capacity. Modern philosophy begins with Descartes. *The Discourse on Method*, which he published in 1637, was of epochal importance. The starting point of Descartes' philosophy – his method of inquiry – is methodical doubt. It is *de omnibus dubitandum* or universally doubting the existence or reality of everything. But Descartes comes to something whose existence he cannot doubt. A man's body may be illusory; sense perceptions might be wrong; but thought is different. How could a man think if he did not exist? *Cogito ergo sum*: "I think, therefore, I am." Beginning with methodological doubt, the self became the indisputable starting point of Descartes' philosophy. Now, why is the *cogito* so evident? Descartes concludes that it is only because it is very clear and distinct. He therefore adopts as a general rule *the principle that all things that we conceive very clearly and very distinctly are true.*[30] Such are the ideas of god, of the self, of space, time and motion, the axioms of mathematics, and the freedom of the will; these are for Descartes, *innate*; that is, the soul derives them not from sensation and experience but from its own essence and rationality. Based on such a theory of knowledge, Descartes hoped to build a universal philosophical edifice, and the geometrical spirit of Cartesianism dominated the ensuing age.

3. The Impact of the Scientific Revolution on Historiography

How did the Scientific Revolution of the seventeenth century influence historiography? In what way did it affect its fortunes? The impact of the Scientific Revolution was both beneficial and inimical to historiography.

Beneficial Effects

Change in the Mental Outlook of the Western Man

The rise of science brought about a great change in the mental outlook of the Western man. Bertrand Russell writes: "In 1700 the mental outlook of educated men was completely modern; in 1600, except among a very few, it was still largely medieval."[31] The change manifested itself in an increasing faith in reason. The idea of a world planned and created by a supreme being gave way to the idea of an orderly universe and of a physical world governed by natural laws which could be discovered by human reason. The confidence in reason and in the limitless potentialities of science encouraged a massive secularization of life and thought and a new faith in man and his capabilities. Man was lifted up, as it were, with a new confidence; there was no limit to what he might do.

Idea of Progress

Most characteristic of the self-confidence instilled into man by the Scientific Revolution was the repeated assertion of the idea of progress. The essence of the idea of progress is that human intelligence, building upon the achievement of the past, was steadily creating a better world. The idea would be fully developed by the thinkers of the Enlightenment, but it had already started influencing men's thoughts. In 1688, Fontenelle, a brilliant popularizer of science, in his *Digression on the Ancients and the Moderns* affirmed the steady progress visible in modern times. Abbe St. Pierre's *Observations on the Continual Progress of Universal Reason* (1737) expressed much the same idea of human progress. The idea of progress was to develop into a powerful influence on the writing of history. The idea invested history with a meaning by showing that human society was not static but had always grown from lower to ever higher states of civilization. The study of the past now seemed to acquire a new relevance. Men became interested as never before in knowing the way in which mankind from a primitive beginning had attained its present civilized state.

Collection of Source Materials, Development of the Auxiliary Sciences, Periodization, Improvement of Methodology

The change of outlook brought about by the rise of science had a parallel impact on the study of the past. It was marked by an eager collection and publication of a wide range of source materials by a growing body of scholars. Ludovico Muratori wrote a year-by-year account of Italian history in seventeen volumes in addition to collecting twenty-five large folios of Italian source materials (1723–1751). Collection and publication of vast bodies of source materials – manuscript documents – made it absolutely necessary to devise techniques for authenticating such documents. Hence there developed the so-called 'auxiliary sciences' such as *epigraphy, diplomatics* (the science of deciphering ancient writings and the identification of different types of documents), and *numismatics*. A growing concern with matters like *periodization* was also visible. After Bodin's work on history, Joseph Scaliger produced another work entitled *On the Restoration of Chronology* (1583). Periodization was made more precise by the German Christian Cellarius, who divided his *Tripartite History* (1685–96) of the world into 'ancient', 'medieval', and the 'new' ages.

Historiography gained from the Scientific Revolution particularly in the matter of *method*. Bacon's explicit rejection of the deductive in favor of the inductive method, his call for the expurgation of the intellect of all prejudices and dogmas, and Descartes's advocacy of methodic doubt as the first step in any serious inquiry would in due course revolutionize historical methodology. Particularly suited to historical inquiry was the method Descartes had devised—the method of analyzing every entity or complex conception into its constituents until the irreducible elements are clear and distinct ideas. Historical methodology in like manner would break up a document into its component units of ideas in inquiring what really had happened.

Undoubtedly, the critical spirit was growing. Daniel Papebroch, the Jesuit scholar who succeeded Bolland, was asserting the important truth that the oldest authority might not necessarily be the best—that the quality of the source had to be considered.[32] Pierre Bayle's epochal *Historical and Critical Dictionary* (1697) is a masterpiece of skeptical thought, a product of the impact of the Scientific Revolution. Bayle's method was to collate authorities, expound contradictory opinions, and follow reason to its conclusion.[33] The *Historical and Critical Dictionary* was to become "the fountainhead of the Enlightenment".[34]

Inimical Effects

The benefits for historiography were the unintended results of the Scientific Revolution. On the other hand, the rise of science contained in it – in the works of two of its greatest proponents – ideas inimical and damaging to history. R.G. Collingwood writes that by relegating history to the realm of memory, Francis Bacon left it in an unenviable, even precarious, position; and, by questioning the very validity of historical knowledge, Descartes left history perilously adrift. It had now to fight for its life.

Collingwood analyzes the position accorded to history by Bacon and Descartes.[35] Francis Bacon was himself a historian, and to him the value of history lay in conferring wisdom on men. Yet, Bacon's thinking betrayed a lack of the true historical spirit. He divided his map of knowledge into the three realms of poetry, history and philosophy, ruled over by the three faculties of imagination, memory and understanding. Memory presides over history. Collingwood informs us, however, that the position of history thus defined was not safe, but precarious. It had freed itself from the errors of medieval thought, but it had still to find its own function.

Actually, Bacon's definition of history as the realm of memory was wrong, because the past only requires historical investigation so far as it is not and cannot be remembered. If it could be remembered there would be no need for historians.[36]

The task of the historian is not to remember the past as it is in Bacon's thinking, but to reconstruct it by using archeological and other data much as the natural scientists were using data as the basis of scientific theories. Collingwood informs us that Bacon's own contemporary, William Camden, was doing that kind of historical reconstruction.

Descartes, like Bacon, distinguished poetry, history and philosophy, and added divinity to the list. Of these he applied his new method to philosophy alone, with its three main divisions of mathematics, physics and metaphysics, for it was only here that he hoped to attain certain and secure knowledge. Poetry was more a gift of nature; divinity depended on faith in revelation; "history, however interesting and instructive...could not claim truth, for the events which it described never happened exactly as it described them."[37] Not only did the Cartesian reformation of knowledge neglect historical thought but there was in it a strong anti-historical tendency. This was because Descartes did not believe history to be a branch of knowledge at all. A passage in his *Discourse on Method* questioned the very validity and utility of historical knowledge. The Cartesians were, for this reason, at best indifferent to history and sometimes even hostile to it.

Collingwood examines each of the four arguments advanced against history by Descartes:

The first is *historical escapism*. To Descartes the historian is a traveler who by living away from home becomes a stranger to his own age. The true answer to such an 'escapist' view of history, says Collingwood, is to show that the historian can genuinely see into the past only so far as he stands firmly rooted in the present. But such an answer had to wait until further advances were made in the theory of knowledge. What makes true historical knowledge possible is the fact that the historian does not abandon the standpoint of his own age.

The second objection that Descartes raises is that *historical narratives are not trustworthy accounts of the past*. Here is Collingwood's rejoinder to Descartes's historical Pyrrhonism:[38] To say that historical narratives relate events that cannot have happened is to say that we have some criterion, other than the narratives that reach us, by which to judge what could have happened. Descartes here is adumbrating a genuinely critical attitude in history which if fully developed would be the answer to his own objection.

The third is Descartes's *anti-utilitarian idea of history.* He asserts that untrustworthy narratives cannot really assist us to understand what is possible and thus to act effectively in the present. Collingwood observes that Descartes was quite right in rejecting the utilitarian conception of history as Hegel would do later when he wrote in the introduction to his *Philosophy of History* that the practical lesson of history is that no one ever learns anything from it. But Descartes in his condemnation of history forgot that the old Graeco-Roman conception revived by the Renaissance historians, that the value of history was a practical value, was dead by the time he criticized it. As Collingwood tells us, the French philosopher did not see that the historical work of his own day in the hands of men like Buchanan and Grotius was actuated not by any pragmatic consideration but by a sheer desire for truth.

Descartes's *fourth* objection is that *historians distort the past by making it more splendid than it really was.* Collingwood subtly remarks that in saying that historical narratives exaggerated the grandeur and splendor of the past, Descartes was actually propounding a criterion by which they could be criticized and by which the truth they concealed or distorted could be rediscovered. But instead of laying down a method or code of rules for historical criticism, he seems to have been obsessed with demonstrating that no such improvement in historical method was possible.

Descartes's work, in brief, threw doubt on the validity as well as the value of history. Clio had to be vindicated.

4. Cartesian Historiography

After Descartes the position of history was precarious. But the immediate effect of Cartesianism was the rise of a new school of historiography. Descartes's historical skepticism did not discourage the historians; rather they seem to have taken it as a challenge, an invitation to devise their own methods which would demonstrate that critical history was possible. During the latter half of the seventeenth century a new school of historical thought arose which

Collingwood calls Cartesian historiography.[39] The phrase is a paradox but its aptness cannot be questioned. It is all the more surprising that those who picked up the Cartesian gauntlet were ecclesiastical historians.

Cartesian historiography was based, like the Cartesian philosophy, on systematic skepticism and thorough-going recognition of critical principles. The main idea of this new school was that the testimony of written authorities must not be accepted without submitting it to a process of criticism based on at least three rules of method:[40] (a) the first was Descartes's own implicit rule that no authority must induce us to believe what we know cannot have happened; (b) the second rule was that different authorities must be confronted with each other and harmonized; and (c) according to the third rule, written authorities must be checked by non-literary evidence. Historians were now learning to treat their authorities in a thoroughly critical spirit.

The best examples of this school were Tillemont and the Bollandists. Tillemont (1637–1698) was a French Jansenist priest who began to make historical and literary researches at the age of eighteen. His two great works are the *Ecclesiastical History* (16 volumes) dealing with the first six centuries of Christianity, and the *History of the Roman Emperors* (6 volumes) during much the same period. Both are highly objective accounts and among the first of modern historical works to include a critical discussion of sources for each period. Tillemont's was the first attempt to write Roman history with systematic attention paid to reconciling the statements of different authorities. Tillemont's works were among the chief sources used by Gibbon for his *The Decline and Fall of the Roman Empire.*

The Bollandists were Belgian Jesuit scholars under the guidance of Bolland. They searched the libraries of the monasteries of Europe for fresh materials. They set themselves to rewrite the lives of saints on a critical basis, purging away all exaggeratedly miraculous elements. They went more deeply into the problem of sources and the way traditions had grown up. It is to this period (1660–1720) and especially to the Bollandists that we owe the idea of dissecting a tradition, allowing for the distortion of the medium through which it has reached us. Thus was the old dilemma between either accepting a tradition *en bloc* as true or rejecting it as false solved.[41]

The *Acta Sanctorum* (1643), a cooperative historical endeavor of the Bollandists, was the result of this fresh historical perspective.

Almost contemporary with this effort was the great historical endeavor of the congregation of St. Maur in Paris. From 1688, *The Acts of the Saints of the Benedictine Order* began to appear in publication. The leader of the great enterprise was Dom Jean Mabillon who in the course of an attempt to establish a more critical and scholarly type of historiography founded the science of paleography or diplomatics. Diplomatics is the study of the ancient modes of handwriting; it is the science of deciphering ancient documents like manuscript folios, charters, treaties, etc. chiefly in order to distinguish their authenticity. The composition of Mabillon's treatise *De re Diplomatica* (1681) was occasioned by a dispute with Daniel Papebroch, the leading Bollandist of the day, over the procedure to be adopted in establishing the authenticity of charters (grants conferring privileges to medieval cities). Papebroch advanced practical principles that involved the rejection of a series of documents which Mabillon, from his lifetime's work on such sources, regarded as genuine. In reply, Mabillon carefully described the sorts of tests which should be applied to a charter before it could be safely used as evidence. The Jesuit scholar showed how such documents could be properly assessed through detective work on the parchment, the writing material, the style of writing, the technical terms employed, the abbreviations, the form of seals, the system of chronology, the content of the document, the kind of language employed and the way of introducing and concluding the main text. Such scientific scrutiny enabled experts to detect forgeries, date authentic documents, and to guess where they were drawn up. In a way it was an extension of the philological methods employed by humanists like Valla. *De re Diplomatica* established the method of source criticism – the study of the form of documents – on a firm foundation. Papebroch graciously acknowledged Mabillon's magisterial command of his methods.

The work and achievement of the ecclesiastical historians illustrate the extent to which the skeptical challenge to the status of historical knowledge had influenced the practice of the historian. True, the historian's proof cannot be of mathematical precision, but it was accepted that with a disciplined use of his sources he could establish a degree of probability beyond all doubt. Rightly has the period from 1660 to 1720 been described as the grand age of scholarly research,[42] and as the age of erudition.[43] Detailed studies were now being made of the possibilities of coins, inscriptions, charters and other non-literary documents. Systematic collection of such sources began and they were used to check and illustrate the narratives and descriptions of literary historians. It was during this period that John Horsby of Morpeth made the first systematic collection of Roman inscriptions in Britain, following the lead of Italian, French and German scholars.

Yet it is well to remember that the great achievements of the ecclesiastical historians were practical rather than theoretical. Mabillon had answered the skeptics by an improvement of method rather than by an alternative theory of knowledge. The sharply anti-historical tendency of the Cartesian school could be met only by a vindication of Clio at the theoretical level. This was what Vico did and he did it by a powerful attack on the Cartesain theory of knowledge which led to the general discredit and downfall of the Cartesian philosophy.

III. VICO: THE NEW SCIENCE OF HISTORY

Son of a poor bookseller of Naples, Giambattista Vico grew up in circumstances of extreme poverty. He attended various schools but often skipped his classes because his mediocre teachers could offer him nothing more than an arid Scholasticism. Vico was largely self-taught. In 1699 he obtained at the University of Naples a chair of rhetoric but not the more prestigious and better paid chair of law which he actively sought. His son, Gennaro, succeeded to the father's chair—the only satisfaction of a life which otherwise was unlucky throughout.

Vico had in fact shared the Cartesian contempt for history until 1708. It was the inaugural oration for that year at the university that marked a definite change. From that time onwards the *Scienza nouva* began to take shape. To bring it out in print Vico had to sell the only jewel that the family possessed, a family ring.

1. Anti-Cartesianism: Vico's Theory of Knowledge

What Vico attempted in the *Scienza nouva* (1725) was to bring about the convergence of history and the more systematic social sciences so that their interpretation could form a single science of humanity. The task called for the establishment of history itself on a theoretical as well as on a critical basis. This constructive work called for an attack on Cartesian philosophy, which had relegated history to a realm where, Descartes had held, no certain and secure knowledge could be attained. Vico set out to vindicate historical knowledge by impugning, not the validity of mathematical knowledge, but the Cartesian theory of knowledge with its implication that no other kind of knowledge was possible. *History, for the first time, was to get an epistemological basis different from that of the natural sciences.*

Vico asserted that man can know history – events and institutions and mental achievements – for the simple reason that one can know the things that one actually makes. He attacked the Cartesian principle that the criterion of truth is the clear and distinct idea. Far from being a foundation of truth it is only a subjective or psychological criterion. The clarity and distinctness of an idea has nothing to do with its truth or falsity. The fact that I think my ideas clear only proves that *I believe them*, not that they are true. Nothing is easier than for one to think one's beliefs self-evident, when in fact they may only be baseless fictions. What we need, Vico contends, is a principle by which we can distinguish what can be known from what cannot, i.e., a doctrine of the necessary limits of human knowledge.[44]

Vico finds this principle in the doctrine that *verum et factum convertuntur*. It means that *the condition of being able to know anything truly*, to understand it as opposed to merely perceiving it, *is that the knower himself should have made it.* On this principle nature is fully intelligible only to god, but mathematics is intelligible to man, because the objects of mathematical knowledge are fictions or hypotheses which the mathematician has constructed. Any piece of mathematical thinking begins with a fiat: *let* ABC be a triangle and *let* AB = AC. It is because by this act of will the mathematician makes the triangle, because it is his *factum*, that he can have true knowledge of it.[45]

It follows from the *verum-factum* principle that *history which is emphatically something made by the human mind is especially adapted to be an object of human knowledge.* Vico regards the historical process as a process whereby human beings build up systems of language, custom, law, government, etc. He thinks of history as the history of the genesis and development of human societies and their institutions. Here, we have for the first time a completely modern idea of what the subject matter of history is. The plan of history is a wholly human plan, but it does not preexist in the shape of an unrealized intention to its own gradual realization. Man, like god, is a real creator, bringing into existence the fabric of human society out of nothing, and every detail of this fabric is therefore a human *factum*, eminently knowable to the human mind as such.[46]

How does historical knowledge arise?—knowledge just as certain, dependable and useful as Descartes had ascribed to mathematics and physics? The historian reconstructs in his own mind the process by which the things of history have been created by men in the past. There is a kind of preestablished harmony between the historian's mind and the objects which he sets out to study. This harmony is not based on a miracle; it is based on a common human nature uniting the historian with the men whose work he is studying.

The new attitude towards history is profoundly anti-Cartesian, because Cartesian skepticism – the relation between ideas and things – did not arise in the world of history as it did in the physical sciences. This is because history, as conceived by Vico, is concerned with the actual structure of society in which we live, the manners and customs, which we share with the people around us. *In order to study these we need not ask whether they really exist.* The question has no meaning. Descartes, looking at the fire, asked himself whether in addition to his own idea of a fire there was also a real fire. For Vico, looking at such a thing as the Italian language of his own day, no parallel question could arise. The distinction between the idea of such a historical reality and the reality itself would be meaningless. The Italian language is exactly what the people who use it think it is. *For the historian, the human point of view is final.* "History is a kind of knowledge in which questions about ideas and questions about facts are not distinguishable; and the whole point of Descartes's philosophy consists in distinguishing those two types of question."[47]

2. Vico's Idea of History[48]

Meeting Descartes's skeptical challenge at the epistemological level Vico had stood historical knowledge on the bedrock of the *verum-factum* principle, that is, man can have true knowledge of the things he himself has made. The things of history – language, custom, law, government, etc – are things made by the human mind, for which reason they are especially adapted to be an object of human knowledge.

After thus proving that history was a philosophically justifiable form of knowledge, Vico proceeded to show that historical problems could be solved and historical knowledge extended by a clear conception of historical method. The rules of method which Vico laid down contained his idea of history and the errors that historians had to guard themselves against. These rules, as explained by Collingwood, may be outlined as follows.

Recurrence of Periods in History

Certain Periods of History have the Same General Character

Vico held that certain periods of history had a general character, coloring every detail, which reappeared in other periods. Vico instanced the general resemblance between the Homeric period of Greek history and the European Middle Ages, both of which he called by the generic name of *heroic periods*. Their common features were such things as government by a warrior aristocracy, an agricultural economy, a ballad literature, a morality based on the idea of personal prowess and loyalty, and so forth. To learn more than what Homer could tell us about the Homeric age, therefore, we should study the Middle Ages.

Similar Periods Tend to Recur in the Same Order

Vico showed that these similar periods in history tended to recur in the same order. Every heroic period is followed by a classical period, where thought prevails over imagination, prose over poetry, industry over agriculture. This in turn is followed by a decline into a new barbarism, which Vico calls the barbarism of reflection in which thought has exhausted its creative power and only constructs meaningless cobwebs of artificial and pedantic distinctions.

Recurrence of Periods not Cyclical but Spiral

The recurrence or movement of periods is not cyclical but spiral;

for history never repeats itself but comes round to each new phase in a form differentiated by what has gone before. Thus the Christian barbarism of the Middle Ages is different from the pagan barbarism of the Homeric age. The Middle Ages of Europe are distinctively an expression of the Christian mind. Because history is always creating novelties, the cyclical movement becomes a spiral movement in Vico which does not permit us to forecast the future. The true historian never prophesies.

Errors that Historians Are Liable to Commit

After presenting such an idea of history Vico goes on to enumerate certain prejudices or errors against which historians should always be on their guard. They are like the 'idols' in Bacon's *Novum Organum*. Vico distinguishes five such sources of error.

Magnificent Opinions Concerning Antiquity

Historians usually commit the error of exaggerating the wealth, power, grandeur, etc of the period they happen to study. Collingwood affirms that this prejudice is real. He cites the example of how many are reluctant to believe that Roman London had only about 10,000 to 15,000 inhabitants. (This is a fact that Collingwood himself has proved from archeological evidence). They would rather it had 50,000 to 100,000 because they have magnificent opinions about antiquity.

Conceit of Nations

Every nation in dealing with its own past history has a prejudice in favour of painting it in the most favourable colours. Histories of England, says Collingwood, written by and for English people do not enlarge on British military failures.

Conceit of the Learned

A special form of prejudice is what Vico calls the conceit of the learned. The historian thinks that the people about whom he is thinking were like himself scholars and students and in general people of reflective intellect. The academic mind fancies that the persons in whom it is interested must have been academic persons themselves. Actually, Vico held, the most effective men in history have been the least academically minded. Historical greatness and reflective intellect are very rarely combined.

The Fallacy of Sources or the Scholastic Succession of Nations

The fallacy of sources consists in thinking that when two nations have a similar idea or institution one must have learned it from the other. Vico holds that this kind of error denies the original creative power of the human mind, which can rediscover ideas for itself without learning them from another. The warning, Collingwood thinks, is a right warning. Even when it could be shown that one nation has taught another, as China has taught Japan, Greece Rome, Rome Gaul, and so on, the learner invariably learns not what the other has to teach but only the lessons for which its previous historical development has prepared it.

Error of Thinking the Ancients Better Informed than Ourselves

The historian may commit the error of thinking the ancients better informed than ourselves about the times that lay nearer to them. Collingwood illustrates this particular error by pointing out that the scholars of King Alfred's time knew much less about Anglo-Saxon origins than we do. Vico's warning is of great importance because the historian does not depend on an unbroken tradition for his knowledge, but can reconstruct by scientific methods a picture of a past age. This is an explicit denial that history depends on what Bacon called memory, or on the statements of authorities.

Positive Methods by which True Historical Knowledge can be Derived

Not content with negative warnings, Vico goes on to positively indicate certain methods by which the historian can transcend mere reliance on the statements of authorities. He reminds us that historical knowledge is not to be passively received but actively pursued. Vico's observations here, says Collingwood, are commonplaces to the historian of today, but in his own time they were revolutionary.

Language

Vico shows how linguistic study can throw light on history. The historian aims at the reconstruction of the mental life, the ideas, of the people he is studying. Now, Vico says that the stock of words of a people shows what their stock of ideas was. The way in which a people use an old word metaphorically in a new sense when they want to express a new idea, shows what their stock of ideas was before that new one came into existence. Thus Latin words like *intellegere* and *disserere* show how when Romans needed words for 'understanding' and 'discussing', they borrowed from an agricultural vocabulary the words for 'gleaning' and 'sowing'.

Mythology

Vico makes a similar use of mythology. The gods of primitive religion represent a semi-poetical way of expressing the social structure of the people who invented them. Thus, in Graeco-Roman mythology, Vico saw a representation of the domestic, economic and political life of the ancients. These myths were the way in which a primitive and imaginative mind expressed to itself what a reflective mind would have stated in codes of law and morality.

Tradition

Vico propounds a new method of using tradition. Tradition is to be taken not as literally true but as a confused memory of facts distorted through a medium whose refraction we can define to a certain extent. All traditions are true, though none of them mean what they say. In order to discover what they mean, we must know what kind of people invented them and what such a kind of people would mean by saying that kind of thing.

The Study of Savage Minds

According to Vico in order to find the key to this reinterpretation of tradition we must remember that minds at a given stage of development will tend to create the same kind of products. Savages, at all times and in all places, are savages in mind; by studying modern savages, we can learn what ancient savages were like, and thus find out how to interpret the savage myths and legends that conceal facts of remotest ancient history. Children are savages of a kind, and children's fairy tales may help in the same direction. Modern peasants are unreflective and imaginative persons, and their ideas throw light on the ideas of primitive society.

Influence of Vico

When the *Scienza nouva* was published in 1725, Vico had complained bitterly of the universal indifference towards his masterpiece. As Collingwood observes, Vico's ideas were too far ahead of his time to have immediate effect. First, he developed a philosophy of history which could deliver a counterattack on the scientific and metaphysical philosophy of Cartesianism, demanding a broader basis for the theory of knowledge. Secondly, Vico carried historical criticism to a stage hitherto unattained. He showed that historical thought could be constructive as well as critical. The extraordinary merit of his work came to be recognized two generations later when German scholars rediscovered him and, then, all Europe praised him. Goethe was impressed, Michelet translated the *Scienza nouva* and called its author his intellectual forerunner. August Comte hailed Vico as an influence in the formation his laws of the three states or ages of mankind. Karl Marx owed much to Vico though the two differed sharply over the question of religion. Today, many scholars see in Vico the forerunner of the sciences of anthropology and ethnology. He has been increasingly recognized as one of the important figures in European intellectual history, and *Scienza nouva* has been accepted as one of the landmark works in that history.

5

I. THE EIGHTEENTH CENTURY ENLIGHTENMENT AND ITS INFLUENCE ON HISTORIOGRAPHY

1. The Enlightenment

The "Age of Reason", the phrase generally applied to the eighteenth century, came in the wake of the Scientific Revolution. The descriptive phrase "reflects the conviction of this age that man could, by the exercise of his power of reason, pluck the mystery out of the universe and lead his fellows into a future of ever-increasing happiness."[1] Another phrase, "intellectual revolution" refers to the application of reason and science to all the studies of man in society—history, politics, economics, education. The questions arising in these different fields were analyzed and sought to be answered in a way which echoed the methods used by the scientists in their studies of the natural phenomena. In short, intellectual revolution refers to "the change from the concept of a mysterious world directed by the inscrutable will of God to one in which the complex phenomena of life could be regarded as orderly processes, subject to laws which the mind of man was competent to discover."[2] The Scientific Revolution, faith in reason, and the intellectual revolution combined to produce an atmosphere of victory for man. The term which characterized this victory was the English 'Enlightenment', the French *Eclaircissement* and the German *Aufklarung*. Whatever the language, the word signifies "a victory brought by the forces of light over those of darkness."[3] Bacon and Descartes, Newton and Locke, may be called the precursors of the Age of Reason or the Enlightenment. These men provided the massive pillars for the erection of a towering new philosophical edifice that began to crowd out the Christian – both Catholic and Protestant – view of man and the world.[4]

The Enlightenment was marked by the rise of an independent secular class of popular philosophers and writers—Adam Smith, Cesare Beccaria, Immanuel Kant, Voltaire, Hume, Lessing, Gibbon, Montesquieu, Turgot, Condorcet, Diderot, Rousseau, Holbach, d'Alembert. They ranged over the fields of knowledge which had once been the province of the Church, and presented a different view of the world, of the nature of man, of society, religion and history. In France such intellectuals were called *philosophes.* They deliberately effected a revolution in the fundamental beliefs of mankind. "The Enlightenment," the German philosopher Kant wrote in 1784, "is the liberation of man from his self-imposed minority."[5]

2. The Influence of the Enlightenment on Historiography: The Idea of Progress

Revolt against Religion[6]

A movement to secularize every department of human life and thought, the Enlightenment was a revolt against religion. Voltaire regarded himself as the leader of a crusade against Christianity and superstition. Religion was considered as a function of what was backward and barbarous in human life. To the thinkers and historians of the Enlightenment, religion was a thing devoid of all positive value whatever; it was just sheer error; the invention of an unscrupulous, calculating, hypocritical class of beings called priests, an instrument of domination over the mass of men. Terms like religion, priests, Middle Ages and barbarism were, for the *Aufklarung* men, terms of abuse. In Vico's philosophical theory, the religious attitude towards life was destined to be superseded by a rational or philosophical one.

Secularization of History

Enlightenment historiography set itself definitely against Church historiography. Bossuet's *Universal History,* presenting the empires of the ancient world as stages in the preordained march of mankind towards the Roman Church, was the last serious effort of the kind.

Theological interpretations went out of fashion when Bayle's *Critical Dictionary,* followed half a century later by the *Encyclopaedia* of Diderot and d' Alembert, challenged the authority of tradition and assailed inherited beliefs. There was everywhere a massive secularization of interests which left its imprint on historiography too. History came to be viewed not as the preordained implementation of a providential plan, but as a record of human effort. The atmospheric change could be felt in the historical classics of Voltaire, Hume, Montesquieu, Robertson and Gibbon.[7]

Stress on the Need for History

Though the Enlightenment conception of history entertained certain unhistorical notions, it unmistakably stressed the need for history. The rejection of all divine plans in the story of the development of man meant a replacement of the genesis story of the creation and fall (of man) by a plausible account of the origin of mankind. This intellectual need of the *philosophes* of the Enlightenment called for history – an account of the past – if only to show the barbarism of the former ages and the superiority of their own. Indeed, the development of the idea that the study of history is a natural, inevitable kind of human activity dated from the eighteenth century.

Unity of Human History

Encouraged by the progress of the sciences, Enlightenment historiography ventured to formulate general rules governing the development of human societies. It was marked by

> a sense of the unity of all human history, including an interest in the continents outside Europe; a capacity for bold generalizations about the salient features of particular periods or societies; and a preference for topics connected with the progress of human civilization.[8]

Condorcet's historical sketch of the progress of the human mind, written in 1794, subdivided all known history into nine periods, each starting with some great invention or geographical discovery. Voltaire declared that his subject was the history of the human mind; he wanted to know the steps by which man passed from barbarism to civilization.

Idea of Progress

Inspired by the progress of the natural sciences and reassuringly confident of the growing power of reason, the *philosophes* of the Enlightenment took a roseate view of the future. Their confidence and hope found expression in theories of endless progress for mankind, which became an integral part of Enlightenment historiography. Fontenelle and Abbe St. Pierre had written about the steady and continual progress visible in modern times. The idea of progress formed the theme of Turgot's *Discourses on Universal History* delivered at the Sorbonne in Paris (1750). The German writer, Gotthold Lessing, wrote a brief sketch, *On the Education of the Human Race* (1777), and concluded that history reveals a definite law of progress, even if occasional retrogressions hamper the march of mankind towards its lofty goal. But the loftiest expression of the idea of progress is Marquis de Condorcet's *A Sketch of a Tableau of the Progress of the Human Spirit* (1794). A classic in the literature of progress, the book is a vision of the coming glory of the human race. The author foresaw a time, which he called the tenth epoch of human history, when men would devote themselves only to rational knowledge and science and when the sick society – the society of unreason – would be cured by scientific laws. Scientific laws would train and control human nature; crime would be eradicated and men would become moral; women would be freed from subjection to men, slaves from their masters; there would be no subjection of peoples, no war.

Condorcet was a French noble who had sacrificed wealth, rank and privilege for the success of the French Revolution. Yet, the revolutionaries were out for his blood, for he had, like Tom Paine, voted against the execution of Louis XVI. Throughout the composition of his great work he was hiding himself from the police. Once he had finished writing that testament of human progress, he took poison to cheat the guillotine.

History was bound in the long run to be greatly influenced by the idea of progress. The idea helped to provide the structure of a new world view. As Herbert Butterfield has written,

> ...it was no longer a case of one generation succeeding another on the same virtually unchanging stage...all the

centuries still forming only a rope of sand. Here was something which made it possible to give shape and structure to the course of ages. In a way it contributed a meaning to history, and gave point to the temporal succession, making change more than kaleidoscopic, and turning time itself into a generative thing.[9]

The idea of progress made it appear that world history had something like an objective, one which lay within history itself. It turned men's eyes to the future rather than to the past; yet, the study of what had gone before was now taken up with greater interest as though the subject had acquired a new relevance. Men became exceptionally interested in lengthy surveys—in studying the way in which mankind, from a primitive beginning, had come to its present civilized state.[10]

Philosophies of History

Again, we have, from the time of Voltaire, 'philosophies of history' instead of the theologies of history of the Christian pattern. A scientific account of the origin of the world takes the place of the chapter on the creation in the *Book of Genesis*. The historians of the Enlightenment extended their horizon by including China, India and Persia in their survey; they provided depth to history by bringing into their works the whole social and cultural history of the world and not merely confining it to politics.[11]

II. ENLIGHTENMENT HISTORIANS

1. Montesquieu (1689–1755)

A French noble, Montesquieu sought laws in history. His *Considerations on the Causes of the Grandeur and Decadence of the Romans* and *The Spirit of Laws* were early attempts at philosophies of history. In *Considerations*, Montesquieu traced the fortunes of the Roman civilization from its birth to death exposing one of the basic processes of history—the inevitable dissolution that follows full development of civilizations and states. Here is found mentioned, perhaps for the first time, the concept of causation in history. It is not fortune, says Montesquieu, but moral and physical causes which govern the rise, the maintenance and overthrow of monarchies. "All that occurs is subject to these causes; and if a particular cause, like the accidental result of a battle, has ruined a state, there was a general cause which made the downfall of this state ensue from a single battle."[12] The decline of Rome was due first to the change from a republic to an empire. The empire centred all rule in one city and one man, destroying the division and balance of powers under the republic, and the vigor of the citizens and the provinces. To this prime cause were added other factors such as the spread of supine servility among the masses, the desire of the poor to be supported by the state, the weakening of character by wealth, luxury and licence, the influx of aliens and so on. To Montesquieu, the individual genius in history, however great, is only an instrument of the 'general movement'—what Hegel calls *zeitgeist* or 'spirit of the time'.

The Spirit of Laws

Montesquieu's greatest work, *The Spirit of Laws*, was an essay on the relations between physical forces and social forms and on the interrelations between the components of civilization. It tried to lay the foundations of scientific sociology. The origin and character of laws, Montesquieu maintains, are first determined by the soil and climate of the habitat, and then by physiology, economy, government, religion, morals and manners of the people. "Laws in their most general signification are the necessary relations arising from the nature of things."[13] "Law in general is human reason."[14] Like Ibn Khaldoun and Bodin before him, and Buckle after, Montesquieu asserted that climate is the first and the most powerful factor in determining a people's economy, its laws and its national character. He demonstrated his assertion with instances. The prohibition of drinking wine in Arabia and Carthage was a law of the climate. Such a law would be improper in cold countries. Likewise, climate and marriage are interrelated. Women in hot countries are marriageable much earlier than in colder climates, and age much earlier. In such conditions polygamy prevails.

Custom is the best law since it is a natural adaptation of character to situation. And customs are more directly the result of climate than laws are. Since habit determines custom, and custom determines national character, the form of government would vary with the complex of all three. A small territory is ideal for a republic; a large area must submit to monarchical rule. Knowing that absolute monarchy would eventually lead to despotism, Montesquieu favored a mixed government of monarchy, aristocracy and democracy. From this came his most influential proposal: a system of *checks and balances* based on a *separation of powers*—separation of the legislative, executive and judicial powers in a government. Such a government, Montesquieu thought, existed in England, the reason why Englishmen enjoyed liberty.

Assessment

Montesquieu had worked on *The Spirit of Laws* for twenty years and when it came out in print in 1748 it was soon recognized as a major event in French literature. Twenty-two editions came out during 1750–52 and the work was translated into all the languages of Europe. The Jesuits and the Jansenists, usually at odds, united in condemning the book as a subtle repudiation of Christianity. The book had defects. The author had in fact accepted too readily the unverified accounts of travelers and often generalized too recklessly. Such defects were the result of approaching history with a philosophy to be proved by it.[15] Voltaire rightly pointed out that Montesquieu had exaggerated the influence of climate. He thought it more likely that England had gone Protestant because Anne Boleyn was beautiful than because Henry VIII felt cold. Though Montesquieu rightly observed the differences between nations and cultures, Collingwood observes that he misunderstood the essential character of these differences by imagining that they were entirely due to differences in climate and geography. Man, in other words, is regarded as part of nature, and the explanation of historical events is sought in the facts of the natural world. History so conceived would be the natural history of man or anthropology, where human institutions appear not as free inventions of human reason but as the necessary effects of geographical and climatic conditions, as the life of plants. The intimate relation between any culture and its natural environment is a fact; but what determines the character of that culture is not the facts of that environment, in themselves, but what man is able to get out of them.[16]

But the virtues of *The Spirit of Laws* were great. It tried to find some system in laws and their variations in place and time, to enlighten rulers and reformers by considering the sources and limits of legislation. In this enterprise, Montesquieu powerfully advanced the historical method for the comparative study of institutions. Voltaire concluded his criticism by saying: "Europe owes him eternal gratitude."[17] Elsewhere he said: "Humanity had lost its title deeds [to freedom], and Montesquieu recovered them."[18]

Montesquieu had great influence. Gibbon, Blackstone and Burke profited from *The Spirit of Laws* and *Considerations*; Frederick the Great and Catherine the Great frequently consulted the former; the framers of the American constitution took from Montesquieu not only the principle of the separation of governmental powers but that of the exclusion of cabinet members from the Congress. *The Spirit of Laws* became almost the bible of the moderate leaders of the French Revolution. "All the great modern ideas," said Faguet, "have their commencement in Montesquieu."[19]

2. Voltaire (1694–1778)

Born of middle class parents and educated by the Jesuits, Francois Marie Arouet de Voltaire was the greatest luminary of the Age of Enlightenment. He was poet, dramatist, novelist, essayist, political thinker, historian and philosopher. Author of about a hundred books, Voltaire's correspondence alone runs into 107 volumes. A crusader against tyranny and bigotry, he is noted for his caustic wit, satire and critical capacity. Says Will Durant: "Italy had a Renaissance, and Germany had a Reformation, but France had a Voltaire; he was for his country both Renaissance and the Reformation, and half the Revolution."[20]

The History of Charles XII

Of Voltaire's historical works, *The History of Charles XII* (the king of Sweden) was the first to come (1731). Examining masses of state papers and consulting men who had moved close to the 'Lion of the North', the author had bestowed scholarly care upon the work and succeeded in producing a well-documented narrative. Voltaire showed how the very prodigality of Charles had injured Sweden. He concluded that Charles was an extraordinary rather than a great man. The work sold like fiction and some critics claimed that there was too much fiction in it. R.N. Bain, a learned historian, has called it "a romance", vivid in narrative, inaccurate in detail.[21]

The Age of Louis XIV

Voltaire published in 1751 a great historical work, *The Age of Louis XIV.* The book's accuracy owed itself to the arduous and conscientious care with which its material had been collected; but the author had a higher aim. "My chief object," Voltaire had written as early as 1739, "is not political or military history, it is the history of the arts, of commerce, of civilization – in a word, of the human mind."[22] The book marked a revolution in historiography in that it effected a shift of emphasis from politics, diplomacy and war to commerce, art, literature and science. Voltaire ranked scientists, philosophers, dramatists, poets and artists – that is, those who excelled in the agreeable – higher than the heroes of war. He idealized the Sun King chiefly because he had encouraged and honored poets, artists, scientists and philosophers. The work was the first modern attempt at integrated history. It was a new start—history conceived as the biography of civilization.

The New History: Essay on the Morals and Character of the Nations from Charlemagne to Louis XIII

Voltaire knew that history as written by many was no more than a confused mass of minute events without connection and sequence, a mass that overwhelmed the mind without illuminating it. He mourned the distortions of the past by current prejudices, which he said made history "nothing but a pack of tricks that we play upon the dead."[23] Proper history makes for perspective, discovering in events the history of the human mind, society and culture. In 1738, he had laid down a new principle: one must write history as a philosopher. In such a mood he worked intermittently for twenty years.

In 1757 came out the seven volumes of the great *Essay.* "I want to know," wrote Voltaire, "what were the steps by which men passed from barbarism to civilization."[24] By this he meant the passage from the Middle Ages to modern times. He commended Bishop Bossuet's philosophic endeavor in seeking a unifying theme or process in history, but he thoroughly disagreed with Bossuet in finding that theme in a Providential Plan. Similarly, he protested against Bossuet's confining his 'universal' history to the Jews and Christians and treating Greece and Rome chiefly in relation to Christianity. He could not tolerate the Bishop's neglect of China and India and his conception of the Arabs as mere barbarian heretics.

The book's fourteen introductory chapters presented a cosmopolitan perspective of history by touching upon the civilizations of China, Persia, Arabia, India and the classical world of Europe. Was there not a widespread civilization in Mesopotamia? Our historian was moved by the antiquity, extent and excellence of civilization in China which placed the Chinese above all the other nations of the world. China and India, he said, had invented nearly all the arts before Europe possessed them. The anti-Christian warrior was happy to find that there were great cultures antedating Christianity by millenniums. He ranged himself on the side of the Encyclopaedists in a war against the Catholic Church. The Spanish Inquisition and the massacre of the heretical Albigensians were to him the vilest events in history. He anticipated Gibbon in charging Christianity with weakening the Roman state and propagating absurd doctrines among ignorant and credulous people. Voltaire, the Enlightment historian, found little of value in medieval Christian Europe: he saw no nobility in Charlemagne, no sense in Scholasticism, no grandeur in Gothic architecture. On the other hand, he recognised Europe's debt to Arab science, medicine and philosophy..

Philosophical History

Voltaire's two masterpieces, *The Age of Louis XIV* and the monumental *Essay*, deal with universal history in a philosophical interpretative manner. Voltaire himself said of the latter work: "Mankind dictated it and truth acted as the scribe."[25] What he had written was the onward march of the human mind in the arts and the sciences. His wide conclusions were: civilization preceded 'Adam' and 'Creation' by millenniums; human nature is fundamentally the same in all the ages and climes but is differently modified by climate, government, religion and custom; chance and accident play an important role in generating events; history is made less by the genius of individuals than by the instinctive operation of human multitudes upon their environment; in this way are produced, bit by bit, the manners, morals, economies, laws, sciences and arts that constitute civilization and produce *the spirit of the times.* "My principal end," wrote Voltaire, "is always to observe the spirit of the times, since it is that which directs the great events of the world."[26]

History, a Remedy

In his *Recapitulation,* Voltaire came to the sad conclusion that "All history, in short, is little else than a long succession of useless cruelties...a collection of crimes, follies, and misfortunes..."[27] with occasional interludes of happy times. Yet he believed that history could play a powerful role in the enlightenment of men and in the creation of a rational humane society, the remedy the Age of Reason suggested to cure the ills of mankind. If we cannot change human nature, we can modify its operations by remoulding education and making saner customs and wiser laws. If ideas have changed the world, why may not better ideas make a better world? Voltaire's seven volume *Essay* may be taken as a plea for the dissemination of reason as a patient agent in the progress of mankind.[28]

Assessment

Many critics picked in the *Essay* errors of fact and the Jesuits had no difficulty in exposing its distorting bias. Voltaire replied to his critics that he had stressed the sins of Christianity because others were still defending them. Bias apart, Will Durant writes:

> Perhaps with all his illuminating conception of how history should be written, Voltaire mistook the function of the historian; he sat in judgement on each person and event, and passed sentence on them like some Committee of Public Safety pledged to protect and advance the intellectual revolution.[29]

Yet he says that the merits of the *Essay* are numberless.

> Its range of knowledge was immense, and testified to sedulous research. Its bright style, weighed with philosophy and brightened with humour, raised it far above most works of history between Tacitus and Gibbon. Its general spirit alleviated its bias; the book is still warm with love of liberty,

toleration, justice and reason. Here again, after so many lifeless, credulous chronicles, historiography became an art.[30]

3. David Hume (1711–1776)

The Philosophical Position: Anti-Cartesianism[31]

Collingwood observes that it was of great significance that so determined and profound a thinker like David Hume should have deserted philosophical studies in favor of historical at about the age of thirty-five. Hume, Berkeley and Locke completed the destruction of Cartesianism begun by Vico and reoriented philosophy in the direction of history. Locke attacked the Cartesian theory of knowledge: (a) He denied the Cartesian conception of *innate ideas* which was an anti-historical conception and insisted that knowledge is empirical, i.e., coming through experience. If all knowledge is based on experience, it is a historical product; (b) Lockian empiricism denied *abstract ideas* claiming that all ideas are concrete. Such a philosophical or epistemological position was particularly helpful to history where knowledge consists not of abstract generalizations but of concrete ideas; (c) The Lockian school held a conception of human knowledge as falling necessarily short of absolute truth and certainty, but *capable of attaining* (in Locke's words) *such certainty as our condition needs.* Such a position when interpreted and extended by Hume became a solid basis for historical knowledge though not for natural sciences like mathematics and physics. What Locke calls 'our condition' is the actual state of human affairs, or the way in which men live and talk and act. Hume applied the principles of his philosophy to the case of historical knowledge. He showed that the Cartesian objections to historical thought were invalid. He demonstrated that history was a legitimate and valid type of knowledge, more legitimate in fact than others because history did not promise more than it could perform and because it did not depend on any metaphysical hypotheses. Hume shows that historical knowledge such as that, for example, the assassination of Caesar, to be a system of reasonable beliefs based on testimony.

Hume, the Historian

A product of the Scottish Enlightenment, David Hume had at the age of twenty-eight written the brilliant philosophical piece, *The Treatise of Human Nature.* But he had such a high conception of history and a great longing to write it that at about thirty-five years of age he left his own field of philosophy to become a historian. He demonstrated the absurdity of the idea that human society had originated in a 'social contract'. In an essay called "Of the Study of History", Hume referred to the subject as an "agreeable entertainment" more interesting than fiction. He declared that "a man acquainted with history may, in some respect, be said to have lived from the beginning of the world."[32] He hoped to discover in his adopted subject the causes of the rise and fall of nations and to see in it all the human race pass in review before him.

Hume's *History of England* in six volumes was published between 1754 and 1762. The work covered the story of Britain from Julius Caesar's invasion of the island to the glorious revolution of 1688. It was largely a work of interpretation rather than of exhaustive research. Indeed, Hume once referred to research as the 'dark industry'. The volume, which appeared first was the history of James I and Charles I (1603 – 1649). It raised a furore because Hume's sympathy for Charles I and the Earl of Stafford was too much for the anti-Stuart passion bred by the Whig domination. Hume admitted that Charles I had overstepped the royal prerogative and deserved to be dethroned; but he pictured the English Parliament as likewise overreaching its privilege and equally guilty of the Civil War. The six volumes had a tremendous popular success and even the first book, mentioned above and which had the least sale, brought the author 2000 pounds. Voltaire reviewed Hume's *History* and thought the author quite impartial and later pronounced it the best history perhaps ever written in any language.

4. William Robertson (1721–1793)

It is a marvel that William Robertson, a minister of the Scottish Presbyterian Church, became the complete Enlightenment historian. True to the Enlightenment theory, Robertson thought of history as the development of human society and civilization, a conviction exemplified by his *The History of America.* His *History of Scotland* rejected everything that smacked of fable and conjecture. Robertson's most famous work is *The History of the Emperor Charles V* (1769). It is important not only for its attempt to deal with social as well as political matters, but also for the extensive scholarly apparatus it provides.

5. Edward Gibbon (1737–1794)

Born in 1737, Edward Gibbon was so sickly and shy that he spent most of his time with books in his grandfather's library. At the age of fifteen, he was sent to Magdalen College, Oxford. There he turned a Catholic. The mortified father sent him to Lausanne, where a Calvinist pastor, Pavilliard, cured him of his Catholic faith. But it was no gain for Protestantism, for contact with the French Enlightenment undermined his faith in Christianity itself. He met Voltaire and read his *Essay*; he read Montesquieu and Hume. These completed his initiation into the Enlightenment. At Lausanne he had met and loved Suzanne Curchod, but his love was frustrated by the disapproval of his father. Quite early in life Gibbon had aspired to be a historian and had made elaborate preparations. And now he cast about for a subject that would lend itself to philosophy and literature as well as to history. It was in 1764 when he was musing amidst the ruins of the Capitol in Rome that the idea of working on the decline and fall of the Roman empire first occurred to him.

Sources

Gibbon's scholarship was immense. He made detailed studies of roads, coins, weights, measures and laws. The critical Bury has commented: "If we take into account the vast range of his work, his accuracy is amazing."[33] But the very vastness of the work prevented him from consulting unprinted original sources and kept him confined to printed material. He frankly relied in part on secondary authorities like Ockley's *History of the Saracens*, and Tillemont's *History of the Emperors* and *Ecclesiastical History*. Gibbon declared his sources in honest detail, and thanked them.

The Decline and Fall of the Roman Empire

The first of the six volumes of *The Decline and Fall of the Roman Empire* appeared in 1776. It was well received and soon went into a second edition. Gibbon dated the decline of the empire from the accession of Commodus (AD 180), the son of Marcus Aurelius, and here the great history began. Without being openly hostile to

Christianity, the author, however, asserted that the rise of that creed contributed to the decline of the Roman Empire. Christianity sapped the faith of the people in the official religion, thereby undermining the state, which that religion supported and sanctified. The Christians formed a secret society hostile to military service, and diverted men from useful employment to concentrate on heavenly salvation. Unlike the pagans, they were intolerant, dooming all others as vicious and damned, and openly predicting the fall 'Babylon', i.e., Rome. The Christian community gradually formed an *imperium in imperio*. Gibbon followed Voltaire in reducing the number of Christians martyred by the Roman government, putting that number at 2000 at most. He concluded that "the Church of Rome defended by violence the empire she had won by fraud."[34] Such assertions aroused criticism of inaccuracy, unfairness, insincerity. Gibbon in a *Vindication* admitted some inaccuracies, but denied wilful misrepresentations, gross errors and servile plagiarisms.[35]

The second and third volumes were received quietly. Gibbon interpreted the conversion of Constantine as an act of statesmanship. Constantine recognized that the aid of supernatural religion was a precious aid to morality, social order and government. Gibbon honored Julian the Apostate with hundred and fifty eloquent and impartial pages. Volume 4, writes Durant, included masterly chapters on Justinian and Belisarius, and a chapter on Roman law, which won high praise from jurists. In Volume 5, Gibbon treated the rise of Islam and the Arab conquest of the eastern Roman empire, lavishing upon the Prophet and the martial Khalifs all the impartial understanding that had failed him in the case of Christianity.[36] In Volume 6, the Crusades gave the author another stirring theme and the capture of Constantinople by Muhammad II in 1453 provided the climax and crown of the work. When in June 1787, the labour of twenty years ended, Gibbon felt relieved, but the relief left him sad that he had "taken an everlasting leave of an old and agreeable companion...."[37]

Characteristics of Gibbon's History

Style

The Decline and Fall is written in a style marked by subtle suggestions and transparent irony. Gibbon wrote, comments Will

Durant, like an orator. His pomposity fitted well with the reach and splendor of his theme—the thousand year crumbling of the great Roman empire. Thus Durant: "The venial sins of his style are lost in the masculine march of the narrative, the vigour of the episodes, the revealing portraits and descriptions, the magisterial summations that cover a century in a paragraph, and marry philosophy to history."[38]

Philosophical History

The Decline and Fall is one of the masterpieces of rationalist, philosophical historiography. Gibbon wrote that "An enlightened age requires from the historian some tincture of philosophy and criticism."[39] Without reducing history to laws or formulating a philosophy of history, he took a stand on some basic issues: he confined the influence of climate to the early stages of civilization; he rejected race as a determining factor in history; and he acknowledged within limits the influence of exceptional men. Child of the Enlightenment, Gibbon accepted the reality of human progress, the idea that conferred a purposefulness on the study of long stretches of the past. He wrote in Volume 4 of *The Decline and Fall*, "that every age increases the real wealth, the happiness, the knowledge, and perhaps the virtue of the human race."[40] Yet he judged history, as he wrote in Volume 1, to be "indeed little more than the register of the crimes, follies, and misfortunes of mankind."[41] This is because human nature remains unchanged. Cruelty, suffering and injustice have always afflicted mankind, and always will, for they are written in the nature of man.

Exclusion of Cultural History

If Voltaire concentrated on cultural history, Gibbon excluded it altogether. "Wars and the administration of public affairs," he said, "are the principal subjects of history."[42] Art, science and literature, Arabic science and philosophy, the rise of industry and the condition of the lower classes – such ingredients of culture and civilization – find no place in Gibbon's volumes.

Verdict on the Middle Ages

The rationalist influence of Voltaire, Montesquieu and Hume could further be noticed in Gibbon's view and treatment of the Middle Ages. Gibbon saw nothing of value in that long stretch of time but crudity and superstition. His verdict on the Middle Ages is contained in a famous sentence: "I have described the triumph of barbarism and religion."[43] He merely saw a steady decline from the peak of pre-Christian Rome to the dawn of the modern age when the spark of reason lit again the torch of learning.

Judgement on the Byzantine Civilization

Gibbon's treatment of the Byzantine civilization is said to be equally partial and prejudiced. In the judgement of Bury, "He [Gibbon] failed to bring out the momentous fact that till the twelfth century the Eastern Roman Empire was the bulwark of Europe against the East; nor did he appreciate its importance in preserving the heritage of Greek civilization."[44]

Judgement on Christianity

Finally, the charge of intentional hostility to Christianity has been brought against Gibbon. Following Voltaire's lead in his treatment of the Christian religion, Gibbon pointed out the exclusiveness and intolerance of the Christians of the Roman Empire, their hostility to the official religion of the empire as well as to military service, their posture as an independent and an increasing power in the heart of the Roman state, and their open prediction of the fall of Rome—all these were tantamount to undermining the Roman system. We must admit that much of what Gibbon wrote about Christianity was historically true, but we must also point out that he was not completely impartial and that he failed to appreciate the great spiritual ferment that Christianity represented. He was fully a historian of the Enlightenment.

As a last word on Gibbon, Barthold Niebuhr says: "Gibbon's work will never be excelled."[45]

6. Drawbacks of Enlightenment Historiography

Unhelpful Attitude towards the Past

Convinced that the past, particularly the Middle Ages, had been dark and that they were of the new dawn – the age of light – the

Enlightenment historians tended to turn away from history altogether, or at least neglect long stretches of it. Thus Jean d' Alembert wanted to do away with much of the past. Again, the Marquis de Condorcet, an early prophet of the doctrine of endless progress of mankind and a pioneer historian of the European civilization, was a prominent member of a French parliamentary commission that in 1792–93 deliberately destroyed some of the royal records as comprising relics of past servitude. To condemn the past in the light of the present is unhistorical. Such a tendency led to two fundamental weaknesses. First, Enlightenment historiography, writes Arthur Marwick, "was remarkably innocent of any sense of human development and change...."[46] Failing to see that times change and ages differ, both Voltaire and Gibbon somewhat despised the men of the Middle Ages as of a lower standard of civilization and behavior than that of eighteenth century high society. By reason of this fundamentally unhistorical attitude the great historical works of the Enlightenment treated the Middle Ages scrappily and with little respect. Secondly, the great histories of the Enlightenment were interpretative works, not always based on detailed scholarly research. "Woe to details," exclaimed Voltaire, "they are a sort of vermin that destroys big works."[47]

To the above may be added the following drawbacks which Collingwood picks out in Enlightenment historiography:

Polemical and Anti-historical Attitude of Enlightenment Historiography

The historians of the Enlightenment, observes Collingwood, assumed an extremely violent and one-sided attitude towards religion. Terms like religion, priest, Middle Ages and barbarism, were for them not historical or sociological terms with a definite scientific meaning, but simply terms of abuse. It did not occur to them that such terms like 'religion', and 'barbarism' have a conceptual significance with a positive function in human history.

> A truly historical view of human history sees everything in that history as having its own *raison d'etre* and coming into existence in order to serve the needs of men whose minds have corporately created it. To think of any phase in history as altogether irrational is to look at it not as a historian but as

a publicist, a polemical writer of tracts for the times. Thus the historical outlook of the Enlightenment was not genuinely historical; in its main motive it was polemical and anti-historical.[48]

Lack of Improvement in Historical Method

Collingwood further observes that writers like Voltaire and Hume did very little to improve the methods of historical research. They took over the methods devised by men like Mabillon and Tillemont and the Bollandists, and even these methods they did not use in a really scholarly spirit. They were not sufficiently interested in history for its own sake to persevere in the task of reconstructing the history of obscure and remote periods. Voltaire openly proclaimed that no securely based historical knowledge was attainable for events earlier than the fifteenth century. Hume's *History of England* is a very slight and sketchy piece of work until it comes to the same period, the age of the Tudors. Their narrow conception led them into the error of thinking certain periods as non-rational.

Backward-looking and Forward-looking Developments of Enlightenment Historiography

Collingwood discerns in Enlightenment historiography a backward-looking historical development showing past history as the play of irrational forces; and a forward-looking political development forecasting and endeavoring to bring about a millennium in which the rule of reason shall have been established. The first tendency is exemplified by Gibbon, the typical Enlightenment historian, who found the motive force of history in human irrationality itself, just as Montesquieu had placed it in climate and geography. His narrative, Gibbon said, displayed the triumph of barbarism and religion. There must be something for barbarism and religion to triumph over. Gibbon found it in a golden age – the period of the Antonines – when, as he believed, human reason ruled over a happy world. It is with such a golden age in the past that Gibbon began his monumental work.[49] The second or the forward-looking aspect of the Enlightenment movement is represented by Condorcet. His classic *A Sketch of a Tableau of the Progress of the Human Spirit* looked forward to an

Utopian future when tyrants and their slaves, priests and their dupes, would have disappeared, and people would behave rationally in the enjoyment of life, liberty and the pursuit of happiness.

Apocalyptic Nature of Enlightenment Historiography

Collingwood shows how the historiography of the Enlightenment was apocalyptic to an extreme degree. The very word 'enlightenment' suggests it. The central point of history is the sunrise of the modern scientific spirit. Before that everything was superstition and darkness, error and imposture, all unworthy of historical study. The story of them is a tale told by an idiot full of sound and fury signifying nothing.[50]

Lack of Conception of Historical Origins, Processes, Causation

The historians of the Enlightenment, continues Collingwood, do not seem to have had any conception of historical origins, or processes, or historical causation. Pure reason cannot come into existence out of pure unreason. But from the point of view of the Enlightenment, the sunrise of the scientific spirit was a pure miracle, unprepared by the previous course of events and uncaused by any cause. This inability to explain or expound historically what they regarded as a most important event in history was due to the fact that, in general, they had no satisfactory theory of historical causation. Consequently, throughout their historical work, their account of causes is superficial to absurdity. It was these historians, for example, who invented the grotesque idea that the Renaissance in Europe was due to the fall of Constantinople and the consequent expulsion of scholars; and a typical expression of this attitude is the remark of Pascal that if Cleopatra's nose had been longer the history of the world would have been different. It betrays a bankruptcy of historical method which in despair of genuine explanation acquiesces in the most trivial causes for the vastest effects.[51]

In short, Enlightenment historiography adapted the conception of historical research which had been devised by the church historians of the late seventeenth century and used it deliberately in an anti-clerical spirit. No attempt was made to lift history above the level of propaganda; the crusade in favor of reason was regarded as a holy war; and Montesquieu judged correctly when he remarked that in spirit Voltaire was a monastic historian writing for the glory of his order.

7. Merits of Enlightenment Historiography

Against such drawbacks Collingwood sets certain definite advances that the historians of the Enlightenment made. With all their intolerance and unreason, they were fighting for tolerance. They were again bringing to an altogether new prominence, the history of the arts, sciences, industry, trade and culture in general. Though they were superficial in their search for causes, they did at least search for them, and thus implicitly conceived history as a process in which one event led necessarily to the other.

> There was thus a leaven at work in their own thought which was tending to disrupt their own dogmas and transcend their own limitations. Deep down beneath the surface of their own work lay a conception of the historical process developing neither by the will of enlightened despots nor by the rigid plans of a transcendent God, but by a necessity of its own, an immanent necessity in which unreason itself is only a disguised form of reason.[52]

6

THE ROMANTIC REACTION AGAINST RATIONALISM

1. Romanticism

The *philosophes* of the Enlightenment had treated certain ages of the past like the Middle Ages as primitive and barbaric and as such unworthy of serious historical investigation. They had also held a conception of human nature as something uniform and unchanging. These two tendencies had to be combated and the horizon of history widened before any further progress in historical thought could be made. The two thinkers who made substantial advance in these directions were Rousseau and Herder.[1]

The assumption of the *philosophes* that faith and feeling must submit to reason provoked a romanticist reaction which looked upon life and its interpretation as based more on feeling than on thought. Romanticism is the establishment of human life on a pure basis of feeling. To the romanticist, the medium of thought itself was feeling. The skepticism, rationalism and intellectualism of the Age of Reason came to be challenged everywhere by faith and feeling, imagination and mystery, sentiment and romance. In the new 'age of feeling' sensibility and emotional expression became an ideal and a fashion.

2. Rousseau (1712–1778)

Jean Jacques Rousseau was the inspirer, the messiah of the Romantic movement. A child of the Enlightenment, Rousseau became the father of the Romantic movement. His gospel exalted feeling above thought. Romanticism was Rousseau's call back to naturalness and freedom, a call for originality, for direct experience and unhindered expression. Rousseau, said Madame de Stael, "invented nothing, but he set everything on fire."[2] His books were the best expression of the Romantic idea, and they had an incalculable influence on political thought, philosophy, literature, education and history. A man of the people, Rousseau's fundamental theory was the inherent virtue of the natural man. In the first of his two *Discourses* (1750), a prize-winning essay, Rousseau challenged the Age of Reason by asserting that civilization, i.e., the arts and the sciences, had corrupted the morals and character of men. In the second, *On the Origin of Inequality* (1754), he went to the extent of declaring that "a thinking man is a depraved animal."[3] Inequality had its origin in private property which begot civil society and from these followed all the curses of civilization. Rousseau impugned the Enlightenment and its hopeful belief in human progress by asserting that progress is nothing but degeneration. Reacting against the classic mode of restraint, order, reason and form, Rousseau's novel, the *New Heloise* (1761) proclaimed the primacy of feeling, thus setting the tune for Romantic fiction—the literature of feeling, passion and sentiment. The novel became so popular that printing fell far behind demand. The *Social Contract* of only hundred and twenty-five pages opened with the cry: "Man is born free, and he is everywhere in chains." The chains are the bonds that civil society has put upon him and by breaking which alone can man regain his freedom and happiness. Sovereignty lies with the people and law should be the expression of the general will, of the deep instinctive conscience of the community. Again, Rousseau produced in *Emile* a classic in education. Its object was to show that it was possible to preserve and develop man's natural goodness by right education.

Influence of Rousseau

The Romantic tide swept Europe from 1760 to 1859, between Rousseau and Darwin. A literature of feeling, sentiment and passion flowed from Germany, England and France. Goethe bathed his *Werther* in love, nature and tears, and made Faust say "feeling is all"; Schiller hailed Rousseau as liberator and martyr and compared him with Socrates.[4] Philosophy was moved. Kant's *Critique of Pure Reason* was suffused with Rousseau. The German philosopher hung a picture of Rousseau on his study wall and declared him the

Newton of the moral world.[5] Herder said, "Come Rousseau and be my guide."[6]

3. Herder (1744–1803)

Rosseau had no direct relation to history, but Johann Gottfried von Herder, the harbinger of the Romantic movement in Germany, became also an innovator in the philosophy of history and culture. It was through Herder that the Romantic movement became so influential among historians.

Herder's ideas on history are contained in two works. The first, *One More Philosophy of History,* published in 1774, opposed rationalism in historiography. Its theme was elaborated in a second and larger work, "a massive masterpiece,"[7] entitled *Ideas for the Philosophy of the History of Mankind,* published between 1784 and 1791. Divided into four parts, it is "one of the epochal, seminal books of the eighteenth century,"[8] containing as Collingwood says, "a marvellous quantity of fertile and valuable thoughts."[9] In this second work Herder attempted to demonstrate that nature and history obey a uniform system of laws. Let us look at Herder's philosophy of history.

Man, an Evolutionary Product of Nature[10]

Herder, like Darwin later, thought of man as an evolutionary product of nature, each stage in the evolution designed to prepare for the next. But because man is an end in himself, the process reaches a culmination with him. Nature's purpose in creating man, her best product, is the creation of a rational and social being with capacity for religion, humaneness, and so on. Herder saw human life as closely related to its setting in the world of nature. Man is a product of his environment and, as such, his history, like that of a worm, is interwoven with the fabric which he inhabits. History as a whole is a purely natural history of human forces, actions and instincts.

Racial Division of Mankind[11]

The stage next to the evolution of the human being is the division or differentiation of mankind into various races, each race closely related to its geographical environment. A race once formed is a specific type of humanity; it will have permanent physical and mental characteristics of its own, depending not on its environment but on its inbred peculiarities (like a plant formed in one environment remains the same when transplanted into another). The sensuous and imaginative faculties of different races are genuinely different; and each race has its own conceptions of happiness and its own ideal of life.

Historical Organism[12]

From among the several races there arises a higher type of human organism, namely the historical organism. It is a race whose life instead of remaining static has developed in time to higher and higher forms. The favored centre in which this historical life has arisen is Europe, owing to its geographical and climatic peculiarities. In Europe alone is human life genuinely historical, whereas in China or India or among the natives of America, there has been no true historical progress. Europe is thus a priviledged region of human life.

National Culture and National Character

Herder's philosophy of history and culture caused a ferment of fundamental thinking in Germany known as Romanticism, and sowed the seeds of a cultural nationalism nurtured later by Beethoven, Goethe, Schiller, Kant, Fichte, Hegel, Schliermacher and many others. The whole movement was based on the primacy of feeling and emotion; and from Germany, the most 'romantic' of all countries, the influence spread throughout Europe.

Herder's philosophy of national culture and national character was rooted in Romanticism. Herder declared that all true culture or civilization must rise from native roots – from the life of the common people, the *volk* – and not from the cosmopolitan life of the upper classes. Each people, he held, had its own attitudes, spirit or genius. A sound civilization must express the national character or *volksgeist* of a people which is different from that of other peoples. Each nation should develop its genius in its own way without being changed or distorted by outside influences.[13]

Each civilization, Herder asserted, is a biological and spiritual entity, a plant, an organism with its own birth, maturity, decline and death. Each national culture is a unique entity with its own inherent character, its own language, religion, moral code, literature and art. Nations and ages are organic unities in which all things are fused into something like a unique 'personality' by the governing influence of a spirit—morals, laws and artistic production so interrelated in a given culture that they cannot be transplanted from one nation to another. They all sprang from their central spiritual source, which was unlike anything else in the world.[14] It is this national culture that moulds national character. It follows, then, that each civilization, each national culture, each age, should be studied and judged in its own context, without moral prepossessions based on another environment and age.

Romantic Love of the Middle Ages

Herder, like Rousseau, assumed that man is by nature good and that primitive societies are relatively excellent and happy. Representing a reaction against eighteenth century rationalism and seventeenth century formalism, Herder, and the Romantics in general, hearkened back to the Middle Ages as the age of imagination and feeling, of popular poetry and art, of rural simplicity and peace. The *philosophes* of the Enlightenment had treated the Middle Ages with contempt, as an age of barbarism and superstition; Herder and, following him, the Romantics, looked back upon the Middle Ages with respect and even nostalgia, finding in them a fascination, a colorfulness, or spiritual depth which they missed in their own time. In art, the 'Gothic' which Rationalists thought barbarous had a strong appeal for romantics.[15]

4. Herder: Collingwood's Critique

Collingwood writes that Herder's book is one of the richest and most stimulating on its subject but that the wealth of ideas therein is developed in a loose and hasty manner. Herder was not a cautious thinker and was not critical of his own ideas.

Herder, says Collingwood, was the first thinker to recognize that there are differences among men in respect of physical and mental peculiarities which account for the differences among the civilizations of the world. The peculiar characteristics of, say, the Chinese civilization, then, are to be ascribed to the unique nature of the Chinese. The different kinds of men once (racially) formed, if placed in the same environment, will exploit the resources of that environment in different ways and thus create different kinds of civilization. The determining factor in history, then, is race. *The recognition that civilizations differ because human nature is not uniform was an important advance made by Herder in the understanding of history.* Human thought and behavior do not conform to a uniform pattern throughout the world and throughout the historical periods. It clearly meant that *different ages and different peoples should not be judged from contemporary moral and cultural standpoints.* But the gain was only partial, for the racial conception of the diversity of cultures was not genuinely historical. Says Collingwood:

> The psychological characteristics of each race were regarded as fixed and uniform, so that instead of the Enlightenment conception of a single fixed human nature we now have the conception of several fixed human natures. Each of these is regarded not as an historical product but as a presupposition of history. There is still no conception of a people's character as having been made what it is by that people's historical experience; on the contrary its historical experience, is regarded as a mere result of its fixed character.[16]

Collingwood now mounts a frontal attack on Herder. It is not true, says that critic, that Europe alone has a history. The racial theory, a crucial step in Herder's argument, should not be accepted without scrutiny.

> The racial theory of civilization has ceased to be scientifically respectable. Today we only know it as a sophistical excuse for national pride and national hatred. The idea that there is a European race whose peculiar virtues render it fit to dominate the rest of the world, or an English race whose innate qualities make imperialism a duty, or a Nordic race whose predominance in America is the necessary condition of American greatness, and whose purity in Germany is indispensable to the purity of German culture, we know to be scientifically baseless and politically disastrous. We know that physical anthropology and cultural anthropology are different studies; and we find it difficult to see how any one can have confused them. Consequently we are not inclined to

be grateful to Herder for having started so pernicious a doctrine.[17]

Collingwood further enlightens us that Herder's racial-cultural doctrine is fatal to a true understanding of history. The doctrine means that the differences in civilization are derived not from the historical experience of each race but from its innate psychological peculiarities. *Herder's differentiations between different cultures are not historical differentiations* like that between, say, medieval and Renaissance culture, but non-historical differentiations like that between a community of bees and a community of ants.[18] It means that a culture cannot be improved by improving the mind; it is possible only by improving the breed! "Once Herder's theory of race is accepted," says Collingwood, "there is no escaping the Nazi marriage law."[19]

Assessment

Aesthetic rather than intellectual, poetical and intuitive rather than careful and logical, Herder flung out brilliant and valuable thoughts on history without patiently developing them into a systematic whole. Because he was not self-critical, he did not see the ill effects of his own ideas. Yet it was Herder's achievement to have perceived and insisted that human thought and behavior did not conform to a uniform pattern throughout the world or throughout the historical periods. He taught historians to reject that vicious practice of judging past ages from contemporary moral and cultural standpoints. He undoubtedly had an influence on practising historians who learnt from him the 'historical sense' – the gift of 'feeling' oneself into the past – the thing that the *philosophes* had lacked.

5. Impact of Romanticism on Historiography: Beneficial Effects of Romanticist Historiography

Widening of the Scope of History

H.E. Barnes writes that the Romanticists had a broader, sounder and more truly historical conception of cultural and institutional development than the rationalist historians as a group. Romanticism humanized history by divesting it of its pragmatic role as the orator and teacher of prudence and virtue. With humanization came a vast widening of the scope of history. The romantic love of the mysterious and the unknown contributed to a new interest in strange and distant societies and civilizations such as the Chinese, Indian, Persian, Arabic and Egyptian, and in distant historical epochs. This was because Rousseau's thought, as Collingwood informs, implied an enormous widening and enrichment of the historical outlook. Whereas in Enlightenment theory *reason* had come into the world at a comparatively recent date, the *general will,* as Rousseau conceived it, had always existed and had always been operative. "The principle upon which Rousseau explained history, therefore, was a principle which could be applied not only to the recent history of the civilized world but to the history of all races and all times."[20] The whole of human history of whatever quality, now became intelligible, at least in principle. Again, Collingwood shows how Rousseau's conception of education elaborated in *Emile,* helped to further enrich the scope of history. That conception called upon the teacher to understand the life of the child, sympathize with it, treat it with respect and help it to develop in a way proper and natural to itself.[21] The conception, applied to history, required historians to regard past ages with sympathy and respect instead of – like Enlightenment historians – contempt and disgust. They must find in such ages the expression of genuine and valuable human achievements.[22] Romanticist sympathy for primitive times and for the Middle Ages became an asset which vastly enriched the historical outlook.

History as Progress

Collingwood observes that this love of the past did not develop into a futile nostalgia for the past as such, owed to another conception of Romanticism—*the conception of history as a progress,* a development of human reason or the education of mankind. It invested the past with a positive value for it meant that past ages in history necessarily led to the present, that a given form of civilization can exist only when the time is ripe for it, and that it is but a necessary phase in the historical process. For a Romanticist historian a past age like the Middle Ages was important doubly—partly because it was of permanent value in itself, as a unique achievement of the human mind; and partly as taking its place in a course of development leading on to things of still greater value.[23] Thus, Romanticist historiography, unlike its Enlightenment counterpart, thought of the whole past as one and, therefore, no part of it was to be neglected as unworthy of study. Collingwood concludes: "The scope of historical thought was vastly widened, and historians began to think of the entire history of man as a single process of development from a beginning in savagery to an end in a perfectly rational and civilized society."[24]

New Way of Looking at History: Genetic Relationism

The Enlightenment historians had looked upon the Middle Ages as a period of barbarism, superstition and intellectual error. Against them Herder, for the first time, advanced the Romanticist view that everything, *relatively,* is right *in its own historical context.* Walter Scott typified in his novels this Romantic desire to see the past from inside, "as it really was", in the celebrated words of Ranke. Portraying the manners and morals, the mores and attitudes, of a vanished Scottish Highland society, Scott's *Waverly* novels had a profound direct influence on Ranke and other historians. This new way of looking at history has been called 'genetic relationism'. 'Genetic' stands for the stress laid on origins and the notion of every phase developing out of a previous phase; and 'relationist', because of the insistence that every person, every activity, every institution, must be seen *in relation* to the age in which it is set.[25]

Emphasis on National Culture and National Character

Enlightenment theory had held that human nature remained the same in all ages and among all peoples; working against it, the Romanticists emphasized the differences between different ages and different national groups. Vico had contributed substantially to the appreciation of cultural differences between different ages and different nations. It meant that it was unhistorical to import ideas or judgements into the history of earlier ages and different peoples. Rousseau and Herder laid the emotional and philosophical basis of the nationalist creed. Herder held that each national culture was a unique biological entity with its own inherent character – the national character – expressed in its language, literature, art and moral code. This 'national character' according to Herder, greatly influenced the history of a nation. He insisted that a historian should understand this national character and sympathize with it. Read his injunctions to historians: "First sympathize with the nation, go into the era, into the geography, into the entire history, feel yourself into it."[26] Modern nationalism is a powerful sentiment and it powerfully influenced the historiography of the nineteenth century.

Nostalgic Love of the Middle Ages

The sympathy and admiration felt by the Romanticists for the Middle Ages led to an imitation of the mystic and often capricious standards of those past centuries. Interest in medieval poetry, mystery and romance led to an eager collection of medieval ballads and other specimens of medieval culture. The life of chivalry, the crusades, the wars of Christian kings against the Moors, and romantic adventures and travels became the popular themes of historical writing.

The Historical Novel

Romanticist insistence on feeling and passion linked literature and historiography more closely than ever. The new bond led to the creation of a new kind of historical romance typified in the novels of Walter Scott. Placing his characters in exciting and turbulent historical situations, Scott insightfully depicted, reinterpreted and presented with living force the manners and loyalties of a vanished Scottish Highland society. Scott's historical novel created a new sensation in England by establishing ties with the past. It soon became a literary fashion for the other countries to emulate.

Baneful Effects of Romanticist Historiography

Herbert Butterfield writes that in many respects the influence of the Romantic movement in Europe in the late eighteenth century and the first half of the nineteenth came to be regarded as unfortunate.[27]

Mystification of Life and of History

Influenced more by the Romantic poets than by serious investigators of truth, it was unfortunate that the Romanticists in a way mystified human life and history. Holding each nation to be a unit of human culture, Romantic historiography exhorted historians to feel themselves into that culture. Attempting to make history attractive, Romantic historians deliberately indulged in much that was fanciful and even fantastic. Believing that the deeper mystical happenings could not be satisfactorily analyzed by rational methods, they romanticized all national activity. Giving importance to such things as castles, cathedrals, adventure, warfare, chivalry, crusades and so forth, they neglected other vital aspects of life. Holding a view of life and of history not very different from that of the Church, the Romanticists thought of happenings on this earth as so indeterminate and subject to the principle of fatality that pursuit of rational causes was often regarded as futile.

Dangerous Theories of Race and Culture

The Romanticist-nationalist view of history propped up dangerous theories of race and culture which provided the ideological basis, the *raison d'etre*, for the phenomenon of modern Western imperialism. What in truth was a naked power impulse to exploit the weak and defenceless peoples of the world now put on a scientific, religious or ethical garb. The 'White' or the 'Aryan' race being simply better specimens of the *homo sapiens* are more fit to survive than the non-Whites whom they had conquered in war—so ran the scientific argument borrowed from the Social Darwinist. The Christian missionary assumed the task of saving the soul of the conquered heathens in the colonies. Imperialism in its ethical garb found pretext in the 'White man's burden' or 'civilizing mission' of bringing the light of civilization to the non-Whites. Hitler's drive to preserve the racial purity of the so-called Aryan Germans took a grisly toll of Jewish lives.

Chauvinist Historiography

The romanticist emphasis on national peculiarities and national character inspired the spirit of nationalism which in its turn provided the most powerful impetus to historiography in modern times. The nineteenth century, the greatest age of nationalism, was also the greatest age of history writing. But this beneficial effect turned baneful when each nationalist historian began to eulogize his nation and culture in a bid to emphasize the superiority of his own nation over the other. Exaggerated nationalism developed into chauvinism and jingoism which corrupted historiography itself.

6. Philosophy of History

Meaning of Philosophy

Philosophy may be taken to mean speculative thought aimed at comprehending phenomena that are not amenable to the scientific methods of observation, analysis and experiment. Science is the analytical description of parts; philosophy is the synthetic interpretation of the whole. Concerned with problems of matter, science gives objective, verifiable knowledge; philosophy deals with such problems as human existence, the meaning of life, the nature and destiny of man—problems on which no conclusive data are at hand. Philosophy is the queen of sciences, the mother of all knowledge, the adviser to men, the teacher of wisdom. It is the love of truth.

Philosophy of History

Philosophy, concerned as it is with the problem of human life, will necessarily have much to do with history which is the study of man in society. The phrase philosophy of history was coined by Voltaire. But he meant by it not the philosophy of history, but a kind of philosophical history. He complained that history, as written by many, was only a confused mass of minute details without connection and sequence, a mass that overwhelmed the mind without illuminating it. Hundred and fifty years before Benedetto Croce who believed that history should be written only by philosophers, Voltaire, the philosopher, was to write history. His two masterpieces, *The Age of Louis XIV* and *The Essay on the Manners and Customs of Nations from Charlemagne to Louis XIII* dealt in a philosophical interpretative manner with universal history. Since Voltaire's time, the term 'philosophy of history' has come to mean the deeper philosophical problems involved in history, a search for its meaning. At this point, we must distinguish two rather different types of philosophy of history: the critical philosophy of history and the speculative philosophy of history. The two are, of course, related branches of philosophical inquiry into the subject of history.

The Speculative Philosophy of History

The speculative philosophy of history is concerned with finding a pattern or meaning or intelligibility in the past itself,[28] often "as the expression of some universal or cosmic design and having an ultimate goal."[29] It represents a search for unity in the bewildering complexity of events, an aspiration to comprehend the mechanism of growth and decay. It tries to discern laws and patterns of historical development. Speculative philosophy attempts to determine the fundamental factors that direct historical forces and ends up in the formulation of overarching theories of history. Such theories have had great influence on history writing. Hegel, Comte, Marx, Spengler, Croce and Toynbee have more or less viewed history as the past, and as a process that goes on independently of the working historian. In nature and character, speculative philosophy is formal and synthetic.

The ancient Greeks held a cyclical view of history—of similar events and movements endlessly recurring in human history. In contrast to the cyclical view, the Hebrew tradition represented by Judaism and Christianity advanced a specific unilinear view—the whole historical process culminating in the end of the world and a last judgement of all mankind. Paul, Eusebius and Augustine seized upon the concept of a meaning, a plan, and elaborated a Christian view according to which human history conformed to a divine plan the end of which was the end of history itself and the establishment of the kingdom of god. But the Christian view of history was eschatological and prophetic rather than historical because it looked to what was to come in the next world, rather than in this one.[30]

Vico's *Scienza nouva* (1725) advanced a secular view of the evolution of human societies. The Scientific Revolution of the seventeenth century and the limitless potentialities of science had already encouraged thinkers to advance ideas of general and indefinite progress. The idea of progress became the favorite doctrine of the Enlightenment. It was believed that progress was inherent in the historical process. Most of the Enlightenment historians – Hume, Robertson, Gibbon, Voltaire, Turgot and Condorcet – retained the Judeo-Christian teleological view that history was moving and progressing towards a goal. But they consciously shed its theological aspect, rationalized the historical process, and secularized its goal. History became not the realization of god's purpose, but progress towards perfection of man's estate on earth. The idea of progress became the central theme of Turgot's *Discourses on Universal History* (1750). But in Condorcet's *Tableaux of the Progress of the Human Spirit* (1754), the idea became the vision of an earthly paradise—the secularized version of the Kingdom of God.

The true heirs to the Judeo-Christian tradition in the philosophy of history were the German idealist philosophers, notably Kant, Herder, Schelling, Fichte, and above all, Hegel. They discerned in history not merely a universal pattern of development, common to every human society, but the unfolding of a universal providential plan, a plan in which the unit of change was a collective entity, a people or a nation or state.[31] For Hegel the moving spirit of history was the dialectical progression and self-realization of the 'absolute spirit' or human freedom, from primitive times to the civilization of his own day. Hegel's was a purely idealistic system maintaining that all history was the history of thought.

The confident optimism of the nineteenth century had come to assert that history was scientific knowledge providing the basis for the understanding of mankind, such as the natural sciences were doing for the understanding of nature. Positivists and social theorists like Auguste Comte, Henry Thomas Buckle and Herbert Spencer saw science as the highest stage of human development. Comte and Buckle used the concept of the philosophy of history to discover general laws governing the course of history. But the philosophy that went farthest in this direction was Marxism. Marx and Engels borrowed Hegel's dialectical method but employed it to erect a purely materialistic system of thought. Called historical materialism, the Marxian system seeks the essence of historical process in the material conditions of human life. The motivating force for the development from one historical stage to the other is the 'class war'. This dialectical process of the class struggle would end up in the establishment of a classless society.

After Marx, grand theorizing in history seemed to go out of fashion. Objection was raised to the philosophy of history on the ground that such theorizing was against the proper functions of history. Philosophy of history was based on thought, not facts. For this reason, perhaps, Charles Omen considered the philosophers of history as the enemies of history. G.M. Trevelyan categorically stated that for history there was no philosophy of history.

But in the early twentieth century there was a renewed interest in historical philosophy. Oswald Spengler and Arnold Toynbee, though not philosophers like Hegel or Marx, aimed at revealing some of the general laws behind the rise and decline of civilizations. But unlike their nineteenth century forerunners, they were more convinced of the ultimate decline of cultures and civilizations than their apotheosis. In the atmosphere of gloom left by the First World War, Oswald Spengler's *The Decline of the West* pronounced the judgement that Western civilization, reaching its height at about 1800, was doomed to a miserable decline. The law of history was the cyclical law of rise, growth and decay of cultures. Arnold Toynbee's immense work, *A Study of History*, tried to understand the genesis, growth and decline of civilizations in terms of what he calls the 'challenge and response' mechanism. In the growth stage, a civilization successfully responds to a series of ever new challenges. When the efforts to answer the challenges fail, civilizations die.

Critical Philosophy of History

The critical philosophy of history may be said to have originated in the attempt of Niebuhr and Ranke to develop history as a systematic discipline and present it as a science. Unlike the speculative philosophy of history, the critical philosophy is concerned with the actual activities of the historian himself, i.e., the historian's attempt to reconstruct the past. Analytical in nature, the critical philosophy inquires into the logical, conceptual and epistemological problems of historiography.

Historiography had gained from the Scientific Revolution in the matter of method. The critical spirit was growing. Tillemont, the Bolandists and Jean Mabillon had devised certain rules of method to determine the authenticity of documents. Far more important was the definite advance made by Vico. His *Scienza nouva* met Descartes's condemnation of history at the philosophical level and established it as an epistemologically justifiable form of knowledge. According to his *verum-factum* doctrine man can fully understand only what he himself has created. It followed that civil society being man's creation, history was ideally fit for human understanding. The Italian philosopher had also laid down certain rules of method for historical investigation and suggested positive methods by which the historian can transcend exclusive reliance on written sources and extend the frontiers of historical knowledge.

Yet the most important step in the critical philosophy of history – step towards the creation of an autonomous discipline of history

– was taken by Barthold Niebuhr and Leopold von Ranke who together developed the modern scientific methodology of historical investigation. In the manner of the natural scientist who formed his theories through strict observation and inductive discovery and correlation of evidence, so through an impartial and critical study of sources, the historian was to present a complete knowledge of the past as it had actually happened.

The great problem that critical philosophy is called upon to resolve is whether by a scientific study of the evidence, i.e., of the sources, it is possible to show, to lay bare 'what actually happened', as Ranke thought was possible. The problem touches upon almost every aspect of historiography, that is, the historian's activity—the nature of historical facts and their significance, the problem of objectivity or the subjective element in history writing, causation, the nature of historical explanation, generalization in the writing of history, and the problem of value judgement. The critical philosophy of history is the grammar, the science of history.

By the 1880s there set in a kind of reaction against the Rankean scientific and positivistic approach to history. Windelband, Rickert and Wilhelm Dilthey in Germany tried to maintain the distinctiveness of history as a separate kind of knowledge making it more fit to be classed with cultural or human studies. Dilthey showed that unlike science which studied the processes of nature, history studied man as an intelligent being acting according to conscious intentions and choices. History for Dilthey is 'mind-affected', a quality of which nature does not partake. This view found adherents in Collingwood, Croce and Oakeshott. Reacting against the positivistic practice of merely collating events recorded by their sources, Collingwood held that the proper study of history involved going beyond external occurrences to the thoughts which lay behind them. Going perhaps a step further, Croce and Oakeshott treated all history as contemporary history, as the present knowledge of the historians.[32]

7. Hegel (1770–1831)

Georg Wilhelm Frederick Hegel was the most influential philosopher of the Romantic-Idealist historical movement which began with Herder. Hegel's lectures at the University of Berlin "notoriously dull but finally meaningful, drew larger and larger audiences, until students came from almost every country in Europe – and beyond – to hear him."[33] *The Philosophy of History*, containing Hegel's historical thought, was first delivered as lectures in 1822–23.

Distinctive Features

Hegel proposed a philosophy of history different from a philosophical reflection on history as in Voltaire, with history itself raised to a higher power to become philosophical. It was to be a "history not merely *ascertained* as so much fact but *understood* by apprehending the reasons why the facts happened as they did."[34]

Influences behind Hegel

Hegel's historical thought owed much to his predecessors—Herder, Kant, Schiller, Fichte and Schelling.[35] Hegel owed to Herder the idea of a universal history outlining the developmental pattern of mankind as a progress from primitive times to the present day civilization. Hegel follows Kant when he says that the plot of this story is the development of freedom, i.e., the moral reason of man as exhibited in an external system of social relations; in fine, it is to be the story of how the state came into being. And like Schiller before him, Hegel asserts that since the historian knows nothing of the future, history culminates in the actual present, not in a future utopia. Hegel is in line with Fichte in regarding man's freedom as the development of the consciousness of his freedom, and the development itself as a process of thought or logical development. Lastly, following Schelling, Hegel's philosophy of history would exhibit not merely human process but a cosmic process, a process in which the world comes to realize itself in self-consciousness as spirit. Hegel showed extraordinary skill in weaving these threads of thought into a coherent philosophical system.

Nature and History are Different

Hegel insists that nature and history are different. The processes of nature are not historical but cyclical and repetitive: each sunrise, spring and high tide is like the last; the law governing the cycle does not change as the cycle repeats itself with no development; nothing is constructed or built up. History, on the contrary, never repeats itself, for it moves not in cycles but in spirals. If wars reappear, it is not repetition, for every new war is in some ways a new kind of war, different from the last one. "Thus," says Collingwood, "Hegel's conclusion is right, that there is no history except the history of human life, and that, not merely as life, but as rational life, the life of thinking beings."[36]

Reason, the Mainspring of the Historical Process

If history is the history of rational human life, all history is the history of thought. It follows then that reason is the mainspring, the underlying force, of the historical process. The historical process consists of human actions, human actions come by the will of man, and the will of man is nothing but man's thought expressing itself outwardly in human action. Human actions as events are knowable to the historian as the outward expression of thoughts. Hegel's philosophy of history was purely idealistic.

Historical Process is a Logical Process

Since all history is the history of thought exhibiting the self-development of reason, the historical process is ultimately a logical process. Historical transitions are logical transitions set out on a time scale. This means that the developments that take place in history are never accidental, they are necessary. The actual or the real is rational and *vice versa*, meaning that the real is the only logical and necessary result of its antecedents.

Historical Process is a Dialectical Process

The greatest philosophical achievement of Hegel was the systematic development of the dialectical method. First suggested by Plato, the dialectic, literally meaning the art of conversation, had been thought of by Fichte as the mechanism through which the historical process developed. Hegel conceived of the dialectic as the unifying metaphysical process underlying the apparent diversity of the world, of the historical phenomena. This process is essentially the necessary emergence of higher and more adequate entities out of a conflict between their less developed and less adequate anticipations. It is a process of progressive evolution through contradiction. A cannot be not-A. But Hegel would modify it thus: A *may become* not-A, as water may become ice or steam.[37] All reality, Hegel contended in his *Logic*, is in the process not of being, but of becoming.[38] All reality, all thoughts and things, are in constant evolution for an idea or situation potentially contains its opposite which struggles against it and unites with it to take another transient form. The dialectical structure is one of exposition, opposition and reconciliation; of thesis, antithesis and synthesis.

The Hegelian system makes dialectics the moving principle of history. Every historical process is of necessity a dialectical process. Each historical age would be characterized by dominant ideas of a certain type—the 'thesis'; each historical age being short of perfection, must also contain within it exactly contradictory ideas—the 'antithesis'; antithesis working against thesis would ultimately produce a 'synthesis'—the predominant idea of a new age. The historical process is a dialectical process in which one form of life, for example Greek, generates its own opposite, in this case Rome, and out of this thesis and antithesis arises a synthesis, in this case the Christian world.

Hegel contends that it is not merely a dialectics of change, it is a dialectics of progression. He found the fundamental meaning of the historical process in *the development of the consciousness of freedom*. Despotism tried to suppress the human hunger for freedom (democracy); the hunger broke out in revolt; the synthesis of despotism and democracy was constitutional monarchy. The German philosopher detected a dialectical progression of the consciousness of freedom from the despotism and slavery of the Oriental world, to the citizenship rights of the Greek and the Roman world, and to the individual liberties of the Germanic nations of his day. History or the past, then, is a grand design unfolding in four stages: Oriental, Greek, Roman and Germanic.

The Hegelian system is a totality of continuous development. The dialectical progression has as its aim the self-development of the Absolute Idea, which, according to most interpreters of Hegel, is the totality of everything which exists. It is a development which would culminate in the form of the Absolute Truth. In politics it means the emergence of the perfect state.

Apotheosis or Glorification of the State

To Hegel the theme of the historical process is the development of man's consciousness of freedom exhibited in an external system of social relations, i.e., the state. On the question of the state and government he expressed himself in such conservative terms that the liberals of Germany denounced him as a time-serving place-seeker, and the 'philosopher laureate' of a reactionary government.[39]

History for Hegel is the passage from primitive tribal life with all its inadequacies to the more adequate, fully rational state. "Freedom is the essence of life, as gravity is the essence of water. History is the growth of freedom; its goal is that the spirit may be completely and consciously free."[40] The famous Hegelian pattern of the dialectical development of the state, that is, human freedom, is as follows: for the Oriental world (China, India, Persia), only one – the despot – was free; in the slave-holding societies of Greece and Rome, some – the citizens – were free; only in the constitutional monarchies of Hegel's own day was there the institutional possibility of all being free.[41] It is in this modern stage that the rational spirit becomes conscious of its freedom, organizes that freedom in the state, and so makes all men free. It must have been in this sense that Hegel propounded his dictum that "the rational is real, and the real is rational." The state is man's highest achievement, the actuality of concrete freedom— freedom through reason. Such a state he saw in Prussia which he exalted claiming that there was more liberty there than in ancient Greece.

For Hegel the rational state is the nation-state, the largest social unit which he recognized. He had no time for Kantian style confederalism in the interests of peace. He maintained against Kant that to eliminate war in a world of nation-states is impossible. On the other hand, Hegel saw war itself not as a threat to civilization, but as ethically progressive, raising people from the selfish particularism of civil society to the 'universal'.

Zeitgeist and the Genius

In the dialectic of history contradictions are resolved, opposition transformed into fusion, centrifugal diversities transformed toward a unifying centre, often by the *zeitgeist* (the Spirit of the Times) or by the work of exceptional men (genius).[42] These two forces – time and the genius – are the engineers of history, and when they work together they are irresistible. Hegel inspired Carlyle in his belief in the role of heroes in history. Napoleon was no mere conqueror for the sake of conquest; he was the conscious or unconscious agent of Europe's greater need for unity and consistent laws. But the genius is wasted if he does not embody and serve the *zeitgeist.* Such individuals would know what the times required, *what was ripe for development.* If the genius is borne on such a tide like Galileo or James Watt or Napoleon, he will be a force for growth, even if he brings misery for an entire generation. The genius is not born for happiness, and periods of happiness and harmony are blank pages in the history of the world, for in such periods the antithesis is in abeyance and history sleeps.[43]

8. Criticism of Hegel

Much of Hegel's philosophy of history was complex, mysterious and obscure, and conveyed in abstruse language. The envious Schopenhauer unkindly epitomized Hegel's philosophy as "a monument of German stupidity."[44]

History as a Logical Process and Knowledge of it as 'a priori'

Hegel's idea of history as a logical process developed in time, and our knowledge of it as *a priori* has aroused much protest and even hostility. But Collingwood reminds us that Hegel only tells that historical knowledge is not purely or wholly empirical but that it contained *a priori* elements also.[45] Seen from outside, history consisted of empirical events and actions without necessary connections; but events and actions are the outside expressions of thought, and the thought behind the events – not the events themselves – formed a chain of logically connected concepts. What Hegel insists is that the historian must first work empirically by studying documents and other evidence, but he must then look at the facts from the inside and tell us what they look like from that point of view.

Confusion of Opposition and Distinction

Benedetto Croce has termed Hegel's philosophy of history as a gigantic blunder produced by confusing two quite different things, namely, opposition and distinction.[46] Croce says that concepts are related by opposition and stand in a dialectical and necessary relation to each other. But the individual things that are the results of concepts are never related to each other by way of opposition; they are related only by way of distinction, difference, and the relations between them are not identical. In history which is the history of individual actions and persons and civilizations, there is consequently no dialectic, whereas Hegel's whole philosophy turns on the principle that the historical process is a dialectical process. Collingwood reminds us that Croce's objection implies that in talking of history we should never use words like opposition or antagonism, and synthesis or reconciliation. We ought not to say that despotism and liberalism are opposite political doctrines, we ought only to say they are different. Empirically, that is, outwardly, we may talk of the colonization of New England without using any dialectical language; but when we try to see these events as a deliberate attempt on the part of the Pilgrim Fathers to establish a Protestant idea of life, we are talking about thoughts and we must describe them in dialectical terms. We must speak of the opposition between the congregational idea of religious institutions and the episcopal idea, and admit that the relation between the two is a dialectical relation.

The Idea that History Ends in the Present

The Swiss writer Eduard Fueter, has bitterly criticized Hegel for his doctrine that history ends not in the future but in the present.[47] According to him this only means the glorification and idealization of the present, and a denial that any further progress is possible—in effect, a pseudo-philosophica justification for a rigid and unintelligent conservatism. Collingwood says, here again, Hegel, like Fichte, is right. For the historian the future is a closed book and history must end with the present for the simple reason that he cannot have sources and evidence for the things that have not happened. As Hegel puts it, the future is an object not of knowledge but of hopes and fears; and hopes and fears are not history.

Overemphasis on Political History

After declaring that all history is the history of thought, Hegel in his *Philosophy of History,* restricts the field to political history.[48] He neglected art, religion and philosophy—fields where the highest form of thought operated. This, observes Collingwood, is a serious defect. He points out that, as a matter of fact, nearly half of Hegel's collected works is devoted to the study of art, religion and philosophy. Says Collingwood: "The *Philosophy of History* is an illogical excrescence on the corpus of Hegel's works."[49] Political history is not the whole of history. True history is that which integrates political development with economic, artistic, religious and philosophical developments, and the historian should not be content with anything short of a history of man in his concrete reality.

Influence of Hegel

Hegel raised history to a level not hitherto attained. Not long after his death two competing groups of Hegelianism emerged: the Right or the 'Old Hegelians', conservative and Christian, interpreted the dialectical process as culminating in the Prussian state and the Absolute as equivalent to the traditional Protestant conceptions of God. The Old Hegelians produced no major figures and after enjoying the support of the Prussian state went into rapid decline and were fully eclipsed by the 1860s. The Left or 'Young Hegelians', on the other hand, interpreted the dialectic in a revolutionary and atheistic sense, arguing that existing reality, including the prevailing political order was inadequate and needed to be made more rational, a change necessarily entailed by the dynamic logic of the dialectic. To this school belonged David Strauss, Ludwig Feuerbach and Karl Marx, and Marx was to effect a major breakthrough in historical and social studies.

7

I. ROMANTIC–NATIONALIST–LITERARY HISTORIOGRAPHY

1. Romanticism, Nationalism and Literature

Rousseau's stress on feeling and passion and Herder's doctrine of the 'genius of a nation', of national culture and national character, together formed the philosophical basis of nationalism. Herder held that each national culture was a unique entity with its own inherent character – the national character – expressed in its language, literature and art, and in its moral code. This national character, the Romanticist believed, determined the history of a people.

Modern nationalism is a powerful sentiment. The national spirit is essentially spiritual in character. It is the will of a people to live together—the *vouloir vivre collectiff* (the wish to live together).[1] This sentiment of unity is usually produced by community of race, language and religion, geographic unity, common political aspirations, and above all, common historical development. The nation-state has become the normal form of political organization in the modern world. The deep emotional basis of Romanticism not only stimulated nationalism but linked literature and historiography more closely than ever. Indeed, men like Macaulay and Carlyle even looked upon history as literature. The literary approach to history, predominating a great part of nineteenth century historiography, was informed by noble and liberal sentiments.

To evoke the spirit of a nation's past is a task which the Romantic historian does best. The nationalist emphasis on peoples rather than states had the effect of transforming the exclusive idea of political history more comprehensive, embracing the material and spiritual development of man in society. The spirit of resurgent nationalism gave a strong impetus to historical studies and supplied a powerful motive for historical investigation in so far as peoples endeavored to trace the roots of their national identity. For this reason, the nineteenth century, which was the century of nationalism in Europe, was also the century of great history writing. Its historical output was so vast that any survey of it is bound to be narrowly selective.

2. The Romantic School—History as National Epic: Thierry (1795–1856) and Michelet (1798–1874)

Augustine Thierry epitomized the vivid Romanticist way – which had been prepared by Rousseau, Herder and Scott – of recreating the past. Thierry was convinced that the past was not dead and that its actors were as much men of feeling and passion as those of the present. He learnt from Scott, "that master of historic divination,"[2] that the past could be brought to life and seen in colour and relief by the power of imagination. He ends a chapter with the emphatic words: "These men have been dead for seven hundred years. But what of that? For the imagination there is no past."[3] To clothe the past with flesh and blood the historian must have imagination, a power to feel into the past, and a keen sympathy with the masses. The 'Considerations on the History of France' which Thierry added to his work on the Merovingians (1840) may be regarded as a testament of Romantic history. Thierry expected the true historian of France to seek out the roots of the interests, ideas, passions, irresistible emotions, and the hopes and desires of the French people as a whole through the centuries and to link these with those of their ancestors. Such a history alone could portray the mass which always acts impulsively, rarely gives the appearance of wisdom, and yet sweeps everything before it.[4]

Thierry's *Norman Conquest of England*, written in the Romantic spirit, had an unprecedented success. It was its ardent sympathy with the people combined with supreme literary distinction that secured it a warm welcome. Thierry hoped to explain English history from the Norman conquest to the accession of Henry Tudor in 1485, by the simple formula of racial antagonism between the Norman conquerors and the conquered English. His theory of racial cleavage and his open partiality for all conquered peoples so misleads him as to exalt Archbishop Thomas Becket as the champion of the vanquished Anglo-Saxons and the martyr to their cause. Thierry's sympathy with the crowd is so spontaneous that Brunetiere has called him the most democratic and the most socialistic of historians.[5] Chateaubriand said of Thierry: "History will have its Homer, and I am the first of his admirers."[6]

The true historian of France that Thierry sought was found in Jules Michelet whose two great works became two great epics, one of France and the other of the Revolution. The only child of a poor but educated Paris printer, Michelet grew up in grinding poverty. He found in Vico's *Scienza nouva* what he had sought—a philosophical interpretation of civilization, that is, of man civilizing himself in society. "The master's emphasiz on the contribution of the masses to civilization, his conviction that the social life of a people mirrored in its law and poetry, and his use of etymology as a key to human origins struck notes of delightful response."[7]

A translation of the *Scienza nouva* soon followed which introduced Vico's masterpiece not only to France but to Europe. Appointed to teach history and philosophy at the Ecole Normale, Michelet wrote a school textbook of history, *Summary of Modern History* (1827), which surveyed the development of European civilization from the fifteenth century to the French Revolution. G.P. Gooch writes that based on original sources and written simply and concisely, the book is a well-kept garden, not a tropical forest. In 1831 appeared an incomparable work, the first complete modern survey of the ancient Roman Republic.

But the two works into which Michelet poured all his spirit and which have secured him a place among the greatest historians of all time are the *History of France* in 11 volumes, and the *History of the French Revolution* in 7 volumes. An immediate sympathy with the past, a passionate and personal love for France and her people, deep erudition and scrupulous attention to neglected primary sources, a powerful imagination, and an incomparable power of expression in a rich poetic style went into the making of Michelet, the historian. But what marks him out from the other historians is his special concern with regard to people. One can have an idea of the particular variety of history that Michelet wrote from the essay, 'The People'[8] written in 1846. For him the sentiment of France was indistinguishable from the sentiment of the people of France. He wrote history from his heart, and before he wrote he lived and experienced it with the most ordinary people, chatting with the peasant in the field and worker in the factory. It was in them that he found the more common traits in the national character. He regarded it as his task to paint a portrait of his people, their personality; and trace that personality to its historical origin, and see it issue forth from the depths of time.

Michelet's *History of France* aimed at resurrecting the life of the past as a whole—the land, the people, events, institutions and beliefs. By 1843, six volumes of the great history had been published, taking the story from the Celtic origins of France to the Renaissance. One of the first to realize the importance of the geographical factor in historical development, Michelet sketched in the *Tableau de France*, in the second volume, each province with its physical features, climate, inhabitants, character, and its contribution to national life. He rejected the doctrine of race, of the influence of conquest, of the providential role of great men. The treatment is national not dynastic, and the narrative is less a record of events than a series of scenes in which each epoch of the country's history is glorified. The most famous of these magnificent tableaux is that which depicts Joan of Arc. The radiant figure of the maid emerging from the dark background of Charles VII's France marks the summit of Michelet's achievement and is one of the glories of French literature. The most original history of France ever written, the first six volumes of the *History of France* are Michelet's most perfect work.[9]

When the sixth book of the grand epic had been completed, Michelet interrupted his work in order to write a passionately partisan *History of the French Revolution*. The book embodied his dream of a regenerated France, free alike from Church and monarchy, based on the principle of justice alone; a France in which the poor and the humble would at last come by their own rights. Michelet invested the Revolution with a *sacro sancti* character. After centuries of oppression, the people emerged, reorganized society and set an example to the world. Voltaire and Rousseau, the "twin apostles of humanity,"[10] had accomplished the Revolution in the mind of France, the first by attacking religious tyranny and the second by founding social right on an impregnable basis. France, in the early days of the Revolution, was the angel of liberty, justice and eternal reason. But the reign of terror delayed the success of the Revolution for half a century and the September massacres left an indelible stain on the honour of France. Gooch has remarked that with the exception of Carlyle, Michelet's book is the most brilliant picture ever painted of the greatest event in modern history,[11] and Aulard has described it the truest, though not the most exact, history of the Revolution.[12] It was the historian's love of the people that accounted for his admiration for the Revolution. The great event was without a hero, without proper names. "From the first page to the last," Michelet wrote at the end of his task, "there is only one hero—the people."[13]

After ten years of toil on the *French Revolution*, Michelet returned in 1853 to his unfinished *History of France.* But misfortunes had begun to darken his spirit and the five later volumes (1855–67), according to most critics, did not attain the excellence of the first six.

Assessment

Romantic historiography, exemplified in the works of Thierry and Michelet, revealed a taste for colorful reconstruction of the past and a keen sympathy with the masses. History became more real, attractive and democratic, and history reading grew on an unprecedented scale. But Romantic historiography contained in it certain defects.

Partiality for the Masses

The first of these is a certain partiality for the masses. Thierry's main achievement was to introduce a new figure, the people, and set it in the foreground of the historical picture. For Michelet, the people meant everything. His *History of the French Revolution* is not only the most eloquent defence of the Revolution, it is the epic of democracy. But Michelet idealized and glorified the masses so much that G.P. Gooch warns us against accepting his judgement of the Revolution without qualification. Says Gooch:

> Whatever was good in the Revolution was the work of the people; whatever was bad was the work of somebody else. The existence of the *canaille*, the ferocious passions of the mob, the hatred and envy which accompanied the vast upheaval, are hardly suggested.[14]

Owing to this partiality for the masses, Michelet showed personality in a people, sometimes exaggeratedly, but the personality of individuals disappeared. When at times it appeared, he could be harsh. Marat was "the ape of Rousseau", Robespierre "a contemptible pedant".[15] And if Michelet is too tender to the masses, he is too harsh, even hostile, towards the Church.

Weak Criticism

Gooch notes that Romantic historians in general were stronger in imagination than in criticism. Thierry, for example, took the chronicles as he found them. The world of the Romantic historians, of Michelet especially, is a world so full of color, passion, poetry, music, exaggeration and symbolism, as sometimes to swallow up the reality of the past. Observations lack precision; errors abound. In the five later volumes of the *History of France* certain defects are more glaring. Drawing generalizations from isolated facts, giving vent to personal prejudices, and referring great events to trivial causes are only some of them. The critical urge was lost in the magical and mystical evocation of the past.

But in recent years Michelet's reputation has revived. He has been recognized as an exponent of total history, using art and architecture, legend and literature, as well as charters, chronicles and archival materials for reconstruction of the past. And not many among the historians would have by their work promoted history reading on such an unprecedented scale as Michelet did.

3. History as Literature: Macaulay (1800–1859) and Carlyle (1795–1881)

Thomas Babington Macaulay stands out among those who wrote history as national epic and literature. As a Cambridge undergraduate he had learnt to detest the Tories and left the university as a convinced Whig. It was as a writer of political and literary reviews that he made a name before he shone forth as a historian.

The Essay 'History'[16]

In the essay 'History', written when only twenty-eight years of age, Macaulay argued that literary talents are not antithetical but complementary to history. This is because history is under the double jurisdiction of reason and imagination. The perfect historian must possess an imagination sufficiently powerful to make his narrative affecting and picturesque. But this imagination he must control so absolutely as to rest it on historical material. The historian should not invent. History should have as its theme those circumstances which have most influence on the happiness of mankind—the changes of manners and morals; the transition of communities from poverty to wealth, ignorance to knowledge, and ferocity to humanity; in short, everything that embraces culture. And these are, for the most part, noiseless revolutions. The perfect historian is he in whose work the character and spirit of the age is exhibited in miniature. By judicious selection, rejection and arrangement he gives to historical truths the attractions of literature.

Essays

Such a conception of history found expression in the *Essays*. The first essay written on Milton in the *Edinburgh Review* when Macaulay was twenty-five won him fame in the literary world. "If Macaulay did not invent the historical essay," writes Gooch, "he found it of brick and left it of marble. His articles glitter like diamonds in the dusty pages of the *Edinburgh Review*."[17] The historical essays are for the most part polemical, delivering violent attacks on the Tory version of English history. Macaulay denounces Cramner, Strafford and Charles I, eulogizes the character and policy of Cromwell, and defends the revolution of 1688. The two Indian essays on Robert Clive and Warren Hastings are among the most magnificent of Macaulay's achievements.

The History of England from the Accession of James II

In 1838 Macaulay had conceived the project of an *History of England from 1688 to 1820*. But when death came in 1859, the five volumes of the *History* had brought the story only up to 1702. Macaulay was moved by a consciousness of Europe's superiority to other continents and England's superiority to other European nations. He summed up England's story since 1688 as "eminently the history of physical, of moral and of intellectual improvement."[18] Macaulay wrote with untroubled certainty about the merits of the age—the triumph of liberty and wealth in England and the triumph of England in the world.[19] And these he attributed to the genius and greatness of the English people. In all these, Macaulay was reflecting the mood of the earlier half of the nineteenth century. No historian could have been in greater harmony with his time and place.

Intending his *History* to live forever, Macaulay took infinite pains to collect and shape his material, and the work is done with greater learning and thoroughness than the *Essays*. For twenty years he laboured to reconstruct "the spirit of an age" with "appropriate images presented in every line."[20] Writing with a dramatist's instinct, Macaulay produced an epic drama, a fast-moving narrative with an incredible wealth of detail. But the labor of producing it killed him. After a few excellent introductory chapters the detailed narrative begins with the accession of James II. Macaulay writes an eloquent paean to the revolution of 1688. From that date according to him, free trade linked with free thought expressed in a free parliament grew to make England the envy of the world. The account of the revolution is a story of liberalism. It was "of all revolutions the least violent, it has been of all revolutions the most beneficient."[21] Two volumes are devoted to William III but the portrait of the 'Deliverer' suffers from an excess of descriptive color.

Macaulay had wanted to produce something which would "for a few days supersede the last fashionable novel on the tables of young ladies."[22] He took it for granted that his *History* would still be read a thousand years after his death and thought himself the world's greatest historian since Thucydides. The ambition seemed to come near realization. Macaulay's *History* proved a classic. It was the greatest historical work in the English language since Gibbon. Hailed as the best narrative history it was translated into the language of every civilized country. A vote of thanks was carried at a meeting "for having written a history which working-men can understand."[23] Macaulay had promoted history reading so much that a traveler in Australia recorded that the three works he found on every squatter's shelf were the *Bible*, Shakespeare and the *Essays*.

Style

The appeal of Macaulay's works owed chiefly to their narrative style—rapid, sparkling, transparent, utterly lucid. The most fascinating storyteller who ever wrote history, Macaulay was a supreme dramatist with the dramatist's instinct for heightening the color and concentrating on the essential. His pictures linger in the memory. In vividness of presentation only Michelet and Carlyle could equal him.

Criticism

The *Essays* and the *History* that dazzled the reader with their style and encouraged history reading, however, contained serious blemishes. G.P. Gooch's criticism is revealing.

Gaps in Knowledge

Prodigious as was Macaulay's knowledge, there were great gaps in it. He knew little of the history of Europe and practically nothing of the Middle Ages. His colossal ignorance of the life and culture of India did not prevent him from despising Indian learning and civilization in unmeasured terms.

Untroubled Certainty and Political Bias

Lord Melbourne once wished that he might be as certain about anything as Macaulay was about everything. Reflecting the confident mood of early nineteenth century Englishmen Macaulay wrote of "the most enlightened generation of the most enlightened people that ever existed."[24] The British historian was so convinced of the finality of his Whig political views that he became the most popular and eloquent interpreter of Whig political wisdom. But to have mixed political partisanship with history writing was harmful to the latter. "He is the greatest of party writers," writes Gooch, "not the greatest of historians. Thus the most brilliant of English historians is one of those who possess the least weight."[25] The 'Whig interpretation' of history had a great influence and, by the time Macaulay came to be criticized, it had become firmly established.

Political bias and partiality could be seen in the exaggeration of virtues and defects. Prejudice and inaccuracy, rampant in the *Essays*, appear in the *History* also. Macaulay pronounces the whole life of Charles I a lie. James II's adultery is portrayed as a disgusting vice, but his hero William III's as a trivial lapse. The historian repeatedly ignores his own advice and warning to his readers against judging the past by the standards of the present. He condemns Elizabeth I for not tolerating Catholicism and criticizes others for offending the canons of his age or of his political party. He pelted opponents with abuse, calling Archbishop Laud a "ridiculous old bigot," and describing the verses of Frederick the Great as "hateful to God and men". There are distortions, too. Malborough is "a prodigy of turpitude"—a miser, a profligate, a traitor, a murderer. John Paget after a thorough inquiry into Macaulay's account of Malborough charges the historian with suppressing documents, transposing dates, parading witness of the most infamous character as pure and unimpeachable, and reviving forgotten and anonymous slanders of the foulest description.[26] John Stuart Mill's comment on Macaulay's volumes on William III seems to be accurate: "pleasant reading but not exactly history."[27] Indeed, Carlyle, himself a literary historian, wrote in his journal: "Four hundred editions could not lend it any permanent value there being no depth of sense in it, and a very great quantity of rhetorical wind."[28]

Like all literary historians Macaulay describes but does not explain. He is totally blind to the invisible world of thought and emotion, concerned, as he seems to be, only with what is on the surface.

Carlyle: History as Biography and Literature

Thomas Carlyle compares favorably with Macaulay in giving tremendous impetus to history reading and in looking upon history rather as literature. But they differed in their aims. Macaulay wrote history to justify his political convictions, Carlyle employed history to illustrate and reinforce his ethical teaching. The son of a dissenting stonemason, Thomas Carlyle's chosen vocation was to thunder against all kinds of pretence and deception, which he did with a historical reference at every step. A stern moralist, he believed not so much in material forces and economic wants as the moving forces of history as in qualities of a spiritual order.

'On History'

In his essay 'On History', published in 1830, Carlyle wrote that history was the first distinct product of man's spiritual nature, his earliest expression of thought. In the same essay, he emphasized the contribution of the great many humble to the making of civilization, the nameless poor who first hammered out an iron spade.

Battles and tumults...pass away like tavern brawls....Laws themselves, political constitutions, are not our Life, but only the house in which our Life is led; nay, they are but the bare walls of the house: all whose essential furniture...are the work...of long-forgotten train of artists and artisans; who from the first have been jointly teaching us how to think and how to act...."[29]

Heroes and Hero-Worship

But this healthy trend in Carlyle succumbed to the temptation to worship the hero and emphasize the role of the individual and to regard history itself as the essence of innumerable biographies. In an essay entitled 'Biography' (1832), he inquired whether the whole purpose of history was not biographic! His narratives increasingly became the biographies of great men rather than the record of the unnumbered and the unnamed. The author of *Heroes and Hero-Worship* (1841) earned ridicule for his dictum that history is biography writ large. In these series of character studies delivered first as lectures, Carlyle's lack of a conception of humanity and his concern only with the individuals – a concern with the 'great' at the cost of the 'great many' – reached a crescendo. "The immense mass of men," testifies Froude, "he believed to be poor creatures, poor in heart and poor in intellect."[30] The unnamed benefactors of mankind in his earlier works now gave place in his esteem to men of elemental energy who overturned crumbling institutions and carved out paths for the others to follow. "Universal History," Carlyle asserted, "the history of what man has accomplished in this world, is at bottom the History of the Great Men who have worked here."[31] He also said, "In all epochs of the world's history we shall find the Great Man to have been the indispensable saviour of his epoch; the lightning, without which the fuel never would have burnt. The History of the world...was the Biography of Great Men."[32] The great man, the hero could be a king, a prophet, or a poet.

The French Revolution

Carlyle's greatest works, works by which he is to be judged, are, however, political and social, known for their literary beauty and insight into human nature. Of such works the most important are—*The French Revolution* (1837), *Oliver Cromwell's Letters and Speeches* (1845), and *Frederick the Great of Prussia* in 6 volumes (1858–65). Of these, it is the *French Revolution* that must engage our attention. The author had to rewrite its first volume whose sole manuscript was used as kindling by John Stuart Mill's maid! Carlyle had learnt from Walter Scott to look upon the past as peopled by living men – not abstractions, not diagrams and theorems – but plain men, and his masterpiece tried to recapture the drama of the Revolution. The theme fitted well with his purpose of denouncing conservatism, Enlightenment and democracy all at once. The book carried a moral that mere shows with nothing real in them are burnt up. The events of the Revolution coming through Carlyle's pen are pageants the reader carries all through his life. Such are the storming of the Bastille, the raid on Versailles, the fete of the federation, the flight to Varennes, the trial and execution of the king, and the fall of Robespierre. Carlyle's portraits of the king and queen, Mirabeau and Lafayette, and Marat, Danton and Robespierre, are so real and done with such remarkable insight into their nature and character as to require little alteration. Selling slowly at first, the book became a tremendous success and continued to sell for more than a generation. The two historical works of the earlier half of the nineteenth century which continued to be universally read in the twentieth are Macaulay's *Essays* and Carlyle's *The French Revolution.* As Gooch observes, it was a piece of great literature, a book brimful of passion and poetry, a supreme achievement of the creative imagination, the most epic of historical narratives. To the author it was far more than a history of events, for it embodied his deepest moral and religious convictions. We hear the impassioned accents of a prophet calling sinners to repentence.[33]

Criticism

As a prose epic Carlyle's *The French Revolution* is unassailable, but as work of history it has no standing. And this for the following reasons:

Less a History, More a Drama

Carlyle's great work on the French Revolution did not at all advance historical knowledge or acquaintance with sources. Gooch observes that Carlyle's book is "less a history than a series of tableaux."[34] The work does not rest on the widest foundations of original sources, for its author only wanted to dramatically portray the drama of a volcanic eruption to teach a moral. His knowledge of the period was extremely limited, he did not search for sources, and he was not accurate. He used unfounded stories and legends. No true historian would have claimed, as Carlyle said to his wife, that his work had come "direct and flamingly from the heart," or as he wrote to John Sterling, that it was a wild, savage book that had come out of his soul, born in blackness, whirlwind and sorrow.[35]

Lack of Explanation

History must explain more than it describes; it must aid understanding by appealing to the intellect, rather than amuse the reader and arouse his passions by appealing to his senses. Explanation always involves the seeking of causal connections; but in literary histories descriptions drive out causal explanations. The introductory chapters of Carlyle's *French Revolution* scarcely attempt to explain the catastrophe that follows, and the narrative ends abruptly with the whiff of grapeshot in 1795. There is little reference to France's relations with Europe, the condition of the provinces, and constitutional and economic problems. "No reader would learn," writes Gooch, "how the Revolution developed and why one stage passed into the other. To exalt the drama is to condemn the history."[36]

Lack of Philosophic Insight

Carlyle, the moralist, lacked philosophic insight. The Puritan prophet thought of the Revolution as purely destructive, "a transcendent revolt against the devil and his works,"[37] a huge bonfire of the rotten feudalism of France. This colossal misconception arose first from the error of isolating the Revolution from the European movements of the eighteenth century, but more importantly, as Mazzini pointed out in an eloquent review of Carlyle's work, from a lack of a conception of humanity. Carlyle could think only of individuals, and not of a people having any collective life or collective aim. He did not know that the Revolution was not purely destructive, that it had heralded a new age, and that constructive work of a permanent character had been accomplished. "No one," writes Gooch, "can begin to understand the Revolution till he realises its dual character. Tried by this test Carlyle fails. He is the greatest of showmen and the least of interpreters."[38]

4. Nationalist Historiography: Droysen, Sybel and Treitschke

The works of the celebrated Prussian school of historians in Germany in the nineteenth century consisting of Droysen, Sybel and Treitschke may be taken as the best example of militantly nationalist historiography. The Prussian school whose spiritual father was Dahlman, stood for a fuller and more virile national life in a unified Germany. The chief task of nationalist historiography in Germany was to teach a larger patriotism with the specific aim of forging a strong united Germany that would have a commanding role to play in the affairs of the world. Nationalist historiography in Germany had accomplished the unification of the country in the minds of Germans before Bismarck's sword and diplomacy accomplished it in fact.

Johan Gustav Droysen (1808–1884)

The eldest of the three figures who made up the Prussian School was Johan Gustav Droysen. Starting as a classical philologist Droysen translated plays of Aeschylus and Aristophanes. He then proceeded to a study of Alexander the Great and his *History of Hellenism* (1843) was revealing in its interpretation of Hellenistic civilization as an amalgam of the East and the West. In 1848 he was a member of the Frankfurt parliament and secretary of its constitutional committee, but resigned from politics when Frederick William IV refused the German crown.

Droysen wrote works on German history and filled his pages with nationalistic fire and emotion. The historian was certain that German unity would come as soon as Prussia woke up to her duty, and it was the aim of his great work, the *History of Prussian Policy* (1855–86) to remind her of it. The fruit of 'thirty years' heroic labor, the book ranks among the greatest achievements of German scholarship. Based largely on manuscript material and containing so much new information, Droysen's book was an interpretation of Prussian policy in terms of German nationalism. His *Basics of*

History (1858) on the theory of history remains important even now.

Heinrich von Sybel (1817–1895)

A pupil of Ranke, Heinrich von Sybel, however, chose to reject his mentor's doctrine of moral neutrality. Sybel taught at several German universities and later in 1875 became the director of the Prussian State Archives. The series of major documentary publications that he sponsored in this capacity was an enduring contribution to historical scholarship. In 1859 he founded and was the first editor of what is still the leading historical journal of Germany, *Historische Zeitschrift* (*Historical Journal*). Through lectures, pamphlets and books he tried to influence contemporary events and played an active part in the political struggles of his time.

Sybel's five-volume *History of the French Revolution,* published in the 1850s was based on material collected from archives at Berlin, Paris, the Hague, London and Vienna. The project kept him occupied for the greater part of thirty years. But prejudice turned the work into a polemic against the Revolution and a warning to his compatriots. Sybel's second great work, the *Founding of the German Empire under William I* in seven volumes has Bismarck for its hero. Deeply held prejudices and a narrow Prussian viewpoint reduced the value and the unquestionable solidity of Sybel's works.

Heinrich von Treitschke (1834–1896)

The greatest of the Prussian school of historians was Heinrich von Treitschke. Gooch writes: "The most eloquent of preachers, the most fervid of apostles, the most passionate of partisans, he most completely embodies the blending of history and politics which it was the aim of the School to achieve."[39]

Born in Saxony, the son of a general in the Saxon army, Treitschke taught at several German universities before succeeding Ranke as professor of history at the University of Berlin in 1874. Treitschke's lectures on German history at Leipzig attracted crowded audiences as Fichte's had done half a century earlier. His one great theme was the unification of Germany, a task which Hohenzollern Prussia was to achieve with sword in hand. He produced one of the greatest historical works of the nineteenth century, the five-volume *History of Germany in the Nineteenth*

Century which traced the German liberal national movement up to 1848. Alone of the Prussian school Treitschke grasps German national life as a whole and admirably delineates the development of culture—of literature, learning and painting. And Gooch assures us that in style and vitality Treitschke equals Mommsen and leaves all other German historians behind.[40] But these great qualities of the work are marred by the political prejudices of the author. The patriot in him loved and hated with elemental fury.

Defects of Nationalist Historiography

History written from a purely nationalistic point of view such as by the Prussian school contained grave defects.

Narrow Didacticism

The nationalist histories of the Prussian school invariably carried a political message and were didactic in nature. Intended for the political education of the nation, they aimed at inculcating a larger patriotism, training virile citizens, avenging national humiliations and redeeming national honour. Droysen's pages pulsate with fire and emotion as his object was to "express and justify the love and belief in the fatherland."[41] And if Ranke had in his famous preface disclaimed any intention to instruct the present from the past, his pupil Sybel was like Machiavelli, determined to extract and apply the lessons of the past. His *History of the French Revolution* carried a moral; it was intended to teach and convince the German Liberals that the French brand of liberty and equality was poison and were no more than appeals to greed and passion, not a demand for justice.[42] Unfettered liberty leads to anarchy, mechanical equality to the destruction of freedom, and the sovereignty of the people to mob rule or military dictatorship. Treitschke wrote history less to record than to teach. Based though on solid research and keeping unchallengeably high intellectual standards, the histories of the Prussian school were largely exhortations to Germans to wake up to their patriotic duty and serve their fatherland. This narrow didacticism detracted from their real worth as histories.

Worship of State Power and Glorification of War

In nationalist historiography, particularly of the Prussian school, national glorification often ended up in the worship of state power and glorification of war. Droysen, who had sat at Hegel's feet, emphasized the power and majesty of the state. A political liberal claiming extensive rights for the individual against the state, Treitschke's aspect so changed as to deny the individual any ultimate rights at all. The Prussian nationalist historians were chauvinist and jingoist. For Treitschke, particularly, the Germans were the best of peoples, and Prussia the chosen nation. Prussia must wield the sword, annex the princely states and knock Austria out of Germany to effect national unification. The sword was not to be sheathed but kept shining against France and any eventual enemy.

Blending of History and Politics

From patriotic history to patriotic politics was but a step. The Prussian school of historians took an active role in founding the German empire and justifying the way Bismarck achieved it. Believing that history had a distinct political role to play they harnessed their studies as historians to the needs of contemporary politics. Sybel candidly confessed to Bluntschli that he was "four-sevenths a politician and three sevenths professor".[43] Treitschke confessed that his blood was too hot for a historian and that the patriot in him was a thousand times stronger than the professor.[44]

Objectivity, the Greatest Casualty of Nationalist History

The test of all good history is objectivity. But the greatest defect of the nationalist histories of the Prussian school is their unconcealed bias and partiality. Droysen's *History of Prussian Policy* is a history seen exclusively through Prussian spectacles, and "Droysen," says Gooch, "read into the sources what was not there."[45] Again, Sybel's *History of the French Revolution* was a work of great merit, but it was disfigured by prejudice and turned out to be a polemic against that great event. His *Founding of the German Empire under William I* attributed every war to the enemy. Gooch warns us that it has to be checked at every point by the testimony of other witnesses. Sybel attacks not only France and Austria, but Catholicism too, which is branded as anti-national. And Treitschke, the most eloquent preacher of nationalism, was also the most passionate partisan, the very opposite of Ranke, the apostle of objectivity. "That bloodless objectivity," Treitschke wrote in a letter to his father, "which does not say on which side is the narrator's heart is the exact opposite of the true historical sense. Judgment is free even to the author."[46] His blood was too hot for a historian, and the pen became a sword in his hand. He hated France far more offensively than Sybel. Political prejudice ruined Treitschke's great work, the *History of Germany in the Nineteenth Century*. The aggressively Prussian standpoint of the work excused in Prussia what was censured in Austria and led to the incredible failure to understand non-Prussian Germany. Attacks on Austria, France, Russia, England, the Jews, socialism and parliamentary government redound his pages. The blaze of patriotism blinded the Prussian school to the need for objectivity. Says Gooch:

> If the purpose of history is to stir a nation to action, Droysen, Sybel and Treitschke were among the greatest of historians. If its supreme aim is to discover truth and to interpret the movement of humanity, they have no claim to a place in the first class. The stream of historical studies, temporarily deflected by their powerful influence, began to return to the channel which Ranke had marked out for it.[47]

And Will Durant sums up the bias of nationalist history:

> The Middle Ages, the Renaissance, and the Enlightenment gave us histories of the world; but the nineteenth century discovered nationalism and corrupted nearly all the historians. Treitschke and von Sybel, Michelet and Martin, Macaulay and Green, Bancroft and Fiske, were patriots first and historians afterward; their country was God's country, and all the world outside it was filled with villains or barbarians. Those historians are just press agents for the politicians, recruiting officers for the army and navy.[48]

Vitiating and dangerous as the Romanticist-nationalist corruption of history was, it was rendered easier by association with a literary approach to history. Scholarly solidity was sacrificed at the altar of literary excellence. Care was bestowed in making historical works more interesting and attractive than truthful and real.

Yet, the Romantic–Nationalist–Literary nexus promoted history writing and history reading as never before.

II. THE BERLIN REVOLUTION IN HISTORIOGRAPHY: NIEBUHR AND RANKE

1. The Weaknesses in the Study of History before Niebuhr and Ranke

Though history had come to be written and great historians had developed from the time of Herodotus and Thucydides, the subject had been treated more or less as a branch of literature or philosophy. The Scientific Revolution of the seventeenth century began to infuse history with a critical spirit. But history in our modern sense of the term, as a scholarly discipline, came to be established only with Niebuhr and Ranke. Till then, according to Professor Arthur Marwick, history writing may be said have suffered from three cardinal weaknesses.[49]

Ignorance of the Idea of Change through Time

The first of these weaknesses was a total ignorance of the idea of change through time. Eighteenth century historians and most of their predecessors had very little real sense of the idea that 'times change' and that each age has peculiar and unique qualities of its own, different from those of another. Voltaire and Gibbon scoffed at the culture of earlier ages. They had little respect for that long stretch of time called the Middle Ages whose standards of civilization and behavior did not come up to the level of the high society of their own times. Gibbon's judgement of the achievements of the Byzantine empire was grossly unfair. This is fundamentally an unhistorical attitude, failing to see that times change, and that the men of the Middle Ages should be studied on their own terms and not treated as an assortment of curiosities.

Non-availability of Primary Sources and the Absence of Accepted Methodological Principles

Secondly, the great historical works of the Enlightenment were less scholarly and more interpretative. Voltaire strove for perspective in history and wrote his *Essay on the Morals and Character of the Nations* in a philosophical, interpretative manner. He had a contempt for details which he thought were vermin that destroyed great works. Hume once referred to research as the 'dark industry'.

Contempt for basic scholarship sometimes resulted in carelessness and inevitable inaccuracy. Good history demands constant intercourse between interpretation and primary research. This lack of contact between the two must be blamed also on the non-availability of primary sources. Important collections of basic historical material belonging to kings or dukes or to the papacy simply were not open to inspection. As a result historians had often to rely on second-hand accounts. Even when scholars made brave efforts to base their works on primary sources when such sources were available, they were thwarted by the absence of accepted methodological principles.

Lack of Organization and Systematization in the Study of History

The third great weakness that beset history in the eighteenth century was the lack of organization and systematization in its study. Nowhere was it taught as an intellectual discipline in a very systematic way. Political favorites rather than genuine scholars filled the chairs of history at Oxford and Cambridge. From 1757 history was taught on a more serious basis at Gottingen in Germany and a chair of history and morals was established at the College de France in 1769. But the subject had yet to be admitted to all the main centers of learning before it could hope to become a true intellectual discipline.

The Favorable Romantic Atmosphere

The men who did most to combat the above weaknesses were first the Danish-born Barthold Niebuhr and then the German Leopold von Ranke. They launched the Berlin revolution in historical studies. The romantic atmosphere in which they worked was congenial to the growth of historical studies. The revolutionary upheavals at the end of the eighteenth century made it impossible for men to believe either in the unchanging character of human nature or in the immutable character of social institutions. It was a time when the hitherto neglected ideas of Vico and Herder were gaining wide currency. Vico's thought stressed in particular the cultural differences between different ages and different nations. Again, in sharp contrast to Enlightenment historical thought, Vico had pointed his finger to the danger of importing ideas or judgments into the history of earlier ages. Herder presented similar ideas. He stressed the influence of the geographical environment in the evolution of national cultures and developed for the first time the concept of 'national character' which he believed greatly influenced the history of a nation. Herder exhorted historians to 'sympathize' with the nation and 'feel' themselves into it. Against the Enlightenment historians he asserted that everything is *relatively* right in its own historical context. Every age has a right to be studied and known.

The Romanticist desire to see the past from inside, "as it really was," in the celebrated words of Ranke, was typified at the time by Walter Scott's novels whose definite aim was to portray the manners and morals of a bygone age. Scott's novels had a profound influence on Ranke and other historians. This new way of looking at history is called genetic relationism or historical relationism—'genetic' because of the stress laid on origins and the notion of every phase developing out of a previous phase, and 'relationist' because of the insistence that every person, every activity, every institution must be seen in relation to the age in which it is set.[50]

2. Barthold Niebuhr (1776–1831) and Leopold von Ranke (1795–1886)

Just at the time when in the Romantic atmosphere a new emphasis was being laid on historical change, historians felt the need for some critical method and began to insist upon a new precision of documentation. At the head of this movement stands the commanding figure of Barthold Georg Niebuhr, the scholar who raised history from a subordinate position to the dignity of an independent science.

Learning much history (instead of fairytales) when sitting on the knees of his father before bedtime, Barthold at ten produced a historical geography of Africa! Determined to be worthy of his father the boy grew up into "a small miracle of knowledge and intellectual maturity".[51] After university he entered the service of the government of his native Denmark but was pressed to transfer his services to Prussia. When in 1810 he resigned his government post, he was urged to deliver lectures at the newly founded University of Berlin. The three sets of lectures – two on Roman history and the one on Roman antiquities – read out to a large and distinguished audience proved an immense success. Out of the first two sets grew the two volumes of the *History of Rome* (1811–12) which marked the birth of modern historical methodology.

Niebuhr's first achievement was that with his experience of government he was able to trace the political, legal and economic institutions of ancient Rome to their origin and to follow their successive changes with great insight.

> He had grasped the truth that the early history of every nation must be rather of institutions than of events, of classes than of individuals, of custom than of lawgivers. The story of Roman development is built round the struggles of patricians and plebeians, who had their origin in the racial differences of conquerors and conquered. The agrarian problem was for the first time fully investigated.[52]

Niebuhr's second great achievement was the critical examination of the sources and credibility of early Roman history. In the quest for a critical method he had been well armed with a knowledge of antiquity and the mastery of twenty languages. More than this he had a thorough comprehension of the philologist Wolf's method in the *Prolegomena to Homer* which led him to believe that the history of early Rome had been enshrined and transmitted in poems – *carmina* – that is, lays or ballads. Extremely skeptical of the historical tradition about early Rome, particularly as found in Livy, Niebuhr sought to place that tradition on its proper footing. This he did by devising a new method of handling sources, the method of *philological criticism*. The method consisted of two operations. First, the analysis of sources (which were largely literary) into their component parts, distinguishing earlier and later elements in them and thus enabling the historian to discriminate between the more and the less trustworthy portions. This is what is now known as *external* or *textual criticism*. And second, the *internal criticism* of the more trustworthy parts, showing how the author's point of view affected his statement of the facts. This would help detect distortions. Niebuhr's power of historical divination was great. He dissected words as anatomists dissected bodies. Applying such methods to Livy's *History of Rome*, Niebuhr argued that a great part of what was usually taken for early Roman history was patriotic fiction of a much later period. He believed that some events in the monarchical period were mythical, others historical. Niebuhr claimed his *History* "to be a work of science rather than a work of art," and that was his excuse for its bad diction and presentation. This most unreadable of historical classics gained an immediate and resounding fame for it completely discredited Livy and the various accounts based on Livy. The work had inaugurated modern historical methodology and won for history the position of an independent science of the first rank.

Neibuhr's influence was very great. Ranke felt that Thucydides, Fichte and Niebuhr were his masters. Grote could not pronounce Niebuhr's name without admiration and gratitude. Waitz admitted that he owed more to Niebuhr's *History of Rome* than to any other book; and Mommsen succinctly summed up Niebuhr's influence when he said that all historians, so far as they are worthy of the name, were Niebuhr's pupils. And Dilthey said of Niebuhr: "No young man should enter a university without having morally elevated himself by contemplating the figure of this great scholar."[53] The ethical standards Niebuhr set for historiography may well compare with the Hippocratic oath. "In laying down the pen," he wrote, "we must be able to say in the sight of God, 'I have not knowingly nor without earnest investigation written anything which is not true.'"[54]

Niebuhr was the first and Ranke the second, in introducing a new critical spirit into the theory and practice of history. Leopold von Ranke was born in Wiche, in Thuringian Saxony, the son of a lawyer. After schooling Ranke entered the University of Leipzig where he studied theology and classical philology. The seven years spent as teacher in the Gymnasium at Frankfurt on the Oder were decisive, for it was there that Ranke turned by accident, from philology to history. In reading Guicciardini and Pavlo Giovio, the budding scholar found their differences too great, to clarify which he wrote his own account of the time. Thus came Ranke's first book, the *Histories of the Latin and Teutonic Peoples 1494–1514*. Another significant incident was his discovery of the difference in the portraits of Louis XI and Charles the Bold in Walter Scott's *Quentin Durward* and in Comines. The effect was immediate and lasting. "I found by comparison," says Ranke, "that the truth was more interesting and beautiful than the romance. I turned away from it and resolved to avoid all invention and imagination in my works and to stick to facts."[55]

Ranke's first book, the *Histories of the Latin and Teutonic Peoples*, was no more than a series of histories relating to the period

1494–1514. Yet it constituted a distinct advance in the objective treatment of history and inaugurated the critical era in historiography. The book owed its unique position to the technical appendix than to the narrative.

Ranke was one who never wearied of expressing his debt to Niebuhr, whose bust occupied the place of honor in his study. He was explicitly applying Niebuhr's principles to modern history and further developing them. The famous discussion of his authorities contained certain maxims which cannot be regarded as altogether new. He says that the nearest witness to an event is the best and that the letters of the actors were of more value than the anecdotes of the chronicler. What is new about Ranke's method is his determination to seize the personality of the writer and to inquire whence he derived his information. "Some will copy the ancients, some will seek instruction for the future, some will attack or defend, some will only wish to record facts. Each must be separately studied."[56] Applying this method Ranke found Guicciardini guilty of copying from other books, inventing speeches, altering treaties, and misrepresenting important facts.

The new methodology constitutes Ranke's inestimable contribution to history writing. Its main features, which represent the Rankean approach to history may be listed as follows:

Insistence on Primary Sources

Niebuhr and Ranke had achieved a methodological revolution marked by a new precision of documentation. Ranke insisted that any piece of historical writing must be firmly based on primary sources. The epochal preface to his first book, the *Histories of the Latin and Germanic Peoples*, announced the kinds of sources he had used:

> The basis of the present work, the sources of its material, are memoirs, diaries, letters, diplomatic reports and original narratives of eye witnesses; other writings were used only if they were immediately derived from the above mentioned or seemed to equal them because of some original information.[57]

Understanding the Past on its Own Terms

In the same preface Ranke announced in memorable words, the spirit in which the book was written.

> To history has been assigned the office of judging the past, of instructing the present for the benefit of future ages. To such high offices this work does not aspire: it wants only to show what actually happened (*wie es eigentlich gewesen ist*).[58]

These statements, as Arthur Marwick writes, set the key for the modern discipline of history, which was now set firmly on its scientific course. Ranke's hope that the exclusive use of primary sources in a detached manner would yield an exact, objective account 'of what actually happened' was to remain the ideal and the aim of all scholarly history; but the ideal would fall just short of realization owing to the inevitable subjective influences in history writing.

Scholarly Apparatus

Again, Ranke explained in the preface that his book would include the full scholarly apparatus—by this he meant references, footnotes, bibliography, etc. Such apparatus would identify the sources on every page of his work. He would then "present the method of investigation of critical conclusions."[59] It was clear that Ranke was presenting history *as a science* for not only did he insist on the use of primary sources, but he provided a method of identifying those sources for the reader's benefit, and a method of investigation of the critical sources.

Publication of Primary Sources

The new methodology based on the critical study of primary sources led to the publication of hundreds of volumes of thousands of manuscripts, charts, memoirs and correspondence. Ranke himself undertook scientific tours to discover and use unknown sources in the archives of Germany, Austria and Spain, and later visited Paris, London and Oxford.

Organisation of Scientific History as an Important Discipline in the Universities

Ranke originated the famous historical seminars and instructed two generations of advanced students in the critical study of historical sources, that is, in the technique of using primary source materials. By the end of the nineteenth century history had been firmly established as an autonomous academic discipline in all the leading universities of Europe and America. It was Ranke's achievement to have founded the science of history and spread its teaching throughout the world.

The 'Historical Journal'

The new elevated status of the subject was signified in 1859 by the launching of the first historical journal, *Historische Zeitschrift.* "We want an organ," wrote Sybel, its founder and first editor, to Waitz in 1857, "to represent a definite scientific tendency and method."[60] A scientific periodical, "Its first task, therefore," its founders declared, "should be to represent the true method of historical research and to point out the deviations therefrom."[61]

3. Ranke's Important Works

None has ever more fully deserved the epithets of the 'father' and 'master' of modern historical scholarship and the 'Nestor of historians' than Leopold von Ranke. He set history on its scientific course and had to his own credit a massive output of scholarship of over sixty volumes. Even a cursory survey of the more important of his works will fill pages.

The book that launched modern historical methodology, the *History of the Latin and German Peoples* (1824), endeavored to establish the unity of the Latin and Germanic nations, dating from the migrations of the Germanic and other peoples and expressing itself in the Crusades and in the common institutions of Latin Christianity. Thus a single process of development for the Europeans, a single life, might be traced. But it was the *History of the Popes* (1834–36) in 3 volumes, that gave Ranke his place among the great historians of the world. Moved by the inner unity of all the Christian churches, the Protestant Ranke treated with sympathy and admiration the great figures and movements of the Catholic parent church. He treated the papacy as a great historical phenomenon, the unifier of European civilization. The kernel of the book is the counter-Reformation of which Ranke was the first authoritative interpreter. A wealth of information is provided, but as Gooch observes, more important was its tranquil, objective treatment—without rancor, without enthusiasm. Between the

Catholic and the Protestant, a more impartial history could not have been written. A monument of historical research, it was a perfect work of art too, its luminous, measured, if not eloquent style producing an effect of rare power.

> The work for the first time revealed his resources of research and judgement, narrative and portraiture. It combined spaciousness with a mastery of detail, a faculty of generalization with minute accuracy. It was quickly translated into every civilized language and became one of the indispensable books of historical literature.[62]

By the side of such an impartial account of Catholicism which no Protestant could have written Ranke placed in five volumes of the *German History at the Time of the Reformation* (1839–43), an account of the origin of Protestantism. Presenting the Reformation essentially as the return to Christian revelation, the author drew the personality of Luther in the warmest hues. Ranke views both the Protestant and the Catholic positions objectively. If he is tender to the Protestant reformers, he is just to the Catholic Emperor Charles V who is pictured with marked sympathy in his ill-fated efforts to preserve the unity of Christendom. The national character of Ranke's work on the Reformation made it an immediate success. Morris Ritter said that the master never reached the same level again, and Treitschke pronounced it Ranke's masterpiece. But G.P. Gooch observes that later research does not accord Luther as high a place as Ranke gave him. Little do we hear of the masses and their conditions. The chapter on the Peasants' Revolt is one of the weakest.

The *Nine Books of Prussian History,* appearing in 1847–48, are a businesslike study of the rise of a great power. Ranke did not feel the same enthusiasm for Prussia as the Prussian school did.

Ranke's *History of France,* written in a European spirit, is admirably free from the German prejudice against the French. The great theme of the book is the growth of absolute monarchy around which are studied the character and policy of Henry IV, and the economic reforms of Sully; the greatness and ruthlessness of Richelieu; and the vanity and greed of Mazarin. Louis XIV's reign receives extensive treatment. The grand monarch's foreign policy is condemned, but the great king's services to literature, science and art are emphasized.

Ranke who had married Clara Graves, an Englishwoman, now began to sketch a *History of England.* The English history had as its object the study of epochs in which the nation's influence on the development of mankind was most marked. Fully conscious of the importance of personality in history, the narrative broadens with Henry VIII. The English king is a man of "incomparable practical intelligence," one who evokes a "mingled sense of aversion and admiration."[63] He shows how under the Tudors great national changes had been dependent on the personal aims of princes. The two revolutions of the seventeenth century and the foundation of the parliamentary monarchy form the focus of the book. Ranke rates Charles I, both as man and ruler, above his father and thinks of him almost as a martyr dying for a cause. The attitude to Cromwell is unsympathetic. Ranke's English history did not enjoy wide popularity, but Gooch rates it a historical classic.

The Origins of the Wars of the Revolution, though not a very important work, is interesting for Ranke's views on the French Revolution. Though hostile to the ideas of the Revolution, says Gooch, the judicial habit never forsakes him. The responsibility for the outbreak is attributed entirely to the opposition of the clergy and the *noblesse* to reform. And the foolish interference of the European powers excited the national pride of France. The conflict was rendered inevitable by the sharp contradiction of two hostile worlds, the clash of the revolutionary with the conservative. It is surprising that while Sybel, the National Liberal, thought it reasonable and legitimate for the sovereigns of Europe to dictate to France, his conservative master does justice to the French point of view.

Ranke's *Hardenburg,* written at the age of eighty-two, is a history of Prussian policy during the French revolutionary wars, woven round the personality of Hardenburg. Here, too, unlike Sybel, he is never unfair to Austria. The chapter on Jena is written without emotion. The work is a solid contribution to the history of the Napoleonic era and reveals the historian's tranquillity when dealing with the history of his country's fate.

Universal History

Think of the audacity of a man of eighty-three, unable to read and write and having to work through two secretaries, sitting down to the task of writing a universal history! At the end of 1880 appeared the first two volumes of the *Weltgeschichte* (*World History*) from which, however, the author excluded the origin of human society as unknown and the peoples of the East as standing aloof from the historical mainstream. The vast collection of Greek and Roman inscriptions and the testimony of archeology were wholly unknown to the author. The first two volumes dealing with Greece and early Rome were not authoritative though their first edition was exhausted in a week. The third volume devoted to the Roman empire also dealt with the origin of Christianity; the fourth further dealt with Christianity; the fifth concerned itself with the migration of the Germanic and other tribes; the sixth extending to the reign of Otto I (AD 962) was the last that the master saw in print. Despite continual suffering Ranke hurried through the seventh volume dictating it in four months. '*Inter tormenta scrispi,*' he wrote to a friend. When he died in May 1886 he had reached the death of Henry IV (AD 1106). As a substitute for the unwritten volumes on the later Middle Ages, Dove (Ranke's pupil and biographer) published the manuscript of his lectures, completed with the help of the notes of his hearers, bringing the story to 1453. Though the *World History* deals mainly with tendencies, the importance of personality is more fully recognized. The master's last dictated words were: "On the summit of deep, universal, tumultuous movements appear natures cast in a gigantic mould which rivet attention of the centuries. General tendencies do not alone decide; great personalities are always necessary to make them effective."[64]

4. Characteristic Features of Rankean History

Objective History Based on the Primacy and Autonomy of Facts

Niebuhr and Ranke believed that they were creating a completely scientific, objective history. Such a position was based on their belief in the primacy, autonomy and sanctity of historical facts. A scrupulous adherence to primary sources and the employment of an infallible method of source criticism would yield the facts of the past which, it was believed, would speak for themselves without any prompting from the historian whose task was 'simply to show how it really was', and 'what actually happened'. Objectivity, the central problem of historical reconstruction, was a special quality claimed by Rankean history. Subjective influences could be done away with – so it was believed – or at least brought down to the minimum if one got the facts straight. Based on the authenticity of the facts themselves, the historian was to present his picture of the past unswayed by the passions and prejudices of the present.

Ranke's works are the best examples of the objective treatment of the past. An important aspect of historical objectivity is impartiality. Now where Prussia or Germany is concerned, Ranke, in contrast to Droysen, Sybel and Treitschke, is never unfair to Austria and France. When writing about the historic conflict between Catholicism and Protestantism he gives both sides proper hearing. Ranke's passion for objectivity could be seen in the passionless tone in which he narrates events. It was a habit with him to write history with the detachment of an onlooker. The detachment is not born of indifference or moral neutrality; it owed to what G.P. Gooch calls the 'judicial temper' which Ranke possessed in an uncommon degree. When, however, judgement is pronounced, it is, says Gooch, the more weighty from its rarity. On the death of Pope Alexander VI he writes: "A limit is set to human crime. He died and became the abomination of centuries."[65]

Prominence Given to Political History

Ranke held firmly to the exclusive idea of political history, *staatengeschichte*. This resulted in an undue prominence given to political, diplomatic, legal and constitutional history, that led to an undeserved neglect of the history of the other aspects of human life. Political development was never conceived by him as integrated with the other works of man in society—social, economic, artistic, religious and philosophical. The narrowly political standpoint resulted in a neglect of the masses and their life, of the pressure of economic forces, of the evolution of society.

Political Conservatism

Ranke's political ideas were very conservative. He wrote in the *Historico-political Review*, (1832–36), of which he was editor, that constitutions were no panacea and certainly did not suit every country. France exported the republican idea to America and the poisonous idea of the sovereignty of the people threatened the stability of every government in Europe. He was well content with the honest and efficient government of Prussia. Universal theories of government were worthless and dangerous. Indeed, Ranke's unflinching opposition to the ideas of the French Revolution lost him his liberal friends.

Ranke's Conception of the Place of Religion in History

Ranke had a high conception of religion in history. He wrote in *Germany at the Time of the Reformation*:

> History is religion or at any rate there is the closest connection between them. As there is no human activity of intellectual importance which does not originate in some relation to God and divine things, so there is no nation whose political life is not continually raised and guided by religious ideas.[66]

But Ranke's faith is not of a kind that solved the problems of history. In his lectures to King Maximilian of Bavaria he declared it impossible to prove a directing will leading mankind or an immanent force driving it towards a goal. All generations were equally justified before god and stood in equally direct relation to him. Recognizing god's purpose in the world's order, Ranke believed that history was a record of divine manifestations, an object lesson in ethics and religion.

Belief in the Role of Personality in History

In all his works – from the first to the last – Ranke was fully alive to the role of personality in history. The deciding factor in history was to him men of action, and the titles of his books and chapters clearly indicate his sense of their importance. For example, the *History of the Popes* (not the *History of the Papacy*), emphasizes the historian's interest in the concrete realities of human character. He did not forget to show how the individual is determined by the milieu, but his last dictated words leave no doubt as to how general tendencies do not alone decide, and how great personalities – 'natures cast in a gigantic mould' – are always necessary to make them effective. This interest in personality enters into the quaiity of Ranke's narrative art. Says Agatha Ramm: "He (Ranke) showed imagination in his reconstruction of motives, sensitivity in the depiction of character, dramatic sense in choosing when to introduce a particular person into the story. His narrative art is well worth study."[67]

Universal History

It was while engaged working on the *Popes* that Ranke wrote that no history can be written but universal history. Historical knowledge certainly arose from the perception of the particular, and each event was unique and had to be understood as a discrete phenomenon. But history itself was not an immense aggregate of particular facts; the particular had to be grasped as a part of universal history. Universal history does not arise from universal concepts, but from the contact of particular nations to one another. No people can live for itself and the character of each can be developed only in contact with the whole. All specialized studies should be related to a larger context, local history to the history of the whole country and this in turn, to the history of an epoch and all the epochs leading to an entire whole which we call universal history. "The final goal—not yet realized," wrote Ranke, "always remains the conception and composition of a history of mankind."[68]

5. Ranke's Seminar

Ranke's lecture courses at the University of Berlin, begun in 1824, continued in 1871, and many have recorded their impressions of the great teacher. But it was more to his historical *Seminar* than to his lectures – famous though they were – that the master owed his pervasive influence. The *Seminar* was commenced in 1833. It trained scholars not only from Europe but also from America. Organized in the master's own study at his home, it was meant for those who chose history as their profession. Ranke's *Seminar* revolutionized historical method by instructing advanced students in the critical study of historical sources. Giesbrecht, a close disciple, wrote after the master's death:

> We, his most intimate disciples whom he collected round him in his home, found opportunity to gaze at close range into the workshop of his untiringly creative mind. Our admiration was aroused by his wide knowledge, his many-sided culture, the rapidity with which he seized points and his genius in

criticism. He would break into joyous laughter when he succeeded in destroying a false tradition or in reconstructing events as they occurred.[69]

Sybel's testimony in his memorial address may well serve as guidance to professors of all time:

> The *Seminar* was founded for those who chose history as their profession. He allowed free choice of theme, but was always ready with suggestions. Sins against the canons of criticism met with a merciless judgement couched in friendly terms. The master encouraged each talent to develop along its own lines.[70]

Ranke and his pupils were models for any age to emulate. Many of these pupils were known for their lifelong devotion to history. When the great historian was surrounded by his children and grandchildren he used to say, "I have another and older family, my pupils and their pupils."[71] His son relates that he was prouder of Sybel's *French Revolution* than of any of his own books. "With Waitz and Sybel," he wrote to Giesebrecht in 1877, "you make my glory as teacher complete."[72] These were only three of the thirty or more historians of wide renown reared by the master.

Of the three, Georg Waitz was the oldest and perhaps the greatest. Waitz found in 1833 his true vocation in Ranke's *Seminar* where he made rapid advance, which his master watched with rapture. The chief work of Waitz's life was the *German Constitutional History* in eight volumes, a magisterial survey of the political, constitutional and legal history of the German peoples from antiquity to the high Middle Ages. So useful is the work, says Gooch, that many a modern historian when confronted with a puzzling chapter in a charter or chronicle finds a helpful discussion in Waitz, together with references to all the other relevant sources. Ranke's pupil was prolific both in discovering new sources and in interpreting them, and like his master he was an immensely successful teacher. Master and pupil died within two days of each other.

The second of Ranke's pupils to obtain a worldwide fame was Wilhelm von Giesebrecht. Giesebrecht learnt from his master not only the secrets of the critical art but also a certain dislike of France as a source of revolutionary contamination. His monumental six-volume *History of the German Imperial Era* embraces three centuries of German history in the high Middle Ages. The whole era is depicted as one of heroism and piety. The book won phenomenal applause for its moral fervor, its decorative style, and its scholarship. Protestants and Catholics in Germany read it with equal delight. There was, however, limitless idealization of the German race—the race which had to fulfil its destiny for its own honor and for the good of mankind!

The youngest and the most brilliant of Ranke's pupils was Heinrich von Sybel. Reaching Berlin in 1834 at the age of seventeen, Sybel was at once admitted to Ranke's *Seminar* and the youngster was never weary of expressing his gratitude to his incomparable master. He testified in 1867: "You have shown me the way to science, you have always been my model. I have no dearer hope that my name will be worthy of a place in the long list of your pupils."[73]

Sybel's first important work, the *History of the First Crusade*, owed to a suggestion of Ranke who had also warned his pupil against the trustworthiness of William of Tyre and Albert of Aachen. Warned, the intrepid young scholar examined a range of sources. When the *First Crusade* came out in print it won many warm praises but the first from Ranke himself who declared that he was proud to possess such a pupil. Both in its critical and narrative aspects the work deserved all the praises it received. A plain tale from the best authorities, the work, though only written when the author was twenty-four, remained a standard account. Sybel's second great work, the *Origin of German Kingship* (1844) asserted that the early Germans were semi-nomadic and tribal, incapable of producing a true state life which eventually arose from the influence of contact with Rome. In the late 1840s Sybel turned from medieval to modern history. This led him straight to the French Revolution and to his involvement with the problems of the Prussian School. It may also be said to mark the end of Sybel's allegiance to Ranke though the pupil kept a lifelong reverence for his incomparable teacher. If Ranke had done his utmost to break the connection of history with contemporary politics, Sybel devoted his energies to renew that connection. Indeed, one of the theses that Ranke's great pupil defended at his doctoral examination was that the writing of history *sine ira et studio* (without ill-will and without favor) was a false ideal.

6. Ranke: An Assessment

Ranke and the Rankean method came to be lauded universally. But G.P. Gooch informs us that this position of unrivaled supremacy was won only after a prolonged struggle against criticism and attack.

Leo, a German historian of note, characterized Ranke's style as a pale copy of Johannes Muller, his philosophy as superstition, judgement as unhistorical, and contemptuously dismissed his writings as "porcelain painting, the delight of ladies and amateurs"; Ranke replied that the criticism was the outburst of an angry schoolmaster confronted by a new method.[74] Those of the dialectical school like Rotteck, Schlosser and Gervinus did not accept Ranke's method or recognize his authority. In direct opposition to the new method Rotteck used his chair as professor of history at Freiburg as judge and wise counsellor while Schlosser spoke of the lofty mission of history, denied the possibility of objective history, despised the abstruse research of Ranke, and spoke with contempt of archives.

In the twentieth century Ranke's reputation has somewhat suffered. The two main features of criticism are:

Exclusive Idea of Political History

The exclusive idea of political history (*staatengeschichte)* and the mania for documentary sources (state papers and diplomatic correspondence) meant the neglect of all other historical material which *ipso facto* limited the scope of Rankean history. Writing history exclusively from the political and the diplomatic standpoint, Ranke neglected the life of the people and the complex influences that make up their culture; overlooked the pressure of economic forces; and lost sight of the evolution of society and the witnesses of noiseless changes. The course of dynasties, treaties and wars steal the show. The Industrial Revolution, technological invention, science, literature—are all ignored. To this neglect of the socio-economic factors must be added Ranke's concentration on individual historical personalities, with a comparative lack of interest in conditions of the masses, in democratic and working class movements. Charles A. Beard writes:

> Persistently neglecting social and economic interests in history, successfully avoiding any historical writing that

offended the most conservative interests in the Europe of his own time, Ranke may be correctly described as one of the most 'partial' historians produced by the nineteenth century.[75]

Ranke's Claim of Unbiased Objective History Deflated

J.W. Thompson strikes at the very heart of Rankean history by questioning its claim to be 'scientific', 'objective' and 'impartial'. A product of his time, a loyal servant of the Prussian monarchy, a defender of Church and State, Ranke wrote what in reality was a complete reflection of his notions, bias and interests, and certainly not 'truth'.

> Ranke misled a whole generation into believing that he was writing "objective" history, that he was at last approximating the truth. Actually, the most that can be said for his method is that it led to greater detachment, finer poise, and a broader outlook than had been customary before him, and this should be glory enough.[76]

Likewise, E.H. Carr, calls the belief of the Rankean positivists in the existence of a hard core of historical facts "a preposterous fallacy".[77] Carr has shown that the facts of the past need not be the same for all and their valuation and interpretation may vary with the individual historian as well as with his time and circumstances. Ranke was in fact unduly optimistic in his belief that an objective, scientific study of the primary sources could yield a true account of the past, of what had actually happened.

Ranke, the Master

The above imperfections are only 'spots on the sun' as scholars like Gooch would like to call them. Ranke's position as the greatest historian of modern times seems to be secure as none has ever come so closely to the ideal of a historian as he did. His powers of work and length of life enabled him to produce a large number of first-rate works than any other historian.

Gooch enumerates three distinct services Ranke rendered to history. First, Ranke established the necessity of historical reconstruction strictly on sources contemporary to the period of history under study, that is, primary sources. Though not the first to use the archives, Ranke was the first to use them well. In the place of memoirs and chronicles which were believed to be the best authorities, Ranke insisted on the use of the papers and correspondence of the actors themselves. Second, Ranke founded the science of evidence by the analysis of authorities, contemporary or otherwise, in the light of the author's temperament, affiliation and opportunity of knowledge, and by comparison with the testimony of other writers. Henceforth every historian must inquire where his informant obtained his facts. Third, Ranke was the first to divorce the study of the past from the passion of the present, and to relate what actually happened—*wie es eigentlich gewesen.* Gooch concludes that Ranke did not make heroes or villains of historical characters, for his own opinion remained locked in his mind.

The above canons of good scholarship remain just as when they were established. Of those who have worshipped at the altar of Clio with their labors, Ranke was undoubtedly the most devoted. Who else has done more to promote historical knowledge and to equip that knowledge to meet the charge of subjectivity? With whom else did the science of history begin? Who else could have said that he was an historian first and Christian afterward?

8

POSITIVISM IN HISTORY: AUGUSTE COMTE, HENRY THOMAS BUCKLE AND KARL MARX

1. Positivism

Positivism is the belief that the method of natural science provides the principal, or even the sole method for the attainment of true knowledge.[1] 'Positive' means beyond the possibility of doubt or dispute. Positivism stands for actual, absolute, dependable knowledge, i.e., knowledge derived by the application of scientific methods of inquiry, as in the natural sciences. The attempt to make historical knowledge scientific had begun in the wake of the Scientific Revolution of the seventeenth century. With the methodological revolution associated with Niebuhr and Ranke, historical understanding started on its 'scientific' and 'positive' course.

Romanticism and Positivism

Positivism in history was a reaction to Romanticism. Romanticism made historical works more imaginative, while positivism viewed all facts and events of the past in their evolutionary order. Romanticism made individuals the center of attraction, conceived of organic connections, and studied the concepts of liberty and progress; positivism rejected individualism and talked of masses, races, societies and tendencies. Romanticism had overthrown instructive, moralizing and serviceable history; positivism insisted on the interdependence of the social factors. Positivism boasted that it made history a science.

Difference between Rankean and Comtean Positivism

Niebuhr and Ranke had launched scientific history. But by 'scientific' history they meant objective or unbiased history, or history strictly in accordance with facts and uninfluenced by subjective feeling or prejudice. This was the sense in which Lord Acton thought of scientific history and called upon the contributors to the *Cambridge Modern History* for complete objectivity and impartiality. It was, again, the sense in which J.B. Bury asserted that history was "simply a science no less and no more."[2] The avowed aim of the Rankean scientific approach to history was the attainment of 'positive' knowledge of the events of the past. For Ranke the function of scientific history was to lay bare the events of the past as nearly as they were without any subjective influence bearing on them; for him ascertaining new facts about the past was an ideal in itself. When this Rankean positive, particular approach to history was making progress, a different positivist approach to history was being pioneered in the 1830s by the French thinker, Auguste Comte. Comte looked upon the scrupulous study of the sources and the ascertainment of facts as only the first stage of the process of understanding history; the second was necessarily the framing of laws analogous to the laws of the natural sciences.

2. The Philosophy of Auguste Comte (1798–1857)

Positivism, as applied to historical knowledge but different from the Rankean type, can be traced back in its origin to Francis Bacon. With the thinkers and historians of the Enlightenment like Hume, Montesquieu and Condorcet it became an attempt to construct a Newtonian 'science of society'. In the nineteenth century Henri de Saint-Simon, the French radical, endeavored to discredit all so-called metaphysical approaches and to establish instead a 'positive philosophy' wherein gravitation would serve as the model of systematic comprehension and of ultimate unity across every branch of knowledge.[3]

It was St. Simon's secretary, Auguste Comte, who became the high priest of positivism. Born at Montpellier, Comte had grown up into a precocious rebel. After working as teacher for some time, he became secretary to St. Simon against whom after seven years, however, his independent spirit revolted. In an authoritarian religious strain he proclaimed himself high priest of humanity. He drove out his own long-suffering wife, and after her death worshipped another's as his 'virgin mother'. Unstable, isolated and ridiculed, but ever optimistic, the founder of positivism and modern sociology died in 1857 in his celebrated rooms at 10 rue Monsieur-le-Prince.

Collingwood defines positivism as "philosophy acting in the service of natural science, as in the Middle Ages philosophy acted in the service of theology."[4] Comtean positivism and its impact on historiography were the direct result of the great strides the natural sciences were making in the nineteenth century. A mathematician by profession, Comte put the sciences in order, coined the word 'positivism', and strove to introduce into the study of society the same method of the natural sciences like physics and chemistry: firstly, ascertaining facts, and secondly, framing laws. Facts were immediately ascertained by sensuous perception; the laws were framed by generalizing these facts by induction.[5] The positivist philosophy would use historical facts as raw materials to yield general laws of human society. Once the facts were meticulously ascertained in the Rankean manner, history, in the Comtean system, like any natural science, must go on to discover their causal connections. Such an intellectual position was the basis of the new science of sociology which Comte founded. The historian was to discover the facts about human life and the sociologist would discover the causal connections between the ascertained facts. The sociologist, writes Collingwood, would thus be a kind of super-historian, raising history to the rank of a science.

Comte explained the aims and principles of his philosophy in two works—the *Course of Positivist Philosophy* (1830–42) in 6 volumes, and the *System of Positivist Politics* (1851–54) in 4 volumes. The basic view presented in these works is that "all phenomena being subject to invariable natural laws, whose precise discovery and reduction to the smallest number possible is the aim of all our effort."[6] Comte's system is called positivism by reason of the definite, explicit, absolute quality asserted in its name—just those qualities that mark laws in the physical sciences. The French philosopher claimed for his positivist approach two things: first, that it was possible to study man in society just the same way as scientists study natural phenomena; and second, that it was possible to discover definite laws of historical and social behavior. In a triumphant spirit Comte formulated his 'law of three stages'. The law states that the history of all human societies and branches of experience must pass through three stages, each with its corresponding historical epoch: the theological–military (ancient), the metaphysical–legalistic (medieval), and the positive scientific–industrial (modern). Comte thought that it would be possible to discover laws of human society through a study of the progress of the human mind. Have not laws governing the world of nature been discovered? An understanding of such laws of society would help the state to control the direction and predict the course of history, and build an Utopia. Comte's philosophy of history is the prospectus of a morally and materially superior life for the human race.

Though Comte's brilliant analysis and original interpretation of history did not appeal to historians in general, his influence was considerable. His treating of all social thought as an interrelated whole had a profound effect on the subsequent development of the various social sciences. To Emile Faguet, Auguste Comte was the most powerful sower of seeds and intellectual stimulator, the greatest thinker that France has had since Descartes. John C. Cairns writes that

> his works testified to a titanic ambition in his generation to show unity where most historians saw diversity, and scientifically to demonstrate the laws of collective progress.... He remains a commanding presence at the crossroads of history and sociology....[7]

3. Henry Thomas Buckle (1821–1862)

Among those who had come under the spell of the Comtean positivist philosophy and who thought that history had to discover general laws of human development, none was more popular or perceptive than Henry Thomas Buckle. A sickly bachelor, an isolated self-taught historian and one-book author, Buckle aspired to accomplish for history what others had done for the natural sciences—collecting multitude of facts and deriving from them general laws of historical development. He intended to rescue history "from the hands of biographers, genealogists and collectors of anecdotes, chroniclers of courts and princes and nobles, and those babblers of vain things..."[8] and to place it on a sound methodological basis. He planned a fifteen-volume work on the comparative history of the European civilizations but died soon after the publication of the second volume in 1861 having developed a fever on a trip to the Middle East. His boldly analytical two-volume *History of Civilization in England* "is in the tradition of the grand schematizers, from Montesquieu to Toynbee and Braudel."[9] The first volume (1857) enjoyed an immediate success as it seemed to have caught the mood of the times with its timely plea that if historians would only search for and discover the hidden regularities of human action, then history would become a true science. Buckle maintained that a certain regularity and predictability of human actions could be discerned as such actions are governed by mental and physical laws. There is nothing in the actions of men and societies which is mysterious, providential or supernatural as to make them impervious to investigation; they are governed by fixed laws. Buckle avers that such an immense social and religious institution as marriage is completely controlled by the price of food and the rise of wages, not by personal feelings or wishes. Again, uniformity has been detected in the aberrations of memory in an invariable order though the cause thereof has not been unraveled. The returns published by the post offices of London and Paris show that year after year the same proportion of letter writers, through forgetfulness, omit to direct their letters. It shows that for each successive period we can actually foretell the number of persons whose memory will fail in regard to a trifling and seemingly accidental occurrence.

Statistics could reveal these uniformities and regularities in human life. Though in its infancy in Buckle's time, statistics, according to him, are a powerful device for eliciting the truth and can throw more light on the study of human nature than all the sciences put together.

Buckle's emphasis on general laws in history and the usefulness of statistics for the induction of such laws were attacked by professional historians, so much so that his *History of Civilization* became a neglected classic. He forgot that there were important areas of human life where statistics do not illuminate. Buckle's book has been more admired by sociologists than historians. Yet, his highly original studies of the intellectual development of England, France, Scotland and Spain have lost none of their force or relevancy, and his belief that "the real history of the human race is the history of tendencies which are perceived by the mind, and not of events which are discerned by the senses," has come to be shared by many contemporary historians.[10]

4. Positivism, an Assessment: The Influence of Positivism on Historiography

Unprecedented Increase of Detailed Historical Knowledge

The influence of positivism on historiography could best be seen in the growth of a new kind of history marked by meticulous care for details. The positivists whether of the Rankean or Comtean type made a fetish of facts and a cult of details and historians set to work to ascertain all the facts they could. The result was an unprecedented increase of detailed and carefully sifted historical material, whether literary, epigraphic or archeological. Collingwood informs us that the best historians like Mommsen or Maitland became the greatest masters of detail, that the ideal of universal history was thought to be a vain dream, and the monograph became the ideal of historical literature.[11]

A Corrective to the Rankean Approach

By tracing the connection between facts, between events, Comtean positivism proved itself to be a valuable corrective to the Rankean approach to history. The Rankeans were so concerned with unique events and exact detail, that at times their work seemed completely shapeless.[12]

Elimination of the Subjective Element

To the Rankean and the Comtean positivists each fact of history is a separate entity capable of being ascertained by a separate act of cognition. Thus there was to be an infinity of minute facts. Each such fact was thought to be independent not only of the rest but of the knower himself, so that all subjective elements in the historian's point of view had to be eliminated. The historian must pass no judgement on the facts; he must only say what they were.[13]

Possibility of Forming General Formulations

The Comtean positivist assertion that human society is amenable to scientific study is of outstanding importance. From positivism sprang modern sociology which seeks general laws in at least specific spheres of human activity.[14] After Comte and Buckle, the effort to seek general laws in historical development was continued by Marx, Spengler and Toynbee. And, if not general laws of human behavior, historians have actually presented general formulations about certain common features of revolutions and about the processes of industrialization. After studying hundred and fifty-eight constitutions known to him, Aristotle was able to pronounce that the most general cause of revolutions is the struggle between the haves and the have-nots. Formulations of such a general nature might be made regarding imperialist conquests, movements of populations, rise of dictatorships and so on.

Criticism of Positivism

Unhistorical Approach

Historians have been reluctant to accept the positivist approach, suspecting it as basically unhistorical. This is because, the historian, as Arthur Marwick observes, must start off from the particular and the unique; he must be more interested in what actually did happen than in abstract general laws about human and social behavior.[15]

Historical and Natural Processes Are not Analogous

Positivism, in its Comtean garb, observes Collingwood, was of little service to historiography. The assumption that the historical process is analogous to the natural process was wrong; equally wrong was the belief that the methods of natural science were adequate to the study and interpretation of the historical process. History is a knowledge of individual facts, science the knowledge of general laws. The task that historians had to perform was to discover and state the facts themselves and not to enunciate general laws, a task in which positivism had nothing useful to teach them.[16]

Attention to Small Problems to the Exclusion of Larger Ones

Again, according to Collingwood, the legacy of positivism to modern historiography was a combination of unprecedented mastery over small-scale problems with an unprecedented weakness in dealing with large-scale problems. Positivist insistence on microscopic details barred the historian from treating great events or large problems as such. Mommsen, the greatest historian of the positivistic age, had collected a vast corpus of historical material with incredible attention to detail. But his attempt to write a history of Rome broke down exactly at the point where his own contribution to Roman history began to be important. His *History of Rome* ends at the Battle of Actium.[17] E.H. Carr likewise speculates whether it was the nineteenth century fetishism of facts that frustrated Acton as a historian. Acton lamented that the requirements pressing on the historian threatened "to turn him from a man of letters into the compiler of an encyclopaedia."[18]

Crippling Effect of the Positivist Ban on Value Judgement

Finally, Collingwood shows that the positivist rule against passing judgements had an effect on historians no less crippling. The rule, for one, prevented the historians from discussing the wisdom of a policy, soundness of an economic system, or whether a particular movement in art, science or religion was an advance or not. Because of the positivist ban on value judgement, positivist historians could not understand what the ancients thought about slavery or what the people of the Roman world felt about their practice of emperor-worship. Enquiries such as these were quite legitimate for Romantic historians who tried to get into the inside of things; but such problems were out of the purview of their successors, the positivists. The refusal to judge the facts came to mean that history could only be the history of external events, not the history of the thought out of which these events grew. This was why positivist historiography erroneously identified itself with political history and ignored the history of art, religion, science etc. All the errors of positivist historiography flowed from a certain error in historical theory, namely, the false analogy between scientific facts which are empirical facts, facts perceived as they occur, and historical facts which being now gone beyond recall or repetition, cannot be objects of perception.[19]

5. Karl Marx (1818–1883)

Life and Works

The man who outdistanced all others in developing an approach to history which postulated general laws and broad patterns was Karl Marx. Marx raised positivistic outlook in history to a high philosophical level—historical materialism.

Marx was born in the town of Trier in the Rhineland in Germany, the son of a lawyer. He studied law and jurisprudence at the University of Berlin, but took a keen interest in history and philosophy also. Leaving university in 1841, he became a severe critic of the economic and political order of the day and soon had to leave the land of his birth to France, then to Belgium, and finally to England. He was one of those who formed the First International (1864) and remained thereafter the dominant personality of the socialist movement. Two extremely favorable circumstances of an otherwise difficult and turbulent life were Marx's marriage to Jenny von Westphalen in 1843 and his acquaintance with Friedrich Engels in the same year. Jenny was a devoted wife in life and dedicated assistant in his work. Marx found his friendship with Engels invaluable in his life and struggle. Theirs was one of history's most creatively collaborative endeavors.

The first works to expound the materialist conception of life and history were *The Holy Family* (1845) and *The German Ideology* (1846), both of which Marx wrote in conjunction with Engels. In 1848 appeared *The Communist Manifesto*, which was the first coherent and consistent exposition of the fundamentals of Marxism. It was again a collaborative work of Marx and Engels. Marx's *The Critique of Political Economy* (1859) is a brilliant work of which Engels later wrote: "Just as Darwin discovered the law of development of organic nature, so Marx discovered the law of development of human history."[20] The *Das Capital* (1867–94) was the work of a lifetime and the principal text of scientific communism. When Marx died Engels said: "Mankind is shorter by a head, and that the greatest head of our time."[21]

Dialectical Materialism

The view of life and of history developed by Marx and Engels – indeed, what makes Marxism a unified, compelling and dynamic doctrine – is the philosophy of dialectical materialism. Dialectical materialism seeks the essence of the historical process in the changing material conditions of human life. Closely moving in the circle of the 'young Hegelians', Marx had been attracted by the Hegelian philosophical system, particularly its attempt to interpret reality in terms of intrinsic regularities, its totality and world view, but most of all, by the creatively radical method of the dialectic. By the dialectic Hegel and Marx meant that all things are in movement and in evolution, and that all change comes through the clash of antagonistic elements. It implied that all history and indeed all reality, is a process of development through time, through the single and meaningful unfolding of events, that are necessary, logical and deterministic; and every event happens in due sequence for good and sufficient reason (not by chance); and history could not have happened differently from the way it has happened.[22]

But Marx completely disagreed with the idealistic basis of the Hegelian dialectic with its emphasis on the primacy of 'ideas' in social change. Whereas Hegel had applied the dialectic to the self-development of the absolute idea, Marx contended that the idea itself was the product of another entity, and a more basic one, that of life, and not *vice versa*. The basic element in human life, in society, is materialistic, economic. Men must first live before they can have ideas and it is not primarily by having ideas that men create the social world in which they live. On the contrary, their form of society, especially their economic institutions, predisposes them to have certain ideas.[23] Marx seized upon Ludwig Feuerbach's materialist view that thinking springs from being and not being from thinking, and quickly laid the foundation of his system by applying the doctrine to history. Economic and social conditions are the roots, ideas the trees. In Hegel, the dialectics stood on its head as ideas were held to be the roots, and the resulting human activity to be trees. Marx is reported to have said that he found Hegel on his head, and set him on his feet again. *The German Ideology* categorically announced: "Life is not determined by consciousness, but consciousness by life."[24]

Historical Materialism

Proceeding on the material basis of human life, Marx and Engels erected a philosophical edifice variously called 'dialectical materialism', 'historical materialism' or 'the materialist conception of history'. The main lines of historical materialism may be brought under the following heads.

Economic Determinism

In *The Holy Family*, Marx and Engels had written that "history is *nothing but* the activity of man pursuing his aims."[25] The root of this activity is economic and the doctrine of economic determinism holds that material production is the basis of mankind's history and that no part of that history could be understood without a knowledge of the industry of that period. The forces and relations of economic production determine the kind of religion, philosophies, governments, laws and moral rules men accept. An oft-quoted passage in *The Critique of Political Economy* runs as follows:

> In the social production of their existence, men inevitably enter into definite relations which are independent of their will, namely, relations of production appropriate to a given stage in the development of their material forces of production. The totality of these relations of production constitutes the economic structure of society, the real foundation, on which arises the legal and political superstructure and to which correspond definite forms of social consciousness. The mode of production of material life conditions the general process of social, political and intellectual life. *It is not men's consciousness that determines their existence, but their social existence that determines their consciousness.*[26]

This means that the basic causative factor in history is at all times the economic factor.

Stages of History

Marx argued that history, meaning the past, has unfolded through a series of stages: Asiatic, antique, feudal and modern bourgeois. Each of these stages is determined by the prevailing conditions under which wealth is produced. In a slave-owning economy wealth was produced from the ownership of slaves; in the feudal stage, from the ownership of land; in the bourgeois period from the ownership of factories.[27] Each of these different stages develops an ideology and superstructure suited to its needs.

Dialectical Motion of Society: Class Struggle

The motive force for the development from stage to stage is the ever present 'class struggle' or 'class war'. History is human society in dialectical motion. The dialectical motion is caused by the antagonistic interests of economic classes created by the prevailing mode of production. Class is the one enduring reality in a world of flux. "The history of all hitherto existing society," declared *The Communist Manifesto,* "is the history of the class struggle."[28] Classes themselves are determined by the relationship of particular groups to the specific conditions under which wealth is produced. Class membership is determined by certain common material interests that the individual shares with others, typically a relationship of ownership or non-ownership of the means of production. Since the establishment of private property, society has been divided into two hostile economic classes—the exploiters and the exploited. In the slave-owning ancient world the interest of the slave-owners was opposed to that of the slaves; in the feudal stage, the interest of the feudal lord was opposed to that of the serfs; in our own times the interest of the capitalist class is antagonistic to the interest of the working class. History is a story of class war.

Theory of Surplus Value

In *Das Capital* Marx stated that the primary reason for the antagonism between labor and capital is that the capitalists are able to appropriate the *surplus value* which is created by labor and which, therefore, ought to go to labor. Marx declared labor to be the source of all wealth and the only source of value. Surplus value is the value that labor produces above the cost of tools, raw materials and the cost of its own subsistence. But the capitalists through their ownership and control of the means of production deprive labor the wealth it has created. The modern state is a committee of the bourgeoisie to protect it from rebellion by the proletariat who suffer from this process of exploitation.

Social Revolution

Marx believed in revolution as a powerful accelerator of social progress and argued in *The Critique of Political Economy* that at the end of each historical age a point is reached when new productive forces come into conflict with existing class relations or property relations. The conflict leads to social revolution. There were slave revolts in the ancient world; peasant revolts in the medieval age; and there was social revolution when feudal society gave way to the bourgeois in England in 1642, in France in 1789, in Germany in 1848. There is bound to be social revolution with the development of capitalism and with the ever closer and more elaborate organization of its dialectical antithesis, the proletariat. The final stage is the overthrow of the capitalist class by the proletariat when the latter simply takes over the means of production and abolishes private property. Every stage in this historical process is rendered inevitable by the compulsions of material production.

The New Society

To stabilize the gains of the social revolution, i.e., the overthrow of the capitalist class, a dictatorship of the proletariat will be established. *The Communist Manifesto* envisages an Utopia in which the state will wither away in a classless society in which each will contribute to the social wealth according to his capacity and take from it what he needs.

6. The Impact of Marxism (Historical Materialism) on Historiography

History is said to have been Marx's weakest subject at the Trier High School. The German historian Treitschke wrote that Marx "completely lacked a scholar's conscience" and knew what he wanted to prove before the research started, an observation A.J.P. Taylor echoes when he said that "Marx...decided beforehand what he wanted to discover...."[29] Arthur Marwick thinks of the Marxist scheme as in a very real sense unhistorical as it puts the grand pattern of historical development before exact study of the events of history. Historical inquiry must begin with unique and particular facts. Marwick wonders whether the Marxist scheme looks at the past on its own terms at all, from the inside! Are not historical events used simply as convenient material to illustrate the unfolding of Marxist theory?[30]

Positivism, except of the Rankean type, is a generator of systematic general laws, and contains a predictive quality. Marx held that it was possible to establish laws of social development and thereby predict social change and Marxian dialectic has been profuse in making predictions and in offering explanations of everything that had ever happened or could happen. But John Whittam enumerates Marx's predictions that have not been borne out by facts. The proletariat did not grow progressively poorer—what Marx saw in the 1840s was only the early stage of industrial development. The contradictions within capitalism were overcome time after time. Marx's belief that revolution would occur in an advanced society like Britain or the United States was never realized; Marxist revolutions, when they occurred, occurred largely in peasant societies as in Russia, China, Yugoslavia and Cuba, and in circumstances very different from those envisaged by Marx. His assumption that free trade would spread through the world also proved false, as did his belief that it would assist the cause of internationalism which would prove stronger than nationalism; tariff walls sprang up in the 1870s and the workers of the world did not unite but fought each other for the national cause on the battlefields of Europe. Writes Whittam: "Every historian's knowledge of the past and the present must be so selective as to rule out the possibility of correct predictions."[31]

Evaluations of the above kind notwithstanding, of epochal importance is the pervasive influence that Marx and Engels have exercised and continue to exercise on history writing. The same A.J.P. Taylor has written that because of *The Communist Manifesto*, "everyone thinks differently about politics and society, when he thinks at all," and Edmund Wilson has expressed himself in similar vein about *The Eighteenth Brumaire of Louis Bonaparte*.[32] The Marx–Engels scheme had in fact combined a critique of capitalism with a general theory of historical development. Marx's observations about the iniquities of capitalism in the 1840s were essentially just, exemplified in Engels's *Condition of the English Working Class* (1845). That Marx was not a historian of the usual professional type needs hardly any mention though he showed his skill and perception in writing two brilliant pieces of contemporary history—*The Class Struggle in France* and *The Eighteenth Brumaire of Louis Bonaparte.* But the fact that it was Marxism which most sharply challenged prevailing historiography makes all the difference.

Valuable Corrective

It may be indicated at the outset that the Positivists and the Marxists provided a valuable corrective to the mere accumulation of facts in the Rankean manner which paid little attention to the essential interconnections of those facts. Lenin observed that Marx's

> historical materialism was a great achievement in scientific thinking. The chaos and arbitrariness that had previously reigned in views of history and politics were replaced by a strikingly integral and harmonious scientific theory, which shows how in consequence of productive forces, out of one system of social life another and higher system develops....[33]

Two Basic Contributions

Marx and Engels, like other European thinkers between the Enlightenment and the First World War, shared the belief in human progress, but they fundamentally differed from all others in asserting that the prime mover of progress was the mode of production. It is through the dynamics of dialectical materialism that Marxism has influenced history writing. The central idea of the doctrine is that the essential element in an understanding of human history is the productive activity of human beings, and that changes in the forces and relations of material production cause class conflicts by means of which any society develops. Inquiry into the mode of production, and the analysis by class – the basic social entity – then are the two basic contributions of Marx and Engels to historical studies. Marxists and non-Marxists alike have benefited by this insight of fundamental importance—indeed, the latter seem to have derived greater benefit than the former. Sociologists like Max Weber and historians like C.A. Beard have acknowledged their debt to Marx. In fact, inquiry into the mode of production and class analysis are practices so universal in historical research today that scholars have ceased to acknowledge any particular debt at all! A necessary adjunct to these twin theories is the theory of surplus value which, as an instrument of historical analysis and reconstruction, has been extensively employed to explain political and social changes, i.e., historical changes. Skeptical and imaginative application of Marxism can yield rich dividends. The fact is that historical materialism provides a valuable method. The base–superstructure model of historical analysis is a positive contribution to a proper understanding of the past. The historian may profitably use such general concepts as very useful tools of analysis or as organizing principles.

Stimulating and Liberating Effect of Marxism on Historiography

We cannot accept in full Lenin's claim that the materialist conception of history had discovered "the objective law behind the system of social relations," and had "made it possible for us to examine with the precision of a natural science, the social conditions influencing the life of the masses, and the changes taking place in these conditions."[34]

Arthur Marwick writes that barring much "tedious rubbish" written by Marxist historians and the propagandist histories of allegedly Marxist countries, it must be said that some of the most stimulating of all historical work are being written today by scholars who are avowedly Marxist. Marxism has had a stimulating and liberating effect in confronting the manifold problems of history writing. Marx's influence in some manner or other could be seen in almost everything of importance relating to history published since the late nineteenth century.[35]

Materialist Interpretation Helps Causal Explanation

The materialist conception makes causal explanation in history easier. The point may be illustrated from the interpretative works of some of the French and American historians who made the greatest advances in twentieth century historiography. Thus Charles A. Beard revealed the economic causes of the American constitution and Jeffersonian democracy. The rights of man as proclaimed in the French Revolution and in the constitution of the United States were not eternal truths about the nature of man; their significance could be fully understood only if viewed in the context of demands made by the new commercial groups for the end of feudal restrictions and for free competition in economic affairs. The ideology expressed in such celebrated documents is rooted in class interests. Jean Jaures, the author of *The Socialist History of the French Revolution*, and Albert Mathiez, the author of *The French Revolution*, and the foremost Marxist interpreter of the great event, substantially revised the picture of poverty, misery and economic distress painted by Michelet and Taine as the causative factors of the great upheaval. According to them the Revolution was brought about by a wealthy, confident bourgeois class which having effectively taken over economic power as a result of the rise of capitalism, then wished to extend its dominance to the political and social sphere. But it found its ambitions thwarted by the outmoded political, social and economic structure of the *ancien regime.* In their view the Revolution was the work of a class on the rise. Particularly, it was Mathiez's thesis that the Revolution began as a struggle of the aristocracy and the bourgeoisie which then developed into a conflict that pitted the middle classes against the laboring classes.

There is, again, the austere Georges Lefebvre, another historian of the French Revolution who is also an economic historian. Lefebvre accepted the existence of the class struggle, but his Marxism was of the liberatory sort. His special contribution to a better understanding of the Revolution is the proper place, the autonomous role, that he gives to the peasantry in that seismic upheaval of a people. As David McLellan observes, Marxist interpretation of history is at its strongest in periods of sharp social conflict. The transition from feudalism to capitalism and the phenomenon of European imperialism have been the subjects of impressive analyses.[36]

More particularly, from the standpoint of the development of historical studies, Marx and Engels are important for the following reasons.

Conception of History as Study of Society

With Marxism history became the study of society in the way in which modern social scientists understand the phrase. Marx stated in the *Theses on Feuerbach* that human essence is the ensemble of all social relations. Man exists in society, he is a product of society, a product of a definite form of society.[37] Already, in *The Holy Family,* Marx and Engels had pronounced history to be nothing but the activity of (this social) man pursuing his aims.[38] Such tenets were bound to make history the study of the social phenomenon in its varied manifestations. It ceased to be just a detailed, shapeless and purposeless picture of one thing happening after another.

Emergence of Economic and Social History as Major Disciplines

Hegel's *Philosophy of History* had overemphasized the role of the state, and Ranke and most historians had almost exclusively occupied themselves with political history. The materialist conception – the economic interpretation – of history promptly thrust the state into the background and brought to the fore the forces of economic life. Historical interest now began to seep from political history, that is, from individual rulers and activities of states, down to larger and larger numbers of ordinary people. The two characteristic directions in which the new interest took were the economic and the social.

The increasing awareness of the decisive influence of economic developments upon society led to the rapid development of economic history which was facilitated by the growing availability of economic and demographic statistics. At the beginning of the twentieth century economic history gained institutional recognition in England, France and America and great works of economic history as those of George Unwin and J.H. Clapham came to be written. From economic to social history was but a step as the two aspects of life are so intertwined. Though no clear case for direct influence of Marxism on the writing of social history could be established, Fabian socialists and liberal–radical intellectuals took a prominent part in creating the subject in Britain. Elie Halevy, J.L. Hammond and Barbara Hammond, G.D.H. Cole and Raymond Postgate, and R.H. Tawney are only some of those who enriched this branch of historical studies.

Role of the Masses

The influence of Marxism on modern historiography could be seen in the emphasis it laid on the work of the masses. *The Holy Family* formulated the key position about the leading role of the masses in history, a role which is especially pronounced in revolutionary epochs.[39] With social progress, the scope of their influence was bound to grow. Marx predicted that the socialist revolution would open an era in which the size of the masses would increase. The 'great man' in history, like the political state, is being thrust into the shade by the story of the 'great many'.

The conception of history as the study of society has led in recent years to the composition of a class of subaltern studies—studies relating to the hitherto neglected sections of society.

Total History

By pronouncing that the modes of material production affect all the other aspects of human life, Marxism has provided an organizing principle and is now understood to suggest what has come to be called 'total history.' Total history means a history in which stress is laid on the interrelationship between art, ideas, politics and economics. Henri Berr (1863–1954) in France sought through the journal he founded in 1900, *Review of Historical Synthesis*, to bring together in one great synthesis, all the activities of man in society. In France, again, Lucien Febvre and Marc Bloch hoped through their journal, *Annales*, to project a history more 'total' and more human.

9

THE TWENTIETH CENTURY I

1. Scientific History and the Skeptical Note

By the end of the nineteenth century, history had firmly established itself as an autonomous scientific discipline and several manuals of its methodology and technique – as those by C.V. Langlois and Charles Seignobos – were written. The sole aim of this new science of history, as expressed by Lord Acton in his directive to the collaborators of the *Cambridge Modern History*, was the increase of 'accurate knowledge'. It was even believed that it would one day be possible to produce 'ultimate history'—a history that would need no change once it was written.

But a skeptical note could also be heard.[1] Already, in 1874, Nietzsche had complained that historical thinking had overpowered the creative spontaneous forces of life, and that historians had succumbed to a lifeless scientism. There was, in fact, a critical and highly fruitful reexamination of the theory of history in the years between 1890 and 1914. The reexamination consisted partly of a reaction against the presumed identity of history and the natural sciences, and against mere historical empiricism which had taught historians to be 'neutral in thought and action'.

> The philosophical presuppositions of the scientific historian, as seen in Fustel de Coulanges and Bury, were undermined by Rickert's critical analysis of the logical and methodological difference of history and the natural sciences and by Dilthey's insistence on the necessary psychological involvement of the historian in any understanding of the past.[2]

Likewise, the presuppositions of the scientific historians were challenged by Croce's essay on history as an art (1893), by Trevelyan's plea in defence of Clio as a muse (1903), and Eduard Meyer's critique of scientific history (1903).

There was in the twentieth century a widening of the scope of history. Henri Berr in France tried to do it by making history the synthesizing science among the emergent social sciences. In America, meanwhile, a new history, aiming at its immediate usefulness was being launched by James Harvey Robinson. Again, new subdivisions of history – economic, social and legal – were springing up. In the first decades of the twentieth century, the history of ideas, culture and art began to flourish. Historians were beginning to realize that their traditional modes of analysis could be deepened by the contributions of Durkheim, Weber and Freud. They also knew that scientism and specialization had torn their works from the other humanities, especially literature, and alienated them from the reading public. Spengler after the First World War and Toynbee after the Second won large audiences which, if anything, showed the need for synthesis and meaning in history in an age of specialization. And, finally, Lucien Febvre and Marc Bloch tried to produce what has come to be called 'total history' by bringing together all the activities of man in society.

2. Nature, Function and Purpose of History: Bury and Trevelyan

History had emerged as an autonomous scientific discipline with its own methodological apparatus, but doubts still lingered as to whether it was to be computed as science or art. Should Clio continue her old association with literature and philosophy, or was she to be concerned with finding out causes and effects by scientific research? Are there emotional aspects of past events which could only be comprehended imaginatively as in literature? If history is regarded exclusively as a science will it not keep itself away from the people? The question was not merely about the nature of history, but also of its function and purpose in human life. The following is a short summary of the illuminating debate on the nature, function and purpose of history between two giants—Bury and Trevelyan.

John Bagnell Bury (1861–1927)

A Rankean positivist concerned with the philosophical problems of historical research and a writer of great literary grace, John Bagnell Bury was the author of first rate historical works like the *History of Greece, A History of the Later Roman Empire from Arcadius to Irene* (*AD 395–800*), and *The Eastern Roman Empire from the Fall of Irene to the Accession of Basil I* (*AD 802–867*). Besides being an editor of the *Cambridge Ancient History* series, Bury planned the *Cambridge Modern History* and produced what is still a standard scholarly edition of Gibbon's *The Decline and Fall.* He also wrote two important works of a semi-philosophical nature: *A History of Freedom of Thought* (1913) and *The Idea of Progress* (1920). In 1902 he succeeded Lord Acton as Regius Professor of Modern History at Cambridge. Bury's inaugural lecture at Cambridge on 'The Science of History' epitomized the historicist tradition in England.[3]

History: Scientific Method of Research and Investigation

In his inaugural lecture at Cambridge in 1903, Bury presented history as a science, emphatically reminding his hearers that it was not a branch of literature. Though in the nineteenth century history had come to be recognized as a science, Bury thought it necessary to insist that it was so. This was because history's time-honored association with literature was still acting as "a sort of vague cloud, half concealing from men's eyes her new position in the heavens."[4]

Historical truth required the most exact methods to secure it. Though there had been in the past erudite historians who had a high ideal of accuracy, so long as history was regarded as an art, the sanctions of truth and accuracy could not be very severe. A systematized method which distinguishes a science was beyond the vision of all, except a few like Mabillon. It was Niebuhr and Ranke who supplemented erudition by scientific method. Again, said Bury, the philologist Wolf's *Prolegomena to Homer* exercized a powerful influence on historical research.

National Spirit: Powerful Motive for Historical Investigation

But scientific method for ascertaining the truth alone was not enough. A new transforming conception of history's scope and limits was needed if she was to become an independent science. It was a strange and fortunate accident, said Bury, that the scientific movement in Germany associated with Niebuhr and Ranke should have begun simultaneously with the national movements throughout Europe. The national movement disclosed one of the practical uses of history, as men recognizing the principles of unity and continuity sought the key of their national development not in the immediate, but in the remoter past. The spirit of resurgent nationalism thus supplied a powerful motive for historical investigation. The scientific method, said Bury, controlled, while the national spirit quickened the work of historical research.

Idea of Progress

The practical utility of history could be comprehended only when men grasped the idea of human development, of progress. Started by Leibnitz, the idea of progress, Bury proceeded to inform his audience, was the other transforming conception which enabled history not only to define her scope and become an autonomous discipline, but to become a true solvent of anti-historical doctrines. The doctrine of progress has delivered history from the political and ethical encumbrances and has brought it into line with the other sciences. Abandoning old associates – moral philosophy and rhetoric – history has begun to enter into closer relations with the sciences which deal objectively with the facts of the universe.

The idea of progress, so integral a part of scientific history, involves two other real perspectives. The view that certain periods of history are more important than remoter ages is not only subjective and unscientific, but involves a false perspective. The modern age has no special claim to be counted the most important. History will cease to be scientific if its attention is not distributed, so far as the sources allow, to all periods. Secondly, the exclusive idea of political history, *staatengeschichte,* to which Ranke held so firmly, has been yielding to a more comprehensive definition as to include the story of all the material and spiritual development, of the culture and the works, of man in society from the stone age onwards. The true history, whether of a nation or of the world, is one in which the various manifestations of human intellect and human emotion, and every form of social life are set forth each in relation to the rest, in its significance for growth or decline.

Place of History in National Education

The realization that history, our conception of the past, is itself a distinct factor in guiding and moulding our future evolution, supplies us with the true theory of the practical importance of history. For this reason, it is inevitable that history will come to occupy a larger and larger place in national education. It is therefore of the greatest importance that the history which is taught should be true. True history can come only through the discovery, collection, classification and interpretation of facts through scientific research. And the universities have to preach more loudly "that the advancement of research in history, as in other sciences, is not a luxury...but is a matter of inestimable concern to the nation and to the world."[5] The idea of the future development of man justifies all our historical labor, a labor performed in good faith for posterity.

Bury concluded his inaugural address by affirming that history can best prepare her disciples for stripping the bandages of error from men's eyes by remembering that "she is herself simply a science, no less and no more."[6]

Bury's Change of Position

It is not the same Bury of the Cambridge inaugural lecture that we see in his later years when he grew skeptical about the possibility of establishing historical causality. The turnabout is first seen in his lecture on 'The Place of Modern History in the Perspective of Knowledge' (1904), and later in 'Darwinism in History' (1909) and 'Cleopatra's Nose' (1916). It became such that he stressed the role of contingency, of mere chance, in history. So far as history is individual, everything in it was accidental and nothing necessary.[7] It is what Norman H. Baynes speaks of as "the devastating doctrine of contingency in history,"[8] which, as Collingwood tells us, dimmed Bury's historical insight towards the end of his life. In fact, Bury's mind was torn between two antithetical concepts as to the nature of history, its principles and methods—the indistinguishable identity of history and science, and the essential difference between the two.[9]

George Macaulay Trevelyan (1876–1962)

Grandnephew of the great Macaulay and son of Sir George Otto Trevelyan, George Macaulay Trevelyan duly inherited the Whig tradition of the family. As a student at Cambridge, he was told by John Seely that history was science, and that Macaulay and Carlyle were charlatans. The comment awakened in the youngster an abiding suspicion of 'scientific' historians. Plumb's description of him as "a poet at large in history" is perhaps justified as few people could ever have succeeded more completely in the task of bringing history to the people.[10]

Trevelyan's celebrated essay – 'Clio, a Muse' – was a polemical answer in defence of history as a literary art to J.B. Bury's 'The Science of History'. In a bid to revive the old literary traditions of history which the Rankeans had supplanted, the author arrays reasons why Clio should be regarded a Muse and not a Science.

The 'Scientific' in History

Trevelyan pleads that history cannot perform the two functions expected of a science. First, history has no direct utility in practical fields. Its knowledge cannot help cure a disease or invent a machine. Second, it cannot deduce laws of general applicability, laws of cause and effect, which are certain to repeat themselves in the institutions and affairs of men. The law of gravitation is easily proved because it is universal and simple; but the historical law that starvation brings on revolt has not been proved. Indeed, the opposite statement that starvation leads to abject submission is equally true in the light of past events. Unlike physical matter, a historical event cannot be completely isolated from its circumstances so that one might deduce from it a law of general application. "An historical event cannot be isolated from its circumstances, any more than an onion from its skins, because an event is nothing but a set of circumstances, none of which will ever recur."[11]

One part of the historian's work which can be truly called scientific is the collection of facts and the weighing of evidence as to what events happened. But the same cannot be said of discovering the causes and effects of such events. No complete or a wholly true account of even an event like the French Revolution could be given, for the simple reason that it is impossible to examine accurately the psychology of twenty-five million different persons. We cannot dissect a mind and, even if we can, we cannot apply the results to millions of other minds. Therefore, Trevelyan concluded that "in the most important part of its business, history is not a scientific deduction, but an imaginative guess at the most likely generalisations."[12]

Theme and Function of History

Even if cause and effect could be discovered with accuracy, that would not constitute the highest theme of history. That theme is human achievement. The deeds themselves are more interesting than their causes and effects, and are fortunately ascertainable with greater precision. The story of great events is itself of the highest value. To narrate the story of human achievement is the function of history. In its unchangeable essence, history is a tale—the art of narrative.[13] Trevelyan complains that it is the old art of narrative that the new science of history has criminally neglected, and which is its spinal weakness.

Narration

Narration is not easy. To enter into the real thoughts and feelings of those who are dead and gone is much more difficult than to spin guesswork generalizations of cause and effect. It is a function for which not only the documents, but also insight, sympathy and imagination are required, in order to make the documents tell the truth. The historian must have the warmest human sympathy, i.e., emotional understanding, and the highest imaginative powers, even humor—the sense of the comic in human life. Because Carlyle had these qualities in abundance – qualities which are literary rather than scientific – his flame-picture of the French Revolution, the portraits of its leaders, and accounts of mob psychology, are more true than the cold analysis of the same events and conventional accounts of the same persons, by scientific historians "who with more knowledge of facts, have less understanding of Man."[14]

Value of History

History has no properly scientific value, asserts Trevelyan; its only purpose is educative.[15] The first educative function of history is to nurture in the citizen a capability for understanding great affairs and sympathizing with other men. Producing a new state of mind by removing prejudices is what Leckey's Irish history did—training the mind of both Unionists and Home Rulers to think sensibly.

Besides removing prejudices, history should breed enthusiasm. History, unlike science, serves as an important source of ideas that inspire many. It presents ideals and heroes of other ages to smaller men. For this purpose historical events should both be written and read with intellectual passion. To enable the reader to comprehend the historical aspect of literature and to enhance immeasurably the value of travel are the other educative functions of history.

History Reading

Trevelyan closes with a lament. In the eighteenth century the educated classes in England, though numerically small, loved history reading and no country house of any pretension was without its Clarendon, Robertson, Hume and Gibbon. In the Victorian age, history in England reached the height of its popularity and of its influence on the national mind. This was because the Victorian historians carried on the tradition that history was related to literature. The foundation of a broad national culture based upon a knowledge of history seemed to be securely laid. But the scientific historians preferred to destroy the foundations of literary history and to sever the tie between history and the reading public. They gave it out that Carlyle and Macaulay were 'literary historians' and therefore ought not to be read. Hearing that history was a science, the public left it to the scientists.

To the question whether history is a science or an art, Trevelyan gives a meaningfully ambiguous answer: "...let us call it both or call it neither. For it has an element of both."[16]

Trevelyan might seem to have been somewhat overstating the literary aspect of history and arbitrarily limiting the scope of what is scientifically knowable. Arthur Marwick writes that the development of modern psychology has rendered a substantial part of his arguments invalid and no historian would now presume to discuss the French Revolution or similar themes without acquainting himself with the discoveries of individual and social psychology.

3. Renewed Interest in Philosophy: Spengler and Toynbee

In the first phase of the twentieth century renewed interest in philosophy showed itself in a kind of overarching philosophical history as represented by Oswald Spengler and Arnold Toynbee as well as in a reconsideration of the nature of history as seen in the work of Benedetto Croce and R.G. Collingwood. Spengler and Toynbee were philosophers of history, the theme of their philosophizing being the past itself, for which the First World War in part provided the stimulus. Both tried to detect a grand design in history and aimed at revealing what they thought were the general laws behind the rise and fall of civilizations.

Oswald Spengler (1880–1936)

Oswald Cassandra Spengler, German philosopher of history, owed his sudden renown entirely to his two-volume *The Decline of the West.* Taking his doctorate at Halle in 1904, Spengler taught in school until 1911, when he went to Munich on a small inheritance and devoted himself to writing his masterpiece.

Fate of Civilizations

The first volume of *The Decline of the West* appeared in 1918 and the second, in 1922. Spengler's book of doom owed its phenomenal popularity to the *post bellum neurosis.* The work caught the mood of the times and immediately became popular particularly in defeated Germany and Austria where readers drew some philosophic consolation, even if only negative, from Spengler's global history which had highlighted the hollowness of Allied victory. The brutality of the war and the cynicism of the peace had come as a shock to the robust optimism of the nineteenth century. A philosophic gloom, congenial to prophets of doom, had settled on Europe. Readers admired the ambitiousness and dogmatism of Spengler's attempt to pattern not only the past but also the West's doom-laden future.[17]

The Decline of the West is a study in the philosophy of history. A comparative morphology of the history of civilizations, its thesis is that definite laws of birth, growth and decline determine the history of cultures, and that consequently history is predictable. Count Kaiserling, Dean Inge and Hilaire Belloc had all agreed in the belief that Western civilization was in the throes of decline and was doomed, Professor Flinders Petrie, the great Egyptologist, thought that European civilization had reached its zenith around 1800 and had begun to die with the French Revolution.[18] Taking the same frontierline – AD 1800 – between dynamic creation and corroding decay Spengler pronounced Western civilization to have been set irreversibly on the course of decline. It is the law of history. "He who does not understand," Spengler wrote in the *Decline*, "that this outcome is obligatory and insusceptible of modification must forgo all desire to comprehend history."[19]

Spengler's thesis rests on history whose researches, diggings and discoveries in the nineteenth century had unveiled many a dead civilization. The schoolboy's rule that everything that goes up must come down, is also history's rule. Proud Egypt, beautiful Greece and great Rome – Rome that bestrode the world like a colossus – all lay low. Judea, Phoenicia, Carthage, Babylonia, Assyria, Persia—death is on them all. Will it be different with the modern Europe of Italy, Spain, France, England and Germany? The historian concludes that there is only one thing certain in history, and that is decadence, just as there is one thing certain in life, and that is death.[20]

Spengler's View of History

Human Societies: Separate Social Organisms

An interpretation of universal history, *The Decline of the West* rejects the conception of world history as a unified development in which man rises from a primitive state to ever higher levels. Human societies are separate social organisms obeying the laws of birth, growth and death.

> A civilization (*Kultur*) is born at the moment when out of the primitive psychic conditions of a perpetually infantile (raw) humanity, a mighty soul awakes and extricates itself:...This soul comes to flower on the soil of a country to which it remains attached like a plant. Conversely, a civilization dies if once this soul has realized the complete sum of its possibilities in the shape of peoples, languages, creeds, arts, states and sciences and thereupon goes back into the primitive psyche from which it originally emerged.[21]

Unlike Toynbee who later held that cultures are usually 'apparented' or affiliated to older cultures, Spengler contended that the spirit of a culture can never be transferred to another culture. In particular, he rejected any significant influence of ancient civilization, including Christianity, on Western culture.

Cultures and their Prime Symbols

Spengler exemplified his view of history in eight main cultures—the Egyptian, Babylonian, Indian, Chinese, Graeco-Roman, Arabian, Mexican, and modern Western. Each of these cultures is based on its own major premise or prime symbol, which determines the essential character of its science, philosophy, arts, beliefs, and ways of living, thinking and acting. Cultures vary in their prime symbols. Egyptian culture has stone for its prime symbol; Greek culture the ideal of beauty; Indian culture the salvation of the human soul; and modern Western the cavern or vault.

Cyclical Law of the Rise, Growth and Decay of Cultures

Spengler thinks culture to be the soul of history. The rise, growth and decay of a culture are subject to an immutable law of nature. Each culture has its childhood, youth, manhood and old age, and it dies after having fulfilled its destiny. The death of one culture is the birth of another one. Such a view of history is cyclical.

According to Spengler all cultures pass through four distinct phases in their life cycle. The master images are those of flowering and the seasons. In the pre-culture stage man was naked, carnivorous, nomadic and a beast of prey. The next stage is agricultural. Culture begins with the barbarism of primitive society. Spengler sees it rising from among the peasants who lack historical consciousness and who are dominated by instinct. The next phase, the decisive moment, in the growth of a culture is the creation of a rational religion in which *kulturseele* (the soul of a culture) finds its conscious form. Political organization, arts and the sciences are developed, first in an archaic manner, then blossoming into classical excellence. Art, philosophy, science and poetry are the expressions of culture at the height of its creativity. Winter comes at last and culture gives way to mere civilization, "the thing become succeeding to the thing becoming, death following life."[22] Decadence sets in and culture finally sinks into a new type of barbarism.

'Civilization' Phase: Prelude to the Decay of a Culture

Of particular importance is Spengler's close scrutiny of the last phase of a culture which he calls 'civilization', and which he described as a prelude to its decay and destruction. With the development of large cities and states culture turns into civilization, which means for Spengler that political, economic and technical organization prevails over spontaneity. People become sophisticated, urbanized and parasitical. The cities grow artificial and another class, the masses, appears. Cities become a picture of contrasts – of limitless wealth and utter poverty, of profound knowledge and gross ignorance – and where the sophisticated intellect creates unproductive problems. In the cities, in the machine age, the last act of a cultural drama is enacted—people render themselves the slaves of machines. The motorcar, by its numbers, destroys its own value, for one moves faster on foot. People get disgusted with city life. Leadership passes from the idealist intellectual to the shrewd moneylender, the bourgeois, who begins to control the vote through money power. The press becomes a powerful means of propaganda in the hands of the rich, and democratic processes like parliaments, congresses and elections become a farce staged in the name of the popular will. Through money democracy destroys itself and tyrannical dictatorship – Caesarism – becomes inevitable, and upstarts seize power. That is the last scene of the cultural drama. Finally, the culture collapses and its members become peasants again or even roaming savages. If there is any validity in history, if the past has any light to shed upon the future, it is that Western civilization has entered this last phase of culture, that it is in the throes of decline, and by a metaphysical necessity, will collapse and pass away.

Assessment

Spengler's attempt at a systematic interpretation of universal history is commendable. And the interpretation, in some of its parts, contains a bracing suggestiveness—if only as a shock to progressivist complacency. Spengler's predictions about an imminent brutal Caesarism seemed fulfilled in Hitler's rise to power. But most of his book now stands revealed as fantasy, particularly its ominous warning of an imminent catastrophe to Western civilization. Professional scholars are as critical of Spengler's unorthodox methods, as they are contemptuous of his errors of facts.[23] The value of the *Decline of the West* as a major contribution to social theory also may be doubted, as to analyze and explain human society as an *organism* on the false analogy of biology is futile and misleading. Critics have also found fault with Spengler's theory of the determinism of inevitable decline as well as his repudiation of the Enlightenment, the idea of progress and the democratic liberties attained after centuries of struggle.

Arnold Joseph Toynbee (1889–1975)

Arnold Joseph Toynbee was born in London in 1889. After graduating from Balliol College, Oxford, he held many posts until in 1925 he became Director of Studies at the Royal Institute of International Studies, London, where he worked for full thirty years. Toynbee died in York, England, in October, 1975. Besides his master work, *A Study of History,* Toynbee published numerous smaller works of which *Civilization on Trial* and *The World and the West* sparked widespread debate. Some of his other publications are *Nationality and War, Greek Historical Thought, East to West: A Journey Round the World, Hellenism: A History of a Civilization, Autobiography,* and the year-by-year *Survey of Inter-National Affairs* which are good accounts of contemporary history. The last of this prolific output was *Mankind and Mother Earth.*

A Study of History

Nature, Method and Theme of the Work

Following Spengler's *The Decline of the West,* was another work of its kind, Toynbee's ten-volume *A Study of History,* appearing between 1934 and 1961. It is the most ambitious project in historical synthesis ever attempted by a single author. As Arthur Marwick writes, the immense scope and lofty aims of the work make it a metahistory. The writing of metahistory seeking laws and patterns of historical development and human destiny belongs to the positivistic traditions of the nineteenth century.

Spengler's *a priori,* mechanistic and fatalistic model did not appeal to the British philosopher-historian; he chose the empirical and inductive method in the best British tradition. The procedure is a systematic comparison of twenty-one civilizations since, for our author, the intelligible units of historical study are not nations or periods, but societies or civilizations.

Toynbee's realization that civilization was threatened after 1914 raised in his mind the problem of its origin and development. Why did some civilizations thrive while others, no less advantaged, fail? The specific theme of Toynbee's work is thus a philosophical investigation into the origin, growth and breakdown of civilizations. The monumental *Study* put forward a philosophy of history based on an analysis of the cyclical development and decline of civilizations.

Civilizations are a recent phenomenon in human existence, in human history. The 'Unity of Civilization' and the 'Unity of History' are misconceptions. Civilizations, for Toynbee, have only one point in common—they are a separate category from primitive societies. He likewise dismisses the idea that there is only one civilization, namely, the Western, as also the 'Diffusionist' theory that all civilizations had their origin in Egypt.[24] He charts the rise and fall of twenty-one 'Civilizations' or 'Societies' in six thousand years of history. Of these, fifteen are 'apparented' or affiliated to older or predecessor cultures of the same species, while the Egyptian, the Sumeric, the Minoan, the Sinic, the Mayan and the Andean have emerged direct from primitive life.[25] Again, some civilizations like the Egyptian, Babylonian and Minoan, are dead; others like Polynesian, Eskimo and Nomad, are arrested; while some – the Western Christian, Orthodox Christian, Islamic, Hindu and Far Eastern – are still alive.

Genesis of Civilizations

Toynbee asserts that the genesis of civilizations – the transition from a primitive or static to a dynamic society – owes neither to the race factor nor to the geographical environment as such. Civilization arises from the specific combination of two conditions—the presence of a creative minority, an elite; and an environment neither too favorable as to lead to lethargy and indolence, nor too unfavorable as to negate the necessary impulse to strive for progress. Given these, creation is an outcome of an encounter and genesis is a product of interaction.[26]

At this point Toynbee introduces his famous theory of 'challenge and response', the mechanism by which civilization is produced. All civilizations, according to Toynbee, have emerged from the interplay of challenges and successful responses to them. Challenge means a problem which a society confronts; response is the solution that it offers. Civilization rises when a society successfully responds through its creative minority to each of the series of challenges it confronts. A challenge may be presented by a profound physical change as the progressive desiccation of the Afrasian grasslands in which only one part of the inhabitants – those who retired to the marshes and the jungles of the Nile Delta – were able to evolve a civilization, the Egyptian civilization, by successfully draining the marshes and clearing the jungles. All other civilizations are likewise the response to challenges. Challenge and response is the rhythm of history.

Growth of Civilizations

It is wrong to imagine, Toynbee cautions us, that once a civilization is brought into existence, its growth would be a matter of course. Certain civilizations which achieved existence did not grow. They are cases of arrested civilizations such as the Polynesian, Eskimo and Nomad ways of life. Growth occurs when a response to a particular challenge is not only successful in itself but provokes a further challenge which again meets with a successful response. The Hellenic society, for example, had successfully met the challenge of chaos by settling down in cities rather than in villages. But the very success of the response exposed the Greeks to a second, this time, a Malthusian challenge of over-population. The challenge was met by expansion into a Magna Graecia, i.e., colonization around the eastern Mediterranean. But the expansion was stopped by non-Hellenic peoples and the problem of over-population still remained. In the case of Athens, the required response was made by Athenian statesmen who averted a social revolution by carrying through an economic and political revolution (the Solonian revolution). Now Toynbee argues that for the growth of a civilization, there must be what Bergson calls an *elan vital,* a creative minority, to carry that civilization from its birth through a series of challenges and successful responses.

The growth of a civilization is to be measured by its progress towards self-determination. This consists of a process defined by Toynbee as 'etherealization', which means progressive simplification of techniques—for example, as telegraphy with wires is replaced by telegraphy without wires. All growth originates with creative individuals or creative minorities.[27]

The action of the creative individual is a two-fold motion of

'Withdrawal and Return'—withdrawal for the purpose of personal enlightenment, return for the task of enlightening fellow men. The process is shown in practical action in the lives of great pioneers—St. Paul, St. Benedict, St. Gregory the Great, the Buddha, Muhammad, Dante. The law of Withdrawal and Return is true of creative minorities also. Toynbee cites the example of the behavior of the Athenians in the crisis into which Hellenic society had been thrown by the growth of population. When all Greece went on colonizing for two centuries, Athens hung back only to return as the leader of Greece in challenging the Persian empire. Italy had likewise drawn into herself for about two and a half centuries from the middle of the thirteenth to the end of the fifteenth only to equip herself spiritually to lead Europe in the Renaissance movement.

Decay or Breakdown of Civilizations

On Toynbee's showing, all except the Western civilization have either broken down completely or have shown signs of breakdown. He dismisses all deterministic explanations of the phenomenon of breakdown and rejects the economic interpretations of the decay of the ancient world.[28] Breakdowns of civilizations come by what is false within, by an inner malaise, by a process of suicide, when creative minorities exchange persuasion by compulsion and become 'dominant' minorities. Then the mass of the people – alienated and mindless proletariat – breaks out from the control of its guiding minority in a catastrophic schism and the society (civilization), losing the capacity for self-determination, enters on the road to disintegration.

Some of the ways in which the tragedy of suicide or of the loss of the capacity for self-determination presents itself are: (a) *the nemesis of creativity* of which a notorious example is the error of the Jews in idolizing their spiritual growth of discovering monotheism which persuaded them to believe that they were God's Chosen People. The same nemesis of creativity could be seen in the Hellenistic idolization of the city-state, and Athens's idolization of itself as 'the education of Hellas'; (b) *militarism* whose tragic irony is well expressed in the saying, 'They that take the sword shall perish with the sword.' Militaristic Assyria had been committing slow suicide and had become 'a corpse in the armour' by the time

Media and Babylonia struck their final blow (614–610 BC); Sparta's doom is typical of the Assyrian kind; and (c) the *intoxication of victory* of which an extraordinarily instructive example is the fall of the Hildebrandine Church with its ideal of a Christian Republic.

The disintegration period would be characterized by Schism in the Body Social and in the soul. The Schism in the Body Social shows itself in the presence of dominant minorities (militarists, legalists, administrators, philosophers), internal proletariats (religions like Christianity and Mahayanism), and external proletariats (barbarian invaders). The Schism in the Soul would be characterized by certain ways of feeling, behavior and life, such as abandon and self-control, sense of drift and the sense of sin, the sense of promiscuity issuing in vulgarity and barbarism in manners and art, confusion in language, syncretism in religion, archaism, futurism, detachment, and so on. In the disintegration stage, creative individuals appear as saviors of the disintegrating society. The Savior with the sword establishes a universal state, but all the works of the sword prove ephemeral.

A Study of History: Criticism and Assessment

Arthur Marwick writes: "Toynbee has been acclaimed by the reading public and denigrated by professional historians. In general, there is professional agreement that whatever Toynbee has written in *A Study of History*, it is not history."[29]

A Priori and Positivistic

Despite Toynbee's constantly repeated claim that his methods are exclusively empirical and inductive, they are, in fact, *a priori*. First establishing an *a priori* system, he made the facts fit. History is studied by means of certain general categories like interregnum or time of troubles, internal and external proletariats and Universal State and Universal Church; and general concepts like apparentation and affiliation, challenge and response, and withdrawal-and-return. This owes partly to the fact that *A Study of History* is, as Collingwood informs us, a restatement of nineteenth century historical positivism in the sense that its principles are derived from the methodology of the natural sciences. Toynbee's general conception of history is ultimately naturalistic—regarding the life of a society as a natural and not a mental life. The historian is the intelligent spectator of history in the same way in which the scientist is the intelligent spectator of nature. By reason of this positivistic stance Toynbee never reaches the conception of historical knowledge as the reenactment of the past in the historian's mind. History "is converted into nature, and the past, instead of living in the present, as it does in history, is conceived as a dead past, as it is in nature."[30] He fails to see that the historian is an integral element of the process of history itself, reviving in him the experiences of which he achieves historical knowledge. Professor A.L. Rowse sees in Toynbee's great work a sociological schematism which does harm to the rich unpredictable variety of history. He goes on to say that Toynbee imposes his pattern upon the subject, seeks to be a prophet and provides answers to contemporary problems. But this is neither the province nor the function of history. It is contrary to the nature of history to impose a thesis upon the facts. Thesis history, Rowse categorically states, is false history.

Theodicy, rather than a History

H.E. Barnes writes: "Toynbee's suggestive programme of comparing the rise and fall of civilizations was ruined by his extreme theological premises which made his work a theodicy, rather than a history."[31] His philosophy of history seems to be no more than the glorification of god and the higher religion. Great moments in history were to him not when empires were built or inventions took place, but those when great religions were born. If the first three volumes depict the rise and fall of civilizations as history pure and simple, the later volumes, especially those written after the Second World War, portray the cycles of social advance as informed by god's purposes and are marked by a kind of messianic revivalism. Of the creative individuals who are born into disintegrating societies to save them, Jesus alone has conquered death for he is God incarnate in Man! Toynbee seems to hold that civilizations are largely evolved by spiritual forces and that the eventual culmination of history will be the Kingdom of God.[32] Many critics complained that his conclusions were those of a Christian moralist rather than a historian.

Not Death, but only Change

In fact, Toynbee's very thesis of the rise, growth and dissolution of civilizations has been questioned. It is inconceivable for him that a civilization may develop into new forms while yet remaining itself. For him if a civilization changes it ceases to be itself and a new one comes into being. Now, do civilizations die completely? Is it not that they only change before their apparent dissolution? How then have we come to have the alphabet, the various techniques of control over physical nature, and the arts and the sciences long after their creators have gone? The heritage of culture is transmitted; it may change in form but not wholly in essence. Civilizations do not experience birth or death.

Determinism

In a debate broadcast by the British Broadcasting Corporation (BBC), Toynbee refuted the charge of determinism leveled against him by the Dutch historian Pieter Geyl. The fate of human civilizations, he pointed out, is determined by the manner of response to the challenge posed, and the response is not predetermined. Man has his freedom of will, freedom of choice. Finally, Toynbee's conclusions cannot claim universal applicability. By the time of his death in 1975 none of the central contentions of *A Study of History* was still credible among professional historians.

Merits

Criticism notwithstanding, the merits of Toynbee's great *Study* should not pass unnoticed. A great labor of scholarship, one is astounded by the incredible mass of erudition contained in it. Its workmanship, readability and even poetic quality have been admitted by all. Fritz Stern writes:

> The scholar boggles at it and sees the unsoundness of it, but he must also reckon with the reasons for Toynbee's success, and in passing he might be grateful that it was Toynbee, rather than another philosopher-prophet with less gentle philosophical commitments, who erected the most popular postwar system.[33]

Toynbee's monumental *Study* most sharply broke with the

tradition of a Eurocentric historiography. The manner in which he achieved a really universal history in the place of a narrowly Western-oriented history is all the more significant in the context of the rise to power of the nations of the underdeveloped parts of the world after the Second World War. Analyzing an impressive array of civilizations from the Polynesian to the Andean, and from the Egyptian and the Babylonian to the modern Western Christian, the British metahistorian triumphed over many a limitation of the conventional historian and captured the imagination of the reading public. The *Study* is a healthy counterpoise to the excessive specializing tendency of modern historical research. Finally, Toynbee's comparative study of civilizations can help men appreciate one another's histories and to see in them a common achievement and common possession of the whole human race. Arthur Marwick correctly assesses Toynbee's work in the following words:

> We do not have to swallow whole the entire mystic apparatus of the Toynbee system; but we can perhaps agree that, in such deceptively simple notions as challenge and response, Toynbee has in fact made a very genuine contribution towards our understanding of the past. Toynbee is perhaps a great poet, and a not-so-great historian; but in the mansion of history there are many chambers. It is as helpful to say that Toynbee 'is not a historian' as it is to say that Carlyle is not a historian: no less and no more.[34]

4. The Idealistic View of History

Benedetto Croce (1866–1952) and R.G. Collingwood (1889–1943)

Alongside the great philosophical edifices of history created by Spengler and Toynbee, there was also a philosophical reconsideration of the nature of history. The men who represented this trend were Benedetto Croce and R.G. Collingwood. These two men provided a philosophical justification of the relativist mood in historiography which had shown itself, particularly in America, at the beginning of the twentieth century.

One of the great self-taught students of history, Benedetto Croce was historian, humanist, and foremost Italian philosopher of the first half of the twentieth century. Croce served as minister of education in the Italian Government of 1920–21. An unbending and absolute opposition to Fascism made him the rallying point of all lovers of liberty. Croce published most of his writings and systematically expounded his 'Philosophy of the Spirit' in *La Critica*, a journal of cultural criticism which he had founded in 1903.

One part of the 'Philosophy of the Spirit' was history, which Croce held to be the mediational principle of all the moments of the spirit. This spirit, by which he meant human consciousness, is completely spontaneous, without a predetermined structure. Such is the essence of Croce's *History as the Story of Liberty* (1938). The consciousness of his role as the great moral teacher of Italy accounts for the unmistakable didactic character of his great historical works—*History of Europe in the Nineteenth Century, History of Italy from 1871–1915*, and *History of Naples*. Their lesson was intended for Europe and for the entire Western world. The new Italy, in its democratic form, was inspired by his spirit.

Croce wrote a number of philosophical essays on the nature of history. On the question of whether it was *the idea or the economic imperative, the ideal or the material* that was basic in social and historical studies, he firmly ranged himself on the side of the *ideal*. Insisting that historical and scientific knowledge are fundamentally different, Croce thought that the former was a kind of intellectual intuition.[35] History, he thought, becomes a reality only in the mind of the historian; "all history," in our philosopher's celebrated aphorism, "is contemporary history."[36] It means that the past (history) has existence only in the minds of the contemporaries, and that it consists essentially in seeing through the eyes of the present and in the light of its problems. Thinkers, in the exuberance of thought, sometimes lead themselves to untenable positions. Writes Arthur Marwick:

> Croce, however, was also convinced that historical thinking was also superior to all other kinds of thinking: the relativity of history was not a confession of weakness but an assertion of intellectual and imaginative power. As a historian of Italy Croce was perceptive and liberal-minded; as a philosopher of history he left a confusing legacy, which, in the arrogant

claims it made on behalf of the subject, perhaps restored some self-confidence to puzzled researchers in the age of relativity, but which did not contribute much to the development of historical studies.[37]

Croce was an important influence on Robin George Collingwood. A practising archeologist and historian of Roman Britain, Collingwood held a lecturership in history along with his Chair of Philosophy at Oxford. His *Religion and Philosophy* (1916) was a critique of empirical psychology and an analysis of religion as a form of a knowledge; while the *Speculum Mentis* (1924), a major work, proposed a philosophy of culture based on the unity of the mind and a synthesis of five forms of experience—art, religion, science, history and philosophy. But Collingwood's fame rests primarily on the important contribution he has made to the critical philosophy of history in *The Idea of History* (1945).

Historical Relativism

Based on the Crocean idealist position that all history is the history of thought, Collingwood's pamphlet of 1930, *The Philosophy of History*, contained an elaborate justification of historical relativism. The contention that history is the creation of the historian, Collingwood is aware, is apt to make it arbitrary and capricious, yet he underlines the subjective element in all history in the sense that every age, every man, sees in a particular historical event things which another does not. The pamphlet ends with a fine exposition of the Crocean notion that all history is contemporary history; "every age," writes Collingwood, "must write history afresh."[38]

History as Reenactment of Past Thought in the Historian's Mind

Collingwood's *The Idea of History* proposed history as a discipline in which the historian relives the past in his mind in the context of his own experience. The philosophy of history is concerned neither with "the past by itself", nor with "the historian's thought about it by itself", but with "the two things in their mutual relations."[39] That is the meaning in which the word at present is used. "The history of thought, and therefore all history," Collingwood wrote, "is the re-enactment of past thought in the historian's own mind."[40] A natural process, he contends, is a process of events, an historical process is a process of thoughts. Man is the only subject of historical process since he is the only animal that thinks, and thinks enough to render his actions the expression of his thoughts. But all human actions are not subject matter of history.

> ...so far as man's nature is determined by what may be called his animal nature, his impulses and appetites, it is non-historical; the process of these activities is a natural process. Thus the historian is not interested in the fact that men eat and sleep and make love and thus satisfy their natural appetites; but he is interested in the social customs which they create by their thought as a frame-work within which these appetites find satisfaction in ways sanctioned by convention and morality.[41]

By discovering the thought expressed in an event, the historian comprehends the cause or causes of that event. Collingwood explains that the cause of an event for the historian means the thought in the mind of the person by whose agency the event came about. That thought is the inside of the event, its cause.[42] Unlike the scientist, the historian is only concerned with those events which are the outward expression of thought. Historical knowledge is the knowledge of what man has done in the past, and at the same time it is the redoing, the reenactment of the past—the perpetuation of past acts or events in the present.[43]

As E.H. Carr observes, overemphasis on the role of the historian in the writing of history tends to make history subjective – history as what the historian makes of it – ruling out any objective history at all. Likewise, Collingwood's undue reliance on thought in his analysis of the nature of history has been criticized. Yet Arthur Marwick seems to be a bit too harsh on him:

> Everyone interested in history should know something of Collingwood's ideas. But it must be stressed again that he does not stand in the mainstream of the development of historical studies: full of deep insights, he is no sure guide to what historians actually do or how they think.[44]

The work of Croce and Collingwood did much to instill confidence into the wavering, doubtful mind of the twentieth century historian. *The Idea of History* has vastly improved our understanding of the subject, and its author's attempt to integrate history and philosophy has been recognized as a significant scholarly contribution. Convinced of the importance and dignity of history, Collingwood wrote in his autobiography that we might be standing on the "threshold of an age in which history would be as important for the world as natural science had been between 1600 and 1900."[45]

10

THE TWENTIETH CENTURY II

PART I

1. Historical Relativism

Bury in his later years had in fact come a long way from his Rankean positivist position to one which may be termed 'relativist'. He held that the most 'scientific' history had little chance of being 'ultimate' as new ages adopt different interests and attitudes. In 1910, Carl Becker had in an essay challenged the positivist pretensions of *Cambridge Modern History.* Becker held that no history could make a permanent contribution to knowledge and that historical synthesis could be true only "relatively to the needs of the age which fashioned it."[1] J.B. Black in his study of the Enlightenment historians, *The Art of History* (1928), observed that since historical events cannot be observed directly, they must always be seen indirectly "reflected, so to speak, in the mirror of the present."[2] More than these suggestions a clear theory of historical relativism was being formulated in America in the works of J.H. Robinson and C.A. Beard which deliberately stressed the present-mindedness of history and urged that it must be written with the needs of the present in mind. Historical relativism received its most thorough-going exposition during the inter-war years when Einstein's theories (which held that the 'aspect of things' changed with the position of the observer) combined with a growing skepticism and disillusionment were at the height of their influence. To Beard the aspirations of the scientific historians was only a 'noble dream' while Konyers Read was convinced of the relativity of all history.[3]

J.H. Robinson (1863–1936), C.A. Beard (1874–1948), and Carl Becker (1873–1945)

James Harvey Robinson, an effective teacher at the Pensylvania and Columbia universities, was one of the first to feel dissatisfied with the exclusively political, constitutional and military emphasis of nineteenth century historiography, its neglect of vast areas of human experience, and its lack of relevance to contemporary problems. He sought to replace it with a New History, through his many widely-used textbooks which set forth the intellectual and social trends of a particular age. In his crusade for this 'New History' Robinson could enlist the support of many contemporary historians, the most notable of whom was Charles A. Beard, who collaborated with him on a two-volume text, *The Development of Modern Europe* (1907–08). An outstandingly gifted scholar and one fascinated with the economic aspects of history, Beard wrote the stimulating *An Economic Interpretation of the Constitution* (1913), and the penetrating study, *Economic Origins of Jeffersonian Democracy.* Beard "saw the fathers of the American Constitution as realistic appraisers of man's economic instincts, rather than as liberal-minded idealists."[4]

Preface to 'The Development of Modern Europe'

In their Preface to the two-volume *The Development of Modern Europe*, Robinson and Beard observed that a common defect of historical manuals was their failure to connect the past with the present in right proportion. What is the use of a history which gives preference to the organization of the Achaean League to that of the modern German Empire, or bestows more attention on Charlemagne than on Bismarck? Perspectives have to be readjusted. The authors announced that in their own book they had consistently subordinated the past to the present by laying greater emphasis on more recent history without prejudice to that of remoter periods; and this to enable the reader to catch up with his own times, to read intelligently the foreign news in the morning newspaper.[5] Again, purely political and military events, they said, had been given much less space to accord generous treatment to the more fundamental economic matters and even to the general advance of science.

The New History

Robinson wrote in *The New History* (1912) that "The present has hitherto been the willing victim of the past; the time has now come when it should turn on the past and exploit it in the interests of advance."[6] The New History was to be deliberately present-minded in the sense that it would be immediately useful in explaining the present. In standard outlines and handbooks of history used in schools and colleges the question of selection and proportion is sadly neglected. Robinson illustrates the point from one of many such books where the author, in treating the Italian Renaissance, had chosen barely to mention Francesco Petrarch, but had devoted a twelfth of the available space to the interminable squabbles of southern Italy. The historian must select from among the events those which illustrate some profound historical truth. There is a simple principle by which the relevant and the useful may be determined and the irrelevant rejected: "Is the fact or occurrence one which will aid the reader to grasp the meaning of any great period of human development or the true nature of any momentous institution?"[7] The New History was consciously intended to meet the daily needs of the reader, an aim which would call upon it to avail itself of all those discoveries about mankind made by anthropologists, economists, psychologists, sociologists and scientists—discoveries which have served to revolutionize our ideas of the origin, progress and prospects of the human race. The term 'New History' emphasizes the fact that history should not be regarded as a stationary subject and that it is bound to alter its ideals and aims with the general progress of society.

While Robinson and Beard were crusading for a history that would immediately be useful in explaining the present, Carl Becker, another American historian, was engaged in developing a sub-history—intellectual history. All the three agreed on a relativist view of history. Becker owed to German intellectual historians the idea that each age can be distinguished by a specific mode of thinking, 'a climate of opinion'.[8] Becker's abiding interest in political ideas led him to write two intellectual histories; one of his own country, *The United States: An Experiment in Democracy* (1920), and the other of the Enlightenment thinkers: *The Heavenly City of the Eighteenth Century Philosophers* (1932).

2. Economic History

The increasing concern with the social and economic factors of life visible among the intellectual classes in the late nineteenth and early twentieth centuries, particularly in Britain, owed to the problems of the spreading Industrial Revolution and the emergent Marxian thought. To the already developing pattern of mass democracy were now added modern trade-unionism and the ideas of Socialism in Fabian, Syndicalist and Communist forms. A combination of these factors produced an increasing awarness of the decisive influence of economic developments upon society. Arnold Toynbee's (Sr.) *Lectures on the Industrial Revolution* (1884) highlighted the paradox of a great increase in wealth bringing in its wake an enormous increase in pauperism and poverty, and free, competitive production on a vast scale leading to a rapid alienation of classes. The other problems attending industrialization – recurrent slumps and migration to cities – were targets of criticism from the intellectual Left, particularly the Fabians. Interest in economic history was driven forward by the increasing availability of economic and demographic statistics. The new concern showed itself in a move away from event-based political history, *staatengeschichte*, on which the nineteenth century had almost exclusively concentrated. Also there was now a shift in interest from the individual to the masses.

Although quarantined for some time as a non-discipline, by the beginning of the twentieth century economic history gained institutional recognition in England, France and America. In 1892 the Harvard University appointed the English scholar, William James Ashly, to a chair in economic history. George Unwin's deep-rooted affection for England's common people led to an interest in social and economic history exemplified in *The Industrial Revolution of the Sixteenth and Seventeenth Century* (1904). The German, Werner Sombart's *War and Capitalism* (1913) emphasized the part played by war in stimulating eighteenth century industrialization.

Henri Pirenne (1862–1935)

Henri Pirenne, Belgium's greatest historian, was, says Arthur Marwick, "in every sense a *complete* historian".[9] He was an educator, one of the most eminent medievalists, and a great scholar of Belgian national development. From 1886 to 1930 Pirenne taught at the University of Ghent. He was imprisoned by the Germans (1916–18) for refusing to teach while they occupied Belgium. Pirenne died in 1935.

To Marwick, Pirenne is an example of how a historian's environment influenced his approach to the past. Belgium did not have an independent political existence till after the 1830s, but her towns had a long commercial and economic existence reaching back to the eleventh and twelfth centuries. Not surprisingly, Pirenne started not from political history but from a study of economic institutions.

Pirenne's greatest work, the seven-volume *History of Belgium* (1899–1932) won him international respect. The respect owed to (a) his innovative approach to socioeconomic development in town life and (b) for his contention that Belgian unity was not the result of ethnic identification or political centralization; rather it resulted from the position of Belgium as a centre of industrial and intellectual commerce between Latin and Germanic nations. Among his many other works was one of popularization, *The Economic and Social History of Europe*.

The Pirenne Theses

The first of Pirenne's two celebrated theses contended that the medieval European cities originated in the wake of the revival of trade in the eleventh and twelfth centuries. The thesis first appearing in articles published from 1893 onwards, took its final form in 1925 in *Medieval Cities: Their Origins and the Revival of Trade*. The work was a classic analysis of the revival of urban centers and commercial activity during the late Middle Ages. But a greater controversy that engaged Pirerne's attention was how and why the classical ages gave way to the Middle Ages. The full exposition of his famous thesis on this issue was published after his death in *Muhammad and Charlemagne* (1937). Based on a study of economic rather than on political institutions, the celebrated thesis argued that the Roman Empire and civilization declined not as a result of Germanic invasions but rather because of Arab primacy in the Mediterranean in the eighth century. The medieval European civilization began only with the Carolingians. "Without Muhammad," wrote the great Belgian historian, "Charlemagne would have been inconceivable."[10] Subsequent researches have challenged both the theses as well as Pirenne's almost exclusively economic interpretation of causation in history. However that may be, Pirenne and his followers permanently broadened the channels of medieval history which was more and more becoming a true 'social history'.[11]

George Lefebvre (1874–1959)

Arthur Marwick writes: "If the origins of modern professional history lie in the nineteenth century Germany, the greatest advances, unfortunately all too readily ignored in other countries, have been made by a select few in twentieth century France."[12] One of these few, George Lefebvre, evolved "a quantitative and finally a quasi-psychological approach to history."[13] To the importance of scholarship in history he added a new dictum: *Il faut compter*, that is to say, "It is necessary to count." Leftist and working class in his political leanings, Lefebvre accepted the existence of the class struggle and employed Marxism in historical analysis in a liberating and creative manner.

Lefebvre emphasized the economic and social aspects in history. His greatest work, *Peasants of the North during the French Revolution* (1924), is a study in depth of the French peasantry during the Revolution. To Jean Jaures and Albert Mathiez, the French Revolution was the work of a triumphant bourgeois class. Lefebvre added a new dimension to the character of the Revolution by bringing to the fore the part played by the peasants. He took pains to show that there was a "true peasant revolution which had an autonomy of its own in its origins, development, its crises, and its tendencies."[14] If till the fall of the Bastille on 14 July 1789, the bourgeoisie was disposed to attack neither the clerical tithes nor the feudal obligations, the peasants had begun to rise against the seigneurs as early as the month of March (1789) and to refuse to pay their seigneurial dues. On receipt of the news of the events in Paris, they revolted spontaneously, taking their cause into their own hands—to the great discomfiture of the bourgeoisie who in several places took it upon themselves to suppress the risings. And the point which Lefebvre particularly insists on is that the peasant revolution was most autonomous in its anti-capitalist tendencies. In *Agrarian Problems at the Time of the Terror* (1932), Lefebvre attempted to apply to history the insights of social psychology. He in fact believed that in the future, historians will have increasing use of discoveries in sociology, social psychology and social anthropology.

Sidney Webb (1859–1947) and Beatrice Webb (1858–1943)

Economic history benefited, particularly in Britain, by the growing interest the intellectual classes were showing in working-class movements and in socialism. An early and active member of the Fabian Society (1885) and one of the leading intellectuals of the labor movements, Sidney Webb had already expounded his gradualist views in *Socialism in England* (1880). Equally devoted to the cause of the working classes was Martha Beatrice Potter who had in 1891 published *The Co-operative Movement in Great Britain*. In 1892 the kindred spirits married. The Webbs' lifelong crusade for social justice found intellectual expression in great collaborative works which were authoritative treatises on social and economic history: *History of Trade Unionism* (1894), *Industrial Democracy* (1897), and *English Local Government* (1906–1929) in 10 volumes. The singular aim of these books was to establish the social facts upon which to base social reform. The Webbs played an increasingly influential role in guiding the intellectual development of the Labour Party. In 1932 they visited Russia to study the Soviet way of life. The two-volume book which they published in 1935, *Soviet Communism: A New Civilization?*, expressed admiration for Russia's economic planning but dislike for its system of government.

J.H. Clapham (1873–1946)

The greatest among the economic historians of the English speaking world, Sir John Harold Clapham, pursued his academic career as a lecturer and professor of historical and economic subjects at the Cambridge, Leeds and London universities. The founding father of academic economic history, Clapham's methodology was empirical. Of the new discipline he wrote:

> Economic history is a branch of general institutional history, a study of the economic aspects of the social institutions of

> the past. Its methodological distinctiveness hinges primarily on its marked quantitative interest; for this reason it is or should be the most exact branch of history.[15]

The economic historian must perforce have the statistical sense, inquiring the quantity of the subject of study and the duration involved.

Clapham's first book, *The Woolen and Worsted Industries* (1907) was published in Leeds, the centre of the textile trade. In 1921 appeared a major work, *The Economic Development of France and Germany, 1815–1914*. He was now to devote himself to his greatest work, *An Economic History of Modern Britain*, published in three volumes between 1926 and 1938. Never had the subject been dealt with on such a grand scale. Clapham was more concerned with innovation, industrialization and production than with the social aspect of industrialization; yet he challenged certain legends given currency by social historians like the Hammonds. The legend that 'everything was getting worse for the working man', Clapham attributed to the way in which social historians had ignored the work of statisticians on wages and prices.[16]

But the position he took in the great standard-of-living controversy, and his explanation of population increase as due to falling death rates, says Marwick, would now not be accepted by many historians employing more sophisticated methods.

R.H. Tawney (1880–1962)

Richard Henry Tawney was a social theorist and economic historian of vision, who was also moved by a moral fervor. His connection with the Labour Party and his participation in the adult education programs directly involved him with the working class movement. He spent many years at Oxford teaching and writing; in 1919 he moved to the London School of Economics to teach economic history.

Tawney's *The Agrarian Problem in the Sixteenth Century* (1912) studied the decline of the English peasantry – the once proud 'yeomen of England' – and the unscrupulous rise of the gentry. The book in a way set the historical scene for his emerging critique of contemporary society. He endeavored to know why wealth-making had failed to bring social harmony. *The Acquisitive Society* (1921) outlined his thesis that society had become morally 'sick', unethical and misery ridden. The author made the subtle point that the emergence of liberalism and secularism had freed capitalism of all moral restraints. The mad, capitalist rush for wealth had divorced economic life from its moral context turning members of society into a means to the end of acquiring wealth. Tawney's most famous work, *Religion and the Rise of Capitalism* (1926) drew inspiration from the German sociologist Max Weber's two famous articles on 'The Protestant Ethic and the Rise of Capitalism'. Whereas Weber had established a direct connection in the order of cause and effect between Protestantism and the spirit of capitalism, Tawney's work merely suggested "some of the associations between Protestant ethics and capitalist enterprise and giving full weight to the exceptions and anomalies."[17] The work is said to have influenced Maurice Dobb, the Marxist economist and economic historian. Tawney's methods of historical investigation are often rejected now because he did not stress the use of statistical data. But he did draw attention to the ethical basis of social science. As philosopher of the British Labour Party he worked towards the establishment of social democracy.

3. Social History

A branch of study that stands closest to economic history is social history. Fabian socialists and liberal–radical intellectuals took a prominent part in creating the subject in Britain between the late nineteenth century and the Second World War. Arnold Toynbee's efforts in projecting the harsh effects industrialization had had on the lower classes were continued by J.L. and Barbara Hammond in their pioneering studies: *The Village Labourer* (1911), *The Town Labourer* (1917), and *The Skilled Labourer* (1919). They were all attempts to study the Industrial Revolution in terms of its impact on the working classes. Toynbee and the Hammonds concluded that change into mechanized production had only harmed the working class. *The Village Labourer* analyzed the changes in rural England from the sixteenth to the twentieth century and was a searing indictment of the landlord classes and the policies which destroyed the pre-industrial village; and *The Town Labourer* took a pessimistic view of the social consequences of industrialization in the growing urban areas. Elie Halevy's masterly treatment of most departments of English life in *The English People in 1815* is another important effort in social history. The writings of R.H. Tawney, Sidney and Beatrice Webb, Eileen Power and H.N. Brailsford shaped the continuing identity of this branch of history. G.D.H. Cole and Raymond Postgate's *The Common People* (1938) is an important work in the direction, and E.P. Thompson's *The Making of the English Working Class* is one of the most eloquent expressions of this concern. The works of these authors are primarily concerned with the condition and movements of the lower classes. Different in manner and treatment, Trevelyan's *English Social History* (1944) became very popular. Trevelyan's description of his subject as 'the history of the people with the politics left out' created much misunderstanding and led some people to think of his book as 'polite chat about the past'.

In Germany, Karl Lamprecht's thorough volumes on the cultural development of the German people represented a kind of social history. In France, Marc Bloch's *Original Characters of French History* (1931) tried to explore the intrinsic relationship between man's physical setting and his social institutions, while his *Feudal Society* (1939–40) as an attempt to understand medieval European society has few equals and no superior.[18] He founded with Lucien Febvre the journal *Annales of Economic and Social History.*

4. Some Eminent Professional Historians

The vast majority of practising historians – professionals – whom it is difficult to categorize and group remained unaffected by the new trends and movements in historiography. They continued more or less in the old nineteenth century fashion "to deal exclusively with constitutional and political matters, continued to put the patient accumulation of facts above sweeping interpretation, the study of documents above the use of tools borrowed from other disciplines."[19]

Theodor Mommsen (1817–1903)

Except for three years of his long life Theodor Mommsen belonged to the nineteenth century; yet in a sense he represented a new epoch, a decisive move forward. It is told that this slight, sparrow-like figure, when held up by robbers while travelling in Italy in a party, indignantly told the chief brigand, 'Sono Theodoro

Mommsen!' ('I am Theodoro Mommsen!') and that he suddenly found himself hailed as a hero! Most likely it was Mommsen's fame as the author of the *History of Rome*, and as the scholar who had placed the study of the Roman past on an unshakable foundation that impressed that cultivated brigand.

Deeply committed to liberalism and German nationalism, Mommsen took a firm stand against Treitschke's anti-Semiticism, defending academic freedom from political interference. By far the greatest historian of the positivist age, he was like Maitland a great master of detail, having at his disposal vast masses of carefully sifted material of incredible accuracy collected in obedience to the positivist spirit of ascertaining historical facts. Qualities which Mommsen thought indispensable for a historian were a knowledge of law, linguistics and literature, and an adequate perception—an inborn genius which sees meaning and connections in the complexity of history. He himself possessed these qualities to an extent unsurpassed by any other modern historian.[20]

Mommsen's scholarly output was prodigious. A bibliography of his works lists 1500 items. But the work for which he was universally acclaimed was the *History of Rome* (1854–56) in 3 volumes, a work on which could be traced the influence of the author's own political experience. Using a variety of sources including inscriptions, laws and coins, Mommsen reconstructed the history of the Roman republic from its origins to the rule of Julius Caesar. The treatment exceeded in scope anything that had been done before. But the great history ended at the Battle of Actium. Explanations have been given why Mommsen did not take his history beyond the fall of the republic, explanations emphasizing the present-mindness of history writing. Disillusioned by the muddles and humiliations of the German revolution of 1848–49, Mommsen yearned for a strong man to save Germany from ruin. Hence his idealization of Caesar. But the strong man had not appeared in Germany and nothing, says E.H. Carr, inspired Mommsen to project this problem back on to the Roman scene, and the history of the empire remained unwritten.[21] Or was it his antipathy to autocracy that prompted him to stop?[22] But the artist, the philosopher, and the scientist had united in Mommsen in creative harmony to make the three written volumes a literary masterpiece which won the Nobel Prize in 1902.

In 1885 appeared the monumental *Provinces of the Roman*

Empire from Caesar to Diocletian. It rested on another of Mommsen's finest achievements, his editorship of the *Corpus of Latin Inscriptions*, a collection of Roman epigraphic evidence of lasting significance. His most influential work was the *Roman Public Law* (1871–88), with the later addition of the *Roman Criminal Law* (1899).

F.W. Maitland (1850–1906)

Like Mommsen, Maitland belonged for the most part to the nineteenth century. Some regard him as the greatest English historian. Maitland derived the methods of his profession from the nineteenth century but improved upon them. He published his masterpieces between 1890 and 1900, but those works are still constantly in use.

Maitland's first noteworthy publication was his edition of *Bracton's Note Book* (1895). Bracton was a thirteenth century English lawyer but Maitland's interest in law was informed by a deep perception of social and economic necessities. As Trevelyan remarked, Maitland used medieval law "as the tool to prise open the mind of medieval man."[23] His *History of English Law to 1272* (1895), written in collaboration with Frederick Pollock, is still a standard work. Maitland's insistence on the importance of asking questions was an improvement in method unknown to the nineteenth century Rankean tradition. And anticipating the regressive techniques of the *Annales* school, he recommended working "backwards from the known to the unknown, from the certain to the uncertain."[24] This was precisely the counsel he followed in his epoch-making venture into the social and legal history of early England, *Domesday Book and Beyond* (1897). A professional *par excellence*, Maitland was meticulous and punctilious in his use of sources, preoccupied above all with the problems of *analysis*. All professionals adhered to two of his many aphorisms. History, he said, is a "seamless web"; and "the only generalization is that there are no generalizations." Maitland was a brilliant stylist, but not at all interested in the writing of historical *narrative*.[25]

H.A.L. Fisher (1865–1940)

H.A.L. Fisher is another fine example of a professional historian. A distinguished British educationist, a liberal statesman and Cabinet

Minister (1916–18), Fisher contributed to Acton's *Cambridge Modern History* on the French Revolution. He also wrote two volumes of the *Medieval Empire*, and three on Napoleon, but is best remembered for his two-volume *History of Europe* (1935) from neolithic man to Hitler. The work is, as Professor Marwick remarks, a miracle of compression. Fisher's statement in the preface to this work is the position most professionals have adhered to:

> One intellectual excitement has, however, been denied me. Men wiser and more learned than I have discerned in history a plot, a rhythm, a predetermined pattern. These harmonies are concealed from me. I can see only one emergency following upon another as wave follows upon wave, only one great fact with respect to which, since it is unique, there can be no generalizations, only one safe rule for the historian: that he should recognize in the development of human destinies the play of the contingent and the unforeseen. This is not a doctrine of cynicism and despair. The fact of progress is written plain and large on the page of history; but progress is not a law of nature. The ground gained by one generation may be lost by the next. The thoughts of men may flow into the channels which lead to disaster and barbarism.[26]

Lewis Bernstein Namier (1888–1960)

Sir Lewis Bernstein Namier, a Polish Jew by origin, ranks second only to Maitland among the greatest of British professional historians. Namier read history at Balliol, Oxford, before the First World War. He astonished the historical world by the publication of his two greatest works, *The Structure of Politics at the Accession of George III* (1929), and *England in the Age of the American Revolution* (1930). A.J.P. Taylor has likened the publication of *The Structure of Politics* to the publication of Darwin's *The Origin of Species.* Professor Hale would call the present age in historiography as the 'Age of Namier'. But this academic acclaim failed to gain for Namier a much-desired post at Oxford, and it was much later that he was appointed to a chair at the University of Manchester.

Critique of Whig Interpretation

The Structure of Politics, writes Marwick, was "the greatest single contribution made by a twentieth century scholar to British historical study, and, arguably, one of the most important contributions to the development of historical methodology."[27] *The Structure of Politics* and the *Age of the American Revolution* together demolished the myth popularized by the Whig historians that the misguided George III had attempted – through a vast central machinery of corruption, and in the teeth of the heroic resistance by the Whigs – to establish a personal monarchy in the place of the constitutional monarchy established by the revolution of 1688. By intensive research, Namier, the Tory historian, aimed at showing that the part played by the lofty political ideals which Whig historians loved to flaunt was very little and that the reputed corruption of the power held by the central government was insignificant, and that the corruption that did exist was necessary to the smooth running of the government. Again, he denied the claim that the political disputes of the 1760s revolved round two organized parties, Whig and Tory. In explaining why men entered politics Namier rejected the simple classification of Whig and Tory in favour of personal, family or regional interests. It was self-interest and personal ambition that impelled men to take to politics.

Namier also wrote on the 1848 revolutions and on the diplomatic origins of the Second World War. The massive *History of Parliament* was a collaborative work, while his *Charles Townshend* is a psycho-analytical study based on a mass of unsorted manuscript material.

The Namier Method

Namier's reputation rests as much on his methodology as upon his particular conclusions. To understand how the parliamentary or the political machine worked, Namier examined its component parts and their functioning. To support this technique of *structural analysis* he adopted a relatively new technique of historical enquiry, namely, *prosopography* or collective biography.[28] Discarding the abstract ideals and generalizations of political philosophers and relying on the selfish motivation of human beings, the conservative historian got down to the individual unit and collected evidence on the life, career, connections and behavior of every single Member of Parliament. The quantitative evidence thus acquired was used to test stringently the factors which may have motivated the political actions of an individual or group. Composition of the House of Commons, the electoral process, and the impact of vested interests, and personal grievances of the MPs—were for Namier objects of close study. The results of this rather biographical technique were then welded together into a composite portrayal of the age. As he worked deep into the subject, the historian knew what questions to ask and when to ask them.[29] Namier's works are works of analysis rather than of narration.

Assessment

A legend in his own lifetime, Namier gave his name to a school of historians and a historical method. Those who followed his method included Richard Pares, J.E. Neale and Norman Gash. But it may justly be complained that the method in question, though capable of producing fruitful results, atomizes history. Namier relied too much on Freudian psychology and held a very cynical view of human nature. He went too far in denying that there was anything questionable in the conduct of George III. His technique of structural analysis inevitably ended in elevating personal ambition, petty intrigue and family connections above political principles, public opinion, or party ideology. Namier overemphasizes self-interest as the prime motivating factor in human action and sees all ideas as mere rationalization of selfish conduct. It is a position difficult to agree with.

Friedrich Meinecke (1862–1954)

The giant among German historians of the twentieth century is Friedrich Meinecke. His long life witnessed Germany's triumph in 1870–71 and her tragedy in the two world wars. A student in Droysen's course in historical method and an early admirer of Dilthey, Meinecke tried to broaden historicism by bringing it closer to the philosophical revival of the nineteenth century.[30]

Ever interested in political ideas – in intellectual history – Meinecke, in his two most important historical works, broke with the prevailing genre of political and institutional history. The first of the two, *Cosmopolitanism and the National State* (1908), established Meinecke as one of Germany's leading historians. Its theme was how cosmopolitanism, with its universal morality, had to give way to the concept of *Realpolitik*—policies which best served the interest of the state. Germany's astounding defeat in 1918 turned Meinecke bitter and disillusioned. Thus in the second of his great histories, *Machiavellism* (1924), the author questioned his own earlier assumptions about the state. He traced the idealization of power from the time of the Medicis to the calamity of 1914 by which time, according to Meinecke, the application of Machivellism had reached the danger mark in Germany. Both the works were different in method and treatment from the prevailing type of political and institutional history. Meinecke chose the more readable biographical form, describing the changing attitudes of influential conservatives in the nineteenth century to the concept of the German state.[31] Thus by analyzing the historically most important ideas of the leading statesmen and political thinkers, Meinecke reinterpreted several epochs of modern German history. In his eighty-fifth year he published his last and best known work, *The German Catastrophe* (1946). German defeat in the Second World War had been so catastrophic that Meinecke in this work attempted a historical explanation of the German collapse exhorting his countrymen to return to the humanistic and cosmopolitan ideals of Goethe and his age.[32] From his early veneration for power and the state the great historian had turned to the abiding values of culture.

Meinecke's monumental *The Origins of Historicism* (1936) in two volumes is an analysis of the origins of the kind of historical consciousness which found its fullest expression in Ranke. The work ends with the historical thought of Goethe. In the essay, 'Values and Causalities in History' (1928), he wrote that the two great tendencies acting in unison in history are the search for causality and the comprehension of values. "The search for causality in history," wrote Meinecke, "is impossible without reference to values; the comprehension of values is impossible without investigation of their causal origins."[33] But so shattered were his spirits that in the *German Catastrophe* Meinecke was prone to attribute historical events to blind inexorable chance!

The manner of writing *Ideengeschichte* (history of Ideas or intellectual history) has been criticized as being narrowly intellectualistic in approach and neglectful of the general historic conditions of society.[34] Meinecke is a controversial figure, but his influence as cultural historian was profound.

Trevelyan (1876–1962)

The last of the Whig and literary historians, George Macaulay Trevelyan was the grandnephew of the great Macaulay and the son of George Otto Trevelyan. In 1927 he succeeded J.B. Bury as Regius Professor of Modern History at Cambridge.

Trevelyan's first book, *England in the Age of Wycliffe* (1899) presented that period as a critical one in the evolution of religious and political liberty. In 1904 came an enormously successful textbook, *England Under the Stuarts,* which ran to more than twenty editions. The remarkable trilogy on Garibaldi and Italy which came between 1907 and 1911 glorified the virtue of nationalism. These early works established Trevelyan as one of the best known of British historians. His *British History in the Nineteenth Century* (1922) and *History of England* (1926) were again bestsellers. In the early 1930s came another trilogy, *England in the Age of Queen Anne.* Written against the background of his family, this was Trevelyan's finest and maturest work, an outstanding achievement by any standard of historiography. It is in the tradition of the Whig interpretation of history begun by Macaulay. Trevelyan's last major work, *English Social History,* published at the end of the Second World War, was different in conception and treatment from the usual type written by historians. Pundits have raised their eyebrows at the author's definition of his subject as "the history of the people with the politics left out."[35] The definition is casual and inadequate, but the work itself is not, as some have dubbed it, 'polite chat about the past'; it is a vivid survey of the evolution of English society from Chaucer to Queen Victoria. Social history, as conceived by Trevelyan, has

> its own positive value and peculiar concern. Its scope may be defined as the daily life of the inhabitants of the land in past ages: this includes the human as well as the economic relation of different classes to one another, the character of family and household life, the conditions of labour and of leisure, the attitude of man to nature, the culture of each age as it arose out of these general conditions of life, and took ever-changing forms in religion, literature and music, architecture, learning and thought.[36]

But all was not well for the great author. Namier had in 1929 and 1930 published two great volumes, which not only dented the main theme of Trevelyan's Romanes lectures of 1926 – the continuity of party history – but advocated structural analysis as an alternative to sterile narrative.[37] Then, in 1931, came Herbert Butterfield's *The Whig Interpretation of History* with its strictures on historians who took sides in history. Professional historians, among them Kitson Clark, felt that Trevelyan did not address himself to the right questions.[38] And critics assailed the *English Social History*; the reviewer in *History* complained of an "absence of any satisfactory intellectual construction...a lack of analysis."[39] Arthur Marwick thinks of the *English Social History* as Trevelayn's "greatest disservice to historical studies".[40] Trevelyan's remark to his brother in 1939 that he was a mere survivor indicates the gulf that had grown between himself and others of the profession.

All this may be true, and some may feel that Trevelyan had overemphasized the literary aspect of history. But his success with the general reader was phenomenal. Four hundred thousand copies of the *English Social History*, that 'polite chat about the past', was sold in five years—people at large reading history! Trevelyan's success owed chiefly to his Whig glorification of English virtues which suited the prejudices and beliefs of the upper and middle classes in twentieth century Britian.[41]

Setting aside such overpraise of English virtues, none can doubt his deep involvement with the past and the love that he brought to its study.

5. Modern Empiricists

The British historians who succeeded to Namier's legacy of skepticism Marwick calls 'modern empiricists'. Their work in general is characterized by a belief in the complete autonomy of history; a common-sense unwillingness to accept any dogmatic theorizing and innovations in historical study; belief in the centrality of the political theme and institutions; distrust of facile generalizations and a disposition to research into the realities behind them; a stress on the irrational, the unexpected, the unpredictable, the contingent and the unique; emphasis on documental sources; inclination to revise previously held views; awareness of the importance of quantification in history writing; and skepticism about the possibilities of human control over human destinies.

Marwick remarks that the post-Namier empiricist movement in historiography was a Tory movement so completely negative as to take all purpose out of the study of history.[42]

Kitson Clark

George Kitson Clark (b. 1900) is a professional and revisionist historian. He exploded the contention of the Anti-Corn Law League, active in England in the 1830s and 1840s, that it was the great landed interests that had mainly opposed the repeal of the protectionist Corn Laws. Kitson Clark showed that it was the tenant farmers who were most strongly in favor of protection.

Kitson Clark inspired and sponsored a vast wealth of first-rate scholarly research. Adopting politics as an organizing element, his disciples conducted meticulous research in each case to unravel the 'background'—the economic, social, literary and military conditions. The empirical approach was stressed by reducing general statements to the minimum. But knowing that a strictly empirical course may obscure the whole view of anything, works of synthesis were also provided. Such are Kitson Clark's two invaluable studies of the nineteenth century, *The Making of Victorian England* (1962) and *An Expanding Society: Britain 1830–1900* (1967). The opening chapters of the former book entitled 'The Task of Revision' contains advice and warnings to scholars against sweeping explanations and attribution of an economic motivation to everything. Indignation, however honest, Kitson Clark regards as "a dangerous passion for historians." The most important task of revision, he informs us, is "to rescue real men and women who have been shrunk by historians into the bloodless units of a generalization, or have become the ugly depersonalized caricatures of partisan legend or modern prejudice."[43]

Modern empiricists in general stress the appeal of the irrational. Kitson Clark writes that "in order to understand the springs of action it is important to understand the emotions, the irrational feelings, the prejudices, the experiences which form men's minds."[44] Typical also of the empiricist approach is the acceptance of the need to quantify, to submit to the 'discipline of arithmetic', though not beyond a certain limit. Kitson Clark insists upon the value of popular literature as a guide to contemporary life. And valuable are the two books he has written on the nature and methods of history:

Guide for Research Students Working in Historical Subjects (1960), and *The Critical Historian* (1967). The second of the two makes an impassioned plea for the most exacting critical standards in history. This is because history has utility—the influence that it has on men's life and mind makes it obligatory for us to know as near as possible what actually happened.

G.R. Elton

G.R. Elton (b. 1921) adorned the chair of constitutional history in the University of Cambridge. A revisionist like Kitson Clark, Elton stressed the abrupt nature of certain phases of historical change and emphasized the *discontinuous* nature of Tudor administrative history. The 'Elton thesis', first adumbrated in the late 1940s, found its fullest statement in *The Tudor Revolution in Government* (1953). Elton advanced his thesis of a revolution which in the 1530s, equipped England with a modern, national bureaucracy which could function, and provide political security, irrespective of the personal qualities of the monarch and his deputies. Elton, the empiricist, believed that the motor of historical change is "individuals working in a somewhat unorganized and haphazard manner," and he attached a rather undue importance to Henry VIII's secretary, Thomas Cromwell, who is described as "the most remarkable revolutionary in English history".[45] In the true empiricist fashion Elton elevates the political element in history. In the preface to his textbook *England under the Tudors* (1955), he wrote that what counts for most in history is the history of government. Periodization in history is a problem and labels like 'medieval' and 'modern', though not very meaningful, are convenient terms. Elton's *Reformation Europe* is a good example of a work in which the analytical and the narrative elements in history writing are harmoniously blended. A brilliant stylist, he is only too conscious of the importance of the communication aspect of history writing.

Elton, the true professional Tory historian, is no lover of innovators and metahistorians and those who advocate indiscriminate borrowing from other disciplines. In *The Practice of History* he strongly defends the autonomy of history which has developed a professional expertise all of its own. Truly understanding an age from the inside is a task which the professional historian performs best. Thoughts and ideals are secondary to him; it is action that interests Elton, the historian.

A.J.P. Taylor (1906–1990)

A professional historian of worldwide reputation, A.J.P. Taylor was skeptical and distrustful of theory and was empirical in method. Non-conformist and unconventional, Taylor advanced in his *Germany's First Bid for Colonies 1884–85* (1938) the stimulating thesis that Bismarck's bid for colonies was designed to provoke a quarrel with Britain in order that he could draw closer to France. Refusing to see late nineteenth century imperialism as a purely economic phenomenon, he viewed it rather as a projection of European conflicts.

Taylor's *Bismarck*, stretched the element of the fortuitous and the unexpected in history. Bismarck's achievement, on Taylor's showing, was not the result of a fully worked out plan, but that of an opportunist with a genius for turning events to advantage. The book cannot be accepted *in toto* for there is proof of greater forethought and planning in Bismarck's policies than Taylor allowed for. Taylor's *The Hapsburg Monarchy, 1815–1918* (1941), and *The Course of German History* (1945), observes Marwick, are characterized by strong anti-German bias verging on war propaganda.[46] His interest in diplomatic history culminated in his major survey of the subject, *The Struggle for Mastery in Europe 1848–1918* (1954). A second major survey volume was *English History 1914–1945* in which is found most apparent Taylor's rare personal quality of intuition. To the same category belongs *The Origins of the Second World War* (1961), Taylor's best known and most controversial book. This was because it challenged many orthodox views about the 1930s. Taylor wrote that "it is not part of the historian's duty to say what ought to have been done. His whole duty is to find out what was done and why."[47] True to the professional empiricist tradition, Taylor is seen emphasizing diplomatic sources, stressing the significance of contingency and accident as against advance planning. Denying that *Mein Kampf* was a valuable guide to Hitler's actions, our historian tried to show that the Nazi dictator, instead of following any precise, coherent plan, was only exploiting events and situations. In Taylor's opinion the foreign policies of Hitler and Stalin were traditional and not diabolical. The destruction of the Hitler legend was a duty performed not as "a vindication of Hitler" but as "a service to truth".[48] In many ways the book forces a reappraisal of previously held convictions. Taylor's *The Trouble Makers: Dissent over Foreign Policy 1792–1939* is the book which the author loved most of all his works. It is a collection of lectures given on his radical heroes.

In the writing of history Taylor regards the element of communication as important as research. The historian must

> hold listeners or win readers. For, although history may claim to be a branch of science or of politics or of sociology, it is primarily communication, a form of literature....The historian has to combine truth with literary grace; he fails as a historian if he is lacking in either.[49]

The witty Taylor wrote history in a style and manner of presentation unequalled in his own time.

Philosophy of History

If Taylor has a philosophy of history, it is skeptical and empiricist, and which stresses the irrational, the unpredictable and the unique. History, like poetry and music, has no special utility. In his review of Eric Hobsbawm's *Industry and Empire* he wrote that "things happen because they happen." With inadequate data the historian cannot be sure of what has happened in the past. The skeptical Taylor writes:

> Much of the evidence on which we could base our knowledge of the past has been destroyed or never was recorded. We guess from the few remaining fragments much as a geologist reconstructs a prehistoric monster from a single bone...experts and governments have only the vaguest idea of what has happened and no firm idea of what is likely to happen. There is little chance therefore of our reaching any very solid conclusions about early times when no reliable figures existed and there is not much information of any other kind. The only safe generalization we can make about man's record was propounded by Anatole France: 'He was born. He suffered. He died.' History is the great school of scepticism.[50]

Hugh Trevor-Roper (b. 1914)

The other historian of post-war Britain who comes close to Taylor in reputation is Hugh Trevor-Roper, Regius Professor of Modern History at Oxford from 1957 to 1980.

Archbishop Laud, written when the author was only twenty-seven years of age, is a sympathetic but critical biography of the conservative High Churchman. The book has remained a standard work ever since. In 1947, appeared *The Last Days of Hitler* which is a brilliant reconstruction of the exact circumstances of Hitler's death. It has remained a bestseller. *Hitler's Table Talk* (1953) and the *Borman Letters* (1954) were scholarly editions of important Nazi documents. *The Rise of Christian Europe* (1965) is a series of lectures delivered at the University of Sussex and broadcast over the BBC television. Trevor-Roper discovers a 'general crisis' throughout Europe in the middle decades of the seventeenth century which formed the central theme of an important collection of essays under the title *Religion, Reformation and Social Change* (1967). One of the problems studied in this work is 'The European Witch-craze of the Sixteenth and Seventeenth Centuries'. Likening this craze to the twentieth century anti-Semitism of the Nazis, Trevor-Roper has warned against any facile belief in a steady human progress towards greater rationality.[51]

The Controversialist

Trevor-Roper enjoyed historical controversy. R.H. Tawney's article entitled 'The Rise of the Gentry, 1558–1640' had explained the conflicts of the English Civil War in terms of a declining aristocracy of landowners and a 'rising gentry' of agricultural capitalists, merchants and industrialists. Against this Trevor-Roper published in 1953 his own thesis, 'The Gentry, 1540–1640', in which he espoused the view that it was not so much the rise of the gentry as the decline of a part of it which explains the outbreak and the course of the English Civil War. This part of the gentry which was declining and was mostly of puritan outlook left without royal gifts and patronage or the spoils of law and trade, rose in anger against the corrupt, centralizing 'Court'. While Tawney's view was open to criticism, Trevor-Roper's arguments did not find widespread acceptance among historians.

Primacy of European History

Trevor-Roper may not believe in a steady human progress towards greater rationality, yet the idea of progress does loom large in his historical thinking. The philosophical basis of his rejection of any African history is that life in 'dark countries and dark centuries' provides subject matter for anthropologists and sociologists, not for historians. Again, every age *cannot* be equal in history. This is because history is a movement and a purposive movement, and tribes that have not advanced in civilization cannot have history; if all history is equal, there is no reason why we should study one section of it rather than another.[52] Trevor-Roper has no doubt about the primacy of European civilization in the modern age and he defended European history against the growing preoccupation with African, Asian and Latin American history:

> The new rulers of the world, wherever they may be, will inherit a position that has been built up by Europe, and by Europe alone. It is European techniques, European examples, European ideals which have shaken the non-European world out of its past; out of barbarism in Africa, out of far older, slower, more majestic civilizations in Asia; and the history of the world for the last five centuries, in so far as it has significance, has been European history. I do not think we need make any apology if our study of history is Europe-centered.[53]

6. British Marxist Historians

A small group of Marxist historians in Britain represented a move away from the Tory empiricists. A.J.P. Taylor had gone to the extreme of holding that 'things happen because they happen.' Against this the Marxists sought to demonstrate the meaningful interconnectedness of events. The particular achievement of the Marxists, according to Arthur Marwick, "has been to bring 'the people' back into history; not in the old vague romantic way, but in a manner which makes exhaustive use of every available source and every new methodology."[54]

Christopher Hill (b. 1912)

Born in a Methodist family in the north of England and converted to Marxism at College, Christopher Hill's preoccupation as a historian derived directly from his religious and political non-conformity. Hill found Marxism a valuable tool in the critical analysis even of metaphysical poetry. His historical writings of the 1940s, says Marwick, exhibited a crude Marxist standpoint, but "the books published in the fifties and sixties – *Economic Problems of the Church (*1956*), Puritanism and Revolution (*1958*), Intellectual Origins of the English Revolution* (1965) – will undoubtedly hold a permanent place in the historiography of the English Revolution."[55]

Hill's first widely admired work came in 1956, *Economic Problems of the Church*, which readjusted perceptions of the Reformation permanently. His textbook *The Century of Revolution* (1961) was a very sophisticated Marxist history linking social, economic and political issues in a manner new to school teaching. *Puritanism and Revolution* presented – in the place of the older conception of a 'Puritan Revolution' – a new synthesis of the English Civil War. Asserting that men's ideas were not a pale reflection of their economic needs, Hill explained the English situation:

> The connections of religion, science, politics and economics are infinite and infinitely subtle. Religion was the idiom in which men of the seventeenth century thought...it cannot be ignored or rejected as a simple reflex of economic needs. Any adequate interpretation of the English Revolution must give full place to questions of religion and church government, must help us to grasp the political and social implications of theological heresy."[56]

The Intellectual Origins of the English Revolution, as the name itself suggests, refutes the general belief that the English Revolution had no intellectual origins. Hill has a positive conception of the place of ideas in the historical process. He insists that there can be no revolution without ideas, but ideas are not made by intellectuals. The historian must attach equal importance to the circumstances which gave these ideas their chance. Any body of thought – Luther's, Rousseau's, Marx's own – becomes accepted and grows in popularity because it meets the significant needs of the society in which it comes into prominence. Men challenge conventionally accepted standards only when they have an alternative body of ideas to support them.[57] Echoing Marc Bloch, Christopher Hill calls for a history embracing the total activity of society.

Hill's books had gone very well with the academic world until in 1974 J.H. Hexter made his fundamental attack upon Hill's method of writing history. This was followed by that of the 'revisionist' school of seventeenth-century historians who rejected his view of the period.

E.H. Hobsbawm (b. 1917)

The best known Marxist historian of his generation, Eric Hobsbawm taught history at the Birkbeck College, London, from 1947 for the rest of his career. Hobsbawm's abiding interest in the history and the future of the working class took him to the study of the impact of the Industrial Revolution on the British working class. It was followed by the study of the upper working class, the aristocracy of labor. He did not glorify working class culture seeing it as a reflection of poverty under oppression. Hobsbawm was a founder member of *Past and Present.*

Hobsbawm's 'General Crisis of the European Economy in the 17th Century' is an essay on what the author believes to be "the last phase of the general transition from a feudal to a capitalist economy."[58] Hobsbawm's three works proclaim his special interest in 'the people': *Primitive Rebels: Studies of Archaic Forms of Social Movement in the Nineteenth and Twentieth Centuries* (1959), *Labouring Men* (1964) which is a work about the 'working classes as such', and *Captain Swing* (1969), a collaborative work with George Rude, which rescues the great and moving story of England's last agrarian rising of 1830 from oblivion. And Marwick attests that no textbook is a more flawless example of total history than Hobsbawm's *The Age of Revolution 1789–1848* (1962).

E.P. Thompson (b. 1917)

The works of Edward Palmer Thompson, Britain's leading Marxist historian of the post-war era, have aroused both intense admiration and vigorous criticism. Thompson thinks historical knowledge to be provisional, incomplete and approximate, yet he is determined to write history from the 'bottom up' and rescue the laboring poor "from the enormous condescension of posterity."[59] Thus came many stimulating and challenging writings about class consciousness, class struggle and class formation; about the law as an ideological weapon in the hands of the ruling class; and about the motives of the poor who took direct action to protect their concept of justice and rights. Thompson's perceptive imagination has led to a number of original insights into the lives of ordinary people.

The Making of the English Working Class

Thompson achieved world fame with his *The Making of the English Working Class* (1963). The central thesis of the eight-hundred-page book is the growth of a specifically working class consciousness. Class, our author insists, is not a 'structure' nor a 'category' but a 'historical phenomenon' which actually happens in human relationships: "when some men as a result of common experiences (inherited or shared), feel and articulate the identity of their interests as between themselves, and as against other men whose interests are different from (and usually opposed to) theirs."[60] Thompson devoted considerable attention to the impact of growth of agrarian and industrial capitalism in terms of the social, moral and cultural experience of the poor. Where economic historians were content to assess the quantitative gains of the Industrial Revolution, Thompson sensitively explores the qualitative losses. It is "neither poverty nor disease but work itself which casts the blackest shadow over the years of the Industrial Revolution."[61] The great French historian Elie Halevy's celebrated thesis had asserted that the spread of Methodism had saved England from revolution in the early nineteenth century. In a far more subtle analysis Thompson brought out another historical nuance of the Methodist movement: Methodism could act both as an agent of the *status quo*, and as an *agent of inspired political protest.* Marwick comments that

> *The Making of the English Working Class* is a true work of historical revisionism bringing into proper perspective the aspirations and conscious efforts of working people, too often treated by other historians as an inert and faceless mass, passive to the central forces of history.[62]

Thompson's abiding interest in 'the people' found institutional expression in the Centre for the Study of Social History launched at the University of Warwick. Here he promoted a whole new approach to the study 'from below' of earlier British society particularly in the matter of crime and law enforcement.

Thompson's critics have pointed out that he is not always rigorous in his scrutiny of evidence, that he relies too much on inferences, conjectures and hearsay, that some of his arguments go beyond what his evidence will bear, that his view of class is too subjective, and that he both reads the present into the past and uses historical examples to inspire contemporary struggles.[63]

PART II: TOWARDS TOTAL HISTORY

1. Lucien Febvre (1878–1956), Marc Bloch (1886–1944) and the *Annales* School

During the French Enlightenment Voltaire and Montesquieu had challenged the idea that history was a narrative of the deeds of individual political actors, in favor of a more philosophical account of the past. This eighteenth century 'new history' focused its attention on the manners, customs and beliefs of whole peoples, and the broad patterns of their social and cultural development. A more radical attempt was made about the middle of the twentieth century, again in France, to displace political history from the centre of historical attention. The two men who took the first concrete steps in the direction of a fuller and richer history of man's life in society were Lucien Febvre and Marc Bloch. Already, Henri Berr (1863–1954) had founded the journal *Review of Historical Synthesis* (1900) and planned the hundred-volume *Evolution of Humanity* with the object of bringing together in one great synthesis all the activities of man in society. The great project was to employ the methods and insights of sociology and the other sciences.

The meeting of Lucien Febvre with Marc Bloch at the Strassbourg University after the First World War was a germinal event for twentieth century historiography. Febvre had served in the French army during the war before his appoinment at Strassbourg. With a fertile mind responsive to ideas, he had heard lectures on geography, sociolinguistics, and iconography; he admired Burckhardt, and from reading Marxists like Jaures, had developed an interest in economic struggle; he owed his life-long interest in social psychology to Henry Wallon and Charles Blondel; and he was deeply influenced by Vidal de la Blache's human geography which led him to study history in terms of interaction between the physical and the social worlds. In his enthusiasm for a new kind of history based on an interdisciplinary approach, Febvre found a kindred spirit in Marc Bloch. From Levy-Bruhl the two developed the notion that beyond individual thinkers and their particular expressions of value and belief lay patterned systems of thought – mentalities – which differed radically from age to age; and following Durkheim, the two historians accepted the primacy of the social and the collective in the lives of historical agents.[64]

Leopold Benjamin Marc Bloch was born into a Jewish family at Lyons. Like Febvre he served in the French army during the First World War, received Croix de Guerre for bravery, and was admitted to the Legion of Honour. In 1919 he was appointed to the chair of medieval history at Strassbourg where he was with Febvre till 1936 when he moved to a chair of economic history at the Sorbonne and Febvre to the College de France in Paris. On the outbreak of the Second World War, Bloch was soldier again and personally experienced the French defeat in 1940. In 1943 he joined the French resistance against German occupation, was captured and, after much brutality at the hands of the Gestapo, was executed by a firing squad in 1944. Bloch was patriot, soldier, scholar and historian in whose life the past was not separate from the present. A martyr for liberal humanist virtue, he became a powerful symbol for the immediate post-war generation. Febvre lived on in Rio de Janeiro and inspired later historians like Braudel, who carried on the *Annales* tradition.

Sources: Comparative and Regressive Methods

Bloch did not wholly depend on archival sources and traditional methods of historical inquiry and shared with his colleague Febvre an interest in geography and collective psychology. He sought to borrow from sociology an exactness of method and precision of language; he studied archeology, agronomy, cartography, folklore and linguistics, and employed economic theory and statistical methods in historical investigation. Cardinal to his inquiry procedure was the asking of the right kind of questions first, and seeking around for any scrap of evidence of any kind which may provide answers. He was an early believer in both the comparative and the regressive methods.

> Comparative study...involving comparisons within a single country or between different countries, is of immense value, since in highlighting both similarities and differences it can be a source of new syntheses, new questions and, sometimes, convincing answers. The regressive method involves using evidence drawn from a later age of matters—customs, traditions, place names, field patterns—which may well have endured from an earlier age, in order to illuminate that earlier age.[65]

New Approach

Strassbourg provided Bloch and Febvre with what Peter Burke in *The French Historical Revolution* (1990) describes as "a milieu which favoured intellectual innovation and facilitated the exchange of ideas across disciplinary frontiers."[66] The two historians set their face against the tradition of nineteenth century historiography with its sole emphasis on politics and individual events. Nor did they, and following them the *Annalistes* (*Annales* historians), think that history could be satisfactorily recreated from a patchwork of particular facts. They were vehement in their criticism of narrative histories—what Braudel was to dubb 'the history of events'. In fact, the problem-oriented approach of Bloch and Febvre to historiography, and their attempt to answer big questions by thematic examination of structural change would not fit neatly into a narrative form. They thought that the historian could enhance the knowledge of the past if only he showed a readiness to draw freely from sociology, geography, psychology and economics. Yet, this did not mean any disregard of documents or of scholarly concerns, and both historians insisted on the highest standards of impartiality. To uncover the lives of the peasants, even legal and monastic records were opened, as such records were not consciously meant for posterity, and in which the lives of the state and the real people intersected, as during inquisitions and court cases. The history which Bloch and Febvre wrote was "a history which was open to the social sciences, problem-oriented and analytic rather than a mere story of events, and concerned with economic, social and cultural life as well as with politics."[67]

Febvre's Works

Febvre's first important work, *The Regions of France: Franche-Comte*, was mainly geographical in content. In 1911 appeared *Philip II and Franche-Comte.* A work built upon extensive researches, it emphasized the economic and social history of the region at the expense of the political. Febvre's dissatisfaction with monocausal explanation led him to demonstrate what he called "the multiple action of profound causes."[68] His *The Earth and Social Evolution* (1922), a general work written for Henri Berr's multi-volume series, was a study which rejected Ratzel's geographical determinism but recognized the importance in history of geographical factors. One of the many important points which the author made in this book was that rivers, instead of making 'natural frontiers', serve in fact to bring human groups together in common activities. Febvre's interest in what he himself called 'historical psychology' first manifested itself in his *Martin Luther* (1928). The treatment was so innovative as to make the book a trend-setter. Though on appearance a biography, it was really a study of 'social necessity'—of the links between men and groups. Febvre brought the study of individual and group mentality in bygone ages to a consummation in *The Problem of Unbelief in the Sixteenth Century* published just after the Second World War. A classic, the work was a study of the religious milieu of Rabelais relating a particular intellectual event to the structural conditions for its occurrence—in this case its non-occurrence:

> He argued that it was anachronistic to attribute atheistic beliefs to Rabelais and his contemporaries since the absence of certain linguistic and conceptual tools from their mental resources imposed limits on their capacity to disbelieve.[69]

Bloch's Works

The very first book of Marc Bloch, *The Island of France* (*Paris and the Five Surrounding Departments*) (1913) written when the author was twenty-seven, marked a departure from traditional historiography. In it an account of the soil, the language, the archeological remains and architecture took the place of the usual narration of events. Then came in 1924, *The Royal Touch*, a seminal work and a classic of the twentieth century. The book had path-breaking qualities. It was an inquiry into the medieval belief in the ability of kings to cure the skin disease scrofula or 'the king's evil' just by touch. Bloch was attracted to the theme by his interest in collective psychology, particularly the manner in which the irrational imposes patterns on human behavior. Bloch showed that this supernatural power attributed to royalty in England and France was an important element in maintaining the strength of monarchy in the two countries. But Bloch's investigations into the nature of feudal society formed his main contribution to historical study. That he was disposed to view that society from the standpoint of the peasants rather than of lords and kings had been shown clearly in a short work, *King and Serfs: A Chapter of Capetienne History*. Then came in 1921 a far greater work and a most helpful and thorough-going book of the generation, *French Rural History: An Essay on its Basic Characteristics*. It is a social history of medieval rural France. Henry Loyn writes that Bloch gives a realistic and intelligent picture of the flow of agrarian life in France from its known beginnings to the time of the Revolution. All the new techniques of research were employed to make a successful synthesis of French agrarian life in its varied aspects, whether the shape of the field, the nature of the plough, the harnessing of plough beasts, the evolution of watermill and windmill, field-systems, manuring, and, so on.[70] An admirable piece of historical exposition, *French Rural History* tells us of the disappearance of slavery and the modifications in serfdom. Continuing the innovative work, Bloch published in 1940, *Feudal Society*—the book for which he is now most famous. Drawing upon many types of sources and employing many methodologies, the work is an analysis of the structural relationships which linked society, economy, politics, technology and the psychology of the feudal world. The author's main theme is social change in time.

Historian's Craft

One gets a close insight into Bloch's idea of history from the unfinished manuscript of a book which he left behind and which was published in English as *The Historian's Craft*. Arthur Marwick has described the book as a "very human testimony to a personal faith in history, and a manifesto on behalf of the most advanced school of historical writing of the inter-war years."[71]

The introduction discusses the uses of history and its position among the sciences. Apart from its poetry, history's greatest use is that it aids understanding, and without understanding men cannot act reasonably. The human and social need for history lies in its ability to guide human conduct. History is "a science in infancy...."[72] When even the natural sciences have moved from a position of certainties to one which is more flexible, historians have nothing to feel diffident of the uncertanties of their own task. Bloch hoped to see ever-increasing numbers of historians "arrive at that broadened and deepened history"—the history as conceived by the *Annales* School.[73]

The book contains four chapters and a fragment of the fifth. Defining history as "the science of men in time,"[74] Bloch hastens to stress its aesthetic and humane quality. History is as different from the other sciences as the task of a lute-maker is from that of a drill operator. While the drill operator uses precision tools, the lute-maker is primarily guided by his sensitivity to sound and touch. It is unwise for either to adopt the method of the other.[75] The splitting of history into periods, though convenient, is misleading.

In the first chapter Bloch, like Collingwood, treads the idealist path and regards history as a serious science of men in time, studying the dead and the living, and understanding the present by the past and the past by the present.[76] The "faculty of understanding the living is, in very truth, the master quality of the historian."[77] In the second chapter, on 'Historical Observation', Bloch looks forward to a time when historians, better equipped with linguistic and social-science techniques, will engage in cooperative historical research. The third chapter, 'Historical Criticism', deals with problems of forgery, reliability of records, and the like. Besides enabling the historian to detect fraud and error, it is the critical method that gives the historian his standing as a scientist. In the fourth chapter, Bloch affirms his abiding interest in group psychology. The book closes with an unfinished fragment on causation where preference is shown for Febvre's idea of multiple causation. *Dilexi veritatum* (I have loved truth), was the epitaph Bloch desired to have.

Annales of Economic and Social History (1929)

What Bloch and Febvre aimed at and what they tried to achieve in their own works was a more 'total' and a more 'humane' integrated history—a history more truly representative of the richness of man's life in society. Such a history would draw upon many types of sources and employ many methodologies. The great vehicle for this broader history was the famous journal which they jointly launched in 1929, *Annales of Economic and Social History*, known thereafter as *Annales.* Since such a wide-ranging, total history is beyond the grasp of any one individual, many were to be engaged in analyzing particular aspects of society. A highly innovative venture, the *Annales* movement assumed the proportions of a revolution in historiography.

The first editorial committee of the *Annales* consisted of scholars of different disciplines. In their introductory address to the readers, Bloch and Febvre referred to the gulf which had developed in historical and social studies. The walls that separated them were so high as to hide each other's view:

> While historians apply their good old hallowed methods to the documents of the past, more and more people are devoting their activity to the study of contemporary societies and economies....It is against these deep schisms that we intend to raise our standards....Brought together here, scholars in different disciplines and different specialities, all motivated by the same spirit of exact objectivity, will present the results of their researches in subjects which they have chosen and in which they are expert....Our enterprise is an act of faith in the exemplary virtue of honest labour, backed by solid and conscientious research.[78]

The *Annales* today is probably the most prestigious of all historical journals. With its aim of a more total and more humane history, interdisciplinary approaches, trust in analysis as the key to unlock the reality of the past, fresh methodologies and new conceptual models—the *Annales* tradition gave rise to a school of better historical writing.

2. Fernand Braudel

In Fernand Braudel (b.1902), a protégé of Lucien Febvre, the *Annales* vision of 'total history' came to realization. Bloch and Febvre had written such history for only parts of the past, but

Braudel's venture of recapturing human life in all its variety succeeded in his masterpiece, *The Mediterranean and the Mediterranean World in the Age of Philip II* (1949). A classic, it is the greatest historical work of the twentieth century which instantly raised its author to the top of the French historical profession.

The *Mediterranean* was written in twenty years including the Second World War years which Braudel had to spend in a German prison camp. Already a massive work containing 600,000 words when first published in 1949, it has subsequently been enlarged! It is sought to be an answer to the increasing fragmentation of history. James A. Henretta aptly describes the *Mediterranean* as "a comprehensive, multi-dimensional cubist portrait of the society."[79]

Influences behind the Mediterranean

The post-war *Annales* historians always acknowledged a debt to Febvre and Bloch. "What I owe to the *Annales*, to their teaching and inspiration," wrote Braudel, "constitutes the greatest of my debts."[80] In its ideas and plan of construction, the *Mediterranean* owed much directly to Febvre's *The Earth and Human Evolution* and *Philip II and Franche-Comte.* Starting from the physical environment, the three works move on to economic and social structures and end with a narrative of events. It was to Febvre, his mentor, that Braudel dedicated his *magnum opus* with "the affection of a son". And of Bloch, Braudel said, "I think I can honestly say that no aspect of his thought is foreign to me."[81] The two were alike in their concern with long-term historical trends and in their love of comparative history. The sociologist Emile Durkheim's idea of the superficiality of the history of events and the human geographer de la Blache's social and historical geography were common sources of influence and inspiration for Febvre, Bloch and Braudel. And from Jules Michelet, the French master, the historian of the *Mediterranean* learned to indulge his gift for poetic images, and to write of regions as if they were persons.[82]

Sources

The *Mediterranean* is written on such an immense scale that it is idle to expect the same kind and quality of documentation (in the traditional sense) for the whole. Peter Burke writes that "a large part of the work of the greatest historian of our time is based on secondary sources. It is not in finding evidence but in using evidence that Braudel excels."[83] Part Three, the most conventional part of the great work, is solidly based on documents from the archives of Rome, Genoa, Florence, Paris, and above all from Simancas, where the Spanish state papers are kept. Part Two, according to Burke, is simply illustrated from archive material, while the main source for the geohistory of the Mediterranean (Part One) is the landscape itself.

View of Time and of Historical Change

Braudel is a problem-oriented historian in line with the *Annales* conception. *The Mediterranean* had as its guiding principle a new conception of time, and of historical change in relation to space. The author makes the reader conscious of the impact of space by "making the sea itself the hero of his epic,"[84] and also by repeatedly reminding him of the importance of distance, of communications, in an age when many goods traveled at the pace of mules and it often took two weeks to sail from Marseilles to Algiers. But it is in the treatment of time that Braudel is most original. He argued that historical time is multi-layered, each layer having its own pace or rate at which change occurs in its various phases. His conviction that historical time does not move at a uniform speed is expressed in its division into long-term, medium-term, and the short-term: "geographical time, social time, and individual time."[85] Braudel organized his immense work into three such time-layers or phases, each layer or phase typifying a particular approach to historical delineation. In such a mould of space and time, Braudel tries to see things whole on a global scale, and crossing the disciplinary frontiers, integrates the geographical, economic, political and the cultural into a 'total history'.

Part One of the *Mediterranean,* which is the bottom layer of Braudel's three-phased history, spans the immense, timeless phase of human interaction with the natural world. What the author provides here is what he himself calls 'geohistory'—a kind of historical geography devoted to mountains and plains, islands and coastline, climate, land routes and sea routes. Here, man is in intimate relationship to the earth which bears and feeds him. At this level, which Braudel calls *la long duree* (the long run or the long-term), time is almost stationary or moves at the slowest pace because distance was a reality and communications difficult. This bottom level has "a history whose passage is almost imperceptible, that of man in his relationship to his enviornment, a history in which all change is slow, a constant repetition, ever-recurring cycles."[86] In this span of longest duration, the historian needs the perspective of centuries in order to discern any change at all.

In Part Two of the *Mediterranean,* Braudel distinguishes an intermediate pace of change which he calls the time of *conjoctures* (conjunctures). This is the medium-term or time taken by the broader movements of economies, social structures, political institutions, civilizations and forms of war, which constitute the subject matter of this second phase. Here the duration is that of cyclical movements in prices and wages; the rhythms and phases of demographic, technological and social change; and the trends and tendencies of trade and exchange. Such phases last for five, ten, twenty, perhaps fifty years. Changes in this phase of *structures* have to be studied in terms of *structural changes* in other departments of life. Changes in the policy of Spain, for example, need for their proper comprehension, changes in the government's financial resources.

Part Three of the *Mediterranean* is concerned, after the traditional pattern, with 'events, politics and people'. These take the shortest time span. This is the time sector of political events in history as we understand them, and of individual actors in their various engagements—the fast-moving time of micro-history and the usual concerns of the traditional historian. A fine piece of traditional political and military history of the Mediterranean area in the age of Philip II, Part Three is a substantial work in its own right.

The key to the whole work lies in the hierarchy of relationships between the three time-layers. The collective destinies and general trends of the second (middle) layer operate within the context set by geography and the ever-recurring cycles. The individual actions and political events which form the top layer, operate within the constraints established in the bottom and middle layers. Braudel believed that this decisive reversal of priorities based on a pluralistic view of time, the slow-paced history of structures in particular, was capable of making a vital contribution to social theory.

Relative Unimportance of Events and Individuals

In Braudel's multi-dimensional history events and individuals suffer, so to say, a diminution of stature. In Part Three of the *Mediterranean*, dealing with 'events, politics and people', the author places both individuals and events in a wider context with the aim of revealing their fundamental lack of importance relative to that of environmental factors. The history of events, although "the richest in human interest," is also the most superficial. They are "surface disturbances, crests of foam that the tides of history carry on their strong backs."[87] As with events, so with individuals, particularly great men behind whose intention, choice and determination are forces which are separate from them but which fashion what they do. Real history escapes those who fail to recognize these structural forces which fashion the actions of great men. The failure of Don Garcia de Toledo, Philip II's naval commander in the Mediterranean, and his slowness of action against the Turks, according to Braudel, must be seen in terms of the very difficult environmental conditions in which he had to operate. Don John of Austria, the victor of the naval battle of Lepanto, was 'the instrument of destiny', in the sense that his victory depended on factors which he did not know about. The great battle of Lepanto which the Christians greeted as a glorious victory was, for Braudel, an example of the limitations of the history of events; the Christian victory could not destroy the roots of Turkish power which went deep into the surrounding land masses.

3. A Criticism of the *Mediterranean*

The frightening immensity of the *Mediterranean* makes one feel that 'total history' is impossible beyond the local level as, for example, in Ladurie's *The Peasants of the Languedoc*. Braudel's overarching plan and its execution did not fail to invite criticism.

Neglect of the People as Negation of Historical Process

A serious drawback of Braudel's great history is its comparative neglect of the people. The American humanist–socialist historians Eugene and Elizabeth Genovese find fault with Braudel for failing to allot the people their correct place in his history, and making geography – the Mediterranean region itself – its crucial component. They point out that "the people who inhabit this earth do not fare so well in the story," going on to say that Braudel's great work, with its "structural interpretation, with its anthropological, ecological and archaeological predilections, implicitly negates the historical process itself."[88]

Diminished Status of Political History

True to the *Annales* tradition which had never taken political history seriously, Braudel gives to the *Mediterranean* a mould which, if anything, is not political. Though Part Three of the *Mediterranean* deals with political events, and Part Two contains chapters on empires, the author chose not to give political events their due importance. Indeed, historians of the traditional stamp criticized the *Mediterranean* as history with the politics left out. The neglect of politics in a history which claimed to be 'total' is open to question.[89]

Dethronement of the Individual

The dethronement of politics and of events from their place of importance in Braudel's history meant the dethronement of political and military leaders from their place of eminence. If individuals and events are incapable of breaking the structures that constrain them, how can the structures themselves change?

> Some historians are highly suspicious of Braudel's concern with 'collective destinities and general trends' which they see as impersonal forces producing an almost inhuman history. As John Eliot once put it, Braudel's Mediterranean is a world 'unresponsive to human control.' Just how important are individual decisions or events? This, of course, is one of the oldest debates in the history of history, the debate between those who believe that men make their own history and those who think that fortune or providence or climate or economic trends play a greater role.[90]

Absence of Link between the Three Layers of Time

In Braudel's history we often fail to see a link between the three-tier conception of time. Braudel himself believed that geo-history, social history, and the history of events are all so causally linked that at any given moment we should be able to see them operating simultaneously. But the references in Part Three of the *Mediterranean* to the constraints under which individuals like Don Garcia de Toledo operated do not conclusively prove the point in all other cases. In Le Roy Ladurie's *The Peasants of the Languedoc* we see the way in which the peasants became conscious of the constraints and rebelled against them. Says Peter Burke: "Such a link between structures and events can be found for one social group in one region; it may be asking too much to expect anything comparable in a history of the whole Mediterranean world."[91]

Neglect of Mentalities

Again, Part Two of the *Mediterranean* is criticized for its relative neglect of a favourite *Annales* area of study—collective mentalities or beliefs, attitudes and values of past ages. Braudel is a brilliant historian of material culture, but despite his commitment to 'total history', he has, unlike Febvre and Bloch, little to say about non-material aspects of human life even in the chapter entitled 'Civilizations'. Beliefs did matter in the age of Philip II, but we do not know from Braudel's work whether, for example, Catholic and Muslim beliefs interacted. Social anthropologists have discovered that the concept of honor is a dominant part of the value system in Algeria as in Spain, in Sicilian and Turkish villages.[92]

Static Geohistory

The great trouble Braudel took with geographical history did not save Part One of the *Mediterranean* from criticism. An anonymous reviewer in the *Times Literary Supplement* wrote of insufficient attention paid to animals and plants and their effects on the human and natural environment. Instead of giving us a more dynamic ecohistory, what Braudel has given us is static geo-history.[93]

Determinism

Again, the exaggeration of environmental constraints on human life exposes the *Mediterranean* to the charge of determinism, of "reducing men to inevitable defeat in their natural world."[94] This environmental determinism is different from the economic determinism of the Marxists. Like Febvre and Bloch, Braudel is unwilling to assert the predominance of the economic factor even in the long-term. Like them, he stresses the interaction of economic, social, political and cultural factors. However, the *Annales* group shares the Marxists' interest in structures and the desire to penetrate the surface of events in search of an underlying historical reality.

Braudel fails to offer an alternative conception of historical change to Marx, and his work cannot claim to have the dynamism of Marx's base–superstructure philosophy.[95]

4. The Impact of Braudel's *Mediterranean*: Third Generation *Annalistes*

Just as Braudel owed much to the inspiration and example of the first generation of *Annales* historians, Febvre and Bloch, so his *Mediterranean* made a powerful contribution to the rise of a new kind of history associated with the third generation of *Annales* historians. Peter Burke writes that from the 1950s onwards, an increasing number of French historians turned under this influence from political to social history, and from a preoccupation with events to a concern for structures. That influence can also be seen in the way their works pass from a geographical setting to economic and social structures, and end with a study of *conjoctures*, that is, trends over time, usually of hundred years or more. Outside France, Braudel has led many in Italy, Spain, Poland, Britain and the United States to look at the past in a different way and to interest themselves in his methods. Yet, third generation *Annalistes* also learned from criticisms leveled against Braudel's totalist approach—that it could possibly not be achieved on such a scale as the Mediterranean world. For this reason they developed, with the exception of Chaunu, a micro-history approach to the study of regions. Again, they made inroads into using quantitative techniques besides developing the history of collective mentalities begun by Febvre and Bloch.

Pierre Chaunu, Le Roy Ladurie, Le Goff, Robert Mandrou, Keith Thomas

Of the third generation *Annalistes*, one of the most remarkable was Pierre Chaunu. Chaunu took on the Braudel model, the Atlantic as his subject. His twelve-volume study (1955–60), written with the help of his wife, centres on the rise and fall of the trade between

Seville and the New World of the Americas from 1501 to 1650. Taking a global view of the subject, Chaunu was successful in intergrating space into history and in dealing with the changing problems of communication.

'Total history' on a scale conceived and executed by Braudel or Chaunu was increasingly felt to be impossible. This trend of thought was represented most forcefully by Braudel's most brilliant pupil, Emmanuel Le Roy Ladurie, who succeeded him at the College de France, as Braudel himself had succeeded Febvre. Le Roy Ladurie owed much to Braudel and resembled his teacher in imaginative power, wide-ranging curiosity, and the multi-disciplinary approach. Yet, *The Peasants of the Languedoc* (1966), the brilliant piece of 'total history' which he wrote, was different in its far reduced geographical scale than the *Mediterranean.* It is a regional or local 'total history' – or what Giovanni Levi called micro-history – concerned with the peasants of the Languedoc from the fifteenth to the eighteenth century. Sharing Braudel's ecological determinism, that is, the centrality of the natural world to human history, Ladurie starts with the geography of the Languedoc but does not follow Braudel's three-tier time scale. Instead, he divided history into periods and developed quantitative techniques for sifting masses of evidence to analyze the demographic and economic trends of each period. Each such analysis is followed by Ladurie's account of the conscious response of the peasants to the changing situation in which they found themselves, with particular emphasis on movements of protest and revolt.[96]

Perhaps the most significant development associated with the third generation of *Annales* historians was the emergence of the history of collective mentalities or what may be called cultural history—a favourite *Annales* area of study. Febvre had attacked psychological anachronism: "the false assumption that past people thought about things in the same way that we do,"[97] and advocated historical psychology—enquiries into the way in which men and women in the past thought and felt. Bloch's *The Royal Touch* had shown the way in understanding the mental framework of past ages. Following the example many attempts were made to understand past states of mind. A seminal study in this direction was Robert Mandrou's *Introduction to Modern France: 1500–1640* (1961). Mandrou's work is an historical inquiry into the exaggerated fear that early modern people entertained of natural disasters and

Herodotus

Thucydides

Cato the Elder

St. Augustine

Otto of Freising

A page from
The Anglo-Saxon Chronicle

Title page of *Muqaddimah*

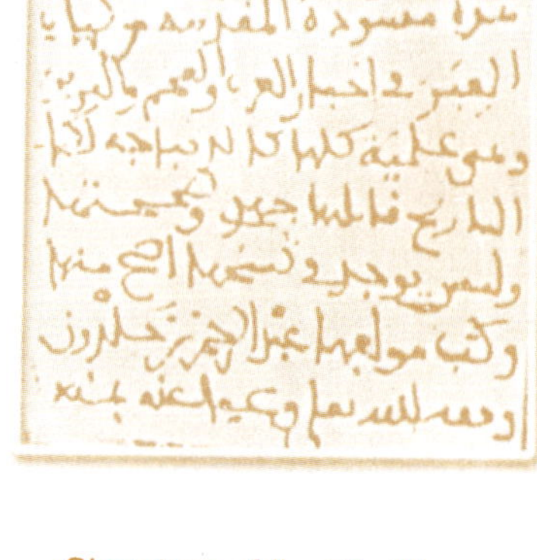

Signature of Ibn Khaldoun

Niccolo Machiavelli

Rene Descartes

Jean Mabillon

Giambattista Vico

Voltaire

Edward Gibbon

Herder

Hegel

Jules Michelet

T.B. Macaulay

Thomas Carlyle

Barthold Georg Niebuhr

Leopold von Ranke

Auguste Comte

Karl Marx

Friedrich Engels

G.M. Trevelyan

Oswald Spengler

Arnold Toynbee

Theodor Mommsen

F.W. Maitland

Fredrich Meinecke

Lucien Febvre

Marc Bloch

Antonio Gramsci

Abul Fazal

Sir William Jones

James Mill

Mountstuart Elphinstone

Jadunath Sarkar

Sardar K.M. Panikkar

R.C. Majumdar

D.D. Kosambi

Romila Thapar

ailments, a fear that issued in morbid hypersensitivity, excessive grief, pity and cruelty.

> In this respect by painting an image of a people locked in fear of their world, Mandrou shared Braudel's social determinism —the idea that the world was shaped by forces extraneous to human-kind. This tradition of understanding past states of mind was continued in the works of various *Annalistes.*[98]

Some other works which were thus deeply influenced by the *Annales* School were Jacque Le Goff's European survey, *Medieval Civilization, 400–1500* (1964), Le Roy Ladurie's *Montaillou* (1975) and *Carnival in Romans* (1980), and the Englishman Keith Thomas's major study, *Religion and the Decline of Magic* (1971). They were all incisive studies of past beliefs and ideas.

Achievements of the Annales Historians[99]

Stuart Clark draws our attention to the tremendous impact the *Annales* historians have made on the character of historical thought. They have broken for ever the timidity and suspicion with which areas of inquiry other than political were regarded; they have advocated that historians must learn from kindred disciplines if they are to deepen and enliven their understanding of the past; they have brought every aspect of human experience within the purview of energetic and innovative scrutiny. The notion of anachronism and the study of past mentalities with which Febvre and Bloch were deeply concerned, and Braudel's structural approach and the notion of the *long duree* have all come to stay. A most significant aspect of the influence of the *Annales* is that it has brought some of the fundamental issues of social theory to the attention of the historian who has now to debate the perennial problems of freedom and constraint in human behavior, and tackle the apparent antithesis between the individuality of events and the generality of structures. This may best be done by setting Braudel's advocacy of structural history in the wider context of French structuralist thought.

5. Structuralism in History

Structuralism in history stands for that approach which pays explicit attention to the analysis and interpretation of historical phenomena and historical change in terms of geographical, economic, and one may add, mental structures and systems. Structural history treats geographical factors, economic systems and time itself as its decisive elements, and views human life as wholly determined by them. It sets aside the autonomy of the historical individual and of the particular historical event, as imaginary and artificial, and treats political narratives as superficial. Lucien Febvre and Marc Bloch and the journal which they founded in 1929 had expressed dissatisfaction with the conventional narrative history of politics, the history of discrete events, and the Rankean cult of detail. Inspired by Henri Berr, they believed in the interdependence of all the social sciences including history. Their approach to the study of the past was particularly marked by a belief in social psychology, human geography (the various ways in which societies reacted to the physical environment), mentalities (collective ideas and beliefs of peoples), and their combined influence on human lives. They were convinced of the primacy of the social and the collective in the life of historical agents. Such an approach may broadly be termed structural. Bloch's *Feudal Society* (1940) was an analysis of the structural relationship which linked the society, economy, politics, technology, and the psychology of the feudal world. Febvre's classic study, *The Problem of Unbelief in the Sixteenth Century* (1942) argued that it was anachronistic to attribute atheistic beliefs to Rabelais and his contemporaries since the structural conditions for atheism were not present in sixteenth century France. Febvre and Bloch's ideal of 'total history' represented by the *Annales* came very near fulfilment in Fernand Braudel's structuralist approach in the *Mediterranean*.

Philosophical–Theoretical–Linguistic Basis of Structuralism

Structuralism in history is to be ultimately traced to the structuralist milieu in French philosophical thought. More distinctly its origins lie in linguistics, specially in the theories of Saussure. Ferdinard de Saussure combated the view that language originated in a kind of nomenclature. He believed that language does not follow reality, but only signifies it. Roland Barthes has shown in his essay 'Historical Discourse' that this Saussurean view radically undermines the naively positivist conception of history as a faithful record of a world of objective facts. The attempt to warrant the claim that 'this happened' in terms of a straightforward narrative of 'facts' is shown to be no more than an assertion of authority on the part of the historian. The factual descriptions that result are therefore not the *source* but the *presuppositions* of meaning. Traditional history imputes meaning to such assertions by its references which are the foundation for its conception of reality.

> Barthes points accordingly to the philosophically crucial importance of those historians—he is surely thinking of the *Annales* group—who abandoned the narrative of events for the analysis of structures and thus make 'not so much reality as intelligibility' the key historiographical problem.[100]

Braudelien Structuralism

Braudel saw the *Annales* history which sought to replace historical positivism, as "a whole new way of conceiving of social affairs,"[101] in which the individual agent (actor) and the individual occurrence (event) were not the central elements in social explanation. The *Annales* viewed events themselves as constituted largely by the force of many different conjunctural and structural circumstances. These circumstances outweigh the reasonings and choices of individual men and women and do so differently in different epochs. For this reason the historian will be in stark error to think of the springs of action as uniform as though, says Braudel, history could be reduced to a "monotonous game, always changing yet always the same, like the thousand combinations of pieces in a game of chess."[102]

Traditional history, Braudel said, had rested on twin beliefs in the dominance of exceptional actor-heroes and in the influence of the instant and the dramatic in men's lives. Braudel felt that the most decisive change wrought by the *Annales* historians was of transcending the individual and the particular event. According to Braudel, it was the task of structural history to uncover the impersonal forces which in reality fashioned men and their destines, and to plot the slower rhythms at which social time in fact moved.[103]

The essence of structuralism in history could be seen in this attempt to uncover those impersonal forces and hidden realities, which mould men's lives and their destinies. And to uncover them, to suit the structural notions of historical change and of the multi-form springs of action, Braudel organized the *Mediterranean*, his masterpiece, on a triad of historical time layers or phases, each with a different pace of change. In a Copernican revolution of historical priorities, he gave to the traditional narration of 'events, politics and people' (Part Three of the *Mediterranean*) the least importance. This is the sector of events and individual actors where time moves fast, a sector which, in the eyes of the structuralist, is of the least historical significance. Of greater moment is the intermediate pace of change, the time of *conjoctures* or time spans of ten, twenty, fifty or even more years when broader movements of economies, social structures, political institutions and civilizations take shape (Part Two of the *Mediterranean*). But the most important sector for the structuralist is the bottom layer of geo-history—of mountains, plains and the sea (Part One of the *Mediterranean*), which Braudel calls *histoire de longue duree* or history of the longest duration because here time is almost stationary or moves at the slowest pace. For this reason it requires the perspective of centuries on the part of the historian to plot any change at all. This is a realm untouched by the traditional narrative history of individual events and men. It is the domain of man's biological, geophysical and climatic circumstances to which ponderous realities Braudel has given the name 'structures'.[104]

To the structuralist this sphere of *longue duree* is where real history is made, for only here are to be found the real actors—the mountains, plains and peninsulas, the sea itself, even time and space. These structures are in Braudel's history personified entities – heroes – to whom he attributes designs and purpose. The action of these geographical agents have results that are profound because they are determinative. These agents, structures, says Braudel, "get in the way of history, hinder its flow, and in hindering it shape it."[105] In this sphere of the *longue duree* men and women are being limited and constrained by the frameworks (structures) in terms of which they are obliged to act. Braudel said: "For centuries man has been a prisoner of climate, of vegetation, of the animal population, of a particular agriculture, of a whole slowly established balance from which he cannot escape without the risk of everything being upset."[106]

Overarching Social Theory of History

Braudel's enthusiasm for structural history must be seen as an attempt to infuse an overarching social theory into history, a theory of the determining effects of structures on those who inhabit them. Such an explanation he believed would be a vital contribution to social history. Changes in climate, vegetation, animal population, and so on – what Braudel called infrastructural changes – were thought to be ultimately responsible for what goes on in the other time sectors of history. A change such as, for example, the biological revolution of the sixteenth century, was "more important than the Turkish conquest, the discovery and colonization of America, or the imperial vocation of Spain."[107] Again, it is in terms of the 'physics' of Spanish policy rather than of any individual will and conscious decision that Braudel explains Spain's orientation towards the Atlantic from the 1580s onwards.[108]

Hostility to the History of Events and of Individuals

Though Braudel talks of interaction between history's various time layers and of balancing the opposition between the instantaneous and the durable in a unitary account, he has a pronounced hostility to events and to history as made by individuals. Events are to him surface disturbances having the evanescent quality of smoke and vapor, single blooms flourishing only for a day, dust on the more solid objects of the past, fireflies incapable of piercing darkness. The world of events is narrow, superficial, ephemeral, provisional and capricious. It is a world of illusion, a world whose reality is as it appears to agents—individuals, not really as it *is*. The world of events and individual actors is one in which "great men appear regularly, organizing things, like conductors organizing their orchestras."[109] This history of the superficial world of individual events and men is not real history but only "that small-scale science of contingence." Real history is the history of the long run, for only here are to be found real actors whose actions have results that are profound and lasting because they are determinative. Just as the destinies of Turks and Christians alike were unknowingly established by common patterns of climate, terrain and vegetation in the Mediterranean region, so Philip II and his advisers were blind to the fact that their actions were responses to seismic shifts in its geohistory.

Assessment of Structuralism

The similarity between *Annales* history and Braudelien structural history was of too general a kind. For Febvre and Bloch, events and structures were complementary aspects of reality, and factors like will and intention were recognized to be important. But in Braudel the decisive elements are the structures which he brings to the foreground of history, and places man in them like a slave or a prisoner tied hand and foot. Braudel is a tireless campaigner against artificial autonomy, as much of the historical event as of the historical individual and the superficiality of political narratives. Much of his argument is true, yet it seems that in his denunciation of traditional history, he exaggerated the importance of geophysical structures most of whose hindrances scientific and technological devices have removed. It has been pointed out that the actual lack of linkages between the three parts of the *Mediterannean* has fostered doubts whether Braudel's triad of time spans could ever accommodate a truly rounded view of human affairs.[110] Historiography would gain if 'structural history' and 'history of events' are brought together in a genuinely holistic explanation of human life.[111]

6. Antonio Gramsci (1891–1937)

The fact that Communist revolution and the growth of revolutionary consciousness materialized not in the heartlands of capitalism but in relatively peasant economies led many Marxists to soften their stand on economic determinism. The trend had been set even before the Second World War by Antonio Gramsci, theoretician of the Italian Communist Party which he himself had founded in 1921. Gramsci died in a Fascist prison hospital in Rome but he has exerted a significant influence through his *Prison Notebooks*.

Gramscian Concept of 'Hegemony'

Gramsci concerned himself with the development of the theoretical implication of Lenin's interpretation of Marx, so as to provide the basis for a re-elaboration of historical materialism in terms of 'a science of history and society'. In the *Prison Notebooks* Gramsci attempts to develop a flexible and humane variant of historical materialism, an original and nuanced Marxist theory of society and social change. Convinced that it was difficult to change advanced societies like those of the industrialized West, Gramsci turned away from the simple notion of superstructure and sponsored the notion of the cultural hegemony of the dominant class. Hegemony he defined as political, intellectual and moral leadership. It consisted in the capacity of a dominant class to articulate its interests and the interests of other social groups, and to become in that way the leading force of a collective will. The theory of hegemony called for a re-evaluation of the social superstructure – politics, law, culture, religion, art, science – that had been given little systematic attention in contemporary Marxist theorizing, owing to its focus on the determining role of the economic base. The superstructure and the economic base form a historic bloc which has to be understood in its entirety. The establishment and maintenance of a historic bloc can be achieved only by the supremacy of a class, which involves both force and consent. Opposing social forces must be dominated, but supremacy cannot be achieved without hegemony, i.e., non-coercive leadership over a coalition of allied forces. The essence of the concept of hegemony is the appropriation of culture by a dominant class for the sake of social control, *not* the identification of culture with sheer class power. The concept relied on the pervasive erosion of old beliefs by overcoming the sources of hegemonic power such as individual will, intellectuals, political parties, churches, schools and the media. The final stage of the socialist revolution must be prepared not through a frontal attack on the state, but by a long and difficult period of 'war of position' during which the working class should be able, through political and ideological struggle, to disarticulate the bourgeoisie and to create a new national popular collective will, in which it will be the hegemonic force.

Gramsci's Influence on Historiography

The concept of hegemony and related ideas – Gramsci's strategy of a Communist revolution – have influenced numerous academic studies of society in general and modern historiography in particular. This concept of the ideological dominance of society has been extensively pursued by scholars of South Asian society and history. Gramscian ideas, it is said, have contributed tremendously to deeper studies of popular religion and popular consciousness. The role that Gramsci assigns to the intellectual class in the revolution has helped Marxist social historians to study leaders of uprisings and politically active intellectuals.

Gramsci began to influence European historiography with the writings of radical social theorists like Earnest Leclan, Chanthal Mouffe and others in the early 1980s. Among European historians influenced by Gramsci, E.P. Thompson ranks foremost. Gramscian ideas are coming into vogue among some Cambridge historians too.

More particularly, Gramsci's thought has had a pronounced influence in Indian historiography, where it was introduced by Bipan Chandra. Using the concept of hegemony in analyzing the colonial state, Chandra called it semi-hegemonic. Gramsci's observation that the subordinate classes are persuaded to hold views and values which are consistent with the continued economic and social dominance of the ruling class, has been tested in the Indian context by Bipan Chandra. The concept of the 'war of position' has been used by Sumit Sarkar, K.N. Panikkar and other historians for a better understanding of peasant movements in India. Gramscian concepts acquired prominence in Indian historiography with the publication of the *Subaltern Studies*. The history of the lower rungs of society, of the inferior classes, began to engage the attention of historians through the study of folk consciousness—mentalities. Particularly, this genre of historiography has addressed itself to the insurgency of the lower classes—of tribals, industrial labor, peasants, hillmen. Gramscian concepts roused a passion to critically study the history of the Indian national movement from the common people's point of view, to assess, perhaps for the first time, the contributions made by the people on their own – independently of the elite – to the making and development of Indian nationalism. Ranajit Guha, the editor of the *Subaltern Studies* series, has gone as far as to assert that, in the freedom movement, there was by the side of elite politics, a domain of people's politics in which the principal actors were the subaltern classes constituting the mass of the population. History writing was enriched through the study of popular consciousness, folk memory, popular religion – the modes of subaltern dissent and protest – themes at which historical inquiry had till then looked askance.

11

POSTMODERNIST CHALLENGE TO HISTORY

What Is Postmodernism?

The *Modern-day Dictionary of Received Ideas* says of postmodernism: "This word has no meaning. Use it as often as possible."[1] No advice has been more faithfully followed for the term can mean anything to anyone. Postmodernism is a maze of ideas and subjects.

But if anything, 'postmodernism' is not to be treated as a method of periodization. The term, says Arran Gare,

> signifies participation in the debate about whether there has been a radical cultural transformation in the world, particularly within Western societies, and if so, whether this has been good or bad. To define the postmodern is not just to define a term. It is to characterize the present age and to assess how we should respond to it.[2]

Gare explains that the postmodern condition is marked by a loss of faith in modernity, progress and Enlightenment rationality; it signifies people's awareness that it is just these conditions that are propelling humanity to self-destruction; it is a special condition in which the whole of modern civilization is being forced to adopt a critical attitude towards itself.[3]

Jean Francois Lyotard characterizes the postmodern condition as "the incredulity towards metanarratives"[4] or metadiscourse. This loss of credulity towards grand narratives is essentially a loss of belief in 'progress'—the idea held to be the moving force of European civilization, especially since the eighteenth century Enlightenment. 'Modernity' had begun with the assumption that progress in reason, knowledge, technology, the arts and economy ensured humanity's cumulative advance towards a final state of perfection. This belief in continual progress received a traumatic shock in the two World Wars, each leaving an appalling trail of destruction, poverty, environmental pollution and human degradation. It may be stated in general terms that postmodernism reflects this loss of faith in modernity which till then had held out hopes of endless development and a roseate future for mankind. And without this faith in the future Western civilization cracks and falls apart. Nietzsche had foreseen a universal disvaluation in preparation, a condition in which nothing would seem to have any meaning.[5]

Poststructuralism and Postmodernism

The thinkers who became most concerned with the crisis of Western civilization were a group of Parisian intellectuals who in one way or the other were associated with the 1968 May movement out of which emerged 'poststructural' or 'postmodern' theory. The best known of these poststructuralists are Barthes, Lacan, Foucault, Derrida, Lyotard, Baudrillard, Deleuze and Guattari. These thinkers have generally aligned themselves with and continued the work of Nietzsche and Martin Heidegger who could be regarded as the true originators of postmodernism. Ben Agger makes a broad distinction between poststructuralism and postmodernism designating the first a theory of knowledge, and the second a theory of society, culture and history. Since it is difficult to draw a line of demarcation between the two movements, they may be treated as one, at least in relation to their impact on history.

Beginning with architecture and then literary theory, the postmodernist trend now embraces every conceivable subject: science, politics, colonialism, late capitalism, classlessness, race, gender, women's studies, feminism, aesthetic theory, literary criticism, environmental pollution, and our special concern—history.

POSTMODERNISM AND HISTORY

PART I THE PHILOSOPHICAL TURN

1. The Postmodern Critique of Enlightenment Humanism

Heidegger, reacting to the humanism of the Enlightenment in his

Being and Time, had shown the way to the postmodern critique of humanism. Philosophical humanism presupposed a conception of 'Man' as a universal category, and French poststructuralists followed Nietzsche in freeing themselves from this conception by demonstrating that the idea itself was historically relative, an invention of the Enlightenment. This is the reason for the poststructuralist critique of humanism to be mainly directed against the Enlightenment, particularly against Immanuel Kant who had explicitly put man at the center of things, and introduced the anthropological question: 'What is man?'[6]

To both Derrida and Foucault man was not a universal category as the *philosophes* of the Enlightenment believed. Both denied the possibility of developing a science of man based on human nature. More important for the student of history is the way poststructuralists impugn Enlightenment humanism's cardinal doctrine of progress—the assumption that science progresses, that knowledge grows cumulatively, and that we know better than our predecessors did. They protest that the knowledge produced are not better forms of knowledge, and that accumulation of knowledge cannot be equated with progress. Foucault and Derrida bracketed their rejection of humanism's belief in *epistemological* progress (growth of knowledge) with a similar rejection of belief in *social-historical* progress. Kant had thought that the law of progress, the progressive character of history, would take man, despite his natural propensity to evil, toward a perfect, free civil society. Hegel had similarly thought of the dialectical development of man's reason culminating and fulfilling itself in the establishment of a fully free civil society. But Derrida and Foucault threw dialectics and the progressive character of history overboard and saw themselves at the end of history not in the Hegelian sense of its culmination and fulfilment but in the Nietzschean sense of its dying.

2. Postmodern Arraignment of History

The poststructural (postmodern) critique of Enlightenment social thought has a fundamental relevance to history. Postmodern thought posed a greater challenge to historical thought than the one voiced by Descartes more than three hundred years ago. In general, the poststructuralists argue that there is no such thing as history. Writes David Hoy in his essay on Derrida:

> The progressive story of man told by speculative philosophers of history is understood to be simply a fiction now bankrupt, a dead metaphor from a defunct rhetoric. 'Philosophy' conceived as the account of the nature of man is itself part of this fiction, and even its hero, since the progress of freedom was equated with the progress of man's reason.[7]

Ever since the Scientific Revolution of the seventeenth century something of the new spirit of the physical sciences had begun to permeate what later came to be called the social or human sciences. The inquiry had begun whether there was a coherent and harmonious pattern of human behaviour. It culminated in a positivist attempt to construct a science of society – of man – until the post-war era when the very idea came to be attacked by men like Sartre. Claude Levi Strauss proposed that history, like everything else, can only be known and transmitted through codes of contrasts—that it offers no exclusive access to either truth or freedom.[8] An outspoken philosophical postmodernist, Lyotard, rejects totalizing perspectives on history and society, what he called *grand narratives* like Marxism that attempt to explain the world in terms of patterned interrelationships. The most influential of such men of thought who held that human behaviour cannot be wholly understood in law-like causal terms is Michel Foucault.

3. Michel Foucault (1926–1984)

A profound thinker and the central figure of French philosophy since Sartre, Michel Foucault shared with Derrida the leadership of poststructuralism.

Foucault's Philosophy of History

History and the Human Subject

The Nietzschean temper of Foucault's thought could best be seen in the iconoclastic spirit of his philosophy of history. Foucault holds that history: (a) has no constant human subject which enables us to identify a coherent or constant human condition or nature; (b) cannot show any rational development, i.e., the gradual triumph of human rationality over human nature; (c) has no overarching purpose or goal, as Hegel and Marx supposed; and (d) being without any constants, its study cannot offer any comfort or consolation either. All these consequences follow from the fact that man is not, as the *philosophes* of the Enlightenment imagined, a universal category. Foucault tells us what effective history is:

> Effective history differs from traditional history in being *without constants.* Nothing in man—not even his body—is sufficiently stable to serve as a basis for this self-recognition or for understanding other men....History becomes effective to the degree that it introduces discontinuity into our very being—as it divides our emotions, dramatizes our instincts, multiplies our body and sets itself against itself.[9]

Course of History[10]

To think of a 'course' of history, of a narrative of human agency from past to present, is an illusion. We think of our present as having been reached by ordered progress in the past as a peak preceded by lowly foothills. Such a progressive view of the past leading up to the peak of the present is an imagined, invented one. What Foucault sees in man's past is not order, but haphazard conflicts, not general agreement but incessant struggle. Struggle is unavoidable since individuals remain caught up in webs of contingency from which there is no escape. As human life is rooted in contingency, discontinuity, inequity and incessant struggle, so are history, knowledge and the human subject.

History as Perspectival Knowledge

The Nietzschean–Foucauldian conception of history holds that the past in its pure form does not exist and what the historian recovers of it can never be its objective reality. Theories, interpretations and explanations can have little to do with the facts of the past since such exercises only reflect the subjective point of view of the historian. Objectivity is a myth, since explanations or interpretations of the same historical phenomenon are liable to yield multiple truths. All that is possible, is to take a view of the past in the perspective of the present. History is perspectival knowledge, an assertion which deprives the past of its hegemony over the present.

Genealogical History

In 'Nietzsche, genealogy, history' (1971), Foucault expresses his admiration for Nietzschean 'genealogy' which, he says "does not fear to be a perspectival knowledge."[11] Genealogical history is not only free from the tyranny of totalizing discourses – great truths, great systems and great syntheses – but it painstakingly rediscovers struggles and fragmented, subjugated, local and specific knowledges. It studies the emergence and descent of cultural phenomena in which old cultural forms receive new functions, like the lazar-houses transformed into lunatic asylums or the monastic cells converted into prison cages. J.G. Merquior observes that genealogical history is pragmatic history which sees *everything from the viewpoint of power* with truth debased as an aid – or a mask – of domination.[12]

History as Discontinuous Process

Along with overarching theories and grand narratives, Foucault rejects all notions of continuity in history. The notion of continuity in history is based on the belief in the continuity of thought and the conception of time in terms of the totalization of the moments of consciousness.[13] But the reality of the past, presents itself in the form of individual, disparate, autonomous events or pieces of happenings—which renders any idea of unity or continuity in history thoroughly meaningless. Homogeneous continuity in thought, mentality and action is only to be seen on the surface of history, beneath which one witnesses rupture, contingencies and discontinuities. It is these latter that must receive the attention of the historian, because history unfolds itself in the form of irruptions and events, and not in the form of stable structures.[14] History is necessarily discontinuous.

4. Characteristics of Foucault's New Kind of History

The history that Foucault wrote was not history of the usual kind. In its themes, method, treatment and conclusions it was a new way of viewing the past. Marked by an opposition to positivism of all kinds in the human sciences, it was an attempt at a highly original merger of philosophy and history, which led to an incisive critique of modern Western civilization and its Enlightenment foundations.

Foucault's Works

In his project of a historico-philosophical critique of modernity, Foucault's eyes turned to certain unusual but fascinating territories of history—madness, sexuality and criminality, and the evolution of social attitudes towards them.

Foucault's first influential work, *Madness and Civilization* (1961), is a book on the birth of the asylum, showing through historical account how the conception of madness has changed corresponding to functions of social changes in law, morals, medicine and criminology. In medieval times madness was regarded as holy; the Renaissance man thought of it as having a share in truth; but in the early modern West, madness became a disease, that is, when reason was firmly separated from unreason. Society administered rationality negatively by isolating the insane, thus imposing its conception of rationality and treatment of madness. In *The Birth of the Clinic* (1963), Foucault scrutinized the rich history of medicine. Foucault's masterpiece, *The Order of Things* (1966), is a history of the variations in the representational presuppositions in the human sciences. *The Archaeology of Knowledge* (1969), may be regarded as Foucault's theoretical manifesto, in which the analyses of the earlier substantive studies are systematized. *Discipline and Punish* (1975), is a book on the birth of the modern prison. It is as well a discourse on the penal establishments, as it is an account of the interaction of knowledge and power, a theme which is further developed in *The Will to Knowledge* (1976). *The History of Sexuality* (1976), was Foucault's last historico-analytical enterprise.

Characteristics of Foucauldian History

Presentist History

One of the characteristic marks of the history written by Foucault is the dominance of the present. Foucault was one with Nietzsche in thinking that an objective study of the past was impossible, that its value lay chiefly in being an aid to the diagnosis of the present. Both held that it was only in the perspective of the present that the past can be explained. Foucault in fact claims to have learnt more from the present than from the past, a view which dethrones the past from its position of hegemony over the present. In such a mood Foucault, the presentist historian, embarks on a critical inquiry into the prehistory of the present in social practices. He studies the evolution of the modern man's ideas of the treatment of such issues as madness, sexuality and criminality in society. Of special interest to him is the rise of rationality in the West as the spirit of modern culture, and its identification with knowledge. Foucault's 'history of the present' turned into an incisive historico-philosophical critique of modern bourgeois disciplinary culture.

Dethronement of the Transcendental Human Subject[15]

The fact that man, the self-contemplating subject, could take himself as his own object was for Descartes the beginning of all solid knowledge. The *philosophes* of the Enlightenment promptly seized upon the idea and duly enthroned reason and the human subject. Reason – rationality – became the theme in modern philosophy, echoed in Kant's celebrated question 'What is the Enlightenment?' (1784). Philosophy continued to be anthropocentric—a philosophy of human experience. Foucault, like other structuralists and postmodernists, was determined to impugn this anthropomorphic view of the world with its idea of a founding, grounding human subject. He was convinced that the clue to an understanding of the ultimate nature of reality cannot be found within natural human experience. Hence his ominous prediction of the 'death of man' at the close of *The Order of Things* which, however, meant only the dethroning of the human subject.

Epistemic Method

Foucault wrote: "My aim was to analyse history in the discontinuity that no teleology would reduce in advance...."[16] In *The Order of Things: An Archaeology of the Human Sciences*, he picked up the label 'archaeology' which "deals with necessary, unconscious and anonymous forms of thought."[17] Foucault called these anonymous forms of thought 'epistemes'. An episteme is the "historical *a priori* which in a given period, delimits in the totality of experience a field of knowledge...."[18] Epistemes are conceptual strata relating to various epochs in Western thought; they have to be unearthed—hence the archaeological model.[19] It is in a way a postulate of knowledge not depending on experience—a kind of paradigm.

Every episteme is autonomous and has its own construction and interiority, a condition which makes relationship between one episteme and another impossible, and as such between the past and the present. The epistemes being so different in nature, continuity between them is impossible. What we get are "enigmatic discontinuities"[20] between four epistemes: pre-classical (up to AD 1650); classical (1650–1800); the modern (1800–1950); and a truly contemporary age taking shape since around 1950. An episteme undergoes mutation when one set of preconceptions gives way to another. Absolute discontinuity is the supreme epistemic law.[21]

Man has so much become the subject-matter of the modern episteme and he is so haunted by history and humanism that he tries to look at reality from his own position. Foucault exhorts us to awake from this 'anthropological slumber' reminding us that "man is an invention of recent date. And perhaps nearing its end…one can certainly wager that man would be erased, like a face drawn in sand at the edge of the sea."[22]

Discourse, Archaeology and the Archive

Foucault continues his discussion on method in *The Archeology of Knowledge*, his theoretical manifesto, in which he drops, so to say, the conception of the episteme in order to assert the primacy of discourse, which is his primary unit of analysis and which is to be understood as a system of possibility for knowledge. The exclusive function of discourse is to serve as a transparent representation of things and ideas standing outside it. The historical discourse simply describes events – irruptive, intersecting events – regardless of any idea of continuous time. It is made up of statements. A statement is always an event, a transferred version of whatever is left in the memory of the author. Statements are produced, manipulated, transformed and exchanged by men in a way that totally destroy or mutilate the past. Between statements there are always irruptions and voids. It is only theory or intentionality of the author that creates discourse by grouping the statements or events.[23]

Foucault presents the concept of discourse almost as a twin to his archaeological model in which he finds many advantages. Whereas the historian of ideas or one who uses documents traces the origin and fate of ideas, the archaeologist fastens on a discourse for itself, regardless of what preceded or followed it. Again, the archaeologist does not look for the psychological and sociological causes of events as the historian of ideas does. Histories of ideas focus on authors, novelty and continuity, but archaeology stresses impersonality, regularities and discontinuities in discourse. Archaeology's main weapon is the concept of statement or enunciation. Statements constituting the nuclei of discourse are like 'events': material, but incorporeal.[24]

Another word – idea – that *The Archaeology of Knowledge* introduces is 'archive'. Foucault's archive is not to be mistaken for the heavy corpus of discourses in a given civilization. It is an historical *a priori*; "the first law of what can be said"; "the system that governs the appearance of statements as unique events."[25] The archaeologist is an archivist and as such does not care who said or wrote what to whom. In a text of 1969 'What is an author?' Foucault dismisses the author in favour of the discourse. Dismissal of the author meant the dismissal of the human subject.[26]

Analysis of Power

Foucault's historical works aimed at a new kind of analysis of power, the element that makes his discourses so fascinating. He saw power as the determinant of what are called truth and knowledge. Texts – whatever their subject – were the products not of individual thought, but were actually the ideological products of the dominant discourse. History is no more than a fiction of narrative order imposed on the irreducible chaos of events in the interests of the exercise of power.[27] Foucault aimed at providing a critique of the way modern societies control and discipline their populations by sanctioning the knowledge claims and practices of the human sciences like medicine, psychiatry, criminology and so on. Arising in the nineteenth century in the wake of the Enlightenment, these social or human sciences have their roots in the drive to dominate and control people. Foucault shows how scientific knowledge is linked to the exercise of coercive power. Universal truth is the name for power disguised as the criterion of all knowledge; reason and science are but instruments and tools of the will to power; particular branches of knowledge are but part of the vast power apparatus. The criterion of truth is might.[28]

Discipline and Punish, Foucault's discourse on the penal establishments, is also an account of the interaction of knowledge and power. Knowledge and power directly imply one another. Power is embedded in the modern social organization; it is an ubiquitous phenomenon in its incidence and operation in society. Foucault wrote:

> In thinking of the mechanism of power, I am thinking of its capillary form of existence, the point where power reaches into the very grain of individuals, touches their bodies and inserts itself into their actions and attitudes, their discourses, learning processes and every day lives.[29]

Of this system of power and control, the modern prison is the crown and symbol.

5. Criticism and Assessment

Foucault had only contempt for what he called 'history of the historians'. But any kind of reading of the past – whether presentist or otherwise – must be true to the facts of the past as far as possible and cannot claim exemption from the usual canons of historical scholarship. And for all his Nietzschean contempt for objective historical truth and his denial that he was writing normal history based on the usual type of sources, Foucault did work as any other conventional historian. But Foucault's history, writes J.G. Merquior, is far from being always sound. Its "conceptual muddle and explanatory weakness…more than outweigh its contributions. Foucault's historical evidence is too selective and distorted, his interpretations too sweeping and too biased."[30]

Foucault's New Methodology

Can Foucault's new method, the archaeology of knowledge and the discursive archive, be accepted as legitimate critical theory, and can the many established ways to knowledge be rejected in its name? Alan Megill aptly comments that Foucault's attempt to articulate a new scientific methodology actually turns out to be an attempt to demolish everything that has hitherto gone under the name of science. And Merquior writes that Foucault's archive, the machine of discursive meaning, is at bottom, a wordplay, with which no meaning remains stable, no truth is better than the next one. For the neo-Nietzscheans there can be little difference between a literary form, a scientific proposition, a daily sentence, and a schizophrenic babble—all are equally valid statements.[31]

Prejudice Leading to False Assumptions

Did Foucault, disposed as he was to accept no truth claims except those of his own theories, get his history right in respect of sources and evidence, interpretations and conclusions?

Lawrence Stone, one of his main critics, concedes that in *Madness and Civilization* Foucault was right in maintaining that widespread confinement of mentally-retarded people in the seventeenth and eighteenth centuries was a retrograde step. But Foucault stands on shaky ground in asserting that the attitude of modern, i.e., rationalist times to lunacy was unprecedentedly repressive. Peter Sedgwick's splendid book, *Psycho-Politics* (1982), has shown how Foucault's anti-modern, anti-bourgeois prejudice leads him to false assumptions. Many attitudes towards mental illness as well as practices in the treatment of insane people which he attributes to the Age of Reason, the chief target of his criticism, were very common in pre-rationalist Europe even from the fifteenth century. In the medical craft throughout the ages, what Sedgwick sees is *continuity*, not Foucault's discontinuity.[32] If absolute discontinuity between epistemes is the supreme law of history, how are we to explain the decisive continuity between the work of Copernicus (of the pre-classical episteme) and the Kepler–Galileo line (of classical episteme since the mid-seventeenth century), which is the fountainhead of modern science?[33]

Of Foucault's archaeological history and its total denial of historical continuity, David Leary remarked, "If one denies any kind of continuity in history...then how is one to explain the possibility of doing history?"[34] A degree of historical continuity is basic to an understanding of the past. Then, Foucauldian genealogies, it is noted, never address such central concerns of our age as science, economics, nationalism and democracy. The historical points that Foucault makes in *The Order of Things* can also be shown to be inaccurate. How could Renaissance magic and humanist science be parts of the same episteme unless one sees little difference between magic and rational thought as Foucault does?

Partisanship: Distorted Evidence and Wrong Conclusions

Discipline and Punish is not only partisan in character, but faulty in points of fact. While Foucault leaves out the French Revolution from his account, Leonard has shown how the Revolution was a specific phase in penal history, and how the revulsion against bloodshed after the Reign of Terror provided a major psychological push for the substitution of imprisonment for the 'spectacle of the scaffold'.[35] Further, Foucault's interpretation of Enlightenment reformism as "a crippling overall disciplinary drive" is open to question and may be cited as one of similar instances of uneven evaluation of historical data.[36]

Circular Analysis, Faulty Explanations

Merquior also finds fault with the nature of explanation offered in *Discipline and Punish*.[37] Foucault thus explains the rapid and universal adoption of imprisonment in penitentiaries: (a) the disciplinary prison made its inmates into a useful working force; and (b) in any case, similar disciplinary institutions were already at work, for example, in the armed forces, the factory, the hospital and the school. Now Foucault's labor-force explanation blames class control on the rising bourgeoisie, while his second explanation blames 'carceral society' on modern culture as a whole, embodied in the Enlightenment. To suggest that the prison sprang from class domination is to forget that it came into force, almost simultaneously, in countries with vastly different class structures. Merquior has termed Foucault's analysis circular with conclusions already present at the beginning, and his method question-begging. His explanations also cannot be properly so called. Foucault's explanation of why prison has failed to deter crime and correct criminals is that its actual purpose is to maintain and promote delinquency by implicitly encouraging recidivism and converting the occassional offender into a habitual criminal.

Assessment

A great commentatorial literature has grown on Michel Foucault and his works. As a social thinker, Foucault was a libertarian anarchist whose history of the present, says Merquior, grossly disfigured the legacy of bourgeois progress.

> In so doing, Foucault proved very adept at a game typical of the most questionable 'counterculture' ideology: the remake of the meaning of modern history so as to serve the prejudices of the ongoing—and profoundly erroneous—revolt against the Enlightenment as a main source and paradigm of modern rational–liberal culture.[38]

Lopsided though it was, Foucault's historical work tried to change our standard conception of social issues like madness and crime as well as our conventional way of thinking about history. Merquior himself commends Foucault's unconventionality in respect of both themes and approach which enables the historian of thought to take a fresh look at many a lost or buried connection. Opening up new perspectives, history has heuristic virtues, and some of his interpretations, says Merquior, are truly suggestive, even casting a genuinely new light on the historical evidence. Mark Poster assesses Foucault's work in the following words: "Foucault offers historians a new framework for studying the past (knowledge–power), a new set of methods for doing so (archaeology and genealogy) and new notion of temporality (discontinuity). Suggestive as it is, his history of history is burdened with several difficulties."[39] Pamela Major Poetzl, an able commentator, has said that the gist of Foucault's most valuable contribution is a new paradigm for the human sciences based on principles analogous to field theory in modern physics.[40]

PART II THE LINGUISTIC TURN

1. The Hermeneutic Method

The positivist test of scientific history was its ability to reveal regularities of human life not only as operative in the past but also predictively applicable. It meant that all successful explanations should conform to the same deductive model of the natural sciences. But the attempt to model the social disciplines on the image of the natural sciences had to confront the fundamental problem of the distinction between the social and the physical sciences. In the sixties of the twentieth century, the difference between the two kinds of explanations – of human behavior and of natural phenomena – came to be increasingly stressed until a hermeneutic approach to the social or human sciences was thought to be preferable. Hermeneutics is the philosophical concern with the theory of understanding and interpretation. The essence of the hermeneutic approach lies in the belief that human (social) actions should be explained from the point of view of the agents performing them. The hermeneutic approach pins its faith on a theory of reading. It axiomatically holds that all knowledge is pragmatically relative to contexts, and that all understanding is based on the interpretation of texts. Belief in the interpretation of texts as the one way of understanding social action finds support in Hans Georg Gadamer's *Truth and Method* (1960).

2. Linguistic Theory behind Postmodern Ideas on History

Clio had already welcomed influences from sister disciplines; she was now to lay herself open to influences from literary criticism and linguistics. Ever since Lorenzo Valla demolished the so-called *Donation of Constantine* in the fifteenth century, and more definitely since Niebuhr recast the early history of Rome in the nineteenth century, there has been a pronounced influence of philology on historiography. This influence centered on the problem of the internal consistency of documents, and their consistency with the other documents originating at the same period—in short, on the problem of reliability. But the linguistic turn in the twentieth century was to bring disturbing, even damaging consequences to historiography.

The challenge to history has again come from France, the land of Descartes. How does language represent reality is a question which has great relevance to the human sciences, particularly history. The linguistic turn in postmodernist theory and its all-too-important relevance to history should be traced back in its origin to the theories advanced early in the twentieth century by the Swiss linguist, Ferdinand de Saussure. Saussure thought that the relation of words to their meanings was usually completely arbitrary, and that words or what he called signifiers were defined not by their relation to the things they denoted, the signified, but by their differential relation to each other. Saussure's theory meant that language does not follow reality, and that it does not reflect the phenomenal world addressed by it. This was cue for Roland Barthes, the French linguistic theorist, who in his essay 'Historical

Discourse' (1968), mounted a frontal attack on history. Barthes showed that the Saussurean view radically undermined the naively positivistic conception of history as a faithful record of a world of objective facts. History as written was only "an inscription on the past pretending to be a likeness of it, a parade of signifiers masquerading as a collection of facts."[41] Objectivity was the product of the referential illusion.

> Verbatim quotations, footnote references and the like were simply devices designed to produce what Barthes described as the 'reality effect', tricking the reader into believing that the historian's unprovable representations of the past were no more than straightforward reporting.[42]

Jacques Derrida: Grammatology as Radical Hermeneutics

In reading and interpreting texts Jacques Derrida has introduced a strategy christened 'deconstruction' which, so far as history is concerned, is as iconoclastic as Foucault's attitude. Derrida's three works – *Speech and Phenomena*, *Writing and Difference*, and *Of Grammatology* – are characterized by a mistrust of all forms of metaphysical thought coupled with the recognition that language is riddled with metaphysical assumptions.

Deconstruction

In his major work, *Of Grammatology*, and in one of his essays. 'Structure, Sign and Play in Discourse of the Human Sciences', Derrida elaborated a method, rather a strategy, of reading texts which he called deconstruction. In deconstruction, Derrida pushed hermeneutics to its limits—even beyond the limits of reason. Deconstruction is the literary activity of making critical readings of the texts of philosophers and writers, revealing their metaphysical assumptions and bringing out unperceived contradictions that undermine their coherence and cogency. Emphasizing such rhetorical devices as pun, ambiguity and metaphor, Derrida deconstructs such oppositions or distinctions as those between speech and writing, mind and body, good and evil, identity and difference, presence and absence, male and female, and so on. Then he shows that although these distinctions or oppositions are supposed to be obvious or value-neutral, their use suggest that in practice one pole in each of the pairs is privileged over the other.[43] Derridean deconstruction reveals such oppositions or dichotomies as hierarchies—for example, male and female, where to be female is to be non-male, thus defining women in terms of their absence of maleness. To take a sociological example—deconstructive reading of the definition of mobility in terms of the occupation of the father would reveal the profound assumptions that exist about the gendered nature of work, as well as about male supremacy. People are apt to think that only men work, thus misrepresenting reality as women also work outside the home for wages.

Undecidability and Dissemination

According to Derrida, one main reason which calls for deconstruction is the undecidability of texts. Undecidability arises when a text does not succeed in its act of representation, that is, in establishing or communicating its message.[44] The French linguist thinks that every text is undecidable in the sense that it conceals conflicts of meaning and intention within it, making it difficult to interpret the meanings of utterances with any certainty at all. As examples of undecidability, Derrida picks single words with opposed meanings where the context does not unequivocally eliminate one or the other meanings. He calls this particular approach 'dissemination'. Dissemination is the activity of illustrating with more and more examples the ultimate illegibility of texts.[45]

Difference and 'Differance'

Derrida's notion of undecidability rests on his notions of difference and 'differance' Derrida believes that it is in the nature of language to produce meanings only with reference to other meanings. He argues that no stable meanings could be established by attempting correspondence between language and the world addressed by language. Meaning is the result of differential significance that we attach to words. The term 'differance' is introduced by Derrida to indicate 'sameness which is not identical', as between male and female. The French literary theorist goes on to argue that in each attempt to fix the play of differance, a binary opposition is assumed, one term of which is taken to be prior to and superior to the other. The privileged first term is taken as the limit or the central concept of a metaphysical system. The second term is made derivative and unimportant in relation to the first, and then effaced or repressed as non-ideal and suggestive of the break-up of the values assured by the first term. Derrida deconstructs ideal limits and exposes the arbitrary nature of what have been taken as absolutes, revealing that 'transcendental essences' which have been taken as absolute points of reference are only arbitrary signifiers.

Reading and Authorial Authority

Deconstruction is both a negative and positive activity in as much as dichotomies or hierarchies, once deconstructively revealed, would be replaced by new 'different' discursive versions. It is claimed that deconstruction prises open inevitable, unavoidable gaps of meaning which readers are free to fill with *their own interpolative sense.* By leaving the reader free to fill in gaps and resolve conflicts of meaning, deconstruction turns reading itself into a strong activity, and not merely a passive reflection of an objective text with singular meaning. The metaphysical basis of the new approach, writes David Hoy, is the contention that linguistic meaning is derived not from the psychological intentions of speakers and authors, but from the structure of language itself. Such a position removes from the speaker or the author any special authority to determine the meaning of what is said or written.[46] Nor is it any part of the interpreter's task to recover a meaning that may have been intended by such agents.

PART III POSTMODERNIST HISTORICAL THEORY versus CONVENTIONAL HISTORY

1. A Crisis of Self-confidence

History as a department of knowledge had from time to time been compelled to tackle problems of its study, research and writing. Clio had to meet a serious crisis of existence itself when in the wake of the Scientific Revolution of the seventeenth century Rene Desecrates in his *Discourse on Method* impugned the validity and usefulness of historical knowledge. Vico's *Scienza nouva* had met this challenge and established the subject firmly on a philosophical, epistemological and critical basis. From the time of Niebuhr and Ranke, the position of history seemed to have been so well established that men began to talk confidently of the nature of the subject and concepts like historical truth and objectivity. But this optimistic belief in the progress of the discipline has come to be rudely shaken, as it were, by the appearance of postmodernist theory, particularly in its linguistic garb, which as Lawrence Stone has aptly said, has thrown the historical profession "into a crisis of self-confidence about what it is doing and how it is doing it."[47] Historians at the end of the twentieth century could only see bleak prospects for their vocation. Says Richard J. Evans:

> Such has been the power and influence of the post-modernist critique of history that growing numbers of historians themselves are abandoning the search for truth, the belief in objectivity, and the quest for a scientific approach to the past. No wonder so many historians are worried about the future of their discipline.[48]

2. Postmodernist Linguistic Theory and its Implications for History

How does language represent reality is a question which history, more than any other social science has to reckon with. What are the implications of postmodernist linguistic theory for history? As expounded by Roland Barthes and Jacques Derrida, that theory is a direct challenge to the historical discipline. The theory that 'language could not relate to anything except itself' means that history as known and written cannot be a record of the past. Since the past no longer exists, the reality of the past could be apprehended only through the texts or documents. Now the texts that the past leaves behind, the postmodernist contends, are as arbitrary in their ascription of meaning as the texts of the historians who use them. Meaning is arbitrarily put there by both the original author of the text and the historian who uses it for his own text or discourse. It follows, then, that texts only reflect other texts. When language is said to be an infinite play of meanings, anything written or spoken becomes a mere arrangement of words, a 'discourse' or 'text' out of which readers may make whatever meaning they care to make, undisturbed by any common measure or denominator to fix meaning. By implication, such a position *takes away from the author all control over the meaning of what he writes, and gives to the reader uncontrolled freedom to interpret what is written.* Meaning may change every time a text is read, for the reader may put meaning into a text, and to postmodernist theory all meanings are equally valid. Thus stated, the postmodern linguistic turn cuts the very ground on which historical studies stand. There cannot be any meaning in the study of the past, if meaning is put there differently by different historians, if the facts of the past are indistinguishable from fiction, if texts do not reflect reality but only other texts.[49] Hostility to history is a marked characteristic of postmodernist thought. Is the historian's ground, gained after centuries of thought and experience, to be surrendered to the postmodernist advance?

It is relieving to learn that voices have been and are being raised against such attacks on history and that many historians have felt the need to repel them. The conservative historian, Geoffrey Elton, reviled postmodernist ideas in copious terms;[50] Arthur Marwick has declared that postmodernist ideas were a menace to historical study;[51] the socialist-radical historian, Raphael Samuel, said that the linguistic, deconstructive turn teaches people to look upon history "not as a record of the past... [but] as an invention, or fiction, of historians themselves."[52] Indeed, the left-liberal historian, Lawrence Stone, "has called upon historians to repel the new intellectual barbarians at the disciplinary gates."[53]

3. Criticism of Postmodernist Historical Theory

It is by way of repelling such vandalistic attacks that Richard J. Evans, professor in Cambridge University, has written a substantial book, *In Defence of History* (1997). A genuine debate on postmodern linguistic and historical theory, the book is at the same time a vindication and vigorous defence of Clio in the face of the postmodernist challenge. In a critical threadbare analysis of postmodernist history in theory and practice, Evans, himself a historian of note, exposes the hollowness of many a postmodernist contention. In an outline, we shall follow Evans in his assessment of the postmodernist attitude towards some of the ideas and concepts that are basic to 'conventional' historiography, such as facts, sources, causation, historical objectivity, and so on.

Facts

Conventional history regards facts as its backbone. That a historian need not be bound by the normal rules of historical facts is exemplified by the postmodernist and feminist historian Diane Purkiss's *The Witch in History*. Evans tells us that instead of taking trouble to collect facts relating to witchcraft to understand that historical phenomenon, Purkiss informs the reader that her purpose is to "tell or retell the rich variety of stories told about the witches."[54] Accounts of witches and witchcraft are picked from verse, drama, and historical and other forms of secondary literature, all treated on an equal basis.

This is because postmodernist theory holds that the sources which are supposed to reflect the reality of the past are always written from somebody's point of view with a specific purpose. In point of veracity they cannot be any different from the texts of the historians who use them, for there is no meaning in either case except what the writers invest them with. A historical source and an account by a poet or a novelist are all forms of discourse treated as of equal validity and importance. Keith Jenkins, the author of two postmodernist critiques of history, argues that "when we study history we are not studying the past but what historians have constructed about the past."[55] Jenkins therefore thinks it more constructive to "get into the minds of the historians than the minds of the people who lived in the past...."[56]

Postmodernist theoretical squabbles are at the expense of historical facts. The difference between primary and secondary sources is abolished, the boundary line between history and historiography is erased, and in effect, the possibility of any objective knowledge of the past is denied. Postmodernist hostility to history cannot be a matter of doubt.

Sources

Postmodernist theory does not look upon a historical source as having a wholly fixed and unalterable meaning. But a historical text, a source, does not lend itself to endless interpretation, for its language sets limits to such extravaganza, and the limits are set to a large extent by the original author.[57] Words are not such arbitrary signifiers and language does reflect the phenomenal world. Says Evans:

> Language and grammar are in fact not completely arbitrary signifiers, but have evolved through contact with the real world in an attempt to name real things. In a similar way, historical discourse or interpretation has also evolved through contact with the real historical world in an attempt to reconstruct it.[58]

The postmodernist theory that language is wholly self-reflective and cannot represent external reality is incorrect. Language can describe things external to itself. It follows that texts or documents of the past are not arbitrary creations, but products of direct interaction with the reality of the past and as such have an integrity which mark them out in importance from discourses and other such secondary material. Evans cites the example of the postmodernist historian Keith Jenkins's book *On 'What is History?'* to expose the hollowness of the argument that there is no difference between a primary source and a secondary source, i.e., a discourse. If someone writes something about this book and if Jenkins feels that what has thus been written is not wholly true, would he not go back to his book itself (the primary account) rather than to some other person's account of it (the secondary material) to clarify the issue?[59]

It is through the primary sources that the past indisputably imposes its reality on the historian. That this imposition is basic in any understanding of the past is clear from the rules that documents should not be altered, or that material damaging to a historian's argument or purpose should not be left out or suppressed. These rules mean that the sources or the texts of the past have an integrity and that they do indeed 'speak for themselves', and that they are necessarily constraints through which past reality imposes itself on the historian.[60]

Causation

Causation is a concept of such fundamental importance to historical understanding that E.H. Carr in his G.M. Trevelyan lectures (1961) declared the study of history to be the study of causes. But postmodernist thinking on the issue of historical causation is different. John Vincent would abandon the search for causes as futile and rather look for explanations.[61] Writing in 1976, Theodore Zeldin thought of causation and chronology as the two tyrants to historians.[62] Hayden White attacked the concept of causation as depriving people of both their freedom of action in the present and of control over the future by trapping them in an inescapable network of causation.[63] Postmodernist theory installs interpretation in the place of empirical research into the causes of specific events.

Since the notion of cause depends on sequential time, some postmodernists attack the latter too. The cause of an occurrence must obviously come before it in time. But the postmodernist historian and philosopher, Ankersmit, says "Historical time is a recent and highly artificial invention of Western civilization," and the writing of historical narrative based on the concept of time, he has declared, is "building on quicksand."[64] The postmodernists would prefer that the idea of sequential time be abandoned in the writing of history.

Richard Evans shows how the very idea of *post*modern is paradoxical in that it is contrary to the assertion that there are no time periods in history. And the postmodernist statement that historical time is a thing of the past, itself uses the historical concept of time which the statement is intended to dismiss.[65] The linear and sequential concept of time is far too powerful a principle to be dispensed with, for it is not an intellectual construct but a matter of everyday experience for people the world over. Time itself may be without boundaries, but in terms of human life it passes, and has limits.

Some postmodernists have argued that we can only know causes from their effects. This, says Evans, is to mistake the process of inquiry for its object. Basic to history is the belief that the past, the present and the future are different, that the three stand respectively in a cause–effect relationship, that what happens today may affect or cause what happens tomorrow, and that the texts and other material objects which we produce today provide the basis on which the future can attempt to know us.[66] In history, as in daily life, the concepts of causality and sequential time cannot be dispensed with.

Historical Objectivity

Postmodernist historical theory maintains that no kind of objective knowledge of the past is possible because all knowledge is relative, all theories are equally valid and that a text is but an infinite play of significations. Hayden White, the postmodernist philosopher and historian, would add that the only reasons we have for preferring one interpretation over another would be moral or aesthetic.

Historical objectivity demands the strict presentation of what actually happened, uninfluenced by any personal feelings or prejudices. It is the knotty problem of the proper relationship between the facts of history and their interpretation. Whatever the postmodernist thinks about historical objectivity, for legitimate interpretation of the past, of the sources, *we need to have some common standards of factuality and evidence.* Evans cites the example of the Paul de Man controversy of 1987 in which deconstructionists who argued for the irrelevance of authorial intentions, as well as those who opposed them, appealed to such common standards.[67]

In 1987, a young Belgian scholar discovered that a leading postmodernist and deconstructionist, Paul de Man, had written about one hundred and eighty anti-Semitic articles for a Nazi-controlled newspaper in Brussels during the German occupation of Belgium from 1940 to 1942. Emigrating to the US after the War, de Man became a very influential literary theorist and led the school of literary deconstructionists at Yale University where he was professor. But he had taken care to keep his wartime collaboration with the Nazis a secret till his death in 1983. When the articles were discovered a raging controversy ensued in which de Man's defenders employed deconstruction to deny the very fact of his collaboration with the Nazis, even arguing that de Man was in fact engaged in resisting Nazism when he wrote the articles in question—which begged the question, why did de Man suppress them after the War? Derrida defended de Man and accused his critics in vehement terms. Evans shows how the theoretical assertion of the endless possibilities of textual interpretation crashed down in practice when Derrida and his supporters argued that to interpret de Man's articles as collaborationist or anti-Semitic was wrong. Postmodernist theory takes away from the author all claims of control over what he wrote; but Derrida denounced in the most polemical terms those he thought were wilfully misunderstanding what he himself said in de Man's defence. If everything was a text as the postmodernists contend, anti-Semitism could not but be a text subject to the infinite play of meanings; then, how could Derrida describe it as 'essentially vulgar'? It is ironic that postmodernists who contend that it is wrong to prioritize elite culture over popular culture bitterly resented the involvement of journalists in the debate. And how could a Nazi-controlled newspaper publish anti-Nazi articles during the War?

The controversy serves to show how deconstruction could be used to justify or rewrite anything. One historian commented: "Although deconstruction should survive the attack of de Man's critics, as a tool for historians it may not survive de Man's defence."[68] The deconstructionists have produced a permissive intellectual climate which encourages scholars to deny that documents have any fixed meaning; to argue that meaning is supplied by the reader, and that there is no ultimate historical reality.

Historical Knowledge and Power

Following Foucault, the postmodernists hold that the main purpose of all historical writing is to gain power for historians or for those they represent in the present. Foucault argued that texts, novels and histories were not the outcome of individual thought but the ideological products of the dominant discourse in every age. History was a fiction in support of the exercise of power, and if one version of the past was more widely accepted than the others, it was only because its exponents had more power than its critics.[69] In postmodernist eyes, conventional history is no more than a dominant bourgeois form of ideology supported and maintained by professional historians. To Keith Jenkins, "history is theory and theory is ideological and ideology just is material interests."[70] Postmodernist history would throw overboard this dominant discourse and its guardians – the privileged professional historians – in the interests of empowering the oppressed social groups. The rules of historical research, and belief in the attainability of historical truth would likewise be done away with. The restructured historical writing and teaching would be based on the belief "that history is propaganda that it is about the present."[71]

Much history may have a present-day purpose and inspiration, but, as Evans asks, is it *that* history is really about, in the end?

4. The Impact of Postmodernism on Historiography

What impact has postmodernism made on historiography? For one, it has not stopped with mere denunciations of conventional history;

it has developed its own genres of historical writing and produced a rich crop of them in a short time. The main features of postmodernist historiography are:

Local Narratives

Local narratives (a term formulated by Lyotard) are a kind of historical work which have come in the wake of the postmodernist rejection of grand or master narratives as hegemonic stories told by those in power. They are generally accounts of forms of resistance —individual stories told by prisoners, students, peasants and others. Subjective in nature, they do not lay claim to objective historical truth or universal validity. Yet, postmodernist theory holds that it is a mass of such local narratives that must constitute history.

Extension of the Range of Historical Knowledge

Richard Evans writes that works of history in which postmodernist influence is already evident have not only extended the range of historical writing but breathed new life into some old and rather tired subjects.[72] For example, historical writing can only benefit from the postmodernist shift of focus from the social bases of nationalist movements to the sources and determinants of national identity. Again, postmodernist critique of social history has had a liberating and enriching influence in that it has shown that there are aspects of social inequality other than class e.g., gender and ethnicity. Moreover, rejecting faith in reason and progress, postmodernist historiography has directed much of its attention towards the irrational, the extraordinary and the magical in human life. Studies of numerous subjects, from popular mentalities to the micropolitics of everyday life, have added substantially to historical knowledge.

History as a Form of Literature

Extremely weak on the critical side, postmodernist historiography has, however, promoted good writing as a normal historical practice. Evans cites four examples.[73] The first two are Simon Schama's *Citizens: A Chronicle of the French Revolution*, and Orlando Fige's *A People's Tragedy: The Russian Revolution 1891–1921*. Though dealing with great 'traditional' subjects, both works interweave small incidents and personal histories of the famous and the obscure making no claims to be certain or definitive. The other two are Natalie Zemon Davis's *The Return of Martin Guerre* and Robert Darnton's *The Great Cat Massacre.* These two works have been sharply criticized for their careless handling of evidence, but their literary treatment of small incidents of everyday life brings alive to the reader the fabric and feel of everyday life in a manner totally unknown to the generalizing social-historical works.

Re-establishment of the Place of the Individual in History

The dethronement of the author and the elevation of impersonal discourses to the centre of historical analysis should not lead us to think that postmodernism would leave little room for the individual actor in history. Ironically, as Evans points out, it has done a great deal to reestablish the place of individual men in history though these are not the 'great men' of the political historians, but the little known men of ordinary life. Postmodernist historiography has in a big way recreated the world of little known individuals. Evans writes:

> One of the very great drawbacks of generalizing social science history, with its reliance on averages and statistics, was its virtual elimination of the individual human being in favour of anonymous groups and trends. To reduce every human being to a statistic, social type, or the mouthpiece of a collective discourse is to do violence to the complexity of human nature, social circumstance and cultural life.[74]

Limited Influence of Postmodernism on Historical Theory and Method

The main theoretical contribution of postmodernism is its exhaustive frontal attack on positivism, thus suggestively holding open the possibility of an empirical social science that does not operate with positivist assumptions. Derrida's intellectual charisma has been enormous and his deconstructive method has spread like wildfire through American humanities departments. The critical Lawrence Stone admits that the "linguistic turn" has "taught us to examine texts with far more care and caution than we did before, using new tools to disclose covert beneath overt messages, to decipher the meaning of subtle shifts of grammar and so on."[75] Summing up what may be called the beneficial effects of the postmodernist advent Evans writes Postmodernist theory has persuaded historians to look more closely at documents and to think about texts and narratives in new ways; it has forced them to be more self-critical and conscious of their own subjectivity; it has helped open many new subjects and areas of research; it has restored individual human beings to history where social science disciplines had more or less written them out; it has shifted emphasiz in historical writing back from historical-scientific to literary models making it more accessible to the public outside the universities; and it has inspired or at least informed, many outstanding historical works in the last decade or more.[76]

But the benefits have been marginal. Postmodernism has had relatively little impact on historical theory and practice. Writing in 1995, the American medievalist, Nancy F. Partner, remarks:

> The theoretical destabilizing of history achieved by language-based modes of criticism has had no practical effect on academic practice because academics have had nothing to gain and everything to lose by dismantling their special visible code of evidence-grounded reasoning and opening themselves to the inevitable charges of fraud, dishonesty and shoddiness.[77]

"The techniques of deconstruction or discourse analysis," declares Arthur Marwick, "have little value compared with the sophisticated methods historians have been developing over the years."[78] Derridean deconstruction, in fact, tends to focus on what is apparently marginal or peripheral in the texts.

Thus it comes to pass that for all the sound and fury with which postmodernism made its appearance, its call for a radical departure in historical thought and practice is clearly out of the question. Evans foresees that like 'cliometrics' or 'social history' or any other innovative wave in historical theory and practice, postmodernist history itself would be content to become yet another sub-specialism rather than revolutionize historical theory and practice as a whole.

12

ANCIENT INDIAN HISTORIOGRAPHY

1. The Lack of Historical Sense

The central defect of the intellectual life of the ancient Indians, in spite of the antiquity and developed character of their civilization, is an almost complete lack of its historical and chronological sense. A.B. Keith writes: "...despite the abundance of its literature, history is so miserably represented...that in the whole of the great period of Sanskrit literature, there is not one writer who can be seriously regarded as a critical historian."[1]

Abundance of Source Material and the Absence of Histories

There existed throughout the subcontinent and throughout the period up to AD 1200, various categories of sources written chiefly in Sanskrit, Pali and Tamil. The Brahmanical *puranas*, the Buddhist Pali canon and the Jain *pattavalis* contain, amid vast masses of religious and social matter, much historical material though their treatment of such material is anything but historical. Hsuan Tsang refers to the archives, official annals and *nilopitu* (state papers) of the Indians. Al-Biruni attests to the existence of similar material in India. And, in the lithic inscriptions, copper plates and coins, ancient India possessed a corpus of historical information unmatched by any country or civilization. Yet the melancholy fact remains that with such material for historical reconstruction, ancient India produced no great historian. No developed civilization in the annals of mankind has been represented so meagrely in its historical literature as the Hindu. The only professedly formal history undertaken in ancient India is the *Rajatarangini* of Kalhana.

2. Explanation of the Absence of Historical Sense

How is this lack of the historical and chronological sense of the ancient Indians to be accounted for? According to Vincent Smith: "Most of the Sanskrit works were composed by Brahmans, who certainly had not a taste for writing histories, their interests being engaged in other pursuits."[2] But the statement almost begs the question since the problem to be resolved is the reason why the ancient Hindu mind veered at a tangent unhelpful to historiography. A.B. Keith has suggested that the "cause of this phenomenon must lie in peculiarities of Indian psychology aided by environment and the course of events," admitting, however, the difficulty of giving an entirely satisfying explanation.[3]

Environment and the Course of Events

Of environment and the course of events, Keith writes that India produced no oratory, which flourished best in an atmosphere of political freedom. Athens is celebrated for its democracy, oratory and history, as Sparta is deficient in all of them. Ancient Rome produced its best orators while it was still a republic, and the Romans wrote history. Again, national feeling and the resultant popular action which are a powerful aid to the writing of history was not evoked in India by all the foreign invasions during the period up to AD 1200 – the Persian, Greek, Saka, Parthian, Kushan and Hun – in the sense in which the Greek repulse of the Persian attacks called forth popular action and evoked the history of Herodotus. The Muhammadan invaders found India without any real national feeling; their successes were rendered possible largely because the Indian chiefs disliked one another far more than they did the *mlechcha* (foreigner).

Belief in the Doctrines of Karma and Rebirth, and Fate

But environmental factors and the course of events cannot explain even partly the absence of the historical sense in ancient India. The presence or absence of that sense must necessarily depend on the beliefs and mental attitudes of a people. The factors which worked against the development of a genuinely historical consciousness among the ancient Indians are to be sought in their religion and philosophy which are often seen integrally related to each other, and which have deeply influenced their basic attitude towards life, their psyche, and their ethos. Of such factors, Keith identifies the doctrines of karma and rebirth, and the operation of almighty fate. The effects of belief in these doctrines are uncalculable, unintelligible, and beyond all foresight. If men's lives were the outcome of actions in their previous births, no one could tell what deed in the remotest past might not come up to work out its inevitable end; and fate might spring surprises on men's plans and actions—favoring or thwarting them. All the three major Indian systems of thought and belief – Hindu, Buddhist and Jain – subscribed to these doctrines.

Impossibility of Progress: Belief in Regression

Keith picks another anti-historical tenet typical of the Indian attitude and shared by the philosophies whether Brahmanical, Buddhist or Jain. It is the impossibility of progress in the world, things happening age after age precisely the same way cyclically in the periodical creation and destruction of the world. Here, the English scholar is somewhat in error which could be corrected in the following manner. The idea of change and the doctrine of progress so cardinal to the idea of history sounded strange to the ancient Indian mind. In India the accepted idea was a fixed order of things or an eternal system of values from which there could only be degeneration. Ancient Indians believed that movement in time – *yuga* succeeded by *yuga* – meant regression for societies, a continuous fall from a state of excellence which would culminate in the worst excesses of the *Kali* era. The idea of regression – the notion that the preceding ages were progressively better than the present – is clearly an idea even more unhistorical than the idea of changeless continuance.

Preference for the General to the Detriment of the Particular

Keith also refers to the tendency of the Indian mind to prefer the general to the particular, which he says is shown in widely differing fields of knowledge. The history of doctrines or of philosophy noting differences and tracing change was foreign to the ancient Indian mind. The names of some great authorities in philosophy or in the other departments of knowledge might be preserved, but little interest was shown in the opinions of predecessors as individuals. A text might be quoted, but not its author. This tendency to prefer the general to the particular developed and froze into a deprecation of individual personality and opinion, rampant anonymity in art, literature and philosophy, a lack of care for accurate knowledge and exact detail, and worship of tradition and authority. Sadly, all such features are anti-historical.

Philosophy of Life-negation

We may add that all the above anti-historical tendencies of the Indian mind noted by Keith might be traced in their origin to an enervating philosophy of life-negation in the place of a positive, man-making philosophy of life-affirmation. It must be stressed that a necessary condition for engaging in historical pursuit – pursuit of knowledge of the past in our sense of the term – is an interest in the problems of the present and the future, an interest which does not seem to have occupied the thoughts of the ancient Indians in the same manner or to the same degree as in the case of other civilized peoples. The present life with all its constituents was thought to be transitory, just a link in an endless chain of births and rebirths—a release from which was sought as its highest goal. The Hindu's highest aim lay not in what was redundantly taught to be the transient, fleeting, withering stubble of life, but in an escape from it. Buddhism advocated that the will to life has to be destroyed in order to achieve *nirvana.*[4] Belief in the transitoriness of things developed into a melancholy view, an unrelieved pessimism, in which human life was seen as a deception, *maya* (illusion), and as in bondage to misery, despair, grief and affliction, and necessarily evil. In contrast, the after-life was shown to be one of release. By the side of the life-temporal as a vale of woe and wickedness was placed what was believed to be the life-eternal the glories of which were emphasized in all possible ways. The first had only a relative value whereas the second had an absolute quality. Knowledge of the life-temporal suffered in comparison with the knowledge of the life-spiritual, *brahmavidya*—knowledge *par excellence.* The idea got itself entrenched in the Hindu mind and anything which aided such knowledge was considered important. Other kinds of knowledge, though useful, could not claim an absolute substantialistic quality. History which was essentially of this world, could flourish only in an atmosphere of life-affirmation. Life-negation and otherworldliness are anti-historical tendencies.

Surrender of Rationality

The elements in the Indian psyche discussed above constricted human volition and freedom and left life helplessly dependent on the transcendental. Understanding the past is a rational process; where rationality itself is at discount, mundane history would be impossible. And every position resigned by reason was sure to be occupied by faith—faith in the contingent, the miraculous and the supernatural, which only prayer, magic and witchcraft could hope to propitiate and control. The habit of the mind which seeks to find natural causes for natural occurrences, if it ever existed, fell out of vogue in India, for nature itself was thought to be capable of being affected by divine or demonic instrumentalities. All three religions – Brahmanical Hinduism, Buddhism and Jainism – favored asceticism not only as a spiritual exercise but as a means of acquiring superhuman magical powers capable of affecting even the course of nature.

3. The Problem of Chronology

Closely related to the comparative lack of a full-fledged historical sense is the comparable lack of a chronological sense which makes it difficult to ascertain precise dates for the events of ancient Indian history. Historical knowledge is the knowledge of past events in the order of their priority and posteriority of occurrence, related to an index of time. Knowledge of events even when accurate, if unaccompanied by the time of their occurrence, is not historical. In ancient Indian history even when a fact is ascertained as such one is left to grope for the date. This chronological difficulty is of two kinds—one, the absence of the dates of events; and the other, the lack, even when the date is indicated, of a basic date of universal applicability such as the Christian or the Islamic era, a date of reference to which the several eras (Vikram, Saka, Gupta, etc.) and innumerable dates in the history of the subcontinent could be converted. In the absence of a proper historical sense, and also perhaps of a unitary religion with a definite founder, no such universal chronology was developed by the ancient Indians. Where the date of an event is given in the regnal years of a monarch, or say after the birth or death of a teacher like the Buddha, one is still adrift on a featureless sea of time as to the occurrence of the event.

A classic example is Asoka's otherwise clear statement that in his eighth regnal year he attacked and conquered Kalinga which still leaves one in doubt as to the date either of his coronation or of the Kalinga war.

Chronology of Events and the Hindu Idea of the Sequence of Actions

The problem of chronology, as that of history in ancient India should be understood in relation to the Hindu conception of time which was generally viewed in terms of the sequence of actions. The punctilious care the Hindu bestows on time in his daily religious and domestic rites has nothing to do with the time factor in its historical sense. At one end of the scale, time is counted in such particles of it as *yama, nadika, vinadika, muhurta,* and so on; at the other, in eons—*Krita, Treta, Dvapara* and *Kali*. For purposes of history one is too small and the other too large. Events of the past are not described as having occurred in their chronological sequence, i.e., as having occurred in specific durations of time as months or years. V.S. Pathak tells us that the arrangement of events in early medieval historical narratives shows a logical development of the theme rather than a historical one. This logical development is shown in five stages: *prarambha* or the beginning; *prayatna* or the efforts; *praptyasa* or the hope of success; *niyatapta* or the certanity of achievement; and *phalagama* or the achievement. Pathak traces the development of these stages in the *Harshacharita* of Bana.[5]

Pathak further tells us that this sequential form of time in place of the chronological owed to the principle of causality and theories of change developed in early times. *Satyam* (reality), according to the major schools of Indian philosophy, was of two kinds: the absolute reality which is beyond change, and the relative reality of *namarupa* (name and shape) which is always in a state of flux. History is concerned with the second kind of reality where changes are to be understood in terms of cause and effect. The theories of causality developed by the *Samkhya*, the *Vedanta* and the *Nyaya* schools judged the development of a thing against its prior and posterior forms, that is to say, in a sequence of changes. Evidently, in this framework, the chronological form of time as dates and years would have been meaningless.[6]

4. Beginnings of the Indian Historical Tradition

Gatha, Narasamsi, Akhyana, Itivrtta, Vamsa and *Vamsanucharita*

Love of the past is an inborn quality of man and the ancient Indians had, in fact, a lively sense of the past though it did not develop into the sense of a worldly, human, historical past. An oral tradition of history, as in the *gatha* and the *narasamsi* (hero-lauds or praises celebrating men) existed in India in a nebulous and amorphous form even in Rig Vedic times. To these were added in the later Vedic Age and after, other forms of quasi-historical compositions—the *akhyana, itivrtta, vamsa* and *vamsanucharita, purana* and *itihasa.* At times the *gatha* and *narasamsi* were welded together and absorbed by the *akhyana,* which simply meant historical narrative such as *Devasuram* and *Pariplavani* mentioned in the *Brahmana* literature. *Itivrtta* meaning occurrence or event, denotes traditional account of men and things of times past. *Vamsa* or royal genealogies and the line of priestly succession is another class of ancient lore. Such stray historical works when collected and systematized developed into the *vamsanucharita,* the material out of which those political parts of the *puranas* were constructed at a later date. This confused mass of myth, legend and history is to be called quasi-history of both the theocratic and mythical kinds.

A class of important court officials in the later Vedic Age (c. 1000–600 BC) were the *sutas,* also called *magadhas,* whose special duty was to compose, collect and preserve *vamsa,* i.e., royal and priestly genealogies. Between 400 BC and AD 400 this oral tradition of history and legend had been given a fixed literary form. The *sutas* disappeared as the proper organization of royal archives at least from the Mauryan times seems to have made the work of the *sutas* and *magadhas* redundant. The *Arthasastra* lists the kinds of records kept by these archives, and Hsuan Tsang and Al-Biruni testify to the existence of such archival material though they are now not extant.

The *Purana* and *Itihasa*

The earliest forms of oral tradition – the *gatha, narasamsi, akhyana, itivrtta* and *vamsanucharita* – seem to have been absorbed by the *purana* and *itihasa.* The *purana* and the *itihasa,* mentioned first in the *Atharva Veda*, occur together in the *Brahmanas*, *Aranyakas* and the *Upanishads*. A question of fundamental importance is whether the *purana* and the *itihasa*, which represent the ancient Indian conception of history, can be regarded as real, genuine history.

Purana means ancient lore. Amarasimha's *Namalinguanusasanam* (*Amarakosa*) informs us:

Sargascha pratisargascha vamso manvantarani cha
Vamsanucharitam chaiva puranam panchalakshanam.

(The evolution of the universe, gradual evolution and recreation of the universe at the end of each *kalpa* or cycle of time, genealogies of gods and *rishis*, the cycles of eons in which mankind is created afresh and systematized genealogies or descent lists of those who are said to have ruled from earliest times, constitute the five characteristics of ancient lore.)

Itihasa means 'verily, thus it happened'. V.S. Apte's *Sanskrit-English Dictionary* (1912) quotes the standard definition of *itihasa*:

Dharmarthakamamokshanam upadesasamanvitam
Purvavrttam kathayuktam itihasam prachakshate.

(What is known as *itihasa* is past events or ancient lore arranged in the form of stories in which duty or moral law, worldly well-being, desire, love and sex, and final deliverance or communion with god, find instructive application.)

Now, for any piece of writing to be treated as history *per se*, R.G. Collingwood prescribes four tests: First, it must partake of the character of *science* in the sense that it should fasten itself on to some problem and attempt to discover things hitherto unknown. Second, it must be *humanistic*, i.e., it should be about man, about actions of human beings in the past. Third, as science it should have an *inquiry procedure*. And, last, it must have a *purpose*, and the purpose of history is *human self-knowledge*, man's knowledge about man.

It will be seen that the definition either of the *purana* or of *itihasa* does not meet any of the above requirements. The definitions do not partake of the character of science for they do not attempt to answer questions; they refer to human actions only faintly and peripherally; again, there is no interpretation of evidence; and last, the *itihasa* categorically states that its object is to instruct man in the attainment of the *purusharthas* (the ends of life as concerned in Hindu philosophy—*dharma, artha, k ıma* and *moksha*).

Historiography in India would have gained immensely if the meaning of terms like *akhyana* (historical narrative), *itivrtta* (occurrence or event) and more especially *itihasa* ('verily, thus it happened'), had been literally and scrupulously applied to human actions in the past. But that was not to be. For the ancients in the West or in China, philosophy meant gaining such wisdom as was necessary for the conduct of life and government. But the Hindu mind, caught up in cosmological and metaphysical webs, did not address itself to the practical problems of life and government so much so that its historical consciousness was never fully awakened until it came into contact with the West. The ancient Indians pictured their past as one in which gods, sages, demons, nymphs and fairies took an active part in the affairs of men. Men who looked up to supernatural agents for grace and redemption easily found in the *itihasa* and *purana* an ideal and a substitute for history. But what these two genres of Indian literature delineated was not what was real about men and women in the past but what was thought to be ideal about them, their aim being moral education by examples and parables. They are not narrative of man's deeds, man's purposes, man's successes and failures. Neither in their content nor purpose were the *itihasa* and the *purana* historical; they represent proto-history or quasi-history of the theocratic and mythical kind.

The Historicity of the 'Puranas'

Though not history proper, the *purana* might contain historical matter alongside much that was mythological. And this is what the *vamsa* or the genealogical part of the *puranas* represents. F.E. Pargiter's two books, *The Purana Text of the Dynasties of the Kali Age* (1913) and *Indian Historical Tradition* (1922), besides presenting an excellent critical study of the puranic texts, also deal with the historicity of their dynastic part.

It is possible, suggests Pargiter, that after the religious hymns were collected in the *vedas*, the ancient secular lore that was left over had been collected in *purana*. Metrical accounts of the dynasties that reigned in northern India after the great Bharata battle (c. 950 BC) gradually grew in a literary Prakrit recited by bards and minstrels. After writing was introduced into India in about the seventh century BC, they must have been written down. There are clear indications that the whole of the *Matsya*, *Vayu* and *Brahmanda*, and portions of the *Vishnu* and *Bhagavata puranas* were originally composed in Prakrit. More precisely, these are Sanskritized versions of older Prakrit *slokas*. All the accounts are in verse in the *sloka* metre, except most parts of the *Vishnu Purana*.

There are instances here and there, of alterations, incorrect statements produced by misreadings, errors in names and numbers, but as Pargiter attests, no instance of deliberate falsification except in the story of the dispute between Janamejaya and the Brahmans. But the case is different with the *Bhavishya Purana*. Its avowed profession announced by the title to treat of future events (*Bhavishya*) is a contradiction in terms. The *Bhavishya* text has been continually tampered with and supplemented even up to the nineteenth century in order to keep its prophecies up to date. The pious fraud, says Pargiter, has left the ancient matter utterly vitiated.

Dynastic Lists

Royal *vamsas* or dynasties is one of the prescribed topics of the *purana,* and it is in these dynastic lists that the historian's chief interest lies. The *Bhavishya* was the first *purana* to give an account of the dynasties of the *Kali* age, and the *Matsya, Vayu* and the *Brahmanda* got their accounts from it. The most important *puranas* as regards royal genealogies are the *Vayu*, *Brahmanda*, *Brahma*, *Harivamsa*, *Matsya* and *Vishnu*. The *Vayu* and the *Brahmanda* have the best texts of the genealogies. The dynastic lists are given in an anti-historical cast since they are uttered as prophecies by Vyasa. The preface says: "Listen as I narrate all *future events*, as Vyasa,...[of] the kings *who are to be*." The royal genealogies are given with the respective reign period in years of each king.

The first four dynastic lists of the *puranas* – those of the Pauravas of Hastinapura and later of Kausambi, the Aikshvakus of Ayodhya, the Barhadrathas of Magadha, and the Pradyotas – though appearing to be legendary, might contain material that is historical. The truly historical part begins with the Sisunagas of Magadha. Here the chief dynastic lists are those of the Sisunagas, Nandas, Mauryas, Sungas, Kanvas and the Andhras. Besides these, the names of a number of races and local dynasties such as the Abhiras, Sakas,

Yavanas, Nagas, Tusharas, Murundas and Pulindas are mentioned. The lists are brought up to the first decades of the fourth century AD for the Guptas are mentioned as reigning over Prayaga, Saketa (Ayodhya) and Magadha, i.e., exactly the territory ruled over by Chandragupta I, before it was extended by his illustrious son and successor, Samudragupta.

The Sisunaga Dynasty: Sisunaga ruling from Girivraja (40 years); his son Kakavarna (36); Bimbisara (28); Ajatasatru (25); Udayin (40), who in his fourth year as king, transferred his capital to Kusumapura on the south bank of the Ganges; and Mahanandin (43).

The Nanda Dynasty: The founder of the Nanda dynasty, Mahapadma Nanda (88 years), and his eight sons ruling in succession (12).

The Maurya Dynasty: The Brahman, Kautilya, uprooted the Nandas and anointed Chandragupta Maurya as king (24 years); Bindusara (25); Asoka (36); Kunala (8); Dasaratha (8); Samprati (9); Salisuka (13); Brahadratha (70).

The Sunga Dynasty: Pushyamitra Sunga, the commander in chief, uprooted Brahadratha Maurya and ruled the kingdom (36 years); Agnimitra (8); Vasumitra (10); and the last Sunga king, Devabhuti, a dissolute youngster (10) was overthrown by his Brahman minister Vasudeva Kanva.

The Kanva Dynasty: Vasudeva Kanva and his successors, known as Sungabhrtya Kanvayana kings, ruled from Pataliputra for 45 years. The kingdom then passed on to the Andhras.

The Andhra Dynasty: Thirty Andhra kings are mentioned who ruled for a total of 460 years. Some of the more important of the Andhra kings are Simukha (23 years); Satakarni (56); Pulomavi (36); Hala (5); Gautamiputra (21); and Yajnasri Satakarni (29).

Historical Value

There can be little doubt that the royal genealogies in the *puranas* embody many genuine historical traditions of great antiquity. Without the puranic account, the reconstruction of a reliable history from the period of the Mahabharata war to the rise of Jainism and Buddhism (c. the tenth to the sixth century BC) – an apparently impossible task accomplished by H.C. Raychaudhuri – would have been well nigh impossible. The puranic dynastic lists for the period from the sixth century BC to the beginning of the fourth century AD, with collateral and corrective information from Buddhist and Jain traditions constitute an invaluable base for the reconstruction of the political history of northern India for the period covered by those lists. Again, the *puranas* are sure to yield valuable information for the cultural history of ancient India. And though the prophetic descriptions of the future evils of the *Kali* age do not provide any direct, authentic information of a historical kind, those gloomy brahmanic forecasts contain an oblique reference to the miseries which the country underwent in lawless, chaotic times such as during the unsettled conditions of northern India in the early part of the fourth century AD.

5. The *Vamsa* and *Charita*

Freed from the *suta* tradition, the *vamsa* form developed a vast body of quasi-historical literature. The Buddhist *Rajavamsa*, *Dipavamsa* and the *Mahavamsa*, the Jain *Harivamsa*, the Hindu *Raghuvamsa*, *Sasivamsa*, the *Nripavali* of Kshemendra, the *Parthivavali* of Helaraja, and the *Rajatarangini* of Kalhana are only some of the *vamsa* genre of a vast body of a semi-historical literature.

Historical Kavya *or* Charita *or Ornate Biographies*

In the early medieval period another kind of historical narrative, the *charita*, a historical epic or ornate biography, came to be developed in the milieu of the royal courts. Asvaghosha's *Buddhacharita* may be cited as perhaps the first known example of the *charita* kind. The *sutas* and such others charged with keeping up the historical tradition were replaced by salaried court poets who wrote royal biographies. Historiography came to be based on court organization, having a real unity between prince, poet, courtier and chronicler; it became an organ for princely propaganda and an instrument for the propagation of the new social values of chivalry, heroism and loyalty.[7]

The historical *charita* or *kavya* is a romance woven around a strong historical kernel. Some of the most famous specimens of this kind are the *Harshacharita*, the *Gaudavaha*, *Vikramankadevacharita*, *Navasahasankacharita*, *Kumarapalacharita*, *Prithviraja-vijaya*, *Somapalavilasa*, and *Ramacharita*.

Bana Bhatta: Harshacharita

The first Indian work which may be regarded as historical is the *Harshacharita* of Bana Bhatta, an incomplete biography of Harshavardhana of Thanesvar and Kanauj, written in the first quarter of the seventh century. It is the model of romance based on a historical kernel. Bana was born in the village of Pritikuta on the River Sone. The mother Rajadevi died while Bana was still a child and his father, Chitrabhanu also died when he was hardly fourteen. Bana then led a difficult life. Summoned by Harsha, Bana was at first reluctant to attend court but obeyed the summons. Harsha received him rather coldly but soon developed the highest degree of confidence in the poet, and honored him.

Contents

The *Harshacharita* is written as a story related by Bana to his kinsmen. The eight chapters of the work running into 265 pages in its English translation, bring us only to the first year of Harsha's reign. The first chapter deals with the family of the author; the second tells us of his introduction to Harsha, while the third goes on to describe Thaneswar. The next five chapters take us through Harsha's ancestry, his sister Rajyasri's marriage to Grihavarman Maukhari of Kanauj, the death of his father Prabhakaravardhana, the murder of Grihavarman and the imprisonment of Rajyasri by the king of Malwa, his brother Rajyavardhana's expedition against the wrong-doer and his easy success, Rajyavardhana's treacherous assassination by King Sasanka of Gauda, Rajyasri's escape and flight to the Vindhyas, her rescue by Harsha and his return to the imperial camp on the Ganges. At this point the work abruptly ends for Bana was not writing history in our sense of the term. V.S. Pathak convincingly argues that the *Harshacharita* was not a fragmentary work but a complete and finished product of art, that Bana never intended to write further than the meeting of Harsha with Rajyasri, and that he had all along been working to achieve this end.[8] Bana's *akhyayika* (narrative) is complete with the recovery of Rajyasri—the royal glory. Bana concludes: "And there, when I was relating to my friends this story which ends with the recovery of Rajyasri, the sun also crossed the sky."[9]

Nature of 'Harshacharita'

Defects

The *Harshacharita* is not history proper, which was a genre unknown to its author. It is a historical prose-romance belonging rather to the *kavya* or court epic category of Sanskrit literature. There is little narrative – that essence of history and prose – its place being taken by flattery and exaggeration and long rhetorical descriptions sometimes running into two or more pages. The work does not seem to be based on any other source than the facts supplied by reporters at the court and information current among the people. Some descriptions indeed look like eye-witness accounts. For the rest Bana seems to have relied on his own knowledge and imagination. He seems to have invented speeches and even situations for his main characters, but as in Thucydides, we may claim for Bana that each such oration may have represented the substance of an address actually given. Bana aimed not at recording events as they happened but at showing a particular objective being attained by his hero, such as redeeming family honor and recovering Rajyasri in both the meanings of the word—his sister as well as royal glory. This master of Sanskrit prose is eloquent of expression, but the language is bombastic, the style florid and often verbose, and the treatment romantic. Bana's pages abound with religious and mythological allusions. The parade of puns or double meanings in the words and veiled allusions in the sentences make the *Harshacharita* difficult reading even as literature, let alone as history. The supernatural and its concomitants – superstitions, omens, dire portents, dreams, throbbing of the eye, and howls of the jackals – find a place in Bana's pages much as they do in Indian life. Manifest impossibilities mar the credibility of the book.

> All at once the trees in the parks put forth untimely flowers, as though to say farewell. Vehemently wept the statues in the halls, beating their breasts with strokes of agitated palms. The warriors, as though their heads had vanished in fear of the near clutching of their hair, beheld themselves headless in their mirrors.[10]

Merits

Yet the *Harshacharita*, though not intended as a history in the usual sense of the word, is securely based on historical facts. These facts can be easily separated from the literary embellishments that cover them and, often confirmed by contemporary inscriptions and other sources, they attest to Bana's devotion to truth. Cowell and Thomas, the English translators of the *Harshacharita*, have observed that Bana's work "is as much based on real events as Scott's *Quentin Durward* or *Waverly*."[11]

Again, in casual references of a peripheral nature, Bana provides other historical information or confirms such information derived from other sources. Thus Skandagupta, commandant of the elephant corps, in warning Harsha against disasters due to mistaken trust and resultant carelessness, refers to the tragic end of Kakavarna, the son of Sisunaga, who had a dagger thrust into his throat; the assassination of Brihadratha Maurya by Pushyamitra Sunga; the murder of Devabhuti, the last of the Sungas, by the daughter of his slave woman at the instance of his minister Vasudeva Kanva; and to the murder of the libidinous Saka Rudrasimha III Western Satrap by Chandragupta II. Then, the introductory verses of the *Harshacharita*, are of great value for literary chronology as they mention a number of works like *Vasavadatta* and *Brihat-katha* and authors like Vyasa, Hala, Harichandra, Pravarasena, Bhasa and Kalidasa, thus fixing their lower chronological limit. This certainty of date has brought an additional value to the *Harshacharita*, particularly as a landmark in literary history.

The intense realism of Bana's pictures of contemporary life, the result of first-hand knowledge, careful observation and deep human sympathy, is not matched by anything similar in Indian literature. Bana describes men and women of all kinds and classes, and speaks of ploughing, rice and wheat crops, sugarcane enclosures, of the Persian wheel, of cut corn heaps ready for the threshing floors, singing herdsmen mounted on buffaloes gay with the tinkle of bells bound to their neck, roaming herds of cows, troops of camel and flocks of sheep under the guardianship of camel boys, travelers blissfully sleeping after drinking the juice of fresh fruits, and of lovely groves where woodrangers taste the coconut juice. Not only the picturesque but also the pathetic catches his eye. Touching are the scenes of Prabhakaravardhana's death and that of his queen's self-immolation in water.

It is not always the eulogy of a courtier but censure too of his proud master that we read in Bana's pages. Listen to the ryots giving vent to their indignation at the damage caused to their crops by Harsha's troops:

> ...others despondent at the plunder of their ripe grain, had come forth wives and all to bemoan their estates, and to the imminent risk of their lives, grief dismissing fear, had begun to censure their sovereign, crying 'Where's the king?' 'What right has he to be king?' 'What a king!'[12]

One might recall Prabhakaravardhana's death-bed advice to the young Harsha: "In their people, not in their kin, are kings rich in relatives."[13] Cowell and Thomas write:

> Bana is not a mere rhetorician; his descriptions of court and village life abound with masterly touches which hold up the mirror to the time. Not even the Pali Jatakas introduce us more directly into the very heart of the period or give us a more life-like picture. The court, the camp, the quiet villages...and the still more quiet monasteries and retreats, whether of Brahmans or Buddhists, are all painted with singular power; and his narrative illustrates and supplements the Chinese traveller's journal at every turn.[14]

6. Vakpatiraja, Padmagupta, Atula, Bilhana, Bhulokamalla and Jayanaka

There are adulatory biographical works bearing many marks of the Indian *kavya* but few of true history. One such is *Gaudavaha* written in the second quarter of the eighth century by Vakpatiraja to celebrate the defeat of a Gauda prince by the author's patron, Yasovarman of Kanauj, who himself was defeated and killed not much later (c. AD 740) by Lalitaditya of Kashmir. The poem is found left unfinished, as the author might not have proceeded after his patron's death. Nor is this to be regarded as a loss to historiography as the written part contains so little historical information that the reader does not even hear of the name of the defeated Gauda king. Of little importance for history, the *Gaudavaha* is of no great significance for literature either.

Again, far from serious history is the *Navasahasankacharita* of Padmagupta, also called Parimala. Written about AD 1005, the eighteen cantos of this work relate a mythical theme but allude at the same time to the history of King Sindhuraja Navasahasanka of Malwa. As the method, so the treatment and the results are not historical.

Atula: Mushikavamsa

Atula's *Mushikavamsa* was introduced to the world of scholarship in 1916 by T.A. Gopinatha Rao. The work, written in the *vamsa* tradition of historical *kavyas*, contains about 1000 *slokas* arranged in fifteen cantos. Intended to be a dynastic history of the Mushika kings of Kolam, the northernmost principality of Kerala, the *Mushikavamsa* is one of the few epics of regional – nay, parochial – history. The author, Atula, may have been the court poet of Srikantha, also known as Rajavarma, who is believed to have flourished towards the end of the eleventh century and in the beginning of the twelfth. In Atula's hands, the history of the Mushika kings begins in mythology and proceeds, without any sense of time and space, through incredible tales and marvels. The ancestors of the Mushikas were Hehayas who after their overthrow in their original home in the Vindhya region, seem to have trekked southward and settled on the west coast around Mount Eli near present-day Cannanore sometime before the sixth century AD. The historical information contained in Atula's poem is squeezed into the last four cantos, the others being filled with mythological tales and accounts of King Nandana's pleasure-seeking life which alone take up four cantos. Of about 118 kings mentioned by Atula, nineteen kings – from Kunchivarman in about the second half of the ninth century to Srikantha in the twelfth century – ruled over Kolam for about 250 years. These nineteen kings whose history spreads over the last four cantos are historical, a fact which is further proved by inscriptions in some of the temples of the locality recording the arrangements made by them for the protection and preservation of temple property.

The evidence of the poem and the inscriptional data from the region put together give us a few scattered glimpses of the life of the period covered by the more historical of the Mushika kings. King Vallabha had a harbor dug and the city of Vallabhapattanam built at the mouth of the River Killa thereby giving a great impetus to seaborne trade. Hinduism, Buddhism and Jainism enjoyed the respect and patronage of the princes and the people. We see

Vallabha visiting amidst his campaigns in Srimulavasa, the famous centre of Buddhistic learning and practice. King Satasoma is credited with the founding of the Chellur temple. Though there are only few references to the life of the ordinary people, Atula's description of well-dressed beautiful women eagerly glancing at the young King Ramaghata Mushika passing through the city with his army suggests a prosperous class of city-dwellers at their ease.[15] And of great significance to social history is the introduction from King Validhara of the matrilineal system of succession in the royal family.

Bilhana (1040): Vikramankadevacharita

Bilhana was born in a Kashmiri Brahman family of scholars and poets. Receiving a traditional Sanskritic education he left his homeland in search of fame and fortune. He was in Mathura, Kanauj, Prayaga, Varanasi, Somnath, Kalyan and Rameswaram but the succor of patronage eluded him. He trekked back and again reached the Chalukya capital, Kalyan, where at last fortune smiled on him when the powerful King Vikramaditya VI appointed him *Vidyapati*. Bilhana rewarded his patron by composing in his honor an epic in eighteen cantos.

The Nature of 'Viramankadevacharita'

V.S. Pathak's excellent study in ancient Indian historiography informs us that the *itihasa-akhyayika* tradition assumed a different complexion when it was brought to the service of the new warrior class of the Rajputs who were eager to be identified with the best traditions of the ancient Kshatriya order. One way in which this tendency expressed itself was the anachronistic and rather childish representation of contemporary Rajput princes in the role of olden heroes. Ranna, the Kannada poet, portrayed Satyasraya Chalukya in the role of Bhima. Somesvara I Ahavamalla was celebrated as Rama in historical narratives, tales and dramas. Vikramaditya VI, Bilhana's patron, was styled Chalukya Rama. Court poets became instruments of princely propaganda.[16] The nostalgic tendency towards the sentimental heroism and chivalry of ancient times found its expression in Bilhana who gave an unreal personality to his hero by describing in epic style the *digvijaya* of Vikrama and his selection in the *svayamvara* by fair Chandralekha to the bitter disappointment of rival kings.

Distortion of History

The *Vikramankadevacharita* must have been written during AD 1083–89. Much cannot be said for Bilhana as a historian. Hailing from Kashmir with its tradition of chronicling events, Bilhana did not perform the duty of a chronicler. We may justly suspect his impartiality. In his case royal patronage can be shown to have compelled him to systematically distort facts.

Pathak argues that to whitewash the unlawful usurpation of the Chalukya throne by his patron, Bilhana invented the story that the god Siva had preordained that Vikrama should succeed his father. As if to confirm this supernatural preordination, the *Vikramankadevacharita* informs us that at the prince's birth flowers fell from the sky and Indra's war drums resounded. Another story is introduced to enhance the moral character of his patron. Vikrama refuses to accept the office of heir-apparent offered by his father pleading that the throne rightly belonged to his elder brother, Somesvara II Bhuvanaikamalla, who is duly anointed *yuvaraja*. Inscriptional data casts grave doubts on Bilhana's account. That account, Buhler writes, "looks as if it had been touched up in order to whitewash Vikrama's character and to blacken that of his enemy."[17] Bilhana then recounts the atrocious acts of Somesvara II as king, including threatening the life of Vikrama. Siva appears in the latter's dreams and expressly commands him to occupy the throne. Inscriptional data, however, give a clear verdict against Vikramaditya VI who, as governor of Gangavadi, fomented internal dissensions and invited foreign invasion against his elder brother.[18]

Vikramaditya VI had rebelled against his elder brother Somesvara and dethroned him, and Bilhana had defended this successful *coup d'etat*; but an allegedly similar attempt by his patron's younger brother, Jayasimha, comes in for condemnation in the poet's hands. Jayasimha was a trusted, loyal and active companion of Vikramaditya VI, and had helped the latter in his struggle against his elder brother Somesvara II. As king, Vikramaditya had assigned the governorship of Banavasi to Jayasimha with the title of heir-apparent, and it was Jayasimha's active help that had enabled Vikrama to subdue internal and external enemies. A record of Jayasimha dated AD 1080 describes him as "an abode of modesty, a cherished companion of Vikramaditya's heart, a beloved younger brother who having won

Chalukya Rama, had mounted up and gained his affection."[19] But suddenly in 1082 Jayasimha is removed from the office of heir-apparent and Vikramaditya's son Mallikarjuna appointed *yuvaraja*. This degradation and consequent humiliation goaded Jayasimha to revolt against his brother. In Bilhana's account of the struggle we read of the kind and considerate nature of Vikramaditya in contrast to the rash, haughty and the ungrateful disposition of Jayasimha on whom charges of all kinds are heaped. Pathak observes that Bilhana's advocacy here "stoops to unprincipled disputation" and that he had "indeed, an unfortunate conception of his duty as a court poet to justify all acts of his patron...."[20]

Finally, Pathak shows that the marriage of the beautiful Vidyadhara princess, Chandralekha to Chalukya Vikramaditya VI is a historical fact, but not the *svayamvara* ceremony as described by Bilhana to have taken place in 1076—for Chandralekha's second son Mahamandalesvara Somesvaradeva was already governor of Kisukad in 1083 and was ruling Banavasi in 1089. In describing both the *svayamvara* and the *digvijaya*, the language of exaggeration is given full rein. When Vikrama, the Rama of the Chalukya family, reached the shores of the western ocean, the latter betrayed signs of fear; the sage Agastya left its shores when its water got mixed up with the blood of the Kerala king. Vikramaditya must have been a soldier-king ruling over a substantial portion of the Deccan in the late medieval period, but not as heroic as Bilhana has potrayed him.

'Vikramankabhyudaya' of Somesvara III

The only historian of royal blood in ancient India was Somesvara III Bhulokamalla (AD 1127–1136), the Chalukya king of Kalyani, and the son and successor of Vikramaditya VI. He is known to fame as the author of *Manasollasa*, an encyclopedic work on royal duties and pleasures completed in AD 1129. The royal author also wrote a biography of his father, entitled the *Vikramankabhyudaya* which, though discovered at Patan before 1925, has not attracted the attention of scholars.[21] It is a historical prose narrative modelled on the famous *Harshacharita* of Bana. But the incomplete manuscript contains only three chapters. A surprisingly redeeming feature of this fragmented work is a graphic description of the geography and people of Karnataka which constitutes the subject matter of the first chapter. The second dwells on the splendor of the capital city, Kalyan. The third and the longest chapter traces the history of the Chalukyas from its mythological beginnings to the sixteenth year of the author's father, Vikramaditya VI, when the latter starts on his *digvijaya.* Here the manuscript abruptly stops leaving an unfinished sentence, "The Brahmanas and the ladies on that day...." The *Vikramankabhyudaya* and the *Harshacharita* are the only historical prose narratives of ancient India available to us.

'Prithviraja-vijaya' (AD *1191) of Jayanaka*

The *Prithviraja-vijaya* is a historical poem which has come down to us in a mutilated form, one-third of it having been lost. It does not mention the author's name, but Har Bilas Sarda has suggested that it was Jayanaka, a Kashmiri poet, who wrote it. The work in its present form contains eleven cantos with a part of the twelfth. It is, as usual, laudatory, celebrating the victory of Prithviraja Chahamana over Muhammad of Ghor in the first battle of Tarain (1191). It must have been written between the first (1191) and the second (1192) battles of Tarain as Prithviraja met with his doom in the second battle. In a process which Pathak calls Ramayanization and divinization of history, Jayanaka portrays Prithviraja in the role of Dasarathi Rama. The Chahamana hero is Rama, Vishnu himself, born for the elimination of evil-doers (*mlechchas*),who are the *rakshasa* followers of Ravana. Again Prithviraja's ministers, Kadambavasa and Bhuvanaikamalla are portrayed as Hanuman and Garuda respectively, and Prithviraja's wife is identified as Sita! At this point, the manuscript of the *Prithviraja-vijaya* breaks off, to the great relief of the reader. In such a divinized history, it was not necessary for the author to provide much political or other information, a task which is better performed by the Jain monks in Prithviraja's service and by the Bijolia inscription. Jayanaka's *Prithviraja-vijaya* is an outrageous distortion of history.

Ramacharita

Ramacharita of the twelfth century AD is one of the best of such works from the historical point of view. Primarily intended to be a biography of Ramapala of Bengal, it also gives a brief account of his two predecessors and successors. The style is artificial, each verse being made to yield two entirely different meanings. It describes in detail the great rebellion against the Palas, of which we know practically nothing from any other source. Though limited in scope in regard to time and locality, the *Ramacharita* may be regarded as a good specimen of historical work delineating contemporary events and a fairly good example of the objective treatment of history.[22]

7. Kalhana: *Rajatarangini*

Kashmir's Tradition of Historical Writing

The *Rajatarangini* (*River of Kings*) is a long Sanskrit narrative poem of eight thousand metrical verses divided into eight cantos, each canto being called a *taranga* or wave by the author. It is a continuous history of the kings of Kashmir from mythical times (1184 BC) to the date of its composition (AD 1148–49). The colophon of the work informs us that its author, Kalhana, was the son of Champaka, the minister of King Harsha of Kashmir (AD 1089–1101). The *Rajatarangini* is the only Sanskrit work so far discovered which may be called a history, and Kashmir the only region of India with a tradition of historical writing. Though essentially a part of India and an inheritor of Indo-Aryan traditions, Kashmir lay exposed to the cultural influence of the western Graeco-Roman, the eastern Mongolian and the northern Scythian or Turk all of which had a definite historical tradition. The mountain fastness which registered the geographical isolation of the region may also have fostered a stronger nationalism, and the persistence of Buddhism with its somewhat keener sense of history than Brahmanism may have aided the development of a tradition of historical writing in Kashmir.

Contents of the 'Rajatarangini'

A work of great scope, the *Rajatarangini* is a storehouse of information. From the holy Brahman and the noble Rajaputra to the humble Domba and the untouchable Chandala, Kalhana depicts all at their tasks. His pen-pictures vivify the past and show how contemporary men and women looked like, what they ate and wore, what they believed, and what they thought of the eternal problem of the relation between the sexes.[23] We hear of the founding of towns, building of temples, shrines and monasteries, and their spoliation by non-believers and iconoclasts; of Avantivarman's Chandala minister Suyya's great engineering feats and irrigation works; of Lalitadatiya's distant wars of conquest; of Meghavahana's curious attempt to spread non-violence also by conquest; of war-lords marching up and down and making havoc; of famines, floods and great fires which decimated the population and rendered the survivors to great misery; of popular risings taking place on such a scale that Kalhana describes Kashmir as "a country which delighted in insurrection."[24]

Political and Administrative Aspects

The *Rajatarangini* is a book of kings. There were self-willed warriors-kings like Lalitaditya and successful benevolent kings like Chandrapida. But the feudatories and the Damaras, the Kayasthas, the Tantrins, the Ekangas and Brahmans reduced the rulers to political imbecility. The Tantrins and the Ekangas, says Kalhana, controlled and exhibited their royal masters "like snakes by snake-charmers" for their own benefit.[25] The priests, in case of difference with the king and the government, "resorted to hunger-strike in a body as a powerful political weapon."[26] The Tantrin, the Ekanga, the Damara, the Kayastha, and the Brahman *purohita parishad* all incur the ire of Kalhana's pen.

Economic Aspect

Though Kalhana does not stress the economic aspect in his chronicle, his descriptions of famine, food prices, taxation, currency and many similar details do not fail to give a picture of the economic life of the times. We have it on his authority that while the courtiers enjoyed "fried meats" and "light wine delightfully cooled and perfumed", the food of the common people was rice and hakh.[27]

Social Scene

Kalhana gives a revealing picture of the social scene. Though slavery as such did not exist, the caste system, as elsewhere in India, acted its part, though with some difference in Kashmir. From Kalhana's account it would appear that caste was no bar to the holding of any civil or military post. The Domba and the Brahman were alike soldiers, and a subject of any caste could raise himself through wealth and influence to the status of Damara.[28] Inter-caste marriages of a kind not heard of elsewhere in India are mentioned. The mother of the warrior-king, Sankaravarman, was the daughter of a 'low'-caste spirit distiller; King Chakravarman (AD 923–33) married an untouchable Domba woman, Hamsi by name, and made her the premier queen; she entered the sacred Vishnu temple of Ramaswamin near Srinagar with a retinue. Going by the evidence of the *Rajatarangini*, the proverbially beautiful women of Kashmir did not know the *purdah* and the harem. The adultery of some queens need only be seen against the polygamy of all the ruling princes.[29] The seclusion and veiling of women was not known even among royalty. The women in general were free, owned immovable property and managed their own estates. Some of them even fought at the head of troops.[30] *Sati* or *anugamana* which means following the husband to death, grew out of a custom of the Scytho-Tartars. The custom survived in Kashmir for several centuries.

Condemnation of Oppression

Kalhana wrote in an age when nothing had been known of the rights of man and the denunciation of monarchy. Yet it was probably his belief in *dharma* that urged him to condemn oppression of many kinds. King Sankaravarman's oppressive acts are listed at length, from plundering temples and the resumption of grants to the exaction of forced labor. And it is commendable in one who had never known want nor had worked for a living to have sympathized with the poor and the downtrodden, denounced forced labor,[31] and expressed his horror of the slave trade of the *mlechhas*.[32]

Kalhana as Historian

In Kalhana, we have in ancient India, the nearest approach to a true historian, the *Rajatarangini* alone being written *as history*. Ancient Indian authors in general were not used to treating past events as purely human, or of their occurrence in any chronological order. In these two respects Kalhana stands for the most part fully vindicated. As R.C. Majumdar remarks, the *Rajatarangini* "shows the high watermark of historical knowledge reached by the ancient Indians."[33]

Kalhana and his Sources

An important test of a true historian is his concern for facts. Kalhana testifies: "That virtuous poet alone is worthy of praise who, free from love or hatred, ever restricts his language to the exposition of facts."[34] Facts that a historian provides depend on the variety and quality of his sources. No historian in the twelfth century could have used a wider variety of sources than Kalhana. Written sources alone included the *Nilamata Purana* of Nila, the patron-saint of Kashmir, the *Nripavali* of Kshemendra, the *Parthivavali* of Helaraja, the compositions of Chavillakara and Padmamihira, and a class of writings called *mahatmyas*, besides eleven works of former savants. To check these literary sources Kalhana used much more original authorities such as ordinances relating to religious foundations and land grants and other privileges, edicts, laudatory inscriptions, coins as well as ancient monuments. He was a master of the topography of the Kashmir Valley. It is surprising that a medieval Indian chronicler should have regarded inscriptions and coins as legitimate sources of history and have explored archeological sources with a diligence that his description of them has guided modern exploration and research. As A.B. Keith has written, local traditions of all kinds and family records, his own personal knowledge and that of his father and many others—all went into the treatment of the events of the fifty years preceding the date of his work. There are precise details of facts, and his assertions as to literary history also are precise.[35] Kalhana took trouble with his sources to detect and remove discrepancies and errors. For he writes that he found in Suvrata's work an irksome style, and that the fault of pedantry and lack of care had filled Kshemendra's *Nripavali* with errors.

The Miraculous and the Supernatural

For the first three *tarangas* or books, Kalhana had to rely heavily on legends, mythology and tradition, or at best semi-historical material, and here we read of flagrant improbabilities and impossibilities which have induced some scholars to treat these three books as unhistorical. We read of a king, Ranaditya, reigning for three hundred years; of Sandhimata, impaled by the king, being brought back to life and becoming successor to King Jayendra. The miraculous and the supernatural find a place even in Book Four:

Cankuna, brought down by Lalitaditya to his court from Central Asia, used a charm which caused the turbulent waters of a river in the Punjab to leave a clear path in the middle for the army to cross!

The fact is that Kalhana shared with his age and clime many superstitions and belief in the miraculous, and his 2333-year survey reaching back to the second millennium BC gave him many opportunities to err. But it also stands to his credit that he sometimes felt ashamed to narrate such nonsense.[36] Referring to the various accounts of the manner in which King Lalitaditya must have met with his death, Kalhana says with ironic humor, that for one who had performed many miraculous deeds, it was proper to have a very miraculous death also. So also, previous writers had represented Mihirakula as having killed three crores of people because he found so many women failing to prove their chastity. Kalhana remarks: "this is what is believed in the opinion of others."[37] To discredit the entire mass of material in the first three books of the *Rajatarangini* would be as unprofitable to us as it would be unfair to its author.

Facts and their Explanation

If with the Karkota dynasty in Book Four, historicity of the *Rajatarangini* rests on firmer foundations, there is in the succeeding books a steady improvement in the quality of the history written. An attempt is made to understand historical events in their context. Explanations do not solely rest on concepts like *dharma* and *karma* but on natural causation, too. In Book Eight, which takes up almost half the work and where Kalhana describes events nearer his own times (AD 1100–1150), the quality of analysis and of causal explanation is of a high order. He attains a high degree of accuracy in point of facts, and of the genealogical and topographical information he provides. And the nearer his own time, the accuracy is the greater for he observed intently the process of current events. Details of the self-immolation of Suryamati and of Sussala's murder imply an eye-witness account.

Chronology of the Rajatarangini

Since history is the study of past events in the order of their occurrence, one of the tests of a true historian is a sense of this order, i.e., of the chronological order. The *Rajatarangini* has for its chronological basis the *Kali*, the *Laukika* and *Saka* eras. In the first three books where he has to rely entirely on tradition, Kalhana avoids giving any date as he could not do so with certainty and accuracy. The first date given is in Book Four, the *Laukika* year 3889 or AD 813–14.[38] There can be little doubt that Kalhana's history after this date is a faithful and accurate record in point of chronology. The work is invaluable for fixing many dates in Indian history as it mentions the names of many authors, poets and playwrights.

Honesty and Impartiality

What distinguishes Kalhana from the common rung of historians is his honest, independent and impartial outlook. At the very outset he had set forth his ideal of a historian. "That man of merit alone deserves praise whose language, like that of a judge, in recounting the events of the past has discarded bias as well as prejudice."[39] Kalhana remained steadfast to his ideal. The *Rajatarangini* is different from court chronicles composing wholesale panegyrics of royal patrons; its author refused to take sides in the factious political struggles of the day, and employed his well-earned freedom to tell the truth. Kalhana presented both sides of most problems, and painted the faults as well as the virtues of the kings and other characters whom he described. Though not given to praise or to blame of individuals and groups, devotion to truth often compels him to censure many, whether king or common man. He severely condemns the deeds of King Sussala; his favorable account of Bhikshachara was not induced by any personal motive; love or hatred did not sway his treatment of King Harsha—telling us the appalling cruelties of this 'Nero of Kashmir' as much as he pities his end. Freedom and detachment enable him to describe fellow Kashmiris as fair, false and fickle. The disorderliness and cowardliness of the soldiers are contemptuously contrasted with the courage and loyalty of the Rajaputras and other foreign mercenaries on whom the king had largely to depend. The Damaras are called robbers, but he has no illusions regarding the Kayasthas whose greed, peculations, oppressions, and disloyalty are frankly exposed. The Brahman historian does not spare the *purohitas* whose pretentious *prayopavesa* (hunger-strikes), ignorance, and arrogance in intervening in matters beyond their skill are ridiculed. And it is to be stressed that Kalhana's strong adherence to Siva does not prevent him from paying his respects to Buddhism.

Didactism

Kalhana's ideal of history is a vivid representation of the past with its great role as the instructor of future generations. A.B. Keith writes that the influence of the epics – particularly of the *Mahabharata* – and of Indian poetics worked towards such an end.[40] The influence of the epics is seen in the general tendency to inculcate morality, in the stress laid on the impermanence of power and riches and the retribution that awaits evil-doers in this or a future life. Then, as Indian poetics required, the dominant sentiment – *rasa* – of the *Rajatarangini* is inner poise, resignation, *santa*.[41] History has no such moral purpose as ancient and medieval historians thought it had.

Kalhana's Philosophy of History[42]

Closely allied to the didactic purpose which Kalhana set before him was his application to history of the basic tenets of the Hindu view of life, sometimes even resorting to them as causal explanations. It is as if an assortment of such concepts – *dharma, punya, papa,* fate, *karma* and *punarjanma,* divine retribution and divine pleasure – provided him with a readymade philosophy of history. Such a philosophy sometimes affected the nature and quality of his explanations. A well-intentioned king may be defeated in his purpose by his own lack of *punya* or that of his subjects. And writing in an age which knew little or nothing of constitutional checks on autocratic power, Kalhana brings in the theory of divine retribution or of divine pleasure as a lesson for rulers.

Style

With a keen historical sense, superb sense of literary form, and elegant, noble and melodious language, Kalhana achieved in the *Rajatarangini* a near marvel in history and literature. The work is pre-eminently a narrative in simple versified prose. Scenes succeed one another in neat orderliness and parable-like sayings, anecdotes and dialogues are skillfully woven into the fabric of the story which lend not merely variety but dramatic power.[43] The account of

Bhoja's terrible journey over the snow-clad mountains to the Dards (AD 1144), the funeral of Ananta, Suryamati's *sati*, and the tragic tale of Harsha's isolation and misery are only some instances of Kalhana's power of simple and deeply affecting narrative. The one great defect of the style was the fatal *double entendre* that serves only to obscure meaning and reality.

8. Ancient Indian Historiography: An Appraisal

'Itihasa–Purana–Kavya' Tradition of Historiography

There is truth in the charge that the ancient Indians, when seen alongside the ancient Greeks, Romans and the Chinese, had no historians and no historical sense. There is little that is genuinely historical in the definition of either the *itihasa* or the *purana*. For this reason the *itihasa–purana* tradition – the way in which the Indians tried to understand their past – was not easily comprehensible to those familiar with the usual Graeco-Roman or even the Islamic traditions of historiography. But the charge that the ancient Indians were an ahistorical people has been objected to, doubtless with a measure of truth. F.E. Pargiter took trouble to bring out this truth. Recently, Romila Thapar has suggested that instead of summarily dismissing the *itihasa–purana* as a fanciful rendering of the past, it may be found to have a firm historical basis if related to the different phases of state formation, i.e., of the transition from a lineage society to a state system.[44] The historical *kavya*, emerging about the beginning of the Christian era, absorbed whatever real history the *itihasa–purana* tradition contained. None too easy for definition or even description, the word *kavya* means a self-contained narrative conveying *rasa*, or experience of sentiment (*vakyam rasatmakam kavyam*). In this modification there was little gain for history, for the *kavya* tradition growing – like that of the *itihasa* and the *purana* – in the habitat of Indian life and culture, was theocratic, mythological and at best quasi-historical. To the theocratic-moral equipage of the *itihasa–purana* tradition, the *kavya* tradition added its own literary outfit. The writers in this tradition did not take trouble to record facts of human life in the past nor to set down such facts as contemporary to them, with the object of preserving them for man's knowledge. In its eagerness for moral edification, ancient Indian historiography threw overboard rationality and allied itself with religion and mythology. No distinction was made between the reliable and the unreliable, the possible and the impossible, the natural and the supernatural. Such normal themes of history as politics, war and strife were to the writers of the *itihasa–purana– kavya* tradition, only superficial expressions of life, below which lay the fascinating drama of man's fulfilment of the sovereign purpose of human existence. The tradition in question tried to grasp this inner story and to understand the meaning of life in terms of the *purusharthas*, the four-fold aims of life.[45] Absorbing a people's need for knowledge of their past, for self-knowledge and identity, the Indian epic tradition produced masterpieces of thought and literature, but at the cost of what we call history. The idea conveyed by the Greek word *istoria* as an inquiry into the human past for man's self-knowledge never occurred to the ancient Indian genius. During the long stretch of time from c. 1500 BC to AD 1200, the *itihasa–purana–kavya* tradition did not show any sign of growth toward real history, the *Rajatarangini* alone being a relieving exception.

Characteristics of Ancient Indian (Hindu) Historiography

Pattern History

Ancient Indian (Hindu) historiography conformed to a certain pattern in respect of theme, mode of treatment, and conclusions drawn. The pattern had little to do with problems of history writing such as chronology, the narration of facts and their explanation. Kalhana alone was an exception.

1. *Theme*: As for theme, the histories of this tradition were the *charitas* or ornate biographies, mostly of kings. Works like the *Harshacharita*, *Vikramankadevacharita* and *Prithviraja-vijaya* are examples. But the *charitas* were not full-fledged biographies written from the historical point of view. The theme would be limited to some aspect of the king's life, usually the attainment of royal glory or victory over an enemy. The conventional *digvijaya* of ancient *chakravartins* and the *svayamvara*, which need not be true to fact, were important features of this pattern.

2. *Causation and causal explanation*: Adhering to the law of

causality enjoined by the medieval Indian philosophers, writers on history seem to have recognized the category of *adrshta* (unseen) causes where the seen causes failed to account for or explain a phenomenon.[46] This meant resort to ideas of supernatural causation resulting in myth-making as in the Agnikula origin of the four Rajput dynasties. Myth-making became so rampant that every dynasty of early medieval India was connected with the solar or lunar lineage with a Kshatriya tradition. Supernatural causation figures even in Kalhana's work. Religiosity and the otherwordly ethos of the Hindu mind enhanced by belief in the doctrines of karma and *punarjanma* and the inscrutability of fate offered an easy way to bypass historical explanations by natural causation. Readymade explanations and incessant recourse to authority and tradition rendered doubt on such topics idle. And fate was always a potent cause.

3. *Facts*: Divine intervention and supernatural occurrences in human affairs, the doctrines of karma and rebirth, and the role of destiny were all intrusive elements which vitiated ancient Hindu historiography. To look for the meaning of human actions outside of those actions is to throw actual facts out of historical focus, persuading the historian not to search for facts at all. Only Kalhana had regard for facts *as facts* and the *Rajatarangini* is exceptional in its sense of sustained narrative and a near-complete freedom from legendary matter. When Bilhana or Atula or Jayanaka describes events, the description itself is without any sense of time and place, giving a mythological cover to what little of real events they cared to set down. Vikramaditya VI Chalukya was Rama whose *digvijaya* obliged Agastya to leave the shores of the ocean; Prithviraja III Chahamana was again Rama, fearful of whose wrath, the ocean gave just enough water to the rainclouds, neither too much to inundate Prithviraja's lands nor too little to scorch it. Fantasy took the place of facts, a trend which assumed an extreme form in the *Navasahasankacharita*, a tenth or eleventh century biography of Sindhuraja Paramara by his Jain court poet, Padmagupta. The author did not think it improper to introduce his historical characters in the garb of animals and supernatural beings and give a fictional character to historical incidents as in fairytales. From the point of view of facts – let alone their accuracy – the *charitas* cannot be considered as historical treatises.

4. *Chronology*: Historical facts can be known as such only in a

chronological framework. But a conception of the past which did not generally look for actual events would not insist on the exact time of their occurrence in dates and years. Keith blames the Indian disregard of chronology to the secondary character ascribed to time by the philosophies.[47] The ancient Indians did develop a chronology of sequence—the beginning, the efforts, the hope of success, the certainty of success, and the attainment of success. But these are only logical stages of development, and unrelated to some point of time—they are too different from the universally accepted meaning of chronology to be able to meet the requirements of history.

5. *Anachronistic portrayal of historical characters*: The vivid sense of the past that the ancient Indians had – say, their nostalgia for the past – had nothing truly historical about it. They took to portraying contemporary history with religious and mythological models, a practice detrimental as much to religion and mythology as it was to history. The result was the anachronistic representation of contemporary kings in the role of the heroes of religion and mythology. We have already seen Vikramaditya VI Chalukya and Prithviraja III Chahamana in the role of the god Rama. Not only individuals, but issues and events were most anachronistically and unhistorically represented. Prithviraja III was Rama incarnate to restore and preserve the religious and social order threatened by Muhammad Ghori and his hosts, who automatically became Ravana and his *rakshasa* followers. If Jayanaka had extended his ridiculously anachronistic portrayal to a date after the second battle of Tarain, he would have had to tell the story not of Rama defeating and killing Ravana—but its opposite.

6. *Meeting the present by the past*: Since for the Hindus the *Kali* age was decadent in comparison with the glory of the preceding ones, it was idle to meet the past by the present. Hence, writes V.S. Pathak:

> these medieval historians tried to understand the contemporary history with the help of ancient forms and ideals. Here in their attempt to study the present in the light of the past, they offer a striking contrast to those modern historians who tend to study the past with direct and perpetual reference to the present.[48]

7. *Language and style*: The proper form of a narrative subject like history is prose, not poetry. Not only that all facts cannot be

expressed in poetry, but a historical narrative, when rendered in poetry, is likely to be colored by dramatic and poetic embellishments. It must be said that verse was as familiar and normal to the ancient Indians as prose was to other peoples and that the *anushtup* metre in Sanskrit could be as matter of fact as prose in the other languages. Yet, ancient Indian historians were poets first and historians last—literary conventions, hyperbolic expressions, and chivalric, dramatic and poetic embellishment overwhelmed the little casual history they cared to write. The *Harshacharita* was not in fact an *akhyayika* or biographical narrative as Bana calls it, but a *kavya* in prose. The *Rajatarangini*, though written in verse, is happily a narrative of historical facts.

It must be said in conclusion that ancient Indian historiography did not make any real advance towards genuine history writing. With the sole exception of Kalhana, who remains a pleasant mystery, the ancient Indians left behind them no great work which we could call history. The modern idea of history, imported from the West, was rightly disinclined to accept the *itihasa–purana–kavya* tradition or any aspect of it as historical, and for the most part, modern historians of ancient India also unceremoniously discarded it.

13

MEDIEVAL INDO-MUSLIM HISTORIOGRAPHY: I. THE SULTANATE PERIOD

The Muslims, like the Christians, had a keener sense of history and a more precise sense of chronology than the ancient Hindus, and it was in the wake of the Muslim conquest of Hindustan that historiography as a deliberate form of cultural expression was introduced into India. The Muslim love of history was continually reinforced from Arab, Turkish and Persian sources. Medieval Muslim historical literature in India was in form, subject and spirit, little different from historical writing elsewhere in the Muslim world. The advent of Islam started a great series of Indian chronicles written by courtiers or officials on the orders of their rulers or in expectation of gaining their patronage. Some of them wrote general or universal histories of the world until gradually a regional and domestic sense emerged, which was reinforced by the deliberate policy of Akbar in severing connections with the outer Muslim world.

1. General Universal Histories of the Sultanate Period (1200–1526)

The practice of writing general or universal histories of the Islamic world had come to prevail between the ninth and eleventh centuries of the Christian era. Such general histories centered on the life of the Prophet as medieval Christian historiography centred on the life of Christ. It was the providential story of Islam which gave meaning to human history.

Shajara-i-ansab-i-Mubarak Shahi

At the beginning of the Turkish Muslim dominion in north India appeared a work which in the words of Peter Hardy epitomized "something of every element of Muslim historiography,"[1] as it existed at the beginning of the thirteenth century in the Muslim world where Persian language and culture were in vogue. Titled the *Shajara,* it was a volume of genealogical tables which its author, Mubarak Shah, presented to Qutb-ud-Din Aibak about 1206. Aibak ordered the tables to be transcribed and bound for his library. The genealogical tables which form the main part of the work contain one hundred and thirty-seven genealogies. The critical approach of Arab historiography to its sources as, for example, the *isnad* criticism rigorosly employed by al-Tabari, is totally absent. Aibak is praised and his career described. The Ghorid victories in Hindustan are explained and the conversion of the infidels which, Mubarak says, followed those victories are also described.[2] The murder of Muhammad Ghori and the subsequent assumption of power by Aibak at Lahore are recounted. The *Shajara* is religious and didactic in nature.

Minhaj-us-Siraj Juzjani: Tabaqat-i-Nasiri

Minhaj-us-Siraj Juzjani belonged to a migrant family and was aristocratic by birth and marriage. A learned man, he held several posts before his final appointment as chief *qazi* at Delhi under Sultan Nasir-ud-Din (1246) after whom the *Tabaqat* is named. Minhaj's sources are 'trustworthy chronicles', personal evidence, hearsay and unspecified accounts. There is no proof that he had adopted *isnad* criticism or the discipline of *hadith* in ascertaining the authenticity of his source material.

The basic form in Minhaj's *Tabaqat-i-Nasiri* is what Franz Rosenthal has categorized as dynastic historiography.[3] A *tabqa* or section which is equivalent to a chapter is given to each dynasty with a sub-chapter to each ruler of that dynasty. So vast is the scope of the work that it gives an account of more than twenty dynasties of the Islamic world from the Nile to the Ganges, and from the patriarchs and prophets to the disasters that had befallen Islam, notably the eruption of the Mongols in the thirteenth century. From the point of view of Indian history, the *Tabaqat* is important for its account of the Ghaznavids, the Ghorids, the Muizzi sultans of Hindustan, the Shamsi Maliks, and the Mongol invasions of India.

The 'universal' history of Minhaj, writes Harbans Mukhia, does not reveal any broad historical perspective. The *Tabaqat* is, in fact, a politico-biographical narrative, describing events as part of the lives of so many individuals. Causal explanation is never attempted, nor an inquiry into the relationship of individual dynasties to the history of the world.[4] The work is a string of fragmented units, each unit, whether dynastic or regnal, is independent of the other. For Minhaj, causation in history lies in human volition, though at times divine will and predestination intrude into his narrative as causing historical events. For example, it was predestined that the states of Hindustan should come under Iltumish. Again, in the second battle of Tarain (1192) almighty god gave the victory to Islam, though almighty god does not figure in the first battle of Tarain (1191) for it was a victory for Prithviraj.[5]

Sarhindi: Tarikh-i-Mubarak Shahi (1428–34)

Yahya ibn Ahamad Sarhindi, the author of the *Tarikh-i-Mubarak Shahi*, appears to have been a courtier of the Sayyid rulers of Delhi after one of whom his work is named. Sarhindi vaguely tells us that he copied his account of past rulers up to the accession of Firuz Tughlaq from 'the different histories', and after that he wrote on the basis of his own memory, observation and reliable information. Employing no critical technique, he has often recourse to the infallible formula that 'God alone knows the truth.' Yet his information is fairly correct.

The *Tarikh-i-Mubarak Shahi* is a bare narrative of mainly political events from the time of Muhammad Ghori to about 1434. It is a reign by reign treatment in strict chronological order of the deeds of the Muslim rulers and nobles of north India. Each reign is complete in itself and stands in no relationship to the preceding or following reign. From the Tughalqs on, the narrative is more detailed and consistent. History for Sarhindi is a recounting of individual events without its having any organic role. He rarely interprets, divine grace taking the place of causal explanation. Mukhia observes that there is only one instance of a full causal explanation – that of the disintegration of Muhammad Tughlaq's empire – and here, among the seven causes adduced, there is not even a casual reference to any divine force or god's displeasure having brought about that event. The causes are all economic, political and military, combined with the rash, impolitic, unwise and cruel measures of Mohammad. Yet, if wanting in critical methods and causal explanation and suffering form a defective idea of history, Sarhindi's work, as Hardy writes, abounds in moral precepts in prose and verse.

Muhammad Bihamad Khani: Tarikh-i-Muhammadi

Bihamad Khani's father was *muqti* of Irich, north of Jhansi, under the 'sultan' of Kalpi. Khani's *Tarikh-i-Muhammadi*, completed in 1439, covers much the same ground as Minhaj's *Tabaqat*, but adds accounts of the subsequent sultans of Delhi, of Timur, and of the struggles of the sultans of Kalpi with their Hindu and Muslim neighbors. The work also includes stereotyped biographies of saints. While Minhaj mainly relies on former histories, Khani paraphrases earlier ones. And, like Minhaj, Khani takes no trouble to examine the veracity of his sources. Both are historians from authority. Peter Hardy writes: "The absence of the discipline of *Hadith* criticism is underlined by the presence of miraculous elements—dreams, visions and war missiles which do not obey the laws of gravity when aimed at the faithful."[6] History for both these authors is didactic—summoning of the wrath of heaven upon vice; and one cannot expect impartiality in histories that are largely theocratic in character. These historians abase the infidel and sanguinely curse him.

2. Particular Histories

Artistic Forms of History Writing: Nizami, Amir Khusrau and Isami

In the tenth century AD a stylistic device developed in Muslim historiography. It was the use of poetry and rhymed prose in historical panegyrics. There were three writers of this kind in the period of the Delhi sultanate.

The first was Hasan Nizami whose *Taj-us-Ma'-athir* written during 1206–1217 purports to tell the glorious deeds of the Ghorid conquerors but does it by recording the minimum of historical facts with a maximum of florid literary effects.[7] In this respect the author is on a par with his Hindu counterparts of old.

The second writer of this literary genre is the famous Indo-Persian poet, Amir Khusrau (1253–1325). Khusrau was in effect the court poet at Delhi from AD 1289 to his death in 1325. He wrote poems each on a particular historical event or group of events limited to a short span of time. The *Qiran us-Saadain* (1285), for example, has for its theme the meeting between Sultan Kaiqubad and his father Bughra Khan in Oudh. The *Miftah-us-Futuh* (1291) celebrates four victories of Sultan Jalal-ud-Din Khalji. The *Ashiqa* (1320) is woven round the tragic love of Duwal Rani, daughter of Raja Karan of Nahrwala, and Khizir Khan, son of Ala ud-Din Khalji. The *Nuh Siphir* (1318) is a panegyric of the court, peoples, languages, and the flora and fauna of Hindustan. The *Tughlaq-nama* is written to celebrate the enthronement and victories of Ghiyas ud-Din Tughlaq over Khusrau Khan. And the prose panegyric, the *Khaza' in us Futuh* (1311) praises the deeds of Sultan Ala ud-Din Khalji and his armies. The didactic nature of medieval historical works shows itself here too. An eminent literary man, Amir Khusrau was no historian. Yet as Syed Husain Askari writes, the poet provides a wealth of information of a political nature not available elsewhere and works like the *Ashiqa, Nuh Siphir* and *Qiran-us-Saadain* are of solid worth for social and cultural history.[8] The information provided is vast and varied—the seasons of north India, buildings constructed at the instance of the sultans, forms of their entertainment, the *chaughan* or the game of polo, Indian languages, custom of *sati*, and the religious beliefs of the Hindus are of undoubted historical interest.[9]

Vainly aspiring to to be a second Firdausi, Isami wrote his historical epic, *Futuh-us-Salatin* (c. AD 1350) as a disappointed man in search of a patron. Muhammad Tughlaq forced him to move from Delhi to Daulatabad with his ninety-year-old grandfather who died on the way. He, however, found a patron in Ala ud-Din Bahman Shah, the arch rebel against Muhammad Tughlaq and the founder of the Bahmani sultanate. Isami's *Futuh-us-Salatin* is a history of the conquest of north India by Muhammad Ghazni and Muhammad Ghori, and of the Delhi sultanate until 1349–50. The sources of the *Futuh* are, by the author's own report—anecdotes, legends, and common reports current among his friends and associates. The arrangement of the work is regnal, chronology defective, and theme political events such as accession of rulers, rebellions, wars, etc. Bitterly hostile to Muhammad Tughlaq, Isami looks upon him "almost as a sadist verging on madness."[10] Accounts of miracles are there—Muhammad Ghazni is led out of the Rann of Cutch on his march back from Somnath by a light projected from the Kaaba. On the eve of the second battle of Tarain, Muiz ud-Din Ghori is given a key in a dream by an old man, with which the invader was to open the gates of Hindustan.

Yet in Isami's treatment of history, human volition becomes the decisive agent. The way Ala ud-Din Khalji gets Jalal-ud-Din Khalji assasinated and Ulugh Khan poisoned, the intrigues of Malik Kafur at the death of Ala ud-Din, and Muhammad Tughlaq's measures are all treated by Isami as historical facts caused entirely by human volition. And Isami's work gives us details of some political events that are not found in other contemporary works. For example, Isami alone informs us that Sultan Muhammad Tughlaq ordered the execution of those soldiers who had survived the disastrous expedition to Qarachil.

Hasan Nizami, Amir Khusrau and Isami so subordinated facts to fantasy and history to art that Peter Hardy is rightly hesitant to class their works "as part of Indo-Muslim historiography, important as they may be as historical evidence."[11]

Manaquib or Fazail History: Afif

Manaquib or *Fazail* historiography consists of highly stylized prose eulogy of a ruler, noble, learned man, or saint. To this class belong the *Sirat-i-Firuz Shahi* (c. AD 1370) by an unknown author, and *Tarikh-i-Firuz Shahi* of Shams ud-Din Siraj Afif. Both are prose panegyrics of Firuz Shah Tughlaq.

Afif was an old courtier under Firuz Shah Tughlaq. His *Tarikh*, a small portion of which is lost, was written not long after Timur's invasion and capture of Delhi in 1399. The work is an excellent report on the administration and welfare activities of Firuz Shah Tughlaq. Afif's observant eyes take note of the power of the nobility and of the *ulama* (a body of professional theologians), the corruption prevalent in the various departments of state and the sultan's indirect encouragement of it. His eulogy of Firuz does not fail to observe the gradual weakening of the Tughlaq state which he blames on the mildness of the Sultan's policies. It is from Afif that we learn of the gross inefficiency prevailing in Firuz's army, and his acquiescing in irregularities in the muster of soldiers. Offices were made hereditary, offences including embezzlement and rebellion were forgiven, and lax control and discipline made a mockery of authority. Afif's report of Firuz's victories of peace are important and interesting. There is the first ever mention in the works of the Sultanate period of the total annual revenue of the state, and there are references to the low prices during the reign. There are details of the buildings erected, dams constructed, canals dug, and gardens laid. The *Tarikh* refers to the establishment of the department of charity and of a hospital, the installation of the astronomical clock and gong invented by the Sultan, his generosity towards servants and respect for Sufis. Afif tells us of how Asoka's pillars at Topra and Meerut were removed and set up one at the new city of Firuzabad and the other near Delhi. Some *shastris* were asked to interpret the inscriptions on the pillars. Though ignorant of the script, the *shastris* had no difficulty in making the epigraphs say that the pillars would be removed from their provenance only by Firuz.

Both works – *Sirat-i-Firuz Shahi* and Afif's *Tarikh-i-Firuz Shahi* – abound in religious and moral precepts and both depict Firuz Tughlak as an embodiment of the virtues they extolled. For such history, sources are of little account. Afif's sources are no more than 'reliable reporters' and 'honorable narrators'. Hardy finds both works defective as historical biographies. Firuz Tughlak, he says, appears as "a tailor's dummy garbed in ideal attributes."[12]

Didactic History: Zia ud-Din Barani (1285–1359)

Barani's *Tarikh-i-Firuz Shahi*, completed in 1357, was written when the author was seventy-four, and it was written in bitterness. Barani belonged to an aristocratic family which for three generations had enjoyed power and position under the Sultans of Delhi. He himself had been a *nadim* (boon companion) of Sultan Muhammad Tughlaq for more than seventeen years. But with the latter's death in 1351, the old historian fell from power and lost his property. Misfortune embittered his feelings against the new class of plebeian upstart officials who had risen to power at the Delhi court. Wounded feelings developed into a hatred against the lower sections of the society which found vent in many a lamentation in the *Tarikh.*[13]

Sources and Chronology

For Barani, as for the other chroniclers of the Sultanate period, history was not exactly a matter of investigated information but one of received knowledge of the past, and of personal testimony and memory. Barani's chief source of information was his own vast knowledge and prodigious memory. Says Nizami: "He records whatever he remembers and he remembers whatever has left a deep impression on his mind."[14] The historian also quotes as his sources the testimony of relatives and other orthodox, god-fearing persons. And, on his own report, Barani based his work on personal observation as he had easy access to the court and ample opportunities of knowing the details accurately. Finally, as Nizami rightly thinks, Barani seems to have availed himself of recorded data as at the opening of every chapter, he gives a list of the maliks and khans, the principal officers and governors of the concerned ruler. Yet, Barani's method was defective as he relied on received truth—truth on authority. Facts were ascertained not by critical doubt and inquiry but by the testimony of religious and virtuous men. *Isnad* source criticism is absent, and the way Barani finds identity between *hadis* and *tarikh,* that is, tradition and history, has led Hardy to the conclusion that his historical approach was theologically conditioned.

Barani does not arrange events in their chronological order. He confuses dates and is very sparing in giving them; and when he does give them, they may be inaccurate. Harbans Mukhia observes that this indifference to chronology cannot be blamed entirely on Barani's failing memory; rather it owed to his belief in the didactic nature of history. History had certain lessons and these lessons would be intelligible even if the events described are disordered chronologicaly.[15]

Historian's Qualifications

Since the foundation of history, as Barani affirms, is 'truthfulness', the historian, he says, should avoid exaggeration and verbose language and be exact in his statements. If he utters lies, salvation would be denied to him. That Barani does not suppress facts or distort them is to be readily admitted. But the speeches that he puts into the mouths of some of the sultans, like those that Thucydides ascribes to his characters, are bound to be imaginary, as Barani composed his *Tarikh* years after the death of the Sultans concerned. Nizami tells us that towards the close of the *Tarikh* Barani becomes a flatterer, finding divine attributes in the person of Firuz Tughlaq.[16]

Idea of History

Barani's idea of history can be read in his preface to the *Tarikh-i-Firuz Shahi*—pragmatic, didactic and aristocratic.

Pragmatic: History, says Barani, is a panorama of human activity unfolded before man to guide his faltering steps in life's journey. Retrospect of the past helps man to rectify the present, by giving him a rare insight into human affairs and the power to distinguish between good and evil, virtue and vice, friend and foe. It is only in history that man can learn from the experience of others.

Didactic: Peter Hardy emphasizes the didactic nature of Barani's *Tarikh* and affirms that Barani wrote it to propagate his own philosophy of history. A full exposition of the duties of a truly Muslim sovereign is to be found in Barani's other work, the *Fatawa-i-Jahandari*. History is didactic as it is to be studied with a view to deriving lessons from it.

Aristocratic: Barani's concept of society as consisting of the royalty and the upper classes had a direct bearing on his idea of history. Nizami writes:

> He looked upon the historical landscape from the foot of the royal throne focusing his attention on the royalty and the governing classes. For him history was their history and authority was their exclusive privilege. He failed to see greatness apart from and independent of kingship.[17]

Aristocratic birth was central to Barani's historical thinking as it was to his life. The thought of the low-born became an obsession with him and his contempt for them was unreserved; they are to be despised and kept in perpetual ignorance and indigence. "Merit for him (Barani) is high birth and vice low birth and neither can be acquired through any amount of effort."[18]

Form and Content

The *Tarikh-i-Firuz Shahi* is, in its basic form, dynastic and regnal. In effect, it is a continuation of Minhaj's *Tabaqat-i-Nasiri* narrating the history of nine sultans from Balban to the first six years of Firuz Tughlaq's reign, thus covering the most important period of the Delhi sultanate. Barani begins with a few references to Iltumish's reign and refers to the frequency of Mongol invasions. Then he goes on to deal with a very significant development in medieval Indian history, that is, the rise of Khalji imperialism and succeeds in communicating its spirit in all its aspects—military, economic and cultural. Though critical of Ala ud-Din Khalji's disregard of the *Shara,* he considers the sultan's market regulations as a near miracle. And Barani gives the best account given by a historian so far of Muhammad Tughlak's character and personality, as well as policy and administration. The interest he shows in the details of administration, land-revenue collection, and economic life is very valuable. *Tarikh* is a compendium of culture, apart from containing lists of historians, philosophers, poets, physicians, saints and religious divines.

Religious and Didactic Nature

Peter Hardy gives several examples of how the religious and didactic purport of the *Tarikh-i-Firuz Shahi* often dictates Barani's explanation of historical situations. Balban keeps the Mongols at bay and subdues revolts by reason of his excellent appointments of god-fearing persons. But since he is too violent towards Muslims and tolerates infidelity in his kingdom, he loses his favorite son Muhammad in battle against the Mongols and the Sultanate passes from his family after his death. Muhammad Tughlaq confronts a sea of troubles because he patronizes unorthdox scholars – particularly those who employ Greek dialectic – and sheds the blood of true Muslims. In contrast, Firuz Tughluq's virtue enables him to enjoy unbroken success. The worldly success of Ala ud-Din Khalji is attributed to the presence near Delhi of Shaikh Nizam-ud-Din Auliya who was a friend of god. To look for the ultimate course of history outside that course is an unhistorical attitude.[19] But it should be stressed that Barani often sought to analyze causes of events on a purely mundane and rational plane as well. Believing that causation in history lies in the nature of the ruler, Barani presents causal explanations in a logical sequence. Harbans Mukhia gives examples: Balban's stern measures to suppress recalcitrant nobles are set against the weakness of Iltutmish's successors; Ala ud-Din Khalji's economic and administrative measures are related to the necessity of reducing the rebellious rural aristocracy to utter poverty; his market regulations were aimed at maintaining a large army at reduced expense, and the large army had to be maintained to meet the Mongol menace and to suppress the rebellious Turkish and Hindu nobles. Barani's attempt to study historical events in their causal relationship represents an advance over that of Minhaj.[20]

Subjectivity

A chief defect of Barani's *History* is its subjectivity. The *Tarikh-i-Firuz Shahi* fails to meet the canons of historical objectivity largely owing to the circumstances of its composition. The author was a man who had fallen from the plentitude of opulence and glory and reduced to indigence and negligence in his old age. "The despair that is in my heart," writes Barani, "flows in tears of blood from my eyes; a wave from the river of blood pours out of my eyes, drips from my pen and stains the paper."[21] Nizami explains this subjectivism by pointing out that Barani found the tragedy of his life writ large in the history of the period he was writing, from which he could not separate his own story. The description of Muhammad Tughalq, for example, almost follows the vagaries of the historian's own psychological moods—at one moment extolling the Sultan to the skies but condemning him and uttering curses on him at the next. Nizami sums up:

> It was not so much the Sultan who was a mass of inconsistencies or a mixture of opposites but the historian himself who was a miserably torn personality. He projected his own psychological states in his assessment of the Sultan's character.[22]

Powers of Recreating the Past

None could deny to Barani powers of recreating the past and getting the reader involved in the life of the period of his description. Even his incidental references to Iltutmish are so vital and significant that they light up the whole epoch and stand in sharp contrast to Minhaj's detailed but soulless account of that monarch. Revealing is his description of Balban as 'a wary old wolf', and his account of the manner in which Ala ud-Din Khalji effected an evenness of price in the market, which astonished all the wise men of the age. Barani arrests the reader's attention most in his portrayal of Muhammad Tughlaq as man and ruler. As Nizami observes, the Sultan and the historian were men of two different worlds. Yet it is Barani and not Isami or Ibn Batuta, the two other contemporary historians, who gives us a graphic, revealing and penetrating study of the dynamic but baffling personality of the Tughlaq monarch.[23] There are exaggerations. The evacuation of Delhi following the transfer of the capital could not have been so complete as to have left no cat or dog, nor could Tughlaq's experiment in token currency have 'turned the house of every Hindu into a mint.' But such exaggerations bring us nearer to the subjects discussed. Says Nizami: "Barani, in fact, had a better sense of history and its spirit than any other Persian chronicler of early medieval period."[24]

Assessment

Barani himself assessed his work as "of solid worth" and "worthy of credence".[25] None would deny that of all the histories written in India during the period of the Delhi Sultanate, Barani's *Tarikh-i-Firuz Shahi* is undoubtedly the most interesting and the most vigorous. He wrote in a simple, vivid, imaginative style shorn of ornamental verbiage, sometimes soaring high in poetic ecstasy. But doubts have been expressed on Barani's *bona fides* as an authoritative historian. Ferishta blames him for withholding the truth, Elliot for omitting or slurring some important events for fear of incurring the displeasure of his patron. And though not deliberately dishonest, Barani's subjectivity may have led to unconscious misrepresentation. Nizami takes a more kindly view and absolves Barani – despite his irremediable subjectivity and bias – from the charge of suppression or distortion of facts. Barani's merit, according to that critic, lies in supplying to his readers not a catalogue of events but glimpses into the spirit of the age.

3. The Chief Features of Pre-Mughal Indo-Muslim Historiography

Subordinate Role of History

Peter Hardy warns us that the comparative abundance of historical literature in early Islamic India should not mislead us into imagining that history was regarded as an independent intellectual discipline. It occupied a subordinate role in Muslim intellectual life. Barani placed history after the religious sciences, as their servant. It was polite education for the princes, but it found no place in the curriculum of mosque schools and colleges.[26]

Past not Seen as a Process

Hardy tells us that history as a process was an idea too early to be conceived. To the medieval Muslim historians of India, history was a sequence of isolated, disconnected events to which meaning was given by God. They saw the past in individual terms and in biographical form. Even the *umma* (the universal Muslim community) was not considered as an organic subject of historical study. Human society was seen as a concourse of atoms, together but not related, colliding but not interacting. Even when god is held ultimately responsible for what happened in history, he is seen as working through individuals, not through classes, social forces, or the spirit of the age.[27]

Theocratic and Providential Historiography

Hardy goes on to indicate that pre-Mughal Indo-Muslim historians, with the possible exception of Barani, looked upon the past not "as a story of change, of process, of becoming. The present follows the past, it is not the outcome of the past."[28] For most of them, history was a spectacle of divine ordination, a story not of human action, but of divine action, in which human beings were mere agents. History was used to glorify Islam. Muslim historians assumed that the only significant history was of the *umma*, and in whatever the *umma* did God's hand could be seen. History is purposeful but its purpose is directed not by human hands. Belief in the omnipresent will of God as directing the course of history makes pre-Mughal Indo-Muslim historiography providential in nature. Since the directing hand is God's and not man's, "Muslim historiography in early medieval India is theocratic rather than humanist."[29]

Didactic History

Didactic history is history that teaches the right morals, and Muslim historians in pre-Mughal India in general had a didactic purpose in revealing the ways of god to man. Rulers were agents of the divine purpose. "By recording the good and bad deeds of the rulers, the Muslim community as a whole and the rulers in particular were to be encouraged, advised and warned."[30] Minhaj, Muhammad Khani, Amir Khusrau, Barani, Sarhindi—all emphasized didactic history which was regarded as a branch of ethics, and a storehouse of morals. Mukhia shows that historians often advanced certain points of view, particularly regarding state policy.[31] Thus Afif seemed to prove from history that only strong rulers were great rulers and Firuz was not one of them. Isami wrote the *Futuh* to show how oppressive Muhammad Tughlaq was; and for Barani one irrefutable lesson of history was the sanctity of high birth.

Lack of Research and Source Criticism

The greatest defect of early Indo-Muslim historiography was its unscholarly, impressionistic nature resulting in an unreal portrayal of the past. For early Indo-Muslim historians, history was what reliable reporters had stated and older books contained. It was history written from 'authority', not an account of discovered knowledge of the past. Research of any substantial kind was absent. Of the medieval Indo-Muslim historian Hardy writes:

> The historian is a scribe rather than a researcher, his work one of transmission rather than creation. He may embellish his material, even chop and cut it about; he does not transmute it in his own mind or 'put it to question'....Absent are the painstaking effort to trace *isnad* or to set down the several different accounts of the same event.[32]

The early medieval historians treated their source materials as authorities to be cited rather than questioned or interpreted. Absent entirely are the *isnad* criticism of al-Tabari or the rejection of legend by Al-Dinawari. The extreme niggardliness of sources and the near-total absence of research and authentication meant that there was to be no increase of historical knowledge, and that the veracity of the knowledge imparted would always be open to question. Early Indo-Muslim historiography only serves to mark the decline in the critical standards of Islamic historiography.

Narrowness of Scope

Lastly, historiography of the Sultanate period suffered from an extreme narrowness of scope. Early Indo-Muslim historians made history revolve round the great men of religion and government—prophets, sultans, nobles and saints. It never came down to the life and conditions of the common man, the poor, the lowly and the lost. The religious orientation of the works had the effect of further narrowing their scope to the campaigns and adventures of Muslim political and military chiefs in an infidel country. The large majority of the population – the Hindus – figured only on the fringe of such works as infidel enemies, to understand whom the great Al-Biruni had stayed back in India and written a marvel of a book.

MEDIEVAL MUSLIM HISTORIOGRAPHY: II. THE MUGHAL PERIOD

In the Mughal period a new kind of historiography – that of official histories or *namahs* – came into vogue in India under Persian influence. Akbar introduced the practice by commissioning officials or others to write the history of his new empire giving them access for this purpose to state archives. The practice continued down to the reign of Aurangazeb who, however, stopped it in his eleventh regnal year. Besides such official histories, biographical works of great historical interest were also produced during the period under survey. And we are not entirely dependent upon chroniclers; we have in some instances contemporary, independent historians.

1. Royal Autobiographers

The Mughal period is important for the memoirs of rulers as well as of private individuals. Though not avowed histories, they are literary works of great historical interest. The most important of them are the *Tuzuk* or *Babur-namah*, the autobiography of Babur, and the *Tuzuk-i-Jahangiri*.

Babur's *Tuzuk* has been rightly recognized as an indisputable historical source of great literary merit. Beveridge considers it one of those priceless records comparable to the confessions of St. Augustine and Rousseau and the memoirs of Newton and Gibbon.[33] Babur claims that he has written "only the plain truth," to have "spoken of things as they happened," and to have "described every good or bad act" of all "with the most perfect impartiality."[34] Yet, as is natural to such accounts of a personal character, value judgements abound, and the historical events in the *Tuzuk* are inextricably mixed up with the author's own opinions, sentiments, judgements and philosophy of life.[35] Events are described in their chronological and geographical setting. Babur ascribed his success in India to the mercy of God, and the weakness of India to her inherent disunity. But the country where he was setting up his dynasty had few pleasures to recommend it. Yet, it had three advantages: its large size, the very pleasant climate during the rains, and the abundance of workmen of every profession and trade. The conqueror informs us that the country from Bhera to Bihar yielded a revenue of fifty-two crores.

Of the people Babur paints a morbid picture. Their sparse clothing catches the foreigner's eye.

> Their peasants and the lower classes all go about naked. They tie on a thing which they call a *langoti*....The women, too, have a *lang* one end of it they tie about their waist, and the other they throw over their head.[36]

"The people of India," Babur wrote, "have no idea of the charms of friendly society, of frankly mixing together or of familiar intercourse."[37] He found the whole of Agra ugly and detestable where however he erected buildings and planted trees. Till the end, the founder of the Mughal empire cherished a desire to go back to his spiritual home—Kabul and Central Asia. The *Tuzuk* makes its author a great writer of Turki prose. The simplicity of its style goes well with its honesty and sincerity. The only defect of the work is its gaps. Elliot and Dowson say:

> Babur's *Memoirs* form one of the best and most faithful pieces of autobiography extant; they are infinitely superior to the

> hypocritical revelations of Timur and the pompous declamation of Jahangir—not inferior in any respect to the Expedition of Xenophon and rank but little below the Commentaries of Caesar.[38]

Emperor Jahangir has also left us an account of himself and his reign in his *Memoirs*, the *Tuzuk-i-Jahangiri*, a work which is not less interesting than that of Babur. Of the three versions of the *Memoirs*, the most authentic is the one which covers the first twelve years of Jahangir's reign written by the emperor himself. Failing health compelled Jahangir to appoint Mutamad Khan, the *bakshi* (military secretary), to do the work under his supervision. The two parts were re-edited in the time of Muhammad Shah by Muhammad Hadi who brought them to the end of Jahangir's reign.

The *Memoirs* are a priceless record of the twenty-two years of Jahangir's reign and are distinguished by their frankness and lucidity. A man of no common ability, Jahangir honestly records his weaknesses and confesses his faults with candor. Calmly but honestly does he tell us that he got Abul Fazal murdered; but he is rather smooth-tongued in the references to his revolt as prince and to his relations with Prince Khusru and Sher Afghan. He does not at all mention his marriage with Nur Jahan. Besides such personal references which are of great value for a study of Jahangir's character, are the many accounts of political, administrative and military transactions. More, the *Memoirs* are rich in details about the social, cultural and spiritual life of the period and in the keen observations of the emperor about men and manners. Also, they contain descriptions of epidemics and certain strange occurrences in the empire.

2. Historiography during the Reign of Akbar (1556–1605)

The Timurid love of history blossomed in Akbar in whose reign four histories were written besides other works of historical interest. Of the four, two were official histories written at the instance of the emperor himself. They are the *Tarikh-i-Alfi* (*Millennial History*), and the monumental *Akbar-namah*. By the time the *Akbar-namah* issued from the hand of the great Abul Fazal, two unofficial histories had been written of the reign of the great emperor—the matter of fact *Tabaqat-i-Akbari* of Nizam ud-Din Ahmad, and the hostile *Muntakhab ut-Tawarikh* of Abdul Qadir Badauni. The two works are important for a proper understanding of Akbar's reign, as they serve as necessary correctives to the overlaudatory account of Abul Fazal.

Tarikh-i-Alfi (1591)

Badauni informs us that in 1582 Akbar ordered the writing of the *Tarikh-i-Alfi* which was to be a comprehensive history of the first millennium of Islam, then drawing to a close. Work on the *Millennial History* began in 1585. The history of the first thirty-five years of Islam after the death of the Prophet was written by a team of seven scholars of all shades of opinion. The board included Nizam-ud-Din Ahmad and Badauni. Mulla Ahmad of Thatta brought the work from the thirty-sixth year to the time of Chengiz Khan when the author was murdered. The rest of the work was brought up to the year 1588–89 by Asaf Khan. In 1591, the millennial year, Badauni on the orders of the emperor, corrected the arrangement of dates etc, in the first two parts. The third volume was likewise corrected by its author, Asaf Khan.

Sources and Chronology

Akbar had ordered that the work should attain a very high degree of objectivity and perfection. He himself supervised the progress of the work. H.M. Elliot and John Dowson have certified that the compilers apparently availed of all the best sources of information open to them, often applying judicious criticism in sifting the most trustworthy information from records which contained many fabulous legends. And Badauni attests that Akbar did not approve of the legendary material being incorporated in the work.[39] The history of Babur is based on the *Tuzuk-i-Baburi*, but that of Humayun and Akbar, as also of Persia, Central Asia and Turkey, are based on information available in the imperial archives, and on those collected from oral evidence of eminent nobles and other people.

The work is arranged strictly in the chronological order. Events are recorded year by year beginning with the first years of Prophet Muhammad's death. While the history of the Indian Timurids has been dealt with at some length, S.A.A. Rizvi feels that adequate justice has not been done to the Sultans of Delhi.

Importance of the Tarikh-i-Alfi

Apart from whatever intrinsic merit the *Tarikh-i-Alfi* may have had, it had a significance for Indian history. Its concluding portions constitute the first official history of Akbar's reign, compiled under the emperor's own supervision. Nizam ud-Din Ahmad based his account of Humayun's reign mainly on the *Millennial History* and extensively drew upon it for his *Tabakat-i-Akbari.* Moreover, Rizvi remarks that the work "prepared the people for adjusting themselves to the new values of life which were gaining increasing importance on account of Akbar's policy of 'peace with all'."[40]

Nizam ud-Din Ahmad: Tabaqat-i-Akbari (1593)

Hailing from a family with an honorable tradition of public service under the first two Mughals, Khwaja Nizam ud-Din Ahmad rose to be *bakshi* or military secretary of the empire under Akbar. His *Tabaqat-i-Akbari* was completed in 1593 and the author died the next year. Badauni writes: "Khwaja Nizam ud-Din left a good name behind him.There was not a dry eye at his death and there was no person who did not on the day of his funeral call to mind his excellent qualities."[41]

Sources

Nizam ud-Din's preface states that history strengthens the understanding of men of education and affords instruction by examples to men of observation. At the outset of his work, he mentions twenty-eight works as his sources. Besides such chronicles, he helped himself with hearsay, reports of individual informants and personal observation. But he never questioned the veracity of the information supplied to him. The sources are copied in summary.[42]

Form and Content

The *Tabaqat-i-Akbari* in three volumes is a history of nine regions and of the first thirty-eight years of Akbar's reign. The nine *tabqa* (regions) are—Delhi, the Deccan, Gujarat, Bengal, Malwa,

Jaunpur, Sind, Kashmir and Multan. Within this regional framework Nizam ud-Din writes dynastic history of each of these regions to the time of its conquest by Akbar. Within a dynasty each reign is a separate unit. But the account of the thirty-eight years of Akbar's reign is written in the form of an annual chronicle, meticulously maintaining the chronological order of events.

The contents of the work comprise information on accession of rulers to the throne, their wars, rebellions of the nobles, etc. but other aspects of political history like politics and administrative measures find almost no mention. Toward the end of the work Nizam ud-Din gives us some information about the length and breadth of Akbar's empire, its revenue, and the 3,200 towns it contained of which 120 were great cities.

Defective Ideas of Historical Causation and Explanation

The regional framework and the dynastic and annalistic treatment of history precluded even a suggestion of tracing causal relationship. Even when the author comes to the reign of Akbar, he confines himself narrowly to the narration of political history. The focus of this narration is Akbar and his conquest and consolidation of Hindustan into a viable empire. It is treated not as a result of any *process* directed by a force within or outside history. Mukhia writes that history for Nizam ud-Din Ahmad is a narration of individual atomized events rather than a study of their causes.[43] For example, the dismissal of Bairam Khan by the budding emperor is treated as just an event. Again, the very important process which culminated in the signing of the *Mahzar* (Petition) is given half a page without going deep into Akbar's religious evolution and the conflict with the *ulama.* So also the introduction of the *karori* system is narrated as a simple event without relating it to the administrative and the institutional change it inaugurated. Yet within these limitations, Mukhia observes a significant departure—the subordination of personalities to events. The emphasis is on events, not on persons.[44]

Assessment

The *Tabaqat-i-Akbari* was treated as a standard history and subsequent writers freely borrowed from it. Erskine regarded its author as "perhaps the best historian of the period."[45] Nizam ud-Din's language and style are simple and his *History* is completely free from value judgements. But Harbans Mukhia, concluding a threadbare analysis of the work has written: "The narration of individual events rather than evaluation...may have been taken for objectivity. For the present day historian, however, this may prove to be its [*Tabaqat's*] chief weakness."[46] Mukhia thinks that the conception of writing regional, provincial histories is Nizam ud-Din's greatest single contribution to the historiography of the sixteenth century.

Mulla Abdul Qadir Badauni (1540–1596): Muntakhab ut-Tawarikh

Background

Badauni regretted having been born at all, but consoled himself that the unfortunate incident took place during the reign of Sher Shah whom he describes as 'destroyer of the infidels', an epithet which in fact was unjust to the great Afghan sovereign. Abdul Qadir was born in August 1540 at Todah, brought up at Bhusawar, while Badaun seems to have been his parental home. He studied first under Shaikh Hatim Sambhali and later under the famous Shaikh Mubarak along with Faizi and Abul Fazal. Faizi testifies to Badauni's vast and varied learning. The historian mentions his second marriage (1567), but not the first. In 1574 Badauni was presented to Akbar at Agra. It was the time when the young, determined emperor was feeling uneasy about the pretentious dominance of the *ulama*. "As learning was a merchandise much in demand," says Badauni, "I had the privilege of being addressed [by His Majesty] as soon as I reached his presence."[47] The intrepid scholar easily challenged the spurious profundity of the *ulama* and Akbar was pleased. Badauni was appointed *imam* (priest) for prayers on Wednesdays on account of his sweet voice, and was given thousand *bighas* of land—a goodly gift.

But the intimacy between the sovereign and the scholar turned into estrangement. Akbar began to suspect that Badauni was a fanatic. The springs of Badauni's bitterness were personal and religious. Abul Fazal who had followed him to court now far outdistanced him in imperial favor. And Badauni saw the faith ebbing from the emperor's heart and thought that it was in danger. The discussions in the *Ibadat Khana* ('Hall of Worship' built by

Akbar for the purpose of discussing religious and philosophical problems) had so planted doubts in Akbar's mind that loss of faith in Islam itself was only a matter of time. The *ulama* were banished, and Akbar assumed supremacy in spiritual matters as well. And disregarding the scholar's religious susceptibilities the emperor thrust on him the task of translating the holy books of the Hindus. Badauni's bitterness found vent in a language which at times verged on obscenity.

Badauni's intense zeal for his faith was inseparable from his hatred of Sufism, the Shias, the Hindus, and the liberalism of Shaikh Mubarak and his sons—Faizi and Abul Fazal. He adopted rigidly orthodox attitudes towards the new flexibility, the more liberal thinking, initiated by Akbar's policies. He criticized everything that Akbar did—not only such religious and social reforms as fixing the age of marriage and establishing poor houses, but administrative measures like the branding of horses and the Mansabdari system. He would condemn Akbar and his program for the benefit of posterity in his *Muntakhab* which he wrote in secret lest he should bring down the wrath of the emperor-prophet. The work must have occupied the author for five years before he completed it in 1596. He died the same year.

Sources

The inducement to write the *Muntakhab,* Badauni announces, was his "sorrow for the faith, and heart-burning for the deceased Religion of Islam."[48] The *Muntakhab ut-Tawarikh* is a history written with a vengeance intended to give a 'true' version of the anti-Islamic 'heresies' and 'innovations' of Akbar's reign.[49] To Badauni, history was a noble science and instructive art, but he warns that taken as a rational science, its study and contemplation might lead the shortsighted "into deviation from the straight path of Muhammad."[50] Badauni mentions only the *Tabaqat-i-Akbari* of Nizam ud-Din Ahmad and *Tarikh-i-Mubarak Shahi* of Sarhindi as the sources from which he derived his information to which, he says, he added something of his own.[51] But he consulted diverse sources like Minhaj's *Tabaqat-i-Nasiri,* Barani's *Tarikh-i-Firuz Shahi,* and Amir Khusrau's *Ashiqa.* The second volume of the *Muntakhab*, which contains Badauni's reactions to the events of Akbar's reign, is written mostly on the basis of his first hand, personal knowledge. To such information he adds his own thoughts and what he thinks to be the thoughts of others. "In this respect," says Harbans Mukhia, "Badauni does not merely adapt information to conform to his object; he creates it."[52] Yet he does not seem to tell untruths to gain his point.

Form and Content

The *Muntakhab* is written in three volumes. The first volume is a formal political history from Subuktagin to Humayun, written in the form of reigns in strict chronological order. But the narrative is disproportionate to the importance of the rulers. Balban gets five pages while a political non-entity like Kaiqubad is honored with eight. Badauni admires Sher Shah, but his reforms do not receive attention at all. The second volume comprises the events of the first forty years of Akbar's reign set in the form of an annual chronicle. The third volume consists of a series of biographical sketches of the *ulama,* the physicians and poets of Akbar's court. There are somewhat detailed accounts of the *karori* system and of the branding of the horses, but the Mansabdari system and the revenue administration receive little attention. But Badauni's account is our chief contemporary source for the religious and philosophical discussions in the *Ibadat Khana*, and the account is given first hand. The historian disliked Akbar's eclecticism and was disgusted with the emperor's patronage of men of different persuasions to the detriment of the Muslims who, he thought, had the sole title to government office and preferment. There are accounts of famine and earthquakes, the *jauhar* at Chitor, and of some of the buildings the author had seen.

Historical Causation

Of causation in history, Badauni thinks that the individual acts not in the background of any historical situation, but according to his nature, motives and will. The source of all action is the individual will which creates historical events. Akbar welcomed Abul Fazal to his court because he expected to find in him a man "capable of teaching the *ulama* a lesson."[53] It is in human volition, the belief that men act of their free will, that Badauni establishes historical causation. It is for this reason that he is so bitter against Akbar and all those who were instrumental in 'corrupting' his mind. For this reason, Badauni's attack on his adversaries is invariably of a very personal nature.[54]

Subjectivity

Perhaps the most important feature of the *Muntakhab ut-Tawarikh* is its chronic subjectivity, for its author wrote under great emotional stress created by what he thought was the organized undermining of Islam by Akbar and his sycophants. His highly personal views and interpretation of historical events were devoid of historical perspective. Value judgements abound and the *shariat,* the mainstay of Muslim life was the sole criterion of judgement for him. Harbans Mukhia shows how his judgements are theologically oriented. Of the one and a half pages given to Hakim ul-Muk Gilani, exactly nine words are devoted to his medical accomplishment, the rest to his postures in disputes between the *ulama* and the physicians. And medicine being a 'rational' science, Badauni thoroughly distrusts its efficacy. His value judgements are entirely negative, emotional and personal, and made always from the religious point of view. He poured his ire into the *Muntakhab* which castigated Abul Fazal, Faizi and Akbar. Badauni's account of Abul Fazal's life is a classic in literary abuse,[55] but it is rendered tolerable when we hear him maliciously condemning to hell Faizi, a friend who had always helped him and never offended him. Faizi

> ...continued to blaspheme in his dying moments, and...at last he barked like a dog, while his face became disfigured, and his lips black, as if he already bore the impress of the damnation that awaited him.[56]

And, yet, the historian claims that it was not his habit to record the faults of others.[57] Akbar and Abul Fazal escaped similar descriptions of their death for Badauni died before them. According to Khafi Khan the publication of the *Muntakhab* was suppressed by Jahangir.

Style

Badauni's feeling conditioned his style, a feeling not harnessed by reason. The language is racy and outspoken, and feeling sometimes carried it to the verge of obscenity. "Consequently," writes Harbans Mukhia, "the *Muntakhab* vibrates with life and emotion and is a very readable, if not an equally reliable, work."[58] Often, the language is pithy, epigrammatic, packed with meaning. Hear this medieval Indian Moliere making fun of physicians: "If knowledge of medicine could prolong life, physicians should never die." And all the world knows Badauni's description of Muhammad Tuglaq's death: "The king was freed from his people and the people from their king."

Assessment

In a final assessment, we have to say that Badauni's *Muntakhab* is not wholly reliable and that it suffers from many faults; but we also have to add that it supplements and corrects the overlaudatory *Akbar-namah.* The bitter historian comes to our aid in regard to some crucial pieces of information which Abul Fazal glosses over as unfavorable to the reputation of Akbar. For instance, Badauni's description of the terrible suffering of the ryots which the *karori* system of land revenue entailed. Again, Badauni's account of Akbar's religious evolution is of inestimable value. He tells us of the emperor's alert mind which speculated on most questions known to man, and of his spiritual yearnings which led him to spend whole nights and long hours of the day in contemplation and meditation. Even in his bitter lament for his faith Badauni does not seem to tell an untruth. Hear him:

> Innovators and schismatics artfully started their doubts and sophistries, making right appear to be wrong, and wrong to be right. And His Majesty [Akbar] who had an excellent understanding, and sought after the truth, but was surrounded by low irreligious persons, to whom he gave his confidence, was plunged into scepticism. Doubt accumulated upon doubt, and the object of his search was lost. The ramparts of the law and of the true faith were broken down; and in the course of five or six years, not one trace of Islam was left in him.[59]

Shaikh Abul Fazal (1551–1602): 'Akbar-namah' and 'Ain-i-Akbari'

The Emperor and the Historian

The greatest among the histories sponsored by kings and financed by the state are Abul Fazal's twin works, the *Akbar-namah* and the

Ain-i-Akbari. Abul Fazal was born in Agra in January 1551, son of Shaikh Mubarak, in a Hejazi family that had migrated to India and settled at Nagaur near Ajmer. Inheriting from his father and grandfather the tradition of mysticism and toleration, of universal learning and cosmopolitanism, under the tutelage of his father Abul Fazal grew into an erudite scholar. Presented to Akbar in 1574 by his brother, the poet Abul Faizi, the young scholar quickly rose to high position at the imperial court with his vast learning and assiduous devotion to the emperor. He was Akbar's *alter ego*, more powerful than the prime minister, and he became the high priest of the *Din Ilahi.* Abul Fazal's gargantuan appetite is said to have called for thirty pounds of food a day. He married four women, including a Hindu. But his power and position had earned him enemies. In 1602 he was cruelly murdered by Bir Singh at the instance of the emperor's son, Prince Salim (later Emperor Jahangir), who admits his crime in his *Memoirs.* Anger and grief consumed Akbar who refused to appear in public for three days. No historian has been so honored by a sovereign.

Form

Abul Fazal was directed by his imperial master to "write with the pen of sincerity the account of the glorious events and of our dominion increasing victories."[60] Few histories could have been written from a wider background of education and experience, few prepared more diligently, elaborately and conscientiously than the *Akbar-namah* and the *Ain-i-Akbari.* Besides being a scholar, Abul Fazal was a man of affairs who could understand the behavior of states and the course of history. He was Akbar's friend and adviser, minister, diplomat and military commander. The work, begun in 1595, was completed and submitted to Akbar in 1602.

In form, the *Akbar-namah* and the *Ain-i-Akbari* are twin complementary works—the *Ain* describing Akbar's experiments and institutions; the *Akbar-namah* endeavoring to explain the spirit behind those institutions. The *Ain*, the descriptive record of Akbar's empire, is divided into five books. The arrangement of the *Akbar-namah* is regnal, each reign being treated as a unit in which each event forms an individual entity. When the author comes to the reign of Akbar, the book assumes the character of an annual chronicle, the events of each year being described strictly in the sequence of their happening.

The second volume of the *Akbar-namah* contains at length Abul Fazal's views on history. The greatest historian of medieval India thought that the study of such history as had been written in the Sultanate period was a waste of time. He was convinced that properly written history embodying the experiences and achievements of man was a positive source of inspiration.[61] He calls history "a unique pearl of science which quiets perturbations, physical and spiritual, and gives light to darkness external and internal."[62] History embodies the knowledge of mankind, other singularities of human existence, and consoles the unfortunate and the grieved. Perhaps thinking of what he himself was doing for Akbar, Abul Fazal writes: "It is evident that of mighty monarchs of old, there is no memorial except in the works of the historians of the age and no trace of them but in the chronicles of eloquent and judicious annalists."[63] Realization of truth, which is the goal of human life, can be achieved only by the light of reason, and reason is nourished by a study of the past. Therefore, in spite of the obvious limitations of history, it was worth cultivating.

View of Indian History

From such a general conception of history, Abul Fazal came to a new and broader view of Indian history inspired as much by his rationalist-liberal attitude as by his master's new conception of the Mughal empire. The empire that Akbar was sedulously building was different in nature from the Sultanate; it was envisioned as a truly Indian empire, a national whole, an empire of partnership with the Hindus, and no longer – as the Sultanate had been – the government of an alien racial and religious group imposed on millions of the native population. Abdur Rashid observes that the political, social and intellectual ferment of the age of Akbar, and the novel character of the empire envisioned and initiated by him called for an academic propaganda to sustain it.[64] And, with his liberal views on religion and politics, none could have performed the task better than Abul Fazal. Representing the need for reason and religious toleration against the entrenched obscurantism of the *ulama*, Abul Fazal provided the moral and intellectual basis for the emperor's unorthodox policies.

Abul Fazal performed his task by: First, effecting a departure from the historiography of the Sultanate period. He employed a rational approach to history. He makes no reference to the generally accepted view of Muslim historians that history only served to enlighten and warn 'believers'.[65] Second, Abul Fazal's assessment of the Indian situation was rational and political whereas that of his predecessors was religious. N.A. Siddiqi writes:

> He refused to agree with the view held by his predecessors that Indian history essentially constituted a record of the struggles between the forces of Islam and Hinduism. For Abul Fazal the conflict was between the Mughal Empire and the Indian Princes, Hindu and the Muslim alike. In essence, it was a conflict between the forces of stability, consolidation and good government under an ideal monarch who was qualified to lead the people in temporal as well as spiritual affairs, and the forces of disintegration and bad government led by the Zamindars.[66]

Third, Abul Fazal again departed from the medieval Muslim view—he did not believe that Indian history should concern itself only with the achievements of the Muslim rulers of India. He widened the scope of that history as no Muslim historian had done by including in the *Ain* an elaborate, sympathetic and careful study of the religious and philosophical systems, and the social customs and practices of the Hindus. He found the source of religious antagonism and bitterness between the Hindus and the Muslims in the belief that the Hindus committed *shirk*, that is, associated the attributes of God with human beings and their images. The charge against the Hindus, Abul Fazal asserted, was baseless. Careful investigation and inquiry show that the Hindus subscribe to the concept of one God. Yet, the misunderstanding was so deep-rooted as to lead to bitter antagonism and even bloodshed. The historian makes a plea for complete religious toleration since persecution of any kind was irrational and futile.[67] After Al-Biruni, it was Abul Fazal who made a systematic attempt to understand Hindu religion and society in proper perspective. His attempt resulted in one of the finest examples of historical objectivity and detachment. Abul Fazal's outlook on Indian history proved to be of abiding value. It went a long way in popularizing the secular nature of the Mughal government under Akbar and his policy of *zulh-i-kull* (peace with all).

Sources and Method

Abul Fazal collected sources of all kinds and Akbar helped him in all possible ways. Records of many events were collected from the Imperial Record Office established by Akbar in his nineteenth regnal year. Royal commands were issued to the provinces that those who from old service remembered with certainty or with the minimum of doubt the events of the past, should copy their notes and memoranda and transmit them to the imperial court. Great pains were taken to procure originals or copies of most of the orders which had been issued to the provinces from the accession. Likewise, the reports which ministers, high officials and military commanders had submitted about affairs of the empire and events in foreign countries were examined. Research also included interrogating the principal officers of state, grandees, dignitaries and the old members of the royal family. All oral statements were reduced to writing.

Abul Fazal expended on the sifting of evidence the same labor and research bestowed on collecting material. Facts were marshalled with the help of the highest scientific experts. Accounts were collated and put to the test of reason. The contradictions and imperfections in the treasures of information amassed were corrected with reference to Akbar's 'perfect memory'. The historian tells us that for each event he took the written testimony of more than twenty intelligent and cautious persons. Every account was put to the most detailed scrutiny and special care was bestowed on the chronology of events. The original draft of the *Akbar-namah* was revised five times before it was submitted to Akbar. No historian in India so far had been so insistent on the need for historical methodology and none brought it to such perfection as Abul Fazal.

Content

The first of the two parts of the *Akbar-namah* deals with Akbar's birth and the reigns of Babur and Humayun, while the second tells us of Akbar's reign to the end of the forty-sixth year. The famous *Ain-i-Akbari* is a detailed, descriptive statistical record of the Mughal empire in the sixteenth century. The *Ain*, according to H.S. Jarret "will deservedly go down to posterity,"[68] for the immense mass of exact information it provides—the extent of Akbar's empire, its resources, condition, population, industry and wealth. Nothing is left out and the accounts are rendered in the smallest detail. The data presented range from "the revenue of a province to the cost of a pineapple, from the organization of an army and the grades and duties of the nobility to the shape of a candle-stick and the price of a curry-comb."[69] Moreover, the *Ain* contains an elaborate account of Hindu culture in its most varied aspects. The sympathy and care with which Hindu society is studied, besides attesting to the author's objectivity and detachment, symbolizes the new enlightened attitude of Akbar's empire. In it are found, too, the 'Happy Sayings of Akbar', and the autobiography of the author. The *Akbar-namah* and the *Ain-i-Akabri* together have bestowed upon posterity the most detailed, complete and authentic account ever left of an empire and of one of the grandest personalities of world history.

Historical Causation

Regarding causation in history, Abul Fazal, like all medieval Indian historians, assumes that men's behavior spring from their nature, and this behavior causes individual events. Akbar is an exception to this rule since he is a semi-divine person whose actions fall beyond the pale of reason and ordinary causation. The categorization of human nature is moral—into good or wicked, or good but susceptible to evil influences. There was little scope for explanation and generalization, since Abul Fazal like most medieval Indo-Muslim historians, thought of history as a collection of individual events or matters relating to individual persons or institutions.

Subjectivity

The first among Abul Fazal's serious limitations as a historian was his subjectivity, which was as intense as that of Barani or Badauni, and which expressed itself in an abject partiality for his patron. All reason, moderation and restraint left him in defending and extolling Akbar who was always right because he could never err. The motives behind Akbar's military expeditions whether against a Rajput prince or a Muslim ruler, are invariably judged to be just and laudable.[70] The explanations and justification do not always fulfil the conditions of historical objectivity. He is unfair and even hostile to Sher Shah as he seems to have thought that the great

Afghan was the enemy of Akbar's father. And though singularly free from rancor and personal recrimination, his old grievance against the *ulama* seeks full vengeance through his powerful pen. His account of Akbar's disgust and breach with the *ulama* cannot be regarded as impartial.[71]

Credulity and Flattery

Credulity and flattery must be reckoned the second great defect of the *Akbar-namah.* The favorite courtier, the trusted friend and secretary of Akbar, could not but have written an official history; but the author's belief in what he thought to be the divine qualities and powers of his patron resulted in the *Akbar-namah* being a panegyric. Like a child, Abul Fazal does believe in Akbar's extraordinary spiritual powers which verge on the supernatural, and his qualities of prescience which amount to prophecy. Siddiqi writes: "It is really painful to keep company with Abul Fazal in these weak moments. The apostle of reason appears to have fallen a victim to credulity and superstition."[72] Harbans Mukhia cites two examples: When the feeble-hearted were depressed for want of rain at a particular time, says Abul Fazal, Akbar engaged in prayer and shortly afterwards there was a downpour. Again, when Akbar plunged his horse into the flooded river, Mahindri, in Gujarat, "by the fortune and miracle of his sacred person," the river became fordable.[73] Most Western scholars judge the author of the *Akbar-namah* as a shameless flatterer of Akbar.

Plagiarism and Suppression of Facts

Lastly, Abul Fazal has been charged of plagiarism—of deriving information from sources which have not been specifically acknowledged. Jarret remarks:

> The sources from which he derived his information are never acknowledged...he not seldom extracts passages word for word from other authors undeterred by fear, or heedless of the charge of plagiarism.[74]

The account of the Hindus in the *Ain*, which draws heavily on Al-Biruni, goes unacknowledged. There are instances, says Mukhia, where Abul Fazal makes changes in words or nuances in the sources by adding or omitting words or phrases.[75] An equally serious charge brought against the author of the *Akbar-namah* is that of suppression of facts—of glossing over certain events and facts unfavorable to the legend of Akbar's ability and wisdom. Thus Abul Fazal is silent on the ruin of large areas of cultivated lands and the terrible suffering of the ryots which the *karori* system of land-revenue settlement entailed. These issues have been recorded by Badauni and corroborated by Nizam ud-Din Ahmad.[76]

Style

The history in which Abul Fazal celebrated Akbar and his elaborate imperial edifice became a literary edifice as well. In the *Ain-i-Akbari* and the *Akbar-namah,* Persian prose achieved two masterpieces. Abul Fazal's inimitable grand style is much admired by the Oriental literati for the force of words, the structure of sentences, and the elegance of periods.[77] But later readers have found the *Akbar-namah* unnecessarily ornate and verbose. Elliot on the authority of Elphinstone, has found fault with that style as rhetorical and unnatural, and the narrative itself as florid, fickle and indistinct, overloaded with commonplace reflections and pious effusions.[78]

Assessment

There is a striking difference of opinion regarding Abul Fazal's veracity as a historian. He is accused of gross flattery, suppression of facts, and dishonesty. His *History* is consequently regarded as not doing justice to Akbar. "Abul Fazal is not for a moment to be compared, either in frankness or simplicity, with Comines, Sully, Clarendon, and other ministers who have written contemporary history."[79]

There is truth in all this criticism. But when every discount has been made, there is much to be said in the historian's favor. The new methodology that Abul Fazal introduced—the extensive collection of original sources and their critical investigation (the first rule that Ranke insists), was the most advanced attempt so far made in Indian historiography. The systematic collection of data by the use of official records, and the rigorous investigation of the authenticity of every piece of information make the *Akbar-namah* a genuine work of research. Among medieval historians Abul Fazal alone can lay claim to a rational, secular and liberal approach to history.[80] The new approach was of abiding value, and had the effect of widening the scope of Indian history in two directions. First, in consonance with Akbar's new concept of a national empire, Abul Fazal's work went a long way in turning medieval Indian history from the narrow confines of a story of the Muslims in India into a national history in which the Hindus and their life and culture found a place. Second, alone of the medieval historians, Abul Fazal left an account not only of the political institutions and administrative arrangements of north India in the sixteenth century, but a description of the country and the manners, customs and popular beliefs of the people. Thus, for the first time, the governed classes were brought to the foreground. The charge that Abul Fazal deified Akbar is true enough. But it must be added that he wove his epic round the personality and achievements of a real hero. He saw in Akbar the ideal monarch whom he made a legend for the Indian people. The halo with which his book surrounds Akbar remains undimmed to this day. An enlightened friend asked Abul Fazal about the *Akbar-namah*: "Will one out of thousands come into existence who will read this glorious volume aright, and be instructed by the new magic of its method?" The author's own assessment of his work could be read in his anwer: "I am preparing a dainty morsel for the Unique One of Time. What have I to do with the crowd?"[81]

3. Historiography from Jahangir to Aurangazeb (1606–1707)

The practice of writing *Memoirs* and official annals as well as private histories continued under Jahangir, Shah Jahan and Aurangazeb though no work could measure up to the *Akbar-namah*. Mutamad Khan's *Iqbal-namah-i-Jahangiri*, written at the instance of the Emperor Jahangir, gives an account of Babur, Humayun, Akbar and Jahangir. For the first seventeen years of Jahangir's reign the author mainly depended on the emperor's own *Memoirs*. *Ma'athir-i-Jahangiri* is an important history of the period, completed in 1630. It was written by a certain Khwaja at the instance of Shah Jahan. The author secured the best available evidence, oral as well as written, and made good use of them.

Inheriting the Timurid love of history, Shah Jahan commissioned Mirza Aminai Qazvini to write the history of his reign. But the emperor disapproved of Qazvini's performance and entrusted Abdul Hamid Lahori with the task. Taking Abul Fazal as his model, Lahori (d. 1654) wrote a detailed account, the *Padshah-namah*, though many of its details were of interest only to the nobles and courtiers of the time. Yet the work gives a deep understanding of the political, social and cultural life of the period. Lahori informs us of the suffering of the peasants caused by the famine of 1630–32 which devastated Gujarat and the Deccan. "Life was offered for a loaf, but none would buy....Men began to devour each other, and the flesh of a son was preferred to his love."[82] This seemingly incredible piece of exaggeration is, however, corroborated by the English Factory Records. And the *Shivbharat* of Shivaji's court poet Paramanand, records: "Reduced to extremity beasts ate beasts and even men ate men."[83] The religious orthodoxy of Shah Jahan's reign is reflected in Lahori's introduction which emphasizes that the one path to salvation is the path of the *Shariat*.[84] Lahori could cover only the first twenty years of Shah Jahan's reign (1627–47), when old age compelled him to entrust the work to his pupil, Waris. Waris added at the end of the work a list of the shaikhs, scholars and poets who flourished during the period.

In the matter of history writing as in other matters of culture, Aurangazeb was not enthusiastic like his predecessors. He is reported have ordered that none was to chronicle the events of his reign. Yet, he did not put a sudden end to the practice of his predecessors, and directed Muhammad Kazim to write an account of his reign. Kazim began work on the *Alamgir-namah* which was to be the official history of the reign of Aurangazeb. But hardly had he brought it to the eleventh year when the emperor withdrew his permission and patronage. Whatever the reason behind the prohibition, the religious spirit was probably a decisive factor in the case of this puritan emperor who had concluded that "the cultivation of internal piety was preferable to the ostentatious display of his achievements."[85]

4. Historiography in India in the Eighteenth Century

Aurangazeb's prohibition could not stop history writing which continued into the eighteenth century and left a sizable output of historical literature. Muhammad Saqi Mustaid Khan's *Ma'athir-i-Alamgiri* was a good history of the reign of Aurangazeb. The author does not mention his sources. But he had access to official records and was an eyewitness to many of the events recounted by him. The work is free from the gross flattery characteristic of official histories.

Khafi Khan: Muntakhab-ul-Lubab

The political and economic decline of the Mughal empire that had begun in the latter half of Aurangazeb's reign became rapid after the emperor's death in 1707. The breakdown of law and order in large parts of the empire, court intrigues and conspiracies, and the factional politics of nobles and groups only hastened the inevitable collapse. *Muntakhab-ul-Lubab* by Khafi Khan, completed in 1733, and the *Ahwal-ul-Khawaqin* by Muhammad Qasim, written around 1738, are two works that give us a more or less faithful account of this historical period. Incidentally, the two works show how histories written of contemporary events could widely differ in treatment.

Sources

Muhammad Hashim or Hashim Ali Khan, better known as Khafi Khan, author of the *Muntakhab-ul-Lubab*, belonged to Delhi. Growing up in Aurangazeb's service since 1688 he was made *diwan* in Farrukh Siyar's reign. He thus possessed personal knowledge of public affairs. Since Aurangazeb had prohibited the recording of the events of his reign, Khafi Khan secretly kept a minute register of all the happenings of the period. He wrote his history based on "personal observations and verbal accounts of men who had watched the occurrences of the time."[86]

Idea of History and the Historian's Duty

Khafi Khan subscribed to the medieval idea of history. History was to him no more than a catalogue of events neatly presented in chronological order, a jumble of facts presented without any coordination or coherence. But he held a high ideal of the duty of a historian. The historian was to be faithful; he should have no hope of profit or fear of injury; he should be free from partiality and animosity; he should know no difference between a friend and a stranger; and he should not write anything except with sincerity.[87] Khafi Khan's passion for truth in historical narrative is clear from the following passage which should serve as an example to all historians:

> I have neither supported friends nor condemned the enemies for fear of harm. I have not followed anything particularly to please any *wazir* or *amir*. I have recorded whatever I myself witnessed and heard from those persons who had access to the assemblies of Farrukh Siyar and the Sayyid brothers and had full knowledge of their activities. After making a thorough investigation about the sifting of information from different sources, I have recorded whatever seemed to me the truth.[88]

Contents

Khafi Khan's *Muntakhab* is a complete history of the Mughals from Babur (1519) to the fourteenth year of Muhammad Shah's reign in 1733. A brief but clear account of Mughal history from Babur to Akbar fills the first part of the work. The major part of the history is concerned with the period from 1605 to 1733. The work is particularly valuable for a full and connected account of the reign of Aurangazeb. The history that Khafi Khan wrote was a brilliant reconstruction of political events based on a great knowledge of facts. Chronology is well ordered, the treatment thorough, the language lucid, and form and expression are remarkably beautiful. The author gives an account of the attempted reforms of the Mansabdari system, and his accounts of the central administration, Maratha affairs, and conditions of *jagirdars* are unique. As one who had served the Mughal government for a considerable period as *amil* (revenue collector), Khafi Khan had authentic knowledge of revenue administration. He himself had only contempt for the post of *amil*, whom he calls wicked, corrupt and cruel. The revenue collector cheats the government and plunders helpless cultivators. Khafi Khan confesses that he himself oppressed the peasantry and destroyed the property of Muslims. His account brings before us the abuses of the *ijardari* system of revenue collection by which the cultivator is ground down to abject misery.

Partiality

For all the pious effusions of Khafi Khan about the duties of the historian, his *Muntakhab* cannot claim complete historical objectivity. His partiality showed itself on religious and ethnic grounds. The author was a Shiah and showed partiality to the Shiah nobles of the court; he was prejudiced against the Turani Sunni nobles except Asaf Jha Nizam ul-Mulk whom he was serving and for whom he was full of praise. He was an ardent admirer of Aurangazeb and agreed with his anti-Hindu policy. And, writing from the Mughal official point of view, he criticized Shivaji to the point of calling him names. The Maratha leader is described as a rebel against the empire and as the murderer of Afzal Khan. Yet he praises the 'mountain rat' very highly and observes that the Maratha leader strictly prohibited harm to "Mosques, the Book of God, or Women."[89]

Khafi Khan and Muhammad Qasim: Differences in the Treatment of History

Muhammad Qasim tells us that he spent some time with the sons of Shah Alam (Bahadur Shah I) in Bihar before he became *bakshi* in the army of the Nizam ul-Mulk whose favor he enjoyed. The information he provides in his *Ahwal-ul-Khawaqin* is based on personal observation. Qasim's work is a history of Aurangazeb's successors up to the date of its composition in 1738–39. Of its two parts, the first deals with political matters from the death of Aurangazeb to Farrukh Siyar's deposition, and the second from Farrukh Siyar's deposition to 1739.

In writing the history of more or less thirty years from 1707, Muhammad Qasim and Khafi Khan differ widely in their views of the deteriorating political situation, and in the treatment of the subject. Muhammad Qasim's analysis of situations with a view to discovering causal connections is a method nearly unknown to Khafi Khan.[90] Qasim traces the source of all troubles to the atmosphere at the imperial court – the profligate life of the emperors, the intrigues of the palace and the cliques of the court – and holds the emperors responsible for the chaos and confusion prevailing in the country. The historian conveys some idea of the extreme helplessness of the people when he says that if kings sit like women in the palace and act on what the effeminate say, then, the one way out for Muslims is to go to Mecca or commit suicide.[91] Qasim comes down heavily on the nobility, the "black-faced, blockheaded sycophants and tale bearers."[92] Khafi Khan, on the other hand, explains the conflicts of the period in terms of the rivalry between the Irani Shiah and the Turani Sunni nobles. The accounts of Muhammad Qasim and Khafi Khan differ in the manner in which Farrukh Siyar was assassinated at the instance of the Sayyid brothers. Khafi Khan, a Shiah, blames the Turani party in order to justify the actions of the Sayyid brothers who were Shiah. Again, the reasons for the estrangement of the Emperor Muhammad Shah and Asaf Jha Nizam ul-Mulk, the *wazir*, who left for the Deccan, differ in the accounts given by Khafi Khan and Muhammad Qasim.

Bhimsen: Nushkha-i-Dilkusha (1709)

There were at the close of the Mughal period Hindu historians who wrote in Persian—Rai Brindaban, Bhimsen and Ishwardas Nagar. Of these Bhimsen was the most important.

Bhimsen was born in 1649 at Burhanpur. A hereditary Kayastha civil officer of the imperial administration, Bhimsen spent much of his time in Mughal cities and camps and saw many places from Cape Comorin to Delhi. He must have carefully made his jottings of the information he had gathered during these journeys. The *Nushka-i-Dilkusha*, Bhimsen's journal completed at about 1709, is a very valuable supplement to the *Ma'athir-i-Alamgiri*. It enjoyed certain advantages over the other histories of the period. A private journal, it was not only free from the defects of official histories but contained information different in nature and quality. The author looked at Aurangazeb's reign through the eyes of a contemporary Hindu. Again, as Jadunath Sarkar succinctly points out, living "near enough to the Mughal officers to learn the events accurately but not near enough to be lying flatterer," Bhimsen "knew the truth and could afford to tell it."[93]

Unlike the official annals, the range of the material that Bhimsen provides is enormous. He has supplied what the official histories of Aurangazeb's reign dearly lacked—the causes and effects of events, incidents in Mughal warfare in the Deccan, state of the country, condition of the people, prices of food, condition of the roads, and the social life of the official class.[94] Bhimsen provides us such data as are vital for an understanding of the true nature of what Sarkar has called the 'Deccan Ulcer' which brought about the advance of the Maratha power and the ruin of Aurangazeb. He tells us that

Aurangazeb's incessant campaigns in the Deccan compelled the inmates of his camp, sick of long separation, to summon their families there. A new generation was thus born (under canvas) which did not know that there were other shelters than a tent. All administration had disappeared. The collector collected the rent committing every oppression, the peasants gave up cultivation, and the *jagirdars* (holders of *jagir*) did not get a penny. Subjected to such exactions the peasants collected arms and horses and joined the Marathas. Bhimsen praises Shivaji's genius for organization.[95]

Eighteenth Century Indian Historiography after Plassey: Siyar U'l Mutakherin[96]

Medieval Indian historical tradition continued into the modern times, i.e., into the years after the establishment of British power in Madras and Bengal. Henry Vansittart, the Governor of Bengal from 1760 to 1764, commissioned Salimullah to write a history of Bengal. Francis Gladwin published an English translation of this work under the title *A Narrative of Transactions in Bengal.* Gladwin himself wrote a history of the reigns of Jahangir, Shah Jahan and Aurangazeb. Another historical work, *Riyazu's-Salatin*, written by Ghulam Husain Salim at the instance of his English employer, gives yet another account of Muslim rule in Bengal. The introductory portion of this work sketched the Hindu period in an incredibly absurd and legendary manner.

Far more important in scope, method and treatment is *Siyar U'l Muntakherin* (*View of Modern Times*) completed in 1783 by Syed Ghulam Husain Khan Tabatabai. Inspired by Warren Hastings, it is a history of India from 1707 to 1780 linking the last years of Mughal rule with the first phase of the British Indian dominion. In particular, the author gives an account of the British wars in Bengal and a critical account of the British government and policy in the Bengal Presidency. R.C. Majumdar rates the work as the best history written by an Indian before modern historiography made its influence felt in this country. There is a pronounced pragmatic and didactic strain in Tabatabai's conception of history. He expatiates on the nature and usefulness of the subject. History gives information about different races of mankind and their institutions. It preserves from oblivion the great deeds of good men. The examples of the meanness, insolence and oppression of evil men serve to put others on their guard and reclaim them from shameful conduct.

5. Mughal Historiography: An Assessment

While some have commended historical works written in India from the sixteenth to the eighteenth centuries, others have condemned them outright. H.M. Elliot condemns all Muslim historians except Ibn Khaldoun. Elliot thinks it "almost a misnomer to style them (Persian accounts) histories" and calls them 'annals' because they are deficient in philosophical analysis and in notices of economic progress, and because their authors had no knowledge of historical criticism.[97] But Major Nasseau Lees pleads that the works of such court historians who were hired to extol the virtues of their patrons, should not however be condemned as of little historical worth. He writes:

> ...a main peculiarity of Muhammadan writers—and which is of the essence of all sound history...is regard for truth.... Where...is the Emperor in modern times who would so truthfully and so frankly record his own follies and vices as the Emperor Jehangir had done in his *Memoirs* or autobiography...? Where is nowadays the empire in which an author could dare to write of his despot rulers in the unmeasured terms in which Abdal Kadir of Badaon had written of the Emperor Akbar? Where in the whole range of the literature of that period of the world history can we find a more valuable and complete compendium of the political, religious, social, commercial, and agricultural institutions of a nation than is contained in the *Institutes of Akbar* compiled by Abul Fazal?[98]

Nature of Mughal Historiography

How did the Mughal historians treat their subject? Did they make any advance in history writing? A survey of the main features of Mughal historiography will help us understand its nature and may provide answers to the above questions.

Secularization

History writing in the Mughal period, it is claimed, marked a change in "form, content and spirit."[99] One great change – an advance – made by Mughal historiography was to have freed itself from religious, theological shackles. History written in the Mughal period, unlike that of the Turko-Afghan period, was not theologically conditioned. Particularly, Abul Fazal refused to regard history as allied to religion and theology, and he tried to link it to philosophy. A more rational approach toward the past began to replace belief in divine ordination, thereby stressing the humanistic aspect. It meant secularization of history. But it must be said that though medieval Indian Muslim historians reiterated that history was 'a noble science and subtle art', they appear to have been unable to expound any particular philosophy of history. They saw in their subject chiefly a didactic and pragmatic value, looking upon it mainly as a collection of examples from which one may learn lessons for a successful and virtuous life.[100] Increasing secularization meant greater focus on human activity – on persons, actions and measures taken, on causes and effects – which slowly began to push the didactic element also out of historiography.

Methodology

Mughal historiography also marked an advance in the methodological direction. Indo-Muslim historiography of the earlier Turko-Afghan period was largely impressionistic, but Mughal historiography, at least in the hands of Abul Fazal, was beginning to use elements of modern historical methodology. Since histories were written from accumulated masses of contemporary records, there was no need to employ the *isnad* method of evaluation and authentication of sources. It was such archival records that Abul Fazal used, but accepting them only after careful sifting and weighing. This was clearly an advance in history writing. Abul Fazal's technique was followed by Abdul Hamid Lahori and Khafi Khan. The use of original sources and their careful sifting ensured a vast improvement in the quality of the history written.

A change in spirit could also be seen in the manner in which Mughal historiography, in the hands of Abul Fazal, was advancing towards the conception of national history instead of remaining a partisan history of the Muslim conquerors of India.

Individual Historian's Freedom

Freedom from theological shackles did not mean freedom for the individual historian who was either an official or a courtier. In the main, Mughal historiography was historiography of the court whose bias it inevitably reflected. The official historians – Abul Fazal, Abdul Hamid Lahori, Muhammad Kazim and Muhammad Saqi Mustaid Khan – writing under the royal nose, could scarcely afford to be independent and critical. Rather, the official historian had to be at times servile. Not only could he not write what he felt to be true, but he often had to write a panegyric of his patron. Badauni wrote a thoroughly independent – though not completely trustworthy – history, but he wrote it in secret and its publication in the time of Jehangir entailed punishment even to the children of the author. Fulsome, nauseating flattery of their patrons is a characteristic of court histories, though Sarkar has observed that such flattery was "more a defect of manner than of fact."[101] There was no falsification of facts in the official histories though credit for positive reforms might be given to the ruler, when it really belonged to some other person. Abul Fazal does not mention Todar Mal's name even once when he deals with the revenue reforms of Akbar's time and makes the emperor the inventor of the *Ain-i-Dahsala.*[102] Mirza Muhammad Kazim's *Alamgir-namah* which covers the first eleven years of Aurangazeb's reign is a courtly panegyric "fulsome in its flattery, abusive in its censure."[103] Private histories of the period like those of Nizam ud-Din Ahmad, Baduani and Bhimsen help to supplement and correct the eulogistic court histories.

Objectivity

Historians of the Mughal period – particularly of the official type – will be found wanting in objectivity which is the marrow of all good history. In fact, subjectivity, expressing itself in partisanship and prejudice, marks the histories of this period, exaggerating the good side of certain men and things while belittling and even concealing their dark side. Abul Fazal is eager to extol Akbar's virtues and gloss over his defects and failures, while Badauni is maliciously hostile toward Akbar. Qazvini and Lahori, engaged by Shah Jahan, were partial to him but prejudiced against Nur Jahan. Muhammad Kazim, while showering praises on Aurangazeb, abused his unfortunate brothers, even perverting their names to suggest foulsome meanings.

Court-centered History

Harbans Mukhia's excellent analytical study of medieval Indo-Muslim historiography outlines its form and indicates its philosophical and metaphysical basis.[104] The basic form of history writing in the Mughal period, as in the Turko-Afghan, is dynastic, and within the dynastic whole each reign is treated as a unit. This made the court and matters connected with the court the focal point of the histories: the accession of rulers, wars of conquest, rebellions and their suppression, and so on. Abul Fazal took a substantial step forward by providing in the *Ain* an impressive array of facts of an administrative, economic and social nature.

Causation

To the medieval Indian historian, events are separate individual units, unrelated to one another. Events occur, according to him, entirely by human will, that is, by individual human volition, which is determined by that individual's nature. Once human will became the basis of the explanation of events, says Mukhia, the ruler's will, in view of his position, assumed pivotal importance in the entire approach. The treatment of historical causation in terms of human volition had the effect of focusing the historian's attention on human action, and of bringing a great deal of realism to historical explanation. But the fact that it was equally basic to medieval historiography to treat history as the narration of unrelated events, limited the explanation to the occurrence of each event. Interrelationship among the events as a whole was not even suspected. There was a lack of historical perspective

Class Origins of Historians

Knowledge of the nature of the medieval historians as a class will greatly aid a better understanding of the histories they have written. Mostly aristocratic in origin and members of the ruling class at some level or the other, the medieval Indo-Muslim historians were indifferent to the conditions of the people. There is little in their histories that enable us to penetrate below the glittering surface to know the life of the great body of the common people, their sufferings and joys. The king, the court and politics riveted their attention. Since they were greatly concerned with the stability of the state system they condemned rebellion of every kind.

Impact of Medieval Indo-Muslim Historiography

In a final assessment of medieval Indo-Muslim historiography, Mukhia discusses its impact on later Indian historiography. He illustrates how some of its features have vitally influenced modern works on medieval India. In the first place, many of the important modern works are set within the dynastic and regnal form, with the imperial court as the focal point and political history as the main theme with small appendages, if at all, of economic and cultural history. Secondly, the absence in modern works of a conscious theoretical framework or a general historical explanation is again a remnant of the medieval Indian historical tradition. While explanation of each event and policy is offered, the interconnections among the events, and between events and the social and state structures are seldom established or analyzed. Again, most modern historians have tended to explain historical causation almost entirely in terms of the personal will or disposition of the ruler. Thus Balban's despotism is explained in terms of his own will; Ala ud-Din Khalji's conquests in terms of his ambitious nature; and Akbar's liberal religious policy in terms of his liberal disposition. In all these, says Mukhia, the influence of the medieval Indian historians' approach is clearly discernible. For a more realistic understanding of medieval Indian history, argues Mukhia, the modern historian of the subject will have to break the pattern imposed on him by medieval historical works, by rejecting their framework. This is evident in K.M. Ashraff's *Life and Conditions of the People of Hindustan* or Irfan Habib's *Agrarian System of Mughal India*.

14

I. INDOLOGY AND THE RECOVERY OF INDIAN HISTORY

1. Paucity of Historical Literature on Ancient India

The earliest and one of the positive results of the British conquest and unification of India – one which kept pace with that process itself – was the recovery of ancient Indian history on modern lines of historiography. Thanks to the medieval Indo-Muslim historians, the history of the seven or eight hundred years prior to the British advent had been duly written and preserved. For this reason the English came to have a fair knowledge of medieval India. But the typical Hindu view of life had kept history encompassing the mundane experience of human beings outside the pale of useful knowledge, and there were no genuine historical records on ancient India that the men of the East India Company could rely upon. The Hindu, as the British found him, had a vague consciousness of the antiquity of his country's culture which, indeed, he was prone to exaggerate, but it was far from a genuine historical consciousness as we understand the term. An Indian of Warren Hasting's time receiving a traditional education, whether Hindu or Muslim, could not have had any idea of the two thousand years of his country's history before the Turkish conquest (AD 1200). How ridiculous an idea of their ancient history that even educated Hindus entertained would be evident from the following example cited by R.C. Majumdar. When the Fort William College was founded in 1800 for giving instruction on India to the officers of the East India Company, a teacher of the college and chief pundit of the Supreme Court named Mrtyunjay Sharma, prepared a historical text in Bengali which was published in 1808. Leaving aside the legendary kings who lived in the *Satya*, *Treta* and *Dvapara yugas* for more than eight lakh years, it referred to the royal dynasties during the four thousand nine hundred and five years which had elapsed since the beginning of the *Kali* age. One hundred and nineteen kings sat on the throne of Delhi during the first four thousand two hundred and sixty-seven years. Except for Yudhishtira and Mahanandi referred to in the *puranas*, the numerous kings that are mentioned in the above text are unknown, with no references to them found in any other work.[1]

It is with Robert Orme's two works that British historiography on India begins. The two works are *A History of the Military Transactions of the British Nation in Indostan from the year 1745* published in 1764, and *Historical Fragments of the Mughal Empire, of the Marathas and of the English Concerns in Indostan from M.Dc. LIX.* Orme was historiographer to the Company from 1769 till his death in 1801. From his study of the Indo-Muslim chronicles of the medieval age, Orme also wrote a fair, though brief outline of the Muslim ruling dynasties in India from the invasion of Muhammad ibn Kasim in AD 712. Francis Gladwin's *History of Hindustan* (1783) covered the reigns of Jahangir, Shah Jahan and Aurangazeb. The second of Orme's works named above contained a brief account of ancient India prefaced with the remark: "The Indians have lost all memory of the ages in which they began to believe in Vishnu, Isvara, Brahma and a thousand deities subordinate to these....The history of these gods is a heap of the greatest absurdities."[2] William Robertson's *Historical Disquisition Concerning the Knowledge which the Ancients had of India* (1792), was an attempt to gather such information on ancient India as preserved in the works of Greek and Roman classical authors from Herodotus and Megasthenes to Pliny and Arrian. Except for such information and merchants' greedy references to 'the wealth of the Indies', as well as Marco Polo's picture of her western fringe, ancient India remained *terra incognita* to the West, a land of marvel and mystery. Here a major thrust of recovery had to be made.

2. The Orientalist or Indological Recovery of Ancient Indian History

It was to this task of reconstructing the lost history of India that the Orientalists or the Indologists addressed themselves. In the absence of genuine historical texts, the work of reconstruction had to rely almost entirely on information obtainable from literature and different kinds of archeological finds like inscriptions, coins, monuments and sculpture.

Influences behind the Indological Quest

Modern Indian historiography began with the writings of the scholar-administrators of the English East India Company. What were the influences behind these men? David Kopf has shown with deep insight that the Company's servants, the more elite among them, came from the intellectual-cultural milieu of the eighteenth century European Enlightenment, a fact which goes far to explain 'the phenomenal Orientalist rediscovery of the Hindu classical age'. Men like William Jones and Henry Colebrooke were as much products of the eighteenth century world of ideas as Voltaire and Gibbon. The Orientalists fully subscribed to the Enlightenment view that differences among large aggregates of human beings as, for example, between Europeans and Asians, are not to be explained by their nature which is constant and universal, but by their custom and culture which bear diverse fruits. Such a position tended toward unity of all human history. This historical and cultural relativism bore fruit not only in a sweet tolerance and a high intellectual regard for non-European peoples, but in a positive appreciation of their histories and cultures. Indeed, Volatire believed that there must have been a widespread civilization in Mesopotamia in times of old, and he had written that India and China had invented nearly all the arts before Europe possessed them.

The impact of the eighteenth century European Enlightenment was combined with the fertilizing influence of European Romanticism which invested non-European civilizations like the Egyptian, Chinese, Indian, Persian and Arabic with an aura of sanctity and positive value. The Romantic love of the mysterious and the unknown had contributed to a new interest not only in distant races, societies and civilizations, but in distant historical epochs. The Orientalist interest in ancient India needs no further explanation.

Moreover, the establishment of British rule in India was roughly coincidental with the development in Europe of a strictly scientific spirit in historical reconstruction. A highly critical attitude in the treatment of the sources had come in the wake of the Scientific Revolution of the seventeenth century, a revolution which had brought about the Enlightenment attitude itself.

Early Indological Efforts

Indology may be defined as the scientific study of data relating to Indian history and culture, a study in which little emphasis is laid on the political aspect. The missionaries – particularly the Jesuits – had begun the Indological quest long before the British efforts in that direction. But the missionary scholars, for all their studies, made no real attempt to know the historical background of the culture of the people among whom they worked, for in them, the religious motive had a preponderance over the historical.

There was already in Bengal, even before William Jones's arrival there, a group of young officers who had been charmed into Indological studies. These early British Orientalists produced works of great interest. One of them, Francis Gladwin, had published the *Institutes of the Emperor Akbar*, an abridged form of Abul Fazal's famous *Ain-i-Akbari.* In 1776, Nathaniel Halhead, at the age of twenty-three, produced the famed *Gentoo Laws* which, two years later, was followed by *A Grammar of the Bengal Languages.* Charles Wilkins who came to India in 1770 had been fascinated by Sanskrit which he mastered, and for that reason, had commended himself to the special favor of Warren Hastings. Jonathan Duncan who served in India from 1772 to 1811, was as avid a scholar as he was an able administrator. True to the Hastings tradition, Duncan consistently encouraged the revitalization of Hindu learning and philosophy.

Apart from personal love and devotion there were two circumstances to which the recovery of India's forgotten past owed its impulse. The first was that the Company officials needed to know the language and culture of the people committed to their charge. Linguistic proficiency was the key to advancement in the Company's service. Second, the young Indologists got a patron in the governor-general himself. Warren Hastings mastered the Persian language, collected Indian paintings and manuscripts, drew inspiration from the *Bhagavad Gita,* and quoted it in his letters to his wife. He encouraged the Indologists, fought for them in the

Supreme Council, and held long discussions with them on their subjects.

William Jones (1746–1794)

Yet the greatest figure in the Orientalist movement was Sir William Jones. Jones's widowed mother, Mary Nix, brought up her son in an intellectual atmosphere and the child Jones grew into a prodigy. In his seventeenth year, Jones went to Oxford. Already he had learnt Hebrew, Greek and Latin, and now at Oxford he learnt Arabic from a Syrian by name Mirza whom he maintained from his own stipend. Arabic drew him to Persian. By 1768, Jones had become well known as an Orientalist. Meanwhile he studied law and, in 1783, was appointed a judge of the Supreme Court at Calcutta.

Asiatic Society of Bengal

In January 1784, supported by Warren Hastings, Jones founded the Asiatic Society of Bengal. The birth of the Asiatic Society was an event of momentous importance. Jones extended to Indology the methods of organized scientific research then spreading in Europe. The Society's unremitting labor bore its first fruits in important translations from Sanskrit literature. In 1784, Wilkins's *Bhagavad Gita*, the first direct translation of a Sanskrit work into English, was completed. In 1787 Wilkins presented his translation of the *Hitopadesa.* Jones himself was studying Sanskrit under Pundit Ramlochan with a devotion which has few parallels. His very first performance in the art of translation, that of *Shakuntala* (1789), was of epochal importance. It immediately caught the imagination of literate Europe and five editions followed in twenty years to cater to the new appetite. The avid scholar quickly followed it up by the translation of the *Gita Govinda*. Jones's translation of *Manusmrti* was published posthumously under the title *The Institutes of Hindu Law.*

Great Discoveries

Indo-European Languages

It was not, however, his translations, but the way he drew the attention of the world in the direction of India's ancient history that made Sir William Jones a seminal figure in the Orientalist movement. Of the eleven annual discourses that Jones delivered before the Asiatic Society, eight were on history and one on science. In the discourse for 1786, Jones announced the first of his outstanding achievements in Indian history, namely, the discovery of the common origin of what came to be known as the Indo-European family of languages. In the discourse, Jones first propounded a theory that India's golden period as a culture lay in a remote, uncharted period of world history, and then he startled the world of scholarship by announcing that Sanskrit was cousin to Old Persian, Greek, Latin and the modern languages of Europe. The theory depended for its validity on the striking affinity that existed between the words of, say, Old Persian, Sanskrit, Greek, Latin, German and English. Some examples:

Old Persian	Sanskrit	Greek	Latin	German	English
pitar	*pitar*	*pater*	*pater*	*vater*	father
matar	*matar*	*meter*	*mater*	*mutter*	mother
bratar	*bhratar*	*phrater*	*frater*	*bruder*	brother
nama	*nama*	*onoma*	*nomen*	*nahme*	name
cta	*stha*	*istemi*	*sto*	*stehen*	stand

*The examples given are not necessarily those cited by William Jones.

D.D. Kosambi shows how the English word *daughter,* German *tochter,* Greek *thygater,* Irish *dear,* Lithuanian *dukte* and Russian *doch* are of common derivation with the Sanskrit *duhitr.*[3] Such correlations are numerous and could not have been accidental. They indicated a common origin. Jones postulated that Sanskrit, Old Persian and most of the European languages must have originated from one mother language which does not exist now.

Aryan Race

From the theory of a common linguistic origin for what came to be called the 'Indo-European family' of languages, Jones made an audacious advance to the theory of a common race. The speakers of the ancient common mother language from which Old Persian, Sanskrit, Greek, Latin and the modern languages of Europe evolved must have belonged to a common nucleus race known to us as Aryan (Wiros, Indo-Europeans). Jones's discovery made the people of northern India kinsmen to the Persians and the Europeans, and Central Asia the cradle of the Indo-European Aryans.

Chandragupta

Equally momentous was the breakthrough in ancient Indian history which Jones effected through a process of synchronism and identification. In the history of Alexander's invasion of India, the classical sources mention an Indian prince called Sandrocottas who ruled the land of Prasii, and whose capital was Palibothra. In his tenth annual address on 28 February 1793, Jones referred to the importance of mythology, tales and even dramas as containing facts of history such as the murder of Nanda and the usurpation by Chandragupta. He then provided a third fact of pivotal importance to the recovery of ancient Indian history. This was the accession of Chandragupta Maurya to the throne of Pataliputra. The identification of the Greek Palibothra with the Indian Pataliputra led to the concomitant discovery of greater moment: Chandragupta Maurya who had the seat of his empire at Pataliputra was none other than the Greek Sandrocottas who ruled from Palibothra and conducted a treaty with Seleukos Nikator. No synchronism and identification has added more chapters to the history of an ancient people. Besides bringing to light the first great empire in Indian history, it supplied for the first time a firm historical date, 325 BC, from which reckoning backward and forward, other dates and periods could be fixed. Simple though it may seem, the synchronism of Chandragupta Maurya with Seleukos Nikator has truly been called 'the sheet anchor of Indian history'.

3. The Development of Indological Studies

After William Jones, Indological studies developed mainly along two lines. The first was the critical study of ancient Indian texts and documents, and the second, archeological discovery and study of old inscriptions, coins and monuments.

Study of Ancient Texts and Documents: Colebrooke and Max Muller

The Asiatic Society became a centre for organized research and hundreds of articles on Indian antiquities were published in its journal. Systematic attempts were made to search for old manuscripts, and translations and critical editions of important texts on Indian history and culture were published in the *Bibliotheca Indica* series.

The Indologist who in importance was second only to William Jones was one who had spoken disparagingly of the Sanskrit-mad Orientalists and their early publications as 'a repository of nonsense'. Henry T. Colebrooke, a mathematician, came to India at the age of eighteen, became himself Sanskrit-mad, and studied the language at Benares. By 1794, Colebrooke's work became so widely recognized that he was chosen as logical successor to Jones.

Colebrooke tackled the grammatical treatises, commentaries, philosophic systems, and above all, the immense literature of the Vedic period. Fascinated with the rediscovery of a Hindu age of splendor, he concentrated his research upon Vedic India. In 1800 Governor-General Wellesley appointed him professor of Sanskrit at the Fort William College. It was then that Colebrooke wrote the famous *Essay on the Vedas or the Sacred Writings of the Hindus* (1805). By the end of his career, Colebrooke had devised a new composite image of the whole Indo-Aryan period as a golden age, an age in which there was no *sati*, no caste, no idolatry, and no polytheism. Instead of being introspective and otherworldly, Colebrooke pictured the early Indians as an outgoing, non-mystical, robust, beef-eating, life-loving, socially egalitarian society. Instead of Oriental despotism, one saw tribal republics. Yet, Colebrooke seems to have failed to realize the importance of the *vedas* for he thought that their study "would hardly reward the labour of the reader much less that of the translator."[4]

About the same time when Colebrooke revealed the oldest product of Indian literature, the *Rig Veda,* to the world, Anquetil Duperron, a French scholar travelling in India, translated (1801–02) Dara Shukoh's Persian translation of the *Upanishads* which acquainted Schelling and Schopenhauer with that product of Hindu philosophy. Eugene Burnouf, the French Orientalist, traced the connection between the languages of the *Rig Veda* and the *Zend Avesta* (the Zoroastrian sacred scripture written in Old Persian). The three German scholars Bopp, Grimm and Humboldt established the intimate relationship among all Aryan languages, the most primitive form of which was shown to be preserved in the language of the *Rig Veda.*

Max Muller (1823–1900), a German Orientalist and language scholar settled at Oxford, acquired a mastery over Sanskrit without the help of a teacher. He then turned to comparative language studies which involved him in the study of the *Zend Avesta*. The *Zend Avesta* led him to the study of comparative religion and to the editing of the whole text of the *Rig Veda* (1845–79) with the commentary of Sayana. His *History of Sanskrit Literature* (1859) mapped out in chronological order all the Sanskrit texts known till then. His interest in mythology on which he wrote appealing essays led him further into the study of comparative religion and to the publication of *The Sacred Books of the East* (1879–1904). A monumental achievement, this collaborative enterprise made available in English, translations of 50 major Oriental non-Christian scriptures.

Eugene Burnouf's *Essai sur le Pali* (1826), i.e., the language of the Buddhist documents, made Buddhism known to the West for the first time as a system of thought. Buddhist and Jain texts came to be treated by Fausbol and Jacobi in the same manner as the Brahmanical texts. Oldenburg's treatise on Buddhism held the field for many years. Rhys Davids was to devote an entire life to the exposition of the literature of Buddhism, and the Pali Text Society was to learn from the examples of the *Sacred Books of the East.*

Discovery and Study of Old Inscriptions, Monuments and Coins: Prinsep and Cunningham

The rediscovery of India's forgotten past could not safely rely on literature alone, for much of that past, as in the case of Egypt, Crete or Troy, lay in epigraphic, archeological or numismatic materials. The Orientalists came from a Europe that had started digging up history or reading it on stones and tablets. With each digging, each reading, the frontiers of man's knowledge of his own development was being pushed further and further. There cannot be anything finer in civilization than this noble curiosity, this restless passion, to discover the development of human life from rude stone-age flints to whole civilizations. The French Champollion, in 1822, had deciphered the Hieroglyphics, read the Rosetta Stone, and begun Egyptology; the English Rawlinson would decipher the Cuneiform in 1851; the German Schlieman and the English Arthur Evans would eventually dig up Troy and Minoa respectively. And typical of the scientific and historical temperament of the nineteenth century was the devotion with which James Prinsep applied himself to the decipherment of Brahmi and Alexander Cunningham to the excavation of Indian archeological sites.

James Prinsep (1799–1840)

The most basic requirement in epigraphic studies, in the decipherment of alphabets, is linguistic proficiency, which fortunately was a particular hallmark of the Orientalists. In 1781, Charles Wilkins had made a beginning in the use of inscriptions to reconstruct the history of the Palas of Bengal. In 1785, he deciphered the Gupta Brahmi characters of some Gaya inscriptions thereby revealing the history of the Maukharis who ruled Gaya in the first half of the sixth century AD. But what puzzled the scholars most were the Asokan inscriptions written in Old Brahmi. Speculations on these inscriptions had continued for nearly fifty years until the Asokan Brahmi found its Champollion in James Prinsep. Prinsep's short life was a saga of devoted scholarship. He was assay-master at the Calcutta Mint, but became the presiding genius of the early period of Indian archaeology. His wide scientific curiosity was driven forward by a burning, irrepressible enthusiasm. Prinsep collected a large number of facsimiles of Old Brahmi characters, yet unread, from inscriptions on rocks, pillars and railings of *stupas*. For seven years, it was his habit, every morning after breakfast, to spread these fascimiles on a table and to gaze at them with undivided attention and undying curiosity—always haunted by the fear that some German scholars would forestall him in deciphering them.[5] Prinsep's labors bore fruit in 1834 when the Old Brahmi alphabet of the Asokan inscriptions yielded its mystery to the key that had suddenly dawned upon him. The achievement parallels in importance to Champollion's reading of the Hieroglyphics and Rawlinson's deciphering of the Cuneiform. A vast, hitherto uncharted realm was added to Indian history. Not only did the legendary forgotten Buddhist emperor become the historical Asoka, but the history of Buddhism in India, lying untapped in the Pali literature, was thrown open to historical investigation. The pattern of research which Prinsep created by his example may be seen in his *Indian Antiquities* (1858), a posthumous edition of his historical, paleographic and numismatic essays.

Alexander Cunningham (1814–1893)

The great pioneer's mantle fell upon the shoulders of Alexander Cunningham, rightly remembered as the creator of the Indian Archaeological Survey. Cunningham had joined the engineering wing of the Bengal Army (1833). A meeting with Prinsep was enough for this young Englishman of nineteen years to be charmed into Indology. In 1837, Cunningham began excavations at Saranath where the Buddha had delivered his first sermon, and where Buddhism as a world historical force had begun to take form. The young archeologist carefully prepared the drawings of the sculptures found in Saranath. In 1850, he excavated Sanchi, site of some of the oldest surviving buildings of ancient India. From 1870 to 1885 Cunningham carried out archeological excavations among many ruins including those at Taxila. Over the years Cunningham had made a large collection of Indian coins, the choicest of which were purchased by the British Museum. In 1870 he was made the director of the Archaeological Department. In 1901, the department received a real boost owing to the interest taken by Lord Curzon.

F.R. Allchin writes that it is not so much the department which deserves notice as Cunningham's own ideas on the scope of Indian archeology. Cunningham contrasts the "closet or scholastic archaeologists" of the old days with what Prinsep called the "field archaeologists or travelling antiquarians" who had appeared.[6] His instructions to his assistants written in 1873 give us a comprehensive account of the scope of archeology.

> Archaeology is not limited to broken sculptures, old buildings and mounds, but includes everything that belonged to the world's history....Architectural remains naturally form the most prominent branch of archaeology....But our researches should be extended to all ancient remains whatever that will help to illustrate the manners and customs of former times.[7]

Cunningham goes on to say that his workers should record evidence not only of sites and ruins, and gather together coins, sculptures or inscriptions, but they should also record finds of stone implements and of dolmens, cromlechs or barrows. They should study the many ancient forms of objects which are still in use today, and they should not be above observing the sort of plough in use, the other implements of agriculture, the types of houses and systems of irrigation, etc. To Cunningham, each such new fact was one of the "fossil fragments of the great skeleton of lost Indian history."[8] Yet, he was not interested in settlement sites.

The founder of Indian archeology also wrote several works on the subject. They include the first volume of the *Corpus Inscriptionum Indicarum*, *Inscriptions of Asoka*, *Coins of India*, *Book of Indian Eras*, *Ancient Geography of India*, *Bhilsa Topes*, *Stupa of Barhut*, and a work on Ladakh. Cunningham's extensive tours also produced the valuable Archaeological Survey Reports in one of which a typical seal from Harappa was published for the first time. Such was the spirit that had been breathed into archeological work that Mackenzie, an avid collector, collected more than 8000 inscriptions from southern India alone. Indian archeology would eventually stride towards its greatest triumph at Mohenjodaro and Harappa where the remains of a highly developed urban life, five thousand years old, would rudely upset the belief that civilization in India began with the Vedic Aryans migrating from the region around the Caspian.

4. The Significance of Orientalist Recovery of Ancient Indian History

Impact on Indian Historiography

It was with the Indological quest that modern methods of historical research and reconstruction – then spreading in Europe – were introduced into India. The Asiatic Society of Bengal which William Jones had consciously modeled on the Royal Society in London ushered in the age of scientific and specialized study in Indian history and culture. More particularly, Jones's revelation of the kinship between the Indo-European languages and peoples almost created the modern sciences of comparative philology, comparative mythology and ethnology; he had demonstrated the importance of linquistic studies in historical inquiry; his identification of 'Sandrocottas' with Chandragupta Maurya and of 'Palibothra' with Pataliputra opened the field for the scientific study of ancient Indian history; and synchronizing the first Mauryan king with Seleukos Nikator he provided the key to resolve many a chronological puzzle that history presented. Prinsep's seminal success with the riddle of Old Brahmi not only solved the problem of the Asokan edicts but set the grand example of epigraphic revelations of Indian history; in the course of the nineteenth century three-fourths of ancient and medieval Indian history would be read from inscriptions. Indian archeology and numismatics, taking shape with the indefatigable Cunningham, were to make history in the years to come. Burnouf's *Essai sur le Pali* opened up another untapped fount of Indian religion and thought – the Buddhist – and roused his great pupil Max Muller to make possible the translation of all the sacred books of the East into English; and Rhys Davids to devote his whole life to the exposition of Buddhist literature. By the end of the nineteenth century, ancient India – that *terra incognita* to the academic world – had been historically charted and mapped.

Revelation of India to the World

The Indologist findings should be reckoned as one of the major breakthroughs effected in the history of knowledge. A.A. MacDonnell writes: "Since the Renaissance there has been no event of such worldwide significance in the history of culture as the discovery of Sanskrit literature in the latter part of the eighteenth century."[9] By a supreme irony of history, even as India was helplessly passing under British rule, the British Orientalists were holding up before the world an image of the Indians as one of the creative peoples of the world with an impressive continuity of development and civilization for more than three thousand years. The literate West often compared the Orientalists with the Italian humanists and praised them in the press for their gift of a new Renaissance in the East. William Jones was accorded the greatest honor of all, as the one who had restored India to its rightful place among the civilizations of the world. His English translation of Kalidasa's *Shakuntala,* rendered into German in 1791, profoundly affected Herder and Goethe, and through the Schlegels, the entire Romantic movement. Colebrooke's *Essay on the Vedas* revealed to Europe the oldest known literary product of the 'Aryan' mind; and Anquetil Duperron's translation of a Persian translation of the *Upanishads* acquainted Schelling and Schopenhauer with what the latter called the profoundest philosophy he had ever read. In fact, the *Upanishads* sent Schopenhauer into a philosophic ecstasy as the

Shakuntala sent Goethe into a poetic one. It was no mean spiritual triumph for a people so physically crushed, and the Orientalists had made it possible.

Seamy Side of Orientalism

The work of the Orientalists had its seamy side which should not be ignored. A cloud of doubt came to be cast on William Jones's notion of the language-race nexus and the theory of the Aryan race has now been generally discarded. The theory however, came to have a somewhat harmful influence on future thought. The belief in the superiority of the White Aryan race became a basic assumption of European imperialism everywhere, and the British imperialist historians of India would duly employ it as the *raison d' etre* of British rule in India.

But the Aryan race theory had a more insidious influence on the writing of Indian history. It came to mean that a superior conquering race of Aryans speaking an Indo-European tongue came invading India through the northwestern passes in the second millennium BC, conquered the indigenous population of mostly Dravidian and Austric origin, inferior in race and culture. The Aryan invasion supposedly effected a racial segregation of the groups through the mechanism of caste and established the superior Vedic Aryan culture which became the foundation of Indian civilization. The interpretation not only contained an explanation of 'upper'-caste superiority,[10] but also the suggestion of an Aryan–Dravidian racial divide. Future revelations and research would cast many of these assertions into the realm of motivated fancy. Again, the race theory in the hands of the European scholar, particularly of the British imperialist historian, also came to mean that everything of value in Indian life and culture, at least above reproach in European eyes, was of European origin. The habit of looking for foreign origins for things of value in a people's life is unhistorical.

Great as were the Orientalist revelations, much of it was fanciful too; and this latter aspect misled some modern Indian historians. The Orientalists, particularly William Jones, had, in the enthusiasm of discovery, romanticized and exaggerated the value of the new revelations, not always warranted by the sources. Jones had found the Sanskrit language "more perfect than the Greek, more copious than the Latin, and more exquisitely refined than either...."[11] He labored to show that the Indian division of the Zodiac was not borrowed from the Greeks or Arabs; he supported the story that Plato and Pythagoras borrowed their philosophical ideas from India and concluded that the six Hindu philosophical schools comprised all the metaphysics of the old Platonic Academy; he endeavored to prove that India had excelled in arithmetic, geometry and logic; he thought that it is possible that Aristotle based his system of logic on Brahmanic syllogisms; and took pains to show that the fertile genius of the Hindus invented the decimal scale, the science of grammar and the game of chess. The rhapsody ended in what was to be his last discourse to the Asiatic Society, which claimed that the whole of the Newtonian theory and part of the Newtonian philosophy may be found in the *Vedas* and even in the works of the Sufis.[12] Such claims were a soothing balm to a wounded, decaying civilization, and nothing could have been more flattering to a conquered, subject people. But the claims bred chauvinism. When, at the turn of the nineteenth century and beginning of the twentieth, nationalist historiography grew in reaction to British imperialist historiography on India, some of the nationalist historians – in their enthusiasm to whip up national feeling by extolling national achievements and virtues – found a ready quiver in Orientalist assertions, and read into the sources things that were not there.

II. BRITISH IMPERIALIST (COLONIAL) HISTORIOGRAPHY ON INDIA

1. James Mill: The History of British India

Ideological Basis

The first important history of India came not from the Orientalists but from their great opponent James Mill, an official of the East India Company in London. To understand the nature and character of British imperialist historical writing on India, it is necessary to acquaint ourselves with the major assumptions, attitudes and purposes of the writers, and the dominant schools of thought to which they belonged. After the battle of Plassey the major question confronting the merchant-conquerors was the method of governance of the newly won empire. During the first phase of empire – in the pre-Mutiny period – three schools of thought competed to control British attitude and policy towards India.

The first of these schools was that of men like Governor-General Warren Hastings and the Orientalists like Wilkins, Jones and Colebrooke who formed a high opinion of early Hindu civilization. They thought that changes in Indian life should be brought about slowly and only with deference to the old institutions of the natives. This view came to be maintained later by Elphinstone, Munroe, Malcolm and H.H. Wilson.

But sympathy for the Indians and their ancient institutions came to be challenged by new ideas and new schools of thought. The eighteenth century was the age of reason, of Enlightenment. Late in that century, the belief that the West had discovered the secret of progress through the employment of reason put India in the category of static or semi-barbaric cultures. Based on this conviction two views were formed as to how Indian society was to be redeemed and reclaimed for civilization. John Shore, who was governor-general after Lord Cornwallis, and Charles Grant, his friend, represented that evangelical viewpoint expressed in the latter's *Observations on the State of Society among the Asiatic Subjects of Great Britain.* Grant urged in the *Observations,* the application of Christianity and Western education to change what he thought was a "hideous state of Indian society."[13] Shore and Grant were actively backed by the missionaries who similarly castigated Indian society and suggested similar remedies. To the much advertized Indian depravity and vice, the evangelical and the missionary found ready remedy in scheme of English education preceded or followed by a general conversion to Christianity. Ironically, they found a ready ally in the rationalist-utilitarian who arrived at the same conclusion by a different route. Benthamite utilitarian philosophy held that the test of anything – any institution whether political, religious or social – is its utility. A thing is valuable if it is useful, if it can perform a useful function. Things that are not useful or institutions that are not conducive to general human welfare are to be reformed or discarded. Reform could be effected through universal education and governmental legislation. The utilitarians believed with evangelical zeal in the efficacy of laws, and of reform on utilitarian lines to remake whole societies and civilizations. To James Mill, Bentham's disciple and the leading utilitarian, Indian culture was static and degraded and the only hope of transforming it lay in an infusion of Western ideas and knowledge to be achieved by proper laws administered by a despotic government. This was the ideological basis of Mill's *History.*

Mill's History

Mill's predominant motive in writing the *History* was his desire to apply the utilitarian doctrine to the governance of India. He saw in the new Indian Empire a fertile field for utilitarian reform toward which arguments were to be supplied by the decadent state of life and culture in India. For this purpose he deliberately attempted an evaluation of the Hindu and Muslim government and civilization in India (the second and the third of the six books of the *History*), and the evaluation was a sweeping condemnation of both. Begun in 1806 when the author was thirty-three, the *History* was published in 1818. It made a great impression. The Court of Directors of the East India Company appointed Mill to a senior post on their London staff. Ricardo praised Mill's work to the skies; Macaulay spoke of it in the House of Commons as "the greatest historical work which has appeared in our language since that of Gibbon."[14] His *Minute on Indian Education* bore its mark. Mill's son, John Stuart Mill, described it as one of the most instructive histories ever written. H.H. Wilson, the leading Orientalist and the severest critic of the *History*, nevertheless judged it as still "the most valuable work upon the subject which had yet been published."[15] The encomiums of Mill's work showed, more than its quality, the British attitude towards the Indians. The radical alteration of Indian society on utilitarian lines recommended by Mill seemed to suit the aims and needs of British imperialism.

Sources and Method

Since Mill had reached his conclusions even before he started work on his *History*, all that he needed was some kind of evidence. Employed in the offices of the East India Company in Leaden Hall Street, London, he had access to every bit of paper from India. Unfortunately he felt no need to benefit by the advances made by the Orientalists in ancient Indian history. He had only contempt for William Jones and the other Orientalists who had learnt the Indian languages and drawn up their accounts from primary sources. Dismissing the Orientalists and their testimony, Mill depended on travelers' reports to point out the vast difference between the professions and practice of the Hindus.

> In the same breath that they extol the wonderful strength of filial piety they speak of the common practice of exposing the infants; a strict morality and ceremonious conduct are followed by a list of the most gross debaucheries.[16]

In his indictment of the Hindus, Mill contravened all rules of historical methodology. Ignorance, prejudice, the quality of the sources and the manner of their treatment combined to give to his *History* its peculiar tone and color. If he felt that the Orientalist account of the Hindus was exaggerated, he should have applied to it a process of criticism to reveal the concealed truth instead of completely dismissing it. For evidence in his indictment Mill relied on Robert Orme's account which was partial; on Buchanan who had tried and failed to learn Sanskrit and was prejudiced against the Indians; on Tennant, a most superficial observer; and on Tytler who had known Indian society only through the criminal law courts. Committed to the view that Hindu society was barbarous, Mill was highly selective in the use of evidence. He cited testimony when it was hostile to the Hindus, such as that of Abbe Dubois, the missionary, of Tytler and other men, but ignored favorable testimony. The massive evidence on the character of the Indians, collected in the parliamentary investigation of 1813, on the whole favorable to the Hindus, went unnoticed. C.H. Philips writes:

> ...he commonly attached the greatest weight to the writers who are least entitled to confidence. In this manner he constructed a damning indictment of Indian society and then went on to prescribe a revolutionary cure to be achieved through the application of government and law on utilitarian principles.[17]

Condemnation of the Hindus

Mill sought "to ascertain the true state of the Hindus in the scale of civilization...."[18] by applying to their life and culture the test of utility. The test turned Book Two of the *History* – filling five hundred pages – into a series of moral judgements. The judgements deal with the ancient history and chronology, classification of society, form of government, laws, revenue system, religion, manners, arts and literature of the Hindus. The worth of the book may be assessed from some samples of the conclusions reached by the author. Mill asserts that the laws and institutions of the Hindus could not have begun or existed "under any other than one of the rudest and weakest states of the human mind."[19] The author speciously argued that if the Hindus had ever been in a high state of civilization, "we know of no such period of calamity, as was sufficient to reduce them to a state of ignorance and barbarity."[20] He declares that "the people of Europe, even during the feudal ages, were greatly superior to the Hindus."[21] "In truth," writes Mill, "the Hindu, like the Eunuch, excels in the qualities of a slave."[22] The condemnation of the Hindu is concluded with a sweeping statement that "human nature in India gained, and gained considerably, by passing from a Hindu to a Muhammadan government."[23] Muslim rule was better than the Hindu, and British rule, though not to be praised in unqualified terms, was better than either.

Influence of Mill's History

The tremendous influence Mill's *History* had on British policy towards India could be seen in the number of times it went to press—1818, 1820, 1826, 1840. In 1848, H.H. Wilson, the leading Orientalist of the day, produced an edition of Mill with elaborate footnotes, and an extension of the story from 1805 to 1834. The persisting influence of the book can be easily explained. It provided, as C.H. Philips observes, the main basis for British thought on the character of Indian civilization and on the way to govern India. Mill's *History* was established as a textbook at Haileybury College from 1805 to 1855, where the Company's civil service recruits were trained, and where a succession of eminent utilitarians or close sympathizers held senior teaching posts. Here, at Haileybury, Mill's catechism worked. His *History* had provided the *raison d'etre* of British rule in India and, trained along lines suggested by the book, the British administrators who came out to India began to entertain illusions of the permanence of that rule. British Indian administration moved into a phase of imperial dogmatism, and complacency of its achievements in India.

Criticism

Mills' *History* had its greatest critic in H.H. Wilson. Referring to the superiority of the Muslims in comparison to the Hindus, so confidently asserted by Mill as a fact, Wilson contended that it was no fact at all. The comparison involved a total disregard of *time and circumstance*. Because, asks Wilson, the British have left the Hindus behind in the march of progress, would one assert that the Britons in the days of Caesar were more civilized than the Hindus of that period?[24]

Wilson then pointed his finger to the evil influence Mill's *History* had on Englishmen. It was destroying all sympathy between the ruler and the ruled, monopolizing all posts of honor and power in India, and producing an unfounded aversion for the Indians. The harsh, illiberal spirit and heavy-handedness of the British Indian administrators originated from the impressions imbibed in early life from the history of Mill. The Mutiny could not have been far in the way. R.C. Majumdar observes: "It would be difficult to name another book, written by one possessing eminent qualifications as a historian, in which so much prodigious labour has been misdirected to produce a historical work which by any canon of criticism does not deserve the name."[25]

2. Mountstuart Elphinstone (1779–1859)

History of Hindu and Muhammadan India

When Mill's *History* was reigning supreme, another history of India was written by a critic of Mill. Mountstuart Elphinstone had come to India as a wild lad of sixteen, but had disciplined himself into a scholar-administrator. In 1827, Elphinstone voluntarily retired from the governorship of Bombay and nothing could induce him to take up another post however high.

Criticism of Mill's History

Deeply in love with India and deeply in love with history, Elphinstone had all along been uneasy about Mill's *History*. In his retirement period he became increasingly critical of Mill and the latter's offensively cynical and sarcastic tone. Mill's work, he felt, though ingenious, original and elaborate, was not candid in its Hindu and Muhammadan parts. Feeling it his duty to combat it, in 1834 Elphinstone began work on the *History of Hindu and Muhammadan India*. In the very year of its publication, 1841,

Elphinstone's *History* came into use at Haileybury for the benefit of the Indian Civil Service cadets and the author was hailed as the Tacitus of India.

Mill had written his *History of British India* on the Enlightenment-utilitarian assumption that human nature was the same everywhere, irrespective of climate and age, and that differences should be accounted for by the custom of the people. This custom, if found useless or harmful, could be changed only by law and government, and the historian's job is to demonstrate it. But cast in the Romanticist mould, Elphinstone held that human nature differed from region to region, period to period, and from people to people. In the true Romantic spirit, he would rather comprehend human nature and recognize its difference from another when cast in different settings or environment than enter into value judgements. Yet, too diffident and cautious, Elphinstone's criticism of his formidable adversary was implied and not open. In answering Mill's sweeping condemnation of the Indians, Elphinstone even allowed a marginal concession:

> Those who have known the Indians longest have always the best opinion of them…all persons who have retired from India think better of the people they have left after comparing them with others even of the most justly advanced of the nations [though] the Hindus have in reality some great defects of character.[26]

Sources, Method and Chronology

Mill's *History* was based solely on European evidence, much of which was casual. Elphinstone rightly felt that a work written using native sources might come to different conclusions. Intending to write a history more full of facts and free from disputes and dissertations, he wrote his account from personal observation and chronicles provided by his friend, William Erskine, the translator of Babur's *Memoirs*. He had intimately known the Hindus for many years, and he made a diligent and careful study of the available literature on Indian history. Guided by the works of William Jones and H.H. Wilson, he dismissed the traditional Hindu conception of the four *yugas* and started the history of the Hindus from the oldest fixed point known till then—the composition of the *Rig Veda*, which he assigned to the fourteenth century BC. Elphinstone tried to fix the later chronology with the help of the dynastic lists given in the *Puranas*. He was also acquainted with Prinsep's decipherment of the Asokan inscriptions. And now, without any difficulty he fixed Chandragupta Maurya's accession towards the end of fourth century BC. Then counting backwards and forwards from this one fixed point, he fixed the approximate dates of the royal dynasties mentioned in the *Puranas* from the Mahabharata war to the Guptas in the fourth century AD. The chronological framework Elphinstone gave to ancient Indian history is much the same as is generally accepted, though occassional modifications have been rendered necessary by archeological discoveries of coins and inscriptions.

Cultural History

But Elphinstone's treatment of the political history of ancient India is meagre and inadequate. There is only a bare enumeration of the succession list of the royal dynasties based on the *Puranas*. Detailed accounts of the invasion of Alexander, and the achievements of Chandragupta Maurya and of Asoka are absent. The absence cannot be blamed on the dearth of sources, as general accounts of them could be found in Graeco-Roman classical writers, ancient Indian literature, and the newly deciphered inscriptions of Asoka. Yet a brief outline of the political history of India south of the Narmada is given. By the side of this meagre treatment of political history is the stress Elphinstone laid on the cultural achievements of the Hindus. Long accounts are given of the administrative system, society, religion, literature, philosophy, arts and sciences, manners and customs, and the trade and commerce of the Hindus. The gradual changes in these are traced with a true historical instinct. Elphinstone also noted the distinction between north and south India in these respects, as Aryan culture penetrated into the south at a considerable later date to merge with the Dravidian, which was already highly developed. It is surprising that he should have given at such an early date, a description of the overseas trade and maritime activities of the Hindus, and their colonization of Java, Bali and other islands. Elphinstone truly laid the foundations of the cultural history of India.

Duff, Erskine and Tod

Elphinstone who loved the Indians and had drawn up an

objectively favorable account of their life and culture inspired others to write on Indian history. He had handed over to James Grant Duff the entire corpus of the Peshwa's state papers and correspondence. In 1825 Duff's two-volume *A History of the Marathas* appeared. Straightforward and sympathetic, Duff's work, says C.H. Philips, is a classic though not much read, and invaluable in that it is based on material that has long since disappeared. A publisher shied away from printing it for fear of not finding enough readers for it and Duff had to print the work at his own expense. William Erskine, another of Elphinstone's followers, completed a translation of the *Babur-namah*, besides providing Elphinstone chronicles for the latter's *History of Hindu and Muhammodan India*. But the most famous of Elphinstone's disciples was James Tod who, between 1812 and 1823, lovingly gathered in three volumes, the *Annals and Antiquities of Rajasthan*. Not even Walter Scott would have stumbled upon material so romantically rich and bearing so much of the pollen and fragrance of the past. Legend and romance have given to the *Annals and Antiquities* such an enduring character that the work would never suffer from want of readers.

3. Persistence of the Mill Tradition

Elliot and Dowson

The British – both the government and the people – were more inclined to take Mill's, and not Elphinstone's view of the Indians. The great Revolt of 1857, they thought, was a further proof of the validity of Mill's argument. It was Henry Elliot who did more than anyone else to perpetuate the tradition of Mill. A product of the Haileybury College, Elliot rose to be Chief Secretary in the Government of India's Foreign Department. Learning Persian, he devoted all his spare time to collecting the chronicles of the Indo-Muslim annalists of the Sultanate and the Mughal periods. Selections from these were translated and published between 1867 and 1877 in eight large volumes as *The History of India as Told by its own Historians*. It was a project in which he received the help of John Dowson, Professor of Hindustani at the University College, London.

Elliot did not write any formal history, but in his preface to the above volumes, he "...poured as great scorn on Muhammadan government in India as Mill had done on the Hindu; in the process pushing into the background the more sober, more sympathetic interpretation of Elphinstone."[27]

Elliot wrote in his preface that the material he had collected on medieval Indian history would "make our native subjects more sensible of the immense advantage accruing to them under the mildness and equity of our rule."[28] The Elliot and Dowson series had great influence on Indian historiography since all the subsequent histories of Muslim rule in India were based on them. Equally important, perhaps more, was the effect that Elliot's preface had on the British Indian officials from the Viceroy down. Writes C.H. Philips: "They were all agreed that the happiness of the governed which might be ensured by strong executive government and the rule of law was more important than self-government."[29] The Mill tradition bred a sense of imperial dogmatism and self-assuredness which crept into the British Indian administration. The British failure to conciliate India must be blamed chiefly on the rigor of the Mill tradition which Elphinstone's more sympathetic interpretation of the country's history could not soften.

Ideas behind Late Nineteenth Century Imperialism

Imperial dogmatism and self-assuredness were only strengthened by certain ideas and pseudo-scientific theories in late nineteenth century Europe. The first of these was the idea of race superiority. The belief, writes James Joll, that the White races are superior to the Black or Yellow was a basic assumption of the confident imperialism of the late nineteenth century.[30] "What is empire but the predominance of race," said Lord Rosebury, a former Prime Minister of England. The belief in race superiority and its relation to imperial domination was nourished by pseudo-scientific evolutionary theories such as the 'survival of the fittest', the Aryan master-race, and Social Darwinism. The very fact that Europeans were able to beat non-Europeans in war showed that in terms of evolution and progress they were more fit to survive than were the non-Europeans. White men are simply better specimens of the human species than are colored men, and this racial superiority carried with it a mandate to rule over those thought to be racially inferior.

The imperialist argument based on the White man's special right to rule was given a moral and humanitarian cover. The Christian missionary was altruistically eager to save heathen souls from the certainty of hell. Ethical imperialism emphasized the humanitarian task of bringing about good government, education, material improvement and moral elevation of the colonial peoples under the White man's care. Rudyard Kipling, in his famous poem, *The White Man's Burden* (1899) put the case comfortably for the Europeans:

> Take up the White Man's Burden
> Send forth the best ye breed
> ...
> To serve your captive's need;
> ...
> Your new-caught sullen peoples,
> Half-devil and half-child.

Some imperialists thought that this benevolent rule of the White men, particularly in the tropics, would last indefinitely, since in their opinion non-Whites were totally incapable of undertaking tasks of leadership and ruling themselves. Tutelage of the civilized over the uncivilized was thought to be a necessity. Lord Curzon, a typical imperialist, expressed the conviction that the world had never seen a greater instrument for accomplishing good than the British empire. In the late nineteenth century, a psychology of imperialism developed which found utterance in such prominent men as Thomas Carlyle, Charles Kingsley, Benjamin Disreali and John Ruskin. John Seely's *Expansion of England* (1883) was so enormously popular as to get into the reading of most middle and upper class school boys.[31] Intellectuals began to speak and write of their country's 'civilizing mission', 'advance of the flag', and 'manifest destiny'—only slight semantic variants of Kipling's 'White man's burden'. Such was the language, such the words and phrases, used to cover up Europe's power impulse—the mad race for empire and spheres of influence dictated by the capitalist search for raw materials and markets and fields of investment.

Holden Furber attests that there was an increasing number of writers who were frankly imperialist as regards India, and anti-imperialist as regards Canada, Australia and New Zealand. They believed in the wisdom of a firm, paternalistic rule in India, and the continuance of the civilizing mission. John Stuart Mill, the apostle of liberty, comforted them by resolving to their satisfaction the paradox of a democratic England despotically ruling India by pointing out that a despot responsible to a free people twelve thousand miles away was better than a despot responsible to none but himself.[32] It was believed too complacently that Indians were unfit for self-government, that British rule was the best for them, and that they were happy under that rule. This was the general attitude of the writers we will consider in the next section. The arrogant tone of British imperialist historiography on India after Elphinstone, and the British treatment of the Indian national movement were conditioned by the tendencies outlined above.

4. The British Imperialist Administrator-historians (c. 1870–1940)

Much of the historical writing on India during the period of British rule came from British Indian administrators. One may form an idea of the main assumptions of such writers by a selective treatment of a few important figures. E.T. Stokes broadly divides them into the two categories of 'popular' and 'philosophic' historians.

Popular Historians

Macaulay returning from India had caught the popular attention by explaining British ascendancy in India in terms of the British national character in its highest examples. He endeavored to demonstrate how individual character moulded history. The fact of a few Englishmen gaining an empire in India was for him a theme which could easily be written in biographical form. Macaulay's *Essay on Clive* drew the picture of the founder of the British Indian empire in heroic proportions. He wrote of "the valour and genius of an obscure English youth" turning the tide of fortune,[33] and the disciplined valor of handfuls of Englishmen led by a genius overcoming and putting to flight vastly superior numbers of Indians. The moral stressed was always the superiority of character. Macaulay's essays on Clive and Warren Hastings were examples to other writers who treated British Indian history largely in biographical terms. Thus the *Rulers of India* series, twenty-eight short studies, edited by William Wilson Hunter, offers a good example of history written as a string of biographical studies. They deal mostly with military campaigns and the careers of successful

British officials, a mere half dozen devoted to Indian rulers. The writers invariably extolled virtues of the British national character. G.B. Malleson who wrote the *History of the Indian Mutiny*, *History of the French in India*, and the *Decisive Battles of India* as well as three volumes in the *Rulers of India* series, explained the British conquest of India in terms of the difference between English and Indian character. The Indian had intelligence, fidelity and individual courage, but was incapable of combination and unity necessary for successful military resistance. Once this defect was compensated by British leadership, Indians became a formidable military force, cooperating willingly and faithfully in the work of conquering their fellow countrymen.

Philosophic Historians

There is another class of British Indian administrators writing on Indian history whom E.T. Stokes calls 'philosophic' historians. Using the new knowledge derived from Sanskrit studies they arrived at conclusions diametrically opposite to that of the Orientalists. Against the traditional view that the British Indian dominion came as a result of a sudden, miraculous accident, this class in general held that it was the result of long working forces and was an inseparable part of the history of Europe and Britain. If the popular historians had tried to interpret British Indian history largely in terms of individual character, the philosophic historians seemed to reduce that history to the interplay of impersonal forces. But whether 'popular' or 'philosophic', they arrived at more or less the same conclusions.

James Fitzjames Stephens

A Haileybury product, James Fitzjames Stephens was a utilitarian trained in the authoritarian tradition and was also Social Darwinist. He was Law Member in India from 1869 to 1872. The above influences issued in a theory which asserted that the strongest always ruled. Stephens was incensed at the old Whig interpretation of British Indian history now voiced by sentimental liberals like John Bright who held that British Indian rule was founded in violence and crime and maintained by an intolerable conception of power. Sharing Mill's dislike of the Indians and their culture, he believed in the forthright imposition of British rule. His book *Liberty*,

Equality, Fraternity (1873) sought to give a firm moral basis to the British rule in India. Stephen's moral argument was that the essential function of Britain in India is similar to that of ancient Rome's in the Mediterranean world. Britain had not only developed the highest ideal of social happiness, but in Bentham's legislative science had devised a scientific instrument of enforcing it. Since only Britain could perform the task of civilizing India within a framework of law, the British Indian government, though only a minority resting on force, had to remain for all the foreseeable future. None could have written a better apology for imperialism.

Henry Maine

Henry Maine, author of the famed *Ancient Law* (1861) and Law Member in India from 1861 to 1869, was not strictly a historian, but his influence in forming an important view of Indian history was great. Maine fully accepted the Aryan theory and believed that even the Indian village community was an Aryan institution surviving in full vigor. But he employed the theory not in India's favor but only as a justification of Britain's dominion. The notion of the common racial stock served only to lessen racial prejudices and render the government of India by the English easier. Maine shared with the other British administrators the contemptuous attitude towards Indian culture. He argued that instead of being in an advanced state of civilization India remained in the "infancy of the human mind prolonged...."[34] In the Cambridge Rede lectures (1875) he said that "the primitive Aryan groups, the primitive Aryan institutions, the primitive Aryan ideas have been arrested in India at an early stage of development."[35] The principle of progress is the continual production of new ideas. Spreading from the Greeks to the Romans, the Germans, the French and the English, this principle was now being communicated to India by the English. Maine's liberalism stopped at India's door. His conclusion did not differ essentially from that of Stephens or the popular writers. E.T. Stokes observes:

> The result of the new intellectual influences was in this way rather to emphasize than diminish the gap between India and Europe, and this historical view provided for Maine, as well as Lyall and Hunter, a rational and dispassionate justification for the continued maintenance of British rule.[36]

J. Tallboys Wheeler

J. Tallboys Wheeler, another administrator-historian, further demonstrated that the attempt to write philosophic history on the basis of the new knowledge derived from Sanskrit studies could reach conclusions as prejudiced as those of James Mill. Wheeler was Assistant Secretary to the Government of India's Foreign Department, and later Secretary to the Chief Commissioner, British Burma. His five-volume *History of India from the Earliest Times* blamed India's failure to develop nationalities on the tyranny of the Brahman priesthood. Devotion to the common weal found amongst all Aryan nations and which certainly belonged to the Vedic Aryans, passed away beneath the blighting influence of Brahmanical oppression. The public spirit which animated the body politic in the Vedic age, and which is essential to the permanence of states and empires came to be narrowed down to the caste, the village, and the family. Political tie, nationality and patriotism—all came to be squeezed into the religious spirit.[37] Wheeler was no kinder to Muslim rule. The Mughal administration "was a monstrous system of oppression and extortion which none but Asiatics could have practised or endured."[38] India, Wheeler concluded, like Charles Grant or James Mill, had been saved from the most hopeless of anarchies only by the introduction of European rule. The Mutiny was a revelation of Asiatic nature and India was utterly unready for any type of representative government. "The would be philosophic historian," comments E.T. Strokes, "ends in this way in the ranks of the most narrow and prejudiced Anglo-Indians."[39]

Alfred Lyall

Alfred Lyall is known through his two series of collected articles *Asiatic Studies* (1882, 1889) and an expanded set of lectures, *The Rise and Expansion of British Dominion in India* (1894). Liberal in outlook and interested in India's religion and culture, Lyall's aim was to correct certain misconceptions about India in England. Burke's oratory had denounced "the oppressors of Indian nationalities, the degraders of ancient nobility, and the dethroners of sovereign princes."[40] Lyall's interpretation endeavored to prove that it was precisely the absence of any permanent organization such as nationalities, aristocracies and long-seated dynasties – in fact, any permanent organization – that ensured the rapid conquest of the country by the British. Like Maine, Lyall maintained that Indian society was "in an arrested state of development, a mere loose conglomeration of tribes, races and castes."[41] Explaining this phenomenon, Lyall advanced the theory that the primeval tribal-units based on kinship and religion into which mankind is distributed everywhere in the world did not, in India, coalesce into larger units based on broader loyalities. Advanced religious and moral conceptions were not unknown in India, but they lacked the persistent backing of a stable political power to extirpate the lower polytheism and establish themselves with a formal ecclesiastical organization and defined theology as the Roman empire and the later monarchies had done in Europe in the interests of Christianity. The one principle of government known in Asia was personal ascendancy. And popular Hindu religious practice assisted not fusion but dispersion; occupational groups came to be organized into the religious institution of caste. Hinduism, unlike Christianity and Islam, was simply a name for the perplexity of diverse practices and beliefs without any organized church and theology to reduce them to order.

Again, John Seely in his *Expansion of England* (1883) had stated that the British conquest of India was unintentional and accidental.[42] Lyall refuted Seely in his *The Rise and Expansion of the British Dominion in India*, and stated that there was nothing miraculous in that conquest. He saw it as part of the powerful wave of European expansion which from the sixteenth century had been steadily overwhelming Asia.

The British rule in India, like its predecessors, was an over-centralized despotism, though far more efficient. Lyall saw decentralization as a necessity and accepted Ripon's local self-government measures and the establishment of provincial assemblies as steps in the right direction. But he could never imagine for a moment that the British should impair their ultimate controlling power over India. Like Mill or Stephens he thought it absolutely necessary to maintain British rule intact for a great transformation of the Indian society.

William Wilson Hunter

Intelligent, perceptive and able, William Wilson Hunter was the leading British historian of India in the last twenty years of the nineteenth century. Hunter's earliest work on India, *Annals of Rural Bengal* (1868), makes him a pioneer in economic studies. His *Indian Mussalman* (1876) is proof of his unusual insight into the mind of the Muslim community in India. He edited the *Rulers of India* series and the *Imperial Gazetteer* took shape under him. But Hunter's most important historical work was his *History of British India*. He died on the eve of completing the second volume of this work.

Hunter's *Annals of Rural Bengal* was an attempt to give a fresh interpretation to Indian history. Hitherto the history of the British period had been presented in the form of the "biographies of the English governors of India, not histories of the Indian people. The silent millions who bear our yoke have found no annalist."[43] He aimed at depicting the historical growth of the peoples of Bengal, and then tracing the early effect of British rule on the state of society. Accepting the notion of a common Aryan stock, Hunter sought to explain why India had not developed strong nationalities like the Aryan races of Europe, a defect which had rendered the foreign conquest by Muslims and Europeans inevitable. Hunter found the answer in the institution of caste, which had its origin in the racial distinction between the conquering Aryans and the aborigines of India. Tracing the successive Aryan migrations into Bengal, he showed how cohabitation between the Aryans and the aborigines had resulted in mixed castes. The refusal of the pure Aryan tribes to mix socially with the latter, and their treatment of them as a helot class had prevented the growth of an homogenous society with a common nationality. Shifting all manual labor on to the mixed castes, the Brahman caste had become slothful and effeminate and had been unable to resist conquest by successive waves of more vigorous peoples. In the *Annals of Rural Bengal* Hunter envisaged the role of the British as one of breaking down all physical, racial and social barriers in preparation for creating a united Indian nation. Previous efforts at uniting India had failed because the material means were inadequate to overcome the physical obstacles.

The *History of British India* purported to show that Britain's Indian connection was not a strange and fortuitous accident, but the outcome of a long process beginning with Britain's own rise to greatness in Elizabethan times. The British achievement "was no sudden triumph but an indomitable endurance during a century and a half (1600–1750) of frustration and defeat."[44] It is national character which Hunter stresses as the dominant factor in the English fortunes in the East. Size had little to do with a European nation's success. "The prize fell successively to states small in area, but of great heart."[45] The history of British rule in India, wrote Hunter, "Stands out as the epic of the British nation.... It will make the world understand the British race—adventurous, masterful, patient in defeat and persistent in executing its designs."[46]

Hunter held that each stage in the history of British rule in India was one of constant readjustment to historical forces Britain had itself set in motion. For this reason alone he believed that a place had to be found for the Western educated classes in India, and that it was impossible to rule modern India through a foreign bureaucracy alone. By the planned introduction of modern life, Britain was to lead India into the modern world with a paternal authoritarian hand.

Vincent Smith (1848–1920)

Vincent Arthur Smith does not belong to the group of what E.T. Strokes calls 'philosophic' historians. Smith was born in 1848 in Dublin, the son of a prominent doctor who was also a well known amateur numismatist and archeologist. Smith joined the Indian Civil Service in 1869, and served in what is now Uttar Pradesh. After retirement in 1900 he taught Indian history at Dublin.

By the time Smith wrote, a vast corpus of new source materials had been brought to light, and the chronology of ancient Indian history had been placed on a firmer footing. In 1904 he produced his famous *Early History of India* incorporating the advances made in the knowledge of India's past. In 1919 appeared the *Oxford History of India.* In the interval between the two books Smith also wrote *The History of Fine Art in India and Ceylon*, and several lesser works. Both the *Early History* and the *Oxford History* were great successes as standard textbooks in Indian colleges and universities.

Pragmatic View and the Subjective Element

Smith shared with the other administrator-historians of India, the pragmatic view that those desirous of knowing modern India and solving its numerous problems must know its ancient history. In the *Early History* he aimed to present the story of ancient India in an impartial and judicial spirit. But he knew fully well that even the most direct evidence is liable to unconscious distortion, as some degree of subjectivity is inevitable for it is impossible for the historian to altogether eliminate his own personality however great may be his respect for the objective fact.[47]

Sympathetic Treatment of Ancient Indian Civilization

Smith, like Elphinstone, is sympathetic in his treatment of ancient Indian civilization. In his *Early India* he rejects a view quite common in his day that all that was good in early India owed to the influence of Hellenistic ideas. Western influence on India was very small.[48] He admires the art of India, though not her literature. Failing to realize, as A.L. Basham observes, that canons of taste differ from culture to culture, Smith writes that the Rajput epics are rude, and Bana's *Harshacharita*, though containing passages of admirable and vivid description, is an "irritating performance, executed in the worst possible taste."[49] For Smith, the Gupta period was "a time not unworthy of comparison with the Elizabethan and Stuart period in England."[50]

Imperialist Strain

But the *Early History* and the *Oxford History* are primarily political histories, and in this aspect Smith becomes an imperialist historian. Here the impartial and the judicial spirit leaves him. The political moral that he draws from ancient Indian history is starkly imperialist. Out of the 478 pages of the *Early History of India* covering the period from 600 BC to AD 1200, sixty-six are devoted to the Indian campaigns of Alexander. Smith writes: "The triumphant progress of Alexander from the Himalayas to the sea demonstrated the inherent weakness of the greatest Asiatic armies when confronted with European skill and discipline."[51] In point of fact, however, King Purushothama or the tribes of northwestern India whom Alexander confronted did not possess the greatest Asiatic armies. The classical writers themselves allude to the war-weary soldiers of Alexander and the military might of the Nandas. Smith concedes that Seleukos's treaty with Chandragupta as "humiliating" to the Greek king. The historian especially admires the India of the Guptas. India had probably never been governed better "after the Oriental manner" than under Chandragupta II.

The *Arthasastra* is criticized for its autocratic and Machiavellian character, and its penal code is stigmatized as "ferociously severe".[52] 'Autocracy' and 'despotism' – the only political forms known to ancient India – are for Smith, forms which do not admit of development, and for this reason, presumably, India has not developed. But the despotic sway of the British over India is benevolent and necessary. The paramount lesson of Indian history is the ever present need for a superior controlling force to check the disruptive forces always ready to operate in India. The description in the *Early History of India* of the condition of northern India after Harsha's death is an unconcealed justification of the continuation of British rule in India. Here Smith gives the reader

> a notion of what India always has been when released from the control of a supreme authority, and what she would be again, if the hand of the benevolent despotism which now holds her in its iron grasp should be withdrawn.[53]

The imperialist strain runs through the later *Oxford History* too:

> ...even now, in the twentieth century, she (India) would relapse quickly into that condition [political disruption] if the firm although mild control exercised by the paramount power should be withdrawn.[54]

Smith tells us that the desire of the Indians for political unity is shown in their acquiescence to British rule, and in the passionate outbursts of loyal devotion to the King Emperor.[55]

E.B. Havell, a pioneer in the sympathetic study of Indian art and the author of *The History of Aryan Rule* in India (1918), believed that the Aryans were responsible for all that is good in India, especially the rural democracy of the *panchayats*, and the rule of law. But unlike other British historians of India he arrived at a different conclusion. Both Englishmen and Indians being Aryans, England should encourage India's aspirations for self-government under the British crown, for they are in keeping with the Aryan tradition. The following passage is Havell's criticism of Smith's approach to early India:

> It must be peculiarly humiliating to [the Indians] to be constantly told by their rulers...that freedom has never spread

her wings over their native land, that they are heirs to untold centuries of "Oriental Despotism"....Whether intentional or not, no greater spiritual injury can be done to a people than to teach them to despise the achievement of their forefathers. To overvalue them can hardly be a mistake.[56]

W.H. Moreland (1868–1938)

William Harrison Moreland may be looked upon as the last important British administrator-historian of India. Born in northern Ireland and educated at Cambridge, Moreland joined the Indian Civil Service as Director of Land Records and Agriculture in what is now United Provinces. His special field was Indian agricultural economy.

Economic Factor

Moreland was one who believed in the primacy of the economic factor in history, and in his writings he always focused his attention on the production and distribution of wealth. "I estimate the various Indian administrations," he wrote in his *From Akbar to Aurangazeb*, "strictly from the economist's point of view."[57] "Economic forces are at the heart of history, and in India agriculture, and the revenue derived from it, is the major economic factor."[58]

British Role in India

Moreland's first book, *Agriculture of the United Provinces* (1904), was followed in 1911 by the *Revenue Administration of the United Provinces.* With the above views on Indian agriculture and land revenue, Moreland did not see any discontinuity between traditional and British India as did the other British historians. There was no discontinuity because he held that the revenue system in ancient India was adopted continually first by the Muslim rulers and then by the English; and that even after a century of British rule, India had remained unaffected by the West. Indian economy largely remained a barter economy unaccustomed to capital as a growing mobile factor of production. The distinct role of the British in India was to act as impersonal agents of economic change. The change itself lay in the introduction of a money economy and of the free productive use of capital. Greater production and trade would destroy the organization of agriculture based on cheap labor and the almost gratuitous services of the 'lower' castes in the villages.

Mughal Economy

The more important of Moreland's works are all on the Mughal economy. In 1918, in collaboration with Yusuf Ali he drew up a detailed study known as *Akbar's Land Revenue System.* It was followed in 1920 by *India at the Death of Akbar.* Moreland's twin criteria for a healthy social order are even distribution of wealth and the encouragement of production. Judged by these standards, the Mughal economic system came under heavy attack for its wastefulness and maldistribution of wealth. *From Akbar to Aurangazeb*, a work, which Moreland published in 1931, defended European activities in India. In the *Agrarian System of Moslem India* (1929), he argued that what the British inherited from the medieval Indian Muslim administration was a *damnosa hereditas*, a legacy of loss, from which they rescued Indian society.[59]

Mooreland and the Indian Nationalists

The early writings of Moreland were academic and research oriented in character, observes J.B. Harrison, which turned more and more into political polemics refuting charges made by the Indian National Congress against the British administration in India. Meeting the charge of over-assessment he wrote in his *Revenue Administration* (1911) that

> the revenue now assessed represents a proportion of substantially less than 10 per cent of the produce of the land—curiously just about what was thought reasonable at the time when Manu wrote, and about one-third of what was considered proper by Akbar.[60]

Agitation against the enhancement of the salt tax brought the rejoinder that in Mughal times salt was much dearer, and the *swadeshi* cry of self-sufficiency met with the comment that when India lived on its own resources its people were ill-fed and badly clothed. The book *From Akbar to Aurangazeb* maintained that if American indigo and British cottons displaced the Indian products, the fault lay in a practice of adulteration, which the Mughals could not eradicate. Indian reaction rightly pointed out that the one object of the learned author in writing his books seemed to be to prove that in the Mughal period the financial and social condition of the people of India was even worse and more deplorable than it came to be under the British.[61]

Moreland's *A Short History of India*, written in collaboration with Atul Chatterjee, rejected in its first section, claims of European origin for Indian science, thought, and arts. The second drew a grim picture of eighteenth century India, torn by factions, economically ruined, degraded in culture and religion—at the moment when power passed into European hands. Uniform praise for British motives and achievements is found in the third section.

Moreland, concludes Harrison, was a true historian though political feelings dominated him, and his vision was somewhat narrowed by his Civil Service training. But that vision was remarkably penetrating and acute, and his analysis of the Mughal land-revenue system and its conditioning factors is masterly.[62]

5. Imperialist Historiography: An Overview

Western Assumptions Regarding India's Past

The evangelical-utilitarian picture of Indian society and culture presented by Charles Grant's *Observations* and James Mill's *History* gave currency to certain historical cliches which influenced not only European historiography on India but even philosophies of history.

The first of these was that of a static, unchanging Indian society. Mill maintained that from the coming of the Aryans to the arrival of the British, Indian society had remained substantially unchanged. This concept of an unchanging society had a direct influence on Hegel's philosophy of history. For Hegel, true history involved dialectical change and development. Indian society, as the German philosopher knew it, remained stationary and fixed, and therefore outside the stream of world history. Mill's division of Indian history into the Hindu, Muslim and British periods has continued to our own days. Christian Lassen (1800–1876) applied the Hegelian dialectic to this periodization of Indian history, with the difference that the three phases of thesis, antithesis and synthesis became in his hands the Hindu, the Muslim and the Christian—not the

British as in Mill. But Lassen could not refute Hegel's assumption of the unchanging nature concerning India's past.[63]

Oriental despotism is the other aspect of this concept of an unchanging society. The basis of Indian society was believed to be the immutable pattern of the Indian village—the village inhabited by people unconcerned with political relationships. To the Western thinker and historian it was this lack of concern with politics, and what was believed to be the absence of private property in land that gave rise to Oriental despotism. Writes Romila Thapar: "The static character of Indian society with its concomitant despotic rulers became an accepted truth of Indian history. The concept of Oriental Despitism began to take shape."[64] The assumption concerning the unchanging nature of India's past was taken over by Karl Marx and worked into the thesis of Asiatic mode of production. The characteristics of the Asiatic Mode of Production were the self-sufficient village economy and the absence of private property in land.

The above concepts became axiomatic to Western thinkers and writers: legalists like Henry Maine, sociologists like Durkheim and Weber, but most of all to the British administrator-historians of India—Stephens, Strachey, Lyall and Hunter. They had special need for such concepts, particularly that of the unchanging character of India's past, for they could then present the British administration as the catalyst in changing Indian society. That was to them the *raison d'etre* of the British rule of India.

Change in the Nature of British Historiography

The evangelical-utilitarian hope in the early nineteenth century of transforming what was thought to be the corrupt and rotten Indian life, within a generation had faded away with the progress of the century. It gave place to the outlook of the Punjab School, expressed in the British determination to do Indians good in spite of themselves. The Indians being unteachable, the British in a spirit of altrüistic resignation would do "What's for their good, not what pleases them," and to "labour, but not to hope for any reward."[65] (Except, one may add, the huge salaries and pensions.) British historiography reflected this shift in aim by moving on from the outright condemnation of Indian life and culture to the edificatory character of British rule.

Justification for the Continuance of British Rule

The so-called change in British attitude towards India was no change at all. The revival and progress of Sanskrit studies instead of lessening the prejudice against India, only served to provide a theoretical justification for the continuance of British rule. Max Muller might speak loosely of "our Aryan brother", "of the debt of Europe to the East, and of the spiritual relationship which now binds India and England together."[66] Western writers on India in general and the British administrator-historians of India in particular, accepted the common Aryan racial bond between the European and the Indian, but went on to offer historical explanations of the present differences between the two. The 'philosophic' among the latter asked themselves why the Indian Aryans failed to develop strong nationalities and institutions as their European cousins did. The evangelical Christan, aiming at conversion, had roundly blamed what he thought to be the degradation and vice of the Hindu to his religion; employing what may be loosely termed as methods of social anthropology, the British administrator-historians attributed the static quality of Indian society to caste. Whatever the explanation, it was to justify the continuance of British rule.

Dominance of the Political Element

But the most important characteristic of British imperialist historiography on India was the dominance of the political element. Here, British prejudice, the tendency to moralize, intense bias and value-loaded statements found free play. The writers had little interest in Indian life and culture, and economic issues were only treated in so far as they had political application. Works written were confined mostly to the British period, and concerned only with British activities. They always presented the British point of view. Short descriptions of Indian manners and customs were included only to emphasize their diversity and reiterate their decadence. Meant mainly for readers in England, the works invariably contained the thrilling story of the British conquest of India, and the consequent benevolence, with the writers and the readers agreeing that the benevolence should continue. It was not strange then that every kind of discrimination was shown in denying self-government to India which Britain had granted to

Canada, South Africa, Australia and New Zealand. One is reminded of Gokhale's meeting with John Morley, the Secretary of State for India, at the India Office in London before the 1909 reforms to plead for establishing parliamentary institutions in India with the object of making India, like Canada, a self-governing colony within the empire. Morley had already observed in the House of Commons that it was wrong to think that because a fur coat was used in the Canadian winter, it was needed in the Deccan also. The liberal Secretary of State even threatened Gokhale that agitation by the National Congress for the realization of colonial self-government would spoil even the expected chance of limited reform.

15

I. INDIAN NATIONALIST HISTORIOGRAPHY

1. The Search for National Identity

After an initial phase of shallow imitation of Western life in dress, manners and customs, an urge began to develop among the really educated Indians to make India more Indian and less English. This class did not want Western civilization to displace their own as Macaulay and the missionaries had wanted; they only wanted the West to revitalize Indian culture as Ram Mohun Roy had desired. They set out to reform their age-old religion and society and rejuvenate their ancient culture. The trend attained the proportions of a renaissance creating among the Indians a sense of self-reliance, self-respect and self-confidence which had been blown out in the Western wind. By degrees India was gaining national self-consciousness which would soon consummate in a desire for freedom from foreign domination. The new consciousness had, however, to be sustained and promoted by a historical consciousness, the knowledge of a people's past.

Bankim Chandra Chatterjee asserted that as a means of creating a sense of unity, national pride and desire for freedom, there was nothing more fundamental than the study and writing of history. India was a subject country because Indian history had not been described and interpreted by Indian historians. In his *Bibidha Prabandha* he says:

> There is no Hindu history. Who will praise our noble qualities if we do not praise them ourselves?...When has the glory of any nation ever been proclaimed by another nation? The proof of the warlike prowess of the Romans is to be

> found in Roman histories. The story of the heroism of the Greeks is contained in Greek writings. The case for Mussulman valour in battle rests only on their own records. The Hindus have no such glorious qualities simply because there is no written evidence.[1]

The deficiency identified by Bankim Chandra was soon to be addressed by Indian historians who wrote in the first half of the twentieth century when the spirit of nationalism provided the ideology for historical investigation and interpretation.

2. Imperialist Attack on Indian Culture and Civilization[2]

The task that the first generation of modern Indian historians had to perform was to defend their culture and civilization against the British imperialist attack. Imperialist prejudice in Indian historiography had first expressed itself in a series of value judgements on Hindu nature and character. James Mill's five-hundred page account of Hindu civilization, the second book of his famous *History*, had the specific objective of proving that it was rude, and that the Hindu excelled in the qualities of the slave. The trend that Mill set was followed by most British historians of India. Even Mountstuart Elphinstone, sympathetic to the Indians, could write passages smacking of those in Mill's *History*. "The most prominent vice of the Hindus," he wrote, "is want of veracity, in which they outdo most nations even of the East."[3]

There were other assumptions. To Elphinstone it appeared strange that "the Arabs should not have overrun India as easily as they did Persia."[4] Vincent Smith's works on India carefully maintained the imperialist assumptions of European superiority in warfare as in his account of Alexander's Indian campaigns. Again, trailing the other British administrator-historians, Smith took pains to prove that endemic political chaos was the normal political condition of India. The inability of the Indians to unite and rule themselves made the permanence of British rule absolutely necessary. They were constantly reminded that freedom had never dawned on their native land.

R.C. Majumdar arrays examples of efforts made to belittle Indian achievements in the past. In the face of the clear testimony of the *Periplus*, Elphinstone assumed that India's foreign trade was conducted by the Greeks and the Arabs. Often, the lowest possible dates were suggested for the *Vedas* and the great epics, and works sometimes hinted and often asserted without evidence that the Indians must have borrowed most, if not the whole, of their culture from the Greeks. Where there was no such possibility, the borrowing must have been from the Babylonians, Assyrians, Persians, and so on.

> Wherever there was the least similarity between Indian and foreign ideas, Indians were taken to be the borrowers. The Epics were supposed to be indebted to Homer's works, Indian drama, mathematics, philosophy, and astronomy were derived from the Greeks, and even Krishna cult was derived from Christ. The very poor evidence on which such theses were boldly enunciated, even by learned scholars, demonstrated a prejudiced mind rather than bad logical deduction or inference.[5]

Here, an observation made by Joseph Needham, the famed author of *Science and Civilization in Ancient China*, may be read with interest:

> We know that the trigonometric sine is not mentioned by Greek mathematicians and astronomers, that it was used in India from the Gupta period onwards (third century)....The only conclusion possible is that the use of sines is an Indian development and not a Greek one. But Tannery, persuaded that the Indians could not have made any mathematical inventions, preferred to assume that the sine was a Greek idea not adopted by Hipparchus, who gave only a cable of chords. For Tannery, the fact that the Indians knew of sines was sufficient proof that they must have heard about them from the Greeks.[6]

One method of undervaluing Indian culture and denigrating the Hindu religion and society was to select and treat only their weak points. Christian missionaries in their writings took special care to highlight the religious superstitions and social abuses of the Hindus. But righteous indignation was one-sided. While justly decrying the barbarous practice of *sati*, witch hunting and the burning of heretics in Europe were forgotten; when the Hindu caste system was justly condemned, slavery, serfdom and the treatment of the 'Blacks' by the 'Whites' were silently passed over.[7]

3. The Meaning, Nature and Content of Nationalist Historiography

Indian nationalist historiography, growing partly in reaction to the pretensions and prejudices of British imperialist historiography on India, was at root concerned with national identity in the pre-colonial period. The search for identity took various forms and covered a wide range of attitudes.

Meaning of Nationalist Historiography

'Nationalist historians' and 'nationalist historiography' are only terms used in a comparative sense, in contrast to the colonial or imperialist attitude of foreign writers – particularly British – in the writing of Indian history. Filled with legitimate national pride, a rising generation of Indian scholars sought to vindicate their national culture against the unfounded charges of European writers. Though there were occasional lapses of the true principles of historical reconstruction, the terms in question should not be taken to mean a body of historical writers or writing whose sole object was the glorification of India's past. R.C. Majumdar restricts the term 'nationalist historians' to those Indians who in reconstructing their country's history aimed at examining or reexamining

> some points of national interest or importance...which have been misunderstood or misconceived or wrongly represented. Such an object is not necessarily in conflict with a scientific and critical study, and a nationalist historian is not, therefore, necessarily a propagandist or a charlatan.[8]

Religion and Society

The imperialist challenge had to be met, and the Hindu religion and its sacred literature, the first target of European attack, were the first to be defended. The defence was perhaps voiced more by reformers than by historians. An extreme school which included men like Rajnarain Bose, Bankim Chandra Chatterjee and Sasadhar

Tarkachudamani and others defended Hinduism in all its forms – including religious superstitions and social evils – claiming that, taken in all the aspects of its development, it formed a highly spiritual force, superior to other faiths. But Dayananda Saraswati, that strange amalgam of liberalism and orthodoxy, defended Hinduism on rational lines. He claimed that the true religion and society of the Hindus are only those purer forms described in the *Vedas.* Idolatry and abuses like caste and *sati* were later accretions not sanctioned by the original faith. Caste was speciously explained as a kind of division of labor, and women in the Vedic period, and even in later times, were shown to have been enjoying a very high status.

Material Culture

The material side of Hindu culture was also defended with equal zeal against European criticism. The results of the new archeological researches and discoveries of both European and Indian scholars were brought forward to disprove the inferiority of Hindu culture. Romesh Chandra Dutt brought together such data in his three volume *Civilization in Ancient India* (1889). R.C. Majumdar calls it the first nationalist history in the best sense of the term. The book is distinguished by its scientific and moderate tone keeping at a distance the extravagant nationalist sentiment of the Indians. Following Max Muller, more or less, Dutt assigned the *Rig Veda* to c. 1200 BC, and his picture of the rude self-assertion and boisterous greed for conquests of the Vedic warriors was one which did not satisfy extreme nationalists and orthodox Hindus. These latter would be content only by the dating of the *Rig Veda* much further back in time. B.G. Tilak, a very able Sanskritist, sought to prove from astronomical data that the Rig Veda was composed in 4000 BC, while A.C. Das pushed the composition of at least some hymns of the *Rig Veda* back to geological epochs. Orthodox Hindu sentiments fancied the Vedic Aryans as a spiritual, pious and contemplative people. The spiritual superiority of Hinduism came to be so loudly asserted that care had to be taken to present the ancient Indians not as a species panting for salvation. Tall claims of scientific and technological achievements were made—claims which included knowledge of even firearms and aeroplanes in ancient India.[9] R.K. Mukherjee's book, *A History of Indian Shipping and Maritime Activity*, was a rejoinder to Elphinstone's doubt whether India's foreign trade was conducted in Indian ships themselves.

While a class of European writers was anxious to prove that Indian culture owed much to foreign sources, some Indian scholars disclaimed with equal vehemence such outside influence. Some of the latter held that India was the original home of the Aryans and that they spread from this country to Europe.

Politics and Adminsitration[10]

The British had repeatedly asserted that India was not a country but a congeries of small states, and that the Indians were not a nation but a conglomeration of peoples of diverse creeds and sects. Against this, R.K. Mukerjee wrote a scholarly thesis, *The Fundamental Unity of India*, which maintained that the religious unity and spiritual fellowship among the Hindus all over India and their ideal of an all-India empire were the basis of Indian nationalism in the past. Again, it was a time when educated Indians were demanding the establishment of representative institutions and a share in the administration of the country. In this respect K.P. Jayaswal had the spurious satisfaction of proving (in his *Hindu Polity*) wrong the thesis of Oriental Despotism. He demonstrated that not only there existed a constitutional form of government, but the entire parliamentary system, including address from the throne and voting of grants, was prevalent in ancient India.

Military

Nationalist historiography likewise sought to explain the easy conquest of India by the British. The explanation offered could not, however, always square up with historical propriety. When the issue at Plassey (1757) was held to be the result of treachery, Buxar (1764) was forgotten. English victory in the Sikh wars was attributed to bribery, but Chilianwala, which was not a British victory, was attributed to the superiority of Sikh military skill. In all this, to prove some points many more had to be forgotten.

Hatred of the British

Nationalist historiography often consciously fanned a hatred of the British government and of individual Englishmen. The calm and moderate tone of Dadabhai Naoroji and R.C. Dutt in their criticism of the British government on economic grounds was not to be heard amongst the diatribes of historians like B.D. Basu. Basu's books are well documented and his charges, supported as they are by facts and figures, are not easy to refute. But, remarks R.C. Majumdar, his scathing comments had the sole objective of arraigning the British before the bar of world opinion. Nationalist bias led to wanton criticism of Macaulay's system of education and Dalhousie's policy of annexing Indian native states. In assessing the work of Clive, Warren Hastings and Wellesly, well-deserved condemnation was coupled with unmerited censure. The very title of the book, *Clive, the Forger*, shows the obvious bias. Siraj ud-Daulah and Mir Kasim became heroes and patriots, Nandakumar a martyr, the Black Hole tragedy a myth, while the massacres of Monghyr were lightly passed over.[11]

Reinterpretation of Indian History

As the freedom struggle developed, nationalist historiography attempted "a deliberate re-interpretation of Indian history in order to infuse enthusiasm in the fight for freedom...."[12] It was the patriot in V.D. Savarkar that renamed the Revolt of 1857 as the 'Indian War of Independence'. Savarkar's book of that title is a typical example of the representation of history from an extremely nationalist point of view. S.B. Chaudhuri's *Civil Rebellions in the Indian Mutiny 1857–59* asserted that the civil rebellions which accompanied the Mutiny gave it the character of a national war of independence. Again, as the British government held out that Hindu–Muslim differences were the chief obstacle in granting dominion status to India, some nationalist historians, realizing the harmful effects of communalism, went out of their way to reinterpret the entire medieval history of India in order to prove that the Hindus and Muslims always behaved like good brothers toward each other, and that they formed one nation. Tarachand's book, *Influence of Islam on Indian Culture* is another attempt in the same direction.[13]

4. Critical Assessment of Indian Nationalist Historiography

Weakness of Nationalist Historiography

Indian nationalist historiography, engaged in an eager search for national identity by meeting European charges against Indian life and culture, at times betrayed a complete lack of historical propriety. Lack of propriety assumed various forms, some of which being inseparable from its nature and content have already emerged in the account given so far. Others may be outlined as:

Methodological Defects

Nationalist historiography in India, as elsewhere, was sometimes guilty of methodological lapses, of deviation from the ideal of objectivity which is the marrow of all true history. It is the inevitable result of making history provide service for current issues. To prove the existence of responsible government in ancient India, Jayaswal put new interpretations on words and passages .in inscriptions and literary texts. A.L. Basham tells us of the manner in which Jayaswal arrived at his conclusions in his famous *Hindu Polity*.

> In order to prove his thesis Jayaswal employed a large range of sources, but used them in the manner of a barrister trying to win a favourable judgement, emphasizing every passage which tended to support his case, and interpreting it in the most favourable light, while virtually ignoring the evidence which went against him.[14]

Chauvinistic Claims

From patrotism to chauvinism is but a step. If the imperialist historians were prone to see everything bad in the Indian past, some of their nationalist counterparts betrayed a tendency to see everything good in it. Emotion and sentiment usurped the place of reason; and detachment, balance, perspective, and objectivity—all became a casualty. Romila Thapar writes:

> There was an unashamed glorification of the ancient Indian past. This was in part a reaction to the criticism of Mill and

other writers and in part a necessary step in the building of national self-respect. The glorious past was also a compensation for the humiliating present.[15]

The Indian origin of the Aryans; the pre-Harappan antiquity of the Vedic culture, denial of foreign influence on Indian civilization, superiority of what was thought to be the essential spiritual quality of Indian culture and art to the essentially materialistic culture and art of the West, and the existence from earliest times of political unity based on a cultural unity were all part of this glorification. The deep conviction in India's past glory sometimes led historians to stretch their arguments to an obnoxious and ridiculous extent. Such is Jayaswal's assertion of the existence in ancient India of constitutional monarchy, parliamentary government, voting of grants, and address from the throne. Such, again, was the claim that ancient India did not lag far behind modern Europe in scientific achievements. We are informed that there were firearms and aeroplanes in the age of the Epics.

Self-contradiction

Nationalist historians could at times be seen asserting or justifying contradictory positions: military power and the values of non-violence; democratic traditions and those of imperial glory; the spiritual superiority of Hinduism and the worldliness of the ancient Indians; and the high status of women in the Vedic period and their secluded life and position of inferiority on social, economic, religious and moral grounds.

Communalism

A by-product of nationalist historiography but one which had dangerous potentialities was communalism. Sensational accounts drawn up by Hindu historians of the heroic struggles of the Rajputs, the Marathas and the Sikhs against the Muslims were a challenge which Muslim historians could hardly afford to miss. It became such that the friend of the Hindu automatically became the enemy of the Muslim and *vice versa*. Enmity was fanned by drama, poetry and novels. Communalism which was to divide the country had its roots in the writing of history, too.

Strength of Nationalist Historiogaphy

Stimulant of Historical Studies

The weakness of nationalist historiography should not blind us to its positive side. Had the author of the *Vande Mataram* lived for three or four more decades he would have been happily surprised at the number of his fellow countrymen engaged in the grand quest of their country's past. Historical study in India received its greatest impetus from the sentiment of nationalism. This was because the nationalist spirit disclosed, as in Europe in the nineteenth century, one of the practical uses of history. Indians sought the key of their national development not in the immediate, but in the remoter past. By supplying a powerful motive for historical investigation the national spirit quickened the work of historical research. To meet the imperialist challenge, the Indian savants plunged themselves into a study of the sources, and India was rich in raw historical materials—monuments, epigraphs, coins and a variety of literary sources. Armed with the newly acquired information they proceeded with the zeal of crusaders to refute the Western charges against their nation and culture. Their researches opened the vast vistas of India's hoary past, and the new-found treasure in its turn filled the mind of the Indians with national fervor and pride, enriched nationalism itself, and quickened the struggle for freedom.

Work Done by Nationalist Historians

Weakness of historical works of an extreme nationalist color were only incidental to the time and the purpose of their composition. A good many historical works of the nationalist category deservedly occupy a high place in the world of scholarship. R.C. Dutt's three-volume *Civilization in Ancient India*, while presenting the nationalist case, is admirably free from the extravagant claims of some of the later Indian nationalist historians. Romila Thapar acknowledges that in spite of weaknesses, nationalist historians played a significant role in the interpretation of ancient Indian history. Because they wrote in conscious opposition to imperialist historiography, the historians were forced to take a fresh look at sources. Once the study of the past was found to have relevance for the present, historiography ceased to be the antiquarian's collection of mere facts, and became narration and interpretation. Although most of the historical writing was confined to dynastic history, the debate on ancient political and cultural life necessitated the study of social and economic history as well.[16]

Growth of Interest in Regional and Local History

Romila Thapar further observes that a valuable offshoot of nationalist historiography was a growth of interest in regional and local history. This in turn led to the discovery of new source materials in local repositories and to greater archeological work in the region. The result of such studies filled many lacunae in historical knowledge and acted as a corrective to some of the earlier generalizations. Evidence of regional variations in the cultural pattern led to the recognition that it was unwise and unhistorical to generalize about the entire Indian subcontinent on the basis of the history of the Ganges heartland. Histories of smaller geographical areas such as Bengal and Maharashtra became common. Neelakanta Sastri's works have brought the history of south India into national perspective.[17]

Economic History

Nationalist historiography had earlier expressed itself in revealing the exploitative nature of British rule in India. William Digby's *Prosperous British India* had shown the way and Dadabhai Naoroji and Romesh Chandra Dutt did laborious work to show that British economic exploitation ruined India's trade and industry and reduced its people to starvation. They imputed the impoverishment of India to the subordindation of its economy to British imperialist economy. The 'drain theory' developed by Naoroji blamed India's poverty to British 'draining' of India's wealth. Romesh Chandra Dutt's two-volume *Economic History of India* (1904) had a revelatory character in that it asserted that the basic cause of India's malady should be sought in the agrarian problem. The economic critique of British imperialism as found in Naoroji and Dutt marked the beginning of economic history in India.

Cultural History

Nationalist historiography had unearthed so vast a corpus of information relating to the multifarious facets of Indian life and culture as to suggest a new approach to the study of India's past. If the material for a continuous narration of ancient Indian political history is lacking, that for the cultural history of the subcontinent is abundant. The idea abumbrated by Rabindranath Tagore caught the imagination of historians. The essence of the cultural approach has perhaps been brought out by Sardar K.M. Panikkar, a nationalist historian, in his introduction to his *Survey of Indian History*.

> Ever since India became conscious of her nationhood...there was a growing demand for a history of India which would try and reconstruct the past in a way that would give us an idea of our heritage. Brought upon textbooks written by foreigners whose one object would seem to have been to prove that there was no such thing as "India", we had each to "discover India for ourselves." I do not think it is an exaggeration to say that it was a spiritual adventure to most of us to gain in some measure an understanding of the historical processes which have made us what we are and to evaluate the heritage that has come down to us through five thousand years of development.[18]

II. SOME MODERN INDIAN HISTORIANS

Under the multifarious influences set in motion by the British conquest and governance of the country, the Indians themselves made, by the end of the nineteenth century, a beginning in writing the history of their country. Valuable preliminary work had been done by genuine scholars like Bhagawanlal Indraji, Bhau Dhaji and Rajendralal Mitra in exploring and editing the core material for history. Then came real histories of which those written till about the 1960s may be said to have been more or less nationalist in character. They were mostly political, dynastic and cultural in nature. Since it is impossible in the space and scope of a textbook to deal with all the historians and their work, only some of them and the more significant of their works are dealt with.

1. R.G. Bhandarkar (1837–1925)

The earliest indigenous modern historian of India was Ramakrishna

Gopal Bhandarkar. Son of a clerk in the Revenue Department, Bhandarkar was teacher, researcher and author besides being a social reformer.

In the realm of political history, Bhandarkar produced two very valuable monographs: *The Early History of the Deccan* (1884) and *A Peep into the Early History of India* (1900). Though the author modestly calls the *History of the Deccan* "merely a congeries of facts,"[19] the work gives a historical account of western India from the earliest times to the Muslim conquest. It is not merely a political history, but one informing the reader of the social, economic and religious conditions of the Deccan during the period covered, as also the state of literature and art. *A Peep into the Early History of India* is a brief survey of the early history of northern India from the beginning of the Mauryan period to the end of the Gupta empire. Again, political history is supplemented by information given on the Brahmanical revival under the imperial Guptas as reflected in the religion, literature and art of the period. Both works are thus integral in approach, treated with a complete mastery of details and command over the critical apparatus.

In one of his numerous papers entitled, 'The Critical, Comparative and Historical Method of Inquiry', as well as in the introduction to the *Peep into the Early History of India*, one gets glimpses of Bhandarkar's ideas on methodology. He tried to attain historical truth and accuracy by subjecting the different kinds of sources used to rigorous scrutiny. He insisted on strict impartiality as of a judge, and condemned the attitude of an advocate or prosecuting counsel in a historian. The scholar's aim should be dry truth. He should in every case determine the credibility of the witnesses before him. None of the current legends should be considered to be historically true, though an effort should be made to find any germ of truth that they may contain.[20] In the matter of analysis and source criticism, Bhandarkar was more meticulous than many European scholars of the time and found much fault with Vincent Smith on this score. Though patriotic he was not anti-British and he did not share the tendency of some Indian scholars to reject foreign influences on the development of Indian civilization and claim high antiquity for some of the occurrences in its history. He seems to have subscribed to the Rankean dictum that the task of the historian was to describe the past as it actually was.

The Bhandarkar Oriental Research Institute at Poona is a worthy and abiding monument to the scholar-historian. Here, in 1919, presiding over the First Oriental Conference, he said: "I close the active years of my life with an assured belief that sound critical scholarship has grown up among us, and that it will maintain its own against aspersions and attacks."[21] We have to prove ourselves worthy of this belief.

2. Romesh Chandra Dutt (1848–1909)

An Indian Civil Service officer, Sanskrit scholar and master of the Indian classics, Romesh Chandra Dutt left behind him a prolific literary output. Dutt was convinced of the importance of literature as source material for India's social history. In the *Literature of Bengal* (1877) he wrote:

> The literature of every country, slowly expanding through successive stages, reflects accurately the manners and customs, the doings and the thoughts of the people. And thus, although no work of a purely historical character has been left behind by the people of Ancient India, it is possible to gain from their works on literature and religion a fairly accurate idea of their civilization and the progress of their intellect and social institutions.[22]

Thus, to discover the Indian mind and to understand Hindu social institutions, Dutt relied mainly on Sanskrit literature. Thus came *A History of Civilization in Ancient India*, in three volumes. The book was, according to Sister Nivedita, "an exposition to India and to the world, of the national glory."[23] It was history of the nationalist kind but free from all extravagant claims. The work was not of original scholarship, yet was fully rational and scientific in treatment. Its balance and restraint did not appeal to the orthodox Hindu who was inclined to think of Vedic life as more spiritual and less wordly.

It is surprising that as early as 1904 an Indian scholar should have published an avowed two-volume economic history. Dutt's *Economic History of India* took over Dadabhai Naoroji's 'drain theory' and further inquired into the nature of British rule. The work is based mainly on parliamentary papers and official reports supported by statistical material. Dutt was the first Indian analyst who diagnosed India's malady to be the agrarian problem. He focused attention on the high incidence of land tax. He pointed out that the two-fold objective of British colonial economy were the production of raw materials for British industries and the consumption of British manufactures in India. He suggested that the government "should cease to act under mandates from Manchester,"[24] and that a policy of protection should be adopted. He attacked the home charges and military expenditure, and suggested retrenchment finance. He pointed his finger to the annual 'economic drain' in the context of the poverty of the Indian people. Dutt's criticism became the economic platform of the national movement.

3. K.P. Jayaswal (1881–1937)

An Oxford product and a lawyer by profession, Kashi Prasad Jayaswal plunged himself headlong into historical research with the sole aim of regenerating national pride based on a consciousness of India's ancient heritage.

Jayswal's most important works are *Hindu Polity* (1918) and *History of India c. AD 150–350.* These two works contained important theses to prove which the brilliant Sanskritist employed a variety of literary, epigraphic and numismatic sources often giving them his own interpretations. Written in the context of the nationalist-democratic movement the *Hindu Polity* turned out to be an immense success. Against the imperialist cliche of Oriental despotism, Jayaswal painstakingly worked out the thesis that India had the earliest and most successful republics, and that it had monarchy of the 'limited' type. Rhys Davids had pointed to the existence of republics in Buddha's time; Jayaswal pushed their existence further back. The *samiti* of the Vedic period was, according to him, a sovereign representative assembly which discussed and decided upon all matters concerning the state. The *sabha* was a body of selected men working under the authority of the *samiti*. The *gana* and *sangha* of the post-Vedic times meant republican communities in which decisions were taken by a collective body by the counting of heads. The democratic procedure in the Buddhist *sangha* led Jayaswal to believe that the ancient Hindu republics introduced resolutions, debated on them and decided by vote of the majority. He even sees provision of a 'quorum' and the practice of 'referendum'. In the second book of the *Hindu Polity*, the author establishes the existence of limited monarchy. He writes: "The fact, if not the theory, was clear that the office of the king was a creation of the people and was held conditionally. Above him there was always the National Assembly, the Samiti, which was...the real soverign."[25]

The *paura* and the *janapada* are for Jayaswal twin political institutions of the city and the country, acting as a powerful check on royal authority. A passage in the *Mahabharata* is interpreted as an address from the throne asking the *paura–janapada* for extra taxes. The council of ministers with the prime minister at its head was another great check on royal absolutism. "It is a law and principle of Hindu Constitution that the king cannot act without the approval of the council of ministers."[26]

In his *History of India*,[27] Jayaswal, the protagonist of Hindu nationalism, made heroes of the Bharasiva-Nagas who are said to have liberated the country from the pernicious and denationalizing effects of the Saka-Kushan foreign rule. This much-too-labored story is based on sources sometimes of doubtful authenticity. Jayaswal's patriotism outran historical probity. Many of his theories are mere castles in the air and have been duly questioned by scholars like U.N. Ghoshal and A.S. Altekar. But his systematic account of ancient Indian republics remained the framework of later researches.

4. Radha Kumud Mukherji (1880–1963)

Born in a respectable family of Bengal, Radha Kumud Mukherji had a brilliant academic career. He chose to be a teacher and served at several universities in India.

Though cast in the nationalist mould, patriotism did not mislead Radha Kumud. In 1912, Mukherji published an important work in ancient Indian history, *The History of Indian Shipping and Maritime Activity from the Earliest Times.* The book traces the maritime activity of the Indians in all its forms from the earliest time to the end of the Mughal period. A monument of patient scholarship, the work is a mine of information from previously uncharted realms informing us of how India stood out as one of the foremost maritime countries plying her ships from the shores of Africa and Madagascar to the farthest reaches of the Malay Archipelago facilitating trade and colonization. The work is based on literary sources in Pali, Sanskrit, Tamil, Bengali, Persian and English and available archeological and numismatic evidence. Lord Curzon, V.A. Smith and K.P. Jayaswal were among those who congratulated the author. Likewise, Mukherji's *Local Self-Government in Ancient India* won praise form Lord Bryce, Lord Haldane and A.B. Keith. *Ancient Indian Education* discussed the evolution and growth of Brahmanical and Buddhist education to the end of the ancient period. *The Fundamental Unity of India* (1914), as F.W. Thomas observed, traced the idea of India's unity "in a variety of geographical and political concepts and in the possession of a common fund of culture."[28] Partition pained the patriotic scholar. In *Men and Thought in Ancient India*, Mukherji presents a view of ancient Indian culture and civilization as in a representative selection: Yajnavalkya, the Buddha, Asoka, Samudragupta and Harsha. *Hindu Civilization*, though intended to be a textbook for universities, is an important work. The monograph entitled *The Gupta Empire* brings together in concise form the moral and material progress of the country achieved in the spacious days of the Guptas. *Ancient India*, again a textbook, is a very well written and profusely illustrated work. There are other works by Mukherji. In fact, no historian has written more exhaustively on ancient India than Radha Kumud Mukherji.

5. H.C. Raychaudhuri (1892–1957)

Hem Chandra Raychaudhuri had shown his brilliance at school and college and as a teacher before he joined the Calcutta University in 1918 and served it till 1952. In 1923, Raychaudhuri published *The Political History of Ancient India from the Accession of Parikshit to the Extinction of the Gupta Empire.* Of this work A.L. Basham writes:

> In so many respects it is the most important work of ancient Indian history written in the last forty years, for since its first publication in 1923 it has gone into six editions, and has been used as a standard text-book in all the colleges and universities of India, largely replacing Smith's *Early History*. Thus it has affected the historical thinking of a whole generation of Indians.[29]

The first of the two parts of Raychaudhuri's book deals with the period from the accession of Parikshit (c. ninth century BC) following the Mahabharata war to the accession of Srenika Bimbisara of Magadha in the middle of the sixth century BC. Here Raychaudhuri accomplished a task which had been thought impossible—reconstruction in a definite chronological order of a sober history of the period from the Mahabharata war to the rise of Buddhism. "We are now enabled by the author's penetrating researches," observed Wieh Geiger, "to start the Indian Chronology from the 9th instead of the 6th or 5th century BC."[30] Raychaudhuri's success was comparable to that of Niebuhr in tracing the historical origins of the Roman state. The second part of the *Political History of Ancient India* covers the period from the accession of Bimbisara to the extinction of the Gupta empire (c. 543 BC to AD 550).

The research that has gone into the making of Raychaudhuri's *Political History*, and the original contributions in every chapter have won the unqualified praise of scholars like de la Vallee Poussin, Wieh Geiger, A.B. Keith, F.W. Thomas, E.W. Hopkins and A.L. Basham. Basham regards him as belonging to the school of Bhandarkar in trying to discover 'dry truth'. With a mind which is not hostage to any pre-conceived notion or philosophy and taking nothing on trust, Raychaudhuri examined the bewildering mass of genealogies, traditions, myths and tales preserved in Brahmanical, Buddhist and Jain writing with extreme care and objectivity and drew conclusions in accordance with the canons of modern historical methodology. His chronology is the only one that has a chance of approximating the truth. Yet Basham detects in Raychaudhuri's writings an undertone of Hindu nationalism.[31]

Another major work, *Materials for the Study of Early History of the Vaishnavite Sect* (1936) won praise from Sir George Grierson, Garbe, and A.B. Keith. Yet another publication of Raychaudhuri resting on solid research work is his *Studies in Indian Antiquities* (1932). Raychaudhuri is also the co-author with R.C. Majumdar and K.K. Datta of *An Advanced History of India*, a useful textbook for college students.

6. G.S. Sardesai (1865–1957)

Govind Sakharam Sardesai was in the service of the state of Baroda as reader and personal clerk to Maharaja Sayaji Rao Gaekwad and also as tutor to the Maharaja's children.

Marathi Riyasat

Sardesai's greatest achievement was the series of books on Maratha history known as *Marathi Riyasat.* The eight volumes of the series told in Marathi the history of the Marathas from the beginning to 1848. The work occupied him for over thirty years. The author had gone through the immense mass of source material on Maratha history. It was a thorough work, though not a critical one. Sardesai does not seem to have taken the trouble of evaluating the sources or assessing the work of the leaders of Maratha history.[32]

Peshwa Daftar and the Poona Residency Correspondence[33]

The long, intimate friendship with Jadunath Sarkar was of immense help and encouragement to Sardesai. When the Maratha historian retired from the Baroda State service in 1925, Sarkar suggested to him to take up the work of editing and publishing the *Peshwa Daftar*. After the third Maratha war and the transfer of power from the Peshwas to the English, the Company got possession of the entire state papers of the Peshwas—a total of 34,972 bundles. Of these, the Marathi bundles written in the *Modi* script, numbered 27,332; the English 7,482; the Persian 29; and the Gujarati 129. These diaries, as they were called, contained information on various aspects of Maratha social and political life. Knowing the value of this material Sarkar prevailed upon the Bombay government to appoint Sardesai as the chief editor of the *Peshwa Daftar*. The Maratha historian and his assistants waded through the sea of papers, selecting, chronologically rearranging and classifying some of them subjectwise for publication. The forty-five published volumes of *Peshwa Daftar* contain 8,650 papers covering 7,801 pages. Vasant Rao writes that Sardesai's introduction to each of the volumes was not of high quality. Soon after the publication of the *Peshwa Daftar*, Sarkar and Sardesai jointly set out to edit and publish the *Poona Residency Correspondence* giving 4,159 letters in 7,193 pages.

New History of the Marathas

Sardesai aimed at presenting a fresh and full treatment of Maratha history in English. He was now eighty. Dauntless, he started writing his *magnum opus,* the *New History of the Marathas.* The eight volumes of the *Marathi Riyasat* are here compressed into three volumes in English.

Sardesai's historical works were purely political in nature with little of the economic and social life of the Marathas of the period. He does not even seem to be interested in the methodology of history. And of style there is little that is pleasing or commendable.

7. Jadunath Sarkar (1870–1958)

An exceptionally brilliant student, Jadunath Sarkar took double honours in English and History and in 1892 passed the M.A. degree examination in English literature. From 1893 to 1926 he was teacher of English and History, and then for two years, Vice-Chancellor of the Calcutta University. He declined a second term because Vice-Chancellorship was a hindrance to his first love—historical research.

Works

Among Indian historians Sarkar was most prolific producing about fifty works of great merit. The works mentioned below are only some of his greatest. *India of Aurangazeb, its Topography, Statistics and Roads* (1901), was not a history proper in the usual sense of the term, but an account of the physical aspects of the country. His *magnum opus* was the full-scale *History of Aurangazeb* written between 1912 and 1924. A historian of tremendous brilliance and one capable of prodigious labor, Sarkar successfully tackled the difficult subject, revealing the puritan emperor's complex personality. The great *History* takes the reader through the War of Succession, the principles and policies of Aurangazeb's administration, the Islamic Church-State in India, the tragic death of Sambhaji, the subjugation of Bijapur and Golconda, the disorder and confusion in northern India during Aurangazeb's twenty-five-year absence in the Deccan, and the death of the emperor. The book concludes with Sarkar's assessment of the impact of Aurangazeb's long reign on India's fortunes. Meanwhile, Sarkar published another work, *Shivaji and his Times* (1919). The third volume of his *History of Aurangazeb* had created a stir in Muslim circles in the country; *Shivaji* caused a similar one in Maharashtra. Sarkar's book showed that the Maratha hero's spectacular success notwithstanding, he had failed to build a nation and that most of his institutions were not quite original. These assertions were damaging to the nationalist historians' theories as well as to the hero himself, and therefore caused resentment in Poona.[34] In 1922 Sarkar edited William Irvine's incomplete work on the later Mughals, and he continued the history from 1738, the point where Irvine had left it. He did this in his *Nadir Shah* (1922), and another monumental work, *The Fall of the Mughal Empire* (1932–50). Beginning with Nadir Shah's departure in 1739, the four volumes of the *Fall of the Mughal Empire* end with the capture of Delhi and Agra by the British in 1803. Sarkar's *Military History of India* was published posthumously in 1960. His works are characterized by unity of conception, of theme and presentation, and are delivered to the reader in direct, easy flowing language and a charming style free from cant, verbosity and affectation.[35]

Critical Historian[36]

Before William Irvine and Jadunath Sarkar, scholars working on medieval India had not cared to know of anything beyond the court chronicles in Persian. Sarkar insisted on getting all original contemporary material including letters and diaries in the various languages. Like Ranke, he went on treasure hunts for first-hand original documents. But his long and tedious journeys had also another end in view. To free himself from dependence on written records alone, he would visit the historical site connected with the subject of his study in order to acquaint himself with its topography and terrain. Like Jules Michelet, Sarkar would see the life of the common people and live for months, as he did in Maharashtra, in the company of the people to see them face to face and to have an insight into their character; he would visit places of pilgrimage not as a devotee but as a scholar, keen on studying the religious and communal life of the people. He would inspect every fort, valley and scene of battle of the Mughal age. Thoroughness in the collection of contemporary sources was followed by a scientific scrutiny for ascertaining their authenticity, by employing modern methods of textual criticism. Sarkar mercilessly exposed the gossip and what he called the opium-eater's tale in Marathi *bakhars* and Rajasthani prose and verse compositions. Great care was then taken in testing the evidence and trying to discover what was true in a maze of contradictory records. He did not allow any part of his work to be affected by consideration for country, race, religion, family and the like. Here is the testament of Jadunath Sarkar, the historian:

> I would not care whether truth is pleasant or unpleasant, and in consonance with or opposed to current views. I would not mind in the least whether truth is or is not a blow to the glory of my country. If necessary, I shall bear in patience the ridicule and slander of friends and society for the sake of preaching truth. But still I shall seek truth, understand truth, and accept truth. This should be the firm resolve of a historian.[37]

Criticism

Yet Sarkar had his critics, though none could challenge the factual basis of his historical edifices nor accuse him of distorting facts. Irresponsible fault-finding apart, A.L. Srivastava cites three instances of criticism and tells us how the critics were silenced when facts were revealed to them.[38] 1. In assessing Aurangazeb's religious policy Sarkar omitted to mention the emperor's Benares *firman* making a grant of land to the Viswanath temple. Sarkar answered that Aurangazeb issued the specific *firman* during the war of succession when he was keen on getting Hindu support in capturing Shuja, and that it had nothing to do with his so-called desire to patronize Hindu religious institutions. 2. Another criticism was that Sarkar's description of Shivaji's murder of Afzal Khan as 'preventive murder' cannot be supported by decisive evidence. The historian answered that Afzal Khan was guilty of gripping Shivaji and striking the first blow on him with his belt dagger. This is clearly attested by Mir Alam, the famous *wazir* of Nizam ul-Mulk of Ahmadanagar, who was also a historian. 3. Sarkar's interpretation of the *jazia* was not considered fair. But Sarkar did not offer his own interpretation of the *jazia*, he had only summed up the 'agreed judgements' of the contemporary Muslim jurists. It was ludicrous, therefore, to attempt to exonerate Aurangazeb and Islam in the same breath. The general charge of bias against Islam and the Muslims brought against Sarkar is answered by C.C. David of Oxford. While reviewing the first volume of the *Fall of the Mughal Empire*, David wrote that the readers of his account of the atrocities of the Maratha raiders in northern India would agree that the belief that Jadunath Sarkar was biased against the Muslim rulers of medieval India was groundless.[39]

Jadunath Sarkar may be compared with Ranke and Momsen. He was unquestionably the greatest Indian historian of his time and one of the greatest in the world. His powerful personality and erudite works have established a tradition of honest and scholarly historiography whose tenets have exerted a healthy influence on many an individual historian.

8. S. Krishnaswami Aiyangar (1871–1953)

Krishnaswami Aiyangar had studied Physics and Mathematics before he changed to history in which he took the M.A. degree in 1899. In 1914 he was invited by the Madras University to head the Chair of Indian History and Archaeology it had created in that year. Aiyangar held this post till 1929.

Contributions of South India to Indian Culture

Professor Aiyangar's *Ancient India* is a collection of lectures on such topics as Gupta history, the Hun problem, the Vakatakas, and the Gurjara empire in north India. In his *Some Contributions of South India to Indian Culture*, Aiyangar emphasized the special character of south Indian culture. This special character could be observed in Brahman orthodoxy in its *vaidik* form and ritual. Modern Hinduism is the product of the union of ritualistic Brahmanism and theism in the form of *bhakti*. Aiyangar goes on to emphasize the considerable share of the south in the expansion of Indian trade and the spread of Indian culture. The distinctive stamp of the south could be observed in the matter of local administration, particularly as developed under the Cholas. And, finally, the south has preserved Indian religion and learning better than the north, a service which largely owed to Vijayanagar.

Problems of Chronology and Origins

Knotty problems of chronology and of 'origins' engaged Aiyangar's attention, and the chronological framework he has provided has been more or less accepted. The Sangam literature, being of a pre-Pallava character, he assigns to the early centuries of the Christian era. The literature of the Saiva and Vaishnava saints he regards as belonging to the age of the Pallavas. The Kalabhra interregnum in Pandya rule he assigns to a period after AD 300. He held that the Pallavas were not foreigners but probably a hereditary line of officers under the Satavahanas on whose decline they conquered the Kanchi region and set themselves up as independent rulers. Aiyangar gives perhaps the best account of the working of the self-governing bodies under the Cholas, and was the first Indian historian to describe the maritime relations of the imperial Cholas, for peace or war, with the Sailendra rulers of Malaya and Sumatra. Finally, in his two-volume *History of Tirupati*, Aiyangar, a Srivaishnava, produced an impartial account of the great shrine as having passed through phases of Jain, Buddhist and Saiva influence before it became a great shrine of Srivaishnava worship.

An Ideal of History

Krishnaswamy Aiyangar's struggle as the editor of the *Journal of Indian History* deserves to be gratefully remembered. Shafaat Ahmad Khan started the journal in 1921, but could not continue after the third volume. Aiyangar took it up but had to struggle hard in the face of financial difficulties until at last he was able to relieve himself of the great responsibility by persuading the Kerala University to take it over. By then, however, he had earned for the journal a recognized position in the world of historical scholarship.

Krishnaswami Aiyangar held that the value of the study of history would be destroyed by the slightest interference with the recording of its actual course, or if it is made to subserve other purposes however noble. For example, we cannot hope to end fanaticism in the character and convictions of the nation's youth by omitting from history all that which tends to promote sectarian fanaticism, and by telling the lying tale that there were no fanatics or acts of fanaticism before us. The right way to proceed is to register the fanatical acts and those influences which were responsible for the perpetration of fanatical deeds, and by pointing out the dire consequences to human society that such deeds entailed.[40]

9. Shafaat Ahmad Khan

Born in a middle class Pathan family of Moradabad, Shafaat Ahmad Khan went to England for higher studies. From 1920 to 1941, he was professor and head of the department of history of the Allahabad University. In 1941, he was appointed High Commissioner for India in South Africa. Khan had taken interest in Muslim communal politics before he became a liberal nationalist subscribing to the Congress ideology. A *persona non grata* with the orthodox Muslims, he fell a victim to communal frenzy when he was stabbed in Simla for his alliance with the Congress. He died not long after.[41]

Principal Works

In Shafaat Ahmad Khan's early death the academic world lost a brilliant historian—perhaps another Jadunath Sarkar. He was a historian of the Ranke–Acton line. The more important of his works are *East India Trade in the Seventeenth Century, Anglo-Portugese Negotiations relating to Bombay 1660–67, Sources for the History of British India in the Seventeenth Century, John Marshall in India, Indian Federation* and *Federal Finance.*

The *Anglo-Portugese Negotiations* is an authentic account of the cession of Bombay by the Portugese to the English. Based on contemporary records the story is told in forceful language. "One of the shrewdest of men," writes Khan of Charles I, "he found himself tricked at every turn of the wheel by the subtle Portugese."[42] In his *East India Trade in the Seventeenth Century*, Khan tries to prove that the theory of mercantalism which was being developed in England had East India trade at its base. England was turning itself into a 'commercial state' imposing a series of restrictive measures against its principal commercial rivals, planting colonies, extending commerce and utilizing the navy for such functions. The narrative, though centred on English trade, brings out the power of the Mughal state which prevented the exploitation of the Indian soil for the Company's political-commercial aggressiveness.[43] Khan was a firm believer in the national unity of India which he stressed in his books *Indian Federation* and *Federal Finance.*

History and Historiography

Shafaat Ahmad Khan outlined his conception of history and

historiography in his two Sayaji Rao lectures on 'History and Historians of British India' delivered at the University of Baroda in 1938.[44] The functions of a historian are those of a judge. He should be free from influence of theories and prepossessions; he should be free alike from the war-cries of the politicians and the special pleadings of the partisan. In a country like India with its clash of races and interests, temptation to partiality and exaggeration are serious. The scholar is cautioned against the temptation to mix up history and politics. Though a historian of the Ranke–Acton line believing in the sanctity of documents, Khan said in conclusion that history was not merely a study of the documents, but involved a deep study of the subconscious impulses of the age. The mystical qualities of a born leader cannot be deciphered from moth-eaten documents and mouldy parchments. History should narrate not only thoughts of the rulers, but also the feelings and sentiments of the ruled.

10. An Explanation of the Lack of Historical Works by Muslims on Medieval Muslim India

British and Hindu historians had written in English on medieval Muslim India but no Muslim historian had worked on that area until the 1920s. Peter Hardy attempts an explanation of this time lag:[45] (a) Despite Syed Ahmad Khan's interest in Indo-Muslim history his principal preoccupation after his return from England in 1870 was religious rather than historical. He and his followers were attempting to arm Islam against Western criticism (and not against either the British or the non-Muslims of India) by interpreting the faith in terms of the science and liberal values of the West. This trend set by Khan continued after his death until the First World War. (b) Hardy suggests that in the years after the Mutiny and the banishment of Bahadur Shah II the problem for the Muslims was one of conciliating the British. It would have been unwise to remind the world of the power which Muslims in India enjoyed in the medieval period, a course which would only serve to provoke British fears of Muslim disloyalty. (c) Furthermore, writes Hardy, Syed Ahmad Khan and the Aligarh school were resolutely non-communal in politics. To study the history of medieval India with its literal reliance on 'authorities' could only provoke Hindus whose cowardly ancestors were, in medieval

Muslim histories, usually being sent to hell, and Muslims whose virile ancestors were always doing the dispatching. Primarily educationists, Khan and the Aligarh school would do nothing to prevent the growth of a sense of nationhood between Hindus and Muslims, transcending religious differences. (d) Finally, before 1914, the history curriculum of the Aligarh University emphasized the study of English and European history rather than medieval Muslim history. Only in Western history could Muslims discover the new world pressing in upon them.

Muhammad Habib

The first modern Indian Muslim to study a subject pertaining to medieval Muslim India was Muhammad Habib. Habib had gone to Oxford and read modern history between 1916 and 1920.

His *Mahmud of Ghaznin* had the definite aim of correcting a tendency among Indian Muslims to adore Mahmud of Ghazni as a saint. Mahmud, according to Habib, represented an Islam which by the eleventh century had become corrupt. Habib sees Mahmud as a hero "enjoying power without morality and waging war in India not for religion but for the greed of glory and gold,"[46] plundering temples which is not sanctioned by the *shariat*. *Jehad* or holy war against the infidel covered the real aim of plunder. It was a cry ready at hand for any ambitious Muslim leader in the Middle Ages to inspire his followers to deeds of heroism, valor and sacrifice. Mahmud does not deserve to be called a true Muslim, for Islam does not sanction what he did in India.

Introduction to the Reprint of Elliot and Dowson

Habib's introduction to a reprint of Elliot and Dowson's *History of India* (Volume 2, 1952) is based upon the "principles of Historical Materialism developed to suit the conditions of the East and in particular of India."[47] These principles emphasized the importance of revolutions in the progress of mankind. Revolution may occur at the production level as when a new invention changes the whole structure of society, or at the ideological level as when the rise of Islam posed a moral challenge to existing social institutions. Those who count most in history are the masses – the worker and the peasant – who from the dawn of history have been exploited by the governing classes who live by depriving the workers of the surplus value of their labor. Force, which in Marx's phrase, "is the midwife of every society pregnant with a new one," though wicked, cannot be dismissed, in human life. "Islam wrought one of the most vital and the most bloodless revolutions in human history....Medina under the Prophet was a working-class republic....There was no governing class and no subject people."[48]

Urban and Rural Revolution in Northern India

Under the heading 'The Urban Revolution in Northern India' Habib says that the Turkish Muslim government of early medieval India was neither foreign nor military. The Ghorian Turks replaced the *thakurs* as the governing class and then enfranchised the Indian city-workers who had been obliged to live outside the city walls by the caste Hindus. The Turks emancipated them and this explains their success in maintaining their rule against foreign (Mongol) and domestic enemies alike. Muhammad Habib writes:

> The post-revolutionary Indians were in no mood to be conquered. The Indian worker with his newly-won freedom...was determined to fight it out in every city and in every street. So India alone was able to stand against the Mongol invasions, which had shattered every state power in east and west. And this new-found strength was entirely due to the urban revolution in northern India.[49]

Habib continues in his rhapsodic vein to inform us that the urban revolution was followed by a rural revolution when the Sultan Ala ud-Din Khalji relieved the 'low'-caste cultivator from the oppression of the 'high'-caste intermediary.

> India would never again become the land of caste privileges it had been for some centuries past...Ala al-din had assured one thing for all time....In all spheres of life, except marriage and personal laws, India would become what the *Manusmriti* so intensely hated "a confusion of castes."[50]

K.M. Ashraf

How fine would Muhammad Habib's story be – the story of an urban revolution followed by a rural revolution sponsored by the Turkish (and Turko-Afghan) rulers of medieval India – were it only true! In dealing with the same period of Muslim Turkish rule in India (1200–1500), K.M. Ashraf does not conjure up any such revolution. He could see no fundamental revolution wrought by Islam in the basic conditions of Indian life.

Ashraf's *Life and Conditions of the People of Hindustan 1200–1500* (1935), deals with the status, habits and standard of life of different classes of people in the area of the Delhi Sultanate, although it leaves out matters like the administration, army, land revenue, transport, education, literature and religion. The work considers the Sultan both as a public and as a private person, the nobility, domestics and slaves, the artisans and cultivators, and goes on to the clothing, food, amusements, virtues and vices of the various classes—emphasizing all the time what is shared by Hindus and Muslims. Secular and non-communal in outlook Ashraf views social classes in economic terms as 'haves' and 'have-nots', not in terms of religious allegiance. He concludes that the introduction of Islam was not a "fundamental revolution in the basic conditions of Indian life.... There was no cultural conflict between the Muslims and the Hindus. In fact the cultural forces were rapidly leading to a complete fusion between the two."[51] Peter Hardy comments: "The picture is not dynamic but static; the work is an essay in dissection of a corpse not in description of a living, moving, changing organism."[52]

Muhammad Nazim

Without any analysis of economic, social or religious factors, without any unity of chronology or theme, Muhammad Nazim's *The Life and Times of Sultan Mahmud of Ghazna* (1931) has few merits. Nazim's one aim is to exonerate Mahmud of Ghazni from the charge of fanaticism and to show that his wars in India were not those of a predatory iconoclast, but part of a programme of conquests and annexations. Mahmud was not a fanatic for he "is never said to have demolished a temple in time of peace,"[53] that is to say, if we may add, when he was not in India! Nazim is certain that Mahmud was not a fanatic, but believing in the religious unity of the state he severely punished all dissenters.[54] Mahmud treated the Hindus as an imperialist rather than as a missionary or a crusader and as such they cannot have any real cause for complaint.

The Hindus rejected Islam as their national religion because of the fundamental and irreconcilable differences between Islam and Hinduism.

Ishtiaq Husain Qureshi

Peter Hardy observes that Ishtiaq Husain Qureshi's *The Administration of the Sultanate of Delhi* (1942) emphasizes the Sultanate's Islamic than its Indian character, and that the approach is strongly communalist.[55] The author treats the Delhi sultanate as a welfare state and believes that it more than satisfied modern ideas of tolerance, benevolence and efficiency. The Hindus were not ill-treated. Qureshi claims that,

> The Hindu population was better off under the Muslims than under Hindu tributaries or under independent rulers....Nor was the Hindu despised socially. The Muslims, generally speaking, have been remarkably free from racial prejudice. There are instances of Muslim nobles marrying Hindu maidens; of free intercourse between Muslim saints and Hindu yogis; of Hindu followers of Muslim saints and *vice versa*...it was Hinduism which protected itself beneath the strong armour of exclusiveness. The Muslim was unclean; his very touch polluted the food of the twice-born Brahman and men of the higher castes; the new-comer was outside the pale.[56]

Zahir ud-din Faruki

A graduate of Aligarh University, Zahir ud-din Faruki went to England to qualify in law. Faruki's *Aurangazeb and his Times* (1935) is an avowed apology for Aurangazeb and is mainly directed against Sir Jadunath Sarkar's *History of Auragazeb.* To Faruki—Aurangazeb was the savior of Islam in India after Akbar had surrendered its outer defences; political and not religious considerations moved Aurangazeb in his treatment of the Hindus; he destroyed Hindu temples and levied *jizya* merely in order to preserve Mughal domination; it was not Aurangazeb who antagonized the Hindus, it was the Hindus who antagonized Aurangazeb; and a truly Islamic monarch could not but be a just monarch. The book is evidently inspired by Amir Ali's *Spirit of Islam.*[57]

S.M. Jaffar

S.M. Jaffar's *The Mughal Empire from Babur to Aurangazeb* (1936), writes Peter Hardy,

> ...is a very clear example of an unresolved tension between Islam and Indian nationalism in some 'South Asian' Muslims in the nineteen thirties....However, should the choice be obligatory...there is evidence in this book that he would choose to be a Muslim first.[58]

Blaming false history for the lack of national unity and communal amity, Jaffar's book offers what the author thinks to be a correct interpretation of the respective policies of Akbar and Aurangazeb. Akbar was a liberal nationalist. His *Din Ilahi* which had national unity as its aim was a political code cleverly designed to attract the entire population. The Hindus, Muslims, Zoroastrians and Christians could find in that chameleon of a faith the tenets and practices of their own respective faith. It was to be a universal religion for India. Yet, Akbar was not an apostate from Islam, for he was not sincere in his *Din Ilahi.*

> In a land where the very word "Muslim" was an eyesore to the natives, Akbar thought it expedient to subscribe to the beliefs of his Hindu subjects in spite of their hollowness....Whereas, in fact, he always concealed his religious identity in byways and corners.[59]

Garlic and onions and the wearing of beads were forbidden not because Akbar was an apostate from Islam but because they were inconvenient in kissing. Jaffar's serious writing at times means fun for the readers.

Jaffar writes about Aurangazeb:

> The lot of the subjugated has never been happier than under the ruling races of Islam....Alamgir was tolerant...and to a fairly high degree, but not so tolerant as Akbar and Dara who, in order to achieve their ulterior political aims, concealed their religious identities and even subscribed to the religion of the ruled....[60]

Jaffar affirms that Aurangazeb would have continued the tolerant policy of his predecessors if he had not discovered that it was impossible to reconcile the Rajputs to his rule. Then he refused to rely on them and rallied around him his own co-religionists with whose help he succeeded in crushing his enemies.

Modern Muslim Historiography on Medieval Muslim India: An Assessment

Tension between the National and Islamic Identities

K.M. Ashraf has written that in medieval India the cultural forces represented by Hinduism and Islam "were rapidly leading to a complete fusion between the two." But in general terms modern Indian Muslim historiography on medieval Muslim India reveals what Peter Hardy calls "an unresolved tension between Islam and Indian nationalism...in the nineteen thirties."[61] It is seen in the works of Muhammad Nazim, Ishtiaq Husain Qureshi, Zahir ud-din Faruki and S.M. Jaffar.

Islamic Apologetic

Peter Hardy observes that modern Muslim historiography on medieval India has chiefly taken the form of an Islamic apologetic justifying the life of medieval Muslims to the modern world. It could be seen in an abundance of value judgements and a desire to establish that whatever Muslims did in medieval India was right if not in terms of religion then in terms of politics.[62]

Medieval Politics

The interest of modern Muslim historians on medieval India is overwhelmingly centered on politics. Muhammad Habib's work on mystics and Faruki's work on Shaikh Ahmad of Sarhind are exceptions. Peter Hardy thinks that Syed Ahmad and Amir Ali are the influence behind this comparative neglect of religion among the English-educated Muslim intelligentsia. Instead of trying to get a sympathetic insight into the religious experience of the medieval Muslim, this school stood for a reinterpretation of the Prophet's thought for today in a militant spirit.[63]

Consciousness of Islam as Way of Life and Thought

The same intense consciousness of Islam as the unique, vital, final way of life and thought seems to have been carried over from medieval Muslim historiography by modern Muslim historians of medieval India. Muhammad Habib wrote even in his Marxian strain that "The Quranic conception of God was, and can still be, a revolutionary force of incalculable value for the attainment of human welfare."[64] Peter Hardy comments:

> There is the same inarticulate premises that the writing of history should justify the ways of Muslims to men. There is the same assumption that history is purposive, teleological; there is the same urge towards a universal schematic view of history....The significant feature of Professor Habib's Marxist interpretation of medieval Indian history is not that Marxism has absorbed Islam but that Islam has absorbed Marxism.[65]

11. Surendranath Sen (1890–1962)

One of the most eminent historians of modern India, Surendranath Sen's chief interest lay in Maratha history. To explore source material in original he made a careful study of the Marathi, Persian and Portuguese languages. Leaving the beaten track of political history he chose institutions for his historical investigation. In this he was a pathfinder for later researchers.

Sen's first major work *The Administrative System of the Marathas*, challenged the British-sponsored view that the Marathas were only plunderers. The work demonstrated that they were capable of building administrative institutions consistent with their social and political traditions. Complementary to the *Administrative System* was the *Military System of the Marathas* which Sen wrote during his residence at Oxford. The subject being a comparatively new field for Indian historians, Sen read the standard English works on military history, particularly those relating to the Peninsular war. He made an extensive tour of Spain and Portugal in search of new material on Maratha history in the Portugese archives, and also to understand how military movements are affected by the terrain. Anil Chandra Banerji writes:

> His labours gave him a rich dividend. Judged as a whole, the *Military System* ranks higher than the *Administrative System* as a scholarly performance....A pioneer work on military history, the *Military System* gives interesting clues to the

understanding of Maratha history and remains without a rival to this day.[66]

Sen's *India through Chinese Eyes* originally formed the theme of his Sir William Meyer lectures at the Madras University. The book threw new light on the subject. Finally, no event in British Indian history had provoked more feeling and bitterness than the Revolt of 1857, that to write an objective, dispassionate account of it was an almost impossible task. But when in 1955, Maulana Azad, free India's Minister for Education, invited Sen to write a new history of the struggle of 1857, he accepted the assignment. Though a government-sponsored work, the author acknowledged that there was no attempt at interference and that his work was "not an 'authorised version' in any sense."[67] *Eighteen Fifty Seven*, Sen's last major work, refused to idealize the Mutiny as a 'national war' except in two regions, Oudh and Shahabad; at the same time it refused to dismiss it as a mere military rising. Apart from the feelings roused, the main methodological difficulty in writing an account of the Mutiny is the 'one-sidedness' of the sources which are overwhelmingly British. Sen had to extract the Indian version from scattered materials, such as the papers of Maulvi Rajab Ali, Munshi Jiwanlal's *Diary* of the events of the Mutiny in Delhi, the account of Kedarnath, etc. Sen's narration is above the pale of controversy and his analysis and assessment have set up a high standard of historical objectivity.

12. Sardar K.M. Panikkar (1895–1963)

A man of ideas and many abilities, K.M. Panikkar had a rich and varied career. But his passion was history which he wrote profusely. Sardar Panikkar died in 1963.

In 1922, while teaching at the Aligarh University, Panikkar wrote the monograph *Sri Harsha of Kanauj*. Panikkar's picture of Harsha is that of an enlightened monarch who "deserves to be considered among India's greatest rulers."[68] *The Origin and Evolution of Kingship in India* (1938) which was a series of lectures delivered at the invitation of the Baroda State aimed at dispelling the notion among European scholars that political thought – the inquiry into the phenomenon of the state – was foreign to the ancient Indian genius. His *Malabar and the Portugese* and *Malabar and the Dutch* (1931) are complementary works tracing the history of Europe's connection with India's west coast from the beginning of the sixteenth to the end of the eighteenth century.

Sardar Panikkar was the first, and perhaps the only Indian, who studied history from the geographical and the geopolitical angle. In his *India and the Indian Ocean* (1945), he claimed that India never lost its independence till it lost command of the sea in the first decade of the sixteenth century. The book proceeds to trace the influence of the Indian Ocean on the shaping of Indian history and to discuss the vital importance of oceanic control to the future of India.

In the introduction to the *Geographical Factors in Indian History* (1955), Panikkar wrote that "geography constitutes the permanent basis of every nation's history,"[69] and that "both the internal policies of a country and its external relations are governed largely by the unalterable geographical conditions and their relationship in space to other countries."[70] The role of the Himalayas and the sea as basic elements in the evolution of Indian life and outlook can hardly be overemphasized. A country like India needs "both a continental view and an appreciation of sea-power."[71]

In 1947 came *A Survey of Indian History* which soon became a popular favorite appearing nine times in print in seven years. In about two hundred and fifty pages the author gives the reader an idea of the national heritage of the Indians through five thousand years of development. Panikkar takes trouble to remove certain misconceptions. Foreign writers have attempted to show that there never was an entity called 'India', and that anything good or great in India must have had a foreign origin. The doctrine of the Aryan origin of Indian civilization which finds no support in Indian literature is the result of the theories of the Indo-Germanic scholars who held that everything valuable in the world originated from the Aryans. Indian civilization had a pre-Vedic origin. The division of Indian history into clearly marked periods – Buddhist-Hindu, Muslim, British – has little meaning. And the *Survey* is not a political or dynastic history, for the Sardar aimed at portraying the life of the people. In this portrayal he emphasizes the Aryo-Dravidian synthesis beginning at the end of the Rig Vedic age that created Indian civilization, a synthesis perfected in the life of the mind, but never attempted on the racial level. In this survey of the national evolution of the Indians, the author perceives an undeniable fact of decadence in Hindu life, a certain undermining of the national vigor, in the ninth, tenth and eleventh centuries. The fact of decadence is attested to not only by the breakdown of northern India before the onslaughts of the Turks but also by the corruption of religion, arrested progress in science, and the obscene literature and temple sculpture of the period. An incurable complacency and overweening pride took the place of thought and progress, a fact noted by the shrewd Al-Biruni.

Panikkar's *Asia and Western Dominance*, published in 1953, took the academic world by storm. Translated into many a European language notwithstanding papal prohibition, the book raised the Sardar to world rank as a historian. It is a critical survey of Europe's contact with Asian states during what the author calls 'the Vasco da Gama epoch of Asian history' (1498–1945). Control of the sea enabled the Europeans to extend their economic and political power over Asia. The imposition of Europe's commercial economy and political dominion eventually brought about a silent revolution in almost every aspect of Asian life. Asia's contact with the West created a mental ferment which roused the continent from its long slumber. The Western-educated intellectuals of Asia assumed leadership of their respective countries and liberated them from Western domination. But the liberation itself, in Panikkar's view, owed to the vitality of the old religion and culture of the different Asian countries which defeated the Christianization attempted by the Western religious missions.

Assessment

Looking at India's past as an Indian, Sardar Panikkar completely broke away from the tradition of British historiography on India. But he was not that type of nationalist historian who praised everything Indian. Using every kind of source and examining even legends, his was not record-oriented research of the orthodox type. Heavy scholarship does not sit upon his works; they are rather moved by bright ideas. Believing that "the history of a country has little value unless it deals with the conscious effort of a people to achieve a civilization, to reach better standards, to live a happier and nobler life,"[72] he gave us a new kind of cultural history holding up the national heritage.

Critics have discerned an amount of subjectivity, a pronounced

Hindu bias, in his assertions though few have been able to challenge their validity in national experience.

> Indian history is of necessity, predominantly the history of the Hindu people, for though other and potent elements have become permanent factors in India, the Hindus still constitute over eighty per cent of her population. Besides, what is distinctly Indian has so far been Hindu. Islamic contribution is not specially related to India and is a part of a world culture to which Muslims belong....In essence, therefore, the history of Indian effort towards the building up and maintenance of a specially Indian civilization has to be the history of the Hindu mind and its achievements.[73]

The following passage questions the charge against Panikkar of bias against the Muslims:

> Even in regard to religion the idea that Hinduism was always held in contempt by the early Muslim rulers would not bear examination. In fact we have ample evidence that even under the most bigoted kings like Allauddin Khilji, the Hindu religious leaders received honour and recognition. From Jain sources we know that Allauddin held religious discourses with Acharya Mahasena who had to be brought from the Karnataka country for the purpose. It is also said that the Digambara Jain, Purna Chandra of Delhi, and the Swetambara ascetic Ramachandra Suri were in favour with the same Sultan. Ghiasuddin Tughlaq had two Jain officers who exercised great influence over him, while Firuz held in high honour the poet Ratnasekhara.[74]

13. K.A. Nilakanta Sastri (1892–1975)

The greatest and the most prolific among the professional historians of south India, K.A Nilakanta Sastri, succeeded Krishnaswamy Aiyangar as professor of Indian history and archeology at the Madras University, a position which he held with distinction till his retirement in 1947. From 1957 to 1971 he was director of the Institute of Traditional Cultures of South East Asia set up by the UNESCO. Sastri died in 1975.

Works

Nilakanta Sastri published about twenty-five historical works. Though his special field was the history of south India he wrote several works of a general nature. Such were the *History of India* in 3 volumes (1950–53), *Life and Culture of the Indian People* (1966), and *An Advanced History of India* (1970). Of these, the second and the third were co-authored with G. Sreenivasachari. Sastri not only edited but wrote several chapters of the collaborative *The Age of the Nandas and Mauryas* (1952), and the second volume of *A Comprehensive History of India: Mauryas and Satavahanas. Aspects of Indian History and Culture* (1974) is one of the two volumes of the more important of the articles written by him, while *South India and South East Asia* (1978) is the other volume of collected articles. *History of Srivijaya* (1949), and *South Indian Influences in the Far East* (1949) won for Sastri a respectable place in Southeast Asian historiography.

Yet, Nilakanta Sastri's special field was South Indian history, a comparatively neglected area of Indian historiography. "Attention has been concentrated too long," wrote V.A. Smith, "on the North, on Sanskrit books, and on Indo-Aryan notions. It is time that due regard should be paid to the non-Aryan element."[75] Even before Smith, Sundaran Pillai had remarked: "The scientific historian of India ought to begin his study with the basin of the Krishna, of the Kaveri, of the Vaigai, rather than with the Gangetic plain, as has been now long, too long, the fashion."[76]

Sastri's predecessor in office in the Madras Univesity, Krishnaswami Aiyangar, had made a beginning in south Indian history. Yet even its general outlines were so little known that Sastri thought they deserved to be set forth at some length. Knowing that the scientific study and interpretation of the sources of south Indian history – epigraphic, numismatic and literary – had got but little beyond the elementary stage, Sastri spent much time and academic labor on working out a dependable chronological framework. But a chronological framework by its very nature could not be built up except by fixing the details of political history. This emphasis on chronology and political history was to become a distinguishing feature of Nilakanta Sastri's works. Not that he was oblivious of the importance of economic, social, religious and cultural history, but the reconstructions of these aspects could be held together only if they could be fitted into a political and chronological mould.

The great corpus of his works on south India include the following: *Pandyan Kingdom* (1929); *Studies in Chola History and Administration* (1933); two volumes of *The Cholas* (1935–37); lengthy chapters on the history of the Chalukyas of Badami and of Kalyani in the *Early History of the Deccan*, (the first two volumes edited by Ghulam Yazdani), were definite contributions to the political history of ancient Deccan; *Foreign Notices of South India from Megasthenes to Ma Huan* (1939), which is a source book enriched with useful notes; the three-volume *Further Sources of Vijayanagar History* (1946), which is a collaborative work with N. Venkataramanayya; the *Tamil Kingdoms of South India* (1948); *A History of South India* (1955); *Historical Method in Relation to South Indian History*, with H.S. Ramanna for co-author; *Development of Religion in South India* (1963); the *Culture and History of the Tamils* (1963); *Cultural Contacts between Aryans and Dravidians* (1967); and *Sangam Literature: its Cults and Cultures* (1972).

The Cholas and A History of South India

Sastri's first significant historical work was the *Pandyan Kingdom.* It was followed by his celebrated works on the Cholas: *Studies in Chola History and Administraiton* and *The Cholas*. A revised edition of this second work, published in one volume in 1955 became Sastri's *magnum opus.* Only with great effort would such masses of details have been collected from the thousands of Chola records, and with great craft and care their confusing evidence would have been systematized to present a meaningful picture of south Indian history during the four centuries of Chola rule. Chronology and politics take up half the work, the other half being devoted to the socio-economic and cultural aspects of Chola rule. But the most significant work which Sastri published during the 1950s was *A History of South India* (1955). The book presents a general survey of the history of south India from pre-historic times to the fall of Vijayanagar. That it has gone into several editions testifies to its undimmed quality. Political history is accorded the highest honor though socioeconomic conditions, literature, religion, philosophy and art receive due attention.

Assessment

"Hitherto," observed Vincent Smith, "most historians of ancient India have written as if the South did not exist."[77] In general histories of India this "integral and not the least interesting part of the history of India"[78] figured in a small way. But the south did not have for Sastri any narrowly regional or isolationist connotation and he was always careful to present its history as an integral part of the history of the subcontinent. "We mean by South India," he wrote, "all the land lying south of Vindhyas *Dakshina* (the Deccan) in the widest sense of the term."[79] Romila Thapar has rightly observed, though in a different context, that such histories of restricted geographical areas have "corrected the tendency to generalize about the entire Indian subcontinent on the basis of the history of the Ganges heartland."[80] Cultural patterns are likely to differ in a geographical area as large as the Indian subcontinent where historical change need not be identical nor occur simultaneously. "Nilakanta Sastri's work on South Indian history," says Thapar, "created a new awareness of the history of the subcontinent by bringing the history of the south into perspective."[81]

14. R.C. Majumdar (1888–1980)

After Jadunath Sarkar the best known of the older generation of Indian historians and one of international fame was Romesh Chandra Majumdar. He was Vice-President of the International Commission for a *History of the Scientific and Cultural Development of Mankind* set up by the UNESCO, and chief editor of the Bharatiya Vidhya Bhavan's monumental eleven-volume *The History and Culture of the Indian People.*

Works

With a rare command over the materials of all the different phases of Indian history in their meticulous detail, and also of the pre-European period of Southeast Asian history and culture, Majumdar passed from area to area until he had authored a corpus of historical works of outstanding merit. The more important of this corpus are: *Corporate Life in Ancient India, Outline of Ancient Indian History and Civilization,* the three-volume *Ancient Indian*

Colonies in the Far East, A History of Bengal, Classical Accounts of India, the collaborative *An Advanced History of India, Penal Settlements in the Andamans, History of the Freedom Movement, The Sepoy Mutiny and the Revolt of 1857,* and contributions to the *History and Culture of the Indian People.*

Majumdar began with his doctoral thesis entitled *Corporate Life in Ancient India* (1918). In the introduction to the printed edition of this lucid, comprehensive work he makes an important point that "religion did not engross the whole or even an undue proportion of the public attention..." of the ancient Indians.[82] His *Outline of Ancient Indian History and Civilization* (1927) is projected on a large canvas. The work went into six editions till 1971. Majumdar's *Early History of Bengal* developed into a substantial cooperative work, *A History of Bengal,* in two volumes (1943). Extending his field, Majumdar embarked on exploring the history and culture of the Indianized states of Southeast Asia. The endeavor bore fruit in a major three-volume work, *Ancient Indian Colonies in the Far East.* Apart from its intrinsic merit, the work is also valuable in having made available to those unacquainted with French or Dutch, a systematic account of ancient Indian effort in Southeast Asia through a thousand years of its history. Majumdar has been charged of a nationalistic (imperialistic) point of view for describing, like Nilakanta Sastri, the Indianized states of Southeast Asia as 'Hindu colonies'. In this connection H.B. Sarkar points out that N.J. Krom, who has furnished a good exposition of that phenomenon of Indianization, used the term 'Hindu-Javanese' in his description of Javan culture, stressing the Indian component of that culture; in the tenth century of the Christian era when Islam was not yet a political or cultural force in the region, one could hardly think of Southeast Asia of the time without the Indian art of writing, literature, law books, statecraft, deification of monarchs, royal paraphernalia, Indian religion, social system, art and architecture.[83] Likewise G. Coedes observes:

> It [South East Asia] has not entered history except to the extent that it was civilized by India. Without India its past would be always unknown: we would know scarcely more about it than we know about the past of New Guinea or Australia.[84]

In view of all this H.B. Sarkar does not think that Majumdar was unjustified in using the term 'colony' in the sense of 'cultural colony' and not 'political domination'.

In his work on the Great Revolt of 1857, Majumdar did not treat that event as a national war of independence. He stressed the point that the most important section that fought the British were the sepoys who were inspired more by the hopes of material gain than by national, political or even religious considerations. He wrote that "the miseries and bloodshed of 1857–58 were not the birth pangs of the freedom movement in India, but the dying process of an obsolete aristocracy and centrifugal feudalism of the medieval age."[85] Yet, Majumdar maintains that the great event of 1857 had an indirect and posterior importance. It became a symbol of challenge to the mighty British power in India and was duly invested with the full glory of the first national war of independence.

Majumdar was co-author with K.K. Datta and H.C. Raychaudhuri of *An Advanced History of India*, intended for advanced students of Indian History. From its first appearance in 1946 up till 1980, it has come out in four new editions and fifteen reprints. The *History and Culture of the Indian People* in eleven major volumes is monumental in its conception, dimension and execution. Majumdar not only edited this work but also contributed many of its more important chapters on political history. Some of the volumes have gone into several editions. With the completion of this great project our historian's life's task ended.

Hindu–Muslim Relations[86]

Writing about Hindu–Muslim relations during the Sultanate of Delhi – in Volume Four of the *History and Culture of the Indian people* – Majumdar sees an uncompromising spirit of animosity between the two communities. Living for generations as close neighbors, reciprocal relations were too superficial and touched merely the fringe of life. The ultra-democratic social ideas of the Muslims, an object lesson of equality and fraternity, did not make any impact on Hindu social rigidity and attitude of inequality among men exemplified in the caste system and untouchability. Nor did the Muslims imbibe the Hindu spirit of tolerance and reverence for all religions. They did not moderate their zeal to destroy the Hindu temples and images of gods. The Hindu was *zimmi*—a being protected by the Muslim state on condition of rendering certain service and suffering certain political and civil disabilities.

History Writing

Majumdar's Heras Memorial lectures (1967) may be taken as a summary of his ideas on history writing. A historian of the Rankean school, he attached the greatest importance to facts. A master of analysis and interpretation, he tried to remove subjectivity from historical explanation. He refused to subordinate facts to yield any principle or illustrate any philosophy or ideology. Majumdar adhered, and urged others to adhere, to the Rankean dictum that the task of the historian was 'merely to show what really happened.' The ascertainment of the truth of the past, so far as it can be ascertained, is the one object, the one sanction, of all historical studies. He felt uneasy about the deteriorating standards and what he thought to be the evils growing in our historical studies. In his Presidential Address prepared for the sixth annual conference of the Institute of Historical Studies held at Srinagar in 1968 which, however, he could not attend, he wrote:

> ...history, divorced from truth, does not help a nation. Its future should be laid on the stable foundations of truth and not on the quicksands of falsehood, however alluring it may appear at present. India is now at the cross-roads and I urge my young friends to choose carefully the path they would like to tread upon.[87]

16

I. THE MARXIST PHASE

The New History[1]

In the post-independence period in India a kind of history developed, which was also deeply rooted in the writings of the nationalist historians, and which owed its birth to an interest in Marxism. By the Marxist Phase (of historians) is not meant that the writers were all Marxists but that they more or less adopted materialistic interpretation as a method of understanding the historical phenomena. Some saw that history, particularly ancient history, can best be studied within the framework of a social science discipline. Their interpretation derived from the historical philosophy of Karl Marx, particularly dialectical materialism. The essence of the new approach lies in the study of the relationship between social and economic organization and its effect on historical events. The new trend called not so much for new evidence as for a re-reading of the sources with a different set of questions in mind. It is best exemplified in the work of Damodar Dharmanand Kosambi, the patriarch of the Marxist school of Indian historiography.

1. D.D. Kosambi (1907–1966)

No single writer after James Mill and Vincent Smith has so deeply influenced the writing of Indian history as Damodar Dharmanand Kosambi. Dying rather prematurely Kosambi left behind him besides several papers and articles, the following major works: *An Introduction to the Study of Indian History* (1956), *The Culture and Civilization of Ancient India in Historical Outline* (1965), *Exasperating Essays: Exercises in the Dialetical Method*, and *Myth and*

Reality: Studies in the Formation of Indian Culture. Of these, the first two works revolutionized Indian historiography.

A New Definition of History

The greatest impediment to any study of ancient India is the lack of reliable records and a dependable chronology to go on. For this reason, Kosambi tells us, the direct procedure of history writing in the old European tradition would be futile. But we may know how men lived in those distant times, times for which formal forms of sources and evidence are absent. Man would not have always lived in the same manner, particularly when he advanced by slow degrees from the food-gathering quasi-animal stage to that of food production, which definitely raised him above a mere animal existence. As Gordon Childe says with aphoristic brevity and precision, 'man makes himself'. Man makes himself by making and using tools and implements in order to live increasingly well at the expense of his environment. It follows then that there must have been a change in his life whenever there was a change in the quantity and quality of his tools or the means of material production. This change is historically verifiable as, for instance, from the "comparatively sudden increase in the human population with every important basic discovery in the means of production."[2] Means of material production determine social organization which cannot be more advanced than the former. This fact of human life, that is, the intrinsic connection between man's life and the means of production at his disposal – the former changing *pari passu* (with equal pace) with the latter – constitutes the theme and method of history. Kosambi now offers his definition of history as "*the presentation, in chronological order, of successive developments in the means and relations of production.*"[3] The definition implies a definite theory of history known as dialectical materialism or Marxism, a classic statement of which appears in Karl Marx's preface to his *Critique of Political Economy.* "Certainly," says Kosambi, "this is the only definition known which will allow a reasonable treatment of preliterate history, generally termed pre-history."[4]

The Comparative Method

To reconstruct ancient Indian history Kosambi employs combined methods or the comparative method and interdisciplinary techniques of investigation. Seeing that India abounded in living survivals of the dead past he would notice material relics of that past laid bare by archeology—houses, grave-goods, instruments of production and utensils of household use, groves, stones marking sacrificial ritual, caves and rock shelters; then the religious and social practice even of modern Indians; and, finally, primitive human types. From such 'primary sources' which no library can provide, he would work back to the productive relations and social organization of people of bygone ages. Certain types of joint burials for him indicated whether the society represented was in the matriarchal, patriarchal or the pre-clan stage. Tribal clusters living in and around highly developed areas and cities suggested to him the absorption of the tribes into all strata of a caste society. The red pigment still adorning the vast majority of the countryside deities in India is a relic of the long-vanished blood sacrifice. Caves and rock shelters may have been occupied successively by prehistoric men, Buddhist monks and practitioners of Hindu cults. And even highly educated Indians today do not suspect that some of the religious and social rites they practise have behind them millennia of continuity.

Kosambi turned his knowledge of Sanskrit and etymological analysis in that language to good account in reconstructing the social background of the Vedic period. Since the language of the Vedic texts pointed to an admixture of the Aryan and non-Aryan elements, he thought it likely that non-Aryans must also have been taken into the fold of the Brahmans whose original seven *gotras* must have been of mixed Aryan and non-Aryan priests.[5] He philologically equated the Hittite *khatti* with the Sanskrit *kshatriya* and the Pali *khettiyo*. Knowledge of mathematics enabled him to weigh with the utmost precision large numbers of punch-marked coins which were in use between c. 500 to 100 BC. Kosambi's extensive field work on microlithic sites and artefacts enabled him to mark the routes which herders, pastoralists and incipient traders would have taken across the western Deccan in the prehistoric period.[6] Geographical, topographical and geomorphological pointers guided him to indicate some of the urban sites and Buddhist monastic centers especially in the western Deccan during the first millennium AD. The study of cultural survivals using ethnological and anthropological material is best illustrated in the pages of *An Introduction to the Study of Indian History*.

From Tribe to Caste

Kosambi maintained that one of the clues to an understanding of the Indian past is the factor of the transition from tribe to caste—from small localized groups to a generalized society. This transition was largely the result of the introduction of plough agriculture in various regions which changed the system of production, broke the structure of tribes and clans, and made caste the alternative form of social organization.[7] Indicative of such a change is the evolution of clan totems into clan names and then into caste names. Brahmanical settlement in various parts of the country was the agency through which plough agriculture was introduced. They led to the assimilation of local cults into the Brahamanical tradition and to the Sanskritization of local folk cults.

Interpretation of Myths

Interpretation of myths is essential to any study of early cultures.[8] The story of Pururavas and Urvasi, Kosambi thought, reflected the institution of sacred marriage in prehistoric societies as well as the ritual sacrifice of the hero by the mother goddess. He believed that societies were largely matriarchal in origin but many changed into patriliny, and myths therefore reflected the transition from the one to the other. Bride-price is for him a survival of matriliny. However, we may observe that the transition may not have uniformly been from matriliny to patriliny since many societies are known to have been patrilineal from the beginning.

The Indus Civilization

The earliest of the transitions from tribe to caste, Kosambi thought, occurred in the Indus Valley. He assumed that the agrarian technology of the Indus people did not know the plough.[9] The river bank, he thought, was cultivated with the harrow. Like those on the Nile and the Euphrates-Tigris, embankments on the Indus stored the flood-water for irrigation and retained the rich river-silt. Again, Kosambi squarely attributes the decline of the Indus civilization to the Aryans who destroyed the agricultural system by breaking the embankments which, he maintains, is symbolically referred to in the Rig Vedic descriptions of Indra destroying Vrtra and releasing the waters. Kosambi believes that the plough was brought by the Aryans who thereby changed agricultural technology. Romila Thapar points out however, that recent evidence on the Indus Valley makes it clear that plough agriculture was practised even in the pre-Harappan period. Indeed, the more commonly used word for the plough in Vedic literature is of non-Aryan etymology.

Aryan Conquest

Kosambi did not subscribe to the theory of an Aryan race,[10] but he did support the idea of an Aryan-speaking peoples settling in northwestern India and spreading gradually into the Ganga Valley, in both cases initially as conquerors. Superior technology in the form of iron tools and the horse seem to be responsible for the dominance of the Aryan speakers. The evidence of bilingualism suggests a long period of coexistence between the Aryans and the indigenous peoples. Kosambi makes an important point when he says that much of the Indian tradition from the earliest Vedic text is already an amalgam of Aryan and non-Aryan, even those of the highest caste. Plough agriculture and iron technology when introduced into the Ganga Valley led ultimately to the growth of urban centers as well as the recognizable forms of caste.

Rise of Jainism and Buddhism

The simultaneous rise of many religious sects in the Ganga Valley implied, for Kosambi, some social need that older doctrines could not satisfy.[11] He analyzes this need by looking for the factors common to all the new religions. Factors such as technological changes, detribalization and urbanism constitute an economic interpretation of the rise of Buddhism and Jainism. The economic changes led to the rise of two classes in the Ganga Valley. The first was a class of land-owning peasants called *grihapatis* or heads of large patriarchal households; and the second was a class of wealthy traders called *shreshtis* meaning the most important persons in a guild or town. The rise of these propertied classes signified the institution of private property. The wealthy peasant and the wealthy trader desired peace above all. Peace could be established only by a universal monarchy seconded by a universal religion. Both Jainism and Buddhism tried to reach out to a wider social range and universal ethic. Since large numbers of cattle were required for sacrifices without payment, the strain upon regular agriculture was intolerable. The sixth century religious reform drove sacrifice of cattle out of fashion and laid a taboo on cattle-killing and beef-eating. That was the economic basis of *ahimsa*. Kosambi argues forcefully that the patronage which the propertied class extended to Buddhism and Jainism rooted the new cults more deeply in society than did the help they received from royal patronage.

Assessment

In an assessment, Romila Thapar writes that the limitations of Kosambi's thought and analysis are marginal to the serious quality of his work. Kosambi presented a view of ancient Indian history which sought answers to the fundamental questions of how and why Indian society is what it is today. In attempting to provide answers to such questions he provided a theoretical framework which was not a mechanical application of Marxism. For example, he did not accept *in toto* the Marxian notion of the Asiatic Mode of Production in relation to the Indian past, and as for the feudal mode of production, he made his own qualifications so far as Indian history was concerned. Based as it was on dialectical materialsm, Kosambi's frame was hammered out of his proficiency in handling a variety of sources, and originality of thought. Fresh evidence may well lead to a reconsideration of his conclusions but his influence is bound to persist much longer.

2. R.S. Sharma (b. 1920)

A front-rank historian of post-independence India, Ram Sharan Sharma is a great scholar who effectively applied the Marxist method of analysis to historical research.

Sudras in Ancient India

Pivotal to any understanding of the nature of social relationships in India throughout its history is the inquiry into the caste—the *varna* system. Sharma's *Sudras in Ancient India* (1958) is a work in which his sympathy for the lower orders of society found early expression. Depending mainly on literary sources, it is a thoroughly scholarly work which examines the relationship of the lower social orders with the means of production and with higher orders from the

Vedic age to the end of the Gupta period. The use of iron for large-scale field cultivation had, by the sixth century BC, transformed the tribal, pastoral and egalitarian pre-class Vedic society into a full-fledged class-divided social order. The new order required large labor power which was procured by force of arms and perpetuated by law and custom, religion and ideology—all interwoven into a social structure called the *varna* system.[12] The Sudra, as the *dharmasastras* were to ordain, was to serve the three higher *varnas*, while Manu would reduce him to slavery. The Indian helot was saddled with all kinds of disabilities – economic, politico-legal, social and religious – and was subjected to a kind of generalized slavery. Sharma writes that "...the *Sudra* skill, together with the agricultural surplus produced by the *Vaisya* peasants, provided the material basis for the development of ancient Indian society, which in this sense was a vaisya-sudra formation."[13] In the Gupta period (c. AD 300–600), the Sudras gained some religious and civic rights and in many respects were placed on a par with the Vaisyas. Many of the Sudras were now peasants with enlarged social and religious rights. Al-Biruni in the eleventh century found it difficult to distinguish the Vaisyas and Sudras. At the same time many Sudra artisans and tribals at lower stages of culture were made untouchables.

Indian Feudalism

Indian Feudalism (1966), was one of R.S. Sharma's books which immediately caught the attention of the academic world and generated debate. For Sharma the political essence of feudalism lay in the organization of the whole administrative structure on the basis of land tenure, and its economic content in the institution of serfdom in which peasants are attached to the soil held by landed intermediaries placed between the king and the actual tillers. Sharma discerns such a development in India in the land grants made to temples, Brahmanas and officials, and links it with the decay of towns, of trade and commerce and the reduced use of money. The process developed unevenly over the country from the Gupta times till about the twelfth century. There were several modes of extracting surplus—taxation, forced labor, the right of sub-in-feudation, and so on. Sharma's sources are the epigraphs of north India which refer to feudal vassals of various ranks.

Urban Decay in India

R.S. Sharma's *Urban Decay in India* (1987) reinforces his arguments regarding the origin and growth of feudalism in India. He furnishes an impressive array of archeological evidence to demonstrate the decline of urban centers in early medieval India. The post-Mauryan period was remarkable for the growth of towns, handicrafts and trade. The towns reached the peak of prosperity during the period from c. 200 BC to AD 300. But after the third century AD urban centers began to decline, a process which continued throughout the Gupta period. An important cause of urban decay was the decline in long-distance trade, which in its turn is to be attributed to the end of the Han (China), Kushana, Parthian and the Satavahana empires, and to the internal dissensions in the Roman empire. A second phase of urban decay, though not as widespread as the first, appeared after the sixth century AD. It covered several important towns in the middle Gangetic plain. This second phase of decay is linked with the decline in the flourishing trade with Byzantium in spices and silk. Throughout the period of the urban decline a process of feudalization marked by large land grants was proceeding apace.

Material Culture and Social Formation in Ancient India

Sharma's *Material Culture and Social Formations in Ancient India* (1983) runs strictly along Marxist lines of historical analysis and interpretation. The book tells us of the transition of the pastoral economy of the Rig Vedic times into the far more developed economy of the later Vedic times (1000 BC to 500 BC) marked by large-scale agriculture, and the use of iron and painted grey ware (PGW). The process had so developed in the Ganga plain that as we come to the age of the Buddha we witness the use of northern black polished ware (NBP), the manufacture of wrought iron, the minting of coins, and wet paddy cultivation with the iron plough-share which doubled production. Change in material production brought with it political and social changes. The large surplus in agricultural production created conditions for the establishment of large rural settlements, growth of trade, use of metallic money, rise of towns, and emergence of large territorial states with a regular system of taxation, well-ordered administrative machinery, and a standing army. Large estates needed large number of dependent laborers as wage earners, for which the *varna* system was created. Tribal society gradually disintegrated into class and occupational groupings. The progress of iron-plough agriculture depended on the augmentation of cattle wealth and hence the Buddhist stress on non-injury to animals. Again, Buddhist teachings recognized the reality of the new social order by favoring money-lending to facilitate trade and slave-keeping to augment agriculture.

Light on Early Indian Society and Economy

In *Light on Early Indian Society and Economy* (1966), Sharma writes on an assortment of subjects pertaining to the social and economic history of ancient India such as traces of promiscuity in ancient Indian society, joint notices of woman and property in the epics and *puranas*, slavery, caste, marriage, land grants, and usury.

R.S. Sharma's works, taken together, have outlined the social and economic history of ancient India.

3. Romila Thapar (b. 1930)

Romila Thapar's life is wholly devoted to creative research on early India in the reconstruction of whose history her contributions are certain to take a crucial place. She was Professor of Ancient Indian History at the Jawaharlal Nehru University where she had a decisive role in building the Centre for Historical Studies.

Asoka and the Decline of the Mauryas

Romila Thapar's brilliant scholarly career began with the publication of *Asoka and the Decline of the Mauryas* (1963). Reprinted several times, this work is in its essentials an original reinterpretation of the history of Asoka Maurya in which his policy of *Dhamma* is seen not as the moral effulgence of an idealistic monarch but as a political and social necessity. Asoka was confronted with a problem which only a statesman could solve. The conquest of Kalinga, induced by strategic and economic reasons, had taken the Mauryan empire to its subcontinental limits leaving only the southern Tamil tip which was only too submissive and friendly to invite imperial attention. The imposition of imperial control over the diverse ethnic and cultural elements of the empire and keeping it intact called for some binding factor. The policy of

Dhamma with its emphasis on social responsibility was intended to provide this factor. It was Asoka's own invention. It was a way of life based on a high degree of social ethics and civic responsibility, a code of social behavior, least sectarian and highly moral.

As to the causes of the break up of the Mauryan empire, Thapar writes that the extremely centralized Mauryan administrative system depended for its proper functioning very much on the personal ability of the ruler. Asoka's death was the signal for the breakdown of the administration and the breaking away of the provinces. The breakdown could have been prevented even in the absence of rulers of exceptional ability by some kind of national consciousness, i.e. the conception of the state as an idea above the king, the government and the social order, and as an entity demanding the loyalty of every citizen. This was simply not existent in Mauryan India.

History of India

Romila Thapar's *History of India*, Volume 1 (1966), is a work intended to reach out to a much wider audience at the popular level of historical understanding. Yet the book presents a view of history marking a departure from earlier works in aim and treatment. The new emphases are clear:

> Political histories and dynastic studies remain an important aspect of historical interpretation but these are viewed in the light of other features which go into the making of a people and a culture. Changes in the political pattern are inextricably entwined in changes in the economic structure and these in turn have a bearing on the social relationships...[14]

and, as it is to be understood, the emergent culture. Beginning with the culture of the Indo-Aryans one thousand five hundred years before Christ, the book takes the reader through three thousand years of the history of the subcontinent to the arrival of the Europeans in the sixteenth century. The aspects of Indian life it touches in a suggestive outline is comparable to the length of time it encompasses. Culture is viewed as rooted in and flowering from the material life of the people. The economic, religious, artistic and literary aspects are portrayed in their interrelation to each other within a framework of political history. Agriculture and industry, rural and urban life, and trade and maritime activity are given especial attention. A systematic study of Indian society through time, the book is a marvel of compression and yet thoroughly scholarly.

Ancient Indian Social History

Romila Thapar's *Ancient Indian Social History* (1978) treats of themes that relate to the study of ancient Indian social life from early times to the end of the first millennium AD. The first of the thirteen essays included in the work, 'Society and Law in the Hindu and Buddhist Traditions', is a kind of parallel, comparative study of Hindu and Buddhist socio-religious systems. The Hindu tradition was generally monarchical and authoritarian in politics and government, discriminatory in law, caste-ridden and inegalitarian in social relations, and inimical to human freedom and individual liberty. In comparison,

> The heterodox (Buddhist and Jain) tradition emphasized the equality of human beings, the equality of all before the law, disapproved of slavery, encouraged the acceptance of a higher status for women, and placed greater value on empirical thinking and education than on the formalism of the brahmanical system.[15]

The essay, 'Ethics, Religion and Social Protest in the First Millennium B.C. in Northern India', looks upon the ethics and religion of Buddhism as means of social protest also. Stress on non-violence, recruitment to the *sangha* from all groups including women, equality of status and compulsory community-living for the monks, and promotion of learning were challenges to the caste segregation, food taboos and educational monopoly of the Brahmanical order. 'Social Mobility in Ancient India with special Reference to Elite Groups', questions the assumption that society in India remained in a more or less frozen condition throughout the period from c. 1000 BC to c. AD 1000. The *varna* concept which was responsible for the assumption was largely a theoretical model and Thapar suggests that in terms of actual, if not in ritual, status there was mobility.

In her Presidential Address to the Ancient History Section of the Indian History Congress (Varanasi, 1969) she called for a reorientation of perspectives in the study of the social history of ancient India and made the following points: First, that archeological evidence does not suggest a massive Aryan invasion or migration; there was only a diffusion of the Indo-Aryan language by small groups of new comers who used iron and the horse.[16] Second, that the origin of caste is not to be seen as a result of the subjugation of the dark-skinned non-Aryans by the light-skinned Aryans, that the essential of caste society could have been present in the Harappan culture, and that on this question the historian must of necessity take the help of social anthropology.[17] And, third, the inclusion of a large amount of non-Aryan practice and belief in the religious aspects of later Vedic literature makes it unlikely that this literature was of purely Aryan composition.[18]

From Lineage to State

Thapar's *From Lineage to State* (1984) is a perceptive analysis of the process of state formation in the middle Ganga Valley in the first millennium BC. Earlier historians had taken the existence of the state for granted without troubling themselves to answer the fundamental question of how it came into existence. Thapar traces the origin of the state system in the Ganga Valley to the transition from a lineage mode of agrarian production to a peasant economy of private holdings and increasing urbanization. She treats Rig Vedic or pre-state society as 'lineage' and not 'tribal' since common ancestry was its binding factor. A lineage society would be mainly pastoral and mobile. A state, in contrast, is neither migratory nor based on lineage descent. It is impersonal. The prime factors towards such a move of state formation were the use of iron, the advance of plough agriculture, the rise of a class of *grihapatis* or peasant proprietors, some of whom were so affluent as to turn over part of the agricultural surplus into trade and commerce and become *shreshtis* or rich merchants. The process led to the establishment of market towns, urbanization, use of coined money, banking and trade. This new society, as it were, called for a new organization to protect and promote its interests, one which the new agricultural and commercial surplus could sustain as taxes. Thus emerged states like Kosala and Magadha which were a far cry from the Kurus and Panchalas of the old lineage system. Among the requisites of the new state system was a treasury built on regular tax collection able to pay its officials and finance a professional standing army. Kinship slowly eroded giving way to impersonal and more formal political ties.

Interpreting Early India

In 'Ideology and the Interpretation of Early Indian History' (the first essay in *Interpreting Early India,* 1992), Romila Thapar challenged two main ideological trends in modern interpretations of early Indian history—the theory of the Aryan race and the notion of Oriental Despotism. Romila questioned the Aryan theory in the light of the evidence supplied by archeology, linguistics and social anthropology. In the same essay she questioned the notion of 'Oriental Despotism' which Western writers had treated as axiomatic in their understanding of India's past. Central to this notion was the unchanging nature of that past. With its emphasis on a static society and absence of change, Karl Marx "worked the theory into his model for Asian Society—that of the Asiatic Mode of Production."[19] The theory had as its main planks absence of private property in land, state monopoly of the irrigation system, absence of urban centers and an effective network of trade, self-sufficient villages at the base, and a despotic king at the apex. Against this Thapar points out that the *Dhamasastras* and the *Arthasastra* list and discuss the laws and regulations for the sale, bequest and inheritance of land and other forms of private property, and the many inscriptions after AD 500 give more precise information relating to private property in land. Archeology has thrown up evidence of the existence of urban centers from the Harappan period onwards, and the details of urban society occurring in the early Pali Buddhist texts and in works like the *Kamasutra* are other striking refutations of the notion of Oriental Despotism. Cities and urban life had as their economic base trade and commerce marked by an extensive use of coins, letters of credit and promissory notes which incidentally testify to a measure of literacy.

Romila Thapar's work in the field of ancient Indian history has immensely widened the historical horizon.

4. Bipan Chandra

Bipan Chandra is another prominent member of the Marxist school of Indian historians.

The Rise and Growth of Economic Nationalism

Chandra's *The Rise and Growth of Economic Nationalism* examines the economic policies of the Indian National Movement before the *swadeshi* agitation carried it to a higher and different plane. Perhaps slightly deviating from the Marxist line of approach and subscribing to what may be called a realist conception of history, Bipan Chandra treats ideas, though secondary to economic forces, as the direct agents of historical evolution.[20] Subscribing to the Marxist position that social relations exist independently of the ideas men form of them, Chandra however holds that "men's understanding of these relations is crucial to their social and political action."[21] This emphasis on ideas leads him to include a wide range of fora – the National Congress, the legislative bodies, the speeches and writings of nationalist leaders, newspapers and journals – as voicing nationalist opposition to British economic imperialism. But he is, however, clear as to the basic capitalist outlook of the Indian national leaders. He writes that "In nearly every aspect of economic life they championed capitalist growth in general and the interests of the industrial capitalists in particular."[22]

Nationalism and Colonialism in India

In his later work, *Nationalism and Colonialism in India*, Bipan says that the independent capitalist class that developed in India after 1857, particularly after 1914, did not develop an organic link with British or other foreign capitalism and it did not become an ally of British rule in India. Indian capitalism was that of a colony with a colonially subordinated and structured economy.

India's Struggle for Independence 1857–1947

In *India's Struggle for Independence 1857–1947* which Bipan Chanda edited and to which he contributed, the authors differed widely from both the imperialist approach of the Cambridge school and that of the Indian nationalist school to the nature of the Indian national struggle. Bipan Chandra assails the Cambridge school's argument that the Indian national movement was not a people's movement but a product of the needs and interests of the elite groups. The nationalist school of historians, though showing awareness of the exploitative nature of colonialism, however ascribe the nationalist movement itself to the spread of the ideas of nationalism and liberty. Bipan Chandra writes that

> unlike the Imperialist School, the Marxist historians clearly see the primary contradictions, as well as the process of the nation-in-the making, and unlike the nationalists, they also take a full note of the inner contradictions of Indian society.[23]

Yet, he adds that the Marxist writers, and Palme Dutt in particular, "tend to see the (national) movement as a structured bourgeois movement...and miss its open-ended and all class character."[24]

Communalism in Modern India

In *Communalism in Modern India* Bipan Chandra denies that the phenomenon of communalism was a mere historical accident or product of dialectical conspiracy.[25] The growth of communalism owed to a multiplicity of forces or causes. He accepts the Marxist thesis that communalism was one of the by-products of colonialism. He writes of "the middle-class or petty bourgeois base of communalism under conditions of relative economic stagnation."[26] Communal politics, he says, is marked by the struggle for individual positions and posts. Communalism often distorted or misrepresented social tension and class conflict into communal conflict. Communalism, he concludes, is an extreme form of reaction to be fought on all fronts and given no quarter. The analysis of communalism in *India's Struggle for Independence: 1857–1947* is more scientific.[27] Communalism, according to Bipan Chandra, remained liberal from 1857 to 1937. But from 1937 it assumed a virulent, extremist or fascist form, based on the politics of hatred, fear psychosis and irrationality. During 1937–47, with the youth and the peasants turning Left, the national movement was radicalized. When the Second World War broke out and the Congress demanded an assurance of complete independence after the war, the British relied entirely on the communal card and recognized the Muslim League as the sole advocate of the Muslims.

5. Irfan Habib (b. 1931)

One of the distinguished historians of the post-independence era, Irfan Muhammad Habib had his initial academic training under the fostering care of his historian father, Muhammad Habib. Habib's contribution to Indian historiography is remarkable in its variety and range.

Interpreting Indian History

Habib's *Interpreting Indian History* underlines the need for explanation and interpretation in historical reconstruction. He thinks that it is interpretation rather than narration that goes to make a historian. To comprehend questions of how and why, one should interpret history. The need for interpretation arises from the fact that the historian in treating events of the past cannot recreate and verify those events. Particularly, the evidence for earlier times is so little as to leave wide blanks. Such blanks could be filled up only by an understanding of how societies operate and what people are motivated by and capable of doing in various situations. Here the historian's personal judgement counts as much as his erudition.

In the same work, Habib examines the kind of 'social formation' established after the Ghorian-Turkish conquest of northern India (1192–1206) on the basis of (a) the form of labor process, i.e., whether slavery, serfdom or wage labor; (b) the extraction of surplus value, i.e., rent, profit; and (c) the system of the distribution of surplus. Based on these categories he finds that in medieval India the labor process was that of petty producer laboring under various constraints; the surplus was extracted by tax which was identical with rent, and that it called for a centralized despotic state sustaining a vast parasitical urban economy. Our historian concludes that medieval Indian economy was a separate social formation different from the feudal economy.[28]

Caste and Money in Indian History

In another work, *Caste and Money in Indian History*, Irfan Habib tries to interpret Indian history in the light of the phenomenon of caste which, he writes, "still remains perhaps the one single most important divisive factor in our country."[29] A rigid form of division of labor, caste formed part of the relations of production. Habib thinks that the chief beneficiaries of this rigorous form of class exploitation were the ruling classes which in the medieval Indian context were the nobility and the *zamindars*.[30]

Problems of Marxist Historiography

In his *Problems of Marxist Historiography*, Irfan Habib observes that Marx has been ill served by some of his followers by their insistance on a rigid universal periodization into Primitive Communism, Slavery and Feudalism, and on a classification of all societies according to that pattern. Nor is it true that Marx held all thought to be just a reflex of the material world.

The Agrarian System of Mughal India

Irfan Habib's greatest work is the *Agrarian System of Mughal India.* The pivot of his thesis is that the principal contradiction in the medieval Indian social formation lay between the centralized ruling class (the state) and the peasantry. This contradiction extended to the relations between the state and the *zamindars* also. This was because the basic motive force, so far as the state was concerned, was the drive for higher tax revenue. The pressure for higher collection of land revenue "devastated the country, antagonized *zamindars* whose own share of the surplus was thereby affected, and drove the peasants to rebellion."[31] Thus we come across in Mughal India the most widespread conflicts between the peasants and the revenue appropriating ruling class.[32] The Mughal state failed to provide any relief to the cultivating peasantry. There followed rapine, anarchy and foreign conquests to which the empire succumbed. The Mughal empire was "its own grave-digger".[33] In the *Agrarian System* Habib postulates the view that economic tyranny rather than religious reaction was the major cause of opposition to Aurangazeb. The *Agrarian System of Mughal India* clearly shows that the historian was disposed to view medieval north Indian society from the standpoint of the peasants rather than that of the government and the *zamindars*.

An Atlas of the Mughal Empire

Irfan Habib made distinctive contributions in a field which Indian historians had consistently neglected—historical cartography. His

An Atlas of the Mughal Empire contains thirty-two pages of maps in addition to three maps in the introductory chapter and sixty-six pages of detailed notes. He has to his credit 'The Economic Map of India, AD 1–300', and has also made cartographic depictions of such themes as 'The Geography and Economy of the Indus Civilization' and 'The Mauryan Empire'.

The Cambridge Economic History of India

Habib's chosen field of inquiry is economic history. In *The Cambridge Economic History of India,* (Volume 1, 1200–1750) which he co-edited with Tapan Chaudhuri and to which he contributed, he discusses the agrarian economy in terms of agrarian production, rural classes, agrarian taxation, and the *iqta* system (forerunner of the *jagirdari).* He estimates the population of the Mughal empire in 1600 between 140 and 150 million, of which 85 per cent were rural and the rest urban.

What we see in Irfan Habib's writing is an urge to understand the common man, especially the peasant and his village in their political, social, economic and cultural settings. Of these the economic setting is central to his analysis.

6. The Marxist Phase of Indian Historiography: An Assessment

Kosambi worked out the general theory of historical development propounded by Marx and Engels into a method, and employed it creatively in the reconstruction of early Indian history. The increasing adoption of this method has wrought a change in Indian historiography that has assumed the proportions of a revolution. Analysis and explanation in terms of economic production and social classes have become basic tenets in historical reconstruction in India.

Broadening of the Scope of History

The Marxist trend has resulted in a major shift of emphasis and has broadened the scope of history from the state to society, from soldiers and statesmen to the people, that is to say, from the political to the economic and social aspects of human life. Large sections of people, hitherto unnoticed, have become legitimate objects of historical inquiry. Works like R.S. Sharma's *Sudras in Ancient India* and Irfan Habib's *The Agarian System of Mughal India* are instances in point. The new paradigm has thrown dynastic history out of fashion and reduced political history itself to the level of a framework, a backdrop, for economic and social history. Idealist and romantic treatment of the past has given way to a search for the economic and social factors of human life—the objective forces of material production and the resultant social relations. The concern with individual roles or with individual achievements or failures is disappearing from history, and with it, much of value judgements, too.

Interdisciplinary Methods

The materialist orientation of history has resulted in the use mostly of primary sources. To study such sources historians try to call to their aid such skills as those of the linguist, sociologist, anthropologist and the statistician. Though the interdisciplinary method has not been attempted in any big way, the data supplied by specialists in the various disciplines have been used extensively in historical reconstruction. Historians now try to integrate literary and archeological evidence wherever possible. The search for material forces of production – pivotal to Marxist historical methodology – has increasingly turned their attention in the direction of archeological evidence, particularly in the study of ancient Indian history. Unlike literary sources, the physical remains of the past are completely free from bias and constitute direct, immediate and tangible evidence allowing a more accurate reconstruction of the past. In the reconstruction of the history of the later Vedic age, the Marxist historians have liberally used archeological evidence (PGW, NBP, etc) along with their reading of the later Vedic texts. A concern with urbanization as centers of production and circulation of wealth is common to Kosambi, Sharma and Thapar who have labored to reconstruct the early history of India. Sharma's *Urban Decay in India* is a work almost entirely based on archeological evidence.

Accounts of Origin

Marxist historiography has been particularly strong in explaining the origins of human institutions. Accounts of state formation in the Ganga Valley by Kosambi, Sharma and Thapar mark a radical advance in historical understanding and should be reckoned a triumph of materialist historiography. The origin and development of caste, that most characteristic institution of the Hindu social order, still awaits a more satisfactory explanation. Oversimplified and readymade explanations will not do. Indeed, Romila Thapar exhorted historians at the Indian History Congress at Varanasi (1969) not to see that complex institution of caste simply as a distinction between light-skinned Aryans and dark non-Aryans but to take the help of social anthropology in the study of its origin and development. No human institution miraculously leaps into existence, and in history there cannot be any other activity and institution than what is human.

Defence of Explanation and Interpretation

The Marxist model has made history writing in India far less narrative and descriptive and more explanatory and interpretative. The change from one to the other has been a conscious exercise in which processes and large movements, not events (as they are understood), assume importance. Some have held that it is interpretation that makes the historian. Irfan Habib's *Interpreting Indian History* contains a theoretical defence of the historian's freedom of interpretaiton.[34] In all interpretation, ideology of some kind plays the leading role. It is through an emphasis on the interpretative aspect of history that the Marxist view has had its impact on Indian historiography.

Critique of Western Understanding

The nationalist historians had questioned some of the oft-quoted cliches current in British imperialist and European writing on Indian history. Continuing that tradition, as it were, the Marxist historians have challenged certain concepts which were axiomatic in the foreigner's understanding of India's past. D.D. Kosambi refused to accept *in toto* the concept of the Asiatic Mode of Production as applicable to Indian history. Marxist historians have in general taken pains to show the existence from the sixth century BC of extensive urban centers and brisk commercial activity down to the Gupta times. R.S. Sharma and Romila Thapar have drawn attention to the prevalence of comparative social mobility, both occupational and territorial, in ancient India. The theory of the Aryan race and the concept of Oriental Despotism have been criticized by Romila Thapar. She has shown the pervasive influence of such misconceptions, as well as of others like 'the unchanging character of Indian society' and 'an arrested state of development' even in the works of leading European sociologists like Durkheim and Weber.

Differences in Conclusions

Historical explanation based on the mode of production and changes therein need not always lead to identical results. Perhaps, unavoidably, some conclusions could only be distant approximations or even pure guesses. Kosambi assumed that the Harappans did not know the plough and that the banks of the Indus were cultivated with the harrow. We may protest that raising dykes and embankments to collect the flood-waters of a great river and producing agricultural surpluses sufficient to feed an entire urban population are operations that argue for explanations based on more developed tools than the surface-scratching harrow. Or, grain must have been imported. Romila Thapar has in fact argued that recent evidence makes it clear that plough agriculture was known to the pre-Aryans and was practised even in the pre-Harappan period since the more commonly used word for the plough in Vedic literature is of non-Aryan etymology.[35] Sharma and Thapar seem to differ to the extent of contradicting each other as regards the attitude of Buddhism to slavery. The former avers that the new religion recognized the reality of the new social order of the sixth century BC by favoring money-lending to facilitate trade and slave-keeping to augment agriculture,[36] but the latter asserts that Buddhism disapproved of slavery.[37]

Economics of Ashimsa

Kosambi and, following him Sharma and others, offer an economic interpretation of the principle of *ahimsa* enjoined by Buddhism and Jainism. The large-scale slaughter of cattle prescribed by the Vedic rituals was an intolerable strain on the new iron-plough agriculture in the Ganga basin which depended on the preservation and augmentation of cattle wealth. Kosambi writes that "Cattle and other animals were requisitioned in increasing number for the *yajna* without payment. This is shown by Pali stories of royal fire sacrifices. The strain upon regular agriculture was intolerable."[38] Buddhist and Jain reform in the sixth century BC completely drove this Brahmanical practice out of fashion by laying a taboo on cattle-killing and beef-eating.

It is difficult to believe, unless supported by quantitative evidence, that cattle were slaughtered at royal sacrifices on such a scale as to decimate the bovine population and to endanger the new iron-plough agriculture. Were the royal sacrificers and those about them so thoughtless and shortsighted as to kill productive animals? The "slaughter of more and more animals at a growing number of sacrifices"[39] would have added up, from time to time, to forbidding quantities of sacrificed meat (the gods to do not eat!), the difficulty of preserving which would have required countless mouths to consume such enormities of beef before it rotted. A more precise citation of the Pali stories instead of an easy saunter around them would have clarified the point. Such evidence should indicate, in the interests of quantitative objectivity, the incidence of royal sacrifices during a given period, say a year, in a given area and the probable (if not precise) number of cattle killed at each such sacrifice. A mathematician like Kosambi should not have neglected the importance of quantities in historical analysis. It is equally unbelievable that the sixth-century reform could have so easily stopped the ritual cattle-killing of the Brahmanists whose hostility to the reformers is only too well known. "The main Vedic sacrifice," writes Kosambi, "was of cattle, natural in a predominantly pastoral society. How completely the sixth-century reform drove this, too, out of fashion is seen by the absolute Hindu tabu upon cattle killing and beef-eating which is still in force...."[40]

A passage in the *Suttanipata* ascribed to the Buddha and quoted by Kosambi reads: "Cattle are our friends, just like parents and other relatives, for cultivation depends upon them. They give food, strength, freshness of complexion and happiness. *Knowing this brahmins of old did not kill cattle.*"[41] (Emphasis added.)

If Brahmans of old did not kill cattle, where, then, was the need for a Jain and Buddhist taboo on cattle-killing? At any rate the Brahmanists could scarcely be believed to have respected a Jain or Buddhist prohibition.

Freedom of Interpretation

Historians of a Marxist persuasion generally concentrate more on the interpretation of events than on their narration. In his *Interpreting Indian History*, Irfan Habib stresses its need and importance. None acquainted with the nature of history will ever doubt the need for interpretation and the historian's freedom thereof. That this freedom should not get beyond the factual basis of history needs to be stressed. The historian should interpret and amplify the facts for the benefit of the reader and not confuse him with a parade of abstruse terms and jargons. The latter course is a temptation which comes when the historian looks for the vanguardism of theory and its vocabulary. Romila Thapar is admirably free from such temptation. But the same cannot be said of some others. Thus Bipan Chandra:

> However, many of them—and Palme Dutt in particular—are not able to fully integrate their treatment of the primary anti-imperialist contradiction and the secondary inner contradictions, and tend to counterpose the anti-imperialist struggle to the class struggle or social struggle. They also tend to see the movement as a structured bourgeois movement, if not the bourgeoisie's movement, and miss its open-ended and all class character.[42]

And Irfan Habib:

> The principal contradictions lay between the centralised ruling class (state) and the peasantry; but there were contradictions too between the state and the *zamindars* which often induced the *zamindars* to use peasants as allies or as canon-fodder in their conflict with state. There were potential contradictions between the menial proletariat and the rest of society, and on the fringes there was a visible conflict between the tribes and advancing caste peasantry. Still more secondary were the contradictions between artisans and town-labour, on the one hand, and the state, on the other.[43]

Perhaps the writers could have better served the interests of the readers than by such exercises in obscurity. Defending the Communist stand on the 'Quit India' movement of 1942, Habib asks: "If Fascist Germany had triumphed, where would the world-working class movement have been today"?[44] Such expressions can hardly serve as explanations.

II. SUBALTERN STUDIES

A Historiography of Protest

A series titled *Subaltern Studies*, appearing in the last two decades of the twentieth century, has introduced an almost new genre of history writing on modern India. Editing the first of the series Ranajit Guha protests that the historiography of Indian nationalism is beset with a prejudiced elitism of two kinds, both sharing the view that the development of the national consciousness and the making of the Indian nation were elite achievements. The first of these – colonial or British imperialist historiography – based on a narrow behavioristic approach, looks upon Indian nationalism as the response of the Indian bourgeois elite to the stimulus provided by British ideas, institutions, opportunities and resources. The second kind – Indian nationalist historiography – on the other hand, pictures Indian nationalism as primarily an idealist venture in which the indigenous elite led the people from subjection to freedom. Neither of these two views can explain Indian nationalism because neither acknowledges the contribution made by the people *on their own*, that is, *independently of the elite*, to the making and development of that nationalism. For this reason, according to Guha, elitist historiography cannot explain such instances of popular initiative asserting itself as the anti-Rowlatt upsurge of 1919 or the 'Quit India' movement of 1942.[45] Guha asserts that parallel to elite politics, there was a domain of people's politics in which the principal actors were the subaltern classes and groups constituting the mass of the population. He feels that elitist historiography which does not recognize this fact should be resolutely fought by developing an alternative discourse based on the recognition of the subaltern domains of politics. That is the *raison d' etre* of subaltern historiography.

Nature of Subaltern Historiography

The *Subaltern Studies* are collections of monographs on diverse, unconnected topics. Their one theme is the insurgency of the lower classes. Subaltern, a term taken from Antonio Gramsci's manuscript writings, means 'of inferior rank' whether of class, caste, age, gender or office. *Subaltern Studies* bring to light the lower sections of the Indian people hitherto neglected by historiography. They are "addressed to a range of topics extending in time from the Mughal period to the nineteen seventies, in theme from communalism to industrial labour, and in manner from the descriptive to the conceptual."[46]

A distinctive feature of subaltern activity being its labor orientation, the *Subaltern Studies* are Marxian in tone, premise (categories) and analysis. The peasant, the factory worker and the tribal – their woes and accumulated grievances breaking out at times in rebellions against constituted authority – become objects of subaltern historiographical treatment. Revolt was the means, the method, by which the lower classes tried to improve their conditions and force themselves on the attention of the elite in colonial India. Guha affirms that the peasant never stumbled or drifted into rebellion. He rebelled consciously and only when he found that his pleadings of various kinds had failed. Insurgency, whether of the worker in the factory, villagers of the plains or of the *adivasis* of the uplands, was a deliberate, desperate way out of an intolerable condition of existence created by wicked landlords, extortionate usurers, dishonest traders, venal police, irresponsible officials and partisan processes of law. Hence revolts and their impact on Indian nationalism form staple theme for the historians of the subaltern genre. Moreover, subaltern consciousness together with the elements of that consciousness – religion, superstition, communalism, and the view that subject classes took of the elites – becomes an object of historical study.

Some Examples of Subaltern Historiography

Close to ten *Subaltern Studies* (SS) volumes have so far appeared. A perusal of the more important titles in the first four collections of the series will give an idea of the historiography that has appeared under that label.

David Arnold brings to light the story of a long series of disturbances and rebellions of hillmen in the Gudem and Rampa hill tracts of Andhra during 1839–1924 (SS 1). Studying the Madras famine of 1876–78 (SS 3), the same author writes of peasant consciousness and peasant action in such crises of subsistence and survival. Arnold complains that the voluminous literature on Indian famine does not treat that phenomenon in terms of human experience, and that peasant experience of dearth and famine has almost invariably been subordinated to the descriptions of state policy and relief administration.

Gyan Pandey gives an account of the peasant revolts of Awadh during 1919–22 and its impact on Indian nationalism (SS 1). Stephen Henningham shows how in Bihar and eastern Uttar Pradesh the 'Quit India' movement of 1942 was a dual revolt consisting of an elite nationalist uprising combined with a subaltern rebellion (SS 2). This combination called forth the enthusiasm and participation of a broad spectrum of society. If, in spite of its drama and intensity the 'Quit India' revolt has not received adequate scholarly treatment, Henningham's explanation is that, for historians operating within the confines of elite historiography "the substance of the 1942 revolt is difficult to swallow and impossible to digest."[47]

Aravind Das demonstrates how erroneous it is to attribute agrarian changes in Bihar during 1947–78 to elite-sponsored land reforms (SS 2). The two major attempts at 'agrarian changes from the above', that is, through *zamindari* abolition and the *bhoodan* movement, were not elite sponsored but responses to peasant discontent. The first followed after years of agitation by Swami Sahajananda Saraswati and the powerful Kisan Sabha, and the second came on the miliant Communist-led peasant upsurge in Telengana. Both were measures to preempt class war in the Bihar country side. Says the author: "Any interpretation of agrarian change primarily as an elite sponsored land reform, amounts therefore to chasing the shadow without trying to grasp the substance."[48]

In 'Agricultural Workers in Burdwan' (SS 2), N.K. Chandra reveals the appallingly poor conditions of the mass of the agricultural laborers and poor peasants in terms of wages and earnings, underemployment and poverty.

Dipesh Chakrabarty studies the condition of the Calcutta jute-mill workers between 1890 and 1940 (SS 2). In another essay on the jute-mill workers during 1920–50 (SS 3), Chakrabarty shows how the elitist attitude has crept into socialist and Communist ranks, leaders treating unions as their 'zamindari', their contact with the workers degenerating into the hierarchical terms of babu–coolie relationship.

Shahid Amin in his essay on Gandhi (SS 3) is concerned to know how the Mahatma's charisma got itself registered in peasant consciousness. He finds that an important element in that charisma was the peasant's belief in superstition and miracles. David Hardiman's essay on the Devi reformist movement among the tribals of south Gujarat (SS 3) affords insights into tribal consciousness and must arrest the attention of the sociologists.

The anti-Partition agitation (1905) did not arouse as much popular enthusiasm in Bengal as did the Non-Cooperation Khilafat movement of 1921–22. Sumit Sarkar informs us (SS 3) that the former did not go beyond the confines of Hindu upper class *bhadralok* groups whereas in the latter "popular initiative eventually alarmed the leaders into calling for a halt."[49]

Ramachandra Guha's essay, 'Forestry and Social Protest in British Kumaun, c. 1893–1921' (SS 4) shows that the Chipko Andolan Movement starting from 1973 in Kumaun against the commercial exploitation of forests has in fact a history beginning from the nineties of the nineteenth century and lasting into the twenties of the twentieth. The reservation of the Kumaun forests in 1911–17 met with violent and sustained opposition from the traditionally 'simple and law abiding hillmen' which culminated in the revolt of 1921 when within the space of a few months the whole administration was paralyzed, first by a strike against statutory labor and then through a systematic campaign in which the Himalayan pine forests were swept by incendiary fires almost from end to end.

Tribal protest as that of Jitu Santhal's movement in Malda, northwestern Bengal (1924–32), is a favourite theme for subaltern historiography (SS 4). In 1924, an anti-landlord tenant agitation developed in Malda under Jitu's leadership and continued till 1932 when the leader was shot. Even *bhadralok* opinion as expressed in the *Amrita Bazar Patrika* was sympathetic to Jitu's revolt but, as Tanika Sarkar shows, in true elitist fashion the responsibility for the revolt was taken away from the tribal leader by imputing it comfortably to the Swarajist agitator from outside.

Gautam Bhadra observes in his 'Four Rebels of 1857' (SS 4) that all the principal modes of historiography on the Great Revolt of 1857 whether 'nationalist' as exemplified by the writings of S.B. Chaudhari or 'radical communist' as represented by Promod

Sengupta and Datta have, with due elitist prejudice, portrayed the great event as an elitist venture. The ordinary rebel, his role and his perception of alien rule and the contemporary crisis—all these have been left out of the historical literature of the Great Revolt. Bhadra's essay rehabilitates four of such rebel characters of 1857: Shah Mal, Devi Singh, Gonoo and Maulvi Ahmadullah Shah. Their stories point to the existence in 1857 of what Gramsci calls 'multiple elements of conscious leadership'.

Assessment

Fine examples of radical scholarship, Marxist and subaltern historiography are bringing historical inquiry to the foundations of Indian society. In its anxiety to highlight the struggles of the workers, the peasants and the tribals, the latter has upset not only conventional historiography but even that of a Marxist perspective. Subaltern historiography essentially belongs to the category of sub-history or local narratives supplementing and enriching mainstream historical accounts and filling up the lacunae in them. Based on a loose, negative elite–subaltern dichotomy, it has no greater theme than popular militancy and consciousness. Its topics are grimly partitioned with no connection or sequence of any kind. A continuous and sustained narrative is outside its purview. Yet, its positive side should not be lost sight of—subaltern historiography is ferreting out innumerable records from their dusty shelves in dark and dingy rooms which stand witness to many a story of faith and struggle. It has reopened for historical examination questions long believed to have been settled. It has restored individual human beings and groups hitherto considered too low for elite historical treatment. These dissevered limbs of subaltern historiography – these sagas of struggle – could be brought together and in many cases woven into mainstream historiography and thereby enrich it.

References

CHAPTER 1

1. For details see Wallbank and Taylor, *Civilization Past and Present*, Vol. 1, 4–7.
2. Ibid., 7.
3. Marwick, *What History Is*, 14.
4. Butterfield, 'Historiography', in *Dictionary of History of Ideas*, Vol. 2, 464.
5. Marwick, *What History Is*, 23–24.

CHAPTER 2

1. Butterfield, 'Historiography', in *Dictionary of History of Ideas*, Vol. 2, 464–66.
2. See Collingwood, *Idea Of History*, 9–10.
3. Stern, *Varieties of History*, 144.
4. Collingwood, *Idea of History*, 12.
5. Butterfield, *Dictionary of the History of Ideas*, 466.
6. Collingwood, *Idea of History*, 20–21.
7. Durant, *Story of Civilization II: The Life of Greece*, 430.
8. *Ibid.*, 431.
9. *Ibid.*, 431–32.
10. *Ibid.*, 432.
11. Barnes, *History of Historical Writing*, 29.
12. Collingwood, *Idea of History*, 19.
13. Durant, *Life of Greece*, 434.
14. *Ibid.*
15. *Ibid.*
16. *Ibid.*, 435.

17. Collingwood, *Idea of History*, 29.
18. *Ibid.*, 29–30.
19. *Ibid.*, 30.
20. *Ibid.*, 25–28.
21. *Ibid.*, 27.
22. *Ibid.*
23. *Ibid.*
24. *Ibid.*, 21–25.
25. *Ibid.*, 22.
26. Butterfield, *Dictionary of the History of Ideas*, 467.
27. Collingwood, *Idea of History*, 23.
28. *Ibid.*, 24.
29. *Ibid.*, 31–33.
30. *Ibid.*, 33.
31. Durant, *Life of Greece*, 613.
32. Thompson and Holm, *History of Historical Writing*, 55.
33. Durant, *Life of Greece*, 615.
34. Thompson and Holm, *History of Historical Writing*, 57.
35. Butterfield, *Dictionary of the History of Idea*, 468
36. Durant, *Idea of Greece*, 615.
37. *Ibid.*, 614–15.
38. *Ibid.*, 615.
39. See Collingwood, *Idea of History*, 33–36.
40. See Thompson and Holm, *History of Historical Writing*, 63–65.
41. Durant, *Story of Civilization III: Caesar and Christ*, 250.
42. *Ibid.*, 251.
43. *Ibid.*
44. Thompson and Holm, *History of Historical Writing*, 76.
45. Durant, *Ceasar and Christ*, 252.
46. Thompson and Holm, *History of Historical Writing*, 80.
47. Durant, *Ceasar and Christ*, 434.
48. *Ibid.*, 434–35.
49. Butterfield, *Dictionary of the History of Ideas*, 470.
50. Thompson and Holm, *History of Historical Writing*, 88.
51. *Ibid.*, 87.
52. See Collingwood, *Idea of History*, 38–40.
53. *Ibid.*, 38.
54. *Ibid.*, 40.
55. Thompson and Holm, *History of Historical Writing*, 112.
56. See Collingwood, *Idea of History*, 40–45.

57. Quoted by Durant, *The Story of Civilization I: Our Oriental Heritage*, 642.
58. Butterfield, *Dictionary of the History of Ideas*, 479.
59. *Ibid.*, 479–80.
60. *Ibid.*, 480–81.
61. Durant, *Ceasar and Christ*, 665.
62. See Barrett, '*Chinese Historiography*', in John Cannon ed., *Blackwell Dictionary of Historians*, 76.
63. Hughes-Warrington, *Fifty Key Thinkers in History*, 293–295.
64. Butterfield, *Dictionary of the History of Ideas*, 480–81.
65. Hughes-Warrington, *Fifty Key Thinkers*, 292.
66. Quoted by Durant, *Our Oriental Heritage*, 719.
67. See Butterfield, *Dictionary of the History of Ideas*, 481.
68. See Barrett, *Blackwell Dictionary of Historians*, 77.
69. See Lach, 'China in Western Thought and Culture', in *Dictionary of the History of Ideas*, Vol. 1, 370–72.
70. Durant, *Our Oriental Heritage*, 718–19.
71. Butterfield, *Dictionary of the History of Ideas*, 480–81.
72. *Ibid.*, 481.
73. *Ibid.*, 481.

CHAPTER 3

1. Thompson and Holm, *History of Historical Writing*, 121.
2. *Ibid.*, 125.
3. *Ibid.*, 125–26.
4. *Ibid.*, 125.
5. *Ibid.*
6. *Ibid.*
7. *Ibid.*, 130.
8. *Ibid.*
9. Durant, *The Story of Civilization IV: The Age of Faith*, 72.
10. *Ibid.*, 73.
11. Butterfield, *Dictionary of the History of Ideas*, 472.
12. Thompson and Holm, *History of Historical Writing*, 150.
13. *Ibid.*, 157.
14. Durant, *Age of Faith*, 488.
15. *Ibid.*, 489.
16. For details see Van Loon, Introduction to *The Story of America*.

17. Thompson and Holm, *History of Historical Writing,* 159–60.
18. *Ibid.*, 168.
19. *Ibid.*
20. *Ibid.* 170.
21. *Ibid.*, 196.
22. Butterfield, *Dictionary of History of Ideas,* 474.
23. Thompson and Holm, *History of Historical Writing,* 198.
24. Butterfield, *Dictionary of the History of Ideas,* 474.
25. Thompson and Holm, *History of Historical Writing,* 250–51.
26. *Ibid.*, 254.
27. See Collingwood, *Idea of History,* 46–56.
28. *Ibid.*, 48.
29. *Ibid.*, 49.
30. *Ibid.*, 55.
31. *Ibid.*, 56.
32. *Ibid.*, 51.
33. Thompson and Holm, *History of Historical Writing,* 336.
34. *Ibid.*
35. *Encyclopaedia of Islam,* Vol. 4, 784.
36. Thompson and Holm, *History of Historical Writing,* 344.
37. Sachau, trans., *Alberuni's India,* 10–11.
38. Ibid., 250.
39. Sarkar, 'Personal History of Some Medieval Historians and their Writings', in Mohibbul Hasan, ed., *Historians of Medieval India,* 168.
40. Thompson and Holm, *History of Historical Writing,* 349–50.
41. Hussain, *Rihla of Ibn Batuta,* xviii–xix.
42. *Encyclopaedia of Islam,* Vol. 3, 829.
43. Rosenthal, trans., Introduction to *Muqaddima,* xxiii.
44. *Ibid.*, 16.
45. *Ibid.*
46. *Ibid.*, 71.
47. Butterfield, *Dictionary of the History of Ideas,* 479.
48. Rosenthal, *Dictionary of the History of Ideas,* 71.
49. Butterfield, *Dictionary of the History of Ideas,* 475.
50. Morgan, 'Ibn Khalduon,' in *Blackwell Dictionary of Historians,* 202; also see Irwin, 'Islamic Historiography,' in *Blackwell Dictionary of Historians,* 211–12
51. *Encyclopaedia of Islam,* Vol. 3, 830.
52. Rosenthal, *Dictionary of the History of Ideas,* 240.

53. *The Blackwell Dictionary of Historians*, 203.
54. *Encyclopaedia of Islam*, Vol. 3, 830.
55. *Ibid.*
56. Toynbee, *Study of History*, Vol. 3, 322.
57. *Blackwell Dictionary of Historians*, 202.
58. Rosenthal, *Dictionary of the History of Ideas*, lxxxvi–lxxxvii.
59. *Blackwell Dictionary of Historians*, 212.
60. Nizami, 'Barani,' in Mohibbul Hasan, ed., *Historians of Medieval India*, 41.

CHAPTER 4

1. Knapton, *Europe 1450–1815*, 75.
2. Butterfield, *Dictionary of the History of Ideas*, 482.
3. Thompson and Holm, *History of Historical Writing*, 481.
4. *Ibid.*, 492.
5. Collingwood, *Idea of History*, 57.
6. Butterfield, *Dictionary of the History of Ideas*, 485.
7. *Ibid.*
8. Collingwood, *Idea of History*, 57.
9. Butterfield, *Idea of History*, 485.
10. *Ibid.*
11. *Ibid.*, 482.
12. Thompson and Holm, *History of Historical Writing*, 491.
13. *Ibid.*, 492.
14. Durant, *The Story of Civilization V: The Renaissance*, 547.
15. *Ibid.*, 551.
16. *Ibid.*, 554.
17. *Ibid.*, 555.
18. *Ibid.*
19. *Ibid.*, 544.
20. Thompson and Holm, *History of Historical Writing*, 498.
21. *Ibid.*, 499.
22. Butterfield, *Dictionary of the History of Ideas*, 483.
23. Durant, *Renaissance*, 545.
24. Haddock, *Introduction to Historical Thought*, 4.
25. *Ibid.*, 5.
26. Knapton, *Europe 145–1815*, 472.
27. *Ibid.*, 465–66.

28. Durant and Durant, *The Story of Civilization VII: The Age of Reason Begins*, 175.
29. *Ibid.*, 182.
30. Russell, *History of Western Philosophy*, 587.
31. *Ibid.*, 588.
32. Butterfield, *Dictionary of the History of Ideas*, 486.
33. Durant and Durant, *The Age of Louis XIV*, 610.
34. *Ibid.*, 609.
35. Collingwood, *Idea of History*, 58–61.
36. *Ibid.*, 58.
37. *Ibid.*, 59.
38. The complete skepticism of Pyrrho of Elis of third century BC.
39. Collingwood, *Idea of History*, 62.
40. *Ibid.*
41. *Ibid.*
42. Butterfield, *Dictionary of the History of Ideas*, 487.
43. For details see 'Historiography' in *Chambers's Encyclopaedia*, Vol. 7, 130.
44. Collingwood, *Idea of History*, 64.
45. *Ibid.*
46. *Ibid.*, 64–65.
47. *Ibid.*, 65–66.
48. *Ibid.*, 66–71.

CHAPTER 5

1. Knapton, *Europe 1450–1815*, 465.
2. *Ibid.* 464–65.
3. *Ibid.* 465.
4. See Manuel, *The Enlightenment*, 1–16.
5. Knapton, *Europe 1450–1815*, 465.
6. Collingwood, *Idea of History*, 76–77.
7. See *Chambers's Encyclopaedia*, Vol. 7, 130–31; also *Encyclopaedia Britannica, Macro VIII*, 945.
8. *Encyclopaedia Britannica, Macro VIII*, 945.
9. Butterfield, *Dictionary of the History of Ideas*, 488.
10. *Ibid.*
11. *Ibid.*
12. Durant and Durant, *The Age of Voltaire*, 345.

13. *Ibid.*, 348.
14. Knapton, *Europe 1450–1815*, 493
15. Durant and Durant, *The Age of Voltaire*, 358.
16. Collingwood, *Idea of History*, 78–79.
17. Durant and Durant, *The Age of Voltaire*, 358.
18. *Ibid.*
19. *Ibid.*, 360.
20. Durant, *Story of Philosophy*, 201.
21. Durant and Durant, *The Age of Voltaire*, 362.
22. *Ibid.*, 464.
23. *Ibid.*, 483.
24. *Ibid.*, 484.
25. Stern, *Varieties of History*, 36.
26. Durant and Durant, *The Age of Voltaire*, 487.
27. *Ibid.*
28. *Ibid.*
29. *Ibid.*
30. *Ibid.*
31. See Collingwood, *Idea of History*, 71–76.
32. Marwick, *Nature of History*, 33.
33. Durant and Durant, *The Story of Civilization X: Rousseau and Revolution,* 807.
34. *Ibid.*, 802.
35. *Ibid.*
36. *Ibid.*, 804.
37. *Ibid.*
38. *Ibid.*, 806.
39. Gibbon, *Decline and Fall of the Roman Empire*, Vol. 6, 656.
40. Durant and Durant, *Rousseau and Revolution*, 807.
41. *Ibid.*, 807.
42. *Ibid.*
43. Gibbon, *Decline and Fall of the Roman Empire*, Vol. 6, 656.
44. Durant and Durant, *Rousseau and Revolution*, 807.
45. *Ibid.*, 808.
46. Marwick, *What History Is*, 35.
47. *Ibid.*
48. Collingwood, *Idea of History*, 77.
49. *Ibid.*, 79.
50. *Ibid.*, 80.
51. *Ibid.*, 80–81.

52. *Ibid.*, 81.

CHAPTER 6

1. Collingwood, *Idea of History*, 86.
2. Durant and Durant, *The Story of Civilization X: Rousseau and Revolution*, 887.
3. *Ibid.*, 29.
4. *Ibid.*, 889.
5. *Ibid.*, 890.
6. *Ibid.*, 889.
7. *Ibid.*, 578.
8. *Ibid.*
9. Collingwood, *Idea of History*, 90.
10. *Ibid.*, 89.
11. *Ibid.*, 90.
12. *Ibid.*
13. Palmer and Colton, *History of the Modern World*, 403.
14. Butterfield, *Dictionary of the History of Ideas*, 489.
15. Palmer and Colton, *History of the Modern World*, 432.
16. Collingwood, *Idea of History*, 91.
17. *Ibid.*, 91–92.
18. *Ibid.*, 92.
19. *Ibid.*
20. *Ibid.*, 86–87.
21. *Ibid.*, 87.
22. *Ibid.*, 87.
23. *Ibid.*, 87–88.
24. *Ibid.*, 88.
25. Marwick, *Nature of History*, 37.
26. *Ibid.*
27. Butterfield, *Dictionary of the History of Ideas*, 489.
28. Marwick, *Introduction to History*, 154.
29. *Blackwell Dictionary of Historians*, 323.
30. *Ibid.*
31. *Ibid.*
32. *Ibid.*, 324.
33. Durant and Durant, *The Story of Civilization XI: The Age of Napoleon*, 648.

34. Collingwood., *Idea of History*, 113–14.
35. *Ibid.*, 114.
36. *Ibid.*, 115.
37. Durant and Durant, *Age of Napolean*, 649.
38. *Ibid.*
39. *Ibid.*, 653.
40. Durant, *Pleasures of Philosophy*, 231.
41. *Blackwell Dictionary of Historians*, 182–83.
42. Durant and Durant, *Age of Napoleon*, 655–56.
43. *Ibid.*, 656.
44. *Ibid.*, 645.
45. Collingwood, *Idea of History*, 117–18.
46. *Ibid.*, 118–19.
47. *Ibid.*, 119–20.
48. *Ibid.*, 121–22.
49. *Ibid.*, 121.

CHAPTER 7

1. Appadorai, *Substance of Politics*, 15.
2. Gooch, *History and Historians of the Nineteenth Century*, 171.
3. *Ibid.*
4. Stern, ed., *Varieties of History*, 70.
5. Gooch, *History and Historians*, 172.
6. *Ibid.*
7. *Ibid.*, 176.
8. For details see, Stern, ed., *Varieties of History*, 109–119.
9. Gooch, *History and Historians*, 178.
10. *Ibid.*, 182.
11. *Ibid.*, 183.
12. *Ibid.*
13. *Ibid.*
14. *Ibid.*
15. *Ibid.*
16. See Stern, *Varieties of History*, 72–89.
17. Gooch, *History and Historians*, 297–98.
18. *Blackwell Dictionary of Historians*, 260.
19. Stern, *Varieties of History*, 71.
20. *Blackwell Dictionary of Historians*, 260.

21. Gooch, *History and Historians*, 302.
22. *Blackwell Dictionary of Historians*, 260.
23. Gooch, *History and Historians*, 301.
24. *Ibid.*, 300.
25. *Ibid.*, 299.
26. *Ibid.*, 303.
27. *Ibid.*
28. *Ibid.*, 303–4.
29. Stern, *Varieties of History*, 93–94.
30. Gooch, *History and Historians*, 327.
31. Stern, *Varieties of History*, 101.
32. *Ibid.*
33. Gooch, *History and Historians*, 324–25.
34. *Ibid.*, 326.
35. *Ibid.*, 325.
36. *Ibid.*, 326.
37. *Ibid.*
38. *Ibid.*, 327.
39. *Ibid.*, 147.
40. *Ibid.*, 153.
41. *Ibid.*, 131.
42. *Ibid.*, 142.
43. *Ibid.*, 144.
44. *Ibid.*, 153.
45. *Ibid.*, 138.
46. *Ibid.*, 150.
47. *Ibid.*, 155.
48. Durant, *Pleasure of Philosophy*, 206.
49. Marwick, *Nature of History*, 35–36; see also *What History Is*, 42–43.
50. Marwick, *Nature of History*, 37.
51. Gooch, *History and Historians*, 15.
52. *Ibid.*, 18.
53. Stern, ed., *Varieties of History*, 46.
54. Gooch, *History and Historians*, 19.
55. *Ibid.*, 78.
56. *Ibid.*, 79.
57. Marwick, *What History Is*, 43.
58. Marwick, *Nature of History*, 37.
59. Marwick, *What History Is*, 43.
60. Gooch, *History and Historians*, 143.

61. Marwick, *Nature of History*, 39.
62. Gooch, *History and Historians*, 87.
63. *Ibid.*, 93.
64. *Ibid.*, 100.
65. *Ibid.*, 78.
66. *Ibid.*, 88.
67. *Blackwell Dictionary of Historians*, 350.
68. Stern, *Varieties of History*, 61.
69. Gooch, *History and Historians*, 114.
70. *Ibid.*
71. *Ibid.*, 117.
72. *Ibid.*
73. *Ibid.*, 128.
74. *Ibid.*, 103–104.
75. Thompson and Holm, *History of Historical Writing*, 186.
76. *Ibid.*
77. Carr, *What is History?*, 12

CHAPTER 8

1. *Blackwell Dictionary of Historians*, 336.
2. Stern, *Varieties of History*, 223.
3. *Blackwell Dictionary of Historians*, 336–37.
4. Collingwood, *Idea of History*, 126.
5. *Ibid.*, 127.
6. *Blackwell Dictionary of Historians*, 337.
7. *Ibid.*, 92.
8. *Ibid.*, 56.
9. *Ibid.*
10. Stern, *Varieties of History*, 121.
11. Collingwood, *Idea of History*, 127.
12. Marwick, *Introduction to History*, 38.
13. Collingwood, *Idea of History*, 131.
14. Marwick, *Nature of History*, 43–44.
15. Marwick, *Introduction to History*, 38.
16. Collingwood, *Idea of History*, 130–131.
17. *Ibid.*, 131–132.
18. Carr, *What Is History*, 15.
19. Collingwood, *Idea of History*, 132–133.

20. *Karl Marx: A Biography*, 319.
21. *Ibid.*, 601.
22. See Palmer and Colton, *History of the Modern World*, 495–502.
23. *Ibid.*
24. Stern, *Varieties of History*, 149.
25. *Karl Marx: A Biography*, 74.
26. *Ibid.*, 315.
27. Marwick, *What History Is*, 45.
28. John Whittam, 'Karl Marx', in John Cannon, ed., *Historian at Work*, 97.
29. *Ibid.*, 86–87.
30. Marwick, *What History Is*, 45.
31. Whittam, 'Karl Marx', 98.
32. *Ibid.*, 87.
33. *Karl Marx: A Biography*, 80.
34. Marwick, *Nature of History*, 44.
35. *Ibid.*
36. *Blackwell Dictionary of Historians*, 271.
37. *Karl Marx: A Biography*, 84.
38. *Ibid.*, 74.
39. *Ibid.*, 75.

CHAPTER 9

1. See Stern, *Varieties of History*, 20–24.
2. *Ibid.*, 21.
3. Stern, *Varieties of History*, 209.
4. *Ibid.*, 211.
5. *Ibid.*, 217.
6. *Ibid.*, 223.
7. Collingwood, *Idea of History*, 149.
8. *Ibid.*, 151.
9. *Ibid.*, 148.
10. *Blackwell Dictionary of Historians*, 418–19.
11. Stern, *Varieties of History*, 230–31.
12. *Ibid.*, 232.
13. *Ibid.*, 234.
14. *Ibid.*, 231.
15. *Ibid.*, 235–37.

16. *Ibid.*, 239.
17. *Blackwell Dictionary of Historians*, 389.
18. Durant, *Pleasures of Philosophy*, 250.
19. *Ibid.*, 260.
20. *Ibid.*, 260–62.
21. Spengler, *Decline of the West*, 153.
22. *Blackwell Dictionary of Historians*, 389.
23. *New Encyclopaedia Britannica*, Micro II, 85.
24. Toynbee, *Study of History*, Vol. 1, 649–50.
25. *Ibid.*, 67.
26. *Ibid.*, 89.
27. *Ibid.*, 254.
28. *Ibid.*, 299.
29. Marwick, *Nature of History*, 88.
30. Collingwood, *Idea of History* 164.
31. Barnes, *History of Historical Writings*, 378.
32. *Encyclopaedia Americana*, Book 26, 889.
33. Stern, *Varieties of History*, 23.
34. Marwick, *Nature of History*, 88–89.
35. *Ibid.*, 73, 81.
36. Carr, *What is History*, 20–21; also see Marwick, *Nature of History*, 81.
37. Marwick, *Nature of History*., 81–82.
38. *Ibid.*, 82.
39. Carr, *What is History*, 21.
40. Collingwood, *Idea of History*, 215.
41. *Ibid.*, 216.
42. *Ibid.*, 214–15.
43. *Ibid.*, 217–18.
44. Marwick, *Nature of History*, 83.
45. *Ibid.*, 85.

CHAPTER 10

1. Marwick, *Nature of History*, 80.
2. *Ibid.*
3. *Ibid.*, 80–81.
4. *Ibid.*, 71.
5. Stern, *Varieties of History*, 257.

6. Robinson, 'The New History', in Stern, ed., *Varieties of History*, 256–57.
7. *Ibid.*, 260.
8. Marwick, *Nature of History*, 72.
9. *Ibid.*, 64.
10. *Ibid.*, 65.
11. *Ibid.*
12. *Ibid.*
13. *Ibid.*
14. Greenlaw, *Economic Origins of the French Revolution*, 75.
15. Black and Macraild, *Studying History*, 60.
16. Marwick, *Nature of History*, 68.
17. *Ibid.*, 67.
18. *Blackwell History of Historians*, 44.
19. Marwick, *Nature of History*, 89
20. Stern, *Varieties of History*, 191–92.
21. Carr, *What is History?*, 36–37.
22. *Blackwell Dictionary of Historians*, 285.
23. Marwick, *Nature of History*, 90.
24. *Ibid.*
25. *Ibid.*
26. Fisher, 'Preface' to *History of Europe*, Vol. 1.
27. Marwick, *Nature of History*, 92.
28. *Blackwell Dictionary of Historians*, 295.
29. *Ibid.*
30. Stern, *Varieties of History*, 267.
31. *Blackwell Dictionary of Historians*, 275.
32. Stern, *Varieties of History*, 268.
33. *Ibid.*
34. *Ibid.*, 267.
35. Trevelyan, *English Social History*, vii.
36. *Ibid.*
37. *Blackwell Dictionary of Historians*, 418.
38. *Ibid.*, 419.
39. *Ibid.*
40. Marwick, *Nature of History*, 61.
41. *Ibid.*
42. *Ibid.*, 225.
43. *Ibid.*, 204.
44. *Ibid.*, 205.

45. *Ibid.*, 206.
46. *Ibid.*, 209.
47. *Ibid.*, 212.
48. *Ibid.*
49. *Ibid.*, 210–211.
50. *Ibid.*, 211.
51. *Ibid.*, 215–216.
52. *Ibid.*, 216.
53. *Ibid.*
54. *Ibid.*, 226.
55. *Ibid.*
56. *Ibid.*, 226–27.
57. *Ibid.*, 227–28.
58. *Ibid.*, 228.
59. *Blackwell Dictionary of Historians*, 411.
60. Marwick, *Nature of History*, 229.
61. *Ibid.*
62. *Ibid.*, 230.
63. *Blackwell Dictionary of Historians*, 411.
64. Clark, 'The Annales Historians', in Quentin Skinner, ed., *Return of Grand Theory in the Human Sciences*, 181.
65. Marwick, *Nature of History.*, 75.
66. Black and Macraild, *Studying History*, 67.
67. Burke, 'Fernand Braudel', in John Cannon ed., *Historian at Work*, 193.
68. Marwick, *Nature of History*, 74.
69. Clark, 'The Annales Historians', 181.
70. Loyn, 'Marc Bloch', in John Cannon, ed., *Historian at Work*, 127.
71. Marwick, *Nature of History*, 77.
72. *Ibid.* 78.
73. *Ibid.*
74. *Ibid.*
75. *Ibid.*
76. See Loyn, 'Marc Bloch', 132–33.
77. Marwick, *Nature of History*, 78.
78. *Ibid.*, 76–77.
79. Black and Macraild, *Studying History*, 73.
80. Cannon, *Historian at Work*, 193.
81. *Ibid.*, 194.
82. *Ibid.*

83. *Ibid.*, 199.
84. *Ibid.*, 192.
85. *Ibid.*, 192.
86. *Ibid.*, 191.
87. For details see Clark, 'The *Annales* Historians', 184.
88. Black and Macraild, *Studying History*, 74.
89. Peter Burke, 'Fernald Braudel', in *Blackwell Dictionary of Historians*, 197.
90. *Ibid.*, 197–98.
91. *Ibid.*, 199.
92. *Ibid.*, 196–197.
93. *Ibid.*, 196.
94. Black and Macraild, *Studying History*, 74.
95. Burke, 'Fernand Braudel', 195–96.
96. *Ibid.*
97. Black and Macraild, *Studying History*, 78.
98. *Ibid.*
99. Clark 'The *Annales* Historians', 186–87.
100. *Ibid.*
101. *Ibid.*, 180.
102. *Ibid.*
103. *Ibid.*, 179–80.
104. *Ibid.*, 182–83.
105. *Ibid.*, 185.
106. *Ibid.*
107. *Ibid.*
108. *Ibid.*
109. *Ibid.*, 184.
110. *Ibid.*, 194.
111. *Ibid.*, 195.

CHAPTER 11

1. Gare, *Postmodernism and the Environmental Crisis*, 4.
2. *Ibid.*
3. *Ibid.*, 1–2.
4. *Ibid.*, 4.
5. *Ibid.*, 5.

6. Hoy, 'Jacques Derrida', in Skinner, ed., *Return of Grand Theory in the Human Sciences*, 46–47.
7. *Ibid.*, 49.
8. Boon, 'Claude Levi Strauss', in Skinner, ed., *Return of Grand Theory in the Human Sciences*, 169–70.
9. Philp, 'Michel Foucault', in Skinner, ed., *Return of Grand Theory in the Human Sciences*, 78.
10. See *Ibid.*, 78.
11. Merquior, *Foucault*, 26.
12. *Ibid.*, 101.
13. Bajaj, *Recent Trends in Historiography*, 103.
14. *Ibid.*, 101.
15. See Merquior, *Faucault*, 17–19; also see Philp, 'Michel Foucault', 67–81.
16. Merquior, *Foucault*, 18.
17. *Ibid.*, 36.
18. *Ibid.*
19. *Ibid.*
20. *Ibid.*, 39.
21. *Ibid.*, 42.
22. *Ibid.*, 51–52.
23. Bajaj, *Recent Trends in Historiography*, 106–107.
24. Merquior, *Foucault*, 81–82.
25. *Ibid.*, 80–81.
26. *Ibid.*, 81.
27. Evans, *In Defence of History*, 195–96.
28. Philp, 'Michel Foucault', 67.
29. Bajaj, *Recent Trends in Historiography*, 108.
30. Merquior, *Foucault*, 144.
31. *Ibid*, 83.
32. *Ibid.*, 26–28.
33. *Ibid.*, 57–58.
34. *Ibid.*, 151–52.
35. *Ibid.*, 102.
36. *Ibid.*, 105.
37. *Ibid.*, 106–107.
38. *Ibid.*, 146.
39. Bajaj, *Recent Trends in Historiography*, 119.
40. Merquior, *Foucault*, 141.
41. Evans, *In Defence of History*, 94.

42. *Ibid.*
43. Hoy, 'Jacques Derrida', 45–46.
44. *Ibid.*, 54–55.
45. Skinner, *Return of Grand theory in the Human Sciences,* 8.
46. Hoy, 'Jacques Derrida', 51.
47. Evans, *In Defence of History*, 4.
48. *Ibid.*, 4.
49. *Ibid.*, 95–96.
50. *Ibid.*, 6–7.
51. *Ibid.*, 7.
52. *Ibid.*
53. *Ibid.*
54. *Ibid.*, 99.
55. *Ibid.*, 97.
56. *Ibid.*
57. *Ibid.*, 106.
58. *Ibid.*, 112.
59. *Ibid.*, 114.
60. *Ibid.*, 116.
61. *Ibid.*, 136.
62. *Ibid.*
63. *Ibid.*, 138–39.
64. *Ibid.*, 141.
65. *Ibid.*
66. *Ibid.*, 157.
67. See *Ibid.*, 232–38.
68. *Ibid.*, 237–38.
69. *Ibid.*, 195–96.
70. *Ibid.*, 204.
71. *Ibid.*, 204–205.
72. *Ibid.*, 243–44.
73. See *Ibid.*, 244–46.
74. *Ibid.*, 189.
75. *Ibid.*, 126.
76. *Ibid.*, 248–49.
77. *Ibid.*, 5.
78. *Ibid.*, 71.

CHAPTER 12

1. Keith, *History of Sanskrit Literature*, 144.
2. Smith, *Oxford History of India*, xiii.
3. Keith, *History of Sanskrit Literature*, 144–47.
4. For Max Weber's view see Thaper, *Interpreting Early India*, 50.
5. See Pathak, *Ancient Historians of India: A Study in Historical Biographies*, 96.
6. *Ibid.*, 29.
7. *Ibid.*, 26.
8. See *Ibid.*, 30–32.
9. *Ibid.*, 32.
10. Cowell and Thomas, trans., *Harshacharita*, 195.
11. *Ibid*, viii.
12. *Ibid*, 208–209.
13. *Ibid.*, 143.
14. *Ibid.*, x–xi.
15. Pillai, ed., Introduction, *Atula's Mushikavamsa*, 23.
16. See Pathak, *Ancient Historians of India*, 58–62.
17. *Ibid.*, 65.
18. *Ibid.*, 67–68.
19. *Ibid.*, 73.
20. *Ibid.*, 73–74.
21. *Ibid.*, 84.
22. Majumdar, 'Ideas of History in Sanskrit Literature' in C.H. Philips, ed., *Historians of India, Pakistan and Ceylon*, 19.
23. Sitaram, trans., *Rajatarangini*, xix.
24. *Ibid.*, 10–11.
25. *Ibid.*, 214.
26. *Ibid.*, xl.
27. *Ibid.*, xxxii.
28. *Ibid.*, xxxiv.
29. *Ibid.*, x.
30. *Ibid.*,1137.
31. *Ibid.*, 201.
32. *Ibid.*, 154.
33. Philip, *Historians of India, Pakistan and Ceylon*, 169.
34. *Rajatarangini*, 706.
35. Keith, *History of Sanskrit*, 161–62.

36. *Rajatarangini*, 716–17.
37. *Ibid.*
38. *Rajatarangini*, xxix.
39. *Ibid.*, 7.
40. Keith, *History of Sanskrit*, 165.
41. *Ibid.*
42. See Thapar, 'The Historical Ideas of Kalhana as expressed in *Rajatarangini'* in Mohibbul Hasan ed., *Historians of Medieval India*, 2–5.
43. Keith, *History of Sanskrit*, 169–72.
44. Thapar, *From Lineage to State*, 19–20.
45. Pathak, *Ancient Historians of India*, 45.
46. *Ibid.*, 145.
47. Keith, *History of Sanskrit*, 147.
48. Pathak, *Ancient Historians of India*, 79–80.

CHAPTER 13

1. Hardy, 'Some Studies in Pre-Mughal Muslim Historiography', in Philips, ed., *Historians of India, Pakistan and Ceylon*, 117.
2. *Ibid.*, 116.
3. Rosenthal, *History of Muslim Historiography*, 77–82.
4. Mukhia, *Historians and Historiography during the Reign of Akbar*, 16.
5. *Ibid.*, 18–19.
6. Hardy, 'Some Studies in Pre-Mughal Muslim Historiography', 119.
7. *Ibid.*, 124.
8. Askari, 'Amir Khusru as a Historian' in Hasan, ed., *Historians of Medieval India*, 31.
9. Mukhia, *Historians and Historiography*, 12–13.
10. *Ibid.*, 35.
11. Hardy, 'Some Studies in Pre-Mughal Muslim Historiography', 125.
12. *Ibid.*, 121.
13. Nizami, 'Zia ud-Din Barani', in Hasan, ed., *Historians of Medieval India*, 41.
14. *Ibid.*, 45.
15. Mukhia, *Historians and Historiography*, 5.
16. Nizami, 'Zia ud-Din Barani', 49–50.
17. *Ibid.*, 40.
18. Mukhia, *Historians and Historiography*, 22.

19. Hardy, 'Some Studies in Pre-Mughal Muslim Historiography', 122–23.
20. Mukhia, *Historians and Historiography*, 20–21.
21. Nizami, 'Zia ud-Din Barani', 43.
22. *Ibid.*, 44.
23. *Ibid.*, 44–45.
24. *Ibid.*, 46.
25. *Ibid.*, 37.
26. Hardy, 'Some Studies in Pre-Mughal Muslim Historiography', 125.
27. *Ibid.*, 126.
28. *Ibid.*
29. *Ibid.*, 126–127.
30. Philips, *Historians of India, Pakistan and Ceylon*, 6.
31. Mukhia, *Historians and Historiography*, 15–16.
32. Hardy, 'Some Studies in Pre-Mughal Muslim Historiography', 125.
33. Suri, 'Babar', in Hasan, ed. *Historians of Medieval India*, 98.
34. *Ibid.*
35. *Ibid.*, 99.
36. *Ibid.*, 101.
37. *Ibid.*
38. Sathianathier, *History of India*, Vol. 2, 208.
39. Rizvi, 'Tarikh-i-Alfi', in Hasan, ed., *Historians of Medieval India*, 118.
40. *Ibid.*, 119.
41. Rashid, 'The Treatment of History by Muslim Historians in Mughal Official and Biographical Works', in Philips, ed., *Historians of India, Pakistan and Ceylon*, 148.
42. Mukhia, *Historians and Historiography*, 145–146.
43. *Ibid.*, 150.
44. *Ibid.*, 151–152.
45. Sathianathier, *History of India*, Vol. 2, 233.
46. Mukhia, *Historians and Historiography*, 153.
47. Mujib, 'Badauni', in Hasan, ed., *Historians of Medieval India*, 107.
48. Rashid, 'Treatment of History by Muslim Historians', 148.
49. Mukhia, *Historians and Historiography*, 111.
50. *Ibid.*, 123–24.
51. *Ibid.*, 121.
52. *Ibid.*, 123.
53. *Ibid.*, 126.
54. *Ibid.*, 126–27.

55. *Ibid.*, 116.
56. Sathianathier, *History of India*, Vol. 2, 234.
57. Mukhia, *Historians and Historiography*, 131.
58. *Ibid.*, 129.
59. Pandey, *A Book of India*, 356–57.
60. Rashid, 'Treatment of History by Muslim Historians', 143.
61. Siddiqui, 'Shaik Abul Fazal', in Hasan, ed. *Historians of Medieval India*, 132.
62. Rashid, 'Treatment of History by Muslim Historians', 146.
63. *Ibid.*
64. *Ibid.*, 146–47
65. Siddiqui, 'Shaik Abul Fazal', 132.
66. *Ibid.*, 136.
67. *Ibid.*, 129–30.
68. Rashid, 'Treatment of History by Muslim Historians', 146.
69. Sathianathier, *History of India*, Vol. 2, 231.
70. Siddiqui, 'Shaik Abul Fazal', 137.
71. *Ibid.*, 138–39.
72. *Ibid.*, 137.
73. Mukhia, *Historians and Historiography*, 80–81.
74. *Ibid.*, 68.
75. *Ibid.*, 69.
76. Siddqui, 'Shaik Abul Fazal', 137–38.
77. Rashid, 'Treatment of History by Muslim Historians', 145.
78. *Ibid.*, 145–46.
79. Elliot and Dowson, *History of India as told by its own Historians*, Vol. 6, 6.
80. Siddiqui, 'Shaik Abul Fazal', 123–24.
81. Rashid, 'Treatment of History by Muslim Historians', 145.
82. Sathianathier, *History of India*, Vol. 2, 407.
83. *Ibid.*, 408.
84. Rashid, 'Treatment of History by Muslim Historians', 150.
85. *Ibid.*, 150.
86. Sarkar, 'Personal History of Some Medieval Historians' in Hasan, ed., *Historians of Medieval India*, 189–90.
87. *Ibid.*, 190.
88. Umar, 'Comparitive Study of Historical Approach of Mohammad Qasim and Khafi Khan', in Hasan, ed., *Historians of Medieval India*, 157–58.
89. Sarkar, 'Personal History of some Medieval Historians', 190.

90. Umar, 'Comparative Study of Historical Approach of Mohammad Qasim and Khafi Khan', 158.
91. *Ibid.*, 158.
92. *Ibid.*, 160.
93. Sarkar, *Studies in Mughal India* 240–41.
94. Sarkar, 'Personal History of some Medieval Historians', 191.
95. *Ibid.*, 192.
96. See Majumdar, *Historiography in Modern India*, 6–7.
97. Sathianathier, *History of India*, Vol. 2, 384.
98. Rashid, 'Treatment of History by Muslim Historians', 141.
99. Sarkar, 'Personal History of some Medieval Historians', 183.
100. Rashid, 'Treatment of History by Muslim Historians', 150–51.
101. Sarkar, 'Personal History of some Medieval Historians', 184.
102. *Ibid.*
103. *Ibid.*, 186.
104. For details see Mukhia, *Historians and Historiography*, 170–176.

CHAPTER 14

1. Majumdar, *Historiography in Modern India*, 9–10.
2. *Ibid.*, 8.
3. Kosambi, *Introduction to the Study of Indian History*, 6.
4. Majumdar, *Historiography of Modern India*, 20–21.
5. *Ibid.*, 23.
6. Allchin, 'Ideas of History in Indian Archaeological Writing: A Preliminary Study,' in Philips, ed., *Historians of India, Pakistan and Ceylon*, 246.
7. *Ibid.*
8. *Ibid.*, 246–47.
9. MacDonnell, *A History of Sanskrit Literature*, 1.
10. Thapar, *Intrepreting Early India*, 81–82.
11. Mukherjee, *Sir William Jones: A Study in Eighteenth Century British Attitudes to India*, 95.
12. *Ibid.*, 117–19.
13. Philips, *Historians of India, Pakistan and Ceylon*, 218.
14. *Ibid.*, 219.
15. *Ibid.*
16. Majumdar, *Historiography of Modern India*, 11.
17. Philips, *Historians of India, Pakistan and Ceylon*, 221.

18. *Ibid.*, 220.
19. Majumdar, *Historiography of Modern India*, 12.
20. *Ibid.*, 12–13.
21. *Ibid.*, 13.
22. *Ibid.*
23. *Ibid.*
24. *Ibid.*, 13–14.
25. *Ibid.*, 14.
26. Philips, *Historians of India, Pakistan and Ceylon*, 225.
27. *Ibid.*, 226.
28. Elliot, *History of India as Told by its own Historians* Vol. 1, xxii.
29. Philips, *Historians of India, Pakistan and Ceylon*, 227.
30. Joll, *Europe Since 1870*, 104.
31. Furber, 'The Theme of Imperialism in Modern Historical Writings on India', in Philips, ed., *Historians of India, Pakistan and Ceylon*, 341.
32. *Ibid.*, 339–40.
33. Stokes, 'The Administrators and Historical Writings on India', in Philips, ed., *Historians of India, Pakistan and Ceylon*, 386.
34. *Ibid.*, 393.
35. *Ibid.*
36. *Ibid.*
37. *Ibid.*, 395.
38. *Ibid.*
39. *Ibid.*, 396.
40. *Ibid.*
41. *Ibid.*, 397.
42. *Ibid.*, 399.
43. *Ibid.*, 394.
44. *Ibid.*, 402.
45. *Ibid.*, 402–403.
46. *Ibid.*, 403.
47. Smith, *Early History of India*, 4.
48. Basham 'Modern Historians of Ancient India', in Philips, ed., *Historians of India, Pakistan and Ceylon.*, 269.
49. *Ibid.*, 270.
50. *Ibid.*, 269.
51. Majumdar, *Historiography in Modern India*, 42.
52. Philips, *Historians of India, Pakistan and Ceylon*, 252.
53. Majumdar, *Historians in Modern India*, 41–43.

54. Philips, *Historians of India, Pakistan and Ceylon.*, 271.
55. Smith, *Oxford History of India*, ix–x.
56. Philips, *Historians of India, Pakistan and Ceylon*, 274.
57. Harrison, 'Notes on W.H. Moreland as Historian', in Philips, ed., *Historians of India, Pakistan and Ceylon*, 316.
58. *Ibid.*
59. *Ibid.*, 316.
60. *Ibid.*, 314.
61. *Ibid.*, 315.
62. *Ibid.*, 317–18.
63. Thapar, *Ancient Indian Social History*, 6–7.
64. *Ibid.*, 6.
65. Philips, *Historians of India, Pakistan and Ceylon*, 409.
66. Stokes 'The Administrators and Historical Writings on India', in Philips, ed., *Historians of India, Pakistan and Ceylon*, 393.

CHAPTER 15

1. Clark, 'The Role of Bankim Chandra in the Development of Nationalism', in Philips, ed., *Historians of India, Pakistan and Ceylon*, 436.
2. Majumdar, 'Nationalist Historians', in Philips, ed., *Historians of India, Pakistan and Ceylon*, 418.
3. Ibid., 418.
4. *Ibid.*
5. *Ibid.*, 419
6. *Ibid.*
7. *Ibid.*, 419–20
8. *Ibid.*, 417
9. *Ibid.*, 421–422
10. *Ibid.*, 422–423
11. *Ibid.*, 424
12. *Ibid.*, 425
13. *Ibid.*
14. Basham, 'Modern Historians of Ancient India', in Philips, ed., *Historians of India, Pakistan and Ceylon*, 283.
15. Thapar, *Ancient Indian Social History*, 12.
16. *Ibid.*, 14.
17. *Ibid.*, 16.

18. Panikkar, *A Survey of Indian History*, viii.
19. Pusalkar, 'R.G. Bhandarkar', in Sen, ed., *Historians and Historiography in Modern India*, 30.
20. Basham, 'Modern Historians of Ancient India', 281.
21. Pusalkar, 'R.G. Bhandarkar', 28.
22. Sen, 'Romesh Chandra Dutt', in Sen, ed., *Historians and Historiography in Modern India*, 322.
23. *Ibid.*
24. *Ibid.*, 324.
25. Sinha, 'Kashi Prasad Jayaswal', in Sen, ed., *Historians and Historiography in Modern India*, 91.
26. *Ibid.*, 92.
27. *Ibid.*, 77–94.
28. Srivastava, 'Radha Kumud Mukherji', in Sen, ed., *Historians and Historiography in Modern India*, 77.
29. Basham, 'Modern Historians of Ancient India', 284.
30. Majumdar, 'Hem Chandra Raychaudhuri,' in Sen, ed., *Historians and Historiography in Modern India*, 98.
31. Basham, 'Modern Historians of Ancient India', 284–85.
32. Rao, 'Govind Sakharam Sardesi', in Sen, ed., *Historians and Historiography in Modern India*, 225.
33. *Ibid.*, 227–29.
34. Srivastava, 'Sir Jadunath Sarkar', in Sen, ed., *Historians and Historiography in Modern India*, 137.
35. *Ibid.*, 139.
36. *Ibid.*, 138–39.
37. See Majumdar, *Historiography in Modern India*, 56.
38. Srivastava, 'Sir Jadunath Sarkar', 141–42.
39. *Ibid.*, 142.
40. Dikshit, 'S. Krishnaswami Aiyangar', in Sen, ed., *Historians and Historiography in Modern India*, 65–66.
41. Prasad, 'Sir Shafaat Ahmad Khan', in Sen, ed., *Historians and Historiography in Modern India*, 147.
42. *Ibid.*, 150.
43. *Ibid.*, 151–52.
44. *Ibid.*, 155–56.
45. For details see Hardy, 'Modern Muslim Historical Writing', 294–97.
46. *Ibid.*, 298.
47. *Ibid.* 299.

48. *Ibid.*
49. *Ibid.*, 300.
50. *Ibid.*, 300–01.
51. *Ibid.*, 301.
52. *Ibid.*
53. *Ibid.*, 302.
54. *Ibid.*
55. *Ibid.*, 302.
56. *Ibid.*, 302–03.
57. *Ibid.*, 303.
58. *Ibid.*, 305.
59. *Ibid.*, 304.
60. See *Ibid.*, 305.
61. Philips, *Historians of India, Pakistan and Ceylon*, 305.
62. Hardy, 'Modern Muslim Historical Writing', 307.
63. *Ibid.*, 308.
64. *Ibid.*, 299.
65. *Ibid.*, 309.
66. Banerji, 'Dr. Surendranath Sen', in Sen, ed., *Historians and Historiography in Modern India*, 354.
67. *Ibid.*, 356.
68. Banerjee, 'Sardar K.M. Panikkar', in Sen, ed., *Historians and Historiography in Modern India*, 330.
69. *Ibid.*, 340.
70. *Ibid.*, 340–41.
71. *Ibid.*, 341.
72. Panikkar, *Survey of Indian History*, 23.
73. *Ibid.*, 237–38.
74. *Ibid.*, 127–28.
75. Sastri, *History of South India*, 11.
76. *Ibid.*, 11–12.
77. *Ibid.*, 2.
78. *Ibid.*, 2.
79. *Ibid.*, 1.
80. Thapar, *Ancient Indian Social History*, 16.
81. *Ibid.*, 16.
82. Sarkar, 'R.C. Majumdar and his work on South and South East Asia: A Panoramic Review', *The Journal of Indian History*, Diamond Jubilee Volume, 1982, Part 1, 316.
83. *Ibid.*, 311.

84. *Ibid.*
85. *Ibid.*, 323.
86. Majumdar, *History and Culture of the Indian People*, Vol. 4, 615–18.
87. Majumdar, 'Indian Historiography: Some Present Trends', in Sen, ed., *Historians and Historiography in Modern India*, xxiii.

CHAPTER 16

1. Thapar, *Ancient Indian Social History*, 16–17.
2. Kosambi, *Introduction to the Study of Ancient Indian History*, 6.
3. *Ibid.*, 1.
4. *Ibid.*, 7.
5. See Thapar, 'The Contribution of D.D. Kosambi to Indology', in *Interpreting Early India*, 94.
6. *Ibid.*, 96.
7. *Ibid.*, 98.
8. *Ibid.*, 98–99.
9. *Ibid.*, 101–02.
10. *Ibid.*, 102.
11. See Kosambi, *Culture and Civilization in Ancient India in Historical Outline*, 96–132.
12. Sharma, *Sudras in Ancient India*, 315.
13. *Ibid.*, 318.
14. Thapar, *History of India*, Vol. 1, 22.
15. Thapar, 'Society and Law in the Hindu and Buddhist Traditions', in *Ancient Indian Social History*, 34.
16. *Ibid.*, 215.
17. *Ibid.*, 220.
18. *Ibid.*, 221.
19. Thapar, 'Ideology and Interpretation of Early Indian History', in *Interpreting Early India*, 7.
20. Singh, 'Bipan Chandra', in Sharma et. al., ed., *Historiography and Historians in India since Independence*, 216.
21. *Ibid.*, 216.
22. *Ibid.*, 217.
23. *Ibid.*, 219.
24. *Ibid.*, 219–20.
25. *Ibid.*, 223.
26. *Ibid.*, 224.

27. *Ibid.*
28. Varma, 'Irfan Habib', in Sharma et. al., ed., *Historiography and Historians since Independence*, 236–37.
29. *Ibid.*, 234.
30. *Ibid.*, 233.
31. *Ibid.*, 237.
32. *Ibid.*
33. *Ibid.*, 239.
34. *Ibid.*, 230–31.
35. See Thapar, *Interpreting Early India*, 101–102.
36. Sharma, *Material Culture and Social Formation in Ancient India*, 165.
37. Thapar, *Ancient Indian Social History*, 34.
38. Kosambi, *Culture and Civilization in Ancient India*, 101–02.
39. Kosambi, *Introduction to the Study of Indian History*, 166.
40. Kosambi, *Culture and Civilization in Ancient India*, 102.
41. *Ibid.*, 103.
42. Bipan Chandra, ed., *India's Struggle for Independence*, 22.
43. Sharma, 'Irban Habib', 237.
44. *Ibid.*, 240.
45. Guha, *Subaltern Studies*, Vol. 1, 3.
46. Guha, Preface to *Subaltern Studies*, Vol. 2.
47. Henningham, 'Quit India in Bihar and the Eastern United Provinces: the Dual Revolt', in Guha, ed., *Subaltern Studies*, Vol. 2, 136.
48. Das, 'Agrarian Change from Above and Below: Bihar, 1947–78', in Guha, ed., *Subaltern Studies*, Vol. 2, 227.
49. Sarkar, 'The Conditions and Nature of Subaltern Militancy: Bengal from Swadeshi to Non Co-operation, c. 1905–22', in Guha, ed., *Subaltern Studies*, Vol. 3, 271–72.

Select Bibliography

Appadorai, A. [1942] 1952. *The Substance of Politics.* Madras: Oxford University Press.

Bajaj, Satish, K. 1988. *Recent Trends in Historiography.* New Delhi: Anmol Publications.

Barnes, H. E. 1937. *A History of Historical Writing,* Oklahoma: Norman.

Black, Jeremy and Donald M. Macraild. 1997. *Studying History.* Basingstoke: Macmillan.

Cannon, John, et. al. eds. 1988. *The Blackwell Dictionary of Historians.* Oxford: Basil Blackwell Ltd.

Cannon John, ed. 1980. *The Historian at Work.* London: George Allen and Unwin.

Carr, E.H. [1964] 1983. *What is History?* London: Macmillan.

Chandra, Bipan. [1979] 1989. *Nationalism and Colonialism in Modern India.* New Delhi: Orient Longman.

—. [1984] 1992. *Communalism in Modern India.* New Delhi: Vikas Publishing House.

Clark, Stuart, 1999. *The Annales Historians, Critical Assessment.* Vol. 1. London: Routledge.

Collingwood, R.G. 1946. *The Idea of History.* Oxford: Oxford University Press.

Cowell, E.B. and F.W. Thomas. trans. 1961. *Harshacharita.* New Delhi: Motilal Banarsidass.

Dictionary of the History of Ideas. 1968. Vol. 1. Charles Scribner's Sons Publishers: New York.

Dictionary of the History of Ideas. 1973. Vol. 2. Charles Scribner's Sons Publishers: New York.

—. 1953. *Pleasures of Philosophy.* New York: Simon and Schuster.

—. 1954. *The Story Civilization I: Our Oriental Heritage.* New York: Simon and Schuster.

—. (n.d.). *The Story of Civilization II: The Life of Greece.* New York: Simon and Schuster.

—. (n.d.). *The Story of Civilization III: Ceasar and Christ.* New York: New York: Simon and Schuster.

—. 1950. *The Story of Civilization IV: The Age of Faith.* New York: Simon and Schuster.

—. 1953. *The Story of Civilization V: The Renaissance.* New York: Simon and Schuster.

—. 1957. *The Story of Civilization VI: The Reformation.* New York: Simon and Schuster.

Durant, Will and Ariel Durant. 1961. *The Story of Civilization VII: The Age of Reason Begins.* New York: Simon and Schuster.

—. 1963. *The Story of Civilization VIII: The Age of Louis XIV.* New York: Simon and Schuster.

—. 1965. *The Story of Civilization IX: The Age of Voltaire.* New York: Simon and Schuster.

—. 1967. *The Story of Civilization X: Rousseau and Revolution.* New York: Simon and Schuster.

—. 1975. *The Story of Civilization XI: The Age of Napoleon.* New York: Simon and Schuster.

Chambers's Encyclopaedia. 1959. Vol. 7. London: George Newnes Limited.

Encyclopaedia Americana. [1929] 1981. Book 25. Danburg: Grolier Incorporated.

Encyclopaedia Americana. [1929] 1981. Book 26. Danburg: Grolier Incorporated.

Encyclopaedia Britannica, Macropaedia. [1768–71] 1993. Vol. 3. Chicago: INC.

Encyclopaedia of Islam. 1979. new edn. Vol. 3. E.J. Brill-Leiden.

Encyclopaedia of Islam. 1979. new edn. Vol. 4. E.J. Brill-Leiden.

The New Encyclopaedia Britannica, Macropaedia 2. Chicago: INC.

Evans, J. Richard. 1997. *In Defence of History.* London: Granta Books.

Fisher, H.A.L. [1935] 1970. *A History of Europe.* Vol. 1. London: Collins, Fontana Library.

Gare, Arran, E. 1997. *Postmodernism and the Environmental Crisis.* London.

Gibbon, Edward. 1962. *The Decline and Fall of the Roman Empire.* Abridgment by D.M. Low in 3 vols. New York: Washington Square Press.

Gooch, G.P. [1913] 1952. *History and Historians of the Nineteenth Century.* London: Longmans Green.

Greenlaw, Ralph. W. ed. 1958. *The Economic Origins of the French Revolution, Poverty or Prosperity?* Boston: D.C. Heath and Co.

Guha, Ranajit, ed. 1982. *Subaltern Studies*. Vol. 1. New Delhi: Oxford University Press.

—. 1982. *Subaltern Studies*. Vol. 2. New Delhi: Oxford University Press.

—. 1982. *Subaltern Studies*. Vol. 3. New Delhi: Oxford University Press.

—. 1982. *Subaltern Studies*. Vol. 4. New Delhi: Oxford University Press.

Haddock, B.A. 1980. *Introduction to Historical Thought*. London: Edward Arnold Publishers.

Hardy, Peter. 1983. *Studies in Indo-Muslim Historical Writing*. London. (n.p.).

Hasan, Mohibbul. ed. 1968. *Historians of Medieval India*. Meerut: Meenakshi Prakashan.

Hughes-Warrington, Marnie. 2000. *Fifty Key Thinkers on History*. London and New York: Routledge.

Hussain, M. 1953. *The Rihla of Ibn Batuta*. Baroda.

Jenkins, Keith. ed. *The Postmodern History Reader*. Routledge, 11 New Fetterlane, London, E.C.4 P4EE, 1997.

Joll, James. [1972] 1983. *Europe Since 1870*. London: Pelican.

Keith, A.B. [1920] 1993. *A History of Sanskrit Literature*. New Delhi: Motilal Banarsidass.

Kearns, Catherine. 1997. *Psychoanalysis, historiography and feminist history*. Cambridge: Cambridge University Press.

Knapton, Ernest John. 1958. *Europe 1450–1815*. Massachusetts: Charles Seribner's Sons.

Kosambi, D.D. [1956] 1985. *An Introduction to the Study of Indian History*. (n.p.).

—. [1972] 1982. *The Culture and Civilization in Ancient Indian in Historical Outline*. New Delhi: Vikas Publishing House.

Macdonell, A.A. [1971] 1986. *A History of Sanskrit Literature*. New Delhi: Motilal Banarsidass.

Majumdar, R.C. 1967. *Historiography in Modern India*. Bombay: Asia Publishing House.

Majumdar, R.C. ed. [1964] 1993. *A History and Culture of the Indian People*. Vol. 4. Mumbai: Bharatiya Vidya Bhavan.

Manuel, E. Frank. ed. (n.d.). *The Enlightenment*. (n.p.).

Marwick, Arthur. 1970. *What History Is and Why It Is Important*. Buckinghamshire: Open University Press.

—. 1977. *Introduction to History*. Milton Keynes: Open University Press.

—. [1984] 1970. *The Nature of History*. London and Basingstoke: Macmillan Press Ltd.

Merquior, J.G. [1985] 1991. *Foucault*. London: Hammersmith.

Munslow, Alun. 1997. *Deconstructing History*. London: Routledge.

Mukhia, Harbans, 1976. *Historians and Historiography during the Reign of Akbar*. New Delhi: Vikas Publishing House.

Palmer, R.R. and Joel Colton. [1950] 1965. *A History of the Modern World*. New York: Alfred Knopf.

Pandey, B.N. ed. [1965] 1982. *A Book of India*. Calcutta: Rupa and Co.

Panikkar, K.M. [1947] 1956. *A Survey of Indian History*. Bombay: Asia Publshing House.

Pargiter, F.E. [1922] 1997. *Ancient Indian Historical Tradition*. New Delhi: Motilal Banarsidas.

—. [1913] 1975. *The Purana Text of the Dynasties of the Kali Age*. New Delhi: Dipa Publications.

Pathak, V.S. 1963. *Ancient Indian Hitorians*. London: Asia Publishing House.

Philips, C.H. ed. [1961] 1967. *Historians of India, Pakistan and Ceylon*. London: Oxford University Press.
1977.

Pillai, Raghavan. ed. (n.d.). *Atula's Mushikavamsa*. Trivandrum: Oriental Research Institute and MSS Library, University of Kerala.

Prepared by the Institute of Marxism-Leninism of the C.P.S.U. central committee, 1973. *Karl Marx, A Biography*. Moscow: Progress Publishers.

Rosenthal, Franz. 1967. trans. *Muqaddima, An Introduction to History*. 2nd edn. New Jersey: Princeton University Press.

Russell, Bertrand. [1947] 1946. *History of Western Philosophy*. London: George Allen and Unwin.

Sachau, Edward. 1983. trans. *India Alberuni's*. New Delhi: National Book Trust.

Sarkar, Jagdish Narayan. 1919. *Studies in Mughal India*. Calcutta: M.C. Sarkar and Sons.

Sastri, K.A. Neelakanta. [1955] 1978. *A History of South India*. Madras: Oxford University Press.

Sastri, K.A. Neelakanta, and Sreenivasachari. 1970. *An Advanced History of India*. Bombay: Allied Publishers.

Sathianathier, R. [1964] 1975. *History of India*. Vol. 1. Madras: S. Viswanathan, Printers and Publishers.

—. [1966] 1976. *History of India*. Vol. 2. Madras: S. Viswanathan, Printers and Publishers.

Sen, S.P. ed. [1973] 1976. *Historians and Historiography in Modern India*. Calcutta: Institute of Historical Studies.

Sharma, Ramesh Chandra, et. al. 1991. *Historiography and Historians since Independence*. Agra: M.G. Publishers.

Sharma, R.S. [1965] 1980. *Indian Feudalism*. New Delhi: Macmillan.

—. 1966. *Light on Early Indian Society and Economy*. Bombay: People's Publishing House.

—. [1983] 1990. *Material Culture and Social Formation in Ancient India*. New Delhi: Macmillan.

—. 1980. *Sudras in Ancient India: A Social History of the Lower Orders down to c. AD 600*. New Delhi: Motilal Banarsidass.

—. [1968] 1987. *Urban Decay in India, c. AD 300 to AD 1000*. New Delhi: Munshiram Manoharlal.

Sitaram, Ranjit Pundit. trans. [1935] 1968. *The Rajatarangini*. New Delhi: Sahitya Academy.

Skinner, Quentin. ed. [1985] 1997. *The Return of Grand Theory in the Human Sciences*. Cambridge: Cambridge University Press.

Smith, V.A. [1924] 1999. *The Early History of India*. New Delhi: Oxford University Press.

—. [1919] 1990. *The Oxford History of India*. Oxford: Clarendon Press.

Spengler, Oswald. 1961. *The Decline of the West*. London: George Allen and Unwin.

Stern, Fritz. [1972] 1956. *Varieties of History*. New York: Vintage Books.

Thapar, Romila. [1963] 1982. *Asoka and the Decline of the Mauryas*. New Delhi: Oxford University Press.

—. [1966] 1976. *A History of India*. Vol. 1. London: Penguin Books.

—. [1984] 1987. *Ancient Indian Social History: Some Interpretations*. New Delhi: Orient Longman.

—. 1984. *From Lineage to State*. Bombay: Oxford University Press.

—. [1992] 1994. *Interpreting Early India*. New Delhi: Oxford University Press.

Thompson, J.W and Bernard Holm. 1942. *A History of Historical Writing*. Vols. 1 and 2. New York: Macmillan Company.

Toynbee, Arnold Joseph. 1965. *A Study of History*. 2 vols. New York: Dell Publishing Company.

Trevelyan, G.M. 1962. *English Social History*. London: The English Language Book Society and Longman.

Van Loon, Henrik. 1959. *The Story of America*. Connectient: Fawcet World Library.

Wallbank, T.W. and A.M. Taylor. 1954. *Civilization Past and Present*. Vol. 1, 3rd ed. Chicago.

Index

A

C

N